THE ENCYCLOPEDIA OF
Demons and
Demonology

Also by Rosemary Ellen Guiley

The Encyclopedia of Angels, Second Edition

The Encyclopedia of Ghosts and Spirits, Third Edition

The Encyclopedia of Magic and Alchemy

The Encyclopedia of Saints

*The Encyclopedia of Vampires, Werewolves,
and Other Monsters*

*The Encyclopedia of Witches, Witchcraft
and Wicca, Third Edition*

THE ENCYCLOPEDIA OF
Demons and
Demonology

Rosemary Ellen Guiley

FOREWORD BY JOHN ZAFFIS

Checkmark Books®
An imprint of Infobase Publishing

The Encyclopedia of Demons and Demonology

Checkmark Books
An imprint of Infobase Publishing, Inc.
132 West 31st Street
New York NY 10001

Library of Congress Cataloging-in-Publication Data

Guiley, Rosemary.
The encyclopedia of demons and demonology / Rosemary Ellen Guiley ; foreword by John Zaffis.
p. cm.
Includes bibliographical references and index.
ISBN-13: 978-0-8160-7314-6 (hardcover : alk. paper)
ISBN-10: 0-8160-7314-7 (hardcover : alk. paper)
ISBN-13: 978-0-8160-7315-3 (pbk. : alk. paper)
ISBN-10: 0-8160-7315-5 (pbk. : alk. paper)
1. Demonology—Encyclopedias. I. Title.
BF1503.G85 2009
133.4'203—dc22   2008052488

Checkmark Books are available at special discounts when purchased in bulk quantities for businesses, associations, institutions, or sales promotions. Please call our Special Sales Department in New York at (212) 967-8800 or (800) 322-8755.

You can find Facts On File on the World Wide Web at http://www.factsonfile.com

Text design by Cathy Rincon
Cover design by Takeshi Takahashi
Composition by Hermitage Publishing Services
Cover printed by Yurchak Printing, Landisville, Pa.
Book printed and bound by Yurchak Printing, Landisville, Pa.

Printed in the United States of America

This book is printed on acid-free paper and contains 30 percent postconsumer recycled content.

For John Zaffis

⫷ Contents ⫸

❧ FOREWORD ❧

I have spent more than 30 years dealing with the shadow side of the paranormal, including negative hauntings and demonic cases. I never actually intended to become so deeply involved, but as most of us in this field are, I was drawn in and called to it.

The first sign of calling came in my teens. I was about 15 years old when I awoke one night and saw my first apparition, my deceased grandfather standing at the foot of my bed. Actually, I did not know him; he had died when I was three years old. But my mother verified my description of him.

Perhaps you could say my calling was "in the blood," as my mother was a twin, and twins have been known to be more psychically sensitive than the average person. Plus, I was related by blood to one of the most prominent investigators of the demonic: Ed Warren, my mother's twin brother and my uncle. Ed and his wife, Lorraine Warren, a clairvoyant, became household names in the paranormal and were in media headlines on some of the most famous modern cases on record. Ed has passed on now, and Lorraine still works in the field.

As a kid I was always fascinated by the work Ed and Lorraine did in the paranormal. I wanted to be part of it too. But Ed was a stickler for the proper education. He refused to allow me to go along on cases before I turned 18, and he spent a lot of time transmitting his knowledge to me. I was impatient back then, but Ed, in his wisdom, knew what he was doing. Dealing with the paranormal, especially the dark side, is not child's play and requires grounding, education, and discernment. I

had to have a base in all of those in order to be properly prepared.

I learned a great deal from my uncle and aunt and eventually went out on my own. I have been privileged to work with some of the best names in the field, both laypersons, like me, and clergy. I have worked on more than 7,000 cases: Many of them have had natural explanations (that is, not paranormal or demonic), and many others have been resolved with intervention. A few of them have been full-blown demonic infestations and possessions. I do not perform exorcisms—that is a role for clergy—but I have assisted at dozens of these rites.

One of the demonic cases brought me face to face with genuine evil: a reptile-like entity that manifested in an infested home, a former funeral parlor in Southington, Connecticut, and came at me down a staircase. The intensity of the evil was astonishing. I had never before experienced anything like it, and I have to admit, I was so shaken that it was several days before I could return to the case. I know from my own experience on this case and others that evil is real, the demonic exists, and dark forces are at work in the world.

As Rosemary Ellen Guiley states in her introduction to this book, the demonic—always fascinating—has acquired a media glamour that has encouraged people to want to become involved as "demonologists." Many of them jump in not properly prepared, not having much understanding of what they are dealing with or the ramifications and consequences of this kind of work. The work is never easy, and there is the constant danger of repercussions. The forces of evil know who you are and will try to prevent you from interfering in their activities. You, your home, your family, and your friends all become targets.

I mentioned earlier the importance of education, how Ed did his best to make sure I was armed with information, knowledge, and insight in addition to experience. If I had had a book like *The Encyclopedia of Demons and Demonology* when I was getting started, I guarantee you that it would have been well thumbed in a hurry. Rosemary Ellen Guiley has gained a well-earned reputation in the paranormal for her thorough research and investigation. I have all of her encyclopedias, refer to them frequently, and recommend them to others. I welcome the addition of this one to my set, and I can tell you that it will be one of my most valuable resources.

I met Rosemary several years ago at a conference in New Jersey hosted by L'Aura Hladik, founder of the New Jersey Ghost Hunters Society. I was already quite familiar with her work. We became good friends and colleagues, assisting each other in our work in whatever ways possible and collaborating on projects. We sometimes have different viewpoints, which add dimension to the overall picture.

Beyond paranormal investigation, there is a need for the average person to become more informed about the demonic. As a whole we are undereducated on the topic. Many of us get our ideas from Hollywood, maybe combined with a few religious teachings. Rosemary points out that many people ignore the topic altogether, hoping that the demonic will just "go away." I assure you, the forces of evil have no intention of disappearing. In fact, we in the field are seeing an increase in intensity and frequency of activity. That is why education is so important. *The Encyclopedia of Demons and Demonology* covers an amazing amount of material and from different perspectives. That is one of the many things I appreciate so much about Rosemary's work: She looks at everything from different angles. Whether you are serious about paranormal investigation or are a casual reader intrigued by a fascinating subject, this book will broaden your knowledge. Everyone who picks up this book will learn something new.

—John Zaffis

✣ ACKNOWLEDGMENTS ✣

I am deeply indebted to John Zaffis and Adam Blai, who have shared their knowledge and expertise on demons and demonology with me. I am also indebted to Philip J. Imbrogno, for sharing his expertise on djinn. Thanks also go to the very talented Richard Cook and Scott Brents for creating some original artwork in this book and especially for putting faces on some most unusual demons.

INTRODUCTION

Dealing with evil has occupied center stage in human affairs since our earliest times. Destruction, chaos, decay, and the ultimate darkness of death have often overshadowed the presence of goodness and light. Human beings have dealt with evil in three principal ways: by meeting it head on in battle, by warding it off before it strikes, and by trying to avoid it altogether through denial.

The how and why of evil have been debated and discussed for centuries in religion, folklore, philosophy, art, literature, and pop culture, all of which attempt to explain why bad things happen, especially to good people. When evil strikes the wicked, we see it as the deserved consequence of evildoing. When evil strikes the righteous, we look for satisfactory explanations, often in vain. Everyone feels the touch of evil at some point in life, regardless of his or her moral striving.

In myth, religion, and folklore the forces of both good and evil are personified. In the pantheons of deities there are gods and goddesses of benevolence and malevolence, and though some are mostly evil, they are seldom completely evil. Their job is to tear things down via disaster, ruination, disease, illness, and death. They are an essential part of the eternal cycle of life, death, and rebirth. Human beings, understandably, seek to avoid these torments as much as possible.

Monotheism creates a sharper polarization between good and evil. The one Creator is all-good but permits evil to exist under the direction of an archfiend. We console ourselves with the explanation that evil serves to test and demonstrate our moral fiber and spiritual worthiness. Our fate in the afterlife—eternal heaven or eternal hell—hangs in the balance.

In Christianity, Satan, the Devil, is the thoroughly evil counterpart to the all-good God. Concepts of the Devil developed over centuries, evolving from the neutral adversary, *satan,* of Hebrew lore, and the once-good angel Lucifer, who chose pride and fell from grace. Every army needs a wholly evil enemy, and Satan obliges Christianity in that sense.

Demons, the lower agents of evil, have many guises and operate under many names and with many purposes. In the pagan view, they are a part of the natural order, entities of moral ambivalence who mostly deceive and interfere. In the Christian view, they are evil—fallen angels who, as Lucifer did, chose pride over obedience to God and were cast out of heaven. They are doomed to eternal hell and serve the Devil, making unending assaults on human beings in an attempt to subvert souls to the Devil's domain.

Outside monotheism, demons have a long history of interfering in the affairs of the physical world and the lives of people, though not always with the goal of subverting souls. They act as tricksters and create annoying disturbances. More seriously, they cause illnesses, insanity, disasters, and bad luck. Some hold long-standing grudges against humanity. The djinn of Arabian lore, for example, say they were the original inhabitants of Earth and were evicted by God in favor of humans. They want their homeland returned, and some of them carry out guerrilla warfare and terrorism against humans to that end.

Whatever the guises, names, and agendas, demonic forces are constantly at play in the world. Thanks to the exaggerations of film and fiction, many Christians think, for example, that demonic attacks occur in the form of hideous beings assaulting people, possessing them, and making green slime run down walls and stairs. While such events do happen, they are relatively rare among all the ways the demonic forces operate. Evil is insidious, a Trojan horse that destroys from within, degrading people's thoughts, intentions, and will to lead the righteous life. Evil often operates through people, in the murder, mayhem, oppression, and violence people wreak on one another.

Several years ago, in my introduction to my *Encyclopedia of Angels,* I affirmed my belief in angels. I also believe in demons. One does not exist without the other. I have had personal experience of both. In my years of researching the paranormal, I have been puzzled by people who adamantly insist that demons do not exist. They readily believe in angels and other representatives of the forces of light and good, but they deny malevolent beings. They would rather not know anything about the demonic in order not to "dignify" it. Some of them naively think that if they do not believe in demons, they will not be bothered by them. "See no evil" means to them "avoiding all evil." Ignorance is their protection.

Ignorance, however, is no protection. Ignorance breeds fear, and fear is evil's greatest weapon. One of the things I have found to be true in my paranormal research, investigation, and personal experience is that what you fear will find you. Demons are the front lines of evil. Denying their existence only makes human beings easier targets.

Consequently, it is important to be informed about demons and evil. One conquers an enemy by knowing it inside and out. To know evil does not mean to embrace it, champion it, or glorify it.

Information shines a powerful light, and it is important that we shine that light into the darkness. My purpose in writing this encyclopedia is to provide one of those lights. The content is not intended to validate any particular religious view. Rather, I have explored numerous avenues of thought on the demonic. There is much diversity but also some common threads and themes. Some common themes, for example, concern the origins and fate of evil. The world in its original state was pristine, perfect, and good. The forces of evil entered the world, often through the actions of humans. Since then, the forces of evil have been having their day, wreaking havoc. At some point, good will vanquish evil, and perfection will be restored. Meanwhile, there are many ways to counter evil, to minimize its impact in the world.

The lore about demons is rich and varied, and the stories of human dealings with demons are colorful and mesmerizing. All of my encyclopedias emphasize the Western tradition, with the inclusion of some cross-cultural entries for comparison. In this volume, I have included entries on many individual demons, including the heavyweights of hell; types and classes of demons; demonized pagan deities; examples of demonic and spirit possessions and exorcisms; expressions of the demonic in folklore, literature, and film; and personalities who have influenced our views on the demonic.

The early church fathers of Christianity tackled the questions of the origins of evil, the existence of the Devil, and the operations of demons, but "demonology" as a study of the demonic did not gel until about the 15th century. By then, the Inquisition, established by the Roman Catholic Church to suppress heresy, was gathering momentum. For the next several centuries, religious and nonsecular authorities on demons wrote with great conviction on the diabolical and the relationship between witchcraft and demons. Thousands of people were accused of witchcraft, which automatically meant being in league with the Devil in order to harm people and destroy everything good. There was little or no evidence to support the claims, but public fears of the demonic were easily warped to believe in wild nights of demonic orgies and blasphemous activities. Some of these ideas linger today, as adherents to Wicca well know.

One demonic activity that fascinates people most is possession. Beliefs about possession are universal and ancient, such as possession by the *zar* of Middle Eastern lore and the *kitsune* of Japanese lore, who demand attention and gifts. Everywhere in the ancient world, possessing demons caused illness and insanity. Jesus gained attention for his ability to heal these conditions by expelling the demons.

The evolution of the Devil in Christianity narrowed the focus on possession; it became the instrument of the Devil's subversion of souls, turning people away from God and the church. The Catholic Church developed formal rites of exorcism to combat this evil.

The Protestant Reformation in the early 1500s was followed in Europe by a period in which Catholics and Protestants used possession as one of their battlegrounds on which to demonstrate religious superiority and sway the faithful. Some of the most famous possession cases on record concerned the alleged possession of nuns—such as at Loudun and Louviers, France—who put on displays of writhing, contorting, shouting obscenities, and other outrageous behavior, all for huge audiences. The exorcisms were more like circus acts than religious proceedings. Sexual repression, revenge, and outright fraud were part of many of these cases, though there were some genuine possessions.

Genuine demonic possession, from a Christian perspective, still exists today. It is rare relative to other forms of demonic interference; however, both religious and lay authorities on the subject say it is on the increase. In the field of lay paranormal investigation, media attention on the demonic has prompted individuals to call themselves "demonologists" and offer their services, sometimes for a fee. Few of them are demonologists in the truest sense of the word. Regardless of religious perspective, becoming a spiritual warrior against evil is a calling, not a profession, occupation, or job description. Real exorcists and deliverance ministers know that battling evil on its own turf is perilous and rarely glamorous.

Outside religion, demons play roles in occultism and magic. They are one of numerous types of entities with whom adepts can traffic. They are conjured, controlled, and assigned tasks. In magical lore, some demons have good dispositions and some do not. They offer humans gifts of wealth, knowledge, power, and pleasure—but always at a price. The greatest price is one's soul.

The Encyclopedia of Demons and Demonology is intended to open further avenues of inquiry on the subject of the dark side. In many respects, it is far more important to be informed about demons than it is about angels. The demonic are masters of deceit and disguise. If you know little or nothing about them, how will you recognize them?

—Rosemary Ellen Guiley

Entries A–Z

Abaddon (Apollyon)   Angel of death, destruction, and the netherworld. The name Abaddon is derived from the Hebrew term for "to destroy" and means "place of destruction." Apollyon is the Greek name.

In MAGIC Abaddon is often equated with SATAN and SAMAEL. His name is evoked in conjuring spells for malicious deeds. Abaddon is the prince who rules the seventh hierarchy of DEMONs, the ERINYES, or Furies, who govern powers of evil, discord, war, and devastation.

Originally, Abaddon was a place and not an angel or being. In rabbinic writings and the Old Testament, Abaddon is primarily a place of destruction and a name for one of the regions of Gehenna (see HELL). The term occurs six times in the Old Testament. In Proverbs 15:11 and 27:20, it is named with Sheol as a region of the underworld. In Psalm 88:11, Abaddon is associated with the grave and the underworld.

In Job 26:6, Abaddon is associated with Sheol. Later, Job 28:22 names Abaddon and Death together, implying personified beings.

In REVELATION 9:10, Abaddon is personified as the king of the abyss, the bottomless pit of hell. Revelation also cites the Greek version of the name, Apollyon, probably a reference to Apollo, Greek god of pestilence and destruction.

FURTHER READING:
van der Toorn, Karel, Bob Becking, and Pieter W. van der Horst, eds. *Dictionary of Deities and Demons in the Bible.* 2nd ed. Grand Rapids, Mich.: William B. Eerdmans, 1999.

Abel de Larue (d. 1582)   French sorcerer believed to be under the influence of a DEMON in the form of a black dog. Living in Coulommiers, France, he was also known as "The Smasher."

Apollyon, from Francis Barrett's The Magus *(AUTHOR'S COLLECTION)*

Abel was placed in a Franciscan monastery by his mother. He became enraged at the instructor of novices for beating him, and he plotted revenge. At his trial, Abel confessed that a black spaniel appeared to him and promised to help him and always go to his aid if he would surrender himself to the dog.

In 1582, Abel was arrested on charges of sorcery and spell casting, which he admitted. The demon never made good on his promise of rescue. Abel was found guilty and sentenced to be hanged and garroted and his body burned. He was executed on July 20, 1582.

FURTHER READING:
Plancy, Collin de. *Dictionary of Witchcraft*. Edited and translated by Wade Baskin. Originally published as *Dictionary of Demonology*. New York: Philosophical Library, 1965.

Abezethibou   One-winged DEMON who lives in the Red Sea, plots against every wind under the heavens, and is the enemy of Moses.

In the Testament of Solomon, Abezethibou states that he once sat in the first heaven, named Amelouth. He was present when Moses was taken before the pharaoh of Egypt and was summoned to the aid of the Egyptian magicians when they sought to discredit Moses. Abezethibou takes credit for turning the pharaoh against Egypt and for inciting the Egyptians to pursue the Israelites in their exodus. When the parted Red Sea falls in on the Egyptians, Abezethibou is trapped with the pillar of air, until the demon EPHIPPAS arrives to take him to King SOLOMON. Solomon binds Abezethibou and Ephippas to the pillar (perhaps a reference to the Milky Way) and commands that they hold it up in the air until the end of time.

FURTHER READING:
The Old Testament Pseudepigrapha. Vols. 1 & 2. Edited by James H. Charlesworth. 1983. Reprint, New York: Doubleday, 1985.

Abigor   DEMON who is a grand duke in HELL. Abigor appears as a handsome man on a horse, holding a standard or scepter. He knows all the secrets of war and sees the future. He teaches leaders how to win the loyalty of soldiers. In hell, he commands 60 LEGIONs of demons.

Abraxas (Abrasax, Abraxis)   Gnostic name for the demigod who rules the 365th (highest and final) aeon, or sphere, ascending to the unknowable God. Christian demonologists put Abraxas in the ranks of DEMONs.

Abraxas also was the name of a sun mounting an ouroborus (a snake biting its tail) held by the highest Egyptian goddess, Isis, the creator of the Sun and mistress of all the gods. Isis mythology found its way into Gnosticism. In addition, Abraxas was associated with the Mithraic mystery religion of Persian origin, the chief rival of Christianity in Rome in its first 400 years. As did Gnosticism, Mithraism featured a complex astrology and numerology. Numerical values of Mithra's and Abraxas' names each total 365.

The Gnostic Abraxas created the material world and also had demonic qualities. He is the supreme power of being, in whom light and darkness are both united and transcended. Orthodox Christians viewed Abraxas as a demon. In turn, Abraxas became a favorite deity of heretical sects of the Middle Ages.

Gnostic talismans made of carved opal show Abraxas as a figure with a human body, the head of a rooster (or occasionally a hawk), and SERPENT legs. His hands hold a shield and a whip, the shield usually inscribed with the name Iao, reminiscent of the Jewish four-letter name of God. He is often mounted on a chariot drawn by four white horses, with both Sun and Moon overhead.

The rooster represents wakefulness and is related to the human heart and the universal heart, the Sun. The human torso embodies the principle of logos, or articulated thought. The snake legs indicate prudence. The shield is symbolic of wisdom, the great protector of divine warriors. The whip denotes the relentless driving power of life. The four horses symbolize the four ethers by which solar power is circulated throughout the universe.

The seven letters of the name of Abraxas represent the seven creative powers and planetary spheres, or ANGELs, recognized in the ancient world. The letters add up to a numerological value of 365, the number of days and powers of the year.

Abigor (DICTIONNAIRE INFERNAL)

Abraxas (DICTIONNAIRE INFERNAL)

Carl G. Jung called Abraxas the "truly terrible one" because of his ability to generate truth and falsehood, good and evil, light and darkness with the same word and in the same deed. In Jungian psychology there is no easy way out of psychic conflict; one must not only fight on the side of the angels but occasionally join the host of the FALLEN ANGELS. According to Jung, fear of Abraxas is the beginning of wisdom, and liberation, or gnosis, is achieved by not resisting.

FURTHER READING:
Hoeller, Stephan A. *The Gnostic Jung and the Seven Sermons to the Dead.* Wheaton, Ill.: Quest Books, 1982.
Hyatt, Victoria, and Joseph W. Charles. *The Book of Demons.* New York: Simon & Schuster, 1974.
The Old Testament Pseudepigrapha. Vols. 1 & 2. Edited by James H. Charlesworth. 1983. Reprint, New York: Doubleday, 1985.

Acaph   See LOUDUN POSSESSIONS.

Achaos   See LOUDUN POSSESSIONS.

Adramelech (Adramalek)   A chieftain of HELL. Adramalech is of uncertain origin. Possibly he was derived from a Samarian Sun god worshipped by the Sepharvites, who burned children as a sacrificial offering to him.

Adramalech is the grand chancellor of DEMONS, president of the DEVIL's general council, and governor of the Devil's wardrobe. Adramelech himself is often portrayed as a peacock (see IBLIS) or as a mule.

He is the eighth of the 10 evil demons of the *sephirot* of the Tree of Life (see KABBALAH). He works under the command of SAMAEL.

FURTHER READING:
Hyatt, Victoria, and Joseph W. Charles. *The Book of Demons.* New York: Simon & Schuster, 1974.

aerial spirits of Solomon   DEMONs associated with the four elements who were commanded by the legendary King SOLOMON. The aerial spirits are both good and evil. They can show anything in the world that is hidden and can fetch, carry, and do anything contained in the four elements of earth, air, water, and fire. They can discover the secrets of anyone, including kings.

The aerial spirits are governed by 31 princes who are aligned to points on a compass. They can be summoned by directing one's self to their compass position. The princes have dukes and myriad ministering spirits or demons under their command. The princes cannot be summoned by magic unless the magician wears their special SEALs as a lamen, or pendant, upon the chest. The conjurations of the aerial spirits are given in a grimoire, the *Lemegeton,* also known as *The Lesser Key of Solomon.*

See SPIRITS OF SOLOMON.

Aeshma   In ZOROASTRIANISM, the DEMON of wrath, rage, and fury. Aeshma's epithet is "of the bloody mace." He is the fiercest of demons and is responsible for all acts of

Adramelech (DICTIONNAIRE INFERNAL)

aggression and malice, whether committed in war or drunkenness. He has seven powers that he can use for the destruction of humanity.

In the hierarchy of Zoroastrian DAEVAS that mirrors a similar hierarchy of divinities, Aeshma is opposed to Asha Vahishta, the Amesha Spenta, or good spirit, who embodies Truth. Aeshma's chief adversary is Sraosha (Obedience), the principle of religious devotion and discipline. Aeshma distracts people from proper worship. He interferes with the souls of the dead as they approach the Chinvat Bridge to the underworld.

The creator God, Ahura Mazda (later Ohrmazd), created Sraosha to counter Aeshma's mischief and protect people from his attacks. Sraosha ultimately will overthrow Aeshma. In medieval texts, Aeshma is made a commander of dark forces by Angra Mainyu (later AHRIMAN). He is swallowed by AZ, the demon of avarice.

Aeshma can be driven away by the recitation of a prayer from the *Vendidad,* a Zoroastrian text. The demon ASMODEUS of Hebrew lore may be based in part on Aeshma.

Agares FALLEN ANGEL and the second of the 72 SPIRITS OF SOLOMON. Prior to his fall, Agares was a member of the angelic order of Virtues. In HELL he is the first duke of the power of the east and rules 31 LEGIONS of DEMONS. He appears as a handsome man riding a crocodile and carrying a goshawk on his fist. He makes those who run stand still, and he can retrieve runaways. He teaches all languages, causes earthquakes, and destroys spiritual dignities.

Agrath In Jewish demonology, a powerful female DEMON. Agrath (beating) and her mother, MAKHLATH,

Agares (DICTIONNAIRE INFERNAL)

are in constant struggle against LILITH. Agrath commands 18 myriads (LEGIONS) of evil spirits and rides in a big chariot. She is most powerful on the nights of Wednesday and Saturday, when she and her mother devour victims, especially people who are out alone.

Ahriman In ZOROASTRIANISM, the DEMON of all demons and the source of all evil. Ahriman originally was a primordial desert spirit who became the personification of evil in Zoroastrianism. As such, he is not immortal, and eventually his reign of terror will be conquered by the forces of good.

There are different legends about the origins of Ahriman as the evil god. In one, Ahura Mazda, the good god, created the universe and twins called Spenta Mainyu (the spirit of Light, Truth, and Life) and Angra Mainyu (the spirit of Darkness, Deceit and Death). The twins fight for supremacy and their battleground is Earth. Over time, Spenta Mainyu became absorbed into Ahura Mazda, and Angra Mainyu became Ahriman.

The battle between the two forces continues and will last for thousands of years, divided into eras. After the fourth era, three saviors will appear, who will destroy Ahriman and all his forces of evil.

In a variation of this legend Ahura Mazda created Angra Mainyu in a moment of doubt when he was making the universe.

According to another legend, Ahriman and Ormazd (a contraction of *Ahura Mazda*) were twins born to Zuvan, the creator deity. Zurvan declared that the firstborn would be supreme ruler. Ahriman ripped himself out of the womb in order to be first. Zurvan was bound by his promise, but he limited the time that Ahriman could rule. At the end of that, Ormazd would take over and reign in goodness and light. The Earth is presently under the rule of Ahriman; that is why there are drought, famine, war, disease, pestilence, and other ills. To aid him in his rule, Ahriman created 99,999 diseases, and six archdemons, called Evil Mind, Tyranny, Enmity, Violence, Wrath, and Falsehood. He also created a female demon named AZ and a dragon. The archdemons struggle against the six archangel *amarahspands,* or "Bounteous Immortals."

Ahriman tried to maim the prophet Zarathustra but failed.

A legend about Ahriman says that he had a son named Zohak, whom he trained to be evil. He told Zohak to kill his own father. He disguised himself, however, and Zohak killed someone he thought was his father. Ahriman, again in disguise, became chef of the palace. Zohak was so impressed with him that he offered to reward him. Ahriman asked only to kiss his shoulders. When he did so, SERPENTS sprang from the spots. Every time Zohak cut them off, they grew back. Ahriman entered in another disguise, as a doctor, and told Zohak that he had to feed the serpents human brains every day. Zohak complied and became Ahriman's pride. The son ruled for a thousand years and finally was destroyed.

RUDOLF STEINER, the founder of anthroposophy, said Ahrimanic forces are intelligent, clever spirits that seek to keep people mired in materialism.

FURTHER READING:
Hyatt, Victoria, and Joseph W. Charles. *The Book of Demons.* New York: Simon & Schuster, 1974.
Mack, Carol K., and Dinah Mack. *A Field Guide to Demons: Fairies, Fallen Angels, and Other Subversive Spirits.* New York: Owl Books/Henry Holt, 1998.

Aim (Aini)   FALLEN ANGEL and 23rd of the 72 SPIRITS OF SOLOMON. In HELL Aim is a strong duke. He appears as a handsome man with three heads: a SERPENT, a man with two stars on his forehead, and a cat. He rides on a viper and carries a blazing firebrand, with which he spreads much destruction and fire. He imparts cunning and gives true answers to questions about "private matters." He governs 26 LEGIONS of DEMONS.

Aiwass   See CROWLEY, ALEISTER.

Aix-en-Provence Possessions (1609–1611)   Sensational case of possessed Ursuline nuns, alleged immoral sex, and a PACT with the DEVIL, which led to the torture and execution of a priest. The Aix-en-Provence case is one of the first in France to produce a conviction based on the testimony of a DEMONIAC. Prior to the 17th century in France, accusations from a demoniac were considered unreliable, since most clerics believed that any words spoken by one possessed by the Devil were utterances from "the father of lies" (John 8:44) and would not stand up to accepted rules of evidence. As with the LOUDUN POSSESSIONS, sexual themes dominated the manifestations of the nuns' POSSESSION.

The central figure—and perpetrator—of the case was Sister Madeleine de Demandolx de la Palud, a high-strung, vain girl from a wealthy and aristocratic Provençal family. Deeply religious from childhood, she was sent in 1605, at age 12, to the new Ursuline convent in Aix-en-Provence. There she was one of only six nuns, all of them from wealthy families. Their spiritual director was Father Jean-Baptiste Romillon.

After about two years, Madeleine became severely depressed and was sent home. There she was visited by a family friend who sought to help her, Father Louis Gaufridi, a handsome priest 20 years her senior. Gaufridi had a much lower class background but was popular among the wealthy. He was personable and entertaining, and his good looks appealed to women.

Thus it was no surprise that 14-year-old Madeleine fell violently in love with him. He visited often, and gossip flew when he once spent an hour and a half with her without her family present. Warnings about this inappropriate behavior were issued to Gaufridi and to Madeleine's mother by the head of the Ursuline convent in Marseilles, Mother Catherine de Gaumer. Still, in 17th-century France, loose behavior by clergy was tolerated, unless WITCHCRAFT was suspected.

In 1607, Madeleine went to the convent in Marseille as a novice. She confessed to Mother Catherine that she had been intimate with Gaufridi. Mother Catherine sent her back to Aix-en-Provence, which was more remote, and where Gaufridi could not visit her.

Nothing happened for nearly two years, and then Madeleine began suffering convulsions, shaking fits, and visions of DEMONS. Before Christmas 1609, she smashed a crucifix during confession. Father Romillon tried to exorcise Madeleine, without success. Meanwhile, her possession infected three other nuns, who began having the same symptoms and lost their speech.

By Easter 1610, the nuns were still afflicted. Father Romillon confronted Gaufridi in June about his affair with Madeleine, which the priest denied. Madeleine, however, had become quite vocal about their indiscretions during her fits. She accused Gaufridi of denying God, giving her a green devil for a FAMILIAR, and having sex with her since she had been 13 (later, she said she was nine when they began their affair). She claimed he gave her a special powder to drink that would cause any babies she bore not to look like him, so he would not fall under suspicion.

Romillon conducted secret EXORCISMS on Madeleine. Five more nuns became infected. One of them, Louise Capeau, became her rival in performance. Exasperated, Romillon took the two young women to see the grand inquisitor in Avignon, Sebastian Michaelis, a man who had gotten on in years but was quite feared: He had sent 18 witches to their death at the stake in Avignon. He was a most determined inquisitor.

Michaelis' approach was a public exorcism of the nuns at the shrine of St. Mary Magdalene in the grotto at Ste-Baume. It failed.

Madeleine and Louise were then sent to another EXORCIST, François Domptius, a Flemish Dominican priest at the Royal Convent of St. Maximin. Louise stole center stage. Three demons who possessed her, Verin, Gresil, and Sonnillon, spoke through her in a deep bass voice. They taunted Madeleine with possession by BEELZEBUB, LEVIATHAN, BAALBERITH, ASMODEUS, and ASTAROTH—all important in HELL—plus 6,661 other demons, for a grand total of 6,666. In response, Madeleine screamed obscenities. The witnesses, including the exorcists, were convinced beyond doubt that the women were genuinely possessed.

On December 15, Verin, speaking again through Louise, identified Gaufridi as the cause of Madeleine's possession. Michaelis sent for Gaufridi, intending that he perform an exorcism, but without explanation to the priest. Gaufridi had no knowledge of exorcisms, and the two nuns mocked him, calling him a magician. He retorted, "If I were a witch, I would certainly give my soul to a thousand devils!"

Michaelis pounced on this and had Gaufridi arrested and jailed in the grotto. While he languished in jail, his quarters were searched for evidence of witchcraft, but nothing was found. Madeleine, not to be outdone by Louise, expanded on her accusations, saying the priest did not pray with a "clean heart" and accusing him of every obscene act possible.

Even so, without hard evidence, there were no grounds to continue to hold Gaufridi. His many friends went to his defense. Michaelis reluctantly freed him, and he returned to his parish in a rage. He undertook a campaign to clear his name, appealing even to the pope. He also sought to suppress the Ursuline convents and jail the offending nuns. Michaelis continued to look for ways to convict him on charges of sorcery.

Michaelis confined Madeleine to the Ste-Baume convent. Her behavior worsened; she may have become manic-depressive. She danced, laughed, had visions, vomited froth, neighed like a horse, sang love songs, disrupted services, and told wild stories of SABBATs at which sodomy was performed and participants ate babies. Beelzebub made her bones crack and disrupted her bowels. After these manic episodes, she would fall into lethargy or a deathlike sleep.

Michaelis at last was able to pressure the Parliament of Aix to bring Gaufridi to trial in civil court in February 1611. Madeleine and Louise were the star witnesses against the priest, recounting in graphic detail their possessions and going into fits before the court. Madeleine alternated this daily display with assertions that she was making everything up. She claimed great love for Gaufridi and actually writhed on the floor imitating the sexual acts they had done. Physicians examined her and agreed she was not a virgin. She displayed the DEVIL'S MARKs on the bottom of her feet and under her left breast. When pricked with a pin, the marks did not bleed or cause her pain. The marks mysteriously disappeared and reappeared repeatedly. Twice she attempted suicide in bouts of deep depression.

While he awaited his turn in court, Gaufridi was kept in heavy chains in a rat-infested dungeon. He was taken before the court in March, weak and dispirited. His body was shaved, and three Devil's marks were found.

At last, the priest surrendered to relentless prosecution and confessed to being "Prince of the Synagogue" and to signing a pact with the Devil in his own BLOOD in exchange for the promise that all women would follow him. He described sabbats, though not as luridly as had Madeleine.

Michaelis was ecstatic at Gaufridi's breakdown and wrote a phony confession of 52 points. Gaufridi rejected it, saying he had been forced under torture to confess. On April 18, 1611, the court found him guilty of sorcery, magic, idolatry, and fornication. He was sentenced to be burned on a pile of bushes, a slower way to die by fire than by being burned on a pile of faggots.

Still, the court was not done with the priest, continuing a relentless interrogation to obtain names of accomplices. Gaufridi became deranged, still denying intimacy with Madeleine but confessing to more sensational crimes. His last appearance before the court was on April 28, at which he said the truth no longer mattered, and he had eaten roasted babies.

Gaufridi was executed on April 30. First, he was subjected to horrible torture. He was defrocked and degraded and subjected three times to the strappado, in which he was strung up on a rope with his hands bound behind his back and dropped, so that his bones were severely and painfully dislocated. Then, he was subjected four times to the squassation, in which heavy weights were attached to his feet, and he was hoisted on a rope and dropped sharply to within inches of the floor. But Gaufridi had no names of fellow witches or sorcerers to give.

He was then forced to ask God for forgiveness and was bound to a wooden sled and dragged through the streets of Aix for five hours. Fortunately for Gaufridi, the bishop of Marseilles had granted him a special dispensation, and he was strangled to death before his body was put on the burning bushes. It was a significant mercy.

As soon as he was executed, Madeleine was "cured." But the Aix-en-Provence affair was not over by any means. Louise continued to have visions of witches, which led to a blind girl's being accused and convicted of witchcraft and burned at the stake on July 19, 1611. The possession infection spread to two other convents, St. Claire's in Aix and, two years later, St. Bridget's in Lille. There, three nuns accused Sister Marie de Sains of bewitching them. Most notable about Sister Marie's testimony, in many ways a copy of Madeleine's performance, was her detailed description of the witches' sabbat: On Mondays and Tuesdays, the witches copulated with devils and each other in a natural fashion; they practiced sodomy on Thursdays and bestiality on Saturdays and sang litanies to the Devil on Wednesdays and Fridays. Sunday, apparently, was their day off. Marie was put away out of sight by the archbishop of Malines, and the Lille possessions died down.

Madeleine's troubles recurred later in life. In 1642, at age 49, she was accused of witchcraft. Her relatives abandoned her, and she was forced to prepare her own defense, with inherited money. She was accused again in 1652, and many witnesses testified against her. Devil's marks were found on her. She was sentenced to pay a large fine and spend the rest of her life in prison. After 10 years, she was released to a relative in Chateauvieux, where she died at age 77 on December 20, 1670.

FURTHER READING:
Baroja, Julio Caro. *The World of the Witches*. Chicago: University of Chicago Press, 1975.

algul   Arabian vampire night DJINN. *Algul* means "horse leech." The algul lives in cemeteries and takes the form of a woman in order to gain the trust of untended children. Although this type of evil djinn lives in cemeteries, it prefers fresh BLOOD. It enters homes to prey upon sleeping children, taking their blood and their breath. It lures untended children into dark places in order to vampirize them. When fresh blood is not available, it drinks the blood of dead infants in cemeteries.

See LILITH.

ACT

Alloces (Allocen, Allocer) FALLEN ANGEL and 52nd of the 72 SPIRITS OF SOLOMON. A duke in HELL, Allocen appears as a soldier who rides a large horse. His lion face is red with flaming eyes, and he speaks in a loud and hoarse voice. He teaches astronomy and the liberal sciences and gives beneficial FAMILIARS. He rules over 36 LEGIONS of DEMONS.

alp In German lore, a vampiric, shape-shifting spirit associated with nightmare DEMONS, the BOGEY, and the sexual predator demons, the SUCCUBUS and INCUBUS. The alp can be either a demon or a malevolent ghost of a dead person. In folklore, children are doomed to become alps if their mothers use horse collars to ease childbirth.

The alp can assume different forms, from seductive humans to animals, such as cats, pigs, birds, and lecherous dogs. It may be disguised as a butterfly released by the breath of the *horerczy,* another vampiric demon.

Regardless of its form, the alp likes to wear a magical hat, which confers upon it invisibility and supernatural power, including the EVIL EYE.

The alp has an odd way of sexually molesting men and women: It enters through the victim's mouth as a mist or a SERPENT. It drinks BLOOD through the nipples of both men and women and consumes the milk of women and cows. It sucks the life breath from victims.

Folklore holds that women can prevent the alp from bothering them at night by sleeping with their shoes at the side of the bed and pointing toward the door.

Amduscias FALLEN ANGEL and 67th of the 72 SPIRITS OF SOLOMON. Amduscias is a great duke of HELL who rules over 29 LEGIONS of DEMONS. He appears first as a unicorn. He will take on human shape if commanded to do so, but this will cause musical instruments to be heard but not seen. Trees sway at the sound of his voice, and he gives people the power to make trees fall and also gives excellent FAMILIARS.

Amenadiel DEMON among the 31 AERIAL SPIRITS OF SOLOMON. Amenadiel is the great emperor of the west and governs 300 great dukes, 500 lesser dukes, and 400,000,300,000,100,000 ministering spirits. Amenadiel's chief dukes are Vadros, Campiel, Luziel, Musiriel, Rapsiel, Lamael, Zoeniel, Curifas, Almesiel, Codriel, Balsur, and Nadroc. Each duke has 3,880 servants. Amenadiel can be conjured anytime day or night, but his dukes will only appear at certain hours.

Amityville Haunting House in Amityville, Long Island, New York, where a family experienced horrifying phenomena in the 1970s. The Amityville Horror® was deemed demonic by ED AND LORRAINE WARREN. The case remains one of the most controversial on modern records and has been the subject of numerous investigations, claims and counterclaims, lawsuits, books and films, intense publicity, and attempts to debunk it.

The haunting phenomena of the house at 112 Ocean Street are believed to be related to a grisly multiple murder on November 13, 1974. Six members of the DeFeo family—parents, two sons, and two daughters—were found shot to death with a .35-caliber rifle. Their estimated time of death was 3:00 A.M. A third son, 23-year-old Ronald "Butch" DeFeo, was charged with the murders. DeFeo pled insanity, based on his history of drug abuse, but he was convicted of six counts of second-degree murder and sentenced to 25 years to life in prison.

The house was empty until December 1975, when it was purchased by newlyweds, George and Kathy Lutz. They were informed of the murders but bought the house anyway. They moved in on December 18, with Kathy's three children by a previous marriage: Daniel, nine; Christopher, seven; and Melissa, five.

According to the Lutzes, they immediately experienced horrible phenomena. Voices told them to "get out"; there were swarms of flies in the cold of winter; Kathy had nightmares about the murders; the apparition of a "demon boy" who could shape-shift into a demonic pig was seen; green slime oozed from walls; a crucifix hanging on a wall was turned upside down; Kathy's face transfigured before George into a horrid hag; mysterious noises sounded in the middle of the night; the apparition of a little girl became Melissa's playmate; unseen presences embraced Kathy; cloven hoofprints appeared in the snow outside the house; locks and doors were damaged; and so on. Their behavior and mood deteriorated. The children could not attend school, and George was unable to work.

The Lutzes tried to bless the house with prayer themselves, but their efforts had no effect. Finally, they were subjected to events that terrified them so badly, they knew they had to get out. The Lutzes never disclosed all that happened on their last terror-filled night, but among the phenomena were bangings and a hooded apparition that appeared on the stairs and pointed at George. They left the house in a rush on January 14, 1976, and went to the home of Kathy's mother, in Deer Park, New York. They left most of their belongings behind and sent a mover to collect them later.

In late February, Ed and Lorraine Warren were contacted by a New York City television producer, who asked them to check the house and story. Parapsychologists and psychical researchers had gone to the house, but what happened there remained a mystery. The producer asked the Warrens to hold a séance at the house.

The Warrens visited the Lutzes where they were staying and obtained keys. The Lutzes refused to reenter the house but asked the Warrens to find and take the deed to them.

On their walk-through, the Warrens found a house evacuated in a hurry. A gingerbread house from Christmas still sat on the dining room table. Laundry was folded, and the freezer was stocked with food. Clothing, jewelry, family photos, and other personal belongings were left in place.

The Warrens conducted a séance and then returned at a later time to conduct a nighttime séance for television. In attendance were 17 people, including two trance mediums, Alberta Riley and Mary Pascarella. Prior to the start of the séance, Ed used religious provocation to test for the presence of DEMONS. Approximately half the persons present were physically assaulted. Ed suffered from intense heart palpitations, which affected him for three weeks.

After returning home to Connecticut, the Warrens said they were assaulted by a demonic force at about 3:00 A.M. Details of the attack were published in their autobiography, *The Demonologist* (1980).

The malevolent presence first assaulted Ed, who was working alone in his office in a cottage attached to the main house. He heard the door open and three footsteps sound. At first, he thought it was Lorraine giving him coffee. Then a howling wind started, building in intensity. The desk lamp dimmed and the temperature in the room plummeted. A smell of sulfur manifested.

Ed armed himself with a vial of holy water and a crucifix and found himself confronted by a triangular, swirling black mass, broad at the top and pointed at the bottom. The mass grew denser, transforming itself into a horrible, hooded figure that moved aggressively toward him. Ed threw the holy water at it and held up the crucifix, commanding it to leave in the name of JESUS Christ. The demon backed off but transmitted an image to Ed of him and Lorraine involved in a deadly automobile accident. It departed.

The demon then visited Lorraine, who was reading in bed with their two dogs present. A loud pounding sounded and the temperature in the room dropped. The sound of wind rose up the stairs. The demon entered the room, and Lorraine was paralyzed, unable to react or scream. She felt herself being drawn into the black mass. She was able to break the paralysis and called out to God for protection. She made the sign of the cross in the air; that stopped the mass from advancing, but it did not depart the home. Ed ran in, and the mass left, going into the next room and up the chimney.

The demonic encounter was not the first that the Warrens said they experienced while pursuing their investigations of places such as the Amityville house. The Warrens determined that the events at Amityville were demonic phenomena, which the Lutzes, who knew nothing of demonology, could not have fabricated. The Warrens took numerous photographs, including one purporting to show the face of the demon boy peering out from a bedroom.

The Lutzes wondered whether something wrong about the house itself might have influenced DeFeo to commit the murders. They moved to San Diego, California, where they struck a deal with the author Jay Anson to write a book. *The Amityville Horror* was published in 1977 and was adapted to film in 1979. Anson never visited the house but wrote the book from taped interviews. It contained numerous errors and embellishments but became a media sensation.

Skeptics used the errors as a way to try to debunk the case. There was no snow in Amityville on the day that the cloven hoofprints were supposed to have been seen. Native Americans refuted Anson's assertion that part of the problem was due to the house's location on a place where Shinnecock Indians had once abandoned mentally ill and dying people. Father Pecoraro said he did not go to the house to bless it (Lutz always asserted that he did). Many more points of controversy surfaced. Even the Warrens and George Lutz acknowledged that Anson's book was not entirely accurate but attributed it to Anson's lack of familiarity with demonology and not any deliberate acts by George Lutz. For years, the case was repeatedly debunked, validated, debunked, and validated.

In 1977, the Lutzes filed a lawsuit against William Weber, DeFeo's attorney, and Paul Hoffman, a writer working on the story; Bernard Burton and Frederick Mars, two clairvoyants who had been to the house; and *Good Housekeeping,* the *New York Sunday News,* and the Hearst Corporation, which had published articles on the haunting. The Lutzes sought $5.4 million in damages for invasion of privacy, misappropriation of names for trade purposes, and mental distress. Weber, Hoffman, and Burton countersued for $2 million, alleging fraud and breach of contract. The Lutzes' claims against the news organizations were dropped.

The Lutzes' case went to trial in district court in Brooklyn, New York, in 1979. The judge dismissed their suit, saying that from testimony, "it appears to me that to a large extent the book is a work of fiction, relying in a large part upon the suggestions of Mr. Weber."

The couple who purchased the house from the Lutzes said nothing unusual happened to them. However, they were so annoyed by the publicity and steady stream of curiosity seekers that they sued Anson, the Lutzes, and the publisher Prentice Hall for $1.1 million. They received a settlement for an unspecified lesser amount. Father Pecoraro, who was consulted by the Lutzes for help, sued the Lutzes and Prentice Hall for invasion of privacy and distortion of his involvement in the case. He received an out-of-court settlement.

The Lutzes stuck to their story for the rest of their lives. They divorced in the 1980s. Kathy died of emphysema on August 17, 2004. George, who had moved to Las Vegas, died on May 8, 2006, of heart disease. Anson died of a heart attack in 1980. Father Pecoraro is no longer living.

The Amityville case has gone on to become a mini-industry, spawning books, films, articles, and Web sites, and endless debates. Books by John G. Jones, *Amityville II* and *Amityville: The Final Chapter,* changed the names of the principles and added other details. Additional films are *Amityville II: The Possession* (1982), *Amityville 3D* (1983), *Amityville 4: The Evil Escapes* (1989, made for television), *The Amityville Curse* (1990), *Amityville 1992: It's About Time* (1992), *Amityville: A New Generation* (1993),

Amityville Dollhouse: Evil Never Dies (1996), and a remake of the original *The Amityville Horror* (2005).

FURTHER READING:
Anson, Jay. *The Amityville Horror.* New York: Prentice Hall, 1977.
Auerbach, Loyd. *ESP, Hauntings and Poltergeists.* New York: Warner Books, 1986.
Brittle, Gerald Daniel. *The Demonologist: The Extraordinary Career of Ed and Lorraine Warren.* Englewood Cliffs, N.J.: Prentice Hall, 1980.
"The Warrens Investigate: The Amityville Horror." Available online. URL: http://www.warrens.net/amityvill.htm. Downloaded November 1, 2006.
Yancey, Tim. "The Amityville Horror: Interview with George Lutz." Available online. URL: http://www.amityvillehorrortruth.com/articles/lutzinterview1.html. Downloaded November 1, 2006.

Amon   FALLEN ANGEL and the seventh of the 72 SPIRITS OF SOLOMON. In HELL, Amon is a strong and powerful marquis. He appears first as a wolf, but on a magician's command, he will take on the shape of a man with a raven's head and dog's teeth. He accurately tells about the past and the future. He makes men and women fall in love with each other, and he settles disputes between friends and enemies. He rules over 40 LEGIONS of DEMONS.

Amorth, Father Gabriele (1925–)   EXORCIST of Vatican City in the Archdiocese of Rome. Dedicated to the abolition of satanic evil, Father Gabriele Amorth has per-

Amon (DICTIONNAIRE INFERNAL)

sonally handled more than 30,000 exorcisms around the world.

Amorth believes that many modern-day pastimes and games—such as conjuring, playing with MAGIC (not illusion), conversing with a OUIJA™, listening to rock music, and having contact with satanic ritual and content—open the door for demonic POSSESSION. He says there are too few priests who believe in casting out devils (although JESUS bequeaths that ability to the apostles in his name: Mark 3:5, 10:8), much less have any training in the rites of EXORCISM.

Amorth was born in Modena, Italy, on May 1, 1925. He received the faculty of exorcist by Cardinal Ugo Poletti, the pope's vicar for the Diocese of Rome, in 1986, studying under Father Candido Amantini, a Passionist priest, who served as chief exorcist for 36 years. When Father Amantini passed away on his saint's day, September 22, 1992, at age 78, Father Amorth succeeded him.

One reporter described Amorth as more like the genial Uncle Fester on *The Addams Family* than the stern priest depicted by Max von Sydow in the film *THE EXORCIST* (Amorth's favorite movie). Amorth's eyes are intense and piercing, encircled by dark rings. Their unwavering gaze appears more than capable of staring down DEMONS. He dresses in black. Amorth works tirelessly at his calling, keeping a full calendar of appointments, reading, lecturing, writing, and, most importantly, ridding sufferers of the evils he sees all around him.

He is most concerned about the rise he perceives in satanic activity through the practice of WITCHCRAFT, participation in satanic groups or rituals, conjuring, attempting to commune with the dead, fortune telling and card reading, listening to rock music with satanic lyrics and a hypnotic rhythm, and dabbling in magic. He has warned against the popularity of the author J. K. Rowling's popular Harry Potter novels, claiming in an interview for a Catholic news source that behind the boy wizard "lies the signature of the king of darkness." He tried unsuccessfully to have the Potter books banned from Italy, claiming that they teach sorcery to children.

Demonic possession can happen in one of four ways, according to Amorth: through a curse by another, by continuing a life of sin, by practicing occultism, and as a test of the victim's faith, most usually the trials endured by the saints that prove their holiness. The possessed person invites SATAN into his or her life by choosing the paths of sin and occultism; the other two ways are foisted upon the unwary.

When a victim of the Devil petitions Amorth for spiritual cleansing, the priest does not wait for proof of demonic presence, as many of his fellow exorcists do, but immediately begins prayers of deliverance and liberation—a small exorcism—even over the telephone or by e-mail. He sees his first efforts as a research tool in themselves, for if the prayers have any impact at all on the victim, then inhuman entities are at work. Early in his career, he despaired of how few exorcists were available, but Amorth is encouraged that the number of practicing exorcists in Italy alone has grown 10-fold to more than 300.

He is involved in the training of those exorcists, especially regarding the changes in the RITUALE ROMANUM, the liturgy of prayers and exhortations in the name of Jesus Christ used to exorcise demons and devils. During the Second Vatican Council under Pope John XXIII, the *Rituale* was scheduled for revision, yet many years passed before Father Amorth and his colleagues saw any of the changes. Others worked on the New Ritual, as it is called, ignoring the input of those who depended on it.

In 2000, Father Amorth outlined his objections to the revised rite. He was especially scornful of strictures on using the New Ritual against evil spells and CURSES—in reality, forbidding its use in such circumstances—and the commands that exorcism not be used unless demonic activity can be absolutely certified. As noted, Father Amorth uses small exorcisms to prove the presence of inhuman spirits and believes this approach to be valuable in terms of diagnosing whether genuine possession has occurred. Most people who think they are demonically possessed are not, he says, and need medical treatment, not exorcism. Amorth and his colleagues submitted carefully worded amendments to the New Ritual, to no avail.

According to Father Amorth, the church hierarchy regards the exorcists as fanatic "demonologues," and it even exhibits hostility toward them and their work. Most insulting to Father Amorth was the refusal by church officials to allow 150 members of the INTERNATIONAL ASSOCIATION OF EXORCISTS, an organization founded by Amorth and representing exorcist priests internationally, to join in a public audience with Pope John Paul II in St. Peter's Square. At the time of the interview, Amorth revealed that entire episcopates refused to acknowledge the need for exorcists, including the countries of Spain, Portugal, Switzerland, and Germany. German bishops went so far as to inform Cardinal Ratzinger, now Pope Benedict XVI, that revisions of the Roman Rite were unnecessary since they would never use it, anyway.

Father Amorth asserted that the church's refusal to acknowledge demonic activity could mean that the Evil One has infiltrated even the innermost circles of the Vatican. He remains steadfast in his faith, noting that while Satan may win battles, the Holy Spirit will win the war.

Father Amorth has written four books: *An Exorcist Tells His Story* (1999), *Gospel of Mary: A Month with the Mother of God* (2000), *An Exorcist: More Stories* (2002), and *Pater Pio: Lebensgeschichte eines Heiligen,* a German biography of Padre Pio published in 2003.

FURTHER READING:

Amorth, Gabriele. *An Exorcist: More Stories.* San Francisco: Ignatius Press, 2002.

———. *An Exorcist Tells His Story.* San Francisco: Ignatius Press, 1999.

Wilkinson, Tracy. *The Vatican's Exorcists: Driving Out the Devil in the 21st Century.* New York: Warner Books, 2007.

amulet   An object believed to have protective power. Amulets are used to ward off DEMONS, evil, disease, bad luck, misfortune, witches, sorcerers, and anything harmful, especially of a supernatural nature.

Amulets to protect people, places, and animals against demonic attack and influence have been used universally since ancient times. Most common are natural stones and crystals. Metals such as iron and silver have special protective powers.

Amulets include objects made and imbued with protective power via prayer or magic and written inscriptions—prayers and CHARMS—carried on the person or placed in an environment. Amulets also can be sounds. Noise, bells, gongs, chants, and songs, as well as fumes, are effective.

Universal Amulets

Some objects have enjoyed widespread use as protections against a variety of evils. Among them are:

Bells Bells are used in many cultures as a powerful way to repel demons, other evil spirits, and the EVIL EYE. Bells are associated with the divine and have been used in magical and religious rites since antiquity. Bells summon people to prayer and clear the air of odious presences.

Bell ringing to drive away evil spirits is described in Assyrian magical texts dating to the first millennium B.C.E.

NICHOLAS REMY said that demons consider bell ringing to be "the barking of those mad witches," and they are repelled by it with great indignation. The revulsion of demons is evidenced in the fact that many bell ringers are struck by lightning, which is under demonic control, Remy said.

Bells are attached to clothing, tied to children and domestic animals, and hung in doorways. Red ties, ribbons, and sashes increase the protective power of the bells.

In lore, bells should be rung during storms, which are caused by witches and demons. On nights when witches were believed to be about, such as Samhain (All Hallows' Eve) and Beltane (also known as Walpurgisnacht), church bells were rung to prevent the witches and their demon FAMILIARs from flying over a village. In witch trials, accused witches testified about being transported through the air to a SABBAT on the back of a demon or the DEVIL and of being thrown off to fall to the ground when a church bell sounded in the night.

When a person dies, church bells traditionally are rung to protect the journey of the dead from demonic attack as it travels into the afterlife.

Fumes Burned incense and herbs and sacrificed animals are not only pleasing to the gods, but repellent to demons. The book of Tobit tells how the archangel Raphael taught a young man, Tobias, to produce fumes from the burned liver of a fish in order to exorcize the demon ASMODEUS.

Salt Salt repels demons and evil things because it is pure in its whiteness, is a preservative, and is linked to life and health. Salt is contrary to the nature of demons, who are intent upon corrupting and destroying. It should be avoided in magical rituals for conjuring demons.

Salt repels witches and the evil eye. A test for bewitchment is the inability of a person or animal to eat anything salted. Inquisitors in the European witch hunts protected themselves by wearing a sacramental amulet that consisted of salt consecrated on Palm Sunday and blessed herbs, pressed into a disk of blessed wax. One means of torturing accused witches was to force-feed them heavily salted food and deny them water.

Salt is a magical remedy for evil spells. An old recipe for breaking an evil spell calls for stealing a tile from a witch's roof, sprinkling it with salt and urine, and then heating it over fire while reciting a charm. In American Ozark lore, women who complain of food being too salty are suspected of being witches. One way to detect a witch is to sprinkle salt on her chair. If she is a witch, the salt will melt and cause her dress to stick to the chair.

In superstition it is considered bad luck to spill, borrow, or run out of salt, perhaps because in times past, salt was a valuable and scarce commodity. Spilling salt makes one vulnerable to the Devil; the bad luck may be negated by tossing a pinch of salt with the right hand over the left shoulder.

In Christianity, blessed salt is mixed with blessed water to make holy water (see below).

Running water Water represents purity and will reject evil. In folklore, crossing running water will enable a person to evade pursuing evil spirits and witches. In the European witch hunts, suspected witches were sometimes "swum," or dunked into deep water with their hands and feet bound. If they floated, it meant that the water rejected them because they were evil, and so they were guilty of WITCHCRAFT. If they sank—and usually drowned—it meant that the water accepted them, and they were innocent.

Crooked paths Crooked paths and bridges confuse all spirits, including evil ones, and will prevent them from accessing a place.

Jewish Amulets against Demons
Major Jewish religious objects with amuletic properties against evil are:

Mezuzah One of the most important amulets is the mezuzah, biblical inscriptions attached to doorposts. The inscriptions are verses in Deuteronomy 6:4–19 and 11:13–20—the delivery of the commandments from the one and only God, and his instructions to obey them—to remind Jews of the principle of monotheism.

The mezuzah may have originated as a primitive charm; by the Middle Ages, it had acquired great power as a protector against demons. Rabbinic leaders tried to give it more religious significance, based on Deuteronomy 6:9: "And you shall write them on the doorposts of your house and on your gates." However, in popular usage, it served primarily to ward off evil.

So powerful was the mezuzah in its ability to keep demons away that Gentiles and Jews alike used it. It was believed also to prevent premature death. Many homes had mezuzot in every room. People also carried small mezuzot as personal protective charms.

Strict procedures were followed for the making of a mezuzah. It was to be written on deer parchment according to an amulet table in the angelic *Sefer Raziel* and under certain astrological and angelic influences. One set of 10th-century instructions were "It is to be written only on Monday, in the fifth hour, over which the Sun and the angel Raphael preside, or on Thursday, in the fourth hour, presided over by Venus and the angel Anael."

Mezuzot were encapsulated in cases. It was forbidden to alter the face of the mezuzah but was permissible to write on the back of the parchment. One popular medieval addition was the name Shaddai, held to be especially powerful in repelling demons. Small windows were cut in the backs of the mezuzot cases so that the name Shaddai would show. Other additions were names of God, other Bible verses, names of angels, and magical symbols. Frequently named angels were Michael, Gabriel, Azriel, Zadkiel, Sarfiel, Raphael, Anael, Uriel, Yofiel, and Hasdiel.

Mezuzot are in still in use as both religious objects and amulets; they guard homes and are worn on the person.

Tefillin Other important antidemonic amulets are tefillin, a pair of black leather boxes containing parchment inscribed with biblical verses. Tefillin are also called phylacteries. One of the pair is a hand tefillin, worn wrapped by a strap around the arm, hand, and fingers. The other is a head tefillin, strapped above the forehead. The tefillin serve as a "sign" and "remembrance" that God led the children of Israel out of Egypt. They are worn during weekday morning prayer services.

Tsitsith The tsitsith consists of fringe attached to outer garment, and survives in the modern day as the fringe on prayer shawls. The tsitsith and the tefillin especially are amulets against accidents, illness, and death. The Talmud states that the "threefold cord" of mezuzah, tefillin, and tsitsith is a powerful combination against evil: "Whoever has the tefillin on his head, the mezuzah on his door, and tsitsith on his mantle, may feel sure that he cannot sin."

Moonlets Moon-shaped amulets were once worn as necklaces by both men and women and were placed on the necks of animals. Other amulets are earrings. The Bible tells of Jacob's burying earrings beneath an oak tree.

Christian Amulets against Demons
Christian amulets against evil include holy objects and chants, including:

Cross and crucifix The cross is one of the oldest amulets in the world, predating Christianity by many centuries.

Its most common form is four arms of equal length rather than in a T shape. The cross has been associated with Sun deities and the heavens and in ancient times may have represented divine protection and prosperity. The cross also is represented by the Y-shaped Tree of Life, the world axis placed in the center of the universe, the bridge between Earth and the cosmos, the physical and the spiritual.

In Christianity, the cross transcends the amulet to become symbolic of the religion and of the suffering of Christ's crucifixion; yet, it still retains aspects of an amulet, protecting against the forces of evil. Even before the crucifixion of Christ, the cross was a weapon against the dark forces. According to legend, when LUCIFER declared war upon God in an attempt to usurp his power, his army scattered God's ANGELs twice. God sent to his angels a Cross of Light inscribed with the names of the Trinity. Upon seeing this cross, Lucifer's forces lost strength and were driven into HELL.

Early Christians made the sign of the cross for divine protection and as a means of identification to each other. In the fourth century, Christ's wooden cross was allegedly found in excavations in Jerusalem by Empress Helena, mother of Constantine I. Helena is said to have found three buried crosses at the site of the crucifixion but did not know which belonged to Christ. She tested all three with the corpse of a man. Two crosses had no effect upon the body, but the third caused it to return to life. Helena sent part of the cross to Constantine, who sent a portion to Rome, where it is still preserved in the Vatican. Helena reburied the rest of the cross. Bits of the cross that were fashioned into amulets became highly prized.

As the church grew in power, so did the cross. According to belief, nothing unholy can stand up to its presence. The cross, and the sign of the cross, will help exorcise demons and devils, ward off the INCUBUS and SUCCUBUS, prevent bewitchment of man and beast, protect crops from being blasted by witches, and force vampires to flee. During the Middle Ages, inquisitors often wore crosses or made the sign of a cross while in the presence of accused witches, in order to ward off any evil spells they might cast with the help of their demons. People crossed themselves routinely, before the smallest task, just in case an evil presence was near. The cross in hot cross buns is a remnant of a medieval custom of carving crosses in the dough of bread to protect it against evil.

In cases of demonic POSSESSION, victims recoil from a cross. Surreptitiously placing a cross behind the head of a DEMONIAC is one of the tests of possession. Demoniacs spit on crosses and destroy them. Some suffer stigmata in the shape of a cross. Other victims recoil from the cross, as in the case of a 16-year-old girl, Clara Germana Cele, in 1906. Cele could not bear to be in the presence of even a small piece of cross, even if it had been wrapped and concealed.

In the Catholic rite of EXORCISM, the priest protects himself and the victim with the sign of the cross. The rite requires that numerous signs of the cross be made on the victim's forehead.

Chant   Gregorian chant, that is, prayers sung in Latin, are used to quell demons in some possession cases, and to cleanse spaces. Demons are believed to find Gregorian chant unbearable.

Benedict medal   The medal of St. Benedict (ca. 480–ca. 457) has always been associated with the cross and is sometimes called the Medal-Cross of St. Benedict. It is the medal of exorcism and protection against SATAN and the forces of evil.

The front of the medal shows St. Benedict with a cross and raven. No one knows when the first medal of St. Benedict was struck. At some point in history, a series of capital letters, V R S N S M V - S M Q L I V B, was placed around the large figure of the cross on the reverse side of the medal. In 1647, a manuscript dating to 1415 was found at the Abbey of Metten in Bavaria, explaining the letters as the initials of a Latin prayer of exorcism against Satan: *Vade retro Satana! Nunquam suade mihi vana! Sunt mala quae libas. Ipse venena bibas!* (Begone Satan! Never tempt me with your vanities! What you offer me is evil. Drink the poison yourself!)

St. Benedict medals are carried on a person and placed in homes, cars, and other places as an amulet against Satan and a reminder to resist temptation.

Holy water   Holy water is a mixture of water and salt blessed by a priest. Salt symbolizes incorruptibility, eternity, and divine wisdom, and water symbolizes purity. Church sites were consecrated with holy water. The Catholic rituals of the benediction and BAPTISM with holy water ensure physical health and the exorcism of evil spirits.

As an extra precaution against demons, salt traditionally is placed in a newborn baby's cradle until the infant can be baptized. At death, salt is left in a coffin to help protect the soul from demons during its transition from Earth to the spirit plane.

See INCANTATION BOWL.

FURTHER READING:
Remy, Nicholas. *Demonolatry.* Secaucus, N.J.: University Books, 1974.
Trachtenberg, Joshua. *Jewish Magic and Superstition: A Study in Folk Religion.* New York: Berhman's Jewish Book House, 1939.

Amy   FALLEN ANGEL and 58th of the 72 SPIRITS OF SOLOMON. Prior to his fall, Amy was a member of the angelic order of powers. He is a president in HELL, where he governs 36 LEGIONS of DEMONs. He possesses perfect knowledge of the liberal sciences and astrology. He gives good FAMILIARs. He appears first as a huge flaming fire and then as a man. Amy reveals hidden treasures guarded by other spirits. In 1,200 years, he hopes to be restored to the "seventh throne," that is, to the place before God that is reserved for the highest of angels. The demonologist JOHANN WEYER called this claim "not credible."

Andra (Indra) In ZOROASTRIANISM, the archDEMON known as the Slayer and Fighter, who turns humans away from virtue. Andra opposes the good spirit, or *amesha spenta,* of Artvahisht. He also punishes the souls doomed to HELL.

Andras FALLEN ANGEL and 63rd of the 72 SPIRITS OF SOLOMON. Andras is a great marquis in HELL who rules over 30 LEGIONS of DEMONS. He appears in the form of an ANGEL with either a raven head or a wooden owl head, rides a black wolf, and carries a gleaming and sharp sword. He creates discord and kills those who are not careful and wary, including the master, servants, and all assistants of any household. He teaches people how to kill their enemies.

Andrealphus FALLEN ANGEL and 65th of the 72 SPIRITS OF SOLOMON. Andrealphus is a mighty marquis, who rules 30 LEGIONS. He first appears as a noisy peacock and then as a human. He can transform people into birds and make them very cunning. He teaches perfect geometry and everything pertaining to measurements, as well as astronomy.

Andromalius FALLEN ANGEL and 72nd of the 72 SPIRITS OF SOLOMON. Andromalius is a great earl in HELL. He appears as a man holding a SERPENT. He returns stolen goods, reveals thieves, discovers wicked deeds and underhanded dealings, and reveals hidden treasures. He rules 36 LEGIONS of DEMONS.

angel A being who mediates between God and mortals. Angels minister over all living things and the natural world, and over all things in the cosmos. They play an important role in MAGIC. Among their duties are battling DEMONS and the DEVIL, and all forces of evil. Angels are sent by God in response to prayer and need.

The term *angel* is from the Greek *angelos,* which means "messenger." Acting as a messenger between realms—humans and God—is one of the angels' primary duties. Angels mete out the will of God, whether it is to aid or to punish humans. They also can act according to their own free will, although they do not sin.

Angels are specific to Judaism, Christianity, and Islam; however, they derive from concepts of helping and tutelary spirits that exist in mythologies the world over. Angels evolved from the mythology of the Jews, influenced by the mythologies of the Babylonians, Persians, Sumerians, Egyptians, and others with whom the Jews had contact. The Jewish angel passed into Christian and Islamic mythology.

The Bible presents angels as representatives of God who exist in a celestial realm and are numberless. They are incorporeal but have the ability to assume form and pass as mortals. They also appear as beings of fire, lightning, and brilliant light, sometimes with wings and sometimes without. Various classes of angels are mentioned in the Bible; by the sixth century, these were organized into hierarchies.

The church fathers of Christianity gave extensive consideration to the duties, nature, numbers, abilities, and functions of angels. Theological interest peaked by the Middle Ages and began to decline in the Renaissance.

Angels are prominent in Jewish magic and preside over every aspect of creation. They are featured in KABBALAH-based magic, which forms a significant part of the Western magical tradition. Angels, along with demons, are involved in rituals given in magical books and GRIMOIRES.

The greatest confrontation between angels and demons will occur in Armageddon, according to the book of REVELATION. Armies of angels led by the archangel Michael will battle and defeat the forces of SATAN.

See THWARTING ANGELS.

FURTHER READING:
The Old Testament Pseudepigrapha. Vols. 1 & 2. Edited by James H. Charlesworth. 1983. Reprint, New York: Doubleday, 1985.

Angels of Mastemoth In the Dead Sea Scrolls, a name for the WATCHERS, FALLEN ANGELS who cohabited with women and begat giants. The Angels of Mastemoth are "Enemy Angels" and "Angels of Darkness." The Qumran text 4Q390 refers to sinners being delivered into the power of the Angels of Mastemoth, who will rule them.

See MASTEMA.

Angra Mainyu See AHRIMAN.

Antaura Greek DEMON of migraine headaches. Antaura is a female demon, who rises up out of the sea, moves like the wind, shouts like a deer, and cries like an ox. She enters into people's heads to cause intense pain. She commands other headache demons to do the same.

Antaura is thwarted by the goddess Artemis, who rules the woodlands and the waxing moon. In lore Artemis diverts Antaura into the head of a bull in the mountains.

Anthony (251–356) Christian saint credited as a founder of monasticism, famous for his temptations by the DEVIL and his DEMONS. *Anthony* means "inestimable." Saint Anthony is also known as Anthony or Antony of Egypt, Anthony of the Desert, and Anthony the Abbott. The account of his life and demonic torments was recorded by his friend St. Athanasius, patriarch of the church at Alexandria, Egypt, in *Vita S. Antoni (Life of St. Anthony).* The temptations of Anthony were a popular subject for medieval artists.

Life
Anthony was born in 251 to Christian parents in the village of Coma (or Koman) south of Memphis in Upper Egypt, during a time of persecutions ordered by the Roman emperor Decius. His fearful parents kept him at home, unread and ignorant of any languages except his own.

His parents died when he was about 20, leaving him a large estate and charged with the care of his younger sister. About six months later, Anthony was moved by the Christian Gospels to change his life radically. He took to heart Matthew 19:21, "Go, sell what thou hast, give it to the poor and thou shalt have treasure in heaven," and so sold all of his estate except what he and his sister needed to live on, and distributed the proceeds to the poor. Then he acted upon Matthew 6:34, "Be not solicitous for tomorrow," and gave away the rest. He placed his sister in a house of maidens and pious women, the first recorded description of a nunnery, and around 272 began a life of solitude.

Anthony's first retreat was in the Libyan desert, not far from his home, where he lived in an abandoned tomb. He usually ate only after sunset, his meal consisting of bread with a little salt, and water to drink. Sometimes he would not eat for three or four days. He slept on a rush mat or the bare floor and spent his days in prayer, reading, and manual labor. He endured fierce demonic assaults.

After emerging triumphant from the temptations, in about 285, Anthony crossed the Nile River to live in the abandoned ruins of a mountain fort, where he stayed in almost total isolation for 20 years. He rarely had human contact except for the man who delivered bread to him every six months, but nevertheless he attracted the faithful and the curious. Anthony finally went down from the mountain in 305, at age 54, to respond to the entreaties of his followers and founded the first monastery, at Fayum.

Anthony spent the remainder of his life working for the Christian cause, punctuated with periods of solitude. In 311, he went to Alexandria to comfort martyrs prior to their executions, somehow escaping arrest himself. He founded another monastery, Pirpir, in the desert and then went to Mount Kolzim to live in a cell in isolation with his disciple, Macarius. He wore a hair shirt and did not bathe. He then joined a company of followers to give them instruction in the monastic life.

In 355, he returned to Alexandria to oppose the Arian heresy, which held that JESUS was not divine but human. He was hugely popular with Christians and pagans alike.

In 356, at age 105, he returned to his refuge at Mount Kolzim. He fell ill and directed his disciples to bury him secretly at Kolzim beside his followers Macarius and Amathas and send his cloak to Athanasius. Anthony then lay down, assured his disciples that his body would rise incorruptible in the Resurrection, and stopped breathing.

In 561, his remains supposedly were discovered and moved first to Alexandria, then to Constantinople, then finally to Vienne, France, during the Crusades.

Demonic Temptations

As soon as Anthony decided to give away his wealth and retreat into the desert, he was beset by the Devil, who spoke to him and tried to lure him back to a life of material comfort and glory. Anthony resisted, and the Devil increased his torments, by day and night, so much so that others became aware of what was happening. Anthony held to his fasting and prayer. Most severe were the sexual seductions attempted. According to Athanasius, his biographer:

> And the devil, unhappy wight, one night even took upon him the shape of a woman and imitated all her acts simply to beguile Antony [sic]. But he, his mind filled with Christ and the nobility inspired by Him, and considering the spirituality of the soul, quenched the coal of the other's deceit. Again the enemy suggested the ease of pleasure. But he like a man filled with rage and grief turned his thoughts to the threatened fire and the gnawing worm, and setting these in array against his adversary, passed through the temptation unscathed. All this was a source of shame to his foe. For he, deeming himself like God, was now mocked by a young man; and he who boasted himself against flesh and blood was being put to flight by a man in the flesh.

The Devil did not give up easily, however, and then appeared in the form of a black boy, who seemed humble and apologetic. He identified himself as "the friend of whoredom" and "the spirit of lust" and acknowledged that Anthony had often bested him. Anthony rebuked

Demons tempting St. Anthony (AUTHOR'S COLLECTION)

him, saying, "Thou art very despicable then, for thou art black-hearted and weak as a child. Henceforth I shall have no trouble from thee, 'for the Lord is my helper, and I shall look down on mine enemies.'" The Devil left.

Once the Devil sent a horde of hyenas to attack Anthony. He told them that if they had genuine power over him, he was ready to be devoured, but if they had been sent by the Devil, they could not harm him. The hyenas departed.

One day while he wove baskets, a man with the feet and legs of an ass appeared with other evil spirits. Anthony repelled them with the sign of the cross and the name of Christ. They fled into the desert, and the ass-footed leader fell and died.

On another occasion, the frustrated Devil arrived with a multitude of demons and beat Anthony so severely that he lay on the ground senseless from the excessive pain; he was found after several days by a friend who arrived with his bread. At first, the friend thought he was dead. Seeing him still alive, the friend carried Anthony to the village church and laid him on the ground. A group of people gathered around and kept vigil as though by a corpse. At midnight, the saint roused and asked to be returned to his tomb.

Anthony said that "the torture had been so excessive that no blows inflicted by man could ever have caused him such torment," according to Athanasius. But worse was to come. The tomb shook as though in an earthquake, and demons in the forms of animals and insects poured in: lions, bears, leopards, bulls, serpents, asps, and scorpions. They made a ferocious racket and feigned as if to attack him. According to Athanasius:

> But Antony, stricken and goaded by them, felt bodily pains severer still. He lay watching, however, with unshaken soul, groaning from bodily anguish; but his mind was clear, and as in mockery he said, "If there had been any power in you, it would have sufficed had one of you come, but since the Lord hath made you weak you attempt to terrify me by numbers: and a proof of your weakness is that you take the shapes of brute beasts." And again with boldness he said, "If you are able, and have received power against me, delay not to attack; but if you are unable, why trouble me in vain? For faith in our Lord is a seal and a wall of safety to us." So after many attempts they gnashed their teeth upon him, because they were mocking themselves rather than him.

After a period of these assaults, the roof of the tomb suddenly opened and a ray of light appeared, and the demons vanished. Anthony was free of pain. He asked God why he was so slow to respond to him. God replied that he wanted to see Anthony's fight. Now that Anthony had won, God said, "I will ever be a succor to thee, and will make thy name known everywhere."

Still Anthony was not free of demonic assault. When he journeyed to the abandoned mountain fort to take up isolation, the Devil tempted him with a beautiful silver dish lying in his path. As soon as Anthony pronounced it a snare of the Devil, it vanished, "like smoke from the face of fire." The Devil next tried real gold strewn about, but Anthony hurried past it.

Anthony would allow no one inside the fort; his followers left his food outside. Often, it was reported, they would hear a horrible din of voices inside, telling Anthony he could not withstand their attack and he should leave. Anthony told them the voices belonged to demons, but he was not troubled by them.

Anthony's Views on Demons

When Anthony emerged from the mountain fort after 20 years in isolation, he was in perfect health and spoke to the public with compelling grace. He taught people about demons. Anthony described them as beings of the air not far from humans, great in number, and with many distinctions among them. They were not originally evil:

> The demons have not been created like what we mean when we call them by that name for God made nothing evil, but even they have been made good. Having fallen, however, from the heavenly wisdom, since then they have been groveling on earth. On the one hand they deceived the Greeks with their displays [of foretelling the future], while out of envy of us Christians they move all things in their desire to hinder us from entry into the heavens; in order that we should not ascend up thither from whence they fell. Thus there is need of much prayer and of discipline, that when a man has received through the Spirit the gift of discerning spirits, he may have power to recognize their characteristics: which of them are less and which more evil; of what nature is the special pursuit of each, and how each of them is overthrown and cast out. For their villainies and the changes in their plots are many.

Anthony said that demons attacked all Christians, and particularly monks, first with evil thoughts, then with sexual seduction, and then with fearsome monsters and animalistic shapes. Demons lie in concealment and enter homes stealthily through the air. They can appear in deceitful guises, including as ANGELs, monks, and holy men, who rouse sleeping people and exhort them to prayer—but then claim that prayer is useless. If lower demons do not succeed, they call in a leader.

He described more examples from his own experiences:

> Once a demon exceeding high appeared with pomp, and dared to say, "I am the power of God and I am Providence, what dost thou wish that I shall give thee?" But I then so much the more breathed upon him, and spoke the name of Christ, and set about to smite him. And I seemed to have smitten him, and forthwith he, big as he was, together with all his demons, disappeared at the name of Christ. At another time, while I was fasting, he came full of craft, under the semblance of a monk, with what seemed to be loaves, and gave me counsel, saying, "Eat and cease from thy many labors. Thou also art a man and art like to fall sick." But I, perceiving his

device, rose up to pray; and he endured it not, for he departed, and through the door there seemed to go out as it were smoke.

Athanasius said he was often beaten by demons, as when he was found in his mountain fort, but when he proclaimed his love of Christ, the demons beat each other.

Once SATAN appeared as a tall man, who knocked at the cell of his door. Satan demanded to know why Christians cursed him undeservedly, for he was weak and they were the source of their own troubles. Anthony called him a liar in the name of Christ, and Satan disappeared.

Christians need have no fear of demons, Anthony said, for they are cowards and liars. They have no power to carry out their threats, but are like actors on a stage. They are overcome with prayer, fasting, the sign of the cross, and faith. Demons, he said, "fear the fasting, the sleeplessness, the prayers, the meekness, the quietness, the contempt of money and vainglory, the humility, the love of the poor, the alms, the freedom from anger of the ascetics, and, chief of all, their piety towards Christ." But if a person reacts with fear to them, the demons will increase their attacks.

He said that demons will often accurately foretell the future, but this is a ploy to make the unwary victim trust them. Demons led Greek oracles astray in this manner.

He recommended a test that would reveal demons:

> Whenever there is any apparition, be not prostrate with fear, but whatsoever it be, first boldly ask, Who art thou? And from whence comest thou? And if it should be a vision of holy ones they will assure you, and change your fear into joy. But if the vision should be from the devil, immediately it becomes feeble, beholding your firm purpose of mind. For merely to ask, Who art thou? and whence comest thou? is a proof of coolness.

Anthony's Exorcism Skills

Athansius gives examples of Anthony's ability to exorcise demons from others. While he was in isolation, people would bang on his cell door to ask for his help. Many times he would not answer, and the people camped on his doorstep, often becoming healed in the process of maintaining a prayerful vigil there.

Sometimes he answered and told people they would be healed by their own prayer and faith. A soldier who had a demon-infested daughter sought his help and was sent away with this advice. When the soldier arrived home, he found his daughter free of demons.

When he was out among the public, Anthony cast out demons by invoking the name of Christ. Once, he was invited aboard a ship to pray with monks. He noticed a rank smell from the fish and meat—he was the only one who did—and discovered a stowaway, a young man who was possessed by a demon. He cast it out.

Another young man was taken to him, so badly possessed that he ate his own excrement. Anthony cast out the demon and made the man whole and healthy again.

Anthony warned others who healed and cast out demons not to boast about it, for they would make themselves vulnerable to demonic attacks.

Importance of Anthony's Experiences

The account of Anthony's triumphs over demons, and his descriptions and advice, laid an important foundation for the Christian perspective on demons. In subsequent centuries, as cases of POSSESSION were treated by the church, the demons performed as described by Anthony, increasing the intensity of their assaults and calling in higher-ranking leaders as assaults continued. They lied, shape shifted, and made accurate prophesies and clairvoyant observations. They were ultimately banished by the name of Christ.

FURTHER READING:

Athanasius, St. *Vita S. Antoni (Life of St. Anthony)*. Internet Medieval Sourcebook. Available online. URL: http://www.fordham.edu.halsall/basis/vita-antony/html. Downloaded on January 31, 2000.

Ankarloo, Bengt, and Stuart Clark, eds. *The Athalone History of Witchcraft and Magic in Europe*. London: Athlone Press, 1999.

Antichrist   The ultimate opponent of Christ. The Antichrist is associated with the Second Coming and the Apocalypse. Originally a man, the Antichrist in more modern times is seen as half-human and half-DEMON, the son of SATAN, brought forth into the world by a woman.

The only references in the Bible specific to the Antichrist are found in the epistles of John. The term is ambiguous and could mean "opponent of Christ," "false Christ," "against Christ," or "instead of Christ." The references assume the Antichrist to be an existing tradition, knowledge that the opponent will precede the Second Coming in an effort to seize control of the world.

The verse 1 John 2:18:22 states, "Who is the liar but he who denies that Jesus is the Christ? This is the antichrist, he who denies the Father and the Son." In 4:3, the author says that "every spirit which does not confess Jesus is not of God. This is the spirit of the antichrist, of which you heard that it was coming, and now it is in the world already." The verse 2 John 7 states, "For many deceivers have gone out into the world, men who will not acknowledge the coming of Jesus Christ in the flesh; such a one is the deceiver and the antichrist."

Here the Antichrist seems more like a spirit or attitude that infects many people, the disbelievers (and thus heretics), and not a single individual.

Other passages in the New Testament mention opponents of Christ without using the term *Antichrist*. The Gospels of Mark and Matthew refer to false prophets, and Paul's 2 Thessalonians 2:3–12 refers to the "Lawless One" or "the man of lawlessness" who will precede the Second Coming:

> Let no one deceive you in any way; for that day will not come, unless the rebellion comes first, and the man

of lawlessness is revealed, the son of perdition, who opposes and exalts himself against every so-called god or object of worship, so that he takes his seat in the temple of God, proclaiming himself to be God. Do you not remember that when I was still with you I told you this? And you know what is restraining him now so that he may be revealed in his time. For the mystery of lawlessness is already at work; only he who now restrains it will do so until he is out of the way. And then the lawless one will be revealed and the Lord Jesus will slay him with the breath of his mouth and destroy him by his appearing and his coming. The coming of the lawless one by the activity of Satan will be with all the power and with pretended signs and wonders, and with all wicked deception for those who are to perish, because they refused to love the truth and so be saved. Therefore God sends upon them a strong delusion, to make them believe what is false, so that all may be condemned who did not believe the truth but had pleasure in unrighteousness.

REVELATION makes reference to other opponents, chiefly the Beasts of the Land and the Sea, and the Dragon or SERPENT, the Devil himself.

The concept of the Antichrist was more fully developed in the second century C.E., chiefly by the church father Irenaeus, who argued that the best defense against the DEVIL is Christ. Christian prayers and the uttered name of Christ cause DEMONs to flee. However, the Antichrist, a human, will appear as an apostate, murderer, and robber. He will have "all the Devil's power," Irenaeus said, and will attract followers and worshippers. The Antichrist ultimately will be defeated, and Satan and his demons will go to everlasting torments in HELL.

Origen, another father of the early church, termed the Antichrist "the son of the evil demon, who is Satan and the Devil." He will be supported in his final confrontation with Christ by Satan and his demons, who were imprisoned at the time of the Passion. Augustine, one of the most influential early fathers, assumed the Antichrist to be a single individual rather than groups of wicked men.

By early medieval times, the Antichrist was increasingly regarded as a person rather than a personification of evil. The Antichrist would be fostered by LUCIFER or would be the form that Lucifer himself would take, at the end of the world. This form became more and more entrenched in theological writings, in folklore, and in theater and literature. One common story line held that Lucifer would beget the Antichrist with a Babylonian whore.

After the Protestant Reformation in the 16th century, the pope was often called the Antichrist, while Catholics said MARTIN LUTHER would beget the Antichrist.

In 1848, the Blessed Virgin Mary, appearing in apparitional visions at La Salette, France, predicted that the seat of Rome would serve the Antichrist: "How I warned and warned that Satan would enter into the highest realms of the hierarchy in Rome. The Third Secret, My child, is that Satan would enter into My Son's Church."

In 1928, Lucifer was a principal demon possessing a woman in Earling, Iowa (see EARLING POSSESSION). Father Theophilus, the EXORCIST, became convinced that the hour of the Antichrist was near. However, he did not think that the Antichrist would be a son of the Devil, but Lucifer himself, who would fashion a body out of earthly matter in order to operate in the world. The Antichrist as son of the Devil is the most popular view in modern times, represented in fiction and in films such as ROSEMARY'S BABY, THE OMEN, and THE DEVIL'S ADVOCATE.

FURTHER READING:
Augustine. *The City of God.* Translated by Marcus Dods, George Wilson, and J. J. Smith; introduction by Thomas Merton. New York: Modern Library, 1950.
Dictionary of Deities and Demons in the Bible. 2nd ed. Edited by Karel van der Toorn, Bob Becking, and Pieter W. van der Horst. Grand Rapids, Mich.: William B. Eerdmans, 1999.
Russell, Jeffrey Burton. *The Devil: Perceptions of Evil from Antiquity to Primitive Christianity.* Ithaca, N.Y., and London: Cornell University Press, 1977.
———. *Lucifer: The Devil in the Middle Ages.* Ithaca, N.Y., and London: Cornell University Press, 1984.
———. *Satan: The Early Christian Tradition.* Ithaca, N.Y., and London: Cornell University Press, 1981.
Vogel, Rev. Carl. *Begone, Satan! A Soul-Stirring Account of Diabolical Possession in Iowa.* Rockford, Ill.: TAN Books and Publishers, 1973.

apple   The fruit of the Tree of Knowledge that led to the fall of Adam and Eve became, during the witch hysteria, one of the favored ways for DEMONS and the DEVIL to enter a person and cause POSSESSION.

Eating almost any food might invite possession, especially if cursed by a witch or sorcerer, but apples were held to be especially dangerous. Demonologists, among them the ruthless Henri Boguet, preached warnings about them.

One famous apple possession is the "Vienna Possession" case, in which a 16-year-old girl claimed that her grandmother sent her demons into an apple and gave it to her to eat. The girl was supposedly afflicted by more than 12,000 demons.

Apples, cultivated in Britain as early as 3000 B.C.E., have had a long association with MAGIC and WITCHCRAFT. In mythology, they are the fruit of heaven, longevity, and immortality. In folklore, they are love charms and have been used in divination and spells to reveal lovers and future spouses and to cause people to fall in love. In 1657, Richard Jones, a 12-year-old boy in Shepton Mallet in the county of Somerset in England, was said to be bewitched by Jane Brooks, who gave him an apple. Jones suffered fits, and neighbors said they saw him fly over his garden wall. Brooks was charged with witchcraft, convicted, and hanged on March 26, 1658.

The apple is associated with enchantment and FAIRIES. According to English folklore, it is bad luck to pick all the apples in a harvest, and some must be left for the fairies. In the Arthurian legends, Avalon, the magical fairy isle where time is suspended, is "Isle of the Apples."

FURTHER READING:
Lea, Henry Charles. *Materials toward a History of Witchcraft.* Philadelphia: University of Pennsylvania Press, 1939.

Armadiel   DEMON among the 31 AERIAL SPIRITS OF SOLOMON. Armadiel rules as a king in the northeast. His 15 chief dukes each have 1,260 servants, who are good-natured but must be summoned at the appropriate hour. Armadiel's 15 major dukes are Nassar, Parabiel, Lariel, Calvamia, Orariel, Alferiel, Oryn, Samiet, Asmaiel, Jasziel, Pandiel, Carasiba, Asbibiel, Mafayr, and Oemiel.

asag (asakku)   A type of Sumerian DEMON that attacks humans and kills them with head and fever diseases.

Asag also is the proper name of a monstrous demon in the Sumerian poem *Lugale.* Asag is the offspring of An, the sky god, and Ki, the earth goddess. He is hideous and has the power to make fish boil in their rivers. His allies are the stones of mountains.

The poem relates how Asag battles the hero god Ninurta and is defeated. This allows Ninurta to organize the world and use stones to construct the mountains so that streams and lakes flow into the Tigris and Euphrates Rivers, thereby aiding irrigation for agriculture.

Aseliel   DEMON among the 31 AERIAL SPIRITS OF SOLOMON. Aseliel is the fourth-ranking spirit under the governance of CARNESIEL in the south, and the east. He has 10 spirit attendants during the day and 20 at night, each of which has 30 servants. All the spirits appear beautiful and act in loving ways.

Asmodeus (Aeshma, Ashmedai, Ashmodai, Asmoday, Asmodius, Hasmoday, Sydonay)   The DEMON of lust, the third of the SEVEN DEADLY SINS, and of jealousy, anger, and revenge, and the 32nd of the 72 SPIRITS OF SOLOMON.

Asmodeus' chief objectives are to prevent intercourse between husband and wife, wreck new marriages, and force husbands to commit adultery. He is also one of the chief demons involved in cases of POSSESSION. Throughout history, he has been regarded as one of the most evil of SATAN's infernal demons. He is usually portrayed as having three heads, those of an ogre, a ram, and a bull, all sexually licentious creatures; having the feet of a cock, another sexually aggressive creature; and having wings and the tail of a SERPENT. He rides on a dragon and breathes fire.

Asmodeus has his roots in ancient Persia. His name is derived from *AESHMA,* one of the seven archangels, or *amarahspands,* of Persian mythology. The Hebrews absorbed him into their mythology, where he attained the highest status and most power of all his legends. According to the

Asmodeus   (DICTIONNAIRE INFERNAL)

Hebrews, he is the son of Naamah and Shamdon. Prior to his fall from heaven, he was part of the seraphim, the highest order of ANGELs. In other Hebrew legends, he is either associated with or the husband of LILITH, the demon queen of lust. Sometimes he is said to be the offspring of Lilith and Adam.

The book of Tobit tells how Asmodeus lusted after a young woman named Sarah and killed each of her seven husbands before the marriages could be consummated. With an eighth suitor, Tobias, in her life, Sarah prayed to God for help. God sent down the archangel Raphael, who instructed Tobias in how to make an incense of the heart and liver of a glanos fish, which would drive away Asmodeus. After Tobias and Sarah were married, Asmodeus appeared in their wedding chamber to kill Tobias, but the incense forced him to flee. He went to Egypt, but Raphael tracked him down and bound him.

According to the pseudepigraphical Testament of Solomon, Asmodeus lives in the constellation of the Great Bear (Ursa Major). He spreads the wickedness of men, plots against newlyweds, spreads madness about women through the stars, ruins the beauty of virgins, and commits murders. He is forever thwarted by Raphael and the smoking liver and gall of a fish, especially the sheatfish, which lives in Assyrian rivers. He has knowledge of the future.

Asmodeus is taken into the presence of King SOLOMON by the Prince of Demons, BEELZEBUB. Sullen, arrogant, and defiant, he tells the king he was born of a human mother and an angel father. He also says that Solomon will have only a temporary hold over the demons; his kingdom eventually will be divided, and demons will go out again among men and will be worshipped as gods because humans will not know the names of the angels who thwart the demons. He admits that he is afraid of water.

Solomon binds Asmodeus with care. He orders the demon to be flogged and orders him to state his activities. Asmodeus says, "I am the renowned Asmodeus; I cause the wickedness of men to spread throughout the world. I am always hatching plots against newlyweds; I mar the beauty of virgins and cause their hearts to grow cold. . . . I spread madness about women through the stars and I have often committed a rash of murders."

Solomon puts him in IRON chains and surrounds him with 10 jars full of water, which make the demon complain bitterly. Asmodeus is forced to make clay vessels for the temple. Solomon also burns the liver and gall of a fish and a branch of storax beneath the demon, quelling his nasty tongue.

Solomon uses his magic ring to force Asmodeus and other demons to build his magnificent temple. After its completion, Solomon tells Asmodeus that he cannot understand why demons are so powerful when he, their leader, could be so easily chained. Asmodeus says he will prove his greatness if Solomon will remove his chains and lend him the magical ring. Solomon does so, only to be hurled far away from Jerusalem. Asmodeus steals the ring, forces Solomon into exile, and becomes king himself. He throws the ring into the sea. But Solomon's lover, the Ammonite Namah, finds the ring in a fish belly, and the king regains his power. He is immediately transported to Jerusalem when he puts on the ring. As punishment, he puts Asmodeus in a jar.

Asmodeus was absorbed into Christian lore, becoming one of the Devil's leading agents of provocation. Witches were said to worship him, and magicians and sorcerers attempted to conjure him to strike out at enemies. GRIMOIRES of magical instruction sternly admonish anyone seeking an audience with Asmodeus to summon him bareheaded out of respect. JOHANN WEYER said Asmodeus rules gambling houses.

According to the *Lemegton,* a major grimoire, Asmodeus is the "first and chiefest" under AMAYMON and goes before all other demons. He gives the ring of virtues and teaches arithmetic, geometry, astronomy, and all handicrafts. When properly summoned, he gives full and true answers to all questions. He can make a person invisible and will reveal all treasures under the guard of Amaymon.

He was one of the infernal agents blamed for the obscene sexual possession of the Louviers nuns in 17th-century France (see LOUVIERS POSSESSIONS).

FURTHER READING:
Henson, Mitch, ed. *Lemegeton: The Complete Lesser Key of Solomon.* Jacksonville, Fla.: Metatron Books, 1999.

Hyatt, Victoria, and Joseph W. Charles. *The Book of Demons.* New York: Simon & Schuster, 1974.

The Old Testament Pseudepigrapha. Vol. 1 & 2. Edited by James H. Charlesworth. 1983. Reprint, New York: Doubleday, 1985.

Astaroth (Ashtaroth)   A male DEMON who evolved from the ancient Phoenician mother goddess of fertility, Astarte or Ashtoreth. Astaroth is also a FALLEN ANGEL and 29th of 72 SPIRITS OF SOLOMON. According to Judaic lore, he was a high-ranking ANGEL, either one of the seraphim or a prince of thrones, prior to his fall.

Astaroth is a grand duke and treasurer of HELL and commands 40 LEGIONS of demons. He is one of the three supreme evil demons, with BEELZEBUB and LUCIFER, in the *Grimoire Verum* and *Grand Grimoire,* which date from about the 18th century. In the *Lemegeton,* he appears as either a beautiful or an ugly angel, riding a dragon and holding a viper. He possesses a powerful stench and stinking breath. Magicians who desire to conjure him must hold a magical ring in front of their faces to protect themselves against his smell.

Astaroth teaches all the sciences and is keeper of the secrets of the past, present, and future. He is invoked in necromantic rituals of divination. When conjured in magical rites, which must be performed on Wednesday nights between 10:00 and 11:00, he will give true answers to questions about the past, present, and future. He discovers secrets and is skilled in liberal sciences. He encourages slothfulness and laziness.

The demon is said to instigate cases of demonic POSSESSION, most notably that of the Loudun nuns in France in the 16th century (see LOUDUN POSSESSIONS). The nuns accused a priest, Father URBAIN GRANDIER, of causing their possession. At Grandier's trial, a handwritten

Astaroth (DICTIONNAIRE INFERNAL)

"confession" of his was produced detailing his PACT with the Devil, witnessed and signed by Astaroth and several other demons.

Astaroth loves to talk about the Creation and the Fall, and the faults of angels. He believes he was punished unjustly by God, and that someday he will be restored to his rightful place in heaven.

Astaroth can be thwarted by calling upon St. Bartholomew for help.

FURTHER READING:
Hyatt, Victoria, and Joseph W. Charles. *The Book of Demons.* New York: Simon & Schuster, 1974.
Plancy, Collin de. *Dictionary of Witchcraft.* Edited and translated by Wade Baskin. Originally published as *Dictionary of Demonology.* New York: Philosophical Library, 1965.

Astovidotu   In ZOROASTRIANISM, the red DEMON who binds the soul at death and separates it from the body. Astrovidotu is often mentioned in association with AESHMA, the principal demon of evil. He is called the "creation of the demons" in Pahlavi texts.

Asyriel   DEMON among the 31 AERIAL SPIRITS OF SOLOMON. Asyriel serves under CASPIEL as a king ruling the southwest. He commands 20 dukes under the day and 20 under the night, each of which has servants who are willing to obey the commands of those who summon them. The eight major dukes of the day under Asyriel are Astor, Carga, Buniet, Rabas, Arcisat, Aariel, Cusiel, and Maguel. The eight under the night are Amiel, Cusriet, Maroth, Omiel, Budar, Aspeil, Faseua, and Hamas.

Aueiran, Isaac de (d. 1609)   Young Frenchman executed for WITCHCRAFT and having a PACT with the DEVIL.

Isaac de Aueiran confessed at his trial that he was 10 or 12 years in age when he was introduced to the Devil. He went to a neighbor's house for fire and was asked by the woman who lived there whether he wanted to see "the grand master of sabbats." He agreed and found himself carried through the air to a distant place, where a SABBAT was in progress and men and women were shouting and dancing. A big black man—the Devil—walked up to him, hit him on the shoulder, and urged him to stay. At the same time, the man made a DEVIL'S MARK upon his hand. One day the black man appeared and took him back to a sabbat, where he ate and danced with the others.

De Aueiran was arrested and tried in Bordeaux and was executed by burning on May 8, 1609.

Aupetit, Pierre (d. 1598)   French priest executed on charges of sorcery and trafficking with the DEVIL. Pierre Aupetit, who lived in Fossas, Limousin, was 50 years old when he was arrested and tried. He was tortured and on the rack and confessed.

Aupetit said that he had attended SABBATs, where witches had kissed the anus of the Devil, who was in the shape of a black sheep. Aupetit had read from a book of spells. He had been given a FAMILIAR, the DEMON BEELZEBUB, and had the demon's little finger. Beelzebub had taught him how to procure the love of any woman or girl of his choosing.

Aupetit also said he had been taught the arts of sorcery by a known sorcerer named Crapouplet, who showed him how to staunch the flow of BLOOD and how to use levers.

Aupetit was burned on May 25, 1598.

FURTHER READING:
Plancy, Collin de. *Dictionary of Witchcraft.* Edited and translated by Wade Baskin. Originally published as *Dictionary of Demonology.* New York: Philosophical Library, 1965.

Autak (Udai, Uda)   In ZOROASTRIANISM, the DEMON who makes men speak when they should be silent, and who interferes in their physical labors. Autak is a female demon who also is associated with incest, and is sometimes associated with DRUJ. She is half human and half monster.

Az (Azi)   In ZOROASTRIANISM, the DEMON of avarice, gluttony, insatiability, and lust. Az is often paired with NIYAZ (want) and is featured also in Zurvanite and Manichaean texts. The pair is considered supremely powerful.

Az is the opponent to Atar, the fire god son of Ahura Mazda (later Ohrmadz), the creator god. In the *Bundahisn* text, Az swallows everything and anything to satisfy his want, but he is never fulfilled. If nothing is available, he will eat his own body. Az is not the demon of death, but he brings about death through his corruption. He is behind everything disastrous that happens to human beings. Az and Ahriman will be the last demons to be defeated by the forces of light and good.

In Zurvanite theology, Az leads the demonic hordes. In Manichaeism, Az is a female demon who is the mother of all demons and sin. She formed the human body and imprisoned the soul in it. She is Hyle, or matter and evil, and tries to make humanity forget its divine origins, thus preventing people from finding their salvation.

Azazel (Azael)   Archdemon of the Judean desert and king of the *seirim*, goatlike spirits.

On the Day of Atonement, Jewish custom called for the offering of two goats. One was sacrificed to Yahweh, and the other, blamed with the sins of the people, was taken alive to the wilderness to be released for Azazel (Leviticus 16:8).

In 3 Enoch, Azazel is one of the WATCHERS who lust after mortal women and descend from heaven to cohabit with them. He taught witchcraft and revealed eternal secrets. As punishment, he was bound by angels and imprisoned in the desert in a place called Dudael until Judgment Day.

Under the name of Azael, he is one of the principal evil angels who cohabited with mortal women. The name

Azazel (DICTIONNAIRE INFERNAL)

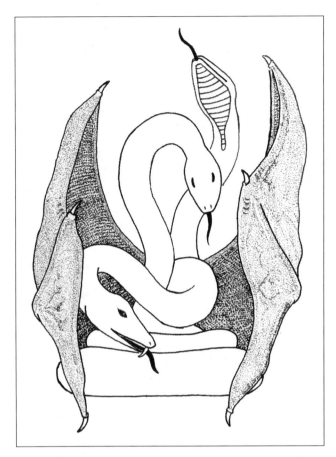

Azhi Dahaka (© SCOTT BRENTS—O.O.O.B., ABRACADABRA LODGE, HELIX MEMBRANE 84390, YELLOW BALL, & T.H.O.G.)

Azael means "who God strengthens." According to lore, Azael slept with Naamah and spawned Assyrian guardian spirits known as *sedim,* invoked in the EXORCISM of evil spirits. As punishment, Azael is chained in a desert until Judgment Day. In magical lore, he guards hidden treasure and teaches WITCHCRAFT that enable men to make the Sun, Moon, and stars move down from the sky.

In 3 Enoch, Azazel (Azael) is one of three primary ministering angels with Azza and Uzza, who live in the seventh (highest) heaven. In later lore, he is fallen and is punished by having his nose pierced.

In Akkadian lore, Azazel is one of the MASKIM, princes of HELL.

In Islamic lore, Azazel or Azazeel was the name of IB-LIS before he disobeyed God by not bowing to humans and was sent from the Earth.

FURTHER READING:
al-Ashqar, Umar Sulaiman. *The World of the Jinn and Devils.* Translated by Jamaal al-Din M. Zarabozo. New York: Al-Basheer Company for Publications and Translations, 1998.
Mack, Carol K., and Dinah Mack. *A Field Guide to Demons: Fairies, Fallen Angels, and Other Subversive Spirits.* New York: Owl Books/Henry Holt, 1998.

Azhi Dahaka (Azhi Dahaki, Azi, Azdaha, Ahi, Zohak)

In Persian and Babylonian lore, a snake DEMON. Azhi Dahaka is Zohak in the Avesta creation myth of ZOROASTRIANISM, as the personification of the Evil One. His name means "biting snake."

Azhi Dahaka was created by Angra Mainyu (later AHRIMAN) and serves him. He has three heads and three jaws, which represent pain, anguish, and death; six or 18 eyes; fangs; and wings. He is filled with spiders, snakes, scorpions, and other venomous creatures that, if set free, would infect the entire world.

Azhi Dahaka also is described in human form with two venomous SERPENTs twining out from his neck, and as a DRUJ, half-human and half-beast. The snakes grew because either Ahriman or IBLIS kissed Azhi Dahaka there. The snakes had to be fed human brains or animal BLOOD.

In Babylonian lore, he was the king of Babel and had a human shape with serpents in his neck.

Azhi Dahaka governs storms and storm clouds and causes drought and disease. He eats cattle. In lore, he turned to eating humans, even the first one created, King Yima. He usurps Yima and rules for 1,000 years until he is vanquished by the Persian king Fereydun. The demon will destroy one-third of the world until he is stopped by Keresapa. In Persian lore, the Persian king Fereydun (Thraetona) binds him in chains under Mount Davand by the Caspian Sea until the end of time. In another version, Azhi Dahaka is chained to a rock in the sun until he dies.

Baal (Bael, Baell)   An agricultural and fertility deity of Canaan turned into a FALLEN ANGEL and a DEMON. Many minor deities of ancient Syria and Persia carried the name *Baal,* which means "the lord." The greatest Baal was the son of El, the High God of Canaan. He was the lord of life and ruled the death-rebirth cycle. He engaged in a battle with MOT (death) and was slain and sent to the underworld. The crops withered, until Baal's sister, Anath, the maiden goddess of love, found his body and gave it proper burial. The Canaanites worshipped Baal by sacrificing children by burning.

According to the Zohar, Baal is equal in rank to the archangel Raphael.

Baal is the first of the 72 SPIRITS OF SOLOMON. He is a king ruling in the east and governs 66 legions of DEMONS. He is triple-headed, with a cat's head and a toad's head on each side of his human head. He speaks hoarsely and imparts invisibility and wisdom.

Baalberith (Balberith)   Major DEMON, one of the spirits possessing Sister Madeleine in the AIX-EN-PROVENCE POSSESSIONS. Baalberith was once a prince in the angelic order of cherubim. According to JOHANN WEYER, Baalberith is the secretary and librarian of the archives in HELL and is a demon of the second order, a master of the Infernal Alliance. He also is a grand pontiff and master of ceremonies. He countersigns or notarizes PACTS with the DEVIL. He tempts men to blasphemy and murder.

In the Aix-en-Provence case, Baalberith volunteered the names of all the demons possessing Sister Madeleine, as well as the names of the saints who could counter them.

Variations of Baalberith's name are Ba'al, Baal Davar, Baal-Peor, Baalam, Baalphegor, Baalsebul, Baalzephon, Bael, Baell, BALAM, Balan, Balberith, Beal, Belberith, Beleth, Belfagor, Belial, Beliar, BELPHEGOR, BERITH, Bileth, Bilet, Byleth, and Elberith. As Berith, he is described as wearing a crown and riding a horse.

A magical ritual for gaining Baalberith's favor for 20 years is as follows: Take a black chicken to a CROSSROADS at night and sacrifice it by cutting its throat. Say, "Berith, do my work for 20 years." Bury the chicken deeply enough so that animals will not dig it up.

Babylonian demon trap   See INCANTATION BOWL.

bacucei   In Greek lore, DEMONS of pride. The *bacucei* incite people to vanity, pomposity, arrogance, condescension, and false humility.

Balam (Balan)   A former member of the angelic order of dominions and now one of the FALLEN ANGELS with 40 LEGIONS of DEMONS under his command. Balam is the 51st of the 72 SPIRITS OF SOLOMON. He is a terrible and powerful king with the heads of a bull, a man, and a ram; the tail of a SERPENT; and eyes of flaming fire. He rides on an angry bear (in some depictions, he is

Balam (DICTIONNAIRE INFERNAL)

Baphomet (AUTHOR'S COLLECTION)

naked) and carries a goshawk on his fist. He speaks hoarsely and gives true answers concerning the past, present, and future. He also can render men invisible and makes them have wit.

Baphomet   Symbol of the satanic goat. Baphomet is portrayed as a half-human, half-goat figure, or a goat head. The origin of the name *Baphomet* is unclear. It may be a corruption of *Mahomet* or *Muhammad*. The English occult historian Montague Summers suggested it was a combination of two Greek words, *baphe* and *metis,* or "absorption of knowledge." Baphomet has also been called the Goat of Mendes, the Black Goat, and the Judas Goat.

In the Middle Ages, Baphomet was believed to be an idol, represented by a human skull, a stuffed human head, or a metal or wooden human head with curly black hair. The idol was said to be worshipped by the Order of the Knights Templar as their source of fertility and wealth. The best-known representation of Baphomet is a drawing by the 19th-century French magician Eliphas Levi, called *The Baphomet of Mendes.* Levi combined elements of the Tarot Devil card and the he-goat worshipped in antiquity in Mendes, Egypt, which was said to fornicate with its women followers—as the church claimed the DEVIL did with witches.

The Church of Satan, founded in 1966 in San Francisco, adopted a rendition of Baphomet to symbolize SATANISM. The symbol is a goat's head drawn within an in-verted pentacle, enclosed in a double circle. In the outer circle, Hebraic figures at each point in the pentagram spell out LEVIATHAN, a huge water serpent DEMON associated with the Devil.

baptism   A spiritual rite of transformation, rebirth, initiation, and EXORCISM. In the Christian tradition, baptism protects a soul against evil and the snares of the DEVIL. In POSSESSION cases, a DEMONIAC who is exorcised must be rebaptized.

Christian baptism is performed with water, in keeping with the tradition established by JESUS' baptism in the river Jordan by John the Baptist. In Catholicism, holy water is sprinkled on the forehead. In some Protestant denominations, baptism is done by complete immersion in water.

Baptisms are part of many magical rituals and may include other elements as well. Baptism by fire and baptism by BLOOD symbolize intense purging and purification; blood also is redemptive, symbolizing the blood shed by Christ on the cross.

In DELIVERANCE ministry, baptism is essential in order to receive the gifts of the Holy Spirit for discernment of spirits and healing.

Demonic Baptism

During the witch hunts of the Inquisition, the Devil was believed to administer a sacrilegious baptism to his followers, usually at a SABBAT, and as part of an infernal PACT. The witches renounced their Christian faith and then adopted a grotesque new name to symbolize their new identity. Isobel Gowdie, a Scottish witch tried in 1662, said that witches were baptized in their own blood and took names such as "Able-and-Stout," "Over-the-dike-with-it," "Raise-the-wind," "Pickle-nearest-the-wind," "Batter-them-down-Maggy," and "Blow-Kate."

According to confessions made by accused witches, children were baptized by the Devil along with adults. Louis Gaufridi, who was executed for his role in the AIX-EN-PROVENCE POSSESSIONS of Ursuline nuns in 1611, confessed to witnessing baptisms at sabbats. He stated:

> I confess that baptism is administered at the Sabbat, and that every sorcerer, devoting himself to the Devil, binds himself by a particular vow that he will have all his children baptized at the Sabbat, if this may by any possible means be effected. Every child who is thus baptized at the Sabbat receives a name, wholly differing from his own name. I confess that at this baptism water, sulphur and salt are employed: the sulphur renders the recipient the Devil's slave while salt confirms his baptism in the Devil's service. I confess that the form and intention are to baptize in the name of Lucifer, Belzebuth and other demons making the sign of the cross beginning backwards and then tracing from the feet and ending at the head.

Such accounts of sabbats and baptisms have been discredited as fables that witnesses were forced to confess to by torture.

FURTHER READING:
MacNutt, Francis. *Deliverance from Evil Spirits: A Practical Manual*. Grand Rapids, Mich.: Chosen Books, 1995.
Summers, Montague. *The History of Witchcraft and Demonology*. London: Kegan Paul, Trench, Trubner, 1926.

Baraqijal   FALLEN ANGEL who teaches astrology. Baraqijal (possibly a variant of *Barakiel*) is named in 1 Enoch as a "chief of ten" leader of troops of fallen angels. In Jubilees he is identified as one of the WATCHERS.

bar egara   A Syrian DEMON that sits on the rooftops of homes and attacks men as they leave to go to work.

Barbatos   FALLEN ANGEL and eighth of the 72 SPIRITS OF SOLOMON. Formerly a member of the angelic order of virtues, Barbatos is a great count, earl, and duke of HELL, where he rules 30 LEGIONS of DEMONS. When the Sun is in Sagittarius, he appears with four kings and three companies of troops. He understands the languages of all animals, especially the singing of birds, the barking of dogs, and the lowing of bullocks. Barbatos can reveal

treasures hidden by magic and can reconcile friends and people in power. He teaches all sciences and knows all things in the past and of the future.

Barbiel (Barakiel, Barbuel, Baruel)   FALLEN ANGEL also described as a good angel.
As a fallen angel Barbiel is the former prince of the orders of virtues and angels. In HELL, he serves under Zaphiel as one of the seven Electors. As a good angel, Barbiel is ruler of October and, when equated with Barakiel, of February.

Barmiel   DEMON among the 31 AERIAL SPIRITS OF SOLOMON. Barmiel is the first and chief spirit under CASPIEL and rules as a king of the South. He commands 10 dukes during the daytime and 20 during the night to do his bidding and the bidding of an EXORCIST. Each duke has 20 servants, except four of the night dukes, who have none. The eight primary dukes of the daytime are Sochas, Tigara, Chansi, Keriel, Acteras, Barbil, Carpiel, and Manoi. The eight primary dukes of the nighttime are Barbis, Marguns, Canilel, Acreba, Morcaza, Baaba, Gabio, and Astib.

Baruchas   DEMON among the 31 AERIAL SPIRITS OF SOLOMON. Baruchas rules as a king in the east and north. His 14 major dukes each have 7,040 servants, all of whom are good-natured and willing to obey commands. The dukes are Quitta, Sarael, Melchon, Cavayr, Aboc, Cartael, Janiel, Pharol, Baoxas, Geriel, Monael, Chuba, Lwnael, and Decariel.

Bathin (Mathim)   FALLEN ANGEL and 18th of the 72 SPIRITS OF SOLOMON. Bathin is a strong and great duke of HELL with 30 LEGIONS of DEMONS under his command. He appears as a man with the tail of a SERPENT, astride a pale horse. He understands the lore of herbs and precious stones. He can transport people from country to country instantly.

Bealphares   DEMON who will tell where treasure is hidden and will fetch gold or silver. Bealphares appears in the likeness of either a fair man or a fair woman and will appear whenever summoned. Bealphares will transport a person from country to country without causing any harm and will answer questions truthfully. He will give all knowledge of the magical arts, grammar, speech and rhetoric, arithmetic, geometry, music, and astronomy.

Beelzebub (Baal-zebul, Beelzeboul, Belzebub)   Prince of DEMONS. Beelzebub, originally an idol of the Canaanites, means "Lord of the Flies." The name is a distortion of *Baal-zebul*, the chief Canaanite or Phoenician god, meaning "Lord of the Divine Abode" or "Lord of the Heavens."
Beelzebub manifests either as a gigantic, ugly fly or as a monstrous being of great height on a giant throne.

In his latter guise, he has a swollen face and chest, huge nostrils, horns, bat wings, duck feet, a lion's tail, and a covering of thick black hair.

Beelzebub has been a feared and formidable demon from the earliest accounts of him. He was the Prince of Demons in Hebrew belief at the time of JESUS. The Pharisees accused Jesus of exorcizing demons in Beelzebub's name, for according to belief, the power to expel unclean spirits was gained through PACTs with demons. The incident is recounted in Matthew (12:24–29), Mark (3:22–27), and Luke (11:14–22):

> And the scribes which came down from Jerusalem said, he hath Beelzebub, and by the prince of devils casteth he out devils. And he called them unto him, and said unto them in parables, How can Satan cast out Satan? And if a kingdom be divided against itself, that house cannot stand. And if Satan rise up against himself, and be divided, he cannot stand but hath an end. No man can enter into a strong man's house, and spoil his goods, except he will first bind the strong man; and then he will spoil his house. (Mark 3: 22–27)

In the pseudepigraphical text the Testament of Solomon, Beelzebub, or Beelzeboul, is the Prince of Demons and is controlled by King SOLOMON with the help of his magical ring. Solomon has the demon ORNIAS fetch Beelzebub to him; Beelzebub resists but succumbs to the power of the ring.

Beelzebub identifies himself as "the ruler of all demons." Solomon orders Beelzebub to explain the manifestation of demons, and he promises to give to the king all unclean spirits bound. He tells Solomon that he lives in the Evening Star (Venus). He alone is the Prince of Demons because he was the highest-ranking angel in heaven and is the only one left of the heavenly angels who fell. He was accompanied by another FALLEN ANGEL, ABEZETHIBOU, who was cast into the Red Sea. Abezethibou will return in triumph when he is ready, Beelzebub says.

Solomon orders him to summon Abezethibou, but Beelzebub refuses to present any demon. However, he says, a demon named EPHIPPAS will appear and raise Abezethibou out of the sea.

Beelzebub says he destroys tyrants, causes men to worship demons, and arouses sexual desire in holy men and "select priests." He also causes wars, instigates murders, and arouses jealousy. He is thwarted by "the Almighty God," Emmanuel (Jesus), and will disappear if anyone uses the oath Elo-i (my God, which Jesus cried on the cross).

Solomon tells Beelzebub to cut blocks of Theban marble for the building of his temple. The other demons protest at this unfitting task for so mighty a demon. Solomon tells Beelzebub that if he wishes his freedom, he will tell the king about other "heavenly things." Beelzebub says that Solomon can strengthen his house by burning oil of myrrh, frankincense, sea bulbs, spikenard, and saffron

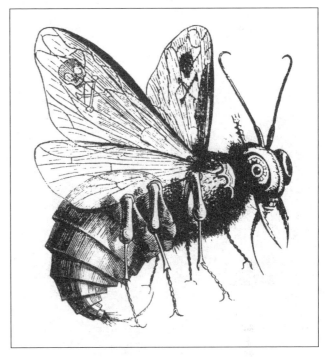

Beelzebub (DICTIONNAIRE INFERNAL)

and lighting seven lamps during an earthquake. Lighting the seven lamps at dawn will reveal the heavenly dragons pulling the chariot of the Sun. Solomon does not believe him and orders the demon to continue cutting marble and producing other demons for interrogation.

The apocryphal text *Gospel of Nicodemus* describes how Beelzebub came to rule in HELL over SATAN. After the crucifixion of JESUS, Satan bragged to Beelzebub that he was going to take Jesus to hell in revenge for all the times he had thwarted Satan. Beelzebub begged him not to do so, for Jesus was too powerful and would upset hell.

Jesus arrived, and Beelzebub pushed Satan from the mouth of hell and barricaded the gate, calling upon all the demons to help him. They could not keep Jesus out. Jesus trampled over Satan and snapped the chains of the imprisoned souls with a single word. He released all the trapped saints, who went immediately to heaven. Beelzebub was powerless against him.

As he left, Satan told Beelzebub, "Satan the Prince shall be subject to thy dominion forever, in the place of Adam and his righteous sons, who are Mine."

In medieval times Beelzebub was regarded as a demon of great power. He was said to reign over witches' SABBATs. Witches denied Christ in his name and chanted it as they danced: "Beelzebub goity, Beelzebub beyty [Beelzebub above, Beelzebub below]." Their Eucharist was bread with *Beelzebub* imprinted on it instead of *Jesus*.

There are many stories of his copulating with witches in wild orgies. The witches were said to gather around the altar in a semicircle and then lie flat on the ground.

They swallowed a foul medicine that made them sweat and then froze them in place. While they were unable to move, Beelzebub copulated with them. A frenzied orgy then began.

When BLACK MASSES were fashionable in high society in the 17th century, Beelzebub's name was chanted during the rites.

According to magical grimoires, a sorcerer conjures Beelzebub at his own risk of death by epilepsy, apoplexy, or strangulation. Once conjured, the demon is difficult to banish. A conjuring spell for him is:

BEELZEBUB	LUCIFER	MADILON
SOLYMO	SAROY	THEU
AMECLO	SAGRAEL	PRAREDUN
VENITE	BEELZEBUTH	AMEN.

Beelzebub also was among the demons blamed for demonic POSSESSION cases, among them NICOLE OBRY in Laon, France, in 1566, and the bewitchment of nuns in the LOUDUN POSSESSIONS and AIX-EN-PROVENCE POSSESSION in France in the late 16th and early 17th centuries, leading to the executions of his accused lieutenants, Fathers Louis Gaufridi and URBAIN GRANDIER.

One of the demon's most notorious acts was the EARLING POSSESSION, in the early 20th century in Earling, Iowa. Beelzebub entered young Anna Ecklund at the behest of her father, Jacob, in retaliation for not engaging in incestuous sex with him. The demon left on December 23, 1928, in a terrible roar of "Beelzebub, Judas, Jacob, Mina [Anna's aunt and Jacob's mistress]" followed by "Hell, hell, hell" and a terrible stench.

Beelzebub rules gluttony, the fifth of the SEVEN DEADLY SINS.

FURTHER READING:
Hyatt, Victoria, and Joseph W. Charles. *The Book of Demons.* New York: Simon & Schuster, 1974.
Mack, Carol K., and Dinah Mack. *A Field Guide to Demons: Fairies, Fallen Angels, and Other Subversive Spirits.* New York: Owl Books/Henry Holt, 1998.
Charlesworth, James H. ed. *The Old Testament Pseudepigrapha.* Vols. 1 & 2. New York: Doubleday, 1983; 1985.

Behemoth   In the Bible a name used for the DEVIL, referring to an impure animal and unclean spirit. *Behemoth* is derived from the Hebrew word *behemet,* meaning "beast" or "large animal."

Job 40:15–24 describes Behemoth as "the first of the works of God," the primal monster of the land:

Behold, Behemoth, which I made as I made you, he eats grass like an ox. Behold, his strength is in his loins, and his power in the muscles of his belly. He makes his tail stiff like a cedar; the sinews of his thighs are knit together. His bones are tubes of bronze, his limbs like bars of iron. He is the first of the works of God; let him

Behemoth (DICTIONNAIRE INFERNAL)

who made him bring near his sword! For the mountains yield food for him where all the wild beasts play. Under the lotus plant he lies, in the covert of the reeds and in the marsh. For his shade the lotus trees cover him; the willows of the brooks surround him. Behold, if the river is turbulent he is not frightened; he is confident though Jordan rushes against his mouth. Can one take him with hooks, or pierce his nose with a snare?

The verse 1 Enoch 60:7–8 a refers to Behemoth and LEVIATHAN as two monsters who will be parted at the final judgment:

On that day two monsters will be parted—one monster, a female named Leviathan, in order to dwell in the abyss of the ocean over the fountains of water; and (the other) a male called Behemoth, which holds his chest in an invisible desert whose name is Dundayin, east of the garden of Eden, wherein the elect and the righteous ones dwell.

Behemoth represents unconquerable strength.

Beherit   DEMON who is a great duke of HELL commanding 26 LEGIONs of lesser demons. Beherit has red skin and appears as a soldier wearing a crown and riding a red horse. He gives true answers about things past, present, and future and can turn metals into gold. A magician must wear a silver ring when conjuring him.

Other names for him are Beal, Beale, Beall, Berithi, Bofry, Bolfri, and Bolfry.

Beherit was named in the LOUDUN POSSESSIONS and was described as having a pleasant and laughing face.

Beleth (Bileth, Bilet, Byleth)   FALLEN ANGEL and 13th of the 72 SPIRITS OF SOLOMON. In HELL, Beleth is a terrible and mighty king who rules over 85 LEGIONS of DEMONS. He once was a member of the angelic order of powers.

Beleth arrives on a pale horse, preceded by many musicians playing trumpets and other instruments. He is very angry when first summoned and must be sent to a magical triangle by a magician pointing a hazel wand to the southeast. He must be treated with great courtesy, but if the magician shows fear, Beleth will forever lose respect for him. The magician must protect himself by wearing a silver ring on the middle finger of the left hand and holding it up to the face. If Beleth refuses to cooperate, the magician must proceed with his commands. According to JOHANN WEYER, a bottle of wine helps to mellow Beleth into cooperation.

Belial (Beliar)   One of the most important and evil DEMONs, who is deceptively beautiful in appearance and soft in voice, but full of treachery, recklessness, and lies. The 68th of the 72 SPIRITS OF SOLOMON, Belial is dedicated to creating wickedness and guilt in humankind, especially in the form of sexual perversions, fornication, and lust. St. Paul considered him to be chief of demons.

Belial's name may be derived from the Hebrew term *beli ya'al*, which means "without worth." In Hebrew lore, Belial was the next angel created after LUCIFER and was partly of the order of angels and partly of the order of virtues. He was evil from the start, one of the first to revolt against God. After his fall from heaven, he became the personification of lies and evil. Belial's name is sometimes a synonym for SATAN or the ANTICHRIST. In the Old Testament, the phrase "sons of Belial" refers to worthlessness and recklessness.

In the Testament of Solomon, a pseudepigraphical text, Belial danced before King SOLOMON and was among the demons who worked under the king's command, ruled by Solomon's magical ring.

In the Dead Sea Scrolls, Belial is described as the leader of the Sons of Darkness, the chief of all devils, dedicated to destruction.

In a Qumrun text called the *Testament of Amran* (Q543, 545–48), Belial is one of the WATCHERS, whose three titles are *Belial, Prince of Darkness,* and *King of Evil.* He is empowered over all darkness and his every way and every work are darkness.

JOHANN WEYER said Belial commands 80 legions of demons and serves as infernal ambassador to Turkey.

According to the magical grimoire the *Lemegeton,* sacrifices and offerings are necessary to invoke him. He appears as a beautiful angel riding a chariot pulled by fire-breathing dragons, and he speaks sweetly. He will break his promises to magicians, but those who manage to gain his true favor are handsomely rewarded with good FAMILIARs and other favors, such as preferences for senatorships or political offices.

FURTHER READING:
Eisenman, Robert, and Michael Wise. *The Dead Sea Scrolls Uncovered.* London: Element Books, 1992.
Hyatt, Victoria, and Joseph W. Charles. *The Book of Demons.* New York: Simon & Schuster, 1974.
The Old Testament Pseudepigrapha. Vols. 1 & 2. Edited by James H. Charlesworth. 1983. Reprint, New York: Doubleday, 1985.

bells   See AMULET.

Belphegor   Moabite god absorbed into Hebrew lore and then Christianity as a major DEMON. The name *Belphegor* means "lord of opening" or "lord Baal of Mt. Phegor." As a Moabite deity, he was known as Baal-Peor and ruled over fertility and sexual power. He was worshiped in the form of a phallus.

In the KABBALAH, Belphegor was an angel in the order of principalities prior to his fall. He is one of the Togarini, "the wranglers." He is an archdemon who is part of the demonic counterparts to the angels who rule the 10 *sephirot* of the Tree of Life; he rules over the sixth *sephirah.* He sits on a pierced chair, for excrement is his sacrificial offering.

In Christian demonology, Belphegor is the incarnation of one of the SEVEN DEADLY SINS, sloth, characterized by negligence and apathy. According to St. Thomas Aquinas, all sins that arise from ignorance are caused by sloth.

Belphegor also rules misogyny and licentious men. He emerged from HELL to investigate the marital state

Belphegor (DICTIONNAIRE INFERNAL)

among humans. For a time, he lived as a man to experience sexual pleasures. Appalled, he fled back to hell, happy that intercourse between men and women did not exist there.

Belphegor appears in the form of a beautiful young girl in order to tempt men. Besides sex and lust, he governs great riches. He is difficult to conjure, but if a person is successful and Belphegor takes a liking to him or her, the demon will bestow great treasures and wealth, as well as the ability to make discoveries and create inventions of all sorts. In hell, he rules inventions and discoveries and serves as infernal ambassador to France.

FURTHER READING:

Hyatt, Victoria, and Joseph W. Charles. *The Book of Demons.* New York: Simon & Schuster, 1974.

Mack, Carol K., and Dinah Mack. *A Field Guide to Demons: Fairies, Fallen Angels, and Other Subversive Spirits.* New York: Owl Books/Henry Holt, 1998.

Benedict (St.) medal   See AMULET.

Berith (Balberith, Baalberith, Beal, Belfry, Bofi, Bolfri, Elberith)   FALLEN ANGEL. Berith appears as a man wearing a soldier's uniform and a golden crown and riding a red horse.

As an angel, Berith was prince of the order of cherubim. As a DEMON, he serves as a master of ceremonies, duke, and grand pontiff in HELL, presiding over 26 LEGIONs of demons. He notarizes PACTs with the DEVIL.

Berith (DICTIONNAIRE INFERNAL)

Berith was important to some alchemists, who believed he had the power to transmute all base metals into gold. He was tricky to conjure, however, and had to be summoned with magic rings bearing his SEAL. He was known for making great promises, but also for being a great liar.

One conjuration spell for Berith calls for bleeding a black chicken at a CROSSROADS on a Monday night. The conjurer promises out loud, "Berith will do all my work for 20 years and I shall recompense him." Alternately, the pledge can be written on parchment with the chicken's BLOOD. Berith will appear and do as commanded—but he will claim his reward, the conjuror's soul, in 20 years' time.

Berith was named as a key demon in the famous AIX-EN-PROVENCE POSSESSIONS in France in 1611.

Bernael   ANGEL of darkness and evil equated with BELIAL. Bernael sometimes is equated with Haziel, who is otherwise a cherub and good angel.

Bidiel   DEMON and wandering duke of the air. Bidiel commands 20 dukes and 200 lesser dukes, plus other servants. The dukes change their offices and locations every year. They appear in the form of beautiful humans and are willing to obey an EXORCIST. The 10 great dukes are Mudiret, Cruchan, Bramsiel, Armomiel, Lameniel, Andruchiel, Merasiel, Charoblel, Parsifiel, and Chremoas.

Bifrons   FALLEN ANGEL and the 46th of the 72 SPIRITS OF SOLOMON. The earl Bifrons has a monstrous appearance but will take on human shape when ordered to do so. He teaches astronomy, astrology, geometry, other mathematical arts, and the knowledge of herbs, precious stones, and woods. He removes dead bodies from their graves and leaves them in other places and lights phantom candles on the graves. He commands six LEGIONs of DEMONs.

Binsfeld, Peter (ca. 1540–1603)   German Jesuit priest, demonologist, and witch hunter.

Peter Binsfeld was born in the village of Binsfeld, Eifel, Germany. His father was a farmer and craftsman. Gifted in childhood, he was sent to Rome for study. He returned to Binsfeld and became prominent in campaigns against the Protestants.

Binsfeld was elected suffragan bishop of Treves (Trier) and became one of the primary witch hunters behind the trials of 306 persons accused of WITCHCRAFT between 1587 and 1594. The region was gripped by a terrible blight on crops, and the public readily blamed their troubles on the evildoing of witches.

Binsfeld authored the *Treatise on Confessions by Evildoers and Witches* (1589), which became a leading inquisitors' handbook and was translated into several languages. He encouraged denouncements—the accused at the Treves trials denounced about 6,000 people—and sanctioned the repetition of torture. He maintained that the DEVIL could not appear in the form of an innocent person, but he did not believe in the DEVIL'S MARK and the shape-shifting ability of witches. He allowed the trials of children under certain conditions.

In the Treves trials, even leading citizens were not immune. The chief judge, Dietrich Flade, was himself accused and burned at the stake, as were two burgomasters and several councilors and associate judges. Numerous clerics were ruined, and the children of the condemned were stripped of all their belongings and sent into exile.

Binsfeld's treatise included a classification of DEMONS and their sins; he was the first person to pair demons with the SEVEN DEADLY SINS: LUCIFER (pride), MAMMON (avarice), ASMODEUS (lechery), SATAN (anger), BEELZEBUB (gluttony), LEVIATHAN (envy), and BELPHEGOR (sloth).

Binsfeld died in Treves of the bubonic plague around 1603.

black book   A magical handbook that provides instructions for trafficking with spirits, including DEMONS and ANGELS; divination; and acquisition and use of supernatural powers. In some cases, possession of the black book itself bestows supernatural powers, wealth, or luck upon its owner. However, use of a black book usually backfires with serious consequences. Some black books are said to be written in BLOOD as a PACT with the DEVIL.

According to a German tale, a black book of unknown origin was passed down through inheritance and came into the possession of some peasants. Its magical powers were released by reading it forward and backward. If anyone failed to read the book backward, the Devil was able to take control of him or her. Once activated, the book enabled people to acquire great wealth and do terrible things to others without punishment. However, there were consequences to using the black book that caused its owners grief. They tried to get rid of the book but could not do so. They sought help from a minister, who successfully nailed the book into a drawer. Such a tale serves to demonstrate the power of Christianity over both occult powers and pagan folk magic.

Black books are more than mysteriously empowered items of folklore, however. In practice, many people and families kept black books as guides for living. They included magical cures and healing recipes, prayers, CHARMS, incantations, blessings, rituals for burial, seasonal and agricultural rites, techniques for divination, and ways to ward off evil and bad luck and attract good luck. The material is a mixture of old folkways and lore and Christian elements. Some black books credit their origins to Cyprianus of Antioch (St. Cyprian), who lived in the fourth century C.E. in Turkey. According to lore, Cyprian was a sorcerer who escaped the domination of DEMONS and the Devil by making the sign of the cross. He converted to Christianity and became a bishop. He ended his life as a martyr.

See GRIMOIRES.

FURTHER READING:
Butler, E. M. *Ritual Magic.* Cambridge: Cambridge University Press, 1949.
Rustad, Mary S., ed. and trans. *The Black Books of Elverum.* Lakeville, Minn.: Galde Press, 1999.

black dogs   Spectral animals associated with demonic powers, death, and disaster. Phantom black dogs are widespread in folklore. They are said to be DEMONS or the DEVIL in shape-shifted form or a demonic animal companion of demons.

Spectral black dogs are often unusually large and have glowing red or yellow eyes. They give out an unearthly, bone-chilling howl. They like to roam remote areas of the countryside. The sight of one is a harbinger of death or disaster.

Sometimes spectral black dogs appear in the middle of lonely roads. If they are struck by a car, they disappear and the vehicle is not damaged.

One famous black dog in English folklore is Black Shuck. *Shuck* derives from an old Anglo-Saxon term, *scucca* or *sceocca,* meaning "demon" or "Satan."

During the European witch hunts, witches were often said to have FAMILIARs in the form of black dogs, or to be visited by their master, the Devil, in the shape of a black dog.

In Arabian lore, black dogs are a favorite form taken by the DJINN. If a djinn becomes attached to a human, it may assume the shape of a black dog in order to get close to that person.

See ABEL DE LARUE; CERBERUS.

Black Mass   An obscene parody of the Catholic Holy Mass at which the DEVIL is worshipped. During the Inquisition, witch hunters and demonologists claimed that witches—or any heretics—frequently performed Black Masses as part of their infernal SABBATs with DEMONS and the Devil. Black Masses have been performed for centuries and occur in contemporary times, but it is doubtful that they have been as prevalent—or as outrageous—as often claimed.

Characteristics
There is no single definitive Black Mass ritual. The purpose is to parody the Catholic Holy Mass by performing it or parts of it backward, inverting the cross, stepping or spitting on the cross, stabbing the host, and performing other sacrilegious acts. Urine is sometimes substituted for the holy water used to sprinkle the attendees, urine or water is substituted for the wine, and rotted turnip slices, pieces of black leather, or black triangles are substituted for the host. Black candles are substituted for white ones. The service is performed by a defrocked or renegade priest, who wears vestments that are black or the color of dried blood and embroidered with an inverted cross, a goat's head, or magical symbols.

One famous form of the Black Mass was the Mass of St. Secaire, said to have originated in the Middle Ages in Gascony for the purpose of cursing an enemy to death by a slow, wasting illness. Montague Summers provides a description of it in *The History of Witchcraft and Demonology*:

> The mass is said upon a broken and desecrated altar in some ruined or deserted church where owls hoot and mope and bats flit through the crumbling windows, where toads spit their venom upon the sacred stone. The priest must make his way thither late attended only by an acolyte of impure and evil life. At the first stroke of eleven he begins; the liturgy of hell is mumbled backward, the canon said with a mow and a sneer; he ends just as midnight tolls.

The Mass of St. Secaire requires a triangular black host and brackish water drawn from a well in which the corpse of an unbaptized baby has been tossed.

History

Magical uses of the Mass and alleged perversions of the Mass are almost as old as Christianity itself. In the second century, St. Irenaeus accused the Gnostic teacher Marcus of perverting the Mass. The Gelasian Sacramentary (ca. sixth century) documents masses to be said for a variety of magical purposes, including weather control, fertility, protection, and love divination. Masses also were said with the intent to kill people; these were officially condemned as early as 694 by the Council of Toledo.

The magical significance of the Black Mass lies in the belief that the Holy Mass involves a miracle: the transubstantiation of the bread and wine into the body and blood of Christ. If the priest, as magician, can effect a miracle in a Holy Mass, then he surely can effect magic in a mass used for other purposes. Priests who attempted to subvert the Holy Mass for evil purposes, such as cursing a person to death, were condemned by the Catholic Church as early as the seventh century.

Magical uses of the Mass increased in the Middle Ages. The beginnings of the organized Black Mass as part of Devil worship coincides with the expansion of the Inquisition and rising public fears about the evil powers of witches. The first witch trials to feature accusations of sabbats, Devil's PACTS, and Black Masses all occurred in the 14th century.

In 1307, the powerful and wealthy Order of the Knights Templar was destroyed on accusations of conducting blasphemous rites in which Christ was renounced and idols made of stuffed human heads were worshipped. The Knights Templar also were accused of spitting and trampling upon the cross and worshipping the Devil in the shape of a black cat. Members of the order were arrested, tortured, and executed.

In 1440, GILLES DE RAIS, a French baron, was arrested and accused of conducting Black Masses in the cellar of his castle in order to gain riches and power. He was charged with kidnapping, torturing, and murdering more than 140 children as sacrifices. He was convicted and executed.

In the 16th and 17th centuries, priests in France were arrested and executed for conducting Black Masses. Many of the masses were theatrical events intended for social shock and protest against the church; the seriousness of the actual "Devil worship" was dubious. For example, in 1500, the cathedral chapter of Cambrai held Black Masses in protest against their bishop. A priest in Orléans, Gentien le Clerc, tried in 1614–15, confessed to performing a "Devil's mass," which was followed by drinking and a wild sexual orgy.

Black Masses figured in high-profile POSSESSION cases, such as the LOUVIERS POSSESSIONS in 1647. Ursuline nuns said they had been bewitched and possessed and were forced by chaplains—led by Abbé Thomas Boulle—to participate nude in Black Masses, defiling the cross, trampling upon the host, and having sex with demons.

The height of the theatrical, anti-Catholic Black Mass was reached in the late 17th century, during the reign of Louis XIV, who was criticized for his tolerance of witches and sorcerers. It became fashionable among nobility to hire priests to perform erotic Black Masses in dark cellars. The chief organizer of these rites was Catherine Deshayes, known as "La Voisin," a witch who told fortunes and sold love philters. La Voisin employed a cadre of priests who performed the masses, including the ugly and evil Abbé Guiborg, who were gold-trimmed and lace-lined vestments and scarlet shoes.

The mistress of Louis XIV, the marquise de Montespan, sought out the services of La Voisin because she feared the king was becoming interested in another woman. Using Montespan as a naked altar, Guiborg said three Black Masses over her, invoking Satan and his demons of lust and deceit, BEELZEBUB, ASMODEUS, and ASTAROTH, to grant whatever Montespan desired. While incense burned, the throats of children were slit and their blood poured into chalices and mixed with flour to make the host. Whenever the mass called for kissing the altar, Guiborg kissed Montespan. He consecrated the host over her genitals and inserted pieces in her vagina. The ritual was followed by an orgy. The bodies of the children were later burned in a furnace in La Voisin's house.

When the scandal of the Black Masses broke, Louis arrested 246 men and women, many of them some of France's highest-ranking nobles, and put them on trial. Confessions were made under torture. Most of the nobility received only jail sentences and exile in the countryside. Thirty-six of the commoners were executed, including La Voisin, who was burned alive in 1680.

Louis kept Montespan out of the trials, but she suffered great humiliation and disgrace. When Louis' queen, Maria Theresa, died in 1683, he married another woman, Madame de Maintenon.

Paralleling the theatrical and antichurch Black Masses were the accusations of Black Masses conducted by witches. In the 14th–18th centuries, inquisitors considered Devil worship in obscene rites to be an integral part of witchcraft. Victims tortured by witch hunters and inquisitors confessed to participating in obscene rituals at SABBATs, in which the cross was defiled and the Devil served as priest. It is doubtful that such sabbats actually took place as described by inquisitors and demonologists. There is no evidence that the Black Mass was part of historical European witchcraft.

The Black Mass continued as a decadent fashion into the 19th century during an occult revival. Joris K. Huysmans' 1891 novel *Là-bas* (*Down There* or *Lower Depths*) features the Gilles de Rais story. It draws upon Abbé Boulle from Louivers—Huysmans even inserted himself as a character—in its exploration of satanic rites and contains a description of the Black Mass.

Durtal, the character who is based on Huysmans, is taken by a woman, Hyacinthe, to a dingy, moldy chapel that once was used by Ursuline nuns, then turned into a livery and a barn to store hay. It has been taken over by satanists. Among the participants is a debauched nun. A choking incense of henbane, datura, dried nightshade, and myrrh is burned. After a mass of obscenities and blasphemies and the desecration of the host, the place erupts in "a monstrous pandemonium of prostitutes and maniacs." Participants, high on the fumes, tear off their clothes and writhe on the floor. Sexual acts are implied but not described by Huysmans; his two characters who are witnesses become disgusted and exit the scene.

The HELL-FIRE CLUB, a fraternal group in London in the late 19th century, was said to perform a Black Mass regularly in worship of the Devil, though it is more likely that the rites were little more than sexual escapades with liberal quantities of alcohol.

In the 20th century, the Black Mass became a staple of Devil worship novels and films. One of the most influential fictions was the 1934 novel *The Devil Rides Out* by Dennis Wheatley, with a black magician character, Morcata, modeled on ALEISTER CROWLEY. The novel was made into a film in 1968 by Hammer Films of England, during a time of occult revival and the birth of Witchcraft, or Wicca, as a religion. Black Masses are not part of modern Witchcraft, or Wicca, which emphasizes rituals composed of ceremonial magic and reconstructed pagan seasonal rites.

The occult revival that began in the 1960s saw the birth of contemporary SATANISM as a religious practice, with varying views on the Black Mass. Satanic cults born of social rebellion also instituted Black Masses as a form of social shock.

Aleister Crowley on the Black Mass

In 1947, a Black Mass was performed at the graveside of Aleister Crowley during his funeral. During life, Crowley was described as practicing "black magic" and performing satanic rituals. However, he stated emphatically that he despised black magic and could never perform a Black Mass, which was an abuse of spiritual power.

Crowley's rituals were "anti-Christian"; that does not make them "satanic." For example, he wrote a Gnostic Mass that remains a central ritual in the Ordo Templi Orientis magical order, of which he was head in England.

In 1933, the London *Sunday Dispatch* newspaper published an article by Crowley on black magic. In it he commented on the Black Mass:

> In Paris, and even in London, there are misguided people who are abusing their priceless spiritual gifts to obtain petty and temporary advantages through these practices.
>
> The "Black Mass" is a totally different matter.
>
> I could not celebrate it if I wanted to, for I am not a consecrated priest of the Christian Church.
>
> The celebrant must be a priest, for the whole idea of the practice is to profane the Sacrament of the Eucharist. Therefore you must believe in the truth of the cult and the efficacy of its ritual.
>
> A renegade priest gathers about him a congregation of sensation-hunters and religious fanatics; then only can the ceremonies of profanation be of extended black magical effect.
>
> There are many ways of abusing the Sacrament. One of the best known of which is the "Mass of Saint Secaire," the purpose of which is to cause an enemy to wither away.
>
> At this "mass," always held in some secret place, preferably in a disused chapel, at midnight, the priest appears in canonical robes.
>
> But even in his robes there is some sinister change, a perversion of their symbolic sanctity.
>
> There is an altar, but the candles are of black wax. The crucifix is fixed the head downwards.
>
> The clerk to the priest is a woman, and her dress, although it seems to be a church garment, is more like a costume in a prurient revue. It has been altered to make it indecent.
>
> The ceremony is a parody of the orthodox Mass, with blasphemous interpolations.
>
> The priest must be careful, however, to consecrate the Host in the orthodox manner. The wine has been adulterated with magical drugs like deadly nightshade and vervain, but the priest must convert it into the blood of Christ.
>
> The dreadful basis of the Mass is that the bread and wine have imprisoned the Deity. Then they are subjected to terrible profanations.
>
> Indescribable
>
> This is supposed to release the powers of evil and bring them into alliance. (It is rather the case of the mouse trying to make a friend of the cat!)
>
> In the congregational form of the Black Mass the priest, having finished his abominations—these are, quite frankly, indescribable—scatters the fragments of the Host on the floor, and the assistants scramble for the soiled fragments, the possession of which, they

believe, will allow them to work their petty and malicious designs.

My most memorable personal experience of the effects of black magic occurred when I was living in Scotland. The machinations of a degraded and outcast member of the Order caused my hounds to die, my servants to become insane. The struggle lasted until the recoil of the current of hated caused the luckless sorcerer to collapse.

The explanation of its effects is that, if you believe passionately enough in your will to do something, then power to achieve it will accrue to you.

The Black Mass in Satanism

When the Church of Satan was founded in 1966, the Black Mass was not included among the rituals. Its founder, Anton Szandor Lavey, said it was outmoded. Church of Satan followers sometimes perform Black Masses as theatrical events.

Other satanic groups have their own practices, and their own versions of the Black Mass. The Temple of Set, founded by Michael Aquino, embraces black magic as a form of self-benefit; elements of the Black Mass are incorporated into some of the rituals. The Order of the Nine Angles, founded by Stephen Brown, incorporates the Black Mass as part of its path of self-development. The blasphemy contained in it has not only mocked Christianity and Christ but also elevates Adolf Hitler as a "noble savior." There are groups of "Traditional Secretive Satanists," who practice the Black Mass, and "Nontraditional Satanists," many of whom place less emphasis on it.

The formats of Black Masses vary with different groups. A Satanic Black Mass is conducted for obtaining and raising magical power. JESUS is cursed and Satan is exalted. A blasphemous mass, where the altar is a nude woman and the vagina is the tabernacle, is performed. If possible, a real host stolen from a Catholic Church is placed in the vagina in the midst of reciting distorted psalms with hot music and all kind of obscenities, cursing Jesus, and honoring Satan. The fake priest ends up having real sex with the woman with the host still in the vagina. A sexual orgy by the participants follows.

Other elements may include drinking urine, blood, or wine from a human skull; shouting obscenities and the names of demons, especially Beelzebub; trampling a cross; reciting blasphemous prayers and psalms; and performing other blasphemous acts. Supposedly, there are some practices of infant sacrifice and cannibalism, but these claims are doubtful. Animal sacrifices are more likely.

FURTHER READING:

Baroja, Julio Caro. *The World of the Witches.* Chicago: University of Chicago Press, 1975.
"Black Mass." Available online. URL: http://www.religion-cults.com/Occult/Satanism/Satanism.htm#Black%20Mass. Downloaded February 2, 2008.
"Black Mass." Available online. URL: http://www.satanheaven.com. Downloaded February 2, 2008.
Crowley, Aleister. "Black Magic Is not a Myth." From the *Sunday Dispatch,* July 2, 1933. Available online. URL: http://www.lashtal.com/nuke/module-subjects-viewpage-pageid-89.phtml. Downloaded February 2, 2008.
The Encyclopedic Sourcebook of Satanism. Edited by James R. Lewis and Jesper Aagaard Petersen. Amherst, N.Y.: Prometheus Books, 2008.
Huysmans, J. K. *La-Bas.* New York: Dover, 1972.
LaVey, Anton Szandor. *The Satanic Bible.* New York: Avon Books, 1969.
Russell, Jeffrey B. *A History of Witchcraft.* London: Thames and Hudson, 1980.
Summers, Montague. *The History of Witchcraft and Demonology.* London: Kegan Paul, Trench, Trubner, 1926.

Blai, Adam Christian (1970–)   Therapist and demonologist. Adam Blai was born in Media, Pennsylvania, on August 23, 1970. After a brief near-fatal illness shortly after birth, he had an uneventful early childhood. A series of hypnopompic and hypnogogic dream experiences started at age five and continued, causing him to develop an interest in meditation, shamanism, and various models of mystical experiences. This led to an interest in psychology with research in brain structure and function, hypnosis, and clinical psychology. Blai has worked in outpatient settings as a therapist as well as in a forensic context, which have afforded experience with the full range of human experience and psychopathology. He has taught at a major state university as well as a small exclusive liberal arts school.

Blai's work in the paranormal started when he was an adviser to a university-based paranormal club, which led to work with the Roman Catholic Church. He is now a member of the INTERNATIONAL ASSOCIATION OF EXORCISTS and speaks from the Roman Catholic perspective on demonology, POSSESSION, and EXORCISM. His casework is predominantly within the church, with additional work on cases with JOHN ZAFFIS and a few other experienced people in the paranormal research field. He has had extensive training in Europe under leading EXORCISTS such as GABRIELE AMORTH and JOSE ANTONIO FORTEA.

Blai researches advances in paranormal activity detection and theory, including the application of the Global Consciousness Project model to extreme paranormal manifestations.

blood   A source of power unleashed in ritual sacrifices to appease gods and conjure DEMONS and other spirits. Blood sacrifices are described in some GRIMOIRES, supposedly derived from ancient rituals calling for animal sacrifices to please God.

Animal Blood

Animal blood is used in folk CHARMS and spells. The blood of a black cat is said to cure pneumonia. A black hen beaten to death with a white cane will provide blood that can be used in sympathetic magic: Smear the blood on a victim or his or her clothing to CURSE the victim with a death as agonizing as that of the hen.

ALEISTER CROWLEY sacrificed animals in his magical rituals. In 1909, while working with his assistant, Victor Neuberg, Crowley had a formidable encounter with a DEMON named CHORONZON. The demon was evoked in a ritual that involved slitting the throats of three pigeons and pouring their blood upon the sand.

Human Blood

Some sources of blood are considered to be more powerful than others. Human blood is identified with the soul and carries the greatest power. Ingesting human blood is believed to confer the powers and strengths of the victim upon the conqueror. Possessing a few drops of a person's blood gives a witch or magician power over that person or enables the magician to harness that person's emotional state. By the principles of sympathetic magic, a person may be bewitched or cursed.

The blood of executed criminals is said to be a powerful protector against disease and bad luck, because of the energy of resentment and fury, which is released upon execution. Spectators at public executions such as beheadings sought to obtain the victims' blood on handkerchiefs or bits of cloth for later use in magical rituals.

Human blood also is used to seal pacts of oath and brotherhood. During the European witch hunts of the Inquisition, it was believed that witches signed blood PACTs with the Devil to pledge servitude and obedience to him. The magical power of a witch could be neutralized or destroyed by burning her blood in fire—hence the common European method of execution by burning at the stake—or a practice called "blooding." The witch was scored above the breast and allowed to bleed, sometimes to death.

Human blood was believed to strengthen the foundations of buildings, and sometimes sacrificial victims were walled up in temples, forts, and other structures.

Menstrual Blood

Menstrual blood, which is linked to the phases of the Moon, is particularly potent. The blood of the Goddess, also called wine, milk, mead, and "wise blood," appears universally in mythologies; it is drunk as a charm for wisdom, fertility, regeneration, immortality, and healing. The blood of ISIS, symbolized in an ambrosia drink, conferred divinity on pharaohs. According to ancient Taoism, red yin juice, as menstrual blood was called, conferred long life or immortality.

Menstrual blood has a long history of being feared by men, and proscriptions have been given against associating with, touching, or having sex with menstruating women, for their blood has the power to harm. Ancient Romans believed the touch of a menstruating woman could blunt knives, blast fruit, sour wine, rust IRON, and cloud MIRRORs. In the Old Testament, Leviticus 18:19 states, "You shall not come near a woman while she is impure by her uncleanness to uncover her nakedness." The Talmud instructs that husband and wife are to be sexually separated during menstruation and for a week later in order to ensure cleanliness.

In Christianity, menstrual blood was believed to spawn DEMONs and to defile altars. Up to the late 17th century, menstruating women were forbidden to partake in communion or, in some cases, even to enter church.

FURTHER READING:
Cavendish, Richard. *The Black Arts.* New York: G. P. Putnam's Sons, 1967.
Guiley, Rosemary Ellen. *The Encyclopedia of Witches, Witchcraft, and Wicca.* 3rd ed. New York: Facts On File, 2008.

bogey In English folklore a horrible evil spirit or hobgoblin, usually big and black, who scares children. The "Bogey-Man" or "Boogie-Man" arrives at night and appears in bedrooms and at the sides of beds. In appearance the bogey often looks like the dark silhouette of a man.

The bogey is called the *bwg* (ghost) in Welsh, *bogle* in Scotland, and *Boggelmann* in German. Among other names are bug-a-boo, boo, bugbear, bock, and boggart. The Irish *puca* is similar. *Bogey* also is another name for the DEVIL.

Botis (Otis) FALLEN ANGEL and 17th of the 72 SPIRITS OF SOLOMON. As a great president and earl of HELL, Botis commands 60 LEGIONs of DEMONs. He appears in the shape of an ugly viper but will take on human form with large teeth and horns when commanded to do so. He carries a sharp sword. He sees past, present, and future and reconciles friends and enemies.

Brossier, Marthe (16th century) Fraudulent POSSESSION case. Used as a vehicle for raising money from the gullible, Marthe Brossier's alleged possession by BEELZEBUB also served as a means for the Catholic Church to try to undercut the religious reform of the Huguenots, members of the Protestant Reformed Church of France. The case stands as the first where accusations of fraud in an alleged possession were backed up by detailed physical evidence.

Reported as both the eldest and the youngest of four daughters of a poor draper in the town of Romorantin, Brossier first showed signs of unusual behavior at the age of 25 in 1598. Still without a husband, she cut her hair, wore men's clothing, screamed, and contorted. She attacked her friend Anne Chevion (also known as Chevreau) in a fit of jealousy, accusing Anne of bewitching her. Although no records exist detailing Anne's fate, other possessed persons in Romorantin successfully used the WITCHCRAFT defense. Brossier's career as a demoniac also may have been influenced by an account of the MIRACLE OF LAON. In any case, she demanded EXORCISM by her local priest and began exhibiting fits, impossible body contortions, a psychosomatic pregnancy, and, as in Laon, ravings by Beelzebub against the heresy of the Huguenots.

Realizing the celebrity potential of her possession, Brossier and her family traveled the Loire valley, stopping in various towns for exorcisms and drawing large audiences. The physician Michel Marescot, who examined Brossier in 1599, unkindly described her tours as "fifteen months spent in carrying of her too [sic] and fro, like an Ape or a Beare, to Angers, Saulmur, Clery, Orleans and Paris."

In Orléans, Brossier obtained a certificate of genuine possession from the local priest. Not everyone was fooled, however, as administrators in Clery and Orléans posted documents forbidding any priest to exorcise "that fictitious spirit." At Angers, Bishop Charles Miron tested Brossier on her reactions to holy water and sacred Latin texts, and she failed both examinations: She did not react to real holy water but to ordinary water, and the Latin, which caused more convulsions, was merely a line from Virgil's *Aeneid*. Bishop Miron ordered Brossier and her family to return to Romorantin and stop playing tricks.

Instead, in early March 1599, Brossier and her father went to Paris. Just a few days prior, the Paris parliament had passed the Edict of Nantes, giving official tolerance to both Catholic and Huguenot beliefs. The Brossiers sought refuge in the Capuchin monastery of Ste. Genevieve, where the monks began to exorcise Brossier immediately and broadcast Beelzebub's anti-Huguenot diatribes. The exorcisms attracted huge crowds, and by the end of March, public feeling was so high that Henri De Gondy, bishop of Paris, intervened to verify Brossier's possessed state. Both theologians and physicians examined Brossier, including Marescot, and all agreed on March 30 that Brossier was not possessed but merely ill; her symptoms were mainly counterfeit.

On March 31, two of the doctors reexamined Brossier and found an insensitive spot between her thumb and index finger. Believing it to be a DEVIL'S MARK, they asked for a postponement of the earlier report and began to exorcise Brossier on April 1. The Capuchins called in another group of doctors on April 2, and on April 3 they proclaimed her genuinely possessed. But their efforts were too late.

Fearing a breakdown of the edict, King Henri IV ordered a halt to the public exorcisms. Brossier was imprisoned for 40 days, and her copy of the Miracle of Laon was confiscated. Her convulsions gradually ceased. On May 24, Parliament ordered Brossier and her father to return to Romorantin, where the local judge was to check on her every two weeks. All was quiet until December, when Alexandre de la Rochefoucauld, the prior of St. Martin-de-Randan in Auvergne and a believer in Brossier's possession, kidnapped her and took her to Avignon and finally to Rome to see the pope, all the while encouraging her anti-Huguenot performances. They arrived just in time for the Papal Jubilee of 1600,

where Brossier contorted and was exorcized for the edification of the tourists.

Upon the advice of Henri IV and other clerics, the French cardinal d'Ossat stopped the Prior's exhibitions, although Brossier continued to perform. According to an account by Palma Cayet in 1605, Brossier was still staging possession fits in Milan as of 1604 and acting as Beelzebub's mouthpiece. That is the last record of her escapades.

FURTHER READING:
Ferber, Sarah. *Demonic Possession and Exorcism in Early Modern France.* London: Routledge, 2004.
Walker, D. P. *Unclean Spirits: Possession and Exorcism in France and England in the Late Sixteenth and Early Seventeenth Centuries.* Philadelphia: University of Pennsylvania Press, 1981.

Bruner (Burner), Theobald and Joseph (19th century)
French case considered a classic example of demonic POSSESSION and EXORCISM. Two brothers, Theobald and Joseph Bruner of Illfurt (Illfurth), Alsace, exhibited all the accepted signs of diabolic interference—contortions, blasphemies, levitation, speaking in unknown languages, revulsion toward holy objects, and clairvoyance—while the DEVIL was successfully driven out through organized rituals.

Theobald (Thiebaut), born in 1855, and Joseph, born in 1857, first began displaying unusual and frightening behavior in September 1865. Confined mostly to their beds for the next two years, the boys would entwine their legs, sometimes every two or three hours, in knots so tight that no human pressure could unentangle them. They would stand on their heads for hours, bend completely backward; become rigid; and undergo attacks of vomiting, expelling great quantities of yellow foam, seaweed, and foul-smelling feathers.

The boys levitated as well, rising upward while remaining seated or in bed. Sometimes their mother, seated on the bed while it rose off the floor, would be thrown into the corner. Their room was unbearably hot, although no stove was lit; only by sprinkling holy water on the bed did the room's temperature return to normal. Furniture flew about the room, the drapes would fall down by themselves, and the windows would burst open. The entire house shook, as if from an earthquake.

More disturbing were the boys' increasing fascination with the Devil and hatred of holy objects. They would draw devilish faces on the walls by their bed and talk to them. Rosaries or sacred relics placed on or under their bed would send the boys into hysterical fits, hiding under the covers and screaming blasphemies. The blessed host was particularly loathsome, and pictures of the Virgin Mary, or even the mention of her name, drove the boys crazy. According to the records kept by the local priest, Father Karl (Charles) Brey, if a "clergyman or pious Catholic visited the house, the possessed children crawled hastily under a table or bed, or jumped out the window." But when someone of less fervent faith entered, the boys were delighted, proclaiming, "That one is one of ours. They should all be like that!"

The final proof of their possession was the boys' ability to speak in foreign languages—English, Latin, and various Spanish dialects—unknown to them and to display paranormal, or clairvoyant, knowledge of outside events. Father Brey told that two hours before one woman died, Theobald knelt in his bed and acted as if he were ringing a mourning bell. On another occasion, Theobald rang his imaginary mourning bell for an entire hour, claiming it was for the death of Gregor Kunegel. Kunegel's daughter happened to be in the house and angrily denied her father's death, protesting that he was not even ill but working as a mason on a new seminary building. Theobald answered that the man had fallen, as indeed he had, and broken his neck.

It was about four years until the Bruners and Father Brey agreed on a diagnosis of demonic possession and convinced Father Brey's bishop to approve an exorcism. Finally, Theobald was sent to the St. Charles Orphanage at Schiltigheim, near Strasbourg, on October 3, 1869. Held by three strong men and forced to stand before the altar, Theobald remained silent for three days (other accounts say two), only drooling a thick yellow froth. On the fourth day, he roared in a horrible voice that he had arrived and was furious. When the nun asked who had come, the Devil in Theobald answered, "I am the Lord of Darkness!" At that point, Theobald was placed in a straitjacket, as he began tearing his clothes and breaking everything in reach. Finally, after the exorcist, Father Stumpf, again called upon the Virgin, Theobald screamed in agony and pitched forward in a deep sleep. When he became conscious, he was himself again and had no memory of the previous three days.

Father Brey himself exorcized Joseph, also in the orphanage, on October 27. After only three hours of frantic struggling and screaming, the Devil released him. As was Theobald, Joseph was surprised to find himself in church and did not remember his ordeal.

Unfortunately, the boys did not live long, peaceful lives. Theobald died two years later, at age 16, while Joseph died in 1882 at age 25.

FURTHER READING:
Oesterreich, Traugott K. *Possession and Exorcism.* Secaucus, N.J: University Books, 1966.

Buer (DICTIONNAIRE INFERNAL)

Buer   FALLEN ANGEL and the 10th of the 72 SPIRITS OF SOLOMON. Buer is a president in HELL, where he governs more than 50 LEGIONS of DEMONS. He appears when the Sun is in Sagittarius. He teaches moral and natural philosophy, the logical arts, and the virtues of all herbs and plants. Buer heals all distempers and gives good FAMILIARS.

Buriel   DEMON and a wandering duke of the air. Buriel has many dukes and servants to do his bidding. All are evil and are hated by other spirits. They must be summoned at night because they hate the day. When they appear, they have the form of a SERPENT with a virgin's head and speak with a man's voice. Buriel's major 12 dukes are Merosiel, Almadiel, Cupriel, Sarviel, Casbriel, Nedriel, Bufiel, Futiel, Drusiel, Camiel, Drubiel, and Nastros.

Busyasta   In ZOROASTRIANISM, the DEMON of lethargy, long sleep, and sloth. Busyasta is a female demon with yellow, jaundiced skin and long claws. She makes men oversleep and neglect their religious duties.

Cabariel Demon among the 31 aerial spirits of Solomon. Cabariel is a prince of the west and north, with 50 attending dukes during the day and 50 more at night. Each duke has 50 servants, who appear when the dukes are summoned. The daytime dukes and servants are good-natured, but the nighttime demons are deceitful, disobedient, and evil. The 10 most important dukes of the day are Satifiel, Parius, Godiel, Taros, Asoriel, Etimiel, Clyssan, Elitel, Aniel, and Cuphal. The 10 most important dukes of nighttime are Mador, Peniet, Cugiel, Thalbus, Otim, Ladiel, Morlas, Pandor, Cazul, and Dubiel.

Cagliostro, Count See Doris Fischer Obsession; Smith, Helene.

Caim (Caym, Camio) Fallen angel and 52nd of the 72 spirits of Solomon. Prior to his fall, Caim was in the order of angels. In hell, he is a great president with 30 legions of demons. He appears first as a black bird or thrush and then as a man carrying a sharp sword. Sometimes he appears as a man adorned with a tuft and a peacock's tail. He answers questions in burning ashes. He is good at settling disputes. He gives men the understanding of the songs of birds, the lowing of cattle, the barking of dogs, and the voice of waters. He gives true answers about the future. Martin Luther reportedly had an encounter with Caim.

Calder, Andrew (1965–) Evangelical Episcopalian priest and exorcist. Andrew Calder is the founder and director of the Georgia Paranormal Research Team, which investigates hauntings and demonic cases. Calder once lived in a haunted home, where he experienced paranormal phenomena. He has worked as a law enforcement officer for city and state agencies, and as a private investigator, specializing in video surveillance. He is an ordained priest with the Communion of Evangelical Episcopal Churches. Calder has appeared on reality television programs in connection with demonic cases and has also been featured in documentaries and docudramas.

Camuel Demon among the 31 aerial spirits of Solomon. Camuel is the third-ranking spirit of the east and rules as the king of the southeast regions of the world. He is attended by numerous spirits, of which 10 daytime spirits and 210 nighttime spirits are significant. His 9 most significant attendants are Camyel, Omyel, Budiel, Elcar, Citgara, Pariel, Cariel, Neriel, and Daniel. Ten of his nighttime servants will also appear during the day: Asimiel, Calim, Dobriel, Nodar, Phaniel, Meras, Aszemo, Tediel, Moriel, and Tugaros. Camuel and his attendants all appear in beautiful form and are courteous.

Carnesiel Demon among the 31 aerial spirits of Solomon. Carnesiel is chief emperor of the east and commands 1,000 great dukes, 100 lesser dukes, and 50,000,000,000,000 ministering spirits. His 12 most important demonic dukes are Myrezyn, Omich, Zabriel, Bucafas, Benoham, Arifiel, Cumeriel, Vadriel, Armany, Capriel, Bedary, and Laphor. Carnesiel can appear day or night. When he does so, he is attended by an entourage of his dukes numbering no fewer than 10 and no more than 300.

Caspiel DEMON among the 31 AERIAL SPIRITS OF SOLOMON. Caspiel is the chief emperor of the south, who rules over 200 great dukes, 400 lesser dukes, and 1,000,200,000,000 ministering spirits. His 12 most important dukes are Ursiel, Chariet, Maras, Femot, Dudarion, Camory, Larmot, Aridiel, Geriel, Ambri, Carnor, and Oriel. Each of the 12 dukes is attended by 2,660 lesser dukes. All of the dukes are stubborn and churlish, but many attend Caspiel when he appears.

Cassian, John (ca. 360–433) Abbot; father of the church. Like St. ANTHONY, who preceded him in the same century, John Cassian was a significant early author on the nature and characteristics of DEMONs and the remedies against them. However, the church ultimately rejected his work as apocryphal.

Life

Cassian probably was born around the year 360; the place is uncertain. Among the possibilities suggested are Gaul, Syria, Palestine, and Scythia. Nothing is known about him until 380, when he, at age 20, and his friend Germanus became monks at Bethlehem, in a monastery near the place of the nativity.

They stayed there until about 385, then left for Egypt, spending about 15 years traveling throughout Lower Egypt and the Nile delta, staying with the most famous monks and anchorites. Cassian kept a journal, recording everything he saw with a vivid style and minute accuracy, a sense of humor, and an eye for the picturesque.

They left Egypt for Constantinople, where Bishop St. John Chrysostom ordained Germanus a priest and Cassian a deacon. In 405, after Chrysostom was deposed, they went to Rome, carrying a letter to Pope St. Innocent I (r. 401–17) from the clergy of Constantinople protesting this act. In Rome, Cassian was ordained a priest. Ten years later, he was in Marseilles (Germanus disappeared in the interim), where he founded and served as abbot of the monastery of St. Victor for men and the convent St. Savior for women.

Asked by a neighboring bishop, Castor of Apt, to compile a summary of all he had observed and learned during his travels, Cassian composed a 12-volume work, *Remedies for the Eight Deadly Sins,* which describes the rules and organization of communities in Egypt and Palestine, and of the means used by the monks in their spiritual combat against the eight chief obstacles to a monk's perfection. (See SEVEN DEADLY SINS.) He was not unduly impressed by extreme asceticism and did not recommend it for the monasteries of the West. Instead, he held that perfection was to be achieved through the charity and love that make humans most like God.

Cassian's next work was *Conferences on the Egyptian Monks,* in which he relates discussions he and Germanus had with the monks. The doctrine he expressed was unorthodox, giving too much importance to free will and not enough to divine grace. *Conferences* was publicly criticized but was still highly popular and influential. Even St. Benedict prescribed it as one of the books to be read aloud by his monks after their evening meal.

About 430, Cassian was commissioned by the future pope St. Leo to write the seven-volume *On the Incarnation of the Lord,* a critique of the Nestorian heresy, which put forth the idea that Christ had existed as two separate beings, one divine and one human. This hastily written book assisted in the condemnation of Nestorius by the Council of Ephesus in 431.

Cassian died in Marseilles, France, on July 23, about the year 433. After his death, *Conferences* was declared apocryphal by a decree attributed to Pope St. Gelasius I (r. 492–96). In 529, Cassian himself was condemned by a church council.

Cassian's Views on Demons and the Devil

Cassian said that there are three origins of all of human thoughts: God, the DEVIL, and ourselves. Thoughts from God lift us up to a higher state of spiritual progress. Thoughts from the Devil try to destroy people with the pleasures of sin and secret attacks and deceitful guises such as purporting to be from "angels of light" who try to show that evil is good.

Cassian's demons, as do those of Anthony, resemble the Greek DAIMONES, who inhabit the air and have supernatural powers. The very air is thick with them, and it is fortunate that they are invisible to people, for the dread of seeing them would drive men to insanity. The demons are similar to humans, with similar thoughts and perceptions, and detect a person's inner weaknesses and vulnerabilities by observing his or her external behavior.

Books 7 and 8 of *Conferences* concern conversations with Abbot Serenus, and there is much discussion of demons. Serenus, through his faith, fasting, and prayer, suppressed his sexual desires and could resist demonic seduction. According to Serenus, demons cannot take over and unite with the inner spirit of humans, but they can seize upon the natural inclinations that reside within and use those to incite impure thoughts. For example, if demons see a natural tendency toward gluttony, they will use that to their advantage. First, demons must take over the mind and thoughts before they can take over a body.

Not every demon can incite every sin within a person, Cassian said. Demons have their specialties and find opportunities to use them. Likewise, the demons cannot incite many sins at the same time but rather focus on one or two in any particular time. Demons also vary in their individual strength and capability. Weaker demons start first and are replaced by stronger demons the more a person is able to resist.

Demons cannot afflict anyone of his or her own free will but only with the permission of God, Cassian said. They are not invincible. They have their own anxieties and uncertainties in their battles against people. When defeated, they retreat in confusion and despair. Cassian said that even by his time, the power of demons had diminished from the time of the first monks in the desert. Those monks could not dare to sleep all at the same time at night, lest demons descend upon them. There are many terms and names for demons, he said, too many to list:

> But it would take too long to search through the whole of Scripture and run through the different kinds of them, as they are termed by the prophets onocentaurs, satyrs, sirens, witches, howlers, ostriches, urchins; and asps and basilisks in the Psalms; and are called lions, dragons, scorpions in the gospel, and are named by the Apostle the prince of this world, rulers of this darkness, and spirits of wickedness.

Importance of Cassian's Views

Cassian reinforced the beliefs that demons are everywhere striving to attack people, that they have the ability to influence people's thoughts and desires, and that they can be thwarted by prayer, fasting, the sign of the cross, and the invocation of the name of Christ.

Cassian added a great deal of force to the connection between demons and MAGIC. The magical arts, taught by the WATCHERS to the "daughters of Cain," were subverted under the influence of demons to profane uses. The "curious arts of wizards and enchantments and magical superstitions" were used to teach people to "forsake the holy worship of the Divinity and to honor and worship either the elements or fire or the demons of the air."

Magic survived the flood because of Ham, the son of Noah, who learned the magical arts from the daughters of Cain. Ham knew that Noah would never allow magical books aboard the ark, so Ham inscribed the secrets on metal plates and rocks that could not be destroyed by the flood waters. Cassian said, "And when the flood was over he hunted for them with the same inquisitiveness with which he had concealed them, and so transmitted to his descendants a seed-bed of profanity and perpetual sin."

FURTHER READING:

Ankarloo, Bengt, and Stuart Clark, gen. eds. *The Athalone History of Witchcraft and Magic in Europe.* London: Athlone Press, 1999.

Cassian, John. *The Conferences of John Cassian.* Translated and annotated by Edgar C. S. Gibson. Available online. URL: http://www.osb.org/lectio/cassian/conf/book1/conf7. html#7.0. Downloaded February 3, 2008.

Cerberus (Kerberos)   Triple-headed dog or doglike creature who guards the entrance to Hades, the Greek underworld. Not originally a "demonic" creature, Cerberus became the model for the Hellhounds of the DEVIL and other BLACK DOGS in folklore.

In classical myth, Cerberus is the offspring of Typhon, a dragon and SERPENT-shaped monster associated with wind and volcanic eruptions. Typhon fathered many of the beasts of Greek legend, including Echidna, a half-woman, half-serpent. Cerberus lives in a den on one side of the river Styx that separates the land of the living from the land of the dead. There, he greets the shades of the newly dead as they are ferried across the river by Charon. Cerberus is unpredictable in his friendliness or hostility; therefore, the dead are buried with honey cake offerings for the shades to give him, which guarantee his friendliness.

As gatekeeper to the underworld, Cerberus also prevents shades from escaping. He figures in numerous myths of descent to the underworld, including the labors of Hercules and Orpheus' foiled rescue attempt of his lover, Eurydice.

In Homeric poems, Cerberus is "the dog." Hades gives Hercules permission to take him up from the river Acheron provided he can quell the beast without weapons. Hercules descends accompanied by Mercury and Minerva, wrestles the dog into submission, and takes him to Eurystheus, king of Tiryns. Saliva drips from Cerberus and creates the poison aconite.

Hesiod, a Greek poet ca. the eighth century B.C.E., was the first writer known to have called Cerberus by a proper name. Hesiod described the beast as having 50 heads.

By the time of the Roman poets, Cerberus had evolved into a three-headed dog with a dragon's neck and tail and serpent's heads along his back. Virgil (70–19 B.C.E.) provided the most detailed description of Cerberus in book 6 of the *Aeneid,* describing the underworld journey of Aeneas:

> Grim Cerberus, who soon began to rear
> His crested snakes, and arm'd his bristling hair.
> The prudent Sibyl had before prepar'd
> A sop, in honey steep'd, to charm the guard;
> Which, mix'd with pow'rful drugs, she cast before
> His greedy grinning jaws, just op'd to roar.
> With three enormous mouths he gapes; and straight,
> With hunger press'd, devours the pleasing bait.
> Long draughts of sleep his monstrous limbs enslave;
> He reels, and, falling, fills the spacious cave.
> The keeper charm'd, the chief without delay
> Pass'd on, and took th' irremeable way.

Cerberus guarding the gates of Hades (AUTHOR'S COLLECTION)

Cesmak (Cheshmak, Cheshmak the Karap) In ZORO-ASTRIANISM, the DEMON of whirlwinds and destruction. In the *Denkart,* Cesmak is a harlot with a body of gold and big breasts. She tries to seduce the prophet Zarathustra (Zoroaster) when he returns from a meeting with Ohrmadz in heaven, but he defeats her.

charm In MAGIC, a spell or "little prayer" for something desirable. Charms may invoke the help of DEMONs. Popular charms are used to secure the love of another person, to find treasure or acquire riches, to have good luck, and so forth. The Catholic Church considers charms to be undesirable and acts that open the door to demonic influence, even POSSESSION, for either the person who makes the charm or the one for whom the charm is intended. The church advises that objects related to charms be destroyed.

See AMULET.

FURTHER READING:
Fortea, Fr. Jose Antonio. *Interview with an Exorcist: An Insider's Look at the Devil, Diabolic Possession, and the Path to Deliverance.* West Chester, Pa.: Ascension Press, 2006.

Choronzon (Coronzon) DEMON or spirit identified in the 16th century by John Dee and Edward Kelly, summoned in a dramatic ritual by ALEISTER CROWLEY in 1909. Dee referred to "Coronzon," or 333, in his Enochian communications with spirits; he did not consider it to be a demon. Crowley called Choronzon the Demon of Dispersions and of the Abyss.

The account of Crowley's evocation is full of drama; it is not known whether the events happened as objective experiences or were experienced as visions. Crowley claimed to have conquered Choronzon to become a full Master of the Temple and Secret Chief.

The evocation was performed in 1909. In November, Crowley and Neuberg went to Algiers on holiday and walked south through the desert to Aumale. There, Crowley was summoned by the voice of Aiwass, the entity who had dictated to him *The Book of the Law,* to "call Me." He had with him the Enochian Keys of Dee and Kelly used to communicate with angels and spirits and felt he had received a divine message to use them. Crowley had successfully used the 19th Key or Call, the most difficult,

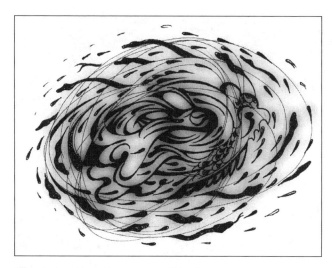

Choronzon (© RICHARD COOK)

to access two of the 30 aethyrs or aires (levels or planes) of expanded consciousness. He decided to access the remaining 28 aethyrs.

Crowley and Neuberg went out into the desert to a mount and ascended it. To make the Call, Crowley held a vermilion-painted Calvary Cross with an engraved topaz set in its axis. The topaz was engraved with a rose of 49 petals. When his clairvoyant visions unfolded, Crowley dictated to Neuberg. They performed one aethyr a day, except for one day when they two performed. They started with the last-numbered aethyr and worked backward toward the first.

Most of Crowley's visions were apocalyptic in nature. In the 15th aethyr, he underwent an initiation to the magical grade of Master of the Temple, a title that could be fully realized only by accessing the other aethyrs. However, Crowley experienced great difficulty in trying to access the next, the 14th aethyr. After making several attempts, he stopped.

He and Neuberg were on their way down the mount when Crowley suddenly was seized with the inspiration to perform a homosexual magic ritual with Neuberg and dedicate it to the Greek god of nature, Pan. They went back to the top of the mount, inscribed in the sand a magic circle protected with names and words of power, and made a crude stone altar. Crowley took the submissive role in the sexual act as a way of eliminating ego. The ritual marked a turning point for him in his view of the importance of sex in magic; he now saw it as a beneficial sacrament.

The ritual also led to a breakthrough in consciousness, for later that evening, Crowley gained access to the 14th aethyr. In his vision, he was informed that in order to attain his cherished goal of becoming a Secret Chief and Master of the Temple, he had to undergo the complete death of his ego and unite his spirit with the ocean of infinity. Only this way, could he cross the Abyss, the

gulf that separates ordinary mortals from the Secret Chiefs.

Crowley was able to resume his explorations of the other aethyrs, where he received revelation after revelation, laden with symbolism. In the 11th aethyr, he was told that in the 10th aethyr he would have to make a conscious crossing of the Abyss, inhabited by a single entity, the demon Choronzon, the "first and deadliest of all the powers of evil," a being composed of "complete negation."

The ritual for crossing the Abyss took place on December 6, 1909, outside the town of Bou Saada. Crowley and Neuberg walked out into the desert until they found a valley that had a suitable floor of fine sand. They formed a circle of rocks, drew around it a magic circle, and then drew a magic triangle. The demon would be invoked into the triangle. The circle would protect Neuberg, who would sit within it, armed with a magical knife and a notebook for recording what happened. Crowley intended to enter the triangle, a dangerous act for a magician. He thus became perhaps the first magician in the Western magical tradition to offer his own body ritually as a vehicle for manifestation of a demon.

Before the start of the ritual, Neuberg took an oath that he would defend the magic circle "with thoughts and words and deeds" and would use the knife to attack anything that entered it, even Crowley.

Crowley apparently was not in the triangle when he invoked the aethyr, but was in a "secret place" out of the sight and hearing of Neuberg. After the invocation, Crowley entered the triangle. To help the demon materialize, he sacrificed three pigeons at the points of the triangle and sprinkled their BLOOD. He took care not to let a drop fall outside the triangle, for that would enable Choronzon to manifest in the universe. When all the blood had soaked into the sand, he secretly recited the Call of the aethyr. He was in full trance.

Neuberg records that he heard a voice, simulating Crowley's voice, call out barbarous names and then blasphemies. Visions appeared within the triangle. First, Neuberg saw the form of a woman prostitute he had known in Paris. The "woman" tried to seduce him, but Neuberg resisted, figuring it was Choronzon in a shape-shifted form. The "woman" then offered submission, which he also rejected. The demon next turned into an old man, then a SERPENT, and then into Crowley, who begged for water. Neuberg held fast within the circle.

Neuberg ordered Choronzon to declare his nature. The demon replied that he spat upon the name of the Most High. He was Master of the Triangle, who had no fear of the pentagram. He gave Neuberg words that the magician took as "great secrets of magic" but turned out to be worthless, a joke played by the demon. Neuberg invoked Aiwass. Choronzon said that he knew the name of the angel and that "all thy dealings with him are but a cloak for thy filthy sorceries."

Ordered again to declare his true nature, Choronzon said his name was *Dispersion* and he could not be bested in argument. He uttered a rapid string of blasphemies that taxed Neuberg's ability to record. While distracting the magician with blasphemies, Choronzon threw sand onto the magic circle. When the outline was sufficiently blurred, he took the form of a naked man and leaped into it, throwing Neuberg to the ground. The two fought furiously. The demon tried to tear out Neuberg's throat with his froth-covered fangs. At last, Neuberg was able to force Choronzon back into the triangle, and he repaired the magic circle.

Man and demon argued. Choronzon threatened Neuberg with all the tortures of HELL, and Neuberg denounced the demon as a liar. After a long time at this, the demon suddenly vanished, leaving Crowley alone in the circle. Crowley traced the word *Babalon* in the sand, and the ritual was over. He and Neuberg built a fire for purification and ritually destroyed the circle and triangle.

Neuberg maintained that he had literally wrestled with Choronzon, and not with Crowley possessed by the demon. Some occultists have posited that Crowley somehow exuded an ectoplasm that enabled the demon to make a form tangible enough to fight with Neuberg. Another explanation advanced is that the entire experience was visionary. Whatever the truth, both Crowley and Neuberg felt that Crowley had beaten the demon and achieved the status of Master of the Temple and Secret Chief. Crowley's new vision of himself was as teacher and prophet who was to indoctrinate the world with the philosophy of *The Book of the Law.*

Associates of Crowley said the ritual permanently damaged him and that he was possessed by Choronzon for the rest of his life.

FURTHER READING:
King, Francis. *Megatherion: The Magickal World of Aleister Crowley.* London: Creation Books, 2004.
Symonds, John, and Kenneth Grant eds. *The Confessions of Aleister Crowley, an Autobiography.* London: Routledge & Kegan Paul, 1979.

chthonic deities   In classical mythology, the dreaded deities of the underworld, who are so feared that they usually are nameless and are called only by euphemisms. They often appear in the form of SERPENTs, which are associated with tombs and death. Chthonic deities originally were ancestral spirits who represented the ghosts of the dead. They were worshipped by propitiation and sacrifice.

As rulers of the underworld, chthonic deities torment souls of the death and reign over chaos, darkness, gloom, and evil spirits (see DEMONs). As Christianity overtook pagan beliefs, the chthonic deities became associated increasingly with evil and the DEVIL.

The greatest and most feared chthonic god is Hades, the Greek King of the Dead, who owns a cap that makes the wearer invisible. Hades is uncompassionate but not evil. He seldom leaves his gloomy realm of the underworld. His name became synonymous with HELL. The Romans also associated him with the minerals of the earth and called him Pluto, the god of wealth.

Hades rules the underworld with his queen, Persephone. According to myth, Persephone was a lovely maiden of spring, the daughter of Demeter, goddess of corn and the harvest. Hades desired her and one day rose up out of a chasm in the earth in his chariot drawn by black horses, kidnapped her, and took her to the underworld. In her grief, Demeter caused all things on Earth to wither and die. Other gods entreated her to relent, but she refused in anger. Finally, Zeus intervened and ordered Hades, his brother, to return Persephone to Earth. Hades acquiesced but first made Persephone eat a pomegranate seed, which bound her to him forever. As a compromise, Persephone returned to Earth each spring, producing a flowering of the planet, and went back to Hades each fall, causing the death of winter.

Other chthonic entities are the three ERINYES (Furies), called Tisiphone, Megaera, and Alecto, who relentlessly pursued and punished the sinners of the Earth; and Thanatos, god of death, and his brother, the god of sleep. From the god of sleep, the "little death," issued dreams, which rose up from the underworld in two forms: true dreams, which passed through a gate of horn, and false dreams, which passed through a gate of ivory. The Greeks and Romans placed a great deal of importance on the meaning of dreams, especially information of a prophetic or oracular nature.

The descriptions of the classical underworld are most vivid in the writings of the Roman poet Virgil and the Greek poet Homer. To Homer, the underworld is a shadowy place where nothing is real. To Virgil, it is more realistic, a place where sinners are tormented and the good enjoy rewards and delights. Virgil gave descriptions of the terrain of the underworld, and the means by which souls entered. A path led to two rivers, the first of which was Acheron, the river of woe, which then emptied into Cocytus, the river of lamentation. There, an old boatman named Charon ferried souls across the waters, but only those whose passage was paid, by coins placed upon the lips of the corpses by the living and who were properly buried. Three other rivers separated the underworld: Phlegethon, the river of fire; Styx, the river of the unbreakable oath sworn to by the gods; and Lethe, the river of oblivion or forgetfulness. (Souls returning to Earth to be reborn were required to drink of the waters of Lethe, so that they would not remember their previous lives.)

The gate of Hades is guarded by a three-headed, dragon-tailed dog, CERBERUS, whose chief job was to prevent any souls from leaving once inside. Hades himself lived in a huge palace somewhere in the gloom of the underworld, surrounded by cold and wide wastes.

Hecate is a powerful goddess with chthonic associations, who became the patron of magic and WITCHCRAFT. Hecate has three aspects: goddess of fertility and plenty, goddess of the Moon, and queen of the night, ghosts, and shades.

Hecate possesses infernal power, roaming the earth at night with the WILD HUNT, a pack of red-eyed hellhounds and a retinue of dead souls. She is visible only to dogs, and if dogs howl in the night, it means Hecate is about. She is the cause of nightmares and insanity and is so terrifying that many ancients referred to her only as "The Nameless One." She is the goddess of the dark of the Moon, the destroyer of life, but also the restorer of life. In one myth, she turns into a bear or boar and kills her own son, then revives him to life. In her dark aspect, she wears a necklace made of testicles; her hair is made of writhing snakes, which, as do the snakes of Medusa, petrify those who gaze upon them.

Hecate is the goddess of all CROSSROADS, gazing in three directions at the same time. In ancient times, sorcerers gathered at crossroads to pay homage to her and such infernal servants as the Empusa, a hobgoblin; the Cercopsis, a poltergeist; and the Mormo, a GHOUL. Three-headed statues of her were set up at many road intersections, and secret rites were performed under a full Moon to appease her. Statues of Hecate carrying torches or swords also were erected in front of homes to keep evil spirits at bay.

Many of the heavenly deities of Mount Olympus have chthonic aspects, such as Zeus and Hermes, but are not feared as much as the underworld deities. Hermes, the swift-footed messenger god, escorts the souls of the dead to the underworld, and souls ready to be reborn back to the land of the living. Demeter also has chthonic aspects, because of her relationship with Persephone.

Church of Satan   See SATANISM.

Cimeries   FALLEN ANGEL and 66th of the 72 SPIRITS OF SOLOMON. Cimeries rules 20 LEGIONs of DEMONs as a marquis in HELL. He also rules spirits in Africa. He appears as a valiant soldier riding a black horse. He teaches grammar, logic, and rhetoric. He finds lost objects and buried treasures.

Colas, Antide (d. 1599)   Woman accused of WITCHCRAFT and having sex with SATAN. Arrested and tried at Dole, France, Antide Colas was examined by a surgeon, Nicolas Milliere, who found a hole below her navel. Colas confessed that the DEVIL, whom she called Lizabet, had intercourse with her through this hole. She also said that when the Devil lay down beside her, if she did not do as he asked, he made her twitch and tremble, and he pricked her left side. Colas was executed by burning in Dole in 1599.

Cole, Ann   A woman involved in a POSSESSION case in Hartford, Connecticut, that astonished her townspeople

and led to the execution of an accused witch. Ann Cole suddenly seemed to acquire preternatural knowledge of the malicious activities of the accused witch, who was a stranger to her. Increase Mather described Cole as "a person of real piety and integrity" in his account in *An Essay for the Recording of Illustrious Providences* (1684).

In 1662, Cole was living in the house of her father—described as "a godly man"—when she began having bizarre fits, "wherein her Tongue was improved by a *Daemon* to express things which she herself knew nothing of," Mather wrote. Sometimes the discourses went on for hours. Cole named persons and described how they intended to carry out "mischievous designs" against her and others, by afflicting bodies and spoiling names.

At times, Cole lapsed into gibberish. Then she began speaking English with a precise Dutch accent, describing how a woman who lived beside a Dutch family had been afflicted by a strange pinching of her arms at night.

One of the persons named by Cole was a "lewd and ignorant" woman named Rebecca Greensmith, who was in jail on suspicion of WITCHCRAFT. Greensmith had denied the charges against her but, when confronted by a written account of Cole's discourses, was astonished and confessed everything. Greensmith said the DEVIL had first appeared to her in the form of a deer or fawn, skipping about her so that she would not be afraid, gaining her confidence. She had sex with the Devil on numerous occasions and had often accompanied him to SABBATs. She denied entering into a satanic PACT but said that the Devil had told her that they would attend a merry sabbat at Christmastime, during which she would sign a pact with him. Greensmith also said that witches had met at a place not far from her house, and that some of them arrived in the shapes of animals and crows.

The confession was sufficient to convict Greensmith, and she was executed, probably by hanging. Her husband was also put to death, even though he said he was not guilty of any wrongdoing. The court apparently thought that since he was the woman's husband, he could not help but be involved in her evil activities.

A man and a woman also named by Cole were given the swimming test of being bound and thrown into water, a common test of a witch's innocence or guilt. They neither floated nor sank but bobbed like buoys, half in and half out of the water. A witness protested that anyone with his or her hands bound to the feet would not sink (and therefore be guilty) and underwent the test himself. He was lowered gently into the water, not thrown in, as were the accused, and promptly sank, proving his innocence.

It is not known how many others named by Cole were tried and executed for witchcraft; some fled Hartford and were never seen again. Ann Cole eventually recovered and had no more fits. She resumed her life as "a serious Christian." It is possible that her fits were a manifestation of latent psychic ability, a clairvoyance. It was a psychic window that opened suddenly, without encouragement, then closed as soon as the cases were laid to rest.

Collin de Plancy, Jacques (1793–1887)

French demonologist, occultist, and author.

He was born Jacques Auguste Simon Collin de Plancy in 1793 in Plancy-l'Abbaye, France. He worked as a printer and publisher in Plancy-l'Abbaye and Paris. Between 1830 and 1837, he lived in Brussels; he then returned to France after practice of the Catholic religion was restored and lived there for the rest of his life. He died there in 1887.

Interested in the occult and superstitions, Collin de Plancy wrote dozens of books under pseudonyms on divination, magic, alchemy, SORCERY, and WITCHCRAFT. About 80 volumes alone were devoted to superstitions. Prolific, he earned a comfortable living.

His most famous, significant, and enduring work is the *Dictionnaire Infernal,* published under his real name in two volumes in 1818. The dictionary profiles DEMONs and gives short summaries of notable cases and trials of witchcraft and sorcery, as well as of ghosts and odd paranormal events. The dictionary went through several editions. In 1863, the artist Louis Breton created a set of 69 drawings, all but five of demons. They were engraved by M. Jarrault, and Collin de Plancy added them to his book. Most of the engravings were republished in S. L. Mac-Gregor Mathers' *The Goetia: The Lesser Key of Solomon,* his translation of a famous grimoire. The illustrated dictionary remains one of the classic works of demonology.

Other notable works by Collin de Plancy are *History of Phantoms and Demons That Have Appeared to Men* (1819, under the pseudonym Gabrielle de Plancy); *Dictionary of Madness and Reason* (1820); *The Devil's Self Portrait, or a Collection of Short Stories and Tales about the Adventures and the Character of Demons, Their Machinations, Their Misfortunes, Their Love Affairs and the Services That They Have Been Able to Render to Men* (1825); and *Legends of the Seven Deadly Sins* (1864).

FURTHER READING:
Collin de Plancy, Jacques. *Dictionary of Witchcraft.* Edited and translated by Wade Baskin. Originally published as *Dictionary of Demonology.* New York: Philosophical Library, 1965.

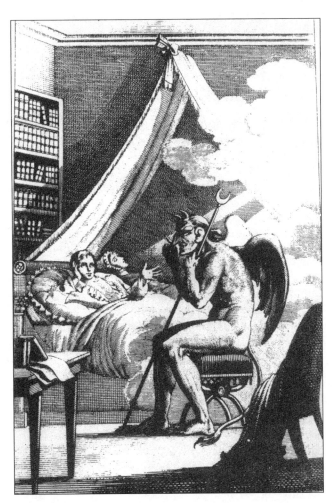

Collin de Plancey conversing with the Devil (AUTHOR'S COLLECTION)

Constantine (2005)

Horror/thriller film about an occult detective and EXORCIST who journeys to HELL to battle DEMONs and confronts LUCIFER. Directed by Francis Lawrence, the film stars Keanu Reeves as John Constantine and Rachel Weisz as Angela Dodson, a detective for the Los Angeles Police Department. The film is loosely based on characters in the comic book series *Hellblazer,* published by Vertigo Comics.

In the movie, Constantine's background is that he was born with the ability to detect ANGELs and demons. Both beings are prohibited from interfering with the free will of humans, but half-breeds, humans mixed with either angels or demons, can do so. Constantine is regarded by his parents as insane. He commits suicide and goes to hell but is restored to life by doctors. He grows up knowing that God and SATAN are both angry with him, and because of his suicide attempt, he is eventually doomed to hell.

The film opens with a young man in Mexico who accidentally finds the Nazi Spear of Destiny and becomes possessed by a supernatural force. He goes to Los Angeles, leaving destruction in his wake. Meanwhile, Constantine, now a heavy chain smoker, has terminal lung cancer. He exorcizes a powerful demon from a teenage girl. A mentally disturbed girl commits suicide in the hospital where Constantine is being treated. Her twin sister, Angela Dodson, goes to the hospital and encounters Constantine. A Catholic, she wants a church-sanctioned funeral for her sister, but the church refuses. Constantine seeks out an audience with the archangel Gabriel, a female entity, to ask why God does not forgive and heal him.

Constantine sees that demons are pursuing Angela, and he discovers that she, as he can, can detect angels and demons. She has repressed this ability, and now he reawakens her to it. She takes him to meet Balthazar, a half-breed who is conspiring with the demon MAMMON to conquer the Earth, a task he can do only with the help of the Spear of Destiny. Mammon takes POSSESSION of Angela.

Constantine struggles in vain to exorcize Angela. Gabriel appears, bitter and disillusioned with humanity, and says she will release Mammon into the world. Constantine slashes his wrists, knowing that Lucifer will appear to collect his soul. When the DEVIL appears, time stops. Lucifer is enraged at Mammon's plans and sends the demon back to hell. He burns Gabriel's wings and the angel is reduced to a human state.

Lucifer removes the cancer from Constantine's lungs and abducts him to hell. Constantine is saved by Divine Light as a reward for his sacrifice of himself. He is returned to Earth and to Angela. The Spear of Destiny appears, and Gabriel taunts Constantine to kill her with it. Instead, he punches her in the face.

Constantine gives the spear to Angela and quits smoking, now in command of his fate.

crossroads   A place of magical power especially for conjuring spirits and DEMONS. The junctions of roads, where forces of energy cross, have been considered to have magical significance since ancient times.

Crossroads are haunted by demons, FAIRIES, and evil spirits who lie in wait for unwary travelers and lead them astray. Crossroads are where witches and sorcerers gather for SABBATs, according to lore. Grass will not grow at crossroads where demons have danced.

Some magical rituals are performed at crossroads, such as necromancy, the appearance of the GOLD-FINDING HEN, conjurations of spirits and demons, and sacrifices of animals. Crossroads also are places of confusion, and lore holds that one can evade evil spirits by running into a crossroads.

Crowley, Aleister (1875–1947)   English magician and occultist. Aleister Crowley was adept at dealing with spirits, including powerful DEMONS. Flamboyant and controversial, he practiced outrageous magic of sex, drugs, and sacrifice, yet made significant contributions to magic.

Life

He was born Edward Alexander Crowley on October 12, 1875, in Leamington Spa, Warwickshire. His father was a wealthy brewer and a "Darbyite" preacher, a member of a fundamentalist sect known as the Plymouth Brethren or Exclusive Brethren. Crowley's parents raised him in an atmosphere of repression and religious bigotry. He rebelled to such an extent that his mother called him "the Beast" after the Antichrist, a name he delighted in using later in life, calling himself "the Beast of the Apocalypse."

Crowley was drawn to the occult and was fascinated by BLOOD, torture, and sexual degradation; he liked to fantasize being degraded by a "Scarlet Woman." He combined these interests in a lifestyle that shocked others and reveled in the attention he drew. He was in his teens when he adopted the name *Aleister.*

In 1887, Crowley's father died and he was sent to a Darbyite school in Cambridge. His unhappy experiences there at the hands of a cruel headmaster made him hate the Darbyites.

Crowley studied for three years at Trinity College at Cambridge but never earned a degree. He wrote poetry, engaged in an active bisexual sex life, and pursued his occult studies—the Great Work—the latter of which was inspired by *The Book of Black Magic and of Pacts* by ARTHUR EDWARD WAITE and *The Cloud upon the Sanctuary* by Carl von Eckartshausen. In his first volume of poetry, published in 1898, Crowley foreshadowed his occult excesses with his statement that God and Satan had fought many hours over his soul. He wrote, "God conquered—now I have only one doubt left—which of the twain was God?"

Crowley was in his third year at Trinity when he formally dedicated himself to magick, which he spelled with a *k* to "distinguish the science of the Magi from all its counterfeits." He also pledged to "rehabilitate" it. He saw magic as *the* way of life, a path of self-mastery achieved with rigorous discipline of the will illumined by imagination.

After leaving Trinity, Crowley took a flat in Chancery Lane, London. He named himself Count Vladimir and pursued his occult activities full-time. Stories of bizarre incidents circulated, perhaps fueled in part by Crowley's mesmerizing eyes and aura of supernatural power. A ghostly light reportedly surrounded him, which he said was his astral spirit. One of his flat neighbors claimed to be hurled downstairs by a malevolent force, and visitors said they experienced dizzy spells while climbing the stairs or felt an overwhelming evil presence.

In 1898, Crowley went to Zermatt, Switzerland, for mountain climbing. He met Julian Baker, an English occultist, who in turn introduced Crowley back in London to George Cecil Jones, a member of the Hermetic Order of the Golden Dawn. At Jones' invitation, Crowley was initiated into the order on November 18, 1898. He took the magical motto *Frater Perdurabo* (I will persevere). He used other names, among them *Mega Therion* (the Great Wild Beast), which he used when he later attained the rank of Magus.

Crowley was already skilled in magic when he joined the Golden Dawn, and its First Order bored him. He received instruction from Allan Bennett, whom he met in 1899, and Samuel Liddell Macgregor Mathers, one of the founders of the Golden Dawn. Mathers taught Crowley Abremalin magic from an old manuscript, *The Sacred Magic of Abra-Melin the Mage,* which Mathers had trans-

Aleister Crowley (© RICHARD COOK)

lated. Mathers believed the manuscript was bewitched and inhabited by an entity. The magic prescribed a rigorous six-month program conducted in complete withdrawal from the world, after which the initiate would make talismans that would draw money, great sexual allure, and an army of phantom soldiers to serve at his disposal. Crowley intended to undergo this rite beginning at Easter 1900 at Boleskin Manor, his house in Scotland.

His plans were disrupted by internal fighting in the Golden Dawn that led to Crowley's expulsion from the order in 1900. He retaliated by publishing secret ritual material.

From 1900 to 1903, Crowley traveled extensively, visiting the Far East and delving deeper into Eastern mysticism.

In 1903, he married Rose Kelly, the first of his two wives. Kelly bore him one child, a daughter, Lola Zaza. Their honeymoon lasted several months. In 1904, they were in Cairo, where Crowley was attempting to conjure sylphs, the elementals of the air. While in Egypt, Crowley engaged in his most significant entity contact, with Aiwass, described later. The contact influenced his life and work, to usher in the Aeon of Horus.

Crowley had a prodigious sexual appetite and had numerous mistresses, some of whom he called "Scarlet Women" and some of whom bore him illegitimate children. He was fond of giving his women "Serpent Kisses,"

using his sharpened teeth to draw blood. He branded some of his women and eventually abandoned all of them to drugs, alcohol, or the streets. Crowley tried unsuccessfully to beget a "magical child." He fictionalized these efforts in his novel *Moonchild* (1929).

Rose descended into alcoholism, and in 1909 she divorced Crowley on grounds of adultery. From late 1914 to 1919, Crowley lived in the United States, where he was unsuccessful in rousing much interest in his message about the Aeon of Horus. He kept a record of his sexual activities, which he titled *Rex de Arte Regia* (The King of the Royal Art). Many of the prostitutes he hired had no idea that he was actually involving them in sex magic. He and his Scarlet Woman of the moment, Roddie Minor, performed sex magic and drug rituals—by then he was addicted to heroin—for the purpose of communicating with an entity, perhaps a demon, whom Crowley called "the wizard Amalantrah," who existed on the astral plane.

In 1916, Crowley initiated himself into the rank of Magus in a bizarre black magic rite in which he crucified a frog.

In 1918, Crowley met Leah Hirsig, a New York schoolteacher, who became his most famous Scarlet Woman. He called her "the Ape of Thoth." They decided to found the Abbey of Thelema, a monastic community of men and women who would promulgate *The Book of the Law*, perform magic, and be sexually free.

In 1920, Crowley found an old abbey in Cefalu, Sicily, which he took over and renamed the Sacred Abbey of the Thelemic Mysteries. It served as the site for numerous sexual orgies and magical rites, many attended by his illegitimate children. Leah bore a daughter, Anne Leah, who died in childhood. In 1921, Crowley decided that he had attained the magical rank of Ipsissimus, equal to God. But in 1923, he was forced out of the abbey after a scandal involving the death of a follower, Raoul Loveday.

In 1929, Crowley married his second wife, Maria Ferrari de Miramar, in Leipzig. Her reputed magical powers led him to name her the "High Priestess of Voodoo." They separated in less than a year when Crowley took up with a 19-year-old woman. Maria entered a mental institution, enabling Crowley to divorce her.

Crowley's later years were plagued by poor health, drug addiction, and financial trouble. He kept himself barely afloat by publishing nonfiction and fiction writings. In 1934, desperate for money, Crowley sued the sculptress Nina Hammett for libel. Hammett had stated in her biography, *Laughing Torso* (1932), that Crowley practiced black magic and indulged in human sacrifice. The English judge, jury, spectators and press were repulsed by the testimony in the trial. The judge stated he had "never heard such dreadful, horrible, blasphemous and abominable stuff." The jury stopped the trial and found in favor of Hammett.

In 1945, Crowley moved to Netherwood, a boarding house in Hastings, where he lived the last two years of his life, asthmatic, dissipated, and bored, consuming large amounts of heroin. He died of cardiac degeneration and severe bronchitis on December 1, 1947. He was cremated in Brighton. At his funeral, a Gnostic Mass was performed and his "Hymn to Pan" was read. His ashes were sent to followers in the United States.

Numerous editions and collections of Crowley's writings have been published. Besides *The Book of the Law*, his other most notable work is *Magick in Theory and Practice* (1929), considered by many occultists to be a superb work on ceremonial magic. *The Equinox of the Gods* (1937) reflects *The Book of the Law*. *The Book of Lies* features 91 sermons and commentaries on each. *The Book of Thoth* (1944) presents his interpretation of the Tarot. The Thoth Tarot deck, inspired by Crowley, is one of the more popular decks in modern use.

Crowley's work continues to inspire people, and Thelemic organizations exist around the world. He has inspired artists in various fields. Posthumously, Crowley has perhaps gained more fame and credibility than he had during his life. He remains controversial to the extreme, vilified as a "satanic occultist" and praised as a brilliant magician.

Entity Contacts

Aiwass On March 18, 1904, Rose suddenly began trance channeling, receiving communications from the astral plane that the Egyptian god Horus was waiting for Crowley. The communicating messenger, Aiwass, was an imposing entity described by Rose as an emissary for the Egyptian trinity of Horus, Osiris, and Isis.

Crowley considered Aiwass to be his Holy Guardian Angel, or divine Higher Self, acting as intermediary for higher beings such as the Secret Chiefs, superhuman adepts of the Golden Dawn. Occultists have debated whether Aiwass was an entity in its own right, or part of Crowley himself. For Crowley, the Holy Guardian Angel was a discrete entity and not a dissociated part of his own personality. Crowley originally spelled the entity's name *Aiwaz*, then later changed the spelling to *Aiwass* for numerological reasons.

Crowley envisioned Aiwass as a male entity, and one distinctly different and more unfathomable than other entities he had encountered. Answers to questions posed by Crowley indicated that Aiwass was

> . . . a Being whose mind was so different from mine that we failed to converse. All my wife obtained from Him was to command me to do things magically absurd. He would not play my game: I must play His.

On April 7, 1904, Aiwass commanded that the drawing room of the Cairo apartment leased by the Crowleys had to be turned into a temple. Aiwass ordered Crowley to enter the temple precisely at noon on the next three days, and to write down exactly what he heard for precisely one hour.

Aiwass (© RICHARD COOK)

Crowley followed the instructions. Inside the "temple," he sat alone at a table facing the southern wall. From behind him he heard the voice of Aiwass, which Crowley described as "a rich tenor or baritone . . . deep timbre, musical and expressive, its tones solemn, voluptuous, tender, fierce, or aught else as suited the moods of the message." The voice was "the Speech in the Silence," he said. Later he called Aiwass "the minister of Hoor-Paar-Kraat," or "the Lord of Silence," an aspect of Horus that was the equivalent of the Greek Harpocrates.

During the dictation, Crowley did not see a visual apparition of Aiwass, though he did have a mental impression of the entity. Aiwass had

> . . . a body of "fine matter" or astral matter, transparent as a veil of gauze or a cloud of incense-smoke. He seemed to be a tall, dark man in his thirties, well-knit, active and strong, with the face of a savage king, and eyes veiled lest their gaze should destroy what they saw.

Further, Aiwass seemed dressed in the garb of an Assyrian or Persian.

Crowley took Aiwass' dictation for three hours on April 8–10, scribbling in longhand to keep pace with the voice. The sessions lasted exactly one hour each. The 65 pages of handwritten material composed the *Liber Legis*, or *The Book of the Law*, which Crowley saw as the herald of the New Aeon or a new religion. Each chapter carried the voice of an Egyptian deity: Nut, the goddess of the heavens, and two aspects of Horus, Ha-Kadit, a solar aspect, and Ra-Hoor-Kuit, or "Horus of the Two Horizons."

For years, Crowley remained in awe of Aiwass. In *The Equinox of the Gods,* he acknowledged that he never fully understood the nature of Aiwass. He alternately called the entity "a God or Demon or Devil," a praeterhuman intelligence, a minister or messenger of other gods, his own Guardian Angel, and his own subconscious (the last he rejected in favor of the Holy Guardian Angel). Crowley also said he was permitted from time to time to see Aiwass in a physical appearance, inhabiting a human body, as much a material man as Crowley was himself.

C. S. Jones, who ran the Vancouver, British Columbia, lodge of the Ordo Templi Orientis, said he underwent a series of magical initiations that revealed to him that Aiwass was in truth an evil demon and the enemy of humanity. Others considered Jones to have become mad.

The Book of the Law became Crowley's most important work. Central to it is the Law of Thelema: "Do what thou wilt shall be the whole of the Law." The law has been misinterpreted to mean doing as one pleases. According to Crowley, it means that one does what one must and nothing else. Perfect magic is the complete and total alignment of the will with universal will, or cosmic forces. When one surrenders to that alignment, one becomes a perfect channel for the flow of cosmic forces.

Besides the Law of Thelema, the book holds that every person is sovereign and shall be self-fulfilled in the Aeon. "Every man and every woman is a star," it states. However, the Aeon of Horus would be preceded by an era of great violence, aggression, and fire.

Aiwass told Crowley that he had been selected by the "Secret Chiefs," the master adepts behind the Golden Dawn, to be the prophet for the coming Aeon of Horus, the third great age of humanity. Crowley genuinely believed that the Aeon of Horus would spread around the world as a new religion—Crowleyanity—and replace all other religions. *The Book of the Law* remained a focus of Crowley's life for the rest of his years.

Crowley insisted that he never understood all of what was dictated. However, the style is comparable to that of some of his other writings, suggesting that the material may have originated in his subconscious. The promised self-fulfillment seemed to elude him. Throughout his life, Crowley believed he had the ability to manifest whatever he desired, including large sums of money, but after squandering his inheritance he was never able to do so.

Vampire demons After returning home to Scotland, Crowley informed the Golden Dawn that he was its new head, but he received no reply. He then determined that Mathers had launched a psychic attack against him, and he responded by summoning BEELZEBUB and his demons to attack in retaliation.

Mathers had prepared himself for six months with magical procedures and rites in order to create a vampiric thought-form demon by channeling the power of Mars, the planet of war and aggression. Mathers entered a trance state and concentrated his will into the psychic vampire, which rose up from his solar plexus. He ordered it to attack Crowley. However, he committed a grievous error in doing the sending himself. In magic, apprentices are often used to do the sending, for if anything goes amiss and the magic boomerangs back, it will be the apprentice who suffers and not the master magician.

Crowley, who was of superior magical skill, took the thought-form, made it nastier, and sent it back to attack Mathers. This warfare supposedly went on for years and was chronicled by journalists around the world.

Mathers' health declined as the attacks continued. When Mathers died in 1918, his widow, Moina, blamed his death on Crowley's psychic vampirism.

Prior to his death, Mathers once described the awful nature of the thought-form vampire demon:

> Only the upper portions of its body were visible when it would appear. Obviously female, it had narrow breasts protruding through some kind of dark raiment. Below the waist nothing existed. The curious eyes were deep-socketed, and glowed faintly with an intense coral-colored luminosity. The head was flat, set low between white, blubbery shoulders, as though it were cut off just below those fearful "eyes." Like tiny useless flippers, the arms seemed almost vestigial. They were like unformed limbs, still in the foetal stage.
>
> But the thing didn't need arms. Its terrifying weapon was an extraordinarily long, coated gray tongue. Tube-like and hollow, it bore a small orbicular hole at its tip, and that lascivious tongue kept darting snake-like in and out of a circular, lipless mouth. Always trying to catch me off guard it would suddenly strike at me, like a greedy missile, attempting to suck out my auric vitality.
>
> Perhaps the being's most terrifying feature was its absolutely loathsome habit of trying to cuddle up like a purring cat, rubbing its half-materialized form against me, all the while alert, hoping to find a gap in my defenses. And when it was sometimes successful—I was not always prepared nor strong enough to maintain the magical barriers—it would pierce my aura with that wicked tongue right down to my naked skin, causing a most painful sensation. This was followed by a total enervation of my body and spirit for a week or more. A listless, dread experience.

Individuals who knew Crowley believed him to be quite capable of creating such a demon.

Choronzon In 1909, after his divorce from Rose, Crowley began a homosexual relationship with the poet Victor Neuberg, who became his assistant in magic. Their most famous workings together took place in 1909 in the desert south of Algiers, when they performed a harrowing conjuration of the demonic Dweller of the Abyss,

CHORONZON. Crowley was inspired to incorporate sex into the ritual, and he became convinced of the power of sex magic. By 1912, he was involved with the Ordo Templi Orientis sex magic occult order, and in 1922 he was invited to head the organization in Britain. He took the magical name BAPHOMET.

Lam In 1918, the same year that Mathers died, Crowley conducted a sex magic ritual called the Almalantrah, with Roddie Minor, known as Soror Ahitha. The working created a portal in the spaces between stars, through which the entity Lam was able to enter the known physical universe. Since then, other entities are believed to enter through this widening portal, and to be the basis for numerous contact experiences with UFOs and extraterrestrials.

One of the revelations of the working was the symbolism of the egg. Crowley and Soror Ahitha were told, "It's all in the egg."

Crowley believed Lam to be the soul of a dead Tibetan lama from Leng, between China and Tibet. *Lam* is Tibetan for "Way" or "Path," which Crowley said had the numerical value of 71, or "No Thing," a gateway to the Void and a link between the star systems of Sirius and Andromeda. Lam was to fulfill the work initiated by Aiwass.

Crowley drew a portrait of Lam and said that gazing on the portrait enables one to make contact with the entity. Some consider Lam to be a demon and the portal to be one accessed by other demons.

See BLACK MASS; SIX-SIX-SIX.

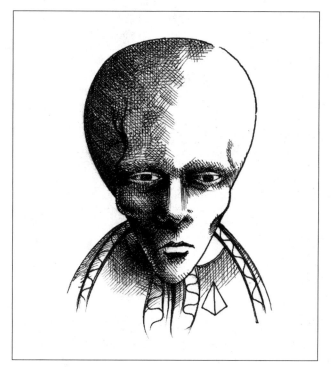

Lam, an entity summoned by Aleister Crowley (© RICHARD COOK)

FURTHER READING:
Crowley, Aleister. *The Holy Books of Thelema.* York Beach, Me.: Samuel Weiser, 1983.
———. *Magic in Theory and Practice.* 1929. Reprint, New York: Dover, 1976.
Hillyer, Vincent. *Vampires.* Los Banos, Calif.: Loose Change, 1988.
King, Francis. *Megatherion: The Magickal World of Aleister Crowley.* London: Creation Books, 2004.
Michaelsen, Scott, ed. *Portable Darkness: An Aleister Crowley Reader.* New York: Harmony Books, 1989.
Stephenson, P. R., and Regardie, Israel. *The Legend of Aleister Crowley.* St. Paul: Llewellyn Publications, 1970.
Sutin, Lawrence. *Do What Thou Wilt: A Life of Aleister Crowley.* New York: St. Martin's Griffin, 2000.
Symonds, John, and Kenneth Grant, eds. *The Confessions of Aleister Crowley, an Autobiography.* London: Routledge & Kegan Paul, 1979.

curse   A SPELL or action to harm, often done by invoking the help of DEMONs, other spirits, and deities. In Christian tradition, a curse can cause demonic problems, including POSSESSION. The person who makes the curse ultimately suffers the effects of it. The term *curse* is derived from the Anglo-Saxon word *cursein,* the etymology of which is not known, which means "to invoke harm or evil upon."

Cursing is common in magical practice and outside Christianity may be considered part of a system of justice in which powerful evil spirits are invoked. The Greeks and Romans used curses as a part of daily life, to gain advantage in business, politics, sports, and love. The Egyptians wrote curses on magical papyri, a practice adopted by Greeks and Romans. From about the fifth century B.C.E. to the fifth century C.E., curse tablets (*tabellae defixonium*) were especially popular in the Hellenistic world.

Tabellae defixonium refers to tablets that fix or pin down, especially in the sense of delivering someone over to the powers of the underworld. The curse tablets were thin pieces of lead (and sometimes other materials) on which were inscribed the victim's name, the curse, magical symbols, and names of various deities or the more generic DAIMONES invoked to carry out the curse. The tablets were buried near a fresh tomb, a battlefield, or a place of execution, all of which were believed to be populated by spirits of the dead en route to the underworld. The curses gave the spirits the power to assault the victim. Curse tablets also were fixed with nails and were thrown into wells, springs, or rivers, also inhabited by spirits. Curses were made for all manner of purposes, including preventing rival athletes from winning competitions, as in this late Roman Empire curse for a chariot race found in Africa:

> I conjure you, daemon, whoever you may be, to torture and kill, from this hour, this day, this moment, the horses of the Green and the White teams; kill and smash the charioteers Clarus, Felix, Primulus, Romanus; do

not leave breath in them. I conjure you by him who has delivered you, at the time, the god of the sea and the air: *Iao, Iasdo . . . aeia.*

Iao and *Iasdo* are variants of *Yahweh,* a Jewish name for God.

Curses in various forms are mentioned 230 times in the Bible. JESUS cursed a fig tree because it had no fruit and he was hungry; the next day the tree was found withered to its roots (Mark 11:12–14). However, Jesus condemned cursing and so did Paul, who urged people to bless those who cursed them.

Curses can affect generations. Families can be cursed by outsiders or become cursed through involvement in sinful activities. Participation in witchcraft or occult activities can curse a person or family, according to Christian tradition. Occult activities can include seeking communication with and knowledge from spirits instead of God and using magic or sorcery to control and manipulate others, including with objects that are cursed.

Curses also can be made against others through ill wishing, negative judgments of others, negative thoughts about one's self, and unhealthy relationships and sexual activities.

DELIVERANCE ministers and EXORCISTs who have the gift of discernment can determine whether or not a person has been cursed and is afflicted by a demon. There are likely to be signs of mental or emotional breakdown, repeated and chronic illness, infertility and miscarriages, financial problems, a tendency to have accidents, and a family history of unnatural and untimely deaths, such as by violence or suicide.

In cases of possession and EXORCISM performed by the Catholic Church, cursed objects are dangerous and must be destroyed. If a victim vomits up a cursed object, the exorcist should not touch it directly; an exorcist who does so should pray and wash his or her hands with holy water. The object should be burned.

In less extreme cases, the effects of a curse can be removed by prayer, attendance at church, reading the Bible, repentance, renunciation, placing crucifixes and religious objects in the home, and attending to a virtuous life.

Cursing Demons in Magic

In ceremonial magic, spirits or demons who refuse to appear when evoked in ritual may be cursed to burn in fire by the magician. This threat is said to terrify the spirits into obedience. The grimoire *Key of Solomon* gives this curse:

> We deprive ye of all office and dignity which ye may have enjoyed up till now; and by their virtue and power we relegate you unto a lake of sulphur and of flame, and unto the deepest depths of the Abyss, that ye may burn therein eternally for ever.

Another curse, called "Curse of the Chains" or "The General Curse" (also called "The Spirits Chains"), in-volves ritual cursing and a sealing of the disobedient demon inside a box bound by IRON chains:

> O spirit N., who art wicked and disobedient, because thou hast not obeyed my commands and the glorious and incomprehensible Names of the true God, the Creator of all things, now by the irresistible power of these Names I curse thee into the depths of the Bottomless Pit, there to remain in unquenchable fire and brimstone until the Day of Wrath unless thou shalt forthwith appear in this triangle before this circle to do my will. Come quickly and in peace by the Names Adonai, Zebaoth, Adonai, Amioram. Come, come, Adonai King of Kings commands thee.

The magician then writes the demon's name and SEAL on parchment which he places in a black wooden box that contains sulfur and other foul-smelling ingredients. He binds the box with iron chains, which imprison the demon. The magician hangs the box on the point of his sword and holds it over a fire, saying:

> I conjure thee, Fire, by Him who made thee and all other creatures of this world to burn, torture and consume this spirit N. now and for evermore.

The magician warns the demon that his name and seal will be burned in the box and then buried. If the spirit still does not appear, the magician works himself up into a greater fury of cursing, calling down the wrath of all the company of heaven, the Sun, the Moon, the stars, and the light of the hosts of heaven. As a final measure, he drops the box into the fire. The demon will find this unbearable and will appear.

Cursed Objects

Any object can be ritually cursed to affect whoever owns it with misfortune, and even death. Sometimes objects are cursed by circumstances. For example, the "screaming skulls" of England are said to be haunted by restless ghosts of the dead. Some of the skulls belong to victims of religious persecution during the 16th-century Reformation initiated by King Henry VIII. Others are those of Oliver Cromwell's supporters, called Roundheads, during the English Civil War in the mid-17th century. Still other skulls are from people who lost their heads in various violent episodes, such as murders. Other cursed objects may house demons that unleash trouble upon the owners of the objects. (See POSSESSION.)

Protection against Curses

Numerous remedies against cursing exist. AMULETs protect against or deflect curses, whether a person has specific knowledge about them or not. Semiprecious stones and jewels have been used since ancient times as amulets against curses and other forms of dark magic, illness, and misfortune. For example, the ancient Egyptians inscribed spells on lapis lazuli. The early Greeks and Romans wore certain carved semiprecious and precious gems as rings and necklaces to ward off curses.

It is assumed in many cultures that one will be cursed by one's enemies for any reason. Spells, CHARMs, and petitions invoke the protection and intervention of benevolent spirits. An individual who has been cursed sometimes visits another witch or sorcerer to break the curse and to curse the curser.

FURTHER READING:

Brier, Bob. *Ancient Egyptian Magic.* New York: William Morrow, 1980.

Butler, E. M. *Ritual Magic.* Cambridge: Cambridge University Press, 1949.

Cavendish, Richard. *The Black Arts.* New York: G. P. Putnam's Sons, 1967.

Fortea, Fr. José Antonio. *Interview with an Exorcist: An Insider's Look at the Devil, Diabolic Possession, and the Path to Deliverance.* West Chester, Pa.: Ascension Press, 2006.

MacNutt, Francis. *Deliverance from Evil Spirits: A Practical Manual.* Grand Rapids, Mich.: Chosen Books, 1995.

daeva (daiva, deva, dev)   In ZOROASTRIANISM, a powerful DEMON. The daevas are the principals of the infernal hordes and are the counterparts and mirror opposites of the *amesha spentas,* good spirits. They personify all diseases, sins, and distresses suffered by humanity. Most of the daevas are male.

In the Gathas, the oldest Zoroastrian texts, the daevas are wrong or false gods, or "gods that are (to be) rejected." In the Younger Avesta, the daevas are vile beings who create chaos and disorder. In later tradition and folklore, they personify all evils imaginable.

The daevas were created from the evil thoughts of AHRIMAN for the purpose of waging war against goodness and humanity. Though spirits, they can appear in human form. Evil men also are called daevas.

When the prophet Zoroaster was born, the daevas went into hiding beneath the earth. They lurk about, ready to attack the vulnerable. They are attracted to unclean places and like to spend time in locations where corpses are exposed.

The daevas originate in the north, the direction of evil. Their gateway to HELL is Mount Arezura, named after a son of Ahriman who was slain by Gayomart.

There are hordes of daevas; little is known about most of them. The most powerful are known by names, along with some of their powers and characteristics.

According to Plutarch, the creator God Ohrmazd made 24 gods and placed them in the cosmic egg. Ahriman made 24 daevas to penetrate the egg so that evil could mix with good. In later Zoroastrian texts, the numbers of daevas are LEGION.

The wicked who follow the daevas are condemned to go to the place of Worst Thought in the afterlife, the same designation given to DRUJ.

The most fearsome of the daevas is AESHMA, who is comparable to ASMODEUS.

FURTHER READING:
Jackson, A. V. Williams. *Zoroastrian Studies.* Whitefish, Mont.: Kessinger, 2003.

daimon   In Greek mythology, a type of spirit or intelligence between gods and humans. *Daimon* means "divine being." *Daimones* can be either good or evil in nature, though even good ones will act in a hostile fashion when angered. A good *daimon* is called an *agathodaimon* and an evil *daimon* is called a *kakodaimon.* Christianity assigned all *daimones* and pagan deities to the infernal ranks of DEMONS.

Daimones include various classes of entities, such as guardian spirits of places, tutelary spirits, genii, ministering spirits and demigods. They also have been associated with the souls of the dead and ghosts, stars and planets, and plants and minerals of the earth. They are ministering spirits (resembling angels), godlike beings, and souls of dead persons. *Daimones* can take over human bodies in the form of POSSESSION (especially for oracular prophecy) and possess humans to cause physical and mental illness. Some are vampiric in nature.

GRIMOIRES for ceremonial MAGIC include instructions for evoking and commanding *daimones*.

FURTHER READING:

Guiley, Rosemary Ellen. *The Encyclopedia of Angels.* 2nd ed. New York: Facts On File, 2004.

Luck, Goerg. *Arcana Mundi: Magic and the Occult in the Greek and Roman Worlds.* Baltimore: Johns Hopkins University Press, 1985.

Dalkiel   Angel of HELL and ruler of Sheol, the underworld, who serves under DUMAH, the angel of the stillness of death. In hell Dalkiel punishes nations. He is equated with Rugziel.

Dantanian   FALLEN ANGEL and 71st of the 72 SPIRITS OF SOLOMON. Dantanian is a mighty duke who appears in the form of a man with many faces of men and women, carrying a book in his hand. He knows human thoughts and can change them at will. He makes people fall in love and can show visions of people anywhere to others. He teaches all arts and sciences. He governs 36 LEGIONS of DEMONS.

Darling Possession (1596)   Fake POSSESSION by Thomas Darling, a 13-year-old boy of Burton-on-Trent, England. Darling, who aspired to become a Puritan minister, claimed to become possessed because a witch cursed him for farting. The case involved the Puritan EXORCIST the REVEREND JOHN DARREL in a peripheral way. An account of the case was written by a "man of trade" named Jesse Bee, who was with Darling during most of his affliction.

Darling began having fits in February 1596. He convulsed, vomited, and had visions of green APPLES and green ANGELS. He lost the use of his legs, except when he had fits. Whenever Bee started to read the GOSPEL OF JOHN, the boy went into fits, which fell into a pattern around certain verses, including 4, 9, 13, 14, and 17.

A doctor examined his urine and pronounced him bewitched. Bee and Darling's aunt discussed the boy's situation, and Bee opined that WITCHCRAFT might indeed be the cause, because Darling had fits upon hearing Scripture read. Darling overheard this conversation.

Soon he thought of a fitting story. He said that the day his fits began, he had been out in the woods and met a "little old woman" with three warts on her face. The woman was 60-year-old Alice Gooderidge, who was already suspected of being a witch, as was her mother. Darling farted, prompting Gooderidge to curse him with a rhyme:

Gyp with a mischiefe, and fart with a bell:
I will go to heaven, and thou shalt go to hell.

Gooderidge then stooped to the ground, and Darling went home, possessed.

Gooderidge was arrested and taken before justices, who had her scratched. Pressured into confessing, the woman acknowledged meeting Darling in the woods on said day but insisted she had mistaken him for another boy, who had once broken a basket of her eggs. She apologized for doing any harm with her words and said she had never said *hell*. She said that when she stooped, the DEVIL appeared in the form of "a little partie-colored dog, red and white." She called the dog Minny and dispatched it to torment Darling.

Darling performed well for a young DEMONIAC. During his fits, he carried on inspired theological debates with the DEVIL modeled on JESUS' temptations by SATAN in the desert. He moaned about dying young at the hands of the Devil. He had a vision of Gooderidge, whom he called "Mother Redde Cap," a common name for witches, and said DEMONS beat her brains out and toads gnawed the flesh from her bones.

The minister at Burton-on-Trent tried unsuccessfully to stop the fits. So did a renowned Puritan minister, Arthur Hildersham, who visited and tried to exorcise the boy with prayer.

Bee's written account was sent to Darrel, who believed that Satan, disguised as an angel of light, was speaking through the boy to deliver what seemed to be divinely inspired messages. At the end of May 1596, Darrel said Darling was possessed of an unclean spirit and recommended fasting and prayer. He did not visit in person, on the grounds that he did not want any glory in the case.

The following day, Darling's friends and family successfully exorcized him, eliciting a flamboyant performance. Darling became entranced, and a "demon" speaking through him said he would go to his master, BEELZEBUB. The great demon appeared, along with the witch, and Darling said he forgave Gooderidge and begged the Lord to forgive her too. He ordered Beelzebub to leave.

This was followed by a vision of an angel, sent by God for comfort, and more conversations with demons, who decided to depart and torment the witch, who was in jail. Interestingly, she reported having a bad night.

Darling came out of trance and lapsed into another one. A voice said, "My son, arise and walke, the evil spirit is gone from thee." Suddenly Darling could use his legs again, which he credited to Jesus. His troubles were not immediately over, for he had a relapse of temptation. After a vision of a dove, he was permanently cured.

Gooderidge was sentenced to a year in jail. Darling confessed to fabricating his possession, then recanted, claiming that his inspired speeches while entranced were indeed from God. In 1599, Darrel was tried on charges of fraud, and both Darling and Bee testified against him.

Darling entered Oxford University, where he maintained his ambition to become a Puritan minister. But, in 1602, he was whipped and had his ears cut off for libeling Vice-Chancellor John Howson, who was persecuting Puritans.

FURTHER READING:
Walker, D. P. *Unclean Spirits: Possession and Exorcism in France and England in the Late Sixteenth and Early Seventeenth Centuries.* Philadelphia: University of Pennsylvania Press, 1981.

Darrel (Darrell), Reverend John (16th century)   English Puritan minister convicted of fraud for exorcising the DEVIL from a man. John Darrel, a successful minister, was caught in religious infighting among moderate Catholics, English Anglicans, and Puritans. His case led the Anglican Church to forbid rites of EXORCISM.

Prior to his fateful case, Darrel was called to exorcize nine people in various cases: Katherine Wright in 1586, Thomas Darling in 1596, and seven possessed children in Lancashire in 1597 (see SEVEN IN LANCASHIRE POSSESSION). He was unsuccessful in dispossessing Wright, and although a witch was accused of causing her POSSESSION, the justice in charge refused to commit the witch and warned Darrel to desist from exorcisms or face imprisonment. In the DARLING POSSESSION, Darrel advised fasting and prayer but was not present during the exorcism so as to avoid personal glory.

The possession of the seven Lancashire children had already led to the execution of Edmund Hartley, originally summoned to cure the children but eventually found to be the witch responsible. Darrel was consulted because the children continued to have fits and convulsions. Assisted by the Derbyshire minister George More, Darrel exorcised the children in one afternoon, emphasizing that the greatest value of such Puritan exorcisms was in refuting the claim by the papists that theirs was the only true church since they could cast out devils.

Darrel's last case was the dispossession of William Sommers of Nottingham, begun in November 1597. Sommers, aged 20, suffered fits and had a lump the size of an egg, which ran about his body. His behavior was obscene, including bestiality with a dog in front of onlookers. Darrel exorcized him before 150 witnesses, but Sommers suffered repossessions, eventually naming witches responsible. Although Sommers did not react consistently to the various witches' presence, Darrel had all 13 arrested. All but two were released, but Darrel claimed that Sommers' accusations were correct, and that Sommers could probably find all the witches in England.

In January 1598, one of the accused witches' powerful families charged Sommers himself with witchcraft, for bewitching a person to death. Sommers confessed to fraud. He demonstrated how he simulated fits, including frothing at the mouth.

Darrel tried to persuade Sommers to withdraw his confession. Called before a church commission set up by the archbishop of York, Sommers went into fits—but the commission was convinced he was genuinely possessed. On March 20, and again at a later date, Sommers reaf-

firmed to church and government authorities that he was indeed faking his fits.

Sommers' flip-flops riled the public, and ministers talked from their pulpits about nothing but witchcraft and the Devil. Fearful of the effect on the people, as well as the increasing power of the Puritans, or Calvinists, the archbishop of Canterbury moved against Darrel. Katherine Wright and Thomas Darling were summoned as witnesses against Darrel and joined Sommers in confessing fraud. Wright and Sommers even accused Darrel of teaching them how to contrive fits. Wright's assertion did not fit the history of her own fits, which had continued periodically for 14 years. Darling recanted on his confession.

Mainly on the basis of Sommers' detailed accusations, the ecclesiastical court found Darrel to be a counterfeit and deposed him from the ministry in May 1599. Darrel languished in prison for several months but was never sentenced. After his release, he went into hiding for at least two years. His career dispossessing people was over.

As a result of Darrel's conviction, the Anglican Church passed Canon 72 of the Episcopal Church, forbidding exorcism as a formal ritual. Although there are Anglican priests today practicing exorcism on an informal basis with the approval of their bishops, most Anglicans—as well as other Protestants—have adopted the beliefs of MARTIN LUTHER: that the Devil can best be driven from a tortured soul by prayer alone, since only God knows when the Devil should leave.

FURTHER READING:
Walker, D. P. *Unclean Spirits: Possession and Exorcism in France and England in the Late Sixteenth and Early Seventeenth Centuries.* Philadelphia: University of Pennsylvania Press, 1981.

Decarabia (Carabia)   FALLEN ANGEL and 69th of the 72 SPIRITS OF SOLOMON. Decarabia is a marquis in HELL with 30 LEGIONS of DEMONS reporting to him. He appears as a star in a pentacle but changes into a man when ordered to do so. He makes magical birds fly before a magician and leaves them as FAMILIARS, singing and eating as ordinary birds do. Decarabia knows the virtues of herbs and precious stones.

deliverance   A form of spiritual warfare that includes EXORCISM of DEMONS, prayer, cleansing, and healing. Deliverance is practiced chiefly by Protestant denominations, especially Pentecostal and charismatic.

Practices of deliverance began in the early years of Christianity, when the apostles and all true believers cast out demons and healed by a laying on of hands. Over time, the practices became more restricted in favor of formal rites performed by priests. Deliverance declined with the advance of psychiatry and psychology but underwent a revival in the 20th century with the growth of Pentecostal and charismatic denominations.

The demonic realm is assumed to operate under a set of rules and to function as a hierarchy with lower-level demons reporting to higher-level demons. When a human being violates the rules, such as by committing a sin, demons then have "legal rights" to assault that person, causing a progression of problems from INFESTATION to OPPRESSION to POSSESSION. Evil acts committed in a place, as well as CURSES against people and places, also give demons legal rights.

Interference includes temptations to sin, physical attacks, obstructions, emotional oppression, and personality changes. Full and true possessions are considered to be rare. *Demonization* is a term used instead of possession.

Different types of demons are recognized.

- Demons with unusual names such as PAZUZU and BEELZEBUB are high in the hierarchy and represent the true demons of HELL. These spirits are in a minority of afflicting demons.
- Other demons take their names from sins such as Envy and Murder. They take advantage of people's weaknesses and foment paranoia.
- Some demons enter on the wake of trauma, especially psychological or emotional.
- Ancestral spirits, who may be genuine restless dead spirits or low-level demons masquerading as the dead, are encountered most often in hauntings and through spirit communications such as mediumship or devices.

Prayers are used to expel demons, but there are no formal rites of exorcism such as those performed in Catholicism only by priests (see *RITUALE ROMANUM*). The cause of demonization must be closed off through repentance and inner healing.

There are symptoms that denote when a deliverance is needed.

- Tormented persons are aware of spirits, such as through voices in their heads urging them to do violent or evil deeds or commit suicide and unusual and extreme nightmares.
- Others observe signs of demonization, such as bodily contortions, unusual changes in voice, severe changes in facial expressions, unpleasant smells, and marked cold.

Widespread belief among Pentecostals, charismatics, and others holds that only pagans, not Christians, are ever in need of deliverance.

Deliverance usually is done by clergy but can be done by others as well, such as mediums and healers and laypersons. Such individuals have been given a chrism, or gift, of discernment by the Holy Spirit, which enables them to perceive whether or not a person is afflicted by evil spirits and to know the identity of the spirits. The identity is helpful in determining the origin or entry point of the demon and in knowing how the demon is affecting the victim.

Deliverance prayers are performed for spiritual protection, light infestation and oppression, and severe demonization. Serious cases are best handled by experienced clergy or trained laypersons who are empowered by the Holy Spirit. Tools include blessed water, oil, and salt.

FURTHER READING:
MacNutt, Francis. *Deliverance from Evil Spirits: A Practical Manual.* Grand Rapids, Mich.: Chosen Books, 1995.

demoniac Person who becomes possessed by a DEMON. A demoniac undergoes a marked change in physical, mental, and emotional symptoms and behavior. Depending on the type of POSSESSION, there may be a pattern to the changes.

In ancient times, demons were blamed for entering a person and taking control of him or her to cause problems. The ancient Jewish historian Josephus said that it was not a demon but the soul of a tormented person that entered a victim. Illnesses and diseases were blamed on demons, especially if a person fell into fits, trances, or bizarre behavior. Natural medical conditions, such as epilepsy, may have been the real causes, but in earlier times, there was little understanding of many illnesses.

Linda Blair as the demoniac Regan in The Exorcist *(1973)* (AUTHOR'S COLLECTION)

The attempted remedy was to undertake an EXORCISM, which would eradicate the problem. Certain empowered individuals had the knowledge, and especially the supernatural power, to help demoniacs.

During the medieval and Renaissance times in Europe, demoniacs said they were cursed by witches and sorcerers (see CURSE) or were overcome by the DEVIL. The Catholic Church used possession to pursue its political agendas. Some cases of demoniacs were false; they faked their symptoms or were swept up in hysterias. (See SPIRIT OF ORLEANS.)

More recently, demoniacs are said to be in "religious altered states of consciousness," or RASC. They exhibit many of the same physical, mental, and emotional symptoms as persons who are swept up in religious or spiritual ecstasies and raptures; however, for them the experience is hellish rather than heavenly: they are under the siege of demons rather than God.

Demoniacs exhibit certain symptoms, among them swellings and contortions of the body, trances, cataleptic states, transfigurations of their faces and voices, unusual behavior, self-battering and mutilation, personality and mood changes, and statements from the possessing demon, often in foreign languages—especially Latin—unknown to the demoniac. The victim shouts obscenities and blasphemies and taunts EXORCISTs and others. In more severe cases, there are uncontrollable hysterics; episodes of supernormal strength; levitation; the vomiting of unusual substances, bile and copious quantities of mucus; clairvoyance; and prophecy. The eyes may roll back into the head. Sexual assault by the demons, poltergeist phenomena, apparitions, and nightmares may happen to the victims.

Demoniacs usually are not steadily possessed but act normally and then are overcome for periods of time. They may be possessed by multiple demons and have to undergo repeated exorcisms over long periods.

Possession is considered life-threatening to a demoniac, though few have actually died under its influence. In 1590, Ann Frank, a nurse in the employ of John Dee, an English occultist, became possessed and attempted suicide. Dee's remedy was to anoint her breast with holy oil and put her under heavy guard. After a month, she succeeded in killing herself by cutting her throat. Frank is one of the few demoniacs on record who actually committed suicide.

In 1976, a young German demoniac, ANNELIESE MICHEL, died while undergoing exorcisms. She was severely emaciated and dehydrated.

FURTHER READING:

Baroja, Julio Caro. *The World of the Witches.* 1961. Reprint, Chicago: University of Chicago Press, 1975.

Goodman, Felicitas D. *The Exorcism of Anneliese Michel.* Garden City, N.Y.: Doubleday, 1981.

Lea, Henry Charles. *Materials toward a History of Witchcraft.* Philadelphia: University of Pennsylvania Press, 1939.

Demon of Jedburgh (1752)   Account of an alleged witch in Jedburgh, Scotland.

In 1752, Captain Archibald Douglas was in Jedburgh on a recruiting campaign. One of his sergeants asked to change quarters because the house he was staying in had a DEMON in a "frightful form" that pestered him at night. Douglas refused the man's request.

Soon the sergeant appealed again to be moved, saying the demon had threatened his life. He said that he had awakened during the night to see the ugly form standing over him. It changed into a black cat, jumped out the window, and flew over the church steeple. The sergeant also had learned that the landlady was said to be a witch and her husband possessed "second sight" (clairvoyance).

That night, Douglas spent the night beside the sergeant, with his gun and sword nearby. At midnight, he was awakened by a noise and saw a large black cat fly in through the window. He fired at it and shot off one of its ears. It vanished.

The next morning, the men saw the landlady, who fainted before them in a pool of BLOOD. They discovered that one of her ears had been shot off. Douglas threatened to turn the woman in to the authorities, but she and her husband begged him to leave them alone. He agreed, on condition that they give up their "wicked ways." It is not known whether the couple did as promised.

The story is possibly a blend of fact and fiction; the telltale wound is prominent in magical folklore in tales of shape-shifting sorcerers, witches, and werewolves.

FURTHER READING:

Grant, James. *The Mysteries of All Nations: Rise and Progress of Superstition, Laws against and Trials of Witches, Ancient and Modern Delusions, Together with Strange Customs, Fables and Tales.* Edinburgh: Leith, Reid & Son, n.d.

demons and demonology   A type of spirit that interferes in the affairs of people. The term *demon* means "replete with wisdom" and is derived from the Greek term DAIMON. The *daimones* were both good and evil and even included deified heroes. In most cultures, demons are troublesome rather than helpful; some are evil. In Christianity, all demons are evil and serve SATAN for the purpose of subverting souls. Demons can cause unpleasant hauntings, often involving INFESTATION, OPPRESSION, and POSSESSION. The study of demons is called demonology. Like ANGELs, demons are numberless.

Historical Overview

Demons universally are considered the cause of all humankind's problems: disease, misfortune, poor health, bad luck, ruined relationships, sin, and soul loss. Since ancient times, they have been said to have sex with humans. They can be sent to torment and possess others. They can be put to productive uses as well and can be summoned and controlled by magic. For example, in ancient Egypt, a

Demon carrying off a child who has been promised to the Devil (AUTHOR'S COLLECTION)

magician who exorcized a possessing demon could command the same demon to perform useful tasks. There are numerous ways to protect against demons and to banish them from places, people, and animals.

Beliefs in demon-caused troubles are ancient and still prevail in many places around the world. Since the mid-20th century, belief in demons and their interferences has risen in the West.

The lore of the ancient Babylonians, Assyrians, and other Middle Eastern cultures teemed with demons. The greatest demonic problem was illness, and demons had to be cast out of a person for healing. In Mesopotamian lore, demons took the form of human-animal hybrids that could walk upright on two legs and were controlled by the gods. Humans could repel demons by magic, such as use of CHARMs and AMULETs (see INCANTATION BOWL).

Demons in Judaism

Judaic demonologies evolved with influences from the lore of the Babylonians, Persians, and Egyptians. In Talmudic tradition, demons are ever-present enemies posing constant dangers to humanity. They were created by God on the first sabbath eve at twilight. Dusk fell before God finished them, and thus they have no bodies. According to another story, demons were spawned by LILITH, the spurned first wife of Adam. King SOLOMON used magic to summon and control demons, or the DJINN, to work for him in building his Temple of Jerusalem.

Demons can have wings and exist between humans and angels, roughly between the earth and the Moon.

They are less powerful than angels. They frequent uninhabited and unclean places, and once they attach themselves to a person or family, bad luck follows.

The Jewish "middle world" teems with numberless demons and angels. Angels of destruction (*malache habbala*) blurred together with the demonic. By the second century C.E., the Hebrews had developed complex systems of both entities. As were angels, demons were seen as having jurisdiction over everything in creation. Rabbinical teachings frowned on demon magic, but beliefs and practices concerning demons were tolerated. By the Middle Ages, rabbinic writings had elaborated upon demons, expanding their classes and duties.

One category of demon, the LUTIN, does possess both body and soul. The lutin were created by sexual unions between Adam and female demons after he parted from Eve.

Another category of demons are created every day from the newly dead, who were believed to linger about in close contact with the living. The spirits of the wicked dead became demons. They are capable of inflicting wounds that only God can heal.

In the development of the KABBALAH, hierarchies of demons were associated with the 10 *sephirot,* or centers, of the Tree of Life. According to the Kabbalah, evil powers emanate from the left pillar of the Tree of Life, especially from Geburah, the *sephira* of the wrath of God. By the 13th century, the idea of 10 evil *sephirot* had developed to counter the 10 holy *sephirot* of the Tree.

Other Hebrew systems of demons distinguish those born of night terrors and those who fill the sky between the Earth and the Moon. There are demons who, with angels, are in charge of the night hours, and interpretations of diseases, and those who have seals that may be used to summon them. This demonic lore later became the core of magical handbooks called GRIMOIRES.

The Old Testament mentions evil spirits but does not feature a primary demonic figure such as the SATAN that emerged in Christianity. "Satan" is more a prosecuting attorney interested in testing humans and is a member of the heavenly court. God sends evil spirits to punish people. Judges 9:22–25 tells of Abimelech, who murdered 70 rivals for the rule of Israel:

> After Abimelech had governed Israel three years, God sent an evil spirit between Abimelech and the citizens of Shechem, who acted treacherously against Abimelech. God did this in order that the crime against Jerub-Baal's seventy sons, the shedding of their blood, might be avenged on their brother Abimelech and on the citizens of Shechem, who had helped him murder his brothers. In opposition to him these citizens of Shechem set men on the hilltops to ambush and rob everyone who passed by, and this was reported to Abimelech.

In 1 Kings 22:19–22, the Lord manipulates human affairs by dispatching a lying spirit, though its nature—good or evil—is ambiguous:

Micaiah continued, "Therefore hear the word of the LORD: I saw the LORD sitting on his throne with all the host of heaven standing around him on his right and on his left (20). And the LORD said, 'Who will entice Ahab into attacking Ramoth Gilead and going to his death there?'

One suggested this, and another that (21). Finally, a spirit came forward, stood before the LORD and said, "I will entice him."

"By what means?" the LORD asked.

"I will go out and be a lying spirit in the mouths of all his prophets," he said.

"You will succeed in enticing him," said the LORD. "Go and do it."

More about demons is found in the rabbinic teachings called the Gemora. (See MAZZIQIN.)

Demons in Apochryphal and Pseudepigraphal Works

The Apochrypha and pseudepigrapha are non-canonical texts written by unknown or pseudonymous authors. Some of the texts have more to say about angels and demons than do the canonical works in the Bible.

The Apochrypha (hidden) consists of 15 books or portions of books written between about 200 B.C.E. and 200 C.E. Demons have minor roles in apochryphal works; the distinguishing exception is the book of Tobit, in which the young man Tobias learns how to exorcize demons from the archangel Raphael, disguised as a man (see ASMODEUS).

Most pseudepigraphal works were written between 200 B.C.E. and 200 C.E., though some were written much later. More information about demons is given in pseudepigraphal works such as Jubilees and Enoch. According to Jubilees, evil originated with bad angels, not with Adam and Eve.

Jubilees says that angels were created by God on the first day. The text does not say specifically when demons were created, but it is implied that they, too, were made on the first day, "along with all of the spirits of his [God's] creatures which are in heaven and on earth" (2:2).

Angels are described only by their classes and duties. One class are the WATCHERS, good angels who were assigned the task of watching over humanity. The Watchers coveted human women and descended to Earth, to create the vampiric, cannibalistic monsters called NEPHILIM. Thus, the demonic and evil powers were created by corrupted angels.

God sends the flood to cleanse the planet, but not all of the Nephilim are destroyed. When the polluted demons start to bother Noah and his sons, Noah appeals to God, who agrees to send angels to bind them all into the place of judgment. MASTEMA, the prince of evil and the only demonic power named in Jubilees, steps forward to ask God to allow one-tenth of the demons to remain on Earth under his jurisdiction. The angels then teach Noah herbal lore for restraining the remaining demons.

The three books of Enoch also tell the story of the Watchers and Nephilim, in more detail. Again, evil comes into being through the fall of the angels. On the Day of Judgment, however, all the demons and evil angels will be cast into the abyss.

Demons in Christianity

In Christianity, demons have their origins in the FALLEN ANGELS who followed LUCIFER, or "morning star," when he was cast out of heaven by God (Isaiah 14:12). In the New Testament, JESUS healed by casting out demons, in keeping with prevailing traditions. By the end of the New Testament period, demons were synonymous with fallen angels, all under the direction of Satan. As Christianity spread, pagan gods, goddesses, and nature spirits were incorporated into the ranks of demons.

The hermits, ascetics, and men who became the early saints of Christianity were constantly beset by evil, including demonic attacks (see ANTHONY). In the early centuries, Christian theologians known as the apostolic fathers grappled with questions about evil. Justin Martyr saw demons as the illicit children of fallen angels and human women. Clement, Ignatius, Polycarp, and Barnabas stressed the Devil rather than his demons. Irenaeus was convinced of the reality of demons and the Devil and advocated EXORCISM as a way to combat them.

Tertullian wrote in more detail about demons, defining them as fallen angels who lusted after women. Demons are quite dangerous, he said, possessing supreme intelligence and knowledge, as well as supernormal abilities such as instant travel.

Demon tempting a woman with the sin of vanity (AUTHOR'S COLLECTION)

Origen agreed with Tertullian, except on the reason for the fall of angels: They fell from the sin of pride rather than lust. Demons were not created evil, he said, but became evil by exercising their free will. They are not pure spirits but have bodies different from human ones. They attack humans in two principal ways: through obsession, with evil thoughts, and through possession, including of animals. Magic is done with the aid of demons, Origen said. He also advocated exorcism, which must be performed according to precise rituals in order to be effective. Under certain circumstances, humans can become demons—a view that later theologians criticized.

From about the third to eighth centuries, theologians built on these early ideas. Jerome and Augustine wrote of shape-shifting demons, including half-human, half-monstrous forms. Augustine in particular never doubted the reality of demons and their evil influences.

For medieval theologians, demons were the tempters of humanity, a system that ultimately worked in favor of humans by proving who was worthy of going to heaven. The Devil and his hordes had no direct access to people except through their free will choices. Thomas Aquinas said that SATAN controls people chiefly through possession, and if demons had no success with a person during life, they made their final assault on the soul at the moment of death.

During the witch trials of the Inquisition, the importance of demons increased. Demons were believed to play a key role, causing possessions, leading people into sin, helping people perpetrate evil deeds, and serving witches as their FAMILIAR spirits in all acts of malevolence. Theologians and witch hunters emphasized the dangers of demons and those who trafficked with them by making PACTs. The Puritan minister Increase Mather said in *Cases of Conscience* (1692), "The Scriptures assert that there are Devils and Witches and that they are the common enemy of Mankind." George Giffard, an Oxford preacher of about the same period, said that witches should be put to death not because they kill others but because they deal with devils: "These cunning men and women which deale with spirites and charme seeming to do good, and draw the people into manifold impieties, with all other which haue familiarity with deuils, or use conjurations, ought to bee rooted out, that others might see and feare."

Characteristics of Demons
Descriptions from antiquity portray demons as shape shifters who can assume any form, animal or human or hybrid, such as the Mesopotamian demons. The Platonists and early fathers and theologians of the Christian Church said that demons condense bodies out of the air or smoke. In Arabian lore, the djinn are made of smokeless fire. Some of the theologians and witch hunters of the Inquisition said that demons have no corporeal form and only give the illusion that they are in human or animal form. They create voices out of air that mimic people.

In Judaic lore, demons are always invisible but can see themselves and each other. They cast no shadows. They eat, drink, propagate, and eventually die, though not exactly as humans do. Their eating and drinking consist of lapping up fire, water, air, and slime. When they die, they dry up and wither away to their primordial state. However, when they have sex, they can assume bodies. They will not copulate in front of any human or another demon.

In Christian lore, demons assume forms that are black, such as dogs (see BLACK DOGS) and other animals and men dressed in black. Because they are evil, they are imperfect, and so they always have a flaw in their appearance, such as a malformed limb or cloven feet. They can also assume beautiful and seductive forms, especially if they are sexual predators.

According to Remy:

When they first approach a man to speak with him they do not wish him to be terrified by any unusual appearance, and therefore they prefer to assume a human shape and manifest themselves as a man of good standing in order that their words may carry more weight and authority; and for this reason they like to wear a long black cloak, such as is only worn by honored men of substance. It is true that many hold their purpose in this last is to conceal the deformity of their feet, which is an ineradicable token and sign of their essential baseness; and that black is, besides, most appropriate to them,

A lion-snake demon (© RICHARD COOK)

Demon (© RICHARD COOK)

of protection. The greatest danger occurs at night when sleeping humans are at their most vulnerable, especially concerning demons that cause nightmares and make sexual attacks. Birth and death are perilous times, as are the nights on which marriages are consummated. At these times, demons are better able to wreak havoc.

During the Inquisition, demons were believed to aid witches by giving instruction on how to cast evil spells and how to poison people, crops, and animals with herbs and other substances. They acted as familiars, taking the form of animals such as birds and insects, to carry out the evil of witches. They participated in SABBATs and pacts. Inquisitors believed that demons influenced women more easily than men, for women, they said, were weaker in will and intellect than men.

Demons send bad weather and pests such as armies of mice and swarms of locusts to destroy crops.

In hauntings and possessions, demons create unpleasant poltergeist phenomena and chaos and attack the living in a progression of increasing intensity. Psychics and mediums perceive them as having grotesque forms. They are often associated with revolting smells. In some cases, demons shape shift into deceitful, desirable forms with charming personalities. Once they have a person under their control, they revert to their original nature. Low-level demonic entities are associated with problems involving talking board use (see OUIJA™).

In possessions, demons will speak through possessed persons, altering the person's voice. Demons have a fondness for profanity and verbal abuse. They cause physical phenomena, such as spitting, vomiting, levitation,

since all their contrivings against men are of a black and deadly nature.

Demons are described as unclean, filthy, and full of abominable stench. They live in dead bodies. If they make their bodies out of air or occupy a living body, they exude a stench. In the body, they swell in the bowels with excrement and waste. They are afraid of cuts, wounds, and blows and can be repelled with threats of them.

They are organized in hierarchies and function as in a military organization, according to GRIMOIRES and Inquisition writings. If lower demons disobey their superiors, they are beaten.

Activities of Demons

Throughout history, the chief activity of demons has been to cause illness and disease. They are the spirits of uncleanness, and the lack of proper hygiene will enable them to enter a person through contaminated food, dirty hands, and foul environments. Widespread beliefs hold that humans are in constant danger of demonic attack in some form, and constant vigilance is required through watchfulness, proper habits, and the use of measures

The demon Harborym (*DICTIONNAIRE INFERNAL*)

unnatural twisting of limbs, supernormal strength, foaming at the mouth, and so on. In rites of exorcism, it is important to know the demon's name.

Demons are exorcized, or expelled, by a variety of methods, from ordering the demon to leave, to magical ritual, to religious ritual.

Sex with Demons

Christianity rejected the idea of sexual intercourse with demons until the 12th century; by the 14th century, it was accepted in theology. Sex with demons became a focus of the Inquisition; witches and those under demonic control were said to copulate wildly with demons, and even with Satan himself (see INCUBUS; SUCCUBUS). The male incubi molested women and the female succubi molested men. Both kinds of demons were said to masquerade as humans in order to seduce their prey. The actual sexual act, however, was held to be painful and vile. Women impregnated by demons were supposed to give birth to monsters.

Witch hunters said that demons enter into marriages with humans. Remy wrote of a 1587 case in which two witnesses, Bertrande Barbier and Sinchen, said they witnessed such a marriage at night in a place where criminals were crucified. Instead of giving the bride a ring, the bridegroom blew his breath into the bride's anus. A roasted black she-goat was served at the wedding feast. This tale is characteristic of the stories fabricated in witch trials and used by inquisitors to convict and execute accused heretics and witches.

In modern cases, demons are opportunistic, assaulting humans weakened by vices, sin, or CURSES or simply being in the wrong place at the wrong time, such as a location where acts of evil have taken place.

Demons in Magic

Demons are invoked in MAGIC. Because demons are unruly, magicians must force them to obey commands for service. Grimoires give the names, duties, SEALS, incantations, and rituals summoning and controlling demons. They are especially useful in DIVINATION, finding lost treasure, and the casting of spells. When evoked, demons are made to take form in a magic triangle, a secured boundary from which they cannot threaten the magician, who is protected by a magic circle.

FURTHER READING:

Ebon, Martin. *The Devil's Bride, Exorcism: Past and Present.* New York: Harper & Row, 1974.

Finlay, Anthony. *Demons! The Devil, Possession and Exorcism.* London: Blandford, 1999.

Flint, Valerie I. J. *The Rise of Magic in Early Medieval Europe.* Princeton, N.J.: Princeton University Press, 1991.

Fortea, Fr. Jose Antonio. *Interview with an Exorcist: An Insider's Look at the Devil, Diabolic Possession, and the Path to Deliverance.* West Chester, Pa.: Ascension Press, 2006.

Goodman, Felicitas. *How about Demons? Possession and Exorcism in the Modern World.* Bloomington: Indiana University Press, 1988.

MacNutt, Francis. *Deliverance from Evil Spirits: A Practical Manual.* Grand Rapids, Mich.: Chosen Books, 1995.

Martin, Malachi. *Hostage to the Devil.* New York: Harper & Row, 1987.

Oesterreich, T. K. *Possession: Demonical and Other Among Primitive Races, in Antiquity, the Middle Ages and Modern Times.* New Hyde Park, N.Y.: University Books, 1966.

The Old Testament Pseudepigrapha. Vols. 1 & 2. Edited by James H. Charlesworth. 1983. Reprint, New York: Doubleday, 1985.

Thomas, Keith. *Religion and the Decline of Magic.* New York: Charles Scribner's Sons, 1971.

Trachtenberg, Joshua. *Jewish Magic and Superstition: A Study in Folk Religion.* New York: Berhman's Jewish Book House, 1939.

Demoriel   DEMON among the 31 AERIAL SPIRITS OF SOLOMON. Demoriel is the emperor of the north, served by 400 great dukes, 600 lesser dukes, and 7,000,008,000,009,000,001 ministering spirits. There are 12 primary dukes, each of whom has 1,140 attending spirits: Amibiel, Cabarim, Menador, Burisiel, Doriel, Mador, Camael, Dubilon, Meclu, Churibal, Dabrinos, and Chomiell.

Denham Exorcisms (1585–1586)   The EXORCISMS of six fraudulent DEMONIACs by 12 Catholic priests, the chief of whom was a Jesuit, William Weston, also known as Edmunds. Most of the exorcisms took place in the home of Sir George Peckham of Denham, Buckinghamshire, England. The "possessions" were fake, part of a conversion campaign against Protestants and a political plot against the Crown.

An account of the exorcisms was written by Samuel Harsnett, chaplain to the bishop of London, Richard Bancroft, and published in 1603. It was entitled *A Declaration of Egregious Popish Impostures, to with-draw the harts of her Majesties Subjects from their allegance, and from the truth of Christian Religion professed in England, under the pretence of casting out devils. Practiced by Edmunds, alias Weston a Jesuit, a divers Romish Priests his wicked associates. Where-unto are annexed the Copies of the Confessions and Examinations of the parties themselves, which pretended to be possessed, and dispossessed, taken upon oath before her Majesties Commissioners for Causes Ecclesiasticall.*

Weston arrived in England in September 1584, during a time of severe persecutions of Catholic clergy. Several Jesuits had been martyred, and some had fled the country. The Act of 1585 made Jesuits and seminary priests guilty of treason simply by being in England. Anyone who harbored them was guilty of felony. And the Witchcraft Act of 1563 made the conjuring of spirits—which included exorcism—punishable by death on the first offense. Nonetheless, Weston and the priests undertook the exorcisms, ostensibly in order to convert Protestants back to Catholicism.

There was a greater factor involved: the Babington plot to assassinate Queen Elizabeth I and replace her with Mary, queen of Scots, and allow the Spaniards to invade England. The first person exorcized by Weston in England was William Marwood, a servant of Anthony Babington, a Catholic nobleman from Derbyshire, who later visited Denham in order to witness the exorcisms of the six demoniacs. Two of the exorcising priests, John Ballard and Anthony Tyrell, were part of the plot; Ballard was a leader of it and convinced Babington to join it. Weston probably knew about it and used the exorcisms to help the plot succeed.

Four of the Denham demoniacs later confessed to faking possessions. If the other two confessed, their records have been lost. Two were Protestants: Sara Williams, 15, a servant at Denham, and her sister, Frideswid or Fid, 17, who took over Sara's chores when she began having fits. Fid fell in the laundry and was persuaded that she had become possessed too. Two were Catholic: Annie Smith, 18, a family friend of the Peckhams, sent to Denham because she was having fits, and Richard Mainey, about 18, an Englishman who had become a Friar Minim in France but left the order because of their strictness and the fact that he disliked fish, their dietary mainstay. He also suffered hysteria.

The demoniacs faked visions, revelations, prophecies, and convulsions. Their DEMONs praised Queen Elizabeth and her courtiers, proclaiming them to be faithful servants of the DEVIL. The exorcisms were witnessed by huge crowds. During the course of the year, at least 500 persons converted, according to the published account.

The exorcisms involved intoxicating, nauseating potions and stinking fumes. The demoniacs were bound to chairs and forced to drink a vile potion of oil, sack, and rue. Chafing dishes of burning brimstone were held under their noses. No wonder that the demoniacs lost their reason, believed themselves to be truly possessed, and babbled about demons. They were shown relics of English saints, bones that they had been coached to identify correctly. The priests put bones into the mouths of Sara and Fid; the girls did not have to fake revulsion that was taken as a sign of demonic horror.

Mainey's demon, Modu, said that Sara and Fid had been bewitched by Goodwife White of Bushy, a woman who was commonly believed to be a witch. The priests captured White's cat and whipped it until it "vanished away." They sent a messenger to Bushy, where White was found in childbed, having lost her baby in childbirth. Fid accused the priests of murder.

Of all the demoniacs, Mainey put on the best show. Prior to Easter 1586, he announced that every Sunday he would have a vision of purgatory, and on Good Friday he would ascend to heaven. Not surprisingly, a large crowd gathered on the appointed day to witness this event. Mainey lay on his bed, preached and prayed in a stern fashion, and then lapsed into a two-hour trance. When he awakened, he sighed and groaned and said:

My time is not yet come: our blessed Lady hath appeared to me, and told me that I must live longer yet: for that

God hath reserved me for a further purpose to doe more good, and to tell of strange wonders.

Mainey had more theatrics in him. The last exorcism occurred on April 23, 1586. Mainey's demon, Modu, appeared and said that he was accompanied by seven other demons, "all of them Captaines and of great fame." They acted out the SEVEN DEADLY SINS. When this gross display was finished, Modu cursed the "popish priests" and said that all of Mainey's visions were false, intended to induce Catholics to worship devils disguised as Christ and "Saffronbag," as he called the Virgin Mary. The demons departed.

On August 4, 1586, Weston and Ballard were arrested by orders of Sir Francis Walsingham, Queen Elizabeth's "spymaster," who had been carefully watching Catholic activities, including the Denham exorcisms. Denham's house was raided, and most of the occupants were arrested. Other priests were jailed. No incriminating evidence against Weston could be found, but nonetheless he was imprisoned in Wisbech Castle for 10 years. Tyrell became an informer for the Crown.

Ballard, Babington, and other conspirators rounded up were tortured and tried at Westminster Hall in London. They were sentenced to be hanged and their bodies drawn and quartered. They were executed in two batches on September 20 and 21. Ballard was among the first to go. Their executions were so bloody and horrific that the crowd witnessing them was revolted. They were hanged but were cut down before they were dead and were butchered alive. Queen Elizabeth also was revolted at the news and ordered the second batch of conspirators to be hanged until they were dead and their bodies then butchered.

The Babington plot thus was foiled and ultimately led to the execution of Mary, queen of Scots in 1587.

Meanwhile, Weston did not sit idle in Wisbech Castle but continued to stir up warring religious factions among English Catholics. In 1602, an inquiry was launched into the Denham exorcisms, followed by the publication of the broadsheet, which may have been part of an effort to smear Weston.

FURTHER READING:
Walker, D. P. *Unclean Spirits: Possession and Exorcism in France and England in the Late Sixteenth and Early Seventeenth Centuries.* Philadelphia: University of Pennsylvania Press, 1981.

Devil   The personification of evil. In Christianity, *Devil* is the proper name for the evil counterpart to God, who rules the torments of HELL and commands armies of DEMONs. The Devil represents darkness, chaos, destruction, suffering, and the complete absence of good, light, and love. The word *devil*, spelled in lowercase, also is a generic term used interchangeably with *demon* to denote a lower-ranking evil entity.

The term *devil* is derived from the Greek *diabolos* (slanderer or accuser), in turn translated from the Hebrew word SATAN. The concept of the Devil as archfiend of evil developed slowly over many centuries, becoming a composite of LUCIFER, the FALLEN ANGEL whose pride and ego cause him to be expelled from heaven; Satan, the tempter of humans; and pagan deities such as Pan and Cernunnos.

In non-Western traditions, evil is expressed through deities, who are seldom completely evil. The gods of a conquered people become devils or evil; Christianity demonized pagan gods as it spread in dominance.

Evolution of the Devil

The Christian Devil evolved from ideas and personifications of evil in Mesopotamian, Egyptian, and classical mythology and in Hebrew demonology. Egyptian gods embody qualities of both good and evil, but the god Set personifies more of the dark side than others. As the evil brother of Osiris, Set represents chaos and destruction. In myth, he slays Osiris, dismembers him, and scatters parts of his body. Osiris' wife, Isis, reassembles them and reanimates the corpse long enough for a sexual union, which produces the son Horus.

Mesopotamian demons are the offspring of gods, such as Tiamat, the goddess of chaos and the primordial waters, and her partner, Apsu, as well as the high god Anu. Demons rule diseases, illnesses, nightmares, plagues, and all misfortunes that befall living things. They are grotesque and deformed and often part-human and part-animal. Protections against them are gained through AMULETS, incantations, and MAGIC.

In ZOROASTRIANISM, the one God, Ahuru Mazda (who became Ohrmazd), generates the twins Spenta Mainyu, who is holy, and Angra Mainyu (who became AHRIMAN), who is evil and destructive. The creation story varies according to the streams of Zoroastrianism. In one, Ahuru Mazda and Ahriman are separated by a void. As does the Christian Devil, Ahriman dwells in darkness on the opposite side of the void and is fated to be conquered by good, Ohrmazd.

Ahriman sees the light of good across the void and lusts for it. He sends his weapons of destruction, which include toads, scorpions, SERPENTs, lust, and chaos, against Ohrmadz. Ohrmadz offers a truce of redemption, but Ahriman refuses it. Orhmadz reveals his fated defeat, which sends Ahriman spinning unconscious into the outer reaches of the void for 3,000 years. He revives with the help of Jeh, a whore, and engages Ohrmazd in battle for 6000 years, foreshadowing the Armageddon of REVELATION. In the first 3,000 years, the forces of good and evil are balanced. In the final 3,000 years, good triumphs over evil. In his assault, Ahriman tears apart the sky and creates the hours of night and darkness, and violence and destruction of life. He creates hordes of demons.

Ahriman corrupts the man and woman who are the ancestors of humanity, Mashye and Mashyane, by tempt-

The Devil tempting St. Patrick (AUTHOR'S COLLECTION)

ing them to believe the lie that he, not Ohrmazd, created the material world. Ohrmazd creates forces of good that bind Ahriman, ultimately enabling the world to be repaired. But in the last phase of the battle, the entire cosmos shakes and much destruction is done. Stars fall from the sky. Ohrmadz either destroys Ahriman or imprisons him forever.

In the Yasht text, Ahriman will be defeated by the coming of a Saoshyant, or Savior. Three saviors will come forward, and the third, a son of Zarathustra conceived by a virgin, will destroy evil and bring forth the reign of righteousness. The world will be restored, the dead will arise, and life and immortality will arrive.

In classical mythology, the gods and goddesses all have both good and evil characteristics; there is no one personification of evil alone. Shades of the dead live in a dull, shadowy realm, Hades, the lowest level of which is Tartarus, a pit or abyss in which the wicked are tormented. Greek philosophy evolved along the lines of moral good and evil, and the distinguishing of the originally ambivalent *DAIMONes* into good demons and evil demons.

The Judaic concept of the Devil developed slowly. The Old Testament tells of different satans, or accusers, rather than a single Satan. One of these is permitted by God to test the faith of Job. The apocalyptic literature placed the harsh and punishing aspects in certain angels, such as MASTEMA, the only significant angel mentioned by name in the book of Jubilees. In Enoch, the WATCHERS are wicked angels whose fall, of their own choice, leads to evil on the earth. The Testaments of the Twelve Patriarchs name BELIAL, or Satan, as the leader of evil angels. SAMMAEL and AZAZEL also are named as leaders of wicked angels, who dwell in darkness. The apocalyptic literature developed a more dualistic idea of evil personified in the Devil as the head of a realm of darkness whose primary role is to seduce, accuse, and destroy.

In Islam, the Devil is not the dualistic counterpart to God, but a high-level being—either an angel or DJINN—who chooses to fall from grace rather than bow to God's first human, Adam. The Devil is most often named SHAYTAN in the Qur'an, an accursed and rejected rebel who has God's permission to use temptation to corrupt souls. He has no power over those who love God. God has no power over his demonic servants, the Shaitan. The Devil is part of God's creation and plan involving punishment and testing. The Qur'an also gives the name of IBLIS as the Devil.

There is no concept of original sin in the Qur'an. Adam and Eve sinned but did not pass on the taint to others. Humans are prone to evil and, therefore, vulnerable to the snares of the Devil. The Devil vows to put all of Adam's descendants under his sway.

In the New Testament of Christianity, the Devil becomes more personal and the great antagonist of God as well as humans. He is a fallen angel, the leader of hordes of fallen angels-turned-demons, and he is the principle of evil itself. He has power over the physical world. His forces of darkness are pitched in war against God's forces of light. JESUS, as the Son of God, goes to Earth in order to defeat him. Revelation forecasts that Christ, in his second coming, will bind the Devil for one thousand years, at which time the Devil will reappear one final time, as the Antichrist, before being destroyed. The dualism of Christianity became firmly established, with a god of light and goodness and a god of evil and darkness.

In 325, the Council of Nicaea confirmed that God was the creator of everything visible and invisible. Therefore, the Devil was originally created good but chose the path of evil.

It was not until later in Christianity that the Devil was seen as the ruler and inhabitant of hell. These concepts were more firmly cemented in literature, such as authored by Dante and John Milton.

By the Middle Ages, the Devil was a real, potent being who possessed terrible supernatural powers and was intent upon destroying humans by undermining their morals. In this pursuit, he was aided by an army of evil demons. This army expanded to include heretics and sorcerers, whose magic posed a threat to the divine miracles of the church. Witches were included, first as associates of sorcerers, then as heretics.

Preachers in the Renaissance and Reformation pounded fear of the Devil into their followers by constantly inveighing against his attempts to pervert people and turn them away from God. Satan's kingdom was the material world. He would tempt people with false riches, luxuries, and carnal pleasures, only to claim their souls for eternal damnation in the end. His chief means of attacking others was through demonic possession. Pacts with the Devil, which date back to the sixth century, became implied; any consort with the Devil automatically meant one had entered into a diabolic pact. John Stearne, the assistant to Matthew Hopkins, England's notorious witch finder of the 17th century, was of the opinion that the preachers' obsession with Satan encouraged witches to worship him.

Appearance of the Devil

Christianity portrays the true form of the Devil as ugly, deformed, and reptilian: a human torso and limbs with reptilian head, clawed hands and feet, a tail, and scaly snakeskin. He has horns, which signify power and association with the dark forces—night, chaos, the Moon, death, and the underworld—and fertility, the latter of which is reinforced by an enormous phallus.

The Devil is a shape shifter, appearing in many guises in order to trick people. His most common human shape was that of a tall black man or a tall man, often handsome, dressed in black. Black is universally associated with fear, evil, the dark, and chaos. Henri Boguet, a 16th- and 17th-century jurist in witch trials, stated that "whenever he (the Devil) assumes the form of a man, he is, however, always black, as all witches bear witness. And for my part I hold that there are two principle reasons for this: first, that he who is the Father and Ruler of darkness may not

Depiction of the Devil from the 1957 film Night of the Demon (AUTHOR'S COLLECTION)

be able to disguise himself so well that he may not always be known for what he is; secondly, as proof that his study is only to do evil; for evil, as Pythagoras said, is symbolized by black."

When not in black, the Devil is most frequently in red.

St. Paul stated that the Devil can appear disguised as an angel of light. His disguises of good also include saints, the Virgin Mary, comely young women, handsome young men, and preachers.

The Devil appears in a multitude of animal shapes, most commonly as a BLACK DOG, SERPENT, goat, or cat. He also has ugly appearances: As the alleged god of witches, he was portrayed as half-human, half-animal, like Pan, with horns, cloven feet, hairy legs, a tail, a huge penis, glowing eyes, and saturnine features.

The Devil appeared to MARTIN LUTHER in the form of a monk with bird claw hands, according to an account written by Georgius Godelmannus in 1591. Godelmannus relates that while he was studying law at the University of Wittenberg, Germany, he heard a story from several of his teachers about a monk who appeared and knocked hard upon the door of Luther. He was invited in and began to speak of papist errors and other theological matters. Luther grew impatient and said his time was being wasted, and the monk should consult a Bible for answers. At that point, he noticed that the monk's hands were like bird claws. Luther showed the monk a passage in Genesis that says, "The seed of the woman shall bruise the head of the serpent." Exposed, the Devil went into a rage, threw about Luther's ink and writing materials, and fled, leaving behind him a stench that lasted for days.

The Devil as Buffoon

In legend, the Devil is often portrayed in a lighter fashion, perhaps to lessen the fear inspired by the clergy. He is called by nicknames such as *Jack, Old Nick, Old Horny,* and *Lusty Dick.* Buffoonish and somewhat dim-witted, he can be easily tricked, as in the numerous versions of the DEVIL'S BRIDGE, in which the Devil builds a bridge in return for the soul of the first to cross the bridge but is fooled when a dog or cat is sent across. In other tales, the Devil shoots off arrows and rocks to try to destroy villages and churches but always misses the mark. He constantly tries to makes PACTs with people in order to get control of their souls but fails.

Devils versus Demons

In both theology and folklore, the distinction between the Devil as Prince of Evil and his hordes of demons often blurs. "The Devil" can refer to both. Joseph Glanvil observed in *Saducismus Triumphatus* (1681), "The Devil is a name for a body politic, in which there are very different orders and degrees of spirits, and perhaps in as much variety of place and state, as among ourselves."

FURTHER READING:

Finlay, Anthony. *Demons! The Devil, Possession and Exorcism.* London: Blandford, 1999.

Pagels, Elaine. *The Origins of Satan.* New York: Random House, 1995.

Rudwin, Maximilian. *The Devil in Legend and Literature.* La Salle, Ill.: Open Court, 1959.

Russell, Jeffrey Burton. *The Devil: Perceptions of Evil from Antiquity to Primitive Christianity.* Ithaca, N.Y., and London: Cornell University Press, 1977.

devil fish   A type of ray fish used by Mexican witches (*brujas* or *brujos*) in the casting of spells. When dried, the devil fish resembles a man with a horned head, tail, and webbed arms. It is considered effective for preventing gossiping of neighbors.

Devil's Advocate, The **(1997)**   Horror film about a young, ambitious attorney who is seduced and deceived by the DEVIL. Directed by Taylor Hackford, the film stars Al Pacino as John Milton, the Devil in disguise, and Keanu Reaves as Kevin Lomax. Charlize Theron plays Lomax's wife, Mary Ann.

Lomax is a defense attorney representing an accused child molester on trial. He knows his client is guilty,

Keanu Reeves as Kevin Lomax, a lawyer who bargains for business success with Al Pacino, as John Milton, the Devil in disguise, in The Devil's Advocate *(1997)* (AUTHOR'S COLLECTION)

but he destroys the prosecution's witness and his client is acquitted. He is immediately approached by Milton, partner in the world's most powerful law firm, Milton, Chadwick & Waters, with a tantalizing job offer. He accepts. He is assigned questionable cases involving guilty people and wins them all. Milton offers to relieve him of cases, but he declines, in a fever of winning at all costs.

Meanwhile, Milton rapes Mary Ann and she has a psychotic break. Lomax commits her to a mental ward, where she commits suicide. He then learns from his mother that Milton is really his father. He confronts Milton and learns the truth, that Milton is also SATAN. Horrified, he tries to shoot Milton, but the bullets do no harm.

Milton tells Lomax that he wants him to have sex with Lomax's half sister, Christabella, to conceive the ANTICHRIST. But Lomax thwarts the plan by committing suicide himself.

The action shifts back to the opening of the child molestation trial, but with a different outcome. Lomax, overcome by his own conscience, decides to step down from representation, even though he is likely to be disbarred. He is approached by a journalist who wants to interview him, saying the story will make him a star. Lomax agrees and exits the courthouse. The reporter shape shifts into Milton and says, "Vanity—definitely my favorite sin."

Devil's arrows   Stones flung by the DEVIL in attempts to destroy towns and churches. According to lore, the Devil usually has bad marksmanship, and the stones miss their mark and stick upright in the air.

The Devil's Arrow is an alignment of three standing stones near Boroughbridge, Yorkshire, England. The stones were quarried, and the reason they were placed in a 570-foot-long alignment is not known. The tallest is 22.5 feet high. The Devil, angry at the people of the nearby town of Aldborough, went up to the top of Howe Hill and fired off three giant arrows of stone, intent on demolishing the town. The stones fell harmlessly to Earth and stuck upright in a straight line.

Also in Yorkshire, a monolith stands up from the graves beside an old Norman church at Rudston. The stone is 25.5 feet high, six feet wide, and about two feet thick, weighing about 40 tons. It may have once marked a pagan sacred site, and the church may have been built around it. The local legend says that the Devil threw the stone at the church in an attempt to destroy it but missed.

FURTHER READING:
Bord, Janet, and Colin Bord. *Mysterious Britain*. London: Granada, 1974.

Devil's book   A black book kept by the Devil listing all persons who have pledged PACTs with him.

In accounts of witch trials during the Inquisition and the writings of demonologists, the Devil held out his book at SABBATs and had his new recruits swear their allegiance to him by placing their hand upon the book. The recruits then signed their names in the book in their own BLOOD. Some witches said that the books also contained spells and CHARMs for evil deeds.

Devil's bridge   An old bridge, especially in England and Europe, said to have been built by the DEVIL or his DEMONS.

According to ancient lore, demons were master architects and builders. King SOLOMON commanded legions of them to build his temples (see DJINN). Medieval folklore held that whenever engineers and architects needed help or ran out of resources, the Devil and his demons would appear—or could be summoned—to lend a helping hand. The infernal beings were called upon most often for help with bridges but also were said to assist with construction of castles.

Devil's bridges are found in Britain, Spain, Germany, Switzerland, and France. There is a Devil's Bridge in Einsiedeln, Switzerland, near the birthplace of Paracelsus. In France, the Pont de Valentre bridge at Cahors was believed to be entirely constructed by the Devil.

St. Cado and the Devil above a Devil's bridge (AUTHOR'S COLLECTION)

The Devil's price for this service was the soul of the first creature who crossed the bridge. Folktales tells of local townsfolk tricking the Devil by sending a cat or dog across first. In the legend of the Devil's Bridge across the Afon Mynach near Aberystwyth, Wales, an old woman spotted her cow on the opposite side of a chasm, unreachable. The Devil appeared in disguise and offered to create a bridge if she would give him the first living thing that crossed over it. She agreed, though she knew she was dealing with the Devil, because she had noticed his cloven hooves. When the bridge was completed, she threw a crust of bread across it and sent her dog to fetch it, sacrificing him to the Devil.

In Somerset, England, the Tarr Steps is a prehistoric stone bridge dating to about 1000 B.C.E. that crosses the river Barle near Winsford. Some of the stones weigh five tons. According to lore, the bridge was built by the Devil in one night to win a wager against a giant who had challenged his power.

Devil's horse   In Ozark folklore, the colloquial name for the praying mantis. It is considered bad luck to disturb a praying mantis, because it might spit tobacco juice into one's eye and cause blindness. In some rural parts, the Devil's horse is thought, falsely, to be poisonous.

Devil's mark   A permanent mark made upon the body by the DEVIL as part of a PACT. Sometimes called a "witch's mark," the Devil's mark was a telltale sign and damning evidence in the witch trials of the Inquisition.

According to demonologists, the Devil always permanently marked the bodies of his initiates to seal their pledge of obedience and service to him. At the moment they renounced their faith, he marked them by raking his claw across the flesh or using a hot iron, which left a mark, usually blue or red, but not always a scar. Sometimes he left a mark by licking people. Branding was done when recruits were initiated at SABBATs and when anyone entered into a formal pledge of allegiance to the Devil.

The marks could be anywhere on the body. In his book *Demonolatry* (1595), NICHOLAS REMY listed brows, left shoulders, hips, breasts, tops of heads, and backs as places bearing marks. Sometimes the marks were made in "secret places," such as under eyelids, in armpits, and in body cavities. According to FRANCESCO-MARIA GUAZZO, an Italian demonologist of the 17th century, in his work *Compendium Maleficarum* (1608):

> And the mark is not always of the same description; for at times it is like the footprint of a hare, or a spider or a dog or a dormouse. Neither does he always mark them upon the same place: for on men it is generally found on the eye-lids, or the arm-pit or lips or shoulder or posterior; whereas on women it is found on the breasts or private parts.

The Devil's mark was considered the proof of WITCH-CRAFT and sorcery. It was believed that every person who trafficked with the Devil had one or more, and it was usually insensitive to pain. Persons accused of witchcraft and brought to trial were thoroughly searched for such a mark, and some had all their body and head hair shaved off in the process. Pins were driven into scars, moles, warts, and skin discolorations. If the person felt little or no pain, or if there was no bleeding, then a Devil's mark was declared.

Inquisitors believed that the mark of SATAN was clearly distinguishable from ordinary blemishes, but in actuality, that was seldom the case. Protests from the victims that the marks were natural were ignored. If no mark was found, or if pricking a mark caused pain, inquisitors declared them Devil's marks anyway, falling back on authoritative statements made by Guazzo and others that the Devil did not necessarily mark everyone, but only those he suspected of turning on him, and some of the marks were painless and others were not. Some inquisitors held that Devil's marks could even be invisible. An innocent person had no way around a determined inquisitor.

Once Devil's marks were found, victims were tortured into confessing how they were acquired. No less than tales of pacts and wild initiatory rites at sabbats would satisfy the inquisitors.

FURTHER READING:
Guazzo, Francesco-Maria. *Compendium Maleficarum*. Secaucus, N.J.: University Books, 1974.
Lea, Henry Charles. *Materials toward a History of Witchcraft*. Philadelphia: University of Pennsylvania Press, 1939.
Remy, Nicholas. *Demonolatry*. Secaucus, N.J.: University Books, 1974.

Devil's Missal   Book said to be used in the performance of a BLACK MASS or infernal SABBAT rites. The Devil's Missal is the unholy replacement for the Bible and is full of CURSEs and blasphemies.

Descriptions of the Devil's Missal were given by accused witches and Devil worshippers during the peak of witch hunts, especially in the 16th and 17th centuries. One account recorded by Pierre de Lancre from a trial in Orléans, France, in 1614 said that

> the Sabbat was held in a house. . . . He [the accused] saw there a tall dark man opposite to the one who was in a corner of the ingle, and this man was perusing a book, whose leaves seemed black & crimson, & he kept muttering between his teeth although what he said could not be heard, and presently he elevated a black host and then a chalice of some cracked pewter, all foul and filthy.

Another man accused in the same trial said:

> Mass was said, and the Devil was celebrant. He was vested in a chasuble upon which was a broken cross. He turned his back to the altar when he was about to elevate the Host and the Chalice, which were both black. He read in a mumbling tone from a book, the cover of

which was soft and hairy like a wolf's skin. Some leaves were white and red, others black.

Madeleine Bavent, one of the chief afflicted nuns in the LOUVIERS POSSESSIONS of 1647, gave this description of the missal:

Mass was read from the book of blasphemies, which contained the canon. This same volume was used in processions. It was full of the most hideous curses against the Holy Trinity, the Holy Sacrament of the Altar, the other Sacraments and ceremonies of the Church. It was written in a language completely unknown to me.

FURTHER READING:
Summers, Montague. *The History of Witchcraft and Demonology.* London: Kegan Paul, Trench, Trubner, 1926.

djinn (genii, ginn, jann, jinn, shayatin, shaytan) In Arabic lore, a type of interfering spirit, often demonlike, but not equivalent to a DEMON. As are the Greek DAIMONes, djinn are self-propagating and can be either good or evil. They possess supernatural powers and can be conjured in magical rites to perform various tasks and services. A djinn appears as a wish-granting "genie" in many Arabic folktales such as those in *The Book of One Thousand and One Nights.*

Early Lore

In pre-Islamic lore, the djinn are malicious, are born of smokeless fire, and are not immortal. They live with other supernatural beings in the Kaf, a mythical range of emerald mountains that encircles the earth. They like to roam the deserts and wilderness. They are usually invisible but have the power to shape shift to any form, be it insect, other animal, or human.

King SOLOMON used a magic ring to control djinn and protect him from them. The ring was set with a gem, probably a diamond, that had a living force of its own. With the ring, Solomon branded the necks of the djinn as his slaves.

One story tells that a jealous djinn (sometimes identified as ASMODEUS) stole the ring while Solomon bathed in the river Jordan. The djinn seated himself on Solomon's throne at his palace and reigned over his kingdom, forcing Solomon to become a wanderer. God compelled the djinn to throw the ring into the sea. Solomon retrieved it and punished the djinn by imprisoning him in a bottle.

According to another story, Solomon took djinn to his crystal-paved palace, where they sat at tables made of iron. The Qur'an tells how the king made them work at building palaces and making carpets, ponds, statues, and gardens. Whenever Solomon wanted to travel to faraway places, the djinn carried him there on their backs.

Solomon forced the djinn to build the Temple of Jerusalem and all of the city as well.

Djinn in Muslim Lore

Islamic theology absorbed and modified the djinn; some became beautiful and good-natured. According to the Muslim faith, humans are created from clay and water, and the essence of angels is light. Djinn were created on the day of creation from the smokeless fire, or the essential fire. They are invisible to most people except under certain conditions; however, dogs and donkeys are able to see them. They were on the Earth before human beings, but it is unknown how long. By some accounts, they were created 2,000 years before Adam and Eve and are equal to angels in stature. Their ruler, IBLIS (also called Shaytan), refused to worship Adam and so was cast out of heaven, along with his followers. Iblis became the equivalent of the Devil, and the followers all became demons. Iblis' throne is in the sea.

As do humans, djinn have free will and are able to understand good and evil. The Qur'an states that the purpose of their creation is the same as that of humans, which is to worship God. They are responsible for their actions and will be judged at the Last Judgment. It is said that HELL will be filled with djinn and humans together.

Conflicting stories about the djinn abound, similar to conflicting stories about ANGELS and demons. According to some accounts, there are three types of djinn:

1. Those who are able to fly. These djinn can be heavy or light, tall or thin, and are shape shifters with very flexible bodies.
2. Those who reside in a given area and cannot travel out of that area. They may live in abandoned houses.
3. Those who manifest as snakes, scorpions, creeping animals, and dogs (especially BLACK DOGS, who are devils or IBLIS) and cats. A cat should not be chased away early in the morning or late at night, lest it be a shape-shifted djinn, who will take revenge.

Muhammad warned the people to cover their utensils, close their doors, and keep their children close to them at night, as the djinn spread out at night and take things. He also warned people to put out their lights, as the djinn could drag away the wicks and start a fire. However, they will not open a locked door, untie a knot, or uncover a vessel. If people find a snake in their house, they should call out to it for three days before killing it. If the snake is a shape-shifted djinn, it will leave.

The djinn can be converted, as sura 72 of the Qur'an indicates: "It has been revealed to me that a company of the Djinn gave ear, then they said 'we have indeed heard a Qur'an wonderful, guiding to rectitude.'" Muhammad converted djinn by reciting the Qur'an to them. However, all djinn are unreliable and deceitful, even if converted.

The djinn will guard graves if commanded to do so by WITCHCRAFT; in Egypt, it is bad luck to open a pharaoh's tomb, for the guarding djinn will harm anyone who violates the sacred space.

Djinn Life

The life span of djinn is much longer than that of humans, but they do die. They are both male and female and have children. They eat meat, bones, and dung of animals. They play, sleep, and have animals.

Descriptions of their appearances vary. They may have the legs of a goat, a black tail, or a hairy body. They may be exceptionally tall and have their eyes set vertically in their heads.

Although they can live anywhere on the planet, they prefer deserts, ruins, and places of impurity like graveyards, garbage dumps, bathrooms, camel pastures, and hashish dens. They also can live in the houses where people live. They love to sit in places between the shade and the sunlight and move around when the dark first falls. They also like marketplaces, and Muslims are warned not to be the first to enter the market or the last to leave it.

In Islam, it is believed that humans are unable to get in touch with the deceased, learn about the future or what happens after death, or be healed, as these phenomena are in God's realm. Djinn have limited powers in these areas. Djinn can appear to humans as the spirits of the dead and communicate with the living through visions and voices. Those who learn the medicinal qualities of plants through the plants' talking to them are actually speaking with devils. It was the djinn who taught humans SORCERY. (See WATCHERS.)

Djinn will eat human food, stealing its energy, unless people say the name *Allah* prior to eating.

Marriage between Humans and Djinn

As do FAIRIES, djinn fall in love with humans and marry them. There is no direct evidence of it, and no children have qualities of both djinn and human. A clan in the United Arab Emirates claims to descend from a female djinn. There is controversy over whether it is lawful to marry djinn, but most Islamic jurists believe it is unlawful. There also seems to be controversy as to whether a mixed marriage will be able to produce children. If the mother is human, the children will be visible and look like humans. If the mother is djinn, the children will be invisible.

Djinn interfere in human relationships. If they fall in love with a human, they try to disrupt marriages and other relationships.

Possession by Djinn

Ordinary human acts can kill or hurt djinn without people being aware of doing so. When that happens, djinn possess the offending people in order to take revenge on them. Others who are vulnerable to possession are those who live alone, for djinn are opposed to community.

As do the *daimones,* pairs of djinn stay with each person. One whispers good; the other whispers evil. The moods of humans can be affected by the djinn, ranging from happiness to sadness for no known reason. Although they are able to affect peoples' minds and bodies, they have no power over the soul or heart.

When possessed, the person appears to be insane and exhibits signs of anger, anxiety, and depression. A woman's voice will sound like a man's, and a man's voice will sound like a woman's. Physical symptoms include nausea after eating, headaches, frequent desire to fight, heavy shoulders, a constant feeling of dissatisfaction, and a desire to commit suicide.

Asking the djinn to leave may not be enough to induce him or her to go, and someone who is trained may be needed to perform an EXORCISM to expel the djinn from the body. (See ZAR.)

Modern Experiences of Djinn

Djinn are still prominent in modern superstitions, and encounters with them occur all the time. They are visible in great numbers to those who can see them. In the Middle East, beliefs about djinn are strong in certain areas. Upper-middle-class people in urban areas tend to look upon djinn beliefs as superstition, but in rural and remote areas, the djinn hold sway.

David Morehouse, a retired remote viewer (clairvoyant) for the U.S. military, relates in his book *Psychic Warrior* how he had temporary visions of djinn due to a head injury. He was among American troops camped with Jordanian troops for training exercises in Jordan at Baten el Ghoul, which means "Belly of the Beast."

> The Jordanians considered it a haunted valley, where the demons came out at night to murder people. It was not unusual to have one's sleep interrupted by the screams and howls of frightened Jordanian soldiers who swore in the light of day that they had seen a demon. . . . Baten el Ghoul was a desolate and jagged valley carved out of the desert that spilled over from Saudi Arabia. There was no life there except arachnids.

Morehouse was accidentally shot in the helmet, an injury that left a huge lump on his head. After this, he experienced djinn:

> Sometime in the night, my eyes opened to a surreal light outside the tent. It was like the light of an eclipsed sun and wasn't coming from any stove. It filled the night sky. The entire Baten el Ghoul and the hills beyond were bathed in the strange bluish gray light; I walked to the edge of the bluff and stared into the valley. Dark figures moved effortlessly across its floor, like apparitions. They poured from the rocks in various heaps and shapes and moved about the clusters of tents. I could hear muffled cries from the Jordanian encampment, and momentarily I thought we were being overrun by thieves or Israelis. Panicked, I turned to run for help. Colliding with one of the figures, I reflexively closed my eyes, except I didn't collide. I walked right through it. Turning around I watched the figure disappear over the edge of the bluff.

After that, the lump on his head disappeared.

FURTHER READING:
Ahmad, Salim. *Revealing the Mystery behind the World of Jinn.* Booksurge.com: 2008.
al-Ashqar, Umar Sulaiman. *The World of the Jinn and Devils.* Translated by Jamaal al-Din M. Zarabozo. New York: Al-Basheer Company for Publications and Translations, 1998.
de Givry, Emile Grillot. *Witchcraft, Magic and Alchemy.* 1931. Reprint, New York: Dover Publications, 1971.
Frieskens, Barbara. *Living with Djinns: Understanding and Dealing with the Invisible in Cairo.* London: Saqi Books, 2008.
Morehouse, David. *Psychic Warrior: Inside the CIA's Stargate Program: The True Story of a Soldier's Espionage and Awakening.* New York: St. Martin's Press, 1996.

Doctor Faustus   See FAUST.

Doris Fischer Obsession   Case of spirit OPPRESSION investigated by the psychical researcher JAMES HERVEY HYSLOP.

In 1914, Hyslop became involved in the case of Doris Fischer, whose real name was Brittia L. Fritschle. The case was first reported by Dr. W. Franklin Prince, an Episcopal minister and psychologist. Fischer suffered an extreme traumatic incident as a child at the hands of her abusive and alcoholic father and had exhibited multiple personalities since she was three in 1892. She also displayed striking psychic tendencies, able to foresee her mother's sudden illness and death. Fischer and her siblings continued to live with their father, but she retreated more and more into the personalities of "sick Doris" and the wicked "Margaret." Fischer was eventually adopted by Prince and his wife. Prince was familiar with the newly recognized syndrome of multiple personality, and he and his wife helped Fischer to regain some normalcy.

For years, Hyslop had postulated that some psychotic states were caused—or at least aggravated—by spirit influence. Although not a spiritualist per se, Hyslop sympathized with the cult's psychic "cures" and believed that spiritual communication was just as important as physiological therapy. With that in mind, Hyslop took Fischer to sit with a medium, Minnie Soule, hoping to find and eliminate the possessive spirits who were destroying the girl's peace of mind.

During the séances, Soule communicated lengthy messages to Fischer from her mother. The medium also heard from Count Cagliostro. Hyslop did not like Cagliostro's presence and encouraged him to leave the séances and Fischer. Later researchers speculate that Cagliostro represented sexual mores that both Hyslop and Fischer suppressed but secretly desired.

Next, Soule heard from the spirit of Richard Hodgson, who confirmed Hyslop's suspicions of spirit influence and promised to help all he could. Finally, Soule received messages from a young Indian spirit calling herself "Minnehaha," or "Laughing Water." Hyslop was skeptical of such a spirit, since Minnehaha is the heroine of Henry Wadsworth Longfellow's poem "Hiawatha." But he went along, impressed with Minnehaha's knowledge of Fischer's case and her claims that she had caused many of Doris' problems. After further communications, Hyslop began to believe that the personality "Margaret" was not an offshoot of Doris' mind but a possessing spirit herself.

Hyslop asked why these spirits hurt Fischer and was told by Soule's communicators that they were evil influences. The controls also told Hyslop that Fischer's case was no different from hundreds of other instances of insanity and multiple personality that could easily be cured through psychic exorcism. By 1915, Hyslop was convinced that Fischer was possessed, and he wrote of his experiences with her in his last book, *Life after Death* (1918).

Hyslop believed that Cagliostro was leader of Fischer's possessing spirits, and he exorcized the count. Whatever other spirits remained were ineffectual, and Hyslop quit the case in the hope that Fischer had been cured. She returned with the Princes to California and resumed a normal life for a while. But she never recovered, finally dying in a mental hospital after years of dealing with her various personalities and psychic disturbances.

The Fischer case was Hyslop's last major investigation, although he never lost interest in the possibility of spirit obsession.

FURTHER READING:
Rogo, D. Scott. *The Infinite Boundary.* New York: Dodd, Mead, 1987.

Dorochiel   DEMON among the 31 AERIAL SPIRITS OF SOLOMON. Dorochiel rules in the west and north as a prince. Forty dukes attend him during the day and 40 more at night. In order to summon the dukes and their servants, a magician must pay attention to the planetary hours when they rule. All are good-natured and agreeable. The 12 dukes of the morning are Magael, Artino, Efiel, Maniel/Efiel, Suriet/Maniel, Carsiel/Suriel, Casiel, Fabiel, Carba, Merach, Althor, and Omiel. The 12 dukes of the afternoon are Gudiel, Asphor, Emuel, Soriel, Cabron, Diviel, Abriel, Danael, Lomor, Casael, Buisiel, and Larfos. The 12 dukes of the early evening are Nahaiel, Ofsiel, Bulls, Momel, Darborl, Paniel, Cursas, Aliel, Aroziel, Cusyne, Vraniel, and Pelusar. The 12 dukes who govern after midnight are Pafiel, Gariel, Soriel, Maziel, Futiel, Cayros, Narsial, Moziel, Abael, Meroth, Cadriel, and Lodiel.

Dozmary Pool   Small lake in the Bodmin Moor in Cornwall, England, associated with the DEVIL. According to lore, the Devil sentenced JAN TREGEAGLE to bail out Dozmary Pool with a limpet shell, a task he could never complete. Similar punishments by the Devil are other tasks that can never be finished.

Dozmary Pool also is associated with King Arthur and is one of the candidate lakes into which the dying Arthur ordered Belvedere to cast his magical sword, Excalibur. A hand arose from the lake to seize the sword and return it to the Lady of the Lake, a FAIRY. The pool is haunted by mysterious lights and the ghosts of men and horses said to have drowned in it, perhaps after losing their way at night across the treacherous moor.

Dregvant   In Persian lore and ZOROASTRIANISM, a wicked and unrighteous DEMON of luxury and vice. *Dregvants* was a name given to the residents of the city of Gilan south of the Caspian Sea, who were considered to be fiends incarnate.

Druj   A female DEMON in ZOROASTRIANISM who represents the principle of wickedness. *Druj* means "falsehood" and "deceit." *Drauga* is the Old Persian version of the name. Druj is associated with AHRIMAN, the principal evil being. In the final confrontation between good and evil, Asha will destroy Druj.

druj   In Persian lore and ZOROASTRIANISM, a class of chiefly female evil beings, sorcerers, monsters, fiends, the unrighteous, and the hosts of HELL. Some of the specific drujes are the following:

- Druj Nasu, the Corpse Fiend, who represents corruption, decomposition, decay, contagion, and impurity. The glance of a dog can expel it from a corpse. It can be expelled from a living person by a bathing and purification ritual lasting nine days.
- AZHI DAHAKA, half-man and half-monster with three heads, six eyes, three jaws, and two SERPENTs growing out of his shoulders. Azhi Dahaka was created by AHRIMAN to wreak destruction in the world. He committed incest with his mother, AUTAK, also a demon.
- Sej, a personification of pestilence and "the fiend who brings about annihilation and misfortune."
- Jahi, a female druj of debauchery, whose name is the root of *jahika,* or "harlot" or "prostitute." AHRIMAN kissed her and caused menstruation to begin in the world. Jahi's name is also associated with wizards and sorcerers.

Dumah (Douma)   Angel of silence, the stillness of death, and vindication; the tutelary spirit of Egypt. In Aramaic, Dumah's name means "silence." He is a prince of HELL; in Babylonian legend, he guards the 14th gate. The Zohar Kabbalistic text describes him as a chief of Gehenna (hell) with tens of thousands of angels of destruction under his command and 12,000 myriads of attendants whose job it is to punish sinners. A small reference in the Talmud holds that even sinners have a day of rest on the sabbath and are released to roam the earth. At evening, Dumah herds them back into hell. Dumah releases all souls of the dead, not just sinners, to the Earth each evening for the first year after their deaths.

dybbuk   In Jewish demonology, an evil spirit or doomed soul that possesses a person's body and soul, speaking through the person's mouth and causing such torment and anguish that another personality appears to manifest itself. The term *dybbuk* (also spelled *dibbuk*) was coined in the 17th century from the language of German and Polish Jews. It is an abbreviation of two phrases: *dibbuk me-ru'ah* (a cleavage of an evil spirit) and *dibbuk min ha-hizonim* (dibbuk from the demonic side of man). Prior to the 17th century, the dybbuk was one of many evil spirits call *ibbur.*

In early folklore, dybbukim were thought only to inhabit the bodies of sick persons. Possessive evil spirits are referred to in the Old Testament. For example, Samuel I describes the possession of Saul and the way David exorcized the spirit by playing the harp. In the book of Tobit the archangel Raphael instructs Tobit in ways of EXORCISM. In the rabbinical literature of the first century, exorcisms called for the ashes of a red heifer, or the roots of certain herbs, to be burned under the victim, who was then surrounded with water. Other methods included incantations in the name of King SOLOMON, repetition of the Divine Name of God, reading from Psalms, and wearing herbal AMULETs.

By the 16th century, the concept of possessive evil spirits changed. Many Jews believed the spirits were transmigrated souls that could not enter a new body because of their past sins and so were forced to possess the body of a living sinner. The spirits were motivated to possess a body because they were tormented by other evil spirits if they did not. Some thought the dybbukim were the souls of people who were not properly buried and, therefore, became demons.

The KABBALAH contains rituals for exorcizing a dybbuk; many are still in use in modern times. The exorcism must be performed by a *ba'al shem,* a miracle-working rabbi. Depending on how the exorcism is done, the dybbuk either is redeemed or is cast into HELL. It usually exits the body of its victim through the small toe, which shows a small, bloody hole as the point of departure.

FURTHER READING:
Winkler, Gershom. *Dybbuk.* New York: Judaica Press, 1982.

Earling Possession (1928)   One of the best-documented demonic POSSESSION cases in the 20th century. The possession of Anna Ecklund also is unusual for the combination of demonic entities within one victim.

Anna was born in the Midwest about 1882 and was raised a devout and pious Catholic. She first began showing the symptoms of possession—revulsion toward holy objects, inability to enter church, and disturbing thoughts about unspeakable sexual acts—at age 14, finally becoming totally possessed in 1908. In the account of Anna's travails, *Begone Satan!,* written in German by the Reverend Carl Vogl and translated into English by the Reverend Celestine Kapsner, O.S.B., Anna's aunt Mina, a reputed witch, caused her possession by placing spells on herbs used in Anna's food. Father Theophilus Riesinger, a native Bavarian and a Capuchin monk from the community of St. Anthony at Marathon, Wisconsin, successfully exorcized her on June 18, 1912, only to have her fall prey to the Devil again after her father heaped CURSES on her and wished her possessed. In 1928, when Anna was 46 years old, Father Theophilus tried again.

Seeking a place where Anna was unknown, Father Theophilus approached his old friend, Father F. Joseph Steiger, parish priest in Earling, Iowa. With great reluctance, Father Steiger agreed that the exorcism could take place in the nearby convent of the Franciscan Sisters. Anna arrived in Earling on August 17, 1928. Trouble started immediately; sensing that someone had sprinkled holy water on her evening meal, Anna threw a fit, purring like a cat, and refused to eat until unblessed food could be served. After that, the devils within her always knew whether one of the nuns had tried to bless the food or drink, and they always complained.

The ancient ritual began in earnest the next morning. Father Theophilus had several of the strongest nuns hold Anna on a mattress laid upon an iron bed, and her clothes were bound tightly around her to prevent her from stripping herself. With Father Theophilus' first exhortations Anna's mouth clamped shut and she fell unconscious, followed almost immediately by an extraordinary feat of levitation. Rising swiftly from the bed, she hung onto the wall above the door like a cat, and it took great effort to pull her down. Although Anna was unconscious and her mouth never moved throughout the sessions, voices issued from within her, accompanied by screams, howls, and unearthly animal noises. Earling citizens, alarmed by the outcries, gathered at the convent, ruining Father Theophilus' hopes of keeping the exorcism secret.

Totaling 23 days, the exorcisms covered three sessions: from August 18 to the 26, from September 13 to 20, and from December 15 to 23. Through it all, Anna's physical state deteriorated to the point of death. She ate no food but only swallowed small amounts of milk or water. Nevertheless, she vomited enormous quantities of foul-smelling debris, often resembling tobacco leaves, and spit prodigiously. Her face became horribly disfigured and distorted, often suffusing with blood as her head swelled and elongated, her eyes bulged, and her lips grew, reportedly, to the size of hands. Her abdomen would swell to the point of bursting, only to retract and become so hard and heavy that the iron bedstead would bend under the enormous weight.

In addition to the physical changes, Anna understood languages previously unknown to her, recoiled at holy words and objects, and revealed clairvoyant knowledge by exposing secret childhood sins of the other participants. The nuns and Father Steiger were so frightened and troubled that none of them could stay in Anna's room throughout the entire exorcism but instead worked in shifts. Father Steiger, taunted by the devils for having agreed to the exorcism in his parish, was especially harassed and suffered an auto accident that the devils had predicted and apparently arranged. Only Father Theophilus, confident of his powers, remained steadfast.

Hordes of lesser devils and avenging spirits, described as like "a swarm of mosquitoes," possessed Anna, but her principal tormentors were BEELZEBUB, Judas Iscariot, and the spirits of her father, Jacob, and his mistress, Anna's aunt Mina. Beelzebub revealed himself first, engaging Father Theophilus in sarcastic theological conversations and acknowledging that the curses of Jacob, Anna's father, sent the devils into her at age 14. Father Theophilus tried to reach Jacob, only to be answered by a spirit identifying himself as Judas Iscariot, who admitted he was there to torment Anna to commit suicide and thereby go to HELL.

Jacob eventually spoke and said that he had cursed Anna for not submitting to his incestuous advances, calling upon the devil to tempt her with every unspeakable sin against chastity. In *Begone Satan!* the author describes Jacob's life as "coarse and brutal," taking Anna's aunt Mina as a mistress while he was still married and repeatedly trying to seduce Anna. At his death, a priest had administered extreme unction, but Jacob ridiculed him. The author continues: "In the judgment after death even all that was pardoned him, but (because) he had cursed his own daughter . . . that ultimately was the guilt of his eternal damnation. And so he was still scheming in hell how he could torture and molest his child. This Lucifer gladly permitted him to do." Whether Anna's virginity really remained intact, even at age 46, or whether she had repressed her sexual contact with her father is unknown.

A high, falsetto voice, present from the beginning among the other voices, revealed itself as that of Mina. God had damned her for living with Jacob and for murdering four children. *Begone Satan!* suggests that the children were Mina's own, but they may also have been multiple abortions. The author describes Mina as any devil's equal for malice and hate, filled with spite and blaspheming the Blessed Sacrament.

The author remarks that the truly amazing aspects of Anna's possession were her basic virtue and pious disposition throughout her ordeal, because "the devil has no power over the free will of a human being." Sensing his eventual triumph, Father Theophilus continued to exhort the devils to depart, and by the latter part of December 1928, they began to weaken and moan, rather than scream, against his efforts. Father Theophilus demanded that when they returned to hell, each should call out his name as a sign of his or her departure, and the devils agreed.

On December 23, 1928, at about 9:00 P.M., Anna suddenly jerked up and stood erect in bed, looking as if she were about to rise to the ceiling. Father Steiger called for the nuns to pull her down, while Father Theophilus blessed her and roared, "Depart ye fiends of hell! Begone Satan, the Lion of Juda reigns!" Anna crumpled back onto the bed as a terrible shout of "Beelzebub, Judas, Jacob, Mina" followed by "Hell, hell, hell" filled the room, repeated several times until the sound seemed to fade into the distance. Anna opened her eyes and smiled, while tears of joy ran down her face and she cried, "My Jesus, Mercy! Praised be Jesus Christ!"

Begone Satan! describes the end: "During the first thrills of joy they were not even aware of the terrible odor that filled the room. All the windows had to be opened, the stench was something unearthly, simply unbearable. It was the last souvenir of the infernal devils for those they had to abandon upon the Earth."

FURTHER READING:
Vogel, Rev. Carl. *Begone, Satan! A Soul-Stirring Account of Diabolical Possession in Iowa.* Rockford, Ill.: TAN Books and Publishers, 1973.

Eligor (Abigor)   FALLEN ANGEL and the 15th of the 72 SPIRITS OF SOLOMON. Eligor is a duke who appears as a goodly knight carrying a lance, a SERPENT, and an ensign. He discovers hidden objects, kindles love and lust, and procures the favor of lords and knights. He marshals armies and causes war. He has 60 LEGIONS of DEMONS under his command.

Emoniel   DEMON and a wandering duke of the air. Emoniel has 100 princes and chief dukes, 20 lesser dukes, and a multitude of servants beneath him. The spirits live mostly in the woods and must be summoned according to their planetary hours. When they appear, they are willing to obey commands. The 12 major dukes are Ennoniel, Edriel, Camodiel, Phanuel, Dramiel, Pandiel, Vasenel, Nasiniet, Cruhiet, Armesiel, Oaspeniel, and Musiniel.

empousai   In Greek lore, a type of female DEMON, related to LAMIAE and similar to the SUCCUBUS. *Empousae* means "forcers in." *Empusa* is sometimes translated into English as "vampire."

The *empousai* are children of Hecate, the goddess of the underworld (see CHTHONIC DEITIES), ghosts, and magic. They appear at her bidding at midday when people make sacrifices to their dead relatives. They are filthy and ugly. They have the hind ends of asses and wear brazen slippers. Sometimes they are described as having one brass leg and one ass leg. They disguise themselves as cows, bitches, or beautiful girls. In the latter form, they seduce men. They enter the human body to consume its flesh and drink its BLOOD.

In *The Life of Apollonius of Tyana,* Philostratus relates a story—probably highly fictitious—about an *empousa* bride. Apollonius, a philosopher and wonder worker of the first century, was credited with great feats of magic and the ability to summon spirits and see the future. Philostratus' biography draws upon the probably fictional memoirs of one of Apollonius' disciples, Damis.

The story concerns a young man of Lycia, Menippus, age 25, smart and handsome. One day as he was walking along the road to Cenchreae, he was met by an apparition—an *empousa*—in the guise of a Phoenician woman. He fell under her spell and fell in love with her, not realizing what she really was. They made plans to marry.

Apollonius was skeptical of her. He attended the wedding and was introduced to her by Menippus. The woman acknowledged she was the owner of all the gold and silver trappings in the house and was the mistress of all the servants. Apollonius told Menippus that his bride was an *empousa* who would devour his flesh and drink his blood. Menippus' bride was offended at this and ordered Apollonius to leave, but he had broken her spell, and all the gold, silver, and servants disappeared.

The woman wept and begged Apollonius not to force her to confess her true identity, but he did. She admitted that she was fattening up Menippus for a kill, and that she loved to dine on young and beautiful bodies because their blood was pure and strong. Thus, was Menippus saved from a gruesome fate.

A similar tale, not quite as demonic in nature, is told by Phlegon of Tralles in *Mirabilia 1,* ca. 140. Philinnion is a young bride who dies and returns as a sexually hungry ghost to visit a man, Machates. Philinnion leaves behind jewelry and underwear. Machates gives her a ring and a golden cup. When the family discovers what is going on, they visit the girl's tomb, to find her bier empty, save for Machates' gifts. The girl herself is lying in the house where Machates is a guest. A learned prophet says her corpse should be burned outside the city limits, and many sacrifices should be made to the chthonic deities. These acts are carried out, and Machates, in despair, commits suicide.

FURTHER READING:
McNally, Raymond T. *A Clutch of Vampires.* New York: Bell, 1984.
Ogden, Daniel. *Magic, Witchcraft, and Ghosts in the Greek and Roman Worlds: A Sourcebook.* New York: Oxford University Press, 2002.
Philostratus. *The Life of Apollonius of Tyana.* Translated by F. C. Conybeare. London: Heinemann, 1912.

Enepsigos   DEMON in the shape of a woman with two heads. Enepsigos has countless other names and can shape-shift into a goddess and other forms. Most often, she takes three forms because she hovers near the Moon (which has three forms: waxing, full, and new). Enepsigos is conjured up as Kronos, Greek god of time.

In the Testament of Solomon, Enepsigos is bound by King SOLOMON with a triple-link chain and is made to prophesy. She predicts that Solomon's kingdom will be divided and the Temple of Jerusalem will be destroyed by the kings of the Persians, Medes, and Chaldeans. The tools in the temple will be used to serve other gods. The vessels used to trap all the demons will be broken by men, and the freed demons will go throughout the world, leading men astray until the Son of God is crucified. This Son shall be born of a virgin and shall be the only one to hold power over all demons. His name is Emmanuel (Emmanouel), the letters of whose name add up to the numbers 644. Solomon does not believe Enepsigos and has her bound in unbreakable chains. But later he witnesses the truth of part of her prophecy, when he is led astray by women to worship pagan gods, and his kingdom is divided by God.

See INCANTATION BOWL.

FURTHER READING:
The Old Testament Pseudepigrapha. Vols. 1 & 2. Edited by James H. Charlesworth. 1983. Reprint, New York: Doubleday, 1985.

Ephippas   Arabian wind DEMON captured by King SOLOMON.

In the Testament of Solomon, Adarkes, the king of Arabia, asks Solomon for his help against a vicious wind demon. The demon appears every morning when a fresh wind starts and blows until the third hour. It kills man and beast and cannot be contained. Adarkes asks Solomon to send someone who can control the demon.

Solomon, however, forgets about the request until he has a problem with the construction of the Temple of Jerusalem. The stone that he wishes for a cornerstone is so heavy that all the artisans and demon laborers cannot move it. Solomon sends a servant out into the Arabian desert to capture the wind demon in a leather flask. The servant places Solomon's magic ring at the neck of the flask, which is a wineskin. When the demon blows into it and fills it up, the servant seals it closed with the ring. The local Arabs do not believe that the boy has actually contained the demon, but when the wind does not blow for three days, they become convinced.

The boy presents the flask to Solomon inside the temple. Solomon is astonished when the flask has the ability to move about on its own and takes seven steps, and then falls on its neck. Speaking from inside, the demon gives his name as *Ephippas* and says he is thwarted by "the one who is going to be born from a virgin and crucified by the Jews" (JESUS).

Ephippas tells Solomon that he has the ability to move mountains, carry houses from place to place, and overthrow kings. Solomon bids him to move the cornerstone. The demon says not only will he do that, but he will also raise up the pillar of air from the Red Sea and place it wherever the king wants. Ephippas inserts the cornerstone at the entrance of the temple. Solomon takes this as a profound sign according to Scripture: Psalm 118:22 says, "The stone which the builders rejected has become the head of the corner."

Ephippas goes out with the demon of the Red Sea, ABEZETHIBOU, to raise up the pillar. They have been outwitted by Solomon, who binds them to the pillar so that they remain suspended in air holding it up until the end of time. The pillar of air may be the same as the "pillar of cloud" referred to in the Old Testament and may mean the Milky Way.

FURTHER READING:
The Old Testament Pseudepigrapha. Vols. 1 & 2. Edited by James H. Charlesworth. 1983. Reprint, New York: Doubleday, 1985.

Erinyes (Furies)   In Greek mythology, three female goddesses, later demonized in Christianity, who punish wrongdoers to death, sometimes causing them to commit suicide. *Erinyes* means "roused to anger."

The Erinyes are Alecto, Megara, and Tisiphone, and they were born from the BLOOD of the castrated god Uranus. They are ugly, winged women with hair, arms, and waists entwined with poisonous SERPENTS. They carry whips and are clothed in the long black robes of mourners or the short skirts and boots of huntress-maidens.

The Erinyes particularly punish those who kill their mothers. They serve in the court of Hades and scourge the shades of sinners. When they play their lyres, mortals wither. They cause insanity and mind-ruining derangement, especially for murderers. They also cause disease, illness, and hunger.

The Erinyes can be placated by rituals of atonement and purification.

See HELL.

Eurynomus   In Greek lore, a high-ranking DEMON of Hades. The Greek geographer Pausanias (second c. C.E.) said in *Description of Greece* that the oracles at Delphi described Eurynomus as a flesh-eating demon who strips corpses down to the bone. His color is black-blue like that of flies, and he has sharp teeth and sits on the skin of a vulture. Later European demonologists described Eurynomus as a "prince of death" who has a body covered with sores, long teeth, and fox-skin clothing.

FURTHER READING:
Collin de Plancy, Jacques. *Dictionary of Witchcraft.* Edited and translated by Wade Baskin. Originally published

The Erinyes in Hades (AUTHOR'S COLLECTION)

as *Dictionary of Demonology.* New York: Philosophical Library, 1965.
Luck, Georg. *Arcana Mundi: Magic and the Occult in the Greek and Roman Worlds.* Baltimore: Johns Hopkins University Press, 1985.

evil eye   A demonic power of causing illness, misfortune, calamity, and death through the eyes.

Evil eye beliefs are universal and date to ancient times. The oldest recorded reference to the evil eye appears in the cuneiform texts of the Sumerians, Babylonians, and Assyrians, about 3000 B.C.E. The ancient Egyptians believed in it and used eye shadow and lipstick to prevent the evil eye from entering their eyes or mouths. The Bible makes references to it in both the Old and New Testaments. It is among ancient Hindu folk beliefs. Evil eye superstitions remained strong into modern times, especially in Mediterranean countries such as Italy, and in Mexico and Central America.

There are two kinds of evil eye, involuntary and deliberate. Most cases of evil eye are believed to occur involuntarily; the person casting it does not mean to do it and probably is not even aware of it. No revenge is sought for this hazard.

A deliberate, malevolent evil eye is called "overlooking" and is a form of witchcraft that can bring about misfortune or catastrophe: illness, poverty, injury, loss of love, even death. In the Middle Ages, witches, who were in league with the DEVIL, were said to give anyone who crossed them the evil eye and to use it to bewitch judges from convicting them.

The evil eye also occurs when someone, especially a stranger, admires another's children, livestock, or possessions or casts anyone a lingering look. Unless immediate precautions are taken, the children become sick, the animals die, the possessions are stolen, or good fortune in business turns sour. If the evil eye cannot be warded off, the victim must turn to an initiate—usually an older woman in the family—who knows a secret cure.

Besides envious glances, the evil eye results from strangers in town or anyone who has unusual or different-colored eyes, for example, a blue-eyed stranger in a land of brown-eyed people. Some unfortunate souls are born with a permanent evil eye, laying waste to everything they see.

The primary defense against evil eye is an AMULET. Most common are frogs, horns, and the "fig," a clenched fist with thumb thrust between the index and middle fingers. Horns and the fig represent a phallus and are associated with the Roman phallic god Fascinus (Priapus). His name is derived from the word *fascinum,* which means "witchcraft." The evil eye is sometimes called fascination. Other amulets include various herbs and stones, red ribbons, and spitting.

FURTHER READING:

Elworthy, Frederick Thomas. *The Evil Eye.* Secaucus, N.J.: University Books/Citadel Press, 1895 ed.

Frieskens, Barbara. *Living with Djinns: Understanding and Dealing with the Invisible in Cairo.* London: Saqi Books, 2008.

exorcism The expulsion of DEMONS and other unwanted spirits from a person or place. Rites of exorcism have been performed since ancient times as remedies against the negative or malevolent influences of spirits, such as the perceived cause of illnesses, bad luck, personal difficulties, OBSESSION, and POSSESSION.

The word *exorcism* is from the Greek *exousia,* meaning "oath," and translates as *adjuro,* or "adjure," in Latin and English. To *exorcise* does not really mean to "cast out" so much as it means to "put the Devil on oath," or petition a higher authority to compel the Devil to act in a way contrary to his wishes.

In Catholicism, exorcism is performed when the church asks publicly and with authority in the name of JESUS Christ that a person or object be protected from the power of the Evil One and withdrawn from his dominion.

In some cultures, demons are exorcised by loud noises, such as beating gongs and bells, and by beating the victim physically, in order to force the demons out of the body. In other methods, rituals for exorcism provide for less extreme measures through the use of holy objects, prayer, and commands.

Exorcism is considered dangerous for victim and exorcist, and even for onlookers, for expelled demons will immediately look for a new host, unless they are properly bound and dispatched.

Demonic Exorcism

In Jewish tradition, demons were exorcised often by casting them into an object or an animal. An exorcism formula in the Talmud for healing demon-caused blindness calls for the blindness (demon) to leave the victim and pierce the eyeballs of a designated dog.

The Jewish historian Josephus, born soon after the Crucifixion of Jesus, wrote of a celebrated exorcist named Eliezar, whom he witnessed in action. Eliezar had a ring attached with certain roots prescribed by the legendary King SOLOMON. The root, called *Baaras,* was probably bo-ara, a highly toxic root that burns with a flamelike color and emits lightninglike rays. Eliezar held the ring under the nose of a DEMONIAC and caused the demons to leave through the breath blown through the nostrils. Eliezar then passed the demons into a bowl of water, which was at once thrown over, dispersing the demons. The technique was in accordance with prevailing beliefs of the time that many illnesses were caused by inhaling demons.

In the New Testament, Jesus and the disciples cast out numerous evil spirits, the most famous of which are LEGION, demons sent by Jesus from a man into pigs (Luke 8:30). According to descriptions in the Gospels and Acts, exorcisms were usually easy to perform. Jesus or an apostle ordered the evil spirit to depart, and the demon immediately complied. Luke 9:38–43 tells of a case in which the disciples had failed to exorcise a boy, and Jesus succeeds in casting out the demon by rebuking him:

> A man in the crowd called out, "Teacher, I beg you to look at my son, for he is my only child. A spirit seizes him and he suddenly screams; it throws him into convulsions so that he foams at the mouth. It scarcely ever leaves him and is destroying him. I begged your disciples to drive it out, but they could not."
>
> "O unbelieving and perverse generation," Jesus replied, "how long shall I stay with you and put up with you? Bring your son here."
>
> Even while the boy was coming, the demon threw him to the ground in a convulsion. But Jesus rebuked the evil spirit, healed the boy and gave him back to his father. And they were all amazed at the greatness of God.

Jesus recommended in one case that prayer and fasting are necessary to expel some demons. In Mark 9:18, Jesus told a man that all things are possible, including the exorcism of his son, to those who believe. Thus, faith can influence the success of exorcism.

Sometimes an expelled demon can return with reinforcements, as Jesus noted in Matthew 12:43–45:

> When an evil spirit comes out of a man, it goes through arid places seeking rest and does not find it. Then it says, 'I will return to the house I left.' When it arrives, it finds

the house unoccupied, swept clean and put in order. Then it goes and takes with it seven other spirits more wicked than itself, and they go in and live there. And the final condition of that man is worse than the first. That is how it will be with this wicked generation.

After the Crucifixion of Jesus, the apostles exorcised in his name. None of them had a specific exorcism ministry or sought out the afflicted; the sick traveled to them for help. Only Christians could successfully performs exorcisms. Acts 19:13–16 describes how seven Jewish exorcists failed to exorcise demons in the name of Jesus and Paul. They were attacked and beaten by the possessed man:

Some Jews who went around driving out evil spirits tried to invoke the name of the Lord Jesus over those who were demon-possessed. They would say, "In the name of Jesus, whom Paul preaches, I command you to come out." Seven sons of Sceva, a Jewish chief priest, were doing this. [One day] the evil spirit answered them, "Jesus I know, and I know about Paul, but who are you?" Then the man who had the evil spirit jumped on them and overpowered them all. He gave them such a beating that they ran out of the house naked and bleeding.

Paul was so successful as an exorcist that even items of clothing he touched could be given to the afflicted, and their possessing spirits would depart (Acts 19:11–12). Acts 16:16–19 tells how Paul exorcised a slave girl of a divining spirit. The spirit enabled her to tell the future and was not "demonic" in the modern sense:

Once when we were going to the place of prayer, we were met by a slave girl who had a spirit by which she predicted the future. She earned a great deal of money for her owners by fortune-telling. This girl followed Paul and the rest of us, shouting, "These men are servants of the Most High God, who are telling you the way to be saved." She kept this up for many days. Finally Paul became so troubled that he turned around and said to the spirit, "In the name of Jesus Christ I command you to come out of her!" At that moment the spirit left her.

The owners of the slave girl were not pleased to have their source of income terminated, and they had Paul and his companion Silas arrested, flogged, and imprisoned.

In the early church, all believers were held to be capable of exorcism. The apostles performed exorcisms for those who sought them out. After they were gone, others carried on the work. There was no special class of exorcists or deliverance ministers, or formal training or ordination; however, it was held that one had to be a true believer in the faith in order to succeed. Origen, a church father anathematized and martyred in 253, said that the plainest of persons, even the illiterate, could perform deliverance or exorcism.

By the third century, the dangers of exorcism were recognized, and the church began approving certain individuals for the task of expelling spirits and healing by laying on of hands. In the mid-third century, Pope Cornelius used the term *exorcist* as an order among the Roman clergy. The ministry of deliverance became increasingly restricted and by the Middle Ages was performed more as formal rites of exorcism. Instead of spontaneous prayers in individual circumstances, priests relied increasingly on standardized prayers and procedures. The focus shifted primarily to demonic possession. The role of exorcist fell to priests. Solemn exorcism became a formal liturgical rite performed only by a priest on a possessed person and only with permission from a bishop. Private exorcisms are performed by ministers and laypersons for various demonic problems and are permitted in the Catholic tradition.

Protestants deemphasized or eliminated exorcism; some, such as Calvinists, held that it pertained only to the early years of Christianity. Exorcism is carried on by some under the name of DELIVERANCE.

In the wake of the abuses of the Inquisition, the Vatican banned five manuals of exorcism in 1709 and in 1725 instituted more controls. In the late 19th century, Pope Leo XIII (r. 1878–1903) reportedly had a vision of demonic spirits trying to attack Rome. He wrote a prayer that is now included in the RITUALE ROMANUM and said at many masses, the prayer to the archangel Michael:

St. Michael the Archangel, defend us in battle, be our protector against the wickedness and the snares of the devil; may God rebuke him, we humbly pray; and do thou, O Prince of the heavenly host, by the power of God, thrust into hell Satan and all the evil spirits who wander through the world for the ruin of souls. Amen.

Church officials became skeptical that possession was genuine and in modern times preferred psychological explanations to demonic ones. However, in 1972, Pope Paul VI affirmed the existence of SATAN and his attempts to pervert humanity.

Pope John Paul II (r. 1978–2005) stated in 1987 that "the devil is still alive and active in the world" and championed exorcism. He reportedly performed three exorcisms himself. The first one was in 1978 and few details are known. The second was performed in 1982 on a young woman named Francesca F., who convulsed on the floor when taken before the pope. He said, "Tomorrow I will say Mass for you," and she was freed of demons. The third exorcism was done in 2000 on a 19-year-old hunchbacked Italian woman. She attended one of the pope's public audiences in St. Peter's Square and shouted obscenities. He took her into a private audience, prayed for her and blessed her, and promised to say a mass for her. However, the woman was not rid of demons.

Pope Benedict XVI, who assumed the papacy in April 2005, is more conservative but has praised exorcists and has encouraged them to pursue their ministry.

In the modern Catholic tradition, major rites of exorcism are performed in which a demon is ordered in the name of Christ to leave the body of a person who is possessed. Lesser rites of exorcism expel demons from a place (see INFESTATION) and relieve a person who is suffering from OPPRESSION. However powerful the demon may be, he ultimately must yield to the power of the Lord. The EXORCIST also calls upon all the saints, the Virgin Mary, and the angels, especially the archangel Michael, an ancient foe of the DEVIL.

Exorcisms are performed once it is determined that a victim is genuinely under the influence of demons. The discernment of an exorcist priest is important. In addition, the church may ask physicians and other medical professionals to rule out natural causes; a psychiatric examination may be desirable but is not necessary. Lesser rites of exorcism, including deliverance, can be carried out by a priest or even a lay demonologist who has been trained by a priest, but the solemn rite of exorcism for possession can be carried out only by a priest, and upon approval by a bishop. The solemn rite is part of the RITUALE ROMANUM, which dates to 1614. Minor revisions were made in 1952. As of the Second Vatican Council (1962–65), it underwent a series of revisions. Since 1999, the exorcism portion was reissued in a new 90-page document, *De Exorcismus et Supplicationibus Quibusdam* (Concerning exorcisms and certain supplications). The rite includes prayers and passages from the Bible and calls upon the demons, in powerful Latin, to depart in the name of Jesus Christ.

The new version eliminates some of the rough medieval language used to describe the Devil. Instead of having the exorcist command the demons or Devil to leave the victim, the exorcist now calls on God to command the demons to leave.

Some contemporary exorcists prefer to use exorcism as a diagnosis of possession and to use more traditional versions of the rites (see AMORTH, FATHER GABRIELE).

Outside Catholicism, priests and ministers perform most demonic exorcisms, but clairvoyants and spiritualists also expel evil spirits. In non-Western traditions, shamans, adepts, and other members of priestly classes perform exorcisms. In occult traditions, exorcisms are performed according to magical rites.

Beating and whipping the possessed in order to expel demons are a common practice and were undertaken in European exorcisms in centuries past. The practice is still in use privately. In 2007, police in Phoenix, Arizona, responded to a report of violence during an exorcism and found a 49-year-old grandfather choking his allegedly possessed three-year-old granddaughter. Police used a stun gun to subdue the man, who lapsed into unconsciousness and died later in a hospital.

The Setting of an Exorcism

According to the *Rituale Romanum*, an exorcism should be carried out in an oratory, chapel, or small room for devotional prayers in a church. There should be few witnesses. Images of the crucifix and the Virgin Mary should dominate the setting. The exorcist should be vested in cassock, surplice, and violet stole. The rite begins with the aspersion of holy water, and the showing of the crucifix to the victim.

In fact, throughout history, exorcisms have been performed in a variety of settings, and some of the more famous cases, such as the LOUDUN POSSESSIONS, were witnessed by thousands of people. In contemporary times, exorcists might perform the rites in the home of the victim.

A special connection exists between the demon and its possessing location, most often the victim's bedroom or personal place. Anything that can be moved is taken out, such as rugs, lamps, dressers, curtains, tables, and trunks, to minimize flying objects. Only a bed or couch remains, accompanied by a small side table to hold a crucifix, candle, holy water, and prayer book. Doors and windows are closed but cannot be nailed shut because air must be allowed to enter the room. Doorways must be kept covered, even if the door is open, lest the evil forces inside the room affect the area outside. Modern exorcists also employ a small tape recorder to validate the procedure. The church forbids the filming of exorcisms to protect privacy.

The exorcist is assisted by one or two other priests, who monitor the exorcist, trying to keep him to the business at hand and not be misguided by the perversions of the demons. They also provide physical aid if necessary. If the exorcist collapses or even dies during the ritual, an assistant takes over.

Other assistants include a medical doctor and perhaps family members. Each must be physically strong and be relatively guiltless at the time of the exorcism, so that the Devil cannot use his or her secret sins as a weapon against the exorcism. The assistants should not be weakened or overcome by obscene behavior and language, blood, excrement, and urine. They must be able to disregard personal insults and be prepared to have their darkest personal secrets revealed.

In non-Catholic exorcisms, rites may be performed in a victim's home, a church, or a sacred setting. In some Pentecostal and charismatic exorcisms, entire congregations participate in the expulsion of demons.

Characteristics of an Exorcism

Prayer and commands are central features of exorcism. Catholic rites are among the most formal. Other rites include a laying on of hands and the use of strong fumes to drive out demons. Hindu priests may blow cow-dung smoke, burn pig excreta, pull their or the victim's hair, press rock salt between their fingers, use copper coins, recite mantras or prayers, cut the victim's hair and burn it, or place a blue band around the victim's neck to exorcise the demonic spirits. Trying another tack, the exorcist may offer bribes of candy or other gifts if the spirit leaves the victim. Early Puritans relied solely on prayer and fasting.

In earlier times and even today, exorcisms may include the physical beating of a sufferer to force the demon to depart or throwing stones at the possessed person. In 1966, members of a fanatic cult in Zurich, Switzerland, ritually beat a young girl to death for being "the devil's bride."

Catholic exorcisms involve only the use of prayer and sacraments. The exorcist demands to know the name of the demon and the time of its departure. Demons seldom work alone, and thus several or even many may possess a person. Initially, they resist. Resistance can last for months or even years, requiring repeated exorcisms. Rarely is an individual freed of demonic influence in a single exorcism. One of Amorth's cases lasted for more than 16 years.

Knowing the names of the demons is helpful but is not essential to the success of an exorcism. Demons are liars, and they are expected to give false names. Sometimes, the names of important and powerful demons are given, even SATAN and LUCIFER. Some names sound nonsensical, and sometimes demons give the names of human beings known for their evil, such as Hitler.

Violence often dominates a demonic exorcism. Furniture bangs, breaks, and levitates; waves of heat and cold pour over the room; and horrible cries emanate from the victim, who may also levitate. Often, the victim suffers real physical pain and distress and must be held down by assistants, who are other exorcists and laypersons. Demons spit, vomit, and engage in other, more disgusting bodily functions as well. They recoil when sprinkled with holy water or touched by a crucifix. Spiritually, the demon and the exorcist engage in battle. While the demon hurls invectives, the exorcist counters with the strongest demands for the demon's departure, vowing pain and penalty if it does not comply. Demons are never insulted, however, for they are FALLEN ANGELS and possess great intelligence and wisdom.

According to MALACHI MARTIN, no two exorcisms are exactly alike, but they tend to unfold in similar stages:

- *The Presence.* The exorcist and assistants become aware of an alien feeling or entity.
- *Pretense.* Attempts by the evil spirit to appear and act as the victim, to be seen as one and the same person. The exorcist's first job is to break this pretense and find out who the demon really is. Naming the demon is the most important first step.
- *Breakpoint.* The moment when the demon's pretense finally collapses in a scene of extreme panic and confusion, accompanied by a crescendo of abuse, horrible sights, noises, and smells. The demon begins to speak of the possessed victim in the third person instead of as itself.
- *The Voice.* Also a sign of the breakpoint, the voice is babel, and it must be silenced for the exorcism to proceed.
- *The Clash.* As the voice dies out, there is tremendous pressure, both spiritual and physical, as the

demon collides with the "will of the Kingdom." The exorcist, locked in battle with the demon, urges the entity to reveal more information about itself as the exorcist's holy will begins to dominate. There is a direct link between the entity and place, as each spirit wants a place to be. For such spirits, habitation of a living victim is preferable to HELL.

- *Expulsion.* In a supreme triumph of God's will, the spirit leaves in the name of JESUS and the victim is reclaimed. All present feel the Presence dissipating, sometimes with receding noises or voices. The victim may remember the ordeal or may not have any idea what has happened.

Demons are expelled when they decide to leave voluntarily or are forced out by the power of the rite. They suffer torment from the prayers and sacraments. Sometimes demons who are high-ranking refuse to leave unless they are cast out by an ANGEL. If God sends an angel, an invisible battle takes place between angel and demon, which causes a great deal of discomfort to the victim until it is over. Successful exorcism depends also on the reform of the victim, in terms of attendance at church and right living. Once expelled, demons cannot return unless the victim expressly invites them back, even unconsciously.

Exorcism of Djinn

Islam considers exorcism of DJINN to be a noble endeavor, practiced throughout the ages by prophets and the righteous. According to the Qur'an, the faithful are obliged to help the oppressed, including those troubled by djinn. The djinn especially like to interrupt Salaah, or formal prayer; occupy homes and steal the essence of food; and cause mental disturbances and physical illness.

There are no formal Islamic rites comparable to those of Catholicism, but exorcisms must follow strict guidelines. The djinn must be rebuked, warned, shamed, and cursed in the same ways permitted against human beings. Measures appropriate against the unfaithful can be applied to djinn. It is permissible for exorcists to listen to what the possessing djinn have to say, but it is forbidden to believe them, for they are deceivers. Djinn will not harm exorcists who act in proper fashion according to the Qur'an, but there are some dangers to exorcists who confront especially powerful djinn (*afrit* or *ifreet*), for they may suffer harm.

Specific prayers and verses from the Qur'an are used; the use of AMULETs and TALISMANs is forbidden. One of the greatest weapons is the Ayatal-kursi, sura 2:255:

Allah! There is no god but He—the Living, The Self-subsisting, Eternal. No slumber can seize Him Nor Sleep. His are all things In the heavens and on earth. Who is there can intercede In His presence except As he permitteth? He knoweth What (appeareth to His creatures As) Before or After or Behind them. Nor shall they compass Aught of his knowledge Except as He willeth. His throne doth extend Over the heavens And on earth, and

He feeleth No fatigue in guarding And preserving them, For He is the Most High. The Supreme (in glory).

Those who recite the Ayatal-kursi every night before going to bed will receive a guardian from Allah who will keep djinn away.

Another qur'anic exorcism weapon are the closing verses from sura 2:285–86. Even the djinn complain about their effectiveness:

> The Messenger believes in what has been revealed to him from his Lord as do the believers. All believe in Allah, His angels, His Books, and His messengers (saying), "We make no distinction between one and another of His messengers." And they say, "We hear and obey, and seek Your forgiveness, Our Lord, to You is the end of all journeys." Allah does not burden a soul beyond its capacity. It gets every good which it earns and suffers for every ill it earns. (Pray): Our Lord, do not condemn us if we forget or fall into error. Do not give us burdens like what you gave to those before us. Our Lord, do not burden us beyond our capacity. Blot out our sins, grant us forgiveness, and have mercy on us. You are our Guardian, so help us against the disbelieving people.

Sometimes djinn must be beaten out of people. The blows are not felt by the possessed person but are felt by the djinn, who howl and scream in agony.

Another technique employed by exorcists is to blow three times into their hands before reciting verses, thus invoking a blessing of the moisture or air touched by divine words remembering Allah.

Words and phrases from proper qur'anic verses can be written in ink made from allowable substances on vessels used for washing and drinking by the possessed; the water also may be sprinkled on the body. Similarly, the essence of the verses can be ingested by eating food prepared with inscriptions written on it (such as bread) or alphabet soup.

The prophet Muhammad acted aggressively against djinn. Once while he was engaged in Salaah, IBLIS went to him and troubled him. Muhammad grabbed him, wrestled him to the ground, and choked him. Muhammad said, "I choked him until I felt the coldness of his tongue on my hand. And if it were not for Sulaymaan's prayer, he would have been tied up so they could could see him." The mention of Sulaymaan (King SOLOMON) refers to Solomon's prayer to Allah for unique power over the djinn, possessed by no one else. If not for that, Muhammad would have had authority to bind Iblis himself.

Muhammad also exorcized djinn by cursing them three times: "I seek refuge in Allah from you! I curse you by Allah's perfect curse!" The same CURSE is used against infidels.

Muhammad exorcized djinn from others by beating the possessed and by ordering the djinn out. A man took his grandson, who became insane through a possessing djinn, to see Muhammad. The Prophet beat the boy's back while saying, "Get out enemy of Allah! Enemy of Allah get out!" The djinn left and the boy was healed.

In another case, a boy suffering with fits was taken to Muhammad. The Prophet blew into his mouth three times and said, "In the name of Allah, I am the slave of Allah, get out enemy of Allah." The boy was healed.

Spirit Exorcism

In some views, possession is not an evil situation but a spiritual one. Exorcism is not a religious expulsion but a firm good-bye, sending the spirit out of its living host and on to its proper realm. Such techniques of persuasion involve the use of psychic force.

Spiritual exorcists may perform several persuasive departures in one day, depending on the individual exorcist's intuitive ability and strength. Working with spirits, the exorcist has come to recognize the sensations associated with such restless entities, usually described as vibrations or a feeling of cold. Some entities emit odors, like stale flowers or worse.

DR. CARL A. WICKLAND and the Anglican clergyman CANON JOHN D. PEARCE-HIGGINS are two of the most famous practitioners of persuasive exorcism. Wickland believed that possession occurred when a discarnate human entity blundered, confusedly, into a living person's aura and became trapped. Using the services of his wife, Anna, a medium, Wickland coaxed the spirit out of its victim and into his wife, through whom he communicated with it.

Canon Pearce-Higgins agreed with Wickland that possession is not demonic but a manifestation of confused, earthbound spirits. He refused to call himself an exorcist. He employed religious services and simple conversation to persuade the spirit to leave. He said that the possessing spirit needs as much help and consolation as the possessed victim.

Exorcism in Magic

Exorcism rites of spirits, demons, ghosts, poltergeists, elementals, and unwanted or negative spirits, energies, or thought forms are part of ritual magic. Literature of the Hermetic Order of the Golden Dawn, one of the leading occult societies in the West, provides information for performing exorcisms. The Golden Dawn flourished from the late 19th century into the early 20th century; its rituals are now public and provide the foundation for many magical practices. An example of a Golden Dawn exorcism follows; it is drawn from material found in GRIMOIRES.

In a record of a personal experience, the Golden Dawn initiate Frater Sub Spe reported that he concluded that he and his wife were possessed by a vampirizing elemental—a low-level spirit—after his wife's bout of influenza left both of them in a state of inexplicable exhaustion and vulnerability. Frater Sub Spe at first thought to consult a fellow adept, but during a state of intense concentration, he was instructed by a nonphysical guide to perform the exorcism himself with the guide's instructions.

A vision of a stately man in black magical robes appeared and responded to the secret Golden Dawn salutes given him by Frater Sub Spe. The magician merged with the body of Frater Sub Spe, taking possession of it and giving instructions via words and impressions.

Frater Sub Spe was told to do the following: turn down the gas, burn incense, trace an invoking Pentagram of Fire toward the east, trace the sigil of Leo in the center of the pentagram, vibrate the Name of Power "Adni ha Aretz," return the coal to the fire, and face East and make the Qabalistic Cross, a ritual gesture, and trace an invoking Pentagram of Earth.

Frater Sub Spe did as instructed, and at the end of the ritual, he ordered the possessing spirit to appear before him:

> As I did so a vague blot, like a scrap of London fog, materialized before me. At the same time I sensed my guide, standing close to my right hand, raising his hand in the attitude of the 1=10 sign [a grade of the Golden Dawn]. I felt him (my guide) mentally order me to command the appearance of the obsessing entity, using the Names JHVH, ADNI, AGLA, AHIH. I did so and the mist thickened and formed a kind of nucleus. My guide then instructed me, "Use the Name of the Lord Jesus." I did so, commanding in that name a fuller manifestation. I saw, at first dimly, as "in a glass darkly," and then with complete clarity, a most foul shape, between a bloated big-bellied toad and a malicious ape. My guide spoke to me in an audible voice, saying "Now smite it with all your force, using the Name of the Lord Jesus." I did so gathering all the force I possessed into, as it were, a glowing ball of electric fire and then projecting it like a lightning flash upon the foul image before me.
>
> There was a slight feeling of shock, a foul smell, a momentary dimness, and then the thing was gone; simultaneously my Guide disappeared. The effect of this experience upon me was to create a great tension of nerves and a disposition to start at almost anything. Afterwards, when going upstairs, I saw floating balls of fire; this may have been hallucination.
>
> Both my wife and myself rapidly recovered our full health. Afterwards, a message came to me that "the unclean spirit is gone out, but it remains to purge away his traces from the house of life."

The great English occultist and ritual magician William S. Gray composed an exorcism ritual for banishing evil within the self, based on the Tree of Life in the KABBALAH. The ritual does not instantly eliminate evil but reduces the influence of evil in daily life, thus benefiting an individual's overall spiritual path and enlightenment.

FURTHER READING:

Davies, T. Witton. *Magic, Divination and Demonology among the Hebrews and Their Neighbors.* First published 1898.

Ebon, Martin. *The Devil's Bride, Exorcism: Past and Present.* New York: Harper & Row, 1974.

Eliade, Mircea. *Shamanism.* Princeton, N.J.: Princeton University Press, 1964.

Fortea, Fr. Jose Antonio. *Interview with an Exorcist: An Insider's Look at the Devil, Diabolic Possession, and the Path to Deliverance.* West Chester, Pa.: Ascension Press, 2006.

Guiley, Rosemary Ellen. *The Encyclopedia of Magic and Alchemy.* New York: Facts On File, 2006.

Ibn Taymeeyah's Essay on the Jinn (Demons.) Abridged, annotated, and translated by Dr. Abu Ameenah Bilal Philips. New Delhi: Islamic Book Service, 2002.

MacNutt, Francis. *Deliverance from Evil Spirits: A Practical Manual.* Grand Rapids, Mich.: Chosen Books, 1995.

Martin, Malachi. *Hostage to the Devil.* New York: Harper & Row, 1987.

Oesterreich, T. K. *Possession: Demonical and Other among Primitive Races, in Antiquity, the Middle Ages and Modern Times.* New Hyde Park, N.Y.: University Books, 1966.

Wickland, Carl. *Thirty Years among the Dead.* North Hollywood, Calif.: Newcastle, 1974. First published 1924.

Wilkinson, Tracy. *The Vatican's Exorcists: Driving Out the Devil in the 21st Century.* New York: Warner Books, 2007.

Exorcism of Emily Rose, The   See MICHEL, ANNELIESE.

exorcist   A person who expels DEMONS. Most exorcists are priests, clergy, or adepts; some laypersons call themselves exorcists. Exorcists use specific prayers and rituals to cause demons to leave people and/or places, either of their own volition or by force.

Beliefs about the ability of spirits to interfere in human life and cause problems, including disease and misfortune, are widespread. JESUS was noted for his ability to exorcise demons. Specially trained persons who cast out demons are found universally since ancient times. According to some beliefs, persons are born with the special ability to battle demons. REGINALD SCOT wrote in the 16th century that a person born with Mars in the ninth house has the power to expel demons from the possessed.

In the Catholic Church, any priest can be an exorcist. While it is desirable that an exorcist lead the most virtuous life possible, even priests who live in mortal sin can function as exorcists, albeit probably not as effectively as their more virtuous counterparts. Since attitudes toward demonic interferences vary, not all dioceses have official exorcists; sometimes, they are concentrated in archdioceses. Priests who perform many exorcisms are likely at some point to be subjected to criticism and ridicule from their peers.

MALACHI MARTIN described the ideal exorcist in *Hostage to the Devil* (1976):

> Usually he is engaged in the active ministry of parishes. Rarely is he a scholarly type engaged in teaching or research. Rarely is he a recently ordained priest. If there is any median age for exorcists, it is probably between the ages of fifty and sixty-five. Sound and robust physical health is not a characteristic of exorcists, nor is proven intellectual brilliance, postgraduate degrees, even in psy-

chology or philosophy, or a very sophisticated personal culture. . . . Though, of course, there are many exceptions, the usual reasons for a priest's being chosen are his qualities of moral judgment, personal behavior, and religious beliefs—qualities that are not sophisticated or laboriously acquired, but that somehow seem always to have been an easy and natural part of such a man.

Priests do not become exorcists by choice. They are called to their duty by receiving the chrism of the Holy Spirit, which gives them discernment of demons and their presences. The discernment is of the utmost importance in determining whether or not a person is possessed and whether demonic influences such as infestation and oppression are present. Some demons are skilled at hiding within a possessed person, and an inexperienced exorcist might be tricked into thinking a person is not possessed or the demons have been expelled.

Priests who are new exorcists receive special personal training from more experienced exorcists. They work in teams to discern POSSESSION, perform the EXORCISM rites, and work with laypersons who assist in the rites. Formal training is offered at the Regina Apostolorum Pontifical Athenaenum, a Vatican-affiliated university in Rome. Students learn the differences between possession and psychological and physical traumas and hear lectures by exorcists, medical professionals, priests, sociologists, law enforcement representatives, and other experts.

Exorcists must develop profound spiritual and inner strength, for they are subjected to demonic attacks designed to interfere in their work or persuade them to leave the work. Some exorcists suffer physical and mental health problems resulting from demonic influences and in a few cases may even become possessed themselves. Martin underscored the dangers of exorcism:

> Every exorcist must engage in a one-to-one confrontation, personal and bitter, with pure evil. Once engaged, the exorcism cannot be called off. There will and must always be a victor and a vanquished. And no matter what the outcome, the contact is in part fatal for the exorcist. He must consent to a dreadful and irreparable pillage of his deepest self. Something dies in him. Some part of his humanness will wither from such close contact with the opposite of all humanness—the essence of evil; and it is rarely if ever revitalized. No return will be made to him for his loss.

In other denominations, ministers sometimes perform exorcisms, and sometimes entire congregations participate in expelling demons, as in Pentecostal churches. In other religions and spiritual traditions and shamanic societies, exorcists are the members of the priestly castes, adepts, and specially trained persons. Members of magical traditions also can be exorcists.

See AMORTH, FATHER GABRIELE; FORTEA, FATHER JOSÉ ANTONIO; INTERNATIONAL ASSOCIATION OF EXORCISTS.

FURTHER READING:
Fortea, Fr. José Antonio. *Interview with an Exorcist: An Insider's Look at the Devil, Diabolic Possession, and the Path to Deliverance.* West Chester, Pa.: Ascension Press, 2006.
MacNutt, Francis. *Deliverance from Evil Spirits: A Practical Manual.* Grand Rapids, Mich.: Chosen Books, 1995.
Martin, Malachi. *Hostage to the Devil.* New York: Harper & Row, 1976.
Wilkinson, Tracy. *The Vatican's Exorcists: Driving Out the Devil in the 21st Century.* New York: Warner Books, 2007.

Exorcist, The (1971)   Novel by William Peter Blatty based on the true story of the ST. LOUIS POSSESSION case. The novel veers away substantially from the real case, but it introduced the horrors of demonic POSSESSION and EXORCISM to a mass audience.

The prologue describes a brief encounter in Iraq, where an archaeologist and cleric are finishing a dig of ancient Assyrian ruins. No names are given, but the reader receives a teaser of evil to come: The cleric, apparently familiar with the ways of the DEVIL, senses that the DEMON PAZUZU has been disturbed by the digging and plans revenge.

Then begins the real story, which opens in a townhouse in the Georgetown section of Washington, D.C., where the divorced actress Chris McNeil and her 11-year-old daughter, Regan, are staying while Chris finishes filming a movie. Strange noises and incidents, most of them in Regan's room, annoy Chris, but she does not pay much attention to them. She asks the servant, Karl, to check the windows and catch the rats she believes are making the scratching noises, but he finds none. Her best friend and the film's director, Burke Dennings, visits often; he is sarcastically funny, self-centered, an alcoholic, and given to obscenities. Other people in the house are Karl's wife the housekeeper, Willie, and Chris' secretary, Sharon, who also tutors Regan.

Portrayed as a bright, happy, affectionate young girl, Regan succumbs slowly to her possession. Alone at home, Regan plays more and more with a OUIJA™ board, talking to a Captain Howdy. At first, the house suffers from an INFESTATION: attack by the demons through the victim's surroundings. Chris hears rapping noises on the ceiling, Regan's room is always cold, the girl's clothing often ends up in a wadded pile on the floor, someone moves her furniture, and there is a foul, burning smell in her room. Other petty incidents occur: Books and objects disappear, and a stuffed mouse is found in the rat traps.

Now Captain Howdy not only talks to Regan but also tells her awful, horrible things, threatening pain and illness. Her bed shakes violently. Then Regan's personality changes; she becomes introverted and argumentative and eventually becomes hostile, disgusting, and obscene. She begins to exhibit superhuman strength, contorting her body in jerking, twisting movements. Strange voices emerge from her body, which is distended and unrecognizable. She slithers like a snake. Her conversations center around sexual and bodily functions.

Linda Blair, as the demonically possessed Regan, suffers at the hands of demons in The Exorcist *(1973).* (AUTHOR'S COLLECTION)

Frantic to find out what torments her daughter, Chris takes Regan from one doctor to another, abandoning her career. The doctors test Regan for everything but find no physical reason for her troubles. Under hypnosis, one psychiatrist tries to talk to what he sees as Regan's other personality. The personality—or demon—identifies himself as Nowonmai, from Dogmorfmocion. Although an agnostic, perhaps an atheist, Chris believes more firmly that her daughter has become possessed and needs a Catholic exorcism.

Meanwhile, in a parallel plot, the psychiatrist priest Father Damien Karras also lives in Washington, D.C., at Georgetown University, counseling the seminarians. Someone has desecrated the nearby Catholic Church; there is excrement on the altar cloth, a huge clay phallus has been attached to the statue of Christ, the statue of the Virgin Mary has been painted to resemble a harlot, and a Latin text describing Mary Magdalene as a lesbian is left on the altar. Father Karras suspects SATANISM—sexual gratification through blasphemous acts—but his training as a doctor prevents him from fully believing the Devil is about.

Besides, Father Karras has become mentally exhausted with his work, burdened not only with the troubles of his patients but with his own overwhelming guilt. He fears he does not love his fellow man as he should, scorning those who are poor or ignorant. He anguishes over his mother, who died poor and alone in a New York slum tenement. Through the movie company, Father Karras meets Chris and Regan. He is tantalized by the evil present in Regan and agrees to help rid her of her demons.

Before Father Karras can obtain permission for an exorcism, Burke Dennings, left alone in the house with Regan, dies mysteriously by falling out the girl's second-story bedroom window and over a steep cliff below. His head is turned completely around, an injury that is practically impossible, even in a severe fall. The demons in Regan eventually admit killing Dennings, explaining that turning his head around was common practice in the murder of witches.

As Regan's condition worsens, she exhibits all the classic signs of true possession. Besides the terrible contortions, foul smells, horrible voices, obscene behavior, and poltergeist phenomena (shaking bed, moving furniture, banging windows, breaking pottery), Regan suffers from incessant hiccuping and skin irritations, eventually displaying stigmata on her chest. The words *help me* appear on her stomach in her handwriting. She recoils from religious objects or uses them blasphemously, often employing a crucifix for masturbation. She taunts Father Karras with paranormal knowledge, impersonating the voices of his mother and an early lover. She uses the clipped British accents of Dennings as well. And most importantly for the church, Regan speaks languages previously unknown to her: French, German, Latin, and maybe Russian. The gibberish she mouths constantly is found to be English, backward. *Nowonmai,* the name of her demon, is "I am no one (won);" *Dogmorfmocion* is "I come from God."

When it seems Regan will die of her ordeal, the church gives its permission for an exorcism. Father Karras is to assist Father Lankester Merrin, an old hand at fighting the Devil and the one who senses the evil of Pazuzu in the book's prologue. The devil in Regan had been calling "Marin" for quite some time, but until Father Merrin arrived, no one had made the connection. The exorcism proceeds according to the ancient *RITUALE ROMANUM,* with Regan spitting, vomiting, and urinating all over the priests as they order the demon to depart. The demon goads both men, flinging their pride, their secret sins, and their guilt in their faces.

Father Merrin cannot survive this final encounter and dies during the exorcism, leaving Father Karras to fight alone. The demon believes he has won, for Father Karras' soul is not strong enough to overcome his guilt. At the climax, Father Karras orders the demon to leave Regan and enter him: Complete possession as a fitting punishment for his sins. The window crashes open, and Father Karras is found dead below. The reader must decide whether the demon accepted Father Karras' offer, but, in any case, Regan regains herself.

In the film version, released in 1973, the young actress Linda Blair gives a wrenching performance as Regan, with Ellen Burstyn as her mother, Chris, and Max von Sydow as Father Merrin. The demonic voices were provided by the actress Mercedes McCambridge, and the theme music, "Tubular Bells," was nominated for an Oscar. Audiences were traumatized by the film, and some persons sought professional help in the fear that they might become possessed themselves.

Exorcist II: The Heretic (1977) was a less successful sequel with Richard Burton as a priest still trying to release Linda Blair from her demonic possession.

Eye Killers   In Southwest Native American lore, monstrous DEMONs who killed by staring at people without blinking. Eye Killers are a variation of EVIL EYE lore.

According to lore, demons were born into the world when women became pregnant by using dildos. Twin Eye Killers, a male and a female, were born after a chief's daughter impregnated herself with a prong from a sour cactus. When born, the Eye Killers were round and tapered at one end, and without limbs. As they grew, they developed owl's heads, SERPENT bodies, and huge, clawed paws. Killing lightning bolts flew from their eyes. It took all of the village shaman's skill to exorcize the demons from the village.

The Eye Killers were a nearly invulnerable force. The only way people could stave them off was to build a fire. However, victims usually would be struck dead before they could make fires.

A hero named Monster Slayer decided he would kill the demons. He went to the cave where they lived and built a large fire in the entrance. Then he called out to the Eye Killers. When they appeared, he threw salt on the fire. The sparks forced the Eye Killers to shut their eyes for a few moments—long enough for the Monster Slayer to club them to death on their heads with his flint club.

FURTHER READING:
Hyatt, Victoria, and Joseph W. Charles. *The Book of Demons.* New York: Simon & Schuster, 1974.

fairies Beings who occupy a middle realm between Earth and heaven. Fairies have magical powers and are sometimes associated with DEMONS and FALLEN ANGELS. In lore, they are capable of bewitchment and POSSESSION, requiring EXORCISM.

Fairy originates from the Latin word *fata,* or "fate," and evolved from *faerie,* a state of enchantment. According to lore, fairies themselves do not like the word; they prefer to be called by more respectful names, such as "the Good Neighbors," "the Gentry," "the People of Peace," "the Strangers," "Themselves," "The Seely (Blessed) Court," and other terms. Fairies are often referred to as "the Little People." In medieval times fairy sometimes described women who had magical powers.

Fairy Origins

Fairy beliefs are universal and ancient, and there are a variety of explanations of their origins. Celtic fairy lore is particularly strong and absorbed Christian elements. In Irish lore, the fairies are descended from the Tuatha de Danaan, the early inhabitants of Ireland. When the Mil invaded, the Tuatha de Danaan used supernatural powers to become invisible and withdraw into the hills. From them arose the gods, demigods, heroes, and the fairies.

Other explanations for the origins of fairies are the following:

- Souls of the unbaptized and pagan dead, trapped between heaven and Earth

- Guardians of the dead, living in an otherworld that exists between the living and the dead. They have the power to take people, and when they do, those people die
- Ancestral ghosts
- Fallen angels cast out of heaven with LUCIFER, sentenced by God to the elements of the earth, where they act as demons
- Nature spirits who are attached to particular places or to the four elements, for example, sylphs of the air, gnomes of the earth, undines of water, and salamanders of fire
- Supernatural creatures who are shape-shifting monsters or half-human, half-monster
- Small human beings, primitive races like the Tuatha de Danaan that went into hiding in order to survive

In more recent times, fairies have been compared to extraterrestrials.

Descriptions and Characteristics

Fairies usually are invisible save to those with clairvoyant sight. They are best seen at dusk. In lore, they do not like to be seen by people and will often punish people who see them accidentally, including striking them blind. If they choose to be visible, fairies can bestow the gift of clairvoyance (and healing) upon mortals.

Descriptions of fairies cover a wide range, from tiny lights to winged creatures and, most often, small people. They tend to be either ugly—even monstrous—or beautiful. They are shape shifters who can assume whatever form they wish, especially to deceive or manipulate people. In Ireland, fairies assume the forms of black birds, especially crows; in French fairy lore, they are sometimes magpies. Black birds, as well as black animals, are associated with demons and the DEVIL.

Some fairies are solitary, like leprechauns, while others live in races and nations. Their homes are often in the earth and are accessed through mounds, caves, burrows, and holes in the ground and under piles of stones and rocks. It is bad luck to disturb these places, and the fairies will take revenge on people who do, causing misfortune, illness, and even death.

The Land of Fairy, also called Elfland, has characteristics of the land of the dead. Time is altered, so that a day in human life might stretch into years in fairyland. There is no day or night but a perpetual twilight. In legend and lore, there is an intermingling of ghosts of the dead and the afterlife with fairies and the Land of Fairy.

Descriptions of European fairies have been collected from oral lore. Robert Kirk, a Scottish Episcopalian minister who was clairvoyant, visited Fairyland and wrote an account, *The Secret Commonwealth,* in 1691–92, still one of the major first-person accounts in existence. A major compendium of fairy lore was written by W. Y. Evans-Wentz in the early 20th century, *The Fairy Faith in Celtic Countries* (1911).

Fairies live much as humans do, working and maintaining families and amusing themselves with food, drink, music, and dancing. They travel in the physical world along paths, tracks, and *raths,* which, as with their homes, must never be disturbed or destroyed by humans. Some of them like to march in processions at night and especially at the "cross quarter" days of the seasons. If someone builds a house atop a fairy track, the fairies will pass right through it, and the occupants will sicken, their crops will fail, and their animals will die. The fairies act as poltergeists, opening closed windows and doors and creating disturbances similarly to haunting ghosts.

Fairies are similar to demons in that many of them do not care for humans, and sometimes they will deliberately fool and attack people. A strong trickster element runs through fairy lore. They are fond of leading travelers astray. They attend human wakes and funerals and eat the banquet food, spoiling it for people.

Fairies kidnap people to their abodes, especially beautiful women they take for wives. In Fairyland, a person who eats their food remains trapped in a netherworld. To be "taken" by fairies means to go to the otherworld, also the land of the dead. If an abduction is temporary, a person sickens and then recovers; if it is permanent, the person dies and stays in the otherworld. Eating fairy food is taboo, for it will alter the body and prevent a person from returning to the world of the living.

Not all fairies are hostile or are tricksters. Some are kind and helpful to people, though on conditions. For ex-

ample, the household brownies will help with chores, as long as occupants are respectful; leave out milk, cream, and food for them; and are not messy. Once food is left for fairies, it must not be eaten by man or beast, for the fairies take the essence of the food, and it is no longer fit for others to consume. If food falls on the floor, the fairies claim it, and it must be given to them.

Fairies have a major weakness: IRON, which repels them and dilutes their supernatural powers. AMULETs made of iron keep fairies away.

Bewitchment and Witchcraft

As do witches, fairies have the magical ability to bewitch people and animals and to blight crops and health. In Irish lore, the Tuatha de Danaan took revenge upon the Mil by blighting wheat crops and spoiling milk. When Christian elements entered fairy lore, it became customary to dip a thumb in fresh milk and make the sign of the cross to ward off fairies.

If a person insults or displeases fairies, they have the power to transform him into a beast, a stone, or something else in nature.

Bewitched and fairy-possessed people and animals, who act strangely, sicken, or fall into trances or even seizures, are called "fairy struck" and "elf shot." The latter term refers to invisible arrows shot into people and animals.

Fairies teach witches their magical lore and casting of spells.

Changelings

Fairies are well known for stealing human babies and substituting their own ugly babies in their place. The taking happens at night when a child is asleep or when it is napping unattended.

Evans-Wentz gives the following quoted oral account from France, about a woman and her three children, as an example:

When she had her first child, a very strong and very pretty boy, she noticed one morning that he had been changed during the night; there was no longer the fine baby that she had put to bed in the evening; there was, instead, an infant hideous to look at, greatly deformed, hunchbacked, and crooked, and of a black color. The poor woman knew that a *fee* [fairy] had changed her child.

This changed infant still lives, and today he is about seventy years old. He has all the possible vices; and he has tried many times to kill his mother. He is a veritable demon; he predicts the future, and has a habit of running abroad at night. They call him the "Little *Corrigan*" [a type of fairy], and everybody flees from him. Being poor and infirm now, he is obliged to beg, and people give him alms because they have a great fear of him. His nickname is Olier.

The woman had two other children, who also were said to be normal at birth but were stolen by the fairies and also became "demonic" hunchbacks. Then she was advised by a wise woman to put a sprig of boxwood blessed by a priest in the cradle, and the fairies would be repelled. She did so for her fourth child, and it was not affected.

The idea of changelings might have explained problems in infants that were not apparent at birth but developed later and even "crib death" or sudden infant death syndrome (SIDS). The affected infants were not unrecognizable or completely different, but they were changed for the worse in noticeable ways.

Possession and Exorcism

Changelings result from possession: An entity steals a soul during sleep. The changelings were thus "fairy-possessed." As the preceding account shows, a changeling had "demonic" characteristics much as a person possessed by a demon does: an altered personality, evil tendencies and acts, supernormal abilities (prophecy), and an altered physical appearance. The hunchback is even called "a veritable demon."

In the case of changelings, the possession was usually permanent. Exorcism remedies exist in fairy lore; how effective they were probably depended on the nature of the problem affecting the infant. One remedy in French lore, for example, was to leave a changeling outdoors. The fairies would hear it cry and take it back, leaving the true child in its rightful place.

Fairies were well known for bewitching milk, and exorcisms of milk once were common in folklore practices. The vessel for containing the milk was exorcized and blessed, and so was the milk poured into it. Demons as well as fairies possessed milk; sometimes little or no distinction was made between one and the other.

The biography of the Irish patron saint Columba, who lived in the sixth century, tells a story about the saint's exorcism of milk. The *Vita Columbae* was written by Adamnan, the abbot of Iona. One day a youth named Columban did the milking and took the pail to St. Columba for exorcism. The saint made the sign of the cross in the air, but the lid flew off and most of the milk spilled. Columba said, "Thou has done carelessly in thy work today; for thou has not cast out the demon that was lurking in the bottom of the empty pail, by tracing on it, before pouring in the milk, the sign of the Lord's cross; and now not enduring, thou seest, the virtue of the sign, he has quickly fled away in terror, while at the same time the whole of the vessel has been violently shaken, and the milk spilled." Columba then ordered a half-full pail to be carried to him for exorcism. When he blessed it, the pail miraculously filled with milk.

One old folk custom in Brittany, France, called for the burning of green branches on the summer solstice. Domestic farm animals were passed through the smoke, which exorcized all evil spirits and fairies and protected them from bewitchment and possession. In the case of cows, it especially guaranteed the abundant supply of milk.

Fairies in Contemporary Lore

Since Victorian times, fairies have been increasingly stripped of their formidable powers and trivialized as little beings with wings, or female ballerinalike figures with wands. The fictitious Tinkerbell, created by the Scottish novelist J. M. Barrie around the turn of the 20th century as part of the Peter Pan stories, also added to the degrading of fairies to inconsequential, little creatures. The continuing portrayal of fairies in popular media is of cute, magical little beings with no demonic associations. The "tooth fairy" who leaves money in exchange for teeth left underneath a pillow is still popular with small children.

FURTHER READING:
Briggs, Katherine. *The Vanishing People.* New York: Pantheon Books, 1978.
Evans-Wentz, W. Y. *The Fairy Faith in Celtic Countries.* 1911. Reprint, New York: Carroll, 1990.
Stewart, R. J. *The Living World of Faery.* Lake Toxaway, N.C.: Mercury, 1995.

fallen angels   Angels who fall from God's grace and are punished by banishment from heaven, becoming DEMONS.

The three versions of the book of Enoch associate fallen angels with the WATCHERS, 200 angels who descend from heaven to cohabitate with women and corrupt humanity and are severely punished by God. 2 Enoch speaks of four grades of fallen angels:

1. SATANAIL, the prince of the fallen one. Satanail was once a high angel who thought he could be greater than God and thus was cast out of heaven on the second day of creation. He is imprisoned in the fifth heaven.
2. The Watchers, who also are imprisoned in the fifth heaven, dejected and silent.
3. The apostate angels, the followers of Satanail who plotted with him and turned away from God's commandments. They are imprisoned in the second heaven, a place of "darkness greater than earthly darkness." There they hang under guard, waiting for the "measureless judgment." The fallen angels are dark in appearance, and they weep unceasingly. They ask Enoch to pray for them.
4. Angels—possibly some of the Watchers—who are sentenced to be imprisoned "under the earth."

In Christianity, LUCIFER is the arrogant, prideful angel cast out of heaven, mentioned briefly in Isaiah as "Son of the Morning" or "Morning Star." One-third of the heavenly host fell with him—133,306,668 angels, according to lore. They fell for nine days. Theologians have posited that a portion of each of the nine orders of angels fell; some said the fallen ones compose a tenth order. The fallen angels become demons who seek to ruin men's souls, a view reinforced by the influential theologian St. Thomas Aquinas. Lucifer later became identified with SATAN.

Archangel Michael evicting Lucifer and his followers from heaven (AUTHOR'S COLLECTION)

falling stars   DEMONs who have no way station in which to rest and so fall from the sky.

In the Testament of Solomon the demon ORNIAS explains to SOLOMON that demons have the capability of flying up to heaven in order to eavesdrop on God and learn his plans. But because they have no place to rest, they become exhausted and fall to Earth like flashes of lightning, burning fields, and cities. People think they are falling stars.

Folklore traditions through history hold that falling stars are the souls of those who have just died or who are descending to Earth to be reborn.

familiar   A spirit that maintains regular contact with a person, sometimes acting in service or guardianship, or providing information and instruction. The term *familiar* is from the Latin term *familiaris,* meaning "of a household or domestic."

Familiars can be either good or evil in nature, and they vary significantly in intelligence and powers. They assume many shapes, such as elementals, animals, birds and insects, and even spirit lovers. The shapes assumed reflect the nature of the spirit, who may be intent on deceit. Personal familiars sometimes attach themselves to a

family bloodline and serve generations. They can possess people and animals and are capable of acting independently of the people with whom they associate.

Familiars are summoned via magical ritual, given, appointed, traded, bought, and sold, or they appear of their own volition. They can be housed in bottles and rings. They have been part of shamanic and SORCERY traditions around the world.

Early Beliefs about Familiars

The Greeks and Romans believed in familiars called DAIM-ONEs, which occupied homes, buildings, and other places and attached themselves to people. Such spirits provided advice and guidance, performed tasks, acted as servants, and did guard duty. Socrates said *daimones* whispered in his ear to warn him of danger and misfortune. Plotinus also was said to have a familiar, who appeared when summoned and obeyed him and was superior to lower-ranking spirits such as the *genii*, guardians of places.

Other early beliefs about familiars cross over into the lore of FAIRIES, elves, brownies, gnomes, and trolls. Spirits that work in mines and guard hidden treasures are sometimes called familiars. The DJINN summoned by King SOLOMON to build his Temple of Jerusalem are comparable to familiars.

Familiars in Magic and Witchcraft

Familiars can be conjured magically for a variety of purposes. In esoteric lore, they are the constant attendants and servants of magicians, wizards, spell casters, and healers. Low familiars are inanimate objects, such as magical books that mysteriously appear. The English magician John Dee acquired a scrying (divining) crystal inhabited by a familiar spirit, which he and his assistant, Edward Kelley, used to communicate with angels and spirits. High familiars assume plant, animal, and human shape. Some familiars assume whatever shape is needed for their purposes. Dee had another familiar, Madimi, who appeared as either a young girl or an adult. She even appeared naked when dealing with a sexual matter.

According to tradition, familiars can be magically locked in bottles, rings, and stones and sometimes sold as CHARMs for success in gambling, love, and business.

In witchcraft lore, familiars are low-ranking DEMONs or IMPs given by the DEVIL to those who commit to PACTs with him. Or witches inherited familiars from other witches. Demonic familiars were said by witch hunters to serve witches in all ways, even sexually. They carried out spells and bewitchments. Most witch familiars were believed to be in animal form; some were spirits kept in bottles and flasks. Even FAIRIES were said to be familiars.

A witch could have multiple familiars. Cats, especially black, were the favored forms. The fear that all cats were witches' familiars led to cat massacres in Europe.

The witch hunter Pierre de Lancre said the highest-ranking witches have familiars in the shape of horned

Low-level demons, or familiars, carrying out tasks for their masters (AUTHOR'S COLLECTION)

frogs that sit on their left shoulder and are invisible to everyone but other witches. Some witches had familiars in human form.

Other common witches' familiars were dogs, toads, mice, ferrets, weasels, birds, wasps, bees, moths, hedgehogs, rabbits, and farm animals, as well as monstrous hybrid creatures. For example, the accused English witch Elizabeth Clark (17th century) confessed to having five familiars, including Vinegar Tom, a creature that looked like a greyhound with an ox's head and could shape shift into a headless child.

Familiars all supposedly had grotesque names that gave away their true demonic identities. Elizabeth Francis, an accused witch in the Chelmsford, England, trials of 1556, had a white spotted cat named *Sathan*. Other names recorded at witch trials were Verd-Joli, Verdelet, Ilemanzar, Greedigut, Jezebel, Abrahel, Grissell, Martinet, Blackman, and Pyewackett.

Witches who were arrested and imprisoned were watched secretly to see whether their familiars came to their aid. Even a fly, ant, or cockroach that went toward a witch was called a familiar. Guards had to watch carefully that familiars—believed to be assassins dispatched by the Devil—did not kill an accused witch before she could be tried.

Witches were said to take great care of their familiars, suckling them with their own BLOOD through "witch's marks," small teats, discolorations, and welts upon their bodies.

Having a familiar was sufficient to condemn a witch to death. In England, the Witchcraft Act of 1604 made it a felony to "consult, covenant with, entertain, employ, feed, or reward any evil and wicked spirit to or for any intent or purpose."

In contrast to the familiars of the witch trials, the literary MEPHISTOPHELES is an elegant familiar, usually assuming the form of a tall man in black who attends his victim, FAUST, in order to subvert his soul. Faust also was accompanied by a black dog familiar.

Many modern Witches, Wiccans, and Pagans have familiars as magical helpers. Many are animals (often cats) whose psychic attunement makes them ideal partners in magic. Some Witches turn pets into familiars, and others send out "calls" on the psychic planes to draw in the right animal. Others create familiars from astral thought forms.

Familiars attend rituals and protect against negative spirits. They are sensitive to psychic vibrations and power and are welcome partners inside the magic circle for the raising of power, the casting of spells, scrying, spirit contact, and other magical work. They also serve as psychic radar, reacting visibly to the presence of any negative or evil energy, whether it be an unseen force or a person who dabbles in the wrong kind of magic. Familiars are given psychic protection by their witches.

Sexual Familiars

Spirits enjoy human sexual intercourse, either by drawing energy from people engaged in it or by assuming or possessing a human form in order to participate in sex directly. Depending on the nature of a familiar, it enjoys the higher spiritual nature of sex or the lustful physical nature of it. A familiar might try to influence a sexual encounter by prolonging it as long as possible. It usually presses on top of a person or lies alongside him or her. A person feels a sexual encounter with a familiar as intense waves of physical pleasure. Familiars can engage in sex by possessing a person's body and generating internal sensations of pleasure, by possessing a person's human lover to manipulate his or her hands and body, and by causing erotic dreams.

The low, demonic types of spirit sexual encounters are with an INCUBUS (male demon) or SUCCUBUS (female demon). During the witch hysteria, witches were said to copulate with demon lovers, and demons masquerading as seductive humans attacked sleeping people at night and raped them.

Problems with Familiars

Frequent contact with familiars can result in nightmares, physical injuries caused by familiars, and also OBSESSION, in which a person sees, hears, and feels an influencing spirit, and POSSESSION, in which the familiar completely takes over a person.

Also, spirits do not always distinguish between truth and falsehood, and so discernment must be applied to whatever information they impart. Familiars can manifest as voices in the head that cause compulsive, aberrant behavior, including self-inflicted wounds, suicide, and violence toward others. Excessive and draining contact with them can create mental, emotional, and physical strain and breakdown.

Familiars that create problems can be banished by ending all engagement with them or, if necessary, by ritual banishment.

See SINISTRARI, LUDOVICO MARIA.

FURTHER READING:

Calmet, Dom Augustin. *The Phantom World: Concerning Apparitions and Vampires.* Ware, England: Wordsworth Editions in association with the Folklore Society, 2001.

Summers, Montague. *The History of Witchcraft and Demonology.* London: Kegan Paul, Trench, Trubner, 1926.

Thomas, Keith. *Religion and the Decline of Magic.* New York: Charles Scribner's Sons, 1971.

Tyson, Donald. *Familiar Spirits: A Practical Guide for Witches and Magicians.* St. Paul, Minn.: Llewellyn, 2004.

Valiente, Doreen. *An ABC of Witchcraft Past and Present.* 1973. Reprint, Custer, Wash.: Phoenix, 1986.

Faust Legend of a learned but arrogant man who makes a PACT with the DEVIL. The Faust legend was based on the legend of THEOPHILUS and circulated widely in Europe in medieval times. It was published as a novel in the mid-1500s after the Protestant Reformation.

The best-known version of the story was published in 1587 by a German publisher, Johann Spies. Translated into English by 1594, the manuscript inspired Christopher Marlowe to write his play, *The Tragicall History of D. Faustus,* around 1601. In the late 18th century, Johann Wolfgang von Goethe wrote his version of Faust.

The Early Story of Faust

Faust, the son of a husbandman, was born in Roda, Weimar, Germany. He was raised in a Christian household. Faust had a superior intellect and earned a doctorate in theology. But he was vain and arrogant. He indulged in gluttony and lust.

Faust began dabbling in MAGIC. One night, he went to a CROSSROADS in the woods, cast a magic circle, and conjured the Devil. The Devil appeared as a griffon or dragon, then as flying lights, then as a burning man, and finally as a gray friar who asked Faust what he wanted. Faust compelled him to agree to go to his house the next morning.

By evening, Faust agreed to a pact presented by the Devil. He agreed to three things:

- Faust would become the Devil's property after a certain number of years.
- He would sign an agreement to this effect in his own BLOOD.
- He would renounce the Christian faith and defy all believers.

In exchange, the Devil would fulfill every lust of Faust's heart and grant him the body and powers of a spirit. In his arrogance, Faust thought the Devil might not be as bad as others said.

The Devil revealed his name as *Mephostophiles* (MEPHISTOPHELES). Faust gave him the following written pact:

I, JOHANN FAUSTUS, Dr.,

Do publicly declare with mine own hand in covenant & by power of these presents:

Whereas, mine own spiritual faculties having been exhaustively explored (including the gifts dispensed from above and graciously imparted to me), I still cannot comprehend;

And whereas, it being my wish to probe further into the matter, I do propose to speculate upon the Elementa;

And whereas mankind doth not teach such things;

Now therefore have I summoned the spirit who calleth himself Mephostophiles, a servant of the Hellish Prince in Orient, charged with informing and instructing me, and agreeing against a promissory instrument hereby transferred unto him to be subservient and obedient to me in all things.

I do promise him in return that, when I be fully sated of that which I desire of him, twenty-four years also being past, ended and expired, he may at such a time and in whatever manner or wise pleaseth him order, ordain, reign, rule and possess all that may be mine: body, property, flesh, blood, etc., herewith duly bound over in eternity and surrendered by covenant in mine own hand by authority and power of these presents, as well as of my mind, brain, intent, blood and will.

I do now defy all living beings, all the Heavenly Host and all mankind, and this must be.

In confirmation and contract whereof I have drawn out mine own blood for certification in lieu of a seal.

Doctor Faustus, Adept
in the Elementa and in Church Doctrine.

Thus began Faust's relationship with Mephostophiles, whom he conjured daily inside his locked study. The DEMON always appeared in the guise of a friar. Mephostophiles indulged Faust with the finest foods and then an endless supply of women.

Faust also plied the demon with questions about the formation of the world, heaven and HELL, and how the ranks of demons came into being as a result of the fall of LUCIFER.

Title page of Christopher Marlowe's The Tragicall Historie of the Life and Death of Doctor Faustus (AUTHOR'S COLLECTION)

After nearly eight years had passed, Faust one day ordered Mephostophiles to summon his lord, BELIAL, but BEELZUBUB appeared instead. Faust asked to be taken on a tour of hell. Beelzebub returned with a bone chair and whisked Faust away.

It seemed Faust fell asleep, and when he awakened, he was in the abyss, which was full of contorted animals, sulfuric stenches, quakes, lightning, flames, and tremendous heat. He also saw many well-known people, including royalty, suffering in the heat. Faust was returned to his own bed, but he was certain he could not withstand hell himself.

Faust then desired to see the heavens, and a coach drawn by two dragons appeared and took him up into the sky, 47 miles up. He looked down upon the earth, and then he was taken into heaven.

In his 16th year of bondage to the Devil, Faust undertook a pilgrimage to Rome, where he had dinner with the pope and stole his goblets and flagons. He then went to Constantinople and visited the Turkish emperor.

Faust had other adventures, including meeting Emperor Charles V and the duke of Bavaria.

Faust entertained a group of students by having Mephostophiles conjure up Helen of Troy.

After Faust had spent 19 years with the Devil, an old man tried to persuade Faust to repent and return to Christianity, but Faust renewed his demonic pact by writing another one in his own blood. He affirmed that in another five years, Lucifer would have full sway over him.

Faust had Helen summoned again and began living with her. In the 23rd year of his pact, she became pregnant and bore a son, whom Faust named Justus Faustus.

When Faust's 24 years were nearly up, he made out a will. As his end approached, he became depressed and fearful of his fate. He regretted his pact. He summoned his students for a final night of dining and company at a village inn and urged them all to follow a good life.

That night between midnight and one o'clock, a great storm arose. A hideous music filled the inn, along with Faust's cries. The students were too frightened to look into his room.

The next morning, Faust was gone. But a hideous sight greeted the students:

> The parlor was full of blood. Brain clave unto the walls where the Fiend had dashed him from one to the other. Here lay his eyes, here a few teeth. O it was a hideous spectaculum. Then began the students to bewail and beweep him, seeking him in many places. When they came out to the dung heap, here they found his corpse. It was monstrous to behold, for head and limbs were still twitching.

Helen and Justus were missing, never to be seen again.

The students obtained permission to bury Faust's remains in the village. They discovered Faust's written record of all that had happened to him—a sober lesson in the consequences of dallying with the Devil.

The story of Faust had different versions and grew in length as time went on. For Faust, there is no redemption; once the demonic pact is made, the price of it must be paid. Other stories of demonic pacts allowed for repentance and redemption, specifically through the intervention of the Blessed Virgin Mary (see MARY OF NEMEGEN).

Goethe's Faust

Goethe began *Faust* in 1774 and worked on it for 60 years, leaving parts of it to be opened posthumously. The story is of a genius who sells his soul to the Devil, then sins, repents, dies, and is redeemed. *Faust* is an aspect of Goethe himself and shows Goethe's knowledge of religion and alchemy and his mystical speculations.

The Prologue in Heaven was probably influenced by Goethe's reading of *Paradise Lost* by John Milton. It presents God with the archangels Michael, Raphael, and Gabriel. Mephistopheles, the Devil, enters as a court jester and asks God about mankind's wretchedness. God mentions Faust, "my serf," and agrees to let Mephistopheles try to sway him. Faust is "doctor" of all knowledge of all the realms, but he has no solace. He projects a noble aspiration of the human spirit, despite his sinister side. He serves as the focal point for the struggle between good and evil as a necessary part of evolution. In Goethe's view, the seeds of good can lie hidden in evil, but at the same time, there can be something satanic in the loftiest feeling or the satanic can even grow out of it.

In part 1, Faust is in despair with weariness and emptiness. He deplores the limitations of book learning and decides to seek real power through magic, but both his immense knowledge and magical power have been rebuffed by the Earth Spirit, the lesser deity that dwells in the earth. He is miffed that he, "godhead's likeness," "more than cherub," has been "withered" by the Earth Spirit's rejection. Faust is about to commit suicide when Easter bells and a chorus of ANGELs interrupt him. Mephistopheles—a symbol of the libido's greed for gold and lust—arrives on the scene with attendant spirits he calls "my airy cherubim." The seduction of Faust through his limitations begins, and Faust sells him his soul. His youthful vigor restored by a witch, he descends into sensuality, which destroys Gretchen, an innocent woman who loves him. Faust attends a witches' sabbat. He watches Gretchen die and prays to the heavenly hosts for protection. A heavenly voice proclaims she is redeemed while Mephistopheles insists she is damned.

As part 2 opens, it seems lifetimes later. Faust wakes in a charming landscape with FAIRIES and Ariel (the same spirit of the air from Shakespeare's play). Mephistopheles next takes Faust to Greece for an inside view of an emperor, lovemaking with Helen of Troy, and frolic among the gods, satyrs, fauns, and nymphs. His steady movement to damnation contrasts with the glories of knowledge and sensuality. After Faust dies, he is buried by angels and DEMONs.

In act 5 of part 2, the heavenly angels confront Mephistopheles and his devils to seize Faust's soul and carry it off. In the epilogue, male and female saints and blessed children sing of God's plan as the ranks of angels comment on the ascent of Faust's immortal essence. Gretchen is heard among the chorus of penitent women, and Faust's soul is received by a Sophia-like "Woman Eternal."

FURTHER READING:
Goethe, Johann Wolfgang von. *The Autobiography of Johann Wolfgang von Goethe*. Vols. 1 & 2. Chicago: University of Chicago Press, 1976.
Goethe, Johann Wolfgang von. *Faust*. Edited by Cyrus Hamlin, translated by Walter Arendt. New York: Norton, 1976.
Gray, Ronald D. *Goethe the Alchemist: A Study of Alchemical Symbolism in Goethe's Literary and Scientific Works*. Mansfield Centre, Conn.: Martino, 2002.
"*Historia* and Tale of Doctor Johannes Faustus." Available online. URL: http://lettersfromthedustbowl.com/Fbk1.html. Downloaded March 7, 2008.
Lukacs, Georg. *Goethe and His Age*. New York: Grosset & Dunlap, 1969.

Fischer, Doris   See DORIS FISCHER OBSESSION.

Flauros (Hauras, Haurus, Havres)   FALLEN ANGEL and the 64th of the 72 SPIRITS OF SOLOMON. Flauros reigns as a duke with 36 LEGIONs of DEMONs under his command. He appears first as a terrible leopard but, if commanded, will change shape into a man with fiery eyes and a terrible countenance. If invoked into the magician's triangle, he will give true answers to questions about the past, present, and future; outside the triangle, he will lie. Flauros will talk openly of divinity, the creation of the world, and the fall of the ANGELs, including his own fall. He will destroy and burn one's enemies but will protect those who invoke him from temptation, spirits, and other dangers.

Focalor (Forcalor, Furcalor)   FALLEN ANGEL and the 41st of the 72 SPIRITS OF SOLOMON. Prior to his fall, Focalor was a member of the angelic order of thrones. In HELL, he reigns as a duke with 31 LEGIONs of DEMONs. He appears as a man with griffin wings. He has the power of the wind and the sea and drowns men and sinks warships. If commanded, he will not harm anyone. Prior to his fall, he was in the order of thrones. After 1,000 years, he hopes to return to the seventh heaven.

Foras (Forcas, Furcas, Fourcas)   FALLEN ANGEL and 31st of the 72 SPIRITS OF SOLOMON. Forcas is a president who commands 29 LEGIONs of DEMONs. He appears as a strong man or as a chevalier. He teaches logic, ethics, and the virtues of herbs and precious stones. He makes

people invisible, discovers hidden treasures and lost objects, and imparts wit, wisdom, eloquence, and longevity.

Forneus   FALLEN ANGEL and 30th of the 72 SPIRITS OF SOLOMON. Forneus is a marquis of HELL, who appears as a sea monster. He teaches rhetoric, art, and languages and confers a good reputation. He causes people to be loved by their enemies. Prior to his fall, Forneus was in the order of thrones and partly in the order of ANGELs. He governs 29 LEGIONs of DEMONs.

Fortea, Father José Antonio (1968–)   One of the foremost demonologists and EXORCISTs of the Catholic Church. Father José Antonio Fortea is also a calligrapher, author, and parish priest.

Fortea was born in Barbastro, Spain, in 1968. His father was an attorney, and Fortea expected to follow in his footsteps. He studied theology at the University of Navarre and received a degree of licentiate in history of the church at the faculty of theology of Comillas. At Navarre, he wrote a thesis, "Exorcism in the Present Age." Not long after that, the bishop there was given a case of POSSESSION and consulted Fortea because of his expertise. Another case arose within a year and a half.

Fortea turned his thesis into a book for the general public, *Interview with an Exorcist: An Insider's Look at the Devil, Demonic Possession and the Path to Deliverance*. He soon found himself to be the only exorcist in Spain. He took training from the Vatican exorcist FATHER GABRIELE AMORTH.

In 1998, he defended the thesis under the direction of the secretary of the Commission for the Doctrine of the Faith of the Spain Conference of Catholic Bishops.

His best-known case is "Marta," a young woman who went into a possessed trance and writhed like a snake on the floor of a chapel near Madrid. The case is still open. In 2005, journalists were able to witness one of her EXORCISMS.

According to Fortea, many of the people who consult him are suffering something related to spirits, such as INFESTATION, but he estimates that fewer than 1 percent are suffering from genuine possession. Phenomena he has witnessed in possession cases include levitation, the ability to speak in foreign languages unknown to the victim, supernormal strength, and knowledge of things impossible for the possessed to know.

FURTHER READING:
Fortea, Fr. José Antonio. *Interview with an Exorcist: An Insider's Look at the Devil, Diabolic Possession, and the Path to Deliverance*. West Chester, Pa.: Ascension Press, 2006.

fox fairy   See HULI JING; KITSUNE.

Fureas (Furcas)   FALLEN ANGEL and 50th of the 72 SPIRITS OF SOLOMON. Fureas is a knight who commands 20

LEGIONs of DEMONs. He appears as a cruel man with a long beard and hairy head, riding a pale horse and carrying a sharp weapon. He teaches rhetoric, philosophy, logic, astronomy, chiromancy (divination of the hands), and pyromancy (divination with fire).

Furfur FALLEN ANGEL and 34th of the 72 SPIRITS OF SOLOMON. Furfur is an earl with 26 LEGIONs of DEMONs under his command. He appears as a hart with a fiery tail. When summoned, he must be placed within the magician's triangle, or what he says—if he speaks at all—will be false. Once in the triangle, he changes form to that of a beautiful ANGEL, who speaks with a hoarse voice. Furfur causes love between a husband and wife. He will give true answers about secret and divine things. He can raise thunder, lightning, and great winds.

Gaap (Goap, Tap) FALLEN ANGEL and 33rd of the 72 SPIRITS OF SOLOMON. Once a member of the angelic order of powers, Gaap is a president and mighty prince in HELL, ruling 66 LEGIONS of DEMONS. He appears when the Sun is in the southern signs, as a human with huge bat's wings and preceded by four powerful kings. Gaap teaches liberal sciences and philosophy; excites love and hatred; makes men insensible; gives true answers about the past, present, and future; and takes FAMILIARS away from magicians. Upon command, he will move people quickly from place to place. Gaap gives instruction in the consecration of things that belong to the divination of his master, AMAYMON.

Gadreel (Gadriel) In 1 Enoch, a FALLEN ANGEL. *Gadreel* means "God is my helper." Gadreel leads Eve astray and teaches men how to make the weapons of war.

galli In Sumerian lore, a group of seven DEMONS who live in Kur, the underworld.

The galli attend Ereshkigal, the sister of Inanna and the goddess of death and gloom. Ereshkigal sits naked on a throne of lapis lazuli in her palace, which is surrounded by seven walls. Anyone, either mortal or god, who enters Kur is doomed to stay. The galli, however, are free to come and go. When they go to the world of the living, they terrorize people and kidnap them to Kur. Galli can exist in favorable form. They do not eat or drink or sexually molest people as many other demons do. However, they despise children.

According to lore, Ereshkigal imprisoned Inanna in the underworld. She escaped, but the galli tracked her down and threatened to take her back unless she found a good substitute. Inanna discovered that her lover, Dumuzi, was

Gaap (DICTIONNAIRE INFERNAL)

93

Galli (AUTHOR'S COLLECTION)

not sad at her death but was celebrating it. In a rage, she killed him with a look and gave him over to the gallı to take her place in Kur. The galli fell upon Dumuzi, tore up his face, and slashed him with an ax. Dumuzi takes the place of Inanna in Kur for six months of the year. During that time, it is winter.

FURTHER READING:
Black, Jeremy, and Anthony Green. *Gods, Demons and Symbols of Ancient Mesopotamia.* London: British Museum Press, 1992.

Gamaliel   ANGEL and DEMON. *Gamaliel* means "recompense of God."

In the Nag Hammadi and other Gnostic literature, Gamaliel is a great aeon, or angellike demigod, whose name is mentioned frequently for graciousness and protection. With ABRAXAS and Sablo, Gamaliel takes the elect into heaven. The occultist Eliphas Levi saw Gamaliel as an evil adversary of the cherubim angelic order, a demon who serves under LILITH.

Gamigin (Gamygyn)   FALLEN ANGEL and fourth of the 72 SPIRITS OF SOLOMON. In HELL, Gamigin is a duke with 30 LEGIONS of DEMONS. He appears in the form of a small horse or ass and then changes into a human. His voice is hoarse. Gamigin teaches liberal sciences and delivers news about people who have died in sin. He can summon the souls of drowned men and those who are in purgatory. These souls appear as aerial bodies before the magician and give answers to questions.

Garadiel   DEMON and wandering duke of the air, who never stays in one place. Garadiel has 18,150 servants, but no dukes or princes beneath him. The number of his attendants varies according to the hours of the day or night. All are good-natured and willing to obey commands.

Gaufridi, Louis   See AIX-EN-PROVENCE POSSESSIONS; BAPTISM; PACT.

Gediel   DEMON among the 31 AERIAL SPIRITS OF SOLOMON. Gediel is the second in command under CASPIEL and has 20 servants during the day and 20 during the night. Each duke has 20 servants. All are courteous and willing to obey the commands of an EXORCIST or magician. Eight principal dukes of the day under Gediel are Coliel, Naras, Sabas, Assaba, Sariel, Panciel, Mashel, and Bariet. Major dukes of the night are Reciel, Sadiel, Agra, Anael, Aroan, Cirecas, Aglas, and Vriel.

Gemory (Gomory)   FALLEN ANGEL and 56th of the 72 SPIRITS OF SOLOMON. Gemory is a powerful duke in HELL with 26 LEGIONS of DEMONS. He appears as a beautiful woman with the crown of a duchess, who rides a camel. He discovers hidden treasures and gives true answers about the past, present, and future. He procures the love of women, especially girls, but also old women.

genie   In pre-Islamic and Islamic lore, a DJINN. The term *genie* is an English translation of *djinn,* which first appeared in print in 1655 and is probably also related to the older Latin term *genius,* a type of guardian or tutelary spirit of people, places, and things that was demonized by Christianity.

Genie became the popular English term for *djinn,* primarily because the French translators of *The Book of One Thousand and One Nights,* a collection of Arabic folktales, used it in place of *djinn.* One of the most familiar tales, "Aladdin's Wonderful Lamp," features a genie released from a magical lamp that fulfills wishes.

In Roman mythology, the genius (pl. *genii*) is present at the birth of a person, remains with him or her throughout life, and shapes the person's character and destiny. If a guardian of a place, the genius serves as the animating force that gives a location its unique power and atmosphere.

In Assyrian lore, the genie is a guardian spirit or minor deity. In art, it is often portrayed as having a role in royal rituals. Genies are anthropomorphic, with animal heads (and sometimes wings) and human torsos and limbs. They guard and purify kings, members of royalty, supernatural figures, and open doorways against malevolent demons and the disorders they cause. In art, they are shown holding a pinecone in the right hand and a bucket of either water or pollen in the left hand. Both bucket and cone have associations of purification. Portrayals of genies were placed in buildings as guardians.

See DJINN.

FURTHER READING:
Black, Jeremy, and Anthony Green. *Gods, Demons and Symbols of Ancient Mesopotamia.* London: British Museum Press, 1992.

Gerasene Demoniac   See JESUS.

ghoul   A DEMON who feeds on the flesh of human beings, especially travelers, children, or corpses stolen out of graves. Ghoulish entities are universal. They are prominent in Arabic lore; the name is from the Arabic terms *ghul* (masculine) and *ghula* (feminine), which mean "demon." There are several types of ghouls in Arabic lore; the most feared is a female type that has the ability to appear as a normal, flesh-and-blood woman. Such a creature marries an unsuspecting man, who becomes her prey.

Ghouls are nocturnal creatures who inhabit graveyards, ruins, and other lonely places. Sometimes they are described as dead humans who sleep for long periods in secret graves, then awake, rise, and feast on both the living and the dead. Ghouls also personify the unknown terrors held by the desert and may be compared to the LAMIAE and LILITH night terror and childbirth demons.

Gilles de Rais (Gilles de Retz) (1404–1440)   Wealthy and distinguished French nobleman executed on charges of child murder, performances of the BLACK MASS, and sacrifices to the DEVIL.

Gilles de Montmorency-Laval, the baron de Rais, distinguished himself in the military as a young man. He took up the side of the dauphin Charles in Charles' dispute with the English over the French throne and was assigned to Joan of Arc's guard. He fought several battles with Joan and accompanied her to Reims for the coronation of the victorious dauphin as Charles VII. The king named him marshal of France. After Joan was captured by the English in 1431 and executed, Gilles returned to his family lands in Brittany.

He had enormous wealth—besides his inheritance, he had married a wealthy woman in 1420—and he lived in a more lavish style than even the king. He employed hundreds of servants, hired 200 knights as bodyguards, and held extravagant parties. Gilles eventually spent all his money and went deeply in debt. He began selling off lands to pay off debt and finance his high-style living. In 1435, Charles officially prohibited him to sell or mortgage more land.

Desperate, Gilles turned to alchemy and began invoking DEMONS in an attempt to gain more riches. Rumors began to circulate that Gilles was involved in far more than alchemy but was kidnapping children for sexual abuse and ritual torture and murder. The duke of Brittany and his chancellor, who were interested in confiscating Gilles' lands if they could have him convicted of heresy, probably encouraged the rumors. Gilles was arrested in September 1440 and charged with abducting and murdering more than 140 children in Black Mass rituals. He was brought to trial in Nantes before both an ecclesiastical court and a civil court.

The church inquisitors brought 47 charges against Gilles. Among them were accusations that he sodomized boys and girls; hung them until they were nearly dead, raped them, and then cut off their heads; and burned, tortured, and dismembered them. He was alleged to have let many bleed to death slowly, having intercourse with them while they died or after they were dead. He supposedly cut out their eyes and organs with a dagger and offered them to the Devil. He was accused of gloating over their pain and suffering.

Gilles refused to plead to the charges, which he said were not true. He was threatened with excommunication and so pleaded not guilty. The ecclesiastical trial lasted 40 days. Gilles was tortured until he confessed not only to committing the crimes but to enjoying them as well. Several of his servants and alleged accomplices also were tortured.

In the civil court parents of missing children testified that their children had disappeared in the vicinity of Gilles' castle. Gilles' personal attendants testified they had witnessed his defiling and murdering children and had counted their heads.

Gilles was condemned for heresy, sodomy, and sacrilege and was found guilty of murder. The civil court sentenced him to death. On October 26, 1440, Gilles was executed. By some accounts, he was hanged. By other accounts, he was strangled and set to burn, the common punishment for witches and sorcerers, and his family was permitted to remove his body and bury it in a Carmelite church.

Glasya Labolas (Caacrinolaas, Caassimola, Glasyalabolas)   FALLEN ANGEL and 25th of the 72 SPIRITS OF SOLOMON. Glasya Labolas is a president in HELL. He appears as a winged dog. He can make men invisible and discern the past and the future. He is the leader of all homicides and incites people to bloodshed. He teaches all arts and science instantly. He commands 36 LEGIONs of DEMONs.

goblin   A wandering sprite who attaches itself to households and both helps and plagues the residents. Goblins are comparable to low-level DEMONs, not inherently evil but mischievous, the equivalent of brownies in England and Scotland, kobalds in Germany, domoviks in Russia. The Greeks called such spirits *kobaloi*, or "rogues" or "tricksters." *Goblin* is a French term. A hobgoblin is a nasty type of goblin, intent on doing harm.

Goblins live in grottoes, but they are attracted to homes that have beautiful children and plentiful wine. When they move in, they help by doing household chores at night and disciplining children—by giving them presents when they are good and punishing them when they are naughty. Goblins have an unpredictable, mischievous

nature, and instead of doing chores at night, they will sometimes keep everyone awake by banging pots and pans, moving furniture, knocking on walls and doors, and snatching bedclothes off sleeping persons. Goblins who become tiresome can be persuaded to leave by scattering flaxseed on the floor. The sprites get tired of cleaning it up every night.

Goblins have become associated with Halloween and are said to roam the night when the veil between the world of the living and the world of the dead is thinnest.

See BOGEY.

Gold-Finding Hen   A ritual for finding gold involving evocation of a DEMON. The Gold-Finding Hen ritual was popular with alchemists in the 18th and 19th centuries. The ritual tells how to hatch a magical hen, a black pullet, that can be commanded to search out hidden gold and other treasures. There are different versions of the ritual in various GRIMOIRES, or magical handbooks.

The *Red Dragon* (1822) tells how to do it with a demon's help. Secure a black hen that has never mated and do so without making the hen cackle. Take it to a CROSSROADS at midnight and trace a magic circle around you with a

Demon torments a greedy treasure hunter. (AUTHOR'S COLLECTION)

cypress rod. Say three times, "Eloim, Essaim, frugativi et appellavi." After making ritual movements, a demon will appear in a scarlet overcoat, a yellow vest, and pale green breeches. His head will be that of a dog, his ears those of an ass; his head will have two horns, and he will have the legs and hooves of a calf. The demon will ask for your orders, which he must obey at all costs. You can direct the demon to find treasures.

FURTHER READING:
Wright, Elbee. *The Book of Magical Talismans/The Black Pullet.* Minneapolis: Marlar, 1984.

Goodman's Ground (Guidman's Grunde)   In Scottish lore, a portion of farmland that is left uncultivated and ungrazed. The offering of Goodman's Ground was intended to avert misfortune, especially diseases among cattle. Other names were the *Halyman's Rig,* the *Goodman's Fauld,* the *Gi'en Rig,* the *Deevil's Craft, Clootie's Craft,* the *Black Faulie,* and *Given Ground.*

Christian Church authorities considered this pagan practice to be an offering to the DEVIL and levied heavy fines on farmers who observed it. Belief in the power of Goodman's Ground was often strong enough for farmers to resist the church and pay the fines, which were seen as preferable to courting disaster and risking the death of their cattle.

The Goodman's Ground played a part in the witchcraft trial of Jonet Wishert in Aberdeen in 1596. It was testified that Wishert was seen in his Goodman's Ground, naked from the waist down, bending over to kiss the Devil's anus.

The last fields dedicated to the "Auld Goodman" were finally ploughed at the beginning of the 19th century as a result of economic pressure.

Goodwin Possessions (1688)   Demonic POSSESSION of children in Boston, exorcized by the Puritan minister Cotton Mather. The possessions were blamed on a woman accused of WITCHCRAFT. Mather wrote about this case in his 1689 book *Memorable Providences,* which was widely read and circulated through Puritan New England and probably influenced public opinions in the SALEM WITCHCRAFT HYSTERIA of 1692–93.

The possessions began in the home of John Goodwin, a mason who lived in South Boston. Affected were four children ranging in age from three to 13. In the summer of 1688, the oldest child, Martha, went to fetch the family's laundry from their washerwoman, an Irish woman named Goodwife Glover. The woman was not well liked; her husband had even accused her of being a witch on his deathbed. Martha thought some of the laundry was missing and complained to Glover, who took offense at the insinuation of theft. Immediately, Martha began suffering fits and seizures. Within a few weeks, all four children were afflicted with physical tortures. Doctors were summoned but were baffled about the cause.

The severity of the tortures increased, but always the children would be able to rest in their beds at night. Other times, they were stricken deaf and dumb and had their limbs, tongues, and mouths pulled about and their skin stretched. They made pitiful, animalistic noises and moans.

Their father, John Goodwin, worried that he had committed some grievous sin that turned his pious "little Bethel" house into a "den for devils." Four ministers were asked to conduct a day of prayer, after which the youngest was permanently relieved of symptoms. Cotton Mather visited the family and prayed for DELIVERANCE and even took Martha into his own home for observation.

One of the boys saw a dark shape wearing a blue cap in the house; the shape tormented him and an invisible hand tried to pull out his bowels. The children said blows of invisible clubs rained down upon them. Voices in their heads urged them to do violent acts, such as strike friends or throw themselves down stairs or strangle themselves. They broke objects and laughed hysterically.

Glover was arraigned and put on trial, charged with witchcraft. Testimony was given that she allegedly had bewitched a person to death six years earlier. She acknowledged that she had been the black shape with the blue cap and invisible hand. Mather visited her twice in prison. He called her a "horrible old woman."

Glover did not deny the charges of witchcraft but said little about her activities as a witch. She acknowledged working with "the Prince," or the DEVIL, and four of his DEMONS. Mather urged her to break her PACT with HELL, but she said she could not do it unless her ANGELS allowed her to do so. She did not want Mather to pray for her, but he did anyway. When he finished, she took out a stone, spit on it, and worried it.

Glover was judged guilty and condemned to execution by hanging. Prior to her death, the almshouse where she had lived was plagued with mysterious banging noises. En route to her execution, she said that the children would not be relieved by her death, for others had a hand in it, and she named one other person.

The three children still afflicted were not relieved at the death of Glover; rather, matters grew worse. John, Jr., saw a specter in the house and was pushed and stabbed by it. The children barked like dogs, yowled like cats, and complained that they felt as though they were in a red-hot oven. Their bodies were covered with bruises and red marks.

The children would have periods of relief for a few weeks, and then the troubles would start again. The afflictions were the worst whenever ministers visited to pray. Martha enjoyed some relief upon her arrival in Mather's home but then declared that the devils found her, and she began suffering again. She vomited weird balls the size of eggs and said she could feel the chains of the dead witch upon her. If Mather read the Bible, her eyes went blank, and she writhed on the floor and howled. She could not say the names of God and Christ. A demon in the form of a spectral horse appeared on many occasions and took her on flights through the air.

The other suspect named by Glover died before she could be brought to trial. Mather and other ministers continued their prayers of deliverance and finally broke the possessions by November 1688. There was one final serious assault on Martha, when she said an invisible rope came about her neck and she choked until she was black in the face. Handprints were seen on her neck.

After that, the assaults of the demons dwindled in frequency and severity. At Christmastime, Martha and one sister were made drunk without having had any alcohol. In her final fit, Martha seemed to be and thought she was dying. The fit ended, and she recovered.

Mather was pleased with the case and considered it a fine example of righteousness overcoming the Devil.

FURTHER READING:
Burr, George Lincoln, ed. *Narratives of the Witchcraft Cases 1648–1706.* New York: Charles Scribner's Sons, 1914.
Middlekauff, Robert. *The Mathers: Three Generations of Puritan Intellectuals 1596–1728.* Berkeley: University of California Press, 1999.

Gospel of John   Biblical text used against DEMONs.
Although the reading of any Scripture sends a possessing demon into a tailspin, the words in the Gospel of John seem to cause the most discomfort. The beginning of the book, especially, sent medieval demoniacs into howling fits and tantrums. The following text appears in the King James version, much as 16th- and 17th-century exorcists would have read it:

> In the beginning was the Word, and the Word was with God, and the Word was God. The same was in the beginning with God. All things were made by him; and without him was not any thing made that was made. In him was life; and the life was the light of men. And the light shineth in darkness; and the darkness comprehended it not.
>
> John 1:1–5

> And the Word was made flesh, and dwelt among us, (and we beheld his glory, the glory as of the only begotton of the Father), full of grace and truth.
>
> John 1:14

If all things are made by God, then the Devil is also God's instrument, perhaps sent to test humans' faith. But can the Devil's claims and boasts be believed? In chapter 8, John tells that Jesus rebuked the Pharisees for not believing in him or his works, saying:

> If God were your Father, ye would love me; for I proceeded forth and came from God; neither came I of myself, but he sent me. Why do ye not understand my speech? even because ye cannot hear my word. Ye are of your father the devil, and the lusts of your father ye will do. He was a murderer from the beginning, and abode

not in the truth, because there is no truth in him. When he speaketh a lie, he speaketh of his own; for he is a liar, and the father of it.

John 8:42–44

The reasoning that any words spoken by the DEVIL were lies acted as a defense for many witches against their accusers. Claims that some poor soul had caused another to be possessed were looked on skeptically by early church inquisitors but not by later ones. Yet Catholic and Protestant exorcists alike believe in the ultimate power of God's word over the work of the Devil; he may be the "father of lies," but when confronted in the name of the Lord, the Devil is forced to yield and speak the truth.

Grandier, Urbain (d. 1634)   Priest framed and executed in the LOUDUN POSSESSIONS of Ursuline nuns in France. Urbain Grandier was brought down by his own arrogant charm and success, Reformation politics, and a spiteful nun he spurned. Burned alive at the stake, he was the only person to be executed in the case.

Grandier, son of a lawyer and nephew of Canon Grandier of Saintes, was born to a life of privilege. A bright and eloquent student, he was sent at age 14 to the Jesuit College of Bordeaux. He spent more than 10 years studying there and took his ordination as a Jesuit novice in 1615. A promising career lay ahead of him.

Grandier's Troubled Rise

At age 27, Grandier had accumulated many influential benefactors and was appointed curé, or parson, at Loudun. He also was made a canon of the collegial church of the Holy Cross. The town was sharply divided between the Protestant Huguenots, who abhorred the church, and Catholics.

Town opinions immediately were divided over Grandier. Women found him appealing and a significant improvement over his aged predecessor. Grandier was young, handsome, sophisticated, and interesting. He was given immediate entree into the highest social circles. He was flattering.

In times past, clerics could get away with quiet sexual escapades and affairs. But in the atmosphere at Loudun, disapproval of scandalous behavior was increasing. Grandier, a wayward priest, should have paid heed to the social climate, but instead he felt entitled to enjoy women, single and married, an attitude that earned him simmering animosity among Loudun's menfolk.

Professionally, he excelled in preaching and in performing his religious duties, which earned him resentment among his peers. He was able to stay out of trouble because he had the support and favor of the town's governor, Jean d'Armagnac.

Grandier, thinking himself to be invulnerable, made arrogant mistakes. He became embroiled in quarrels and did not hesitate to criticize the behavior of others, especially the Carmelites and Capuchins. He disparaged

their relics, a source of income, and caused them a loss of patronage.

One of Grandier's many amorous affairs was with Philippe Trincant, the daughter of Louis Trincant, the public prosecutor of Loudun, who was one of Grandier's staunchest allies. That Grandier, who had his choice of women, jeopardized his relationship with the prosecutor in such an unforgivable way reveals his arrogance. Philippe became pregnant and Grandier abandoned her, creating another great enemy in Louis Trincant. The prosecutor led an informal but growing group of citizens who wished to bring Grandier down for one reason or another.

Grandier then set his sights on Madeleine de Brou, 30, the unmarried daughter of René de Brou, a wealthy nobleman. Madeleine had turned away many suitors, preferring a pious life. Unexpectedly, Grandier actually fell in love with her. He persuaded her to marry him, angering her family and Pierre Menuau, the advocate of King Louis XIII, who had been trying to win Madeleine's hand for years.

Grandier's enemies complained to the bishop, Henry-Louis Chasteignier de la Rochepozay, who lived outside Paris, that Grandier was out of control. He was debauching married women and young girls in his precinct, was profane and impious, and did not read his breviary, among other crimes. The bishop, who despised Grandier, ordered him to be arrested and imprisoned. The case was adjourned, however, and Grandier was given time to clear himself with his superiors.

Instead, accusations of his impropriety were heaped upon him as townspeople came forward. He was accused of having sex with women on the floor of his own church. He touched women when talking to them. Grandier decided to appear voluntarily before the bishop rather than be humiliated by arrest. He was arrested anyway and taken to jail on November 15, 1629.

After two weeks in the cold and dank prison, Grandier petitioned the bishop for his release, claiming he had repented. The bishop's response was to increase his punishment. On January 3, 1630, Grandier was sentenced to fast on bread and water every Friday for three months and was forbidden to perform sacerdotal functions forever in Loudun and for five years in the Diocese of Poitiers. Such a sentence spelled ruin for Grandier, and he announced his intention to appeal the case. He had good odds of winning, for the archbishop was a close friend of Grandier's key supporter, Governor d'Armagnac.

Grandier's enemies appealed to the Parlement of Paris, claiming he should be tried by the nonsecular court. A trial date was set for August. Only six years earlier, a parson had been burned alive at the stake for committing adultery. Grandier's enemies hoped he would have the same fate.

The case went in Grandier's favor. Accusations from the townspeople were recanted, and Philippe's father decided to protect what little remained of his daughter's reputation by keeping silent about her illegitimate child fathered by Grandier. The archbishop remained supportive of Grandier.

Grandier was reinstated as curé, and he must have thought himself to be invulnerable. Friends advised him to be smart and leave Loudun, but he refused, perhaps to spite his enemies.

Grandier's Downfall

The event that sealed Grandier's doom at first seemed trivial. JEANNE DES ANGES, the mother superior of the Ursuline convent at Loudun, invited him to take the vacant post of canon. He declined, citing the press of too many other duties. He had never met Jeanne or been to the convent. Unbeknowst to him, Jeanne was harboring a secret sexual obsession with him, and he had been the object of salacious gossip among the nuns for some time.

Jeanne, a mean and vindictive woman, was stung. The man she appointed to fill the post, Canon Mignon, disliked Grandier. He became privy to the sexual secrets of the nuns, their nervous temperments, and their ghost pranks in their haunted convent. It was soon easy to let them run out of control and become bewitched and beset by DEMONS. Mignon conspired with Grandier's enemies to let it be known that he was responsible for their afflictions.

Grandier shrugged off these stories, confident no one would believe them. As fantastic as they were, the stories found an audience not only among his enemies, but in the fertile political territory of Catholics and Protestants trying to sway the faithful with demonstrations of their spiritual firepower. Nothing played better for the Catholics than demonic possession.

Soon the nuns were giving hysterical performances for swelling crowds, under the exorcisms of Mignon and a Franciscan, FATHER GABRIEL LACTANCE, and a Capuchin, Father Tranquille. Both Lactance and Tranquille were believers in the demonic.

Torture and Death

On August 18, Grandier was convicted and sentenced to be tortured and burned alive at the stake, and his ashes scattered to the winds. The sentence also stated that he would be forced to kneel at St. Peter's Church and the Ursuline convent and ask for forgiveness. A commemorative plaque would be placed in the Ursuline convent at a cost of 150 livres, to be paid for out of Grandier's confiscated estate. The sentence was to be carried out immediately.

Grandier made an eloquent speech of his innocence to the stone-faced judges. So moved were the spectators, however, that many burst into tears, forcing the judges to clear the room. Grandier refused the last services of Lactance and Tranquille and made his final prayers. The exorcists, pushing Grandier's alleged guilt to the maximum, insisted that when he said the word *God* he really meant "Satan."

In anticipation of a guilty verdict and execution, about 30,000 people had flocked to Loudun to witness the spectacle.

Grandier's body was shaved, but his fingernails were not ripped out because the surgeon refused to obey the court. In the interests of moving matters along, that punishment was forgone. He was then prepared for the *question extraordinaire,* the confession of his crimes.

Lactance and Tranquille exorcized the ropes, boards, and mallets of torture, lest the demons interfere and relieve Grandier's suffering. The curé was bound, stretched out on the floor, and tied from his knees to his feet to four oak boards. The outer boards were fixed and the inner boards were movable. Wedges were driven between the pairs so that his legs were crushed. The excruciating crushing took about 45 minutes. At every blow, Grandier was asked to confess, and he refused. The final hammer blows were delivered by Lactance and Tranquille. Grandier's smashed legs were poked, inducing more pain. The exorcists declared that the Devil had rendered him insensible to pain.

For two more hours, Grandier was cajoled to sign the confession prepared for him, but he steadfastly refused, saying it was morally impossible for him to do so. The court finally gave up and sent him off to the stake.

Grandier was dressed in a shirt soaked in sulfur and a rope was tied around his neck. He was seated in a mule-drawn cart and hauled through the streets, with a procession of the judges behind him. At the door of St. Peter's Church, the procession halted and a two-pound candle was placed in Grandier's hands. He was lifted down and urged to beg pardon for his crimes. Grandier could not kneel because of his crushed legs and fell on his face. He was lifted up and held by one of his supporters, Father

Father Urbain Grandier is burned at the stake. (AUTHOR'S COLLECTION)

Grillau, who prayed for him as both of them wept in a piteous scene. The onlookers were ordered not to pray for Grandier, for they would be committing a sin.

At the Ursuline convent, the same procedure was repeated, and Grandier was asked to pardon Jeanne and all the nuns. He said he had never done them any harm and could only pray that God would forgive them for what they had done.

Father René Bernier, who had testified against Grandier, came forward to ask for Grandier's forgiveness and offered to say a mass for him.

The place of execution was the Place Saint-Croix, which was jammed with spectators. Everyone who had a window had rented it out to capacity. More spectators sat on the church's roof. Guards had to fight a way through the throng to reach the 15-foot stake driven into the ground near the north wall of the church. Faggots were piled at the base of the stake.

Grandier was tied to a small iron seat fastened to the stake, facing the grandstand, where his enemies drank wine in celebration. He had been promised strangulation by the noose around his neck prior to the start of the fire.

The Capuchin friars exorcized the site, including the wood, straw, and coals that would start the blaze and the earth, the air, the victim, the executioners, and the spectators. The exorcisms were done again to prevent the interference of demons to mitigate Grandier's suffering and pain. His death was to be as excruciating as possible.

Grandier made several attempts to speak, but the friars silenced him with douses of holy water and blows to his mouth with an iron crucifix. Lactance still demanded a confession, but Grandier gave none. He asked Lactance for the "kiss of peace," customarily granted to the condemned. At first, Lactance refused, but the crowd protested, and so he angrily complied, kissing Grandier's cheek.

Grandier said he would soon meet the judgment of God, and so, eventually, would Lactance. At that, Lactance lit the fire, followed by Tranquille and another exorcist, Father Archangel. The executioner moved quickly to strangle Grandier but discovered that the noose had been secretly knotted by the Capuchins so that it could not be tightened. The friars doused some of the flames with holy water to exorcise any remaining demons. Left to burn alive, Grandier began screaming.

A large black fly appeared, which the exorcists took as a sign of BEELZEBUB, the Lord of the Flies. Grandier's body was consumed in flames. Then a flock of pigeons appeared, wheeling around the fire. Grandier's enemies took this as a sign of demons, and his supporters took it as a sign of the Holy Ghost.

When the fire burned itself out, the executioner shoveled the ashes to the four cardinal points. Then the crowd surged forward to scavenge grisly souvenirs of teeth, bits of bone, and handfuls of ashes, to be used in CHARMS and spells. The relics of a sorcerer were considered to be quite powerful. When all were gone, the satisfied crowd dispersed to eat and drink.

Later, back at the Ursuline convent, Jeanne was exorcized again. She said the fly was the demon Baruch, who had been intent on trying to throw the priests' exorcism book into the fire. She confirmed that Grandier really had prayed to Satan, not to God. She said he suffered an excruciating death thanks to the exorcisms of the priests, and that he was suffering special torments in HELL.

Jeanne and the other nuns were remorseful about Grandier and worried that they had sinned. Soon, however, the priest was forgotten, as the possessions and exorcisms continued. Tranquille and Lactance suffered demonic problems themselves and died.

FURTHER READING:
Certeau, Michel de. *The Possession at Loudun*. Translated by Michael B. Smith. Chicago: University of Chicago Press, 2000.
Ferber, Sarah. *Demonic Possession and Exorcism in Early Modern France*. London: Routledge, 2004.
Huxley, Aldous. *The Devils of Loudun*. New York: Harper and Brothers, 1952.

griffin-demon   An Assyrian guardian against evil spirits. The griffin-demon is a hybrid with a human body and bird head and wings. Figurines of griffin-demons were placed in foundations of houses and palaces to ward off DEMONS.

grimoires   Handbooks of magic that provide instructions for rituals, the casting of spells, the procuring of treasure and love, the procuring of FAMILIARS, and the evocation and control of spirits, including DEMONS and ANGELS, to perform tasks. *Grimoire* is a French term for "grammar book."

Although any handbook of magic could be called a grimoire, the term usually applies to specific texts that claim the magical knowledge of King SOLOMON as their source. The material in grimoires is heavily derivative of Hebrew magical and mystical lore, involving the names, powers, and duties of spirits and the powerful names of God. Other principal sources are Hellenistic Greek and Egyptian magical texts and folk magic.

Most of the principal grimoires were written in the 17th and 18th centuries but claimed to be much older. They were popular well into the 19th century. Printed on cheap paper, grimoires circulated primarily in France and Italy. They are still consulted, but modern magicians have written their own textbooks of magic.

Grimoires give instructions for rituals to conjure and control spirits and cosmic forces for protection, wealth, luck, supernatural power, CURSES on enemies, and so forth. They instruct the magician on what to wear, what tools to use, how to purify himself, and what prayers and incantations to recite at precise astrological times and various hours of the day and night, according to the ruling spirits. They give recipes for fumigations, descriptions of the creation of magic circles, magic triangles, pentacles, AMULETS, TALISMANS, seals and sigils, instructions on sacrifices, and ways to deal with unruly demons, including rites of EXORCISM.

Some grimoires are devoted to theurgy, or white magic, while others concern goetia, or black magic. Some include both. The attainment of treasure and love and the ability to harm one's enemies are prominent throughout the grimoires. Some were printed in red ink and were said to burn the eyes if gazed at too long.

The following are the grimoires of significance:

Key of Solomon   The most important grimoire is the *Key of Solomon*, also called the *Greater Key of Solomon* and the *Clavicle of Solomon*. This text is the source for most other grimoires. The book is attributed to the legendary King Solomon, who asked God for wisdom and commanded an army of demons (DJINN) to do his bidding and build great works. In the first century C.E., the Jewish historian Josephus mentioned a book of incantations for summoning and thwarting demons that was attributed to the authorship of Solomon. Josephus said that a Jew named Eleazar used it to cure cases of POSSESSION. Josephus may have been referring to the *Key*, but some historians believe it was the Testament of Solomon (discussed later) or, more likely, a different text altogether.

The *Key* is mentioned in literature throughout the centuries, and over time it grew in size and content. So many versions of this grimoire were written that the original text is uncertain. A Greek version that dates to 1100–1200 C.E. is part of the collection in the British Museum. From the 14th century on, Solomonic magical works took on increasing importance. Around 1350, Pope Innocent VI ordered that a grimoire called *The Book of Solomon* be burned; later, in 1559, the Inquisition condemned Solomon's grimoire again as dangerous. The *Key of Solomon* was widely distributed in the 17th century. Hundreds of copies of the *Key*, in differing versions, still exist. Supposedly, the original manuscript was written in Hebrew, but no such text is known.

Lemegeton   Another grimoire attributed to Solomon is the *Lemegeton*, or *Lesser Key of Solomon*. The origin and meaning of *Lemegeton* are not known. The book also was known as *Liber Spirituum* (see later discussion) and *Liber Officiorum*. Claims were made that the *Lemegeton* was originally written in Chaldean and Hebrew, but these are doubtful. The earliest perfect examples of it are in French. The material probably is derived in part from the *Testament of Solomon* (discussed later) and also the apocryphal book of Enoch. Part of the *Lemegeton* was published in Latin by the demonologist JOHANN WEYER in 1563, entitled *Pseudomonarchia Daemonum* (*Pseudo-monarchy of demons*). REGINALD SCOT translated part of it into his *Discoverie of Witchcraft* (1584).

The book is divided into four parts: Goetia, Theurgia, the Pauline Art, and the Almadel. The Almadel was mentioned in writing around 1500. Goetia is devoted to evil spirits. Theurgia (or Theurgia-Goetia, as it is also called) is devoted to both good and evil spirits and all aerial spir-

The Devil and a sorcerer exchange copies of a book of black magic and the Gospels. (AUTHOR'S COLLECTION)

its. The Pauline Art concerns the spirits who govern the planets, the signs of the zodiac, and the hours of the day and night. The Almadel concerns 20 chief spirits who govern the four quarters and the 360 degrees of the zodiac. Goetia is the part published by Weyer. Waite speculated that Goetia is the original *Lemegeton* and the other three parts were unknown to Weyer and were added at a later time.

The *Lemegeton* lists 72 FALLEN ANGELS, their titles, seals, duties, and powers, and the angels who can thwart them. The number 72 may have been inspired by the Schemhamphorae, 72 angels who bear the Names of God, which are given in Hebrew Scripture and are expressed at the end of every verse. The verses are used in invocation and in magic. The Schemhamphorae function as names of power. The 72 demons in the *Lemegeton* possess teaching skills for the sciences and art, as well as the ability to cause terrible diseases and disasters. Few have any healing ability.

Testament of Solomon   The Testament of Solomon is a Greek text in the pseudepigrapha written between the first and third centuries C.E. It tells the story of how King Solomon built the Temple of Jerusalem by commanding demons. The text is rich in demonology, angelology, and lore about medicine, astrology, and magic. The author probably was familiar with the Babylonian Talmud.

The text says that stellar bodies are demonic, wielding destructive power over the affairs of humanity. The 36 decans, or 10-degree portions of the zodiac, are called heavenly bodies and likewise are ruled by demons, who cause mental and physical illnesses. There are seven "world rulers," who are equated with the vices of deception, strife, fate, distress, error, power, and "the worst," each of whom is thwarted by a particular angel (with the exception of "the worst").

The testament provides a significant contribution to the legends of Solomon's magical powers and the magical handbooks attributed to Solomon. It is not a grimoire of magical instruction, however.

Grand Grimoire This French grimoire was probably authored in the 17th or 18th century. The earliest edition of it bears no date or place of publication. One version of it claims to date to 1522. Its full title is *The Grand Grimoire, with the Powerful Clavicle of Solomon and of Black Magic; or the Infernal Devices of the Great Agrippa for the Discovery of all Hidden Treasures and the Subjugation of every Denomination of Spirits, together with an Abridgment of all the Magical Arts.* The editor, Venitiana del Rabina, said he translated the work from the writings of Solomon himself, which came into his possession.

The *Grand Grimoire* is a text of black magic. It has the same chief demons as the *Grimorium Verum* and nearly the same subordinate officers but describes different duties for them. The book is especially significant for its feature of a specific PACT between the magician and LUCIFUGE ROFOCALE, the prime minister of LUCIFER, who makes his only appearance in all literature in this grimoire alone. However, his last name, *Rofocale,* may be an anagram of FOCALOR, a demon named in the *Lemegeton.*

The book also includes instructions for necromancy.

Grimorium Verum Drawn from the *Greater Key of Solomon* and written in French, this book probably was written in the mid-18th century. Claims were made that it was translated from Hebrew by a Dominican Jesuit named Plaingiere and was published by "Alibeck the Egyptian" in 1517. Its full title is *Grimorium Verum, or the Most Approved Keys of Solomon the Hebrew Rabbin, wherein the Most Hidden Secrets, both Natural and Supernatural, are immediately exhibited, but it is necessary that the Demons should be contented on their part.*

The *Grimorium Verum* nearly copies the *Key of Solomon* in instructions for preparation of the magician and his tools but provides different instructions for the preparation of the virgin parchment and for the evocation and dismissal of spirits. There is an entirely different hierarchy of demons, who number 30 and who report to three leaders, Lucifer, BEELZUBUB, and ASTAROTH, who have among them six deputy chiefs.

The material also shows influences from *Lemegeton.* It includes the "Admirable Secrets" of the pseudo-Albertus Magnus, or *Little Albert* (see later), which appear in other later grimoires. The *Grimorium Verum* covers the "Genuine Sanctum Regnum," or the true method of making pacts.

Fourth Book Authorship is attributed to the occultist Henry Cornelius Agrippa, but the book, supposedly the fourth volume of Agrippa's monumental three-volume *Occult Philosophy,* was written by an unknown author. It is also known as the *Liber Spirituum* and is in the opening of the *Lemegeton.* The *Fourth Book* appeared after the death of Agrippa in 1535 and rehashes in an informal way much of the material in *Occult Philosophy.* Weyer, a student of Agrippa, rejected it as a forgery, as did other occultists.

As the *Lemegeton* does, the *Fourth Book* gives instructions for communicating with evil spirits. It covers the names of spirits associated with the planets and their characters, sigils, and pentacles. There are rituals for evoking both good and evil spirits and for practicing necromancy.

Waite called the *Fourth Book* "muddled" and said its lack of precision rendered it ineffective as a manual of magic.

Grimoire of Honorius Also called the *Constitution of Honorius,* this text may have been authored in the 16th century but was first published in Rome in 1629. It gained wide circulation during the 17th century. The authorship is attributed to Pope Honorius III (r. 1216–27), who is credited with rites of exorcism. The book shows influences from the *Lemegeton* and claims to be based on the practical Kabbalah, but this connection is tenuous. Rather, it is the only grimoire to introduce significant Christian elements, which earned it the reputation of the blackest of black magic texts. The grimoire is cast as a papal bull in which the pope decrees that the authorities of the church, from cardinals to secular clerks, should have the power of invoking and commanding spirits of all sorts. This power had been vested with the papal office as the successor to St. Peter.

The rituals in *Honorius* combine kabbalistic elements such as the 72 sacred names of God and Christian elements such as confessions, litanies, masses of the Holy Ghost and angels, the office of the dead, the GOSPEL OF JOHN, and various prayers with gruesome sacrifices of animals. The effect is more like a BLACK MASS than anything sacred.

The 1670 edition of *Honorius* includes a rite of exorcism for both humans and animals. The 1800 edition calls for using holy water in human exorcisms. In animal possessions, it prescribes the use of salt exorcized with BLOOD drawn from a bewitched animal.

As a magical text, it is viewed as having little foundation and probably was written for commercial appeal. It is not to be confused with *The Sworn Book of Honorius,* credited to the authorship of Honorius of Thebes, master magician. Waite said that the grimoire "must be avoided, were it necessary at the present day to warn any one against practices to which no one is likely to resort, which belong to the foolish mysteries of old exploded doctrines, and are interesting assuredly, but only as curiosities of the past."

Arbatel of Magic The *Arbatel of Magic* is a slim text written in Latin and published in Basel, Switzerland, in 1575. It was translated into German in 1686. The authorship is not known, but it is speculated the person may have been Italian, because of several obscure references to Italian history. The book refers to "Theophrastic Magic," indicating influences of Paracelsus. It has no connection to the Solomonic writings and does not even mention

Solomon; rather, it has strong Christian elements. Waite considered it representative of "transcendental magic."

The *Arbatel* purports to be a nine-volume work of instructions on the magical arts, but only the first volume, or tome, is extant. It is uncertain whether the other eight tomes were ever written; perhaps, the anonymous author intended to write them but failed to follow through. The first tome is called *Isagoge,* which means "essential or fundamental instruction."

Isagoge comprises Seven Septenaries of aphorisms of a moral and spiritual nature that cite the sources of occult wisdom: God, angels, learned men, nature (stones, herbs, and so forth), apostate spirits, ministers of punishment in HELL (comparable to the avenging classical gods), and the spirits of the elements. The wisdom obtainable from these sources ranges from the low magic of finding treasures to alchemical transmutations to mystical knowledge of God. Meditation, love of God, and living in accordance with the virtues are emphasized as the best means for practicing the magical arts.

Theosophia Pneumatica Also known as *The Little Keys of Solomon,* this grimoire was published in 1686 in German. It possibly was included in the German edition of the *Arbatel of Magic,* a work it follows closely. Of anonymous authorship, the *Theosophia Pneumatica* makes no claims to ancient origins. Like the *Arbatel,* it is Christian in orientation and holds that the exaltation of prayer is the end of the Mystery. The Hebrew term *Talmud*—derived from the verb for "to learn"—is used to describe the aspiring magician. The author also was knowledgeable about alchemy and included references to it.

The only section of the *Theosophia Pneumatica* that differs significantly from the *Arbatel* is the appendix, which contains strong Christian elements and terminology used by the Swiss alchemist Paracelsus. It affirms that all things are threefold in nature after the model of the Father, Son, and Holy Ghost. Man is threefold, having a body, soul, and rational spirit. The body is of the earth. The soul is of the elements derived through the stars, is the seat of understanding, and is the genius for arts and sciences. The rational spirit is from God and is the medium through which divine inspiration enters the physical body. The soul and rational spirit are joined in marriage by God to reside in the body. Regeneration is achieved when the rational spirit overcomes the soul. There are two kinds of death: deterioration of the body and destruction of the soul via poisoned stellar influences. In either case, the rational spirit departs; it may also depart at the will of God. It is not possible to cure certain diseases by which God has chosen to afflict humankind. The unicorn, Quintessence, azoth, and philosopher's stone are all useless. All other diseases can be cured with natural magic and alchemy.

Heptameron Also called *Magical Elements,* this book is attributed to Peter of Abano, an Italian physician who died in 1316 after being condemned to death by the Inquisition. Abano is not believed to be the author. The *Heptameron* probably was written in the 16th century and may have been intended as a supplement to the *Fourth Book.*

The grimoire is a composite work of white and black magic that deals with finding treasure, procuring love, detecting secrets, opening locks, fomenting hatred and evil thoughts, and so on. It is divided into two parts: the evocation of the Spirits of the Air, who are demons, and a set of angelic evocations for each day of the week.

Little Albert Also titled *Marvelous Secrets of the Natural and Cabalistic Magic of Little Albert,* this text was published in 1722. Material from it appear in various grimoires.

The Enchiridion of Pope Leo This book is technically not a grimoire: It offers no instructions for magical rituals but is a collection of charms turned into prayers, accompanied by mysterious figures supposedly taken from rare old manuscripts.

According to the story of the book's alleged origins, Pope Leo III (r. 795–816) gave the Emperor of the West Charlemagne a collection of prayers after his coronation in Rome in 800. The collection had special properties: Whoever carried it about on his person with the proper attitude—respect for the Scripture—and recited it daily in the honor of God would have divine protection for his entire life. He would never be defeated by his enemies and would escape all dangers without harm. The text claims that Charlemagne, who enjoyed great fortune, wrote a letter of thanks in his own hand to Pope Leo III, which is still preserved in the Vatican Library.

This collection of prayers was published as the *Enchiridion* for the first time in Rome in 1523. A second edition is said to have been issued in 1606 and a final edition in 1660. The book was probably composed in the 17th century and given the legend to lend it authenticity. Charlemagne may not have been literate, and no letters of his are extant.

The *Enchiridion's* charms are dressed up as prayers, but few are spiritual in nature; they are instead concerned with material things such as acquiring wealth, happiness, and advantage and protecting ones self against all kinds of dangers, misfortunes, natural disasters, and evils. The text denies any association with magic, but in the fashion of magic, it describes a ritual for its proper use. The book must be kept clean in a bag of new leather. It must be carried on the person, and at least one page of it must be read with devotion every day. Specific pages can be read for various needs. To read from the book, one must face east and kneel, for this, claims the *Enchiridion,* is what Charlemagne did.

Pseudomonarchia Daemonum More a text about demons and demonology than a grimoire, this was written around 1583 by Johann Weyer. It lists 68 of the 72 demons found in the *Lemegeton* but does not give their seals or rituals.

Alberti Parvi Lucii Liber de Mirabilibus Naturae Arcanis Attributed falsely to the authorship of St. Albertus Magnus, this grimoire was published in Lyons, France, with the kabbalistic date of 6516. It gives instructions for making philters, interpreting dreams, discovering treasure, making a hand of glory (a black magic charm), making a ring that confers invisibility, and performing other magical acts.

The following texts were written in the 18th and 19th centuries and are often called grimoires:

The Book of Sacred Magic of Abra-Melin the Mage Authorship is attributed to Abra-Melin (also spelled *Abramelin*), a Jewish kabbalistic mage of Wurzburg, Germany, who supposedly wrote the grimoire for his son in 1458. The manuscript, written in French in the 18th century, claims to be a translation of the original Hebrew manuscript. The book was a major influence in the 19th-century occult revival led by the Hermetic Order of the Golden Dawn. ALEISTER CROWLEY borrowed from it for his own rituals to master demons.

The book comprises three books, all derivative of the *Key of Solomon*. According to lore, Abra-Melin said he learned his magical knowledge from angels, who told him how to conjure and tame demons into personal servants and workers and how to raise storms. He said that all things in the world were created by demons, who worked under the direction of angels, and that each individual had an angel and a demon as familiar spirits. The basis for his system of magic, he said, may be found in the Kabbalah.

The magical system is based on the power of numbers and sacred names and involves the construction of numerous magical squares for such purposes as invisibility, flying, commanding spirits, necromancy, shape shifting, and scores of other feats. Rituals for conjuring spirits, creating magic squares, and making seals and sigils are elaborate and must be followed exactly in accordance with astrological observances.

True Black Magic Also called *The Secrets of Secrets,* this black magic grimoire purportedly was written in the 1600s by a magician named Toscraec, who claimed that it was based on a centuries-old manuscript written in an unknown language. Toscraec said he was only able to translate the manuscript with the help of an angel. It probably was written in the 18th century.

True Black Magic is a goetic adaptation of the *Key of Solomon*. In the book, claims are made that the manuscript was found in the tomb of Solomon, and it was translated from the Hebrew in 1750 by the magus Iroe-Grego. It includes 45 talismans, their properties and uses, and "all magical characters known unto this day." The grimoire quotes Solomon as saying that divine love must precede the acquisition of magical wisdom.

The Black Pullet According to lore, this grimoire was published in Egypt in 1740, but it was probably authored in the late 18th century in Rome or in France. *The Black Pullet* is one of the few grimoires that do not claim to be manuscripts of antiquity. It does not link itself to Solomonic magic but shows influences of the spurious *Fourth Book*. It places particular emphasis on 20 magic talismans and 20 corresponding magic rings, plus two talismans of a magic circle and a magic rod or wand. It disavows all connections to black magic. It has appeared in altered versions as *Treasure of the Old Man of the Pyramids* and *Black Screech Owl*. The 22 talismans have been linked to the 22 trumps of the Tarot.

The Black Pullet tells a colorful story about itself and its alleged origins. The original—and ambitious—French title of the grimoire was *The Black Pullet, or the Hen with the Golden Eggs, comprising the Science of Magic Talismans and Rings, the Art of Necromancy and of the Kabbalah, for the Conjuration of Aerial and Infernal Spirits, of Sylphs, Undines, and Gnomes, for the acquisition of the Secret Sciences, for the Discovery of Treasures, for obtaining power to command all beings, and to unmask all Sciences and Bewitchments, The whole following the Doctrines of Socrates, Pythagorus* [sic]*, Zoroaster, Son of the Grand Aromasis, and other philosophers whose works in the MS. escaped the conflagration of the Library of Ptolemy, Translated from the language of the Magi and that of the Hieroglyphs by the Doctors Mizzaboula-Jabamia, Danhuzerus, Nehmahmiah, Judahim, and Eliaeb, Rendered into French by A.J.S.D.R.L.G.F.*

The Black Pullet claims it is the narrative of an unnamed man who was a member of Napoleon's armed forces sent to Egypt. With several companions, he went to the pyramids outside Cairo, where they all stopped for lunch. They were attacked by Arabs, and all but the author were killed. He was left for dead. When he regained consciousness, he assumed he would soon be dead because he had been abandoned in the desert and delivered a farewell to the setting Sun.

Suddenly, a stone rolled back in the Great Pyramid, and a man walked out. The soldier could tell by his turban that he was a Turk. As luck would have it, the soldier knew the Turkish language and could communicate. The Turk revived him with liquor and took him inside the pyramid, which was revealed to be the magical home of the mysterious man.

The soldier was astonished to find vast halls, endless galleries, subterranean chambers, and piles of treasures, all ministered by spirits. There were blazing lamps and magic suppers. A genius, or FAMILIAR, named Odous was the special attendant of the Turk. The soldier was also shown *The Black Pullet*, a text that was like a version of Aladdin and the magic lamp, but with an inner meaning conferred by the demon ASTAROTH. The magical power was created with talismans embroidered on silk and rings made of bronzed steel.

The Turk said he was the only heir to this magic, which was based on Egyptian hieroglyphs. He told the soldier he was near death. He possessed a magic talisman that enabled him to be fluent in 22 languages. The Turk conveyed to the soldier all the secrets of the book, and then immediately he died on his sofa. The soldier fell into a swoon.

When he recovered, the soldier left the pyramid, accompanied by Odous, who was now under his command, and taking with him *The Black Pullet,* the ashes of the Turk, and piles of treasures. He sailed for Marseilles and settled in Provence, where he spent the rest of his days experimenting with the secrets of the book. He published the book and created a magic talisman that would affect anyone who pirated it with ears six inches longer than Midas'.

The talismans of *The Black Pullet* are, in more modern times, embroidered onto silk but are best engraved on silver, gold, or metals resembling them. They are sometimes used alone rather than in conjunction with the rings.

Once armed with the talismans and rings, the spirits can be commanded. The evocation for Odous is "Thomatos, Benesser, Flianter," which first summons 37 spirits. Address them by saying "Litan, Izer, Osnas," and they will bow down before you. Say "Nanther" as each one does. The command "Soutram Urbarsinens" will cause the spirits to transport you through the air wherever you wish to go, and they will return you home upon the command "Rabiam."

A major section of *The Black Pullet* tells how to procure a GOLD-FINDING HEN.

Red Dragon Published in 1822 but reported to date back to 1522, this is nearly identical to the *Grand Grimoire.* Later editions of *Red Dragon* incorporated the instructions for the Gold-Finding Hen from *The Black Pullet.*

Transcendental Magic This book comprises the occultist Eliphas Levi's own system of magic and was published in 1896. The occultist A. E. Waite called it a grimoire of "absolute science." Levi based his system on the *Key of Solomon,* adding his own views based upon his experiences in magic and alchemy.

The Book of Black Magic and of Pacts Written in 1898 by Waite, the book discusses other grimoires and provides a "Complete Grimoire of Black Magic." Waite draws upon and compares different grimoires in discussing rituals and the fundamentals of magic.

FURTHER READING:
Butler, E. M. *Ritual Magic.* Cambridge: Cambridge University Press, 1949.
Cavendish, Richard. *The Black Arts.* New York: G.P. Putnam's Sons, 1967.
Grillot de Givry, Emile. *Witchcraft, Magic and Alchemy.* 1931. Reprint, New York: Dover, 1971.
Levi, Eliphas. *Transcendental Magic.* 1896. Reprint, York Beach, Me.: Samuel Weiser, 2001.
Mathers, S. L. MacGregor. *The Book of the Sacred Magic of Abra-Melin the Mage.* Wellingborough, England: Aquarian Press, 1976.
Thompson, C. J. S. *The Mysteries and Secrets of Magic.* New York: Barnes & Noble, 1993.
Waite, Arthur Edward. *The Book of Black Magic and of Pacts.* 1899. Reprint, York Beach, Me.: Samuel Weiser, 1972.
Wright, Elbee. *The Book of Magical Talismans/The Black Pullet.* Minneapolis: Marlar, 1984.

grotto A local organized group of Satanists, as well as the regular meeting place of groups of Satanists. The term originated with the Church of Satan, founded in 1966 in San Francisco, which set up grottoes around the United States. In the mid-1970s, the grottoes were dissolved and the church was reorganized as a secret society. Other Satanist organizations also use the term *grotto* for their local chapters.

Guazzo, Francesco-Maria (17th century) Italian friar and demonologist. Francesco-Maria Guazzo is best known as the author of *Compendium Maleficarum* (*Handbook of Witches*), a leading inquisitor's guide published in 1608.

Little is known about Guazzo's life. He joined the Brethren of St. Ambrose ad Nemus and St. Barnabas in Milan. He wrote the *Compendium* over a three-year period in response to a request from Cardinal Federico Borromeo,

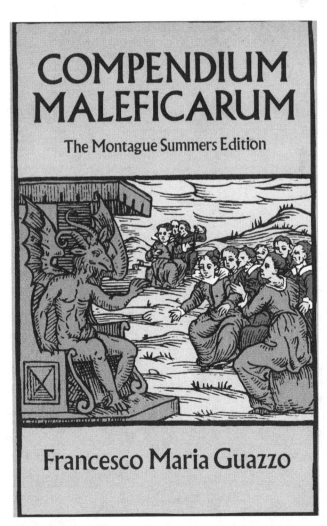

Guazzo's Compendium Maleficarum (AUTHOR'S COLLECTION)

the archbishop of Milan. The book, published in 1608, draws upon the works of other demonologists and repeats some of the superstitions of the time, including the assertion that MARTIN LUTHER was born from the union of the DEVIL and a nun.

Guazzo served as a judge and assessor in WITCHCRAFT trials. In 1605, he was sent to Cleves to advise in a case involving the serene duke John William of Julich-Cleves. The duke accused a 90-year-old warlock, John, of overlooking and ensorcelling him. John confessed that he used CHARMS and runes to afflict the duke with a wasting sickness and "frenzy." He was found guilty and sentenced to be burned at the stake. Before the sentence could be carried out, John committed suicide by slicing his throat with a knife. According to Guazzo, the Devil himself stood at John's side as he died.

The duke asked Guazzo to assist in other witchcraft cases in Germany, and he did.

The *Compendium* became the leading witch handbook in Italy and has been compared to the *MALLEUS MALEFICARUM*. Guazzo never achieved the personal fame of some of his contemporaries such as NICHOLAS REMY or JEAN BODIN, probably because he did not oversee witch trials and interrogations himself.

FURTHER READING:
Guazzo, Francesco-Maria. *Compendium Maleficarum*. Secaucus, N.J.: University Books, 1974.

Gusion (Gusayn)   FALLEN ANGEL and fourth of the 72 SPIRITS OF SOLOMON. In HELL, Gusion is a duke who appears as a cynocephalus (*xenophilus*). He discerns the past, present, and future; answers all questions; confers honor and dignity; and reconciles enemies. He commands 40 LEGIONS of DEMONS.

Hades In Greek mythology, the god who rules the underworld of the dead. Hades is the son of the Titans Cronus and Rhea. With one of his brothers, Zeus, he plots to overthrow their father Cronus, the god of time. Hades; Zeus, god of Olympus; and another brother, Poseidon, god of the sea, drew lots to divide up the world, and Hades fared the worst, getting the underworld.

Hades seeks to increase the population of his kingdom and prevent anyone from leaving. The gates of his abode, also called Hades, are guarded by the three-headed dog CERBERUS. Hades' wife is Persephone, whom he abducted to the underworld.

Hades also is the god of wealth, because of the precious metals mined from the earth; he is also called Pluto (the rich one or the hidden one).

He has a helmet that makes him invisible.

See HELL.

Hagenti (Haagenti) FALLEN ANGEL and 48th of the 72 SPIRITS OF SOLOMON. Hagenti is a president who rules 33 LEGIONs of DEMONs. He appears in the shape of a bull with griffin wings but will change into human form when commanded by a magician. He turns wine into water, transmutes all metals into gold, and imparts wisdom.

Haizmann, Christopher (Christoph) Joseph (17th century) Minor Bavarian painter who announced in 1677 that he had signed a PACT with the DEVIL and was tormented by DEMONs for the rest of his life.

Christopher Haizmann was seized with an "unnatural convulsion" on August 29, 1677. He went to the police and asked for protection, claiming that nine years earlier, he had sold his soul to SATAN. The police granted his request.

Haizmann wrote and illustrated the story of his infernal pact. He stated that the Devil one day had appeared to him as a burgher with a large black dog and asked him why he was distressed and sad. "He would help me out of my distress if I were willing to subscribe myself in ink to him to be his son; he would assist and help me in every possible way," Haizmann wrote.

The painter agreed to a nine-year contract. A pact was drawn up and signed in Haizmann's BLOOD. Over the ensuing years, the Devil appeared to him many times in various grotesque shapes, including that of a dragon with breasts and talons. Satan also sent him visions of HELL, which Haizmann described as "filled with burning flames and terrible stench. In it there was a large cauldron from which came heart-rending moans and groans of human beings; on its edge sat a hellish devil who did nothing but pour flaming resin, sulphur and pitch over them."

When the end of his contract approached, Haizmann grew anxious about his own fate. Sent by the local police to a holy shrine at Mariazell, Haizmann underwent several days of EXORCISM, during which the Virgin Mary recovered the pact from the Devil. Less than a year later, Haizmann, complaining of continuing torment by the

Devil, reappeared at the shrine and underwent another exorcism. This time, the Virgin Mary ripped up the pact.

Haizmann committed himself to a Bavarian monastery but still could not live in peace. He spent the rest of his life tormented by visions of the Devil and his demons. He died in 1700.

A noted Viennese librarian and researcher, the court councilor Dr. Rudolf Payer-Thurn found a document prepared at Mariazell that described Haizmann's exorcism. He showed the document to Sigmund Freud and asked for Freud's analysis of the case. Originally appearing in *Imago* in 1923, Freud's "Eine Teufelsneurose im Siebzehnten Jahrhundert" ("A devil neurosis of the seventeenth century") is considered a key document in Freudian psychoanalysis.

The Mariazell papers, including paintings made by Haizmann during his possession, led Freud to believe the following:

1. Rather feminine self-depictions of Haizmann in his paintings show Haizmann as suppressing homosexual tendencies.
2. Multiple breasts in the paintings show Haizmann's sexual associations with the Devil.
3. The number 9—there is a nine-year gap between Haizmann's pact with the Devil and its implementation, and nine days in which Haizmann resisted the Devil—represents pregnancy fantasies.
4. A penis is painted on the Devil in every picture. This, along with the pregnancy fantasies, show that Haizmann "recoiled from a feminine attitude toward his father which has its climax in the fantasy of giving birth to his child. Mourning for the lost father, heightened by yearning for him, [Haizmann's] repressed pregnancy fantasy is reactivated, against which he must defend himself through neurosis and by degrading his father."
5. Freud found that Haizmann's selling of himself to the Devil bought him peace of mind: "His father had died, he had become melancholy, and the devil, who came along and asked him why he was upset and mournful, promised to help him. . . . Here we have someone who gives himself to the devil in order to be free of an emotional depression."
6. Ultimately, then, Freud reasoned, the Devil is a father figure.

Halahel   In *The Lemegeton,* a DEMON who is part good and part evil, and under the rule of BAAL.

Halpas (Halphas)   FALLEN ANGEL and 38th of the 72 SPIRITS OF SOLOMON. In HELL, Halpas is an earl who appears in the form of a stork and speaks with a hoarse voice. He burns towns; it is also said that he builds towns and fills them with armed men. Halpas takes swords to the wicked and sends men either to battlefields or to other places. He rules 26 LEGIONS of DEMONS.

Harlequin   In European folklore, a GOBLIN figure whose name is sometimes synonymous with SATAN or the DEVIL.

The origin of the name *Harlequin* is uncertain, and it has many variations of spellings, including *erlequin, herlekin, hierlekin, hellequin, hennekin,* and *hellekin. Herlaken* is used as the name for the Devil and the will-o'-the-wisp. Harlican appears in French folklore to describe both IMPS and troublesome children. The Hennekin, sometimes associated with incubi (see INCUBUS), dance at CROSSROADS at night. The Herlethingi are troops of night wanderers who are the dead. In England, such bands were described in the 11th and 12th centuries and sometimes comprised dead aristocrats. They also appeared at noontime. Harlequin (Helequin) is associated with the WILD HUNT as the leader of a pack of ghosts and DEMONS that ride through the air on stormy nights. Harlequin was a frequent clown character in the Italian improvisational theater called commedia dell'arte, popular in the 16th–18th centuries.

FURTHER READING:
Remy, Nicholas. *Demonolatry.* Secaucus, N.J.: University Books, 1974.

Head of the Dragons   DEMON in the form of a three-headed dragon with awful skin.

In the Testament of Solomon, the Head of the Dragons is a three-pronged spirit that is responsible for birth defects and epilepsy. He says he overpowers others through three deeds: He can enter the wombs of women and blind the unborn, turn their ears around backward and make them deaf and dumb, and make men fall down, grind their teeth, and foam at the mouth. He is thwarted by an "angel of the Counselor" (Christ) at Golgotha.

The demon tells King SOLOMON that a great deal of gold lies beneath the foundation of the Temple of Jerusalem, which Solomon has under construction. Solomon finds the gold and binds the demon with his magical ring. He sentences the demon to make bricks for the temple.

FURTHER READING:
The Old Testament Pseudepigrapha. Vols. 1 & 2. Edited by James H. Charlesworth. 1983. Reprint, New York: Doubleday, 1985.

heavenly bodies   DEMONS of the world of darkness who cause all the misery and strife in the world.

The Testament of Solomon identifies two groups of seven or 36 heavenly bodies who are demonic powers of the world. Tsol 8 describes the first group of seven. Interrogated by King SOLOMON, the demons say they live together in Lydia or on Mount Olympus, and they change their position. Their stars in heaven look small, but they are named as gods are. Six of them are thwarted (nullified) by certain ANGELS. The seven are the following:

• Deception, who deceives and causes the most evil heresies. He is thwarted by the angel Lamechiel.

- Strife, who provides weapons for fighting and warfare. He is thwarted by the angel Baruchiel.
- Fate, who causes men to fight instead of make peace with those who are winning. He is thwarted by the angel Marmaroth.
- Distress, who divides and separates men into opposing factions and creates jealousy, and who is followed by Strife. He is thwarted by the angel Balthioul.
- Error, who leads men astray by causing them to kill each other, dig up graves, and do other wicked things. He is thwarted by the archangel Uriel.
- Power, who feeds the greed for power, establishes tyrants, and deposes kings. He is thwarted by the angel Asteraoth.
- The Worst, who tells Solomon he will harm the king by causing him to be bound with the bonds of Artemis. The Worst does not name a THWARTING ANGEL.

Solomon sentences the seven demons to dig the foundation of the Temple of Jerusalem, which is 250 cubits in length.

Tsol 18 describes the second group of 36 heavenly bodies, demons who correspond to the decans (10-degree segments) of the zodiac. When summoned by Solomon, they appear with their heads "like formless dogs." Some have the forms of humans, bulls, or dragons, with faces of birds, beasts, or sphinxes. They call themselves the world rulers of darkness and say the king has no power to harm them or lock them up, but since he has dominion over all the spirits of the air, the earth and beneath the earth, they take their place before him as other spirits do. Solomon instructs them to appear before him in order and explain who they are. The demons are as follows:

- Ruax, who causes headaches and is thwarted by Michael
- Barsfael, who causes pains in the side of the head and is thwarted by Gabriel
- Artosael, who damages the eyes and eyesight and is thwarted by Uriel
- Oropel, who causes sore throats and mucus and is thwarted by Raphael
- Kairoxanondalon, who causes ear obstructions and is thwarted by Ourouel (possibly a variant of Uriel)
- Sphendonael, who causes tumors of the parotid gland and painful stiffening of the body and is thwarted by Sabael
- Sphandor, who paralyzes limbs, destroys the nerves of the hand (possibly carpal tunnel), and weakens shoulders and is thwarted by Arael
- Belbel, who causes perversions and is thwarted by Karael
- Kourtael, who causes colic and bowel problems and is thwarted by Iaoth
- Metathiax, who causes kidney pain and is thwarted by Adonael

- Katanikotael, who causes domestic fights and disharmony. He is thwarted by sprinkling a house with water in which laurel leaves have been soaked and by intoning, "Angel, Eae, Ieo, Sabaoth."
- Saphthoreal, who causes mental confusion and is thwarted by a written CHARM worn around the neck that says, "Iae, Iao, sons of Sabaoth"
- Phobothel, who causes loosening of the tendons and is thwarted by Adonai
- Leroel, who causes chills, fever, and sore throat and is thwarted by the recitation of the words "Iax, do not stand fast, do not be fervent, because Solomon is fairer than eleven fathers"
- Soubelti, who causes shivering and numbness and is thwarted by Rizoel
- Katrax, who causes fatal fevers and is thwarted when a person rubs coriander on his or her lips and says, "I adjure you by Zeus, retreat from the image of God."
- Ieropa, who sits on stomachs and causes convulsions in the bath and who causes seizures and is thwarted when a person repeats three times into the right ear of the afflicted "Iouda Zazabou"
- Modebel, who causes husbands and wives to separate and is thwarted when someone places a written charm bearing the names of the "eight fathers" (Egyptian deities) on doorways
- Mardero, who causes incurable fevers and is thwarted when his name is written in a house
- Rix Nathotho, who causes knee problems and is thwarted when the name *Phouneiel* is written on papyrus
- Rhyx Alath, who causes croup in infants and is thwarted by the name *Raarideris* written and carried on a person
- Rhyx Audameoth, who causes heart pain and is thwarted by Raiouoth
- Rhyx Manthado, who causes pain in the kidneys and is thwarted by the written charm "Iaoth, Ouriel" (Uriel)
- Rhyx Atonme, who causes rib pain and is thwarted with a charm written on a piece of wood from a ship that has run aground that says, "Marmaraoth of mist"
- Rhyx Anatreth, who causes gas and burning bowels and is thwarted by "Arara, Arare"
- Rhyx, the Enautha, who causes people to change their minds and hearts and is thwarted by Kalazael
- Rhyx Axesbuth, who causes diarrhea and hemorrhoids and is thwarted by pure wine that is drunk
- Rhyx Hapax, who causes insomnia and is thwarted when the written charm "Kok; Phedismos" is worn on the temples
- Rhyx Anoster, who causes hysteria and bladder pain and is thwarted when the afflicted takes laurel seeds, mashes them into oil, and massages the preparation

into the body while repeating, "I adjure you by Marmaraoth"

- Rhyx Physikoreth, who causes long-term illness and is thwarted when the afflicted massages the body with salted olive oil while saying, "Cherubim, seraphim, help (me)"
- Rhyx Aleureth, who causes the swallowing of fish bones and is thwarted when a fish bone is put in the breasts of the afflicted
- Rhyx Ichthuon, who causes detached tendons and is thwarted by the words "Adonai, malthe"
- Rhyx Achoneoth, who causes sore throats and tonsillitis and is thwarted by a written charm of "Leikourgos" on ivy leaves made into a pile
- Rhyx Autoth, who causes jealousy and quarrels between people who love each other and is thwarted by a written charm of the letters *alpha* and *beta*
- Rhyx Phtheneoth, who casts the EVIL EYE and is thwarted by an inscribed eye
- Rhyx Mianeth, who holds "a grudge against the body" and causes flesh to rot and houses to be demolished and is thwarted by a written charm, "Melto Ardad Anaath," placed at the entrance to a home

Solomon forces all of these heavenly bodies to bear water for the Temple of Jerusalem.

FURTHER READING:
The Old Testament Pseudepigrapha. Vols. 1 & 2. Edited by James H. Charlesworth. New York: Doubleday, 1985.

Hecataea In Greek lore, frightening DEMONs and apparitions who are considered to be the "children" of Hecate, goddess of the underworld, dark Moon, ghosts, and magic. The Hecataea appear at the goddess' bidding.
See CHTHONIC DEITIES.

Hel In Norse mythology, the goddess and ruler of Helheim, the realm of the dead. Hel is the youngest child of the evil god Loki and the giantess Angrboda. She is usually described as a horrible hag, half-alive and half-dead (half-blue-black and half-flesh-colored), with a gloomy and grim expression. Her face and body are those of a living woman, but her thighs and legs are those of a corpse, mottled and moldering. Hel was cast into the underworld after being abducted by the gods. Her hall in Helheim is called Eljudnir (Sleet-Cold), the home of the dead, and has high walls. Her manservant is Ganglati and her maidservant is Ganglot (tardy).

hell The underworld abode of souls of the dead. In Christianity, hell is the opposite of heaven and is the place ruled by the DEVIL, where DEMONs torment sinners for eternity. Hell is the complete absence of God, light, and love; a place of unbearable fire and horrible tortures. Hell takes its name from HEL, the Norse goddess of the

netherworld. Most concepts of the afterlife segregate the good from the evil, sending them to separate abodes.

Egyptian
Amenti (also Amentet) is the underworld in the Osiris cult of Egyptian myth and religion. *Amenti*, which means "hidden land," is located where the Sun sets in the west. After arriving at Amenti, the soul is taken by the jackal-headed god of death, Anubis, to a judgment hall. Anubis weighs the soul's heart against the feather of truth and light, and the soul is judged by 42 judges. Worthy souls go to the fields of Aalu (also Aaru), which are reached by passing through either 15 or 21 gates guarded by evil demons armed with long knives. The Elysium-like fields were cultivated for food for the dead. Souls who fail judgment and weighing are eaten by a monster named Ammit (Ammut) and sent to a place of torment.

Greek
The Greek underworld of Hades is a realm of shadows. The souls of the dead are colorless shades who wander about in a depressing, gloomy world. According to Homer, they have no blood or bones, twitter like bats, and seek the vitalizing life forces from sacrificed animals and necromantic rituals. In later Greek thought, the good are rewarded and the wicked are punished.

The dead reach the afterlife by crossing the river Acheron, the river of sorrow, in a boat driven by the ferryman Charon. He must be paid for passage, usually in the form of a coin placed under the tongue of the deceased. After passing by the guardian, the three-headed dog CERBERUS, the dead proceed to the place of judgment.

Hades is divided into the Elysian Fields, a paradise for the good, and Tartarus, a hell for the wicked. There are many rivers. Besides the Acheron, major ones are the Cocytus (lamentation), Phlegethon (fire), Lethe (forgetfulness), and Styx (hate), the last of which divides the upper and lower worlds.

Three judges of the underworld, Minos, Rhadamanthus, and Aeacus, weigh souls at a place where three roads meet. The blessed are sent to the Elysian Fields, the wicked are sent to Tartarus, and those who are neither are sent to the Fields of Asphodel.

The wicked are unhappy and suffer, but not at the hand of demons.

Early Christians used the term *Hades* to translate the Hebrew term *Sheol*, the land of the dead.

Zoroastrianism
In Zoroastrianism, hell is created in the middle earth by AHRIMAN, the personification of ultimate evil. In his battle against Ohrmazd, the good god, Ahriman attacks the earth, ripping apart the sky, thereby creating night. He hurtles toward the earth and bores straight through it, making a tunnel. This hole becomes hell, infested with demons. Damned souls are sent here to suffer extremes of heat and cold, loathsome stenches, rotting food, and the torments of demons, who gnaw, swallow, and pierce

Demons whipping sinners in hell (AUTHOR'S COLLECTION)

the damned with spears. The extent of punishment is suited to the crimes and sins of the souls. Souls who are neither wholly good nor wholly evil go to a purgatory-like place, Hamegstan, a shadowy and oppressive realm with extremes of heat and cold. Being sent to hell is not permanent, however. At the Last Judgement, all sin is purged.

After death, the soul spends three days sitting at the head of its body praying for its future. Then, it must cross a river swollen with the tears of weeping loved ones. If too many tears have been shed, the river cannot be crossed. The soul is aided by its guardian angel. If the river is crossed, the soul then arrives at the Chinvat Bridge, or "Bridge of the Requiter," to meet three angels of judgment: Mithra, Srosh, and Rashnu. The deeds of the soul are weighed. Depending on the good or evil reckoning, the bridge is wide and easily crossed, or sharp and narrow, causing the wicked to fall into hell.

One text, The Book of Arda Viraf, describes hell in detail as a gloomy, stinking, fiery, and depressing abode. There are four significant hills: Dush-humat, the place of evil thoughts; Dush-hukht, the place of evil words; Dush-huvarsht, the place of evil deeds; and Chakat-i-Daitih, a desert and dark stinking pit full of demons below the Chinvat Bridge. The deepest pit is Drûgâskan, a place so dark that the sense of sight is lost.

Punishments fit the nature of sins; 85 are described in The Book of Arda Viraf from the sixth century. Eighty-five of its 101 chapters concern hell. The visionary is Arda Viraf, who travels to both heaven and hell with two guides: Srosh the pious and Ataro, an angel. Besides witnessing landscapes and tortures of hell, Arda Viraf sees Angra Mainyu, the deadly world destroyer later known as Ahriman.

Unlike the Christian hell to come, demons do not force the punishments upon the damned; rather, the damned inflict the punishments on themselves, while demons look on. The most common punishment is eating fetid and putrid things for thousands of years until the final resurrection. Other punishments include the eating of their own corpses, flesh, and excrement, menstrual fluids and semen, blood and brains from skulls of the dead, and their own children. Tortures also include hanging (particularly upside-down), dismemberment, decapitation, laceration, mutilation and self-mutilation by cutting, gnawing, devouring, gnashing, piercing, beating, tearing, trampling, stinging, and dragging. The wicked are stabbed and pelted and stretched on racks; they are forced to bear enormous burdens and perform painful and fruitless tasks; are burned and cooked in ovens, cauldrons, and frying-pans; are cast down into heat, cold, smoke, snow, and stench. They endure hunger and thirst, and they are forced to lick hot things or to defecate and masturbate continually; they are submerged in mud and turned into SERPENTs. Their eyes are gouged out and their tongues pulled out; putrid substances are forced into their noses, eyes, and mouths. Their penises are gnawed and their breasts are gnashed and cut off.

Fire is present in the Zoroastrian hell but is not an instrument of torture; instead, hot implements and objects and molten metal are used against the damned.

The mouth of hell, with Lucifer atop and Satan in front of the jaws (AUTHOR'S COLLECTION)

Judaism

Sheol (place of the dead) is a shadowy place under the earth where souls continue their existence in the afterlife. The equivalent Greek term for the Hebrew *Sheol* is *Hades,* but as a place after death, not as a place of punishment. Daniel 12:2, which concerns the coming of the messianic kingdom, expresses the conviction that God will not abandon souls in Sheol: "And many of those who sleep in the dust of the earth shall awake, some to everlasting life, and some to shame and contempt."

All souls go initially to Sheol (with the exception of a few righteous ones whom God takes straight to heaven). In 3 Enoch, two angels of destruction escort "intermediate" souls (those equally good and bad) and wicked souls to Sheol. The intermediate souls are purified in fire in order to be fitting in God's presence. They have spiritual forms that are human faces with eagle bodies. The faces are green because of the taint of their sin and will remain so until they are purified.

The wicked souls, whose faces are as black as the bottoms of pots because of their sins, are taken by an angel to Gehenna (hell) for punishment. Gehenna or Gehinnom (Valley of Hinnom) is associated with the literal valley of Hinnom south of Jerusalem, where human sacrifices were made to MOLOCH. Different accounts exist concerning the creation of Gehenna: it was created by God on the second day, or it existed before the world and its fire was created on the second day. It exists either above the firmament, behind dark mountains, or deep within the earth. Its fire is 60 times hotter than any fire on Earth and is never extinguished. It stinks of sulfur. Sinners go immediately to Gehenna, where they are punished in terrible pain for eternity.

Christianity

In orthodox Christianity, hell has four levels. The first two are limbo regions for pre-Christian souls, now unoccupied, and for the souls of unbaptized children. The third is purgatory, where most mortals go prior to admission to heaven. The duration of their stay depends upon the gravity of their sins. The fourth is hell itself, reserved for eternal punishment of the damned, who have no hope of redemption.

Hell exists in the bowels of the earth. Earthquakes are produced by the convulsions of the damned, according to orthodox belief.

There are three gates to hell: in the inhabited land, in the wilderness, and at the bottom of the sea. In the Middle Ages, caves were considered to be the entry points to hell.

Hell is characterized by extremes of temperature. There are unbearable furnaces and pitch and flames, and extreme cold, ice, and frigidity. The damned are punished according to their sins, and in ways similar to the descriptions of the Zoroastrian hell. Their bodies are tortured and ripped apart by demons; they are subjected to piercings and hanging in agonizing postures, such as by

The gluttonous are punished in hell by being force-fed toads, rats, and snakes. (AUTHOR'S COLLECTION)

their tongues or breasts. They have their organs and flesh devoured; they eat excrement and filth. They have their genitals and breasts mutilated. Worms crawl in and out of their eyes.

Islam

Jahnnam is the Islamic hell, the destination of not only criminals but infidels and those who do not believe in God. The damned are forced to eat bitter fruit from a tree called Zaqqum and endure a host of other tortures. The Qur'an emphasizes the torments of hell for wayward Muslims. The guilty are "bound with chains, their garments pitch, and their faces covered with flames" (sura 14:49–50). For those who oppose God's message, "Hell will stretch behind them, and putrid water shall he drink: he will sip, but scarcely swallow. Death will assail him from every side, yet he shall not die. Harrowing torment awaits him" (sura 14:16–17), and "Garments of fire have been prepared for the unbelievers. Scalding water shall be poured upon their heads, melting their skins and that which is in their bellies. They shall be lashed with rods of iron" (sura 22:19–20).

Visits to Hell

Numerous religious figures and visionaries have visited one or both sides of the afterlife. Zarathustra (Zoroaster) was said to have made midnight trips to both heaven and hell, as did Moses. There is a tradition that JESUS went to hell for three days between his Crucifixion and ascension to heaven. The Bible makes no clear reference to it, but the statement that Jesus went to hell is in the Apostles' Creed. 1 Peter 3:19 says that Jesus went to preach to "the spirits in prison," a reference interpreted as meaning hell.

EMMANUEL SWEDENBORG had numerous out-of-body visits to the afterlife, and ST. JOHN BOSCO visited hell in vivid lucid dreams.

FURTHER READING:

Masters, Anthony. *The Devil's Dominion: The Complete Story of Hell and Satanism in the Modern World.* London: Peter Fraser & Dunlop, 1978.

Ogden, Daniel. *Magic, Witchcraft, and Ghosts in the Greek and Roman Worlds: A Sourcebook.* New York: Oxford University Press, 2002.

Rudwin, Maximilian. *The Devil in Legend and Literature.* La Salle, Ill.: Open Court, 1959.

Russell, Jeffrey Burton. *The Devil: Perceptions of Evil from Antiquity to Primitive Christianity.* Ithaca, N.Y., and London: Cornell University Press, 1977.

***Hellboy* (2004)**   Film about a DEMON conjured by the Nazis, who becomes a fighter for the forces of good. Directed by Guillermo del Toro, the film stars Ron Perlman as Hellboy. The film is based on the comic book character created by Mike Mignola, which debuted in 1993.

In the last days of World War II, the Nazis conjure a young demon in a desperate attempt to avoid defeat. The Allies raid the camp and capture the demon, Hellboy. The demon joins the U.S. government to battle evil. His destiny is to be the Beast of the Apocalypse.

Hellboy has supernormal strength and supernatural powers. He ages slowly and heals quickly. His oversized right arm and hand, called "the Hand of Doom," is impervious to pain yet able to pick up things as small as flies. He uses it as a weapon. Other weapons include holy relics and a large revolver called "the Good Samaritan" that fires custom bullets made of garlic, silver, and holy water.

Hellboy II was released in 2008.

Hell-Fire Club   Satanic order founded in England in the 18th century, more for the purpose of outrageous behavior and sexual play than actual Satanic rites or worship.

The original Hell-Fire Club was founded by Lord Wharton for the purpose of "drinking, gambling and blaspheming." Similar clubs also were in vogue, mostly among the aristocracy, such as the Edinburgh Sweating Club, the Dublin Blasters, and the Demoniacs. In 1721, a royal proclamation banned them, forcing them underground.

The most famous Hell-Fire Club was founded by Sir Francis Dashwood, who owned a large estate in West Wycombe, Buckinghamshire, and who had married a rich widow. Dashwood joined forces with Paul Whitehead to tour erotic archaeological discoveries in Europe and also the private cardinals' rooms at the Vatican. They acquired some GRIMOIRES of spells and conjurations and decided it would be interesting to indulge in magical activity.

Dashwood, Whitehead, and their friends began meeting at the George and Vulture pub in Cornhill. They established as their motto and philosophy *Fais Ce Que Voudras*, "Do What Thou Wilt," which later became part of ALEISTER CROWLEY's "Law of Thelema": "Do what thou wilt shall be the whole of the law."

The group, known first at the Secret Brotherhood and then as the "order of the Friars of Saint Francis of Wycombe," were heavily influenced by Rosicrucianism in their satanic dabblings. They changed their meeting site to a more demonically suited location, Medmenham Abbey, the ruins of a 12th-century Cistercian monastery atop a hill. Dashwood made some additions to the abbey, including an artificial Gothic tower, frescoes on the walls and ceilings, and voluptuous statues. He restored the abbey church by turning it into a common room with a pagan altar. Dashwood and his fellow "monks" spent on the average two days a month at the abbey. Each "monk" had his own cell, to which he could take women. A pleasure boat afforded them trips up and down the Thames River.

The "monks" also conducted rites in caves nearby. The caves stretched to the center of the hill. Three hundred feet down was an underground river, which Dashwood named the River Styx. The caves served as temple rooms, many of which were decorated with Tantric symbols. Supposedly, a secret passage led to the chamber of a girl nicknamed St. Agnes, who served as vestal virgin. There was a labyrinth as well.

The author Hugh Walpole witnessed one of their satanic rites performed covertly in the Sistine Chapel at the Vatican in Rome, which he described in his book *Memoirs of the Reign of King George III*:

> On Good Friday, each person who attends the Sistine Chapel takes a small scourge from an attendant at the door. The chapel is dimly lighted, only three candles, which are extinguished by the priest, one by one. At the putting out of the first, the penitents take off one part of their dress. At the next, still more, and in the dark which follows the extinguishing of the third candle, "lay on" their own shoulders with groans and lamentations. Sir Francis Dashwood, thinking this mere stage effect, entered with the others dressed in a large watchman's coat, demurely took his scourge from the priest and advanced to the end of the chapel, where in the darkness ensuing he drew from beneath his coat an English horsewhip and flogged right and left quite down the Chapel—the congregation exclaiming "Il Diavolo! Il Diavolo!"—thinking the evil was upon them with a vengeance. The consequence might have been serious had Dashwood not immediately fled the Papal dominions.

Dashwood's order lasted for about 35 years.

FURTHER READING:
Masters, Anthony. *The Devil's Dominion: The Complete Story of Hell and Satanism in the Modern World*. London: Peter Fraser & Dunlop, 1978.

Hemah   Angel of wrath, fury, and destruction who governs the death of domestic animals. According to Jewish lore, Hemah lives in the seventh heaven; he is 500 parasangs tall and is made of chains of black and red fire. A parasang is a Persian unit of measurement used to describe the dimensions of the heavens and the distances between them, and the heights of angels. One parasang equals approximately 3.88 miles.

In the Zohar, Hemah is one of three angels in Gehenna (see HELL)—along with Af and Mashit—who punish those who sin by idolatry, incest, and murder. Hemah swallows Moses with the help of his brother angel Af. God intervenes and forces him to spit Moses out again. Moses then kills Hemah.

hobgoblin   See GOBLIN.

horerczy   See ALP.

huli jing (fox fairy)   In Chinese lore, a DEMON that is the malevolent spirit of the returning dead. The *huli jing* rises from its grave and shape-shifts into a seductive woman, scholar, or old man. It seduces victims and vampirizes the victims of the life force during orgasm. When the victim falls ill with tuberculosis, the *huli jing* leaves it for another victim. A female *huli jing* especially likes scholars for their virtuousness.

The *huli jing* has other powers and abilities that make it one of the most feared of all demons in Chinese lore. It can shape shift into dead people, haunt places, and terrify the living. It can take on the appearance of living people. It can transport people through the air and enable them to pass through walls and closed windows. The *huli jing* is invisible during the day but can often be seen at night, especially lurking on the rooftops of homes.

The *huli jing* is responsible for a form of possession that reduces a person to insanity. If madness affects generations of a family, that indicates that an ancestor once injured a *huli jing*. The *huli jing* is so feared that it is treated with great respect; above all, great care must be taken never to harm one. However, if one cuts off the tail, which holds its power, it will leave a home and never return.

One remedy against the *huli jing* is to burn charms written on paper and mix the ashes into tea for drinking. If a female *huli jing* can be given enough wine to become drunk, it will revert to its true form and will vanish.

See *KITSUNE*.

FURTHER READING:
Mack, Carol K., and Dinah Mack. *A Field Guide to Demons, Fairies, Fallen Angels, and Other Subversive Spirits*. New York: Henry Holt/Owl Books, 1998.

Hutriel   An angel of punishment who lives in the fifth camp of HELL and helps to punish the 10 nations. The name *Hutriel* means "rod of God." Hutriel is sometimes equated with Oniel.

Hydriel   DEMON and a wandering duke of the air. Hydriel has 100 great dukes and 200 lesser dukes and their servants beneath him. The 12 chief dukes each have 1,320 servants. All the demons must be summoned according to their appropriate planetary hour. When they appear, each has the form of a SERPENT with a virgin's head and face. Unlike the spirits of BURIEL, they are courteous and obedient. They prefer to be around water and moist places. The 12 major dukes of Hydriel are Mortoliel, Chamoriel, Pelariel, Musuziel, Lameniel, Barchiel, Samiel, Dusiriel, Camiel, Arbiel, Luciel, and Chariel.

Hyslop, James Hervey (1854–1920)   American philosopher, psychologist, educator, and professor of ethics, whose interest in survival after death led him to conduct some of the finest studies of POSSESSION and OBSESSION.

James Hervey Hyslop was born on August 18, 1854, to devout Presbyterians in Xenia, Ohio. His parents expected him to enter the ministry, but instead he studied philosophy and the emerging field of psychology, receiving a bachelor of arts in 1877 from Wooster College, Wooster, Ohio. Despite his religious upbringing, Hyslop professed skepticism about the divinity of Christ by the time he reached college and, after some study, decided to reject the New Testament.

After graduation, Hyslop enrolled at the University of Leipzig, Germany, to study with Wilhelm Wundt, who founded the first formal psychology laboratory in 1879. In Leipzig, he met his wife-to-be, Mary F. Hall, a student of music from Philadelphia. Hyslop returned to the United States two years later, teaching first at Lake Forest University, outside Chicago, then at Smith College in Northampton, Massachusetts. He continued his own education at Johns Hopkins University in Baltimore, completing a doctorate in psychology in 1887, and published several books about logic, ethics, education, and philosophy. From 1889 to 1902, he was professor of logic and ethics at Columbia University in New York City. As was typical of other educated men of the period, Hyslop exhibited eclectic tastes, also exploring geology and biology.

He knew nothing about the psychic until 1886, when an article on telepathy in *Nation* caught his attention. The article concerned a young boy who reportedly saw an apparition of his father and his team of horses going over a bank into a stream some 25 miles away. Hyslop suspected the story was "some illusion of memory or error in judgment as to the facts." He wrote to the author of the article and received answers to his questions that convinced him the phenomenon might be genuine.

At Columbia Hyslop, through his colleagues, became acquainted with the Society for Psychical Research (SPR) in England and the American Society for Psychical Research (ASPR) (founded in 1882 and 1885, respectively) and with the research concerning the British medium Leonora Piper conducted by Richard Hodgson. In 1888, he began a series of sittings with Piper. Initially skeptical, he was astonished when Piper began relaying personal messages from his dead father and various relatives. By his 12th sitting, he was convinced he had communicated with the spirits of his family.

In 1889, the ASPR became a branch of the SPR out of financial need and remained so until the death of Hodgson in 1905. In 1906, the ASPR reorganized as an independent organization, and Hyslop became its president, a position he held until his death in 1920.

Hyslop's most famous case was the THOMPSON/GIFFORD OBSESSION in 1907, in which a metalworker, Frederic L. Thompson, claimed to been taken over by a deceased painter, R. Swain Gifford. After the Thompson/Gifford case, Hyslop continued to work extensively with various mediums, principally Minnie Soule, and ran the operations of the ASPR. He also wrote all the society's papers, as well as magazine and journal articles.

Casework fascinated Hyslop. He investigated the story of S. Henry, a coachman in New Jersey who was tormented by the death of his wife and his increasingly frightening psychical experiences. Henry described feelings of a strange fluid in his stomach, which forced him to breathe in a certain way, then rose to his brain and made him insane. He also wrote that he felt he could leave his body through an opening in the back of his head. Hyslop did not recognize Henry's symptoms as those of kundalini and out-of-body experiences. By 1908, almost two years after Hyslop had first met him, Henry was suffering from delusions and had become insane. Hyslop took Henry to the ASPR in New York, where he hypnotized him and tried to encourage him to forget his troubles. The simple treatment worked. Never having confronted out-of-body experiences before, Hyslop attributed Henry's problems to spirit possession.

In 1909, Hyslop, met Etta De Camp, a medium currently living in New York City who had been psychic since her childhood in Ohio. She was an editor and proofreader for *Broadway* magazine who had never written anything besides letters until 1908. After reading about spirit communications received by W. T. Stead through automatic writing, De Camp decided to try. She reported a tingling in her arm, like an electric shock, and after two or three days began writing copiously.

De Camp experienced terrible headaches and earaches at this time, usually if she tried to resist the writing. She found some relief while in trance but refused to lose conscious control. The scripts made little sense to her, and she complained to the spirits that if they could not write well, they should take someone to her who could. From that point on, the scripts became more coherent. Her first communicator was an Indian brave, who reported that he would hear from a dead man, a writer who wanted someone to finish the stories he left when he died.

Soon, her pencil wrote that the spirit of Frank R. Stockton had arrived and wished to communicate. She felt intense pain, but once Stockton took control of her, the pain subsided. De Camp began writing short stories in Stockton's style, and she showed them to her employer, George Duysters, who introduced her to Hyslop.

Stockton had been popular in the late 19th century, writing whimsical stories for children. His most famous, "The Lady or the Tiger," is still popular. He had a distinctive style, full of humor, cynicism, and bizarre situations. Duysters showed some of the De Camp transcriptions to the late author's editor at *Harper's,* who found them quite real. De Camp also began hearing from her dead father.

De Camp continued to write in Stockton's style, and Hyslop lost contact with her from 1910 to 1912 while he investigated other matters. In 1912, De Camp was near a complete breakdown, and Hyslop agreed to participate in sittings, which would finally reveal Stockton's presence. Through a series of séances with Soule, both Stockton and the recently deceased Duysters revealed themselves, proving again to Hyslop the reality of spirit possession and survival. De Camp wrote of her experiences in *The Return of Frank R. Stockton* in 1913, including all of the transcribed Stockton stories. After initial publicity, De Camp later married and settled down to a private life, hearing no more from Stockton.

A third case involved a woman identified as Ida Ritchie, really Ida Marie Rogers. Rogers claimed to be receiving communications from the great opera singer Emma Ab-

bott, who had died in 1891. Rogers was a budding singer herself and had made remarkable progress for a person with little formal training. When she contacted Hyslop, Rogers said Emma Abbott, her mother, and the late William James, a Harvard philosopher and psychologist and friend of Hyslop's, were all talking to her through automatic writing. Again through sittings with Soule, Hyslop contacted Abbott and Rogers' mother. Their communication indicated great efforts by the spirits to help Rogers' singing career, but she never became a great star.

Hyslop's last major case was the DORIS FISCHER OBSESSION, begun in 1914.

Hyslop reportedly believed his health had been threatened in 1919 by a spirit he was trying to exorcize through sessions in Boston with Soule, and he was ill for several months. He believed firmly that the existence of discarnate spirits had been proved scientifically and dismissed those who did not agree. Hyslop suffered a stroke at the end of 1919 and died June 17, 1920.

FURTHER READING:

Anderson, Roger I., ed. "Autobiographical Fragment of James Hervey Hyslop." *Journal of Religion and Psychical Research* 9, no. 2 (April 1986): 81–92.

———, ed. "Autobiographical Fragment of James Hervey Hyslop Part III." *Journal of Religion and Psychical Research* 9, no. 3 (July 1986): 145–160.

———. "The Life and Work of James H. Hyslop." *The Journal of the American Society for Psychical Research* 79 (April 1985): 167–200.

Rogo D. Scott. *The Infinite Boundary.* New York: Dodd, Mead, 1987.

Iblis In Islam, the DEVIL. *Iblis* is Arabian for "despair." The exact origin and nature of Iblis are uncertain. His name is the primary name for the Devil; he is also described as the chief and father of the DJINN and an ANGEL. He can assume any form, but he is most frequently portrayed as a vain entity who has the head of an ass and is decorated with peacock feathers (see ADRAMELECH).

Iblis is mentioned nine times in the Qur'an; seven of the references concern his fall from God's grace. His other name, Shaytan, is used in context of his rebellion against God.

Sura 18:50 in the Qur'an states that Iblis "was one of the djinn, and he broke the command his Lord." Like other djinn, Iblis was created by God of smokeless fire. Suras 7:12 and 38:76 refer to his creation from fire.

However, the Qur'an also indicates that Iblis was treated as an angel. When Allah created Adam, he ordered all the angels to bow down and worship him. Iblis was among those who refused, claiming that a being made of dust was beneath him, a being of fire. Allah cursed Iblis for his pride and expelled him from heaven. Iblis persuaded Allah to delay further punishment until the Day of Judgment. God gave him the right to roam the earth, tempting people, and to destroy those who yield to temptation. He cannot compel people to sin but only lure them to make the choice. He is aided by the Shaytan, also the name of a type of djinn, who serves under him.

Ultimately, Iblis is doomed to HELL along with the souls he corrupts. He haunts ruins and eats unblessed food until Judgment Day.

Another tradition holds that Iblis was one of the original djinn, taken to heaven as a prisoner. He was made a judge of djinn, a job that he performed well for 1,000 years and poorly for 1,000 years. He was then rehabilitated but refused Allah's command to worship Adam and was punished.

In another legend, in a time before the creation of humankind, Allah sent his angels down to Earth to destroy the djinn, who were rebelling against divine laws. The angels killed most of them and captured Iblis, whom they took up to heaven and educated. The remaining djinn formed a new nation. Iblis, who wanted power, left heaven to become their king. They called him AZAZEL.

In the mystical tradition of the Sufis, Iblis refused to bow to Adam because he could only bow to God. Thus, Iblis represents the perfect lover, a model of loyalty and devotion who would rather be separated from God and God's will than united with God against God's will.

In a 14th-century Syrian legend, Iblis actually assisted in the creation of Adam by gathering sweet and salty matter from the earth.

Another story tells how Iblis tempted Eve. He succeeded in smuggling himself into paradise by promising any animal who carried him in that he would bestow upon it three magical words that would guarantee immortality.

The SERPENT agreed and carried Iblis into paradise hidden in its mouth. Iblis spoke to Eve from within the mouth.

Iblis is both male and female and can impregnate himself. Everytime he celebrates humans' rebelling against God, he lays two eggs that hatch as demons.

FURTHER READING:
Hyatt, Victoria, and Joseph W. Charles. *The Book of Demons.* New York: Simon & Schuster, 1974.
Kelly, Henry Ansgar. *A Biography of Satan.* New York: Cambridge University Press, 2006.
Mack, Carol K., and Dinah Mack. *A Field Guide to Demons: Fairies, Fallen Angels, and Other Subversive Spirits.* New York: Owl Books/Henry Holt, 1998.
Russell, Jeffrey Burton. *Lucifer: The Devil in the Middle Ages.* Ithaca, N.Y., and London: Cornell University Press, 1984.

Icosiel   DEMON and a wandering duke of the air. Icosiel has 100 dukes, 300 companions, and many other servants. His 15 chief dukes have 2,200 servants. He and his demons mainly appear in houses. They can be summoned day and night and will do as commanded. The 15 principal dukes are Mchariel, Pischiel, Thanatiel, Zosiel, Agapiel, Larphiel, Amediet, Cambriet, Nathriel, Zachartel, Athesiel, Cumariel, Munefiel, Heresiel, and Ubaniel.

imp   A small DEMON usually kept inside a bottle or ring. An imp is like a FAMILIAR and is comparable to the DJINN. It is evoked for magical purposes. Imps are both good and evil.

As familiars, imps can take the shape of animals, including insects and birds, which are sent out on tasks at the command of a witch or magician. Witch hunters during the Inquisition accused witches of rewarding their imps for evil deeds by suckling them with their own BLOOD, which the imps sucked from fingers, warts, breasts, or any protuberance on the skin.

In England the Lincoln Imp is a carved stone demon on a column in the Angel Choir at the cathedral in Lincoln, constructed in the 12th century and once the tallest structure in the world. The grinning imp is in a seated position with one leg crossed over the other.

There are different versions of the legend. One version tells in rhyme that one day the Devil was in good spirits and let his young demons out to play. One rode on the wind to Lindum (Lincoln) and ordered the wind to take him into the church, intending to wreak havoc there. The imp started breaking things in the Angel Choir and was turned to stone by angels in punishment.

Another version says that in the 14th century, the Devil sent two imps out to make mischief. First, they went to Chesterfield and twisted the spire of the church there, and then they went to Lincoln Cathedral. They tripped the bishop and smashed tables and chairs and started to destroy the Angel Choir. An angel ordered them to stop. One of the imps defiantly flew up to a stone pillar and began to throw heavy objects at the angel. The angel turned

him into stone, leaving him there forever. The second imp hid in the wreckage and made his escape by latching on to the broomstick of a passing witch. The witch turned him into a black cat to become her familiar.

The Lincoln Imp is associated with both good and bad luck. The imp has been used in jewelry and even worn by royalty. In 1928, the prince of Wales (the future King Edward VII) was given an imp tie pin. The next year, two of his horses won major races, the Grand National and the Epsom Derby.

FURTHER READING:
Kesson, H. J. *The Legend of the Lincoln Imp.* Lincoln, England: J. W. Ruddock & Sons, 1904.

incantation bowl   A terra-cotta bowl inscribed with CHARMS or magical texts, used to trap or drive away DEMONS. Incantation bowls also are known as Babylonian demon or DEVIL traps.

The bowls, about the size of soup tureens, were inverted and buried under the four corners of the foundations of houses and buildings to seal the cracks where demons could sneak in. Their magic was believed to protect against an assortment of evils, including male and female demons, especially the attacks of LILITH and her offspring; illness; WITCHCRAFT; the CURSES of sorcerers; and the EVIL EYE. The bowl either overturned or captured demons.

Incantation bowls were common among the Babylonians and the Hebrews, who were held captive for a time in Babylonia. Their period of usage is uncertain but ranges at least from the second century to the seventh century. Almost all of the bowls that survive are inscribed in Aramaic; a few are inscribed in Persian. The charms are written in ink in a spiral from the rim to the center, and sometimes on the outside of the bowls as well. Some of the centers of bowls have a primitive drawing of a demon in chains. The charms specify protection of homes, families, and possessions. One bowl proclaims a "bill of divorce" from the Devil and all his night monsters, ordering them to leave the community.

Many of the inscriptions call upon powerful ANGELS or King SOLOMON and the power of the seal of his magical ring. The name of the great angel Metatron appears often on incantation bowls in invocations for angelic help. Various titles given him are the *Great Prince of the Whole World, Prince of the World,* and *Great Prince of God's Throne.*

Some Jewish bowls refer to the Angel of Yahweh with this or similar inscriptions: "YYY the Great, the angel who has 11 names."

An example of a charm is the following:

The demon NTY', TTY QLY'. BTY', Nuriel, Holy Rock. Sealed and countersealed and fortified are Ahat, the daughter of Imma; Rabbi, Malki and Dipshi, the sons of Ahat; and Yanai the daughter of Ahat, and Ahat the daughter of Imma, and Atyona the son of Qarqoi, and Qarquoi the daughter of Shilta, and Shilta the daughter of Immi—they are their houses and their children and their property are sealed with the seal-ring of El Shaddai, blessed be He, and with the seal ring of King Solomon, the son of David, who worked spells on male demons and female liliths. Sealed, countersealed and fortified against the male demon and female lilith and spell and curse and incantation and knocking and evil eye and evil black-arts, against the black-arts of mother and daughter, and against those of daughter-in-law and mother-in-law, and against those of the presumptuous woman, who darkens the eyes and blows away the soul, and against the evil black-arts, that are wrought by men, and against everything bad. In the name of the Lord. Lord, Hosts is His name, Amen, amen, selah. This charm is to thwart the demon Titinos. Sealed are the bodies (?) of S QL, the bodies (?) of S QL MYLY MYLY TYGL.

Many bowls were inscribed against LILITH, one of the most feared demons of all. She is often the demon depicted bound in chains in the center of the inscriptions. Inscriptions either cast her out or issue decrees of divorce from her. The first inscription that follows cites the use of IRON, a common means of weakening or binding spirits, especially evil ones:

Bound is the bewitching Lilith with a peg of iron in her nose; bound is the bewitching Lilith with pinchers of iron in her mouth; bound is the bewitching Lilith . . . with a chain or iron on her neck; bound is the bewitching Lilith with fetters of iron on her hands; bound is the bewitching Lilith with stocks of stone on her feet.

Thou Lilith of the desert, thou hag, thou ghoul . . . naked art thou sent forth, unclad, with hair disheveled, and streaming down your back.

See RABISU.

FURTHER READING:
Barker, Margaret. *The Great Angel: A Study of Israel's Second God.* Louisville, Ky.: Westminster/John Knox Press, 1992.
Koltuv, Barbara Black. *The Book of Lilith.* Berwick, Me.: Nicolas-Hays, 1986.
The Old Testament Pseudepigrapha. Vols. 1 & 2. Edited by James H. Charlesworth. 1983. Reprint, New York: Doubleday, 1985.

incubus   A lewd male DEMON who pursues women for sex. In Hebrew mythology, the incubus and his female counterpart, the SUCCUBUS, visit women and men in their sleep, lie and press heavily upon them, and seduce them. They can be conjured by witches, sorcerers, and shamans. During the witch hysteria in Europe, incubi were believed to instruments of the DEVIL, tormenting people for the sole purpose of degrading their souls and perverting them to more vices. Incubus attacks are reported in modern POSSESSION cases.

Incubus is from the Latin word *incubare*, which means "to lie upon." Victims usually feel a heavy weight on top of them that paralyzes them. Sometimes there is a sense of choking or suffocation. The Greeks referred to the phenomenon as *ephialtes,* or "the pouncer." Another Greek term is *pnigalion,* or "suffocation." Pliny called it "suppressions" or "nocturnal illusions."

The Incubus in Jewish Demonology
The existence and activities of incubi are acknowledged in Jewish demonology in relation to a Midrashic legend of Adam's siring demonic offspring. According to the kabbalistic text the Zohar, these unions are continued by men who unknowingly cohabit with spirits in their sleep. The hybrid human-demonic children have a demonic nature and rank high in the echelons of demons, occupying positions of authority and rulership. Thus, demons value intercourse with humans.

The Incubus in the Early Christian Church
According to some of the fathers of the church, among them St. Justin Martyr, Clement of Alexandria, and Tertullian, as well as the Jewish historian Josephus and some Platonist philosophers, the incubi were the SONS OF GOD, angels who fell from heaven because they copulated with women. Their offspring were giants, the Nephilim, who could not have been the progeny of human men and women.

St. Augustine included among incubi the pagan demigods sylvans and fauns, who were exceptionally lascivious and often injured women in their lust, he said.

The Incubus during the European Inquisition
During the witch hunts, demonologists wrote handbooks on witches, the Devil, and demons. They described the appearances, behavior, and characteristics of incubi and remedies against them.

Incubi are especially attracted to women with beautiful hair, young virgins, chaste widows, and all "devout" females. Nuns are among the most vulnerable and could be molested in the confessional as well as in bed. While the majority of women are forced into sex by the incubi, some of them submit willingly and even enjoy the act. It once was a common belief that women were more likely than men to be the sexual victims of demons, because women were inferior to men and less able to resist temptation.

Incubi have enormous phalluses that are so stiff they cause women great pain. According to the French demonologist NICHOLAS REMY, a woman accused as a witch in Haraucourt in 1586 described her demon's penis as as long as a kitchen tool and without testicles or scrotum. Another accused witch, a woman named Didatia of Miremont, said at her trial in 1588 that she was "always so stretched by the huge, swollen member of her Demon that the sheets were drenched with blood." Some incubus penises were described as scaly, like the skin of a reptile.

Incubi are not interested in procreation, only in degrading sex. However, they have the ability to impregnate women. They do not possess their own semen; they col-

Incubus, from Francis Barrett's The Magus *(AUTHOR'S COLLECTION)*

lect it from men in nocturnal emissions, masturbation, or coitus while the demons are masquerading as succubi. The incubi have the power to preserve semen and use it later on one of their victims. Demonic semen is described as frigid and icy cold.

The children that result may be considered the children of the man who unwittingly provided the semen. Some old horror stories held that the children were half-human and half-beast. Remy described monstrous half-demon children with two mouths, two heads, six fingers, two sets of teeth, beards, four eyes, three hands, and three feet. Others were missing limbs or had one eye in the middle of their forehead or in their knee. Some had no human form but were shapeless masses like sponges. Remy recounted an eyewitness description of an incubus child:

> It had a hooked beak, a long smooth neck, quivering eyes, a pointed tail, a strident voice, and very swift feet upon which it ran rapidly to and fro as if seeking for some hiding-place in its stable.

Some of the offspring once were called Adamitici, as though they were descended in an unbroken line from Adam. Because of the defective semen, these infants cried or hissed continually, were emaciated but heavy, and sucked all their nurses dry. They also were attributed the superpowers of pagan demigods and heroes.

Remy said monstrous births were due to the "lustful imagination of a prurient woman" and not to demon se-

men. He cited Empedocles, who said that the likeness of a child is caused by impressions the mother experienced at the time of conception. If a woman had frequent intercourse with an incubus, it affected her imagination, which in turn gave the child a savage appearance.

In a small number of witchcraft cases, claims of molestation by incubi were dismissed as the products of female melancholia or vivid imagination. False pregnancies that arose from this state were chalked up to flatulence.

Witches were said to copulate willingly with incubi, especially at a SABBAT. The inquisitors' handbook the *MALLEUS MALEFICARUM* (1487), stated that "in times long past the Incubus devils used to infest women against their wills," but "modern witches . . . willingly embrace this most foul and miserable servitude." Some incubi served as FAMILIARs to witches, who sent them to torment specific individuals.

Since sex with incubi was expected of witches, many accused witches were tortured until they confessed this crime. In 1485, the inquisitor of Como sent 41 women to their deaths at the stake. Their "confessions" of sex with incubi, among other witchcraft crimes, were corroborated by eyewitness accounts, as well as by hearsay evidence "and the testimony of credible witnesses."

Incubi were believed to be always visible to witches but only occasionally visible to others, even the victims. There were reports of people observed in the throes of passion with no one but themselves visible. Husbands saw incubi as they copulated with their wives but thought they were other men.

Incubi preyed on ordinary people as well as witches. FRANCSCO-MARIA GUAZZO related a story in *Compendium Maleficarum* (1608) about a beautiful noble girl who refused to marry men of her station but instead fell into an affair with an incubus. She freely told her parents of the marvelous sex they had at night and sometimes during the day. One night, the parents, a priest, and others bolted the house doors and went into their daughter's bedroom with lit torches. There they found her in the embrace of a hideous demon, "a horrible monster whose appearance was terrible beyond human imagination." The priest immediately began reciting the GOSPEL OF JOHN. When he said, "The Word was made flesh," the demon shrieked, set fire to all the furniture, and left, carrying with him the roof of the bedroom. The girl immediately gave birth to a "loathsome monster." The midwives built a large fire and burned it.

The church prescribed five ways to get rid of incubi:

- by sacramental confession
- by making the sign of the cross
- by reciting the Ave Maria
- by moving to another house or town
- by excommunication of the demon by holy men

Other remedies included a recitation of the Lord's Prayer and the sprinkling of holy water.

Not all theologians and demonologists agreed that sex with demons was possible. St. Thomas Aquinas said that sex with a demon exceeds their natural powers but is in keeping with their malice and therefore might be permitted by God in accordance with the sins of a person. JOHANN WEYER dismissed incubi and succubi as "purely imaginary, the result of an impaired mind." He also dismissed as "bizarre fiction" the idea that incubi could impregnate a woman by borrowing a man's semen in the guise of succubi. Such stories of demonic seduction were the products of "gullible historians," he said.

Montague Summers compiled quotations from earlier writings and countered in *The History of Witchcraft and Demonology* (1926) that "great Saints and scholars and all moral theologians of importance affirm the possibility of commerce with incarnate evil intelligences."

See SMURL HAUNTING.

FURTHER READING:

Guazzo, Francesco-Maria. *Compendium Maleficarum.* Secaucus, N.J.: University Books, 1974.

The Malleus Maleficarum of Heinrich Kramer and James Sprenger. New York: Dover, 1971.

Remy, Nicholas. *Demonolatry.* Secaucus, N.J.: University Books, 1974.

Summers, Montague. *The History of Witchcraft and Demonology.* London: Kegan Paul, Trench, Trubner, 1926.

Trachtenberg, Joshua. *Jewish Magic and Superstition: A Study in Folk Religion.* New York: Berhman's Jewish Book House, 1939.

Weyer, Johann. *On Witchcraft (De praestigiis daemonum).* Abridged. Edited by Benjamin G. Kohl and H. C. Erik Midelfort. Asheville, N.C.: Pegasus Press, 1998.

infestation   The presence of DEMONs in a place, object, or animal. Infestation occurs when demons are able to take up residence and create disturbances. It is a precursor to more serious demonic problems, such as OPPRESSION and possession.

The Bible does not make direct reference to EXORCISMs of demons from places or animals; however, demonic infestations were well known and accepted in ancient times. Origen, an early father of the church, wrote that the power of the name of JESUS could expel demons from places and animals as well as people.

Infestation can happen as the result of a CURSE or magical spell or ritual, or by the actions of people living in a place. For example, the Catholic Church teaches that using spirit communication devices such as a OUIJA™ board, dabbling in the occult, making a PACT with the DEVIL, or leading a sinful life can create the conditions for infestation. Curses and hexes can allow demons to contaminate an object (see POSSESSED POSSESSIONS).

Infesting demons create chaos and fear through poltergeistlike activity, the manifestation of shadowy figures, and other paranormal phenomena. Victims may hear knocks on the door when no one is present. The knocks usually occur in threes (to mock the Trinity) or in sixes (double three). There are scratching sounds on doors or within walls, hot or cold spots, rooms that just feel "creepy," sounds of baby animals in pain, whisperings, knocks that become pounding on the walls or roof, plumbing that does not turn off, appliances that go on or off without help, and levitation of small objects.

Often such behaviors are attributed to ghosts or poltergeists, especially if there are teenagers in the home. Or they are dismissed out of hand as the products of an overactive imagination. Other mistakes made in this early stage include disbelief by friends, clergy, or family members, leaving the victim frustrated and confused, and turning to a medium or psychic to evaluate the phenomena, because the demonic can easily manipulate the medium's sensitivity.

Sometimes infestations are more subtle, with demons maintaining a low profile in order to gain more oppressive influence over a victim.

Infestations are cleared by minor rites of EXORCISM performed by clergy or trained laypersons. Severely infested objects are destroyed by burning while praying and then scattering the ashes in running water. Mildly infested objects can be exorcized with prayer and a sprinkling of holy water.

FURTHER READING:

Amorth, Gabriele. *An Exorcist: More Stories.* San Francisco: Ignatius Press, 2002.

Fortea, Fr. José Antonio. *Interview with an Exorcist: An Insider's Look at the Devil, Diabolic Possession, and the Path to Deliverance.* West Chester, Pa.: Ascension Press, 2006.

International Association of Exorcists   Roman Catholic organization of priests who perform EXORCISMs. The International Association of Exorcists was founded in 1993 by FATHER GABRIELE AMORTH.

At the first meeting in Rome in 1993, only six exorcists attended. Within a year, 80 exorcists had joined; international membership is now more than 500. Membership is exclusive; a priest must have the permission of his bishop to join. Meetings are held annually in secret.

Father Giancarlo Gramolazzo is president; Amorth serves as honorary president.

The exorcists blame in part the New Age as responsible for a rise in demonic POSSESSION, saying that New Age adherents do not believe in a personal God who reveals himself but in an impersonal God identified with the material world.

Ipos   FALLEN ANGEL and 22nd of the 72 SPIRITS OF SOLOMON. Ipos is an earl and prince who rules 36 LEGIONs of DEMONs. He appears as an angel with a lion's head, goose feet, and a hare's tail; JOHANN WEYER said he appears either as an ANGEL or as an evil and crafty lion. Ipos knows the past and future and imparts wisdom and courage. He makes men witty.

iron Protection against evil, including DEMONs, vampires, witches and evil spirits, and FAIRIES.

Iron repels the DJINN, and LILITH and other childbirth demons and their children. Iron scissors or small implements are placed at beds to ward off demonic attacks. Iron objects placed in coffins and gravesites, and iron nails driven into coffins and graves, prevent vampires and restless ghosts from leaving their graves to attack the living.

Isacaaron DEMON of temptations of the flesh, who played a prominent role in the LOUDUN POSSESSIONS in France in the 17th century. Isacaaron especially possessed and plagued the mother superior, JEANNE DES ANGES, and was blamed for her false pregnancy. The demon jumped from Jeanne into one of her EXORCISTs, Father JEAN-JOSEPH SURIN.

Itzpapalotl Aztec female DEMON and patroness of witches. The name *Itzpapalotl* means "obsidian knife butterfly." She can wear a magic cloak that turns her into a butterfly. Sometimes she appears in a more demonic form, as a female with large butterfly wings edged with obsidian knives, a skull head covered in thick white makeup, a knife for a tongue, fingers with jaguar claws, and toes with eagle claws.

Itzpapalotl once resided in heaven but fell along with the TZITZIMIME. As a demon, she took over the ruling of witches and presides over 13 unlucky signs of the calendar. On those days, she takes a horde of dead witches, who have shape shifted into butterflies and flies, through towns and forests, shrieking and screaming. In order to appease her and her horde, people sacrifice deer.

Jahi   See DRUJ.

James VI and I (1566–1625)   King of both Scotland (as James VI) and England (as James I) and a persecutor of witches, whom he believed to be the servants of the DEVIL. His book, *Daemonologie,* broke no new ground in witch hunting but became a handbook for English demonologists.

James was born in Scotland in 1566 to the violent world of Mary, Queen of Scots and her second husband and first cousin, Henry Stuart, Lord Darnley, who was a vicious and dissipated man. At the time of his conception, Mary was having an affair with her Italian secretary, David Rizzio. Once, Henry attacked Rizzio in Mary's presence in an apparent attempt to cause her to miscarry. Failing that, he and a group of his noblemen murdered Rizzio by hacking him with swords and knives and then heaving him off a balcony.

Mary continued to have affairs and plotted her revenge against Henry. In 1567, she tried to have him killed in a gunpowder explosion. The explosion did not do the job, for Henry was found later in the garden, dead of strangulation.

No one was ever charged with the crime, but his death was rumored to been the result of a plot of the earl of Bothwell, who abducted Mary, raped and impregnated her (she miscarried twins), and then married her. The incident caused an uprising among Scots. Mary abdicated

the throne in favor of one-year-old James, who ruled under regents until 1583, when he began his personal rule as James VI.

Mary later plotted to take the English throne from Elizabeth I, her father's cousin. Elizabeth had her arrested on charges of treason, imprisoned, and then beheaded.

This atmosphere of swirling murder, treason, plotting, and bloodshed was bound to have an impact on James. He took to wearing padded clothing at all times to protect himself against stabbing.

When James took the Scottish throne in 1583, the Scottish clergy, pressured by rising public fears of witchcraft, demanded tougher enforcement of Scotland's witchcraft law, which had been enacted in 1563. James, who believed that witches were evil and posed a threat to God-fearing people, tolerated increasing witch hunts and even participated in some of the trials himself.

James believed that witches tried to kill him on at least three occasions. In the North Berwick witch trials of 1590–92, confessions were made of an alleged plot by witches to murder him and his bride. In 1589, James had agreed to marry by proxy Anne of Denmark, a 15-year-old princess whom he had never met. That same year, she set sail for Scotland from Norway, but her ship was buffeted twice by terrible storms and nearly destroyed. It made port at Oslo, where the passengers where stranded for months. James sailed out to meet the ship. As storms continued, he and Anne were forced to remain in Scandinavia until spring 1590. On their return to Scotland, they were buffeted by yet more storms but managed to make land safely.

The North Berwick witches confessed to raising these storms. James, however, called them "extreme lyars," until one of the accused convinced him of their supernormal powers by repeating to him the private conversation he had had with Anne on their wedding night.

After the North Berwick trials, over which James supervised brutal tortures of the leader John Fian, James made a study of witchcraft in Europe and read the works of the leading demonologists. He was distressed by the arguments that Devil-worshipping witches and their SABBATs were all delusions. He was particularly incensed at the views expressed by REGINALD SCOT in *The Discoverie of Witchcraft* (1854) and by JOHANN WEYER in *De Praestigiis Daemonum* (1563).

Thus, James wrote his own response, *Daemonologie,* published in 1597. *Daemonologie* added no new information about beliefs about witches and increased the public hysteria over witches in Scotland. James affirmed that witches, who received their powers from the Devil, could raise storms, could cause illness and death by burning of waxen images, and were followers of "Diana and her wandering court." He stated that the Devil appeared in the likeness of a dog, cat, ape, or other "such-like beast" and was always inventing new techniques for deceiving others. He defended swimming as a test for witches, in which the accused were bound and thrown into deep water (the innocent sank and usually drowned, and the guilty floated, whereupon they were executed).

James believed in sexual acts with demons but did not believe in impregnation by an INCUBUS. That, he said, was a fabulous tale. He acknowledged that demons could make a woman appear falsely pregnant. The sexual aspects of the nightmare were a "natural sickness," he said, caused by a thick phlegm upon the heart that made people imagine that a spirit was pressing down upon them.

He believed in demonic POSSESSION but doubted the power of the church to cure it permanently. He noted the simplicity of JESUS' instructions for EXORCISM: prayer, fasting, and expelling the demons in his name.

James supported the widely held belief that more women than men were witches because women were inherently weak and predisposed to evil. He accepted the execution of a witch as the therapeutic cure for the victim. He even advocated the death penalty for clients of "cunning men." He defined a witch as "a consulter with familiar spirits."

By 1597, the witch hysteria in Scotland had reached alarming proportions, and there was evidence that over-zealous witch hunters were indicting people on fraudulent evidence. To his credit, James revoked all indictments, and for the remaining years of his rule on the throne of Scotland, executions for witchcraft decreased.

Upon the death of Elizabeth I in 1603, James took the English throne as James I. *Daemonologie* was reissued in London the same year. James also ordered that copies of Scot's *Discoverie* be burned.

In 1604, a new Witchcraft Act was passed by Parliament under pressure from the gentry. The new law stiffened penalties for witchcraft. Under Elizabethan law passed in 1563, WITCHCRAFT, enchantment, CHARMs, or SORCERY that caused bodily injury to people or damage to their goods and chattels was punishable by a year in jail with quarterly exposures in the pillory for the first offense and death for the second offense. A sentence of life in jail with quarterly pillory exposures was given for the divining of treasure and the causing of "unlawful" love and intentional hurt. Bewitching a person to death was a capital offense.

The 1604 law punished crimes of witchcraft with death on the first offense instead of a year in jail or life in jail. In addition, the conjuring or evoking of DEMONs for any purpose whatsoever was made a capital offense.

Passage of the law did not evoke a wave of witch hunts. The first trials of major importance did not occur in England until 1612, trials at Lancaster that saw 10 persons hanged and one pilloried. During James' entire reign of 22 years, fewer than 40 persons were executed for the crime of witchcraft. James pardoned some accused witches because of the weak evidence against them and exposed a number of cases of fraudulent accusations of witches, including the "possession" of a boy in Leicester that sent nine victims to the gallows in 1616. James did not uncover the fraud until after the executions. Though he was sorely displeased with the judge and sergeant, he did not punish them.

The Witchcraft Act of 1604 remained in force until 1736, when it was repealed and replaced by a new law under George II. The 1604 law was used to prosecute the trials of the accused witches in Salem, Massachusetts, in 1692.

In his later years, James' health declined as a result of arthritis, gout, and other diseases. He had a stroke, which severely weakened him, and soon afterward died, on March 27, 1625, while suffering from severe dysentery.

FURTHER READING:
King James I of England. *Demonology.* Edited by G. B. Harrison. San Diego: Book Tree, 2002.
Kittredge, George Lyman. *Witchcraft in Old and New England.* Cambridge, Mass.: Harvard University Press, 1929.
Scot, Reginald. *The Discoverie of Witchcraft.* Yorkshire, England: E. P. Publishing, 1973; 1886 ed.

Jeanne des Anges (1602–1665)   Mother superior of the Ursuline convent in Poitiers, France, who became possessed with major DEMONs in the famous LOUDUN POSSESSIONS case. A mean and vindictive woman, Jeanne des Anges (Joan of the Angels) became the principal DEMONIAC in fraudulent possessions that led to the execution of an innocent priest, URBAIN GRANDIER. She ended her life near sainthood and wrote a vivid account of her experiences in her autobiography, which she modeled on the autobiography of St. Teresa of Avila.

She was born Jeanne de Belciel in 1602 to a noble family. Her father was Louis de Belciel, baron de Coze, and her mother was Charlotte Goumart d'Eschillais. Jeanne evidently suffered tuberculosis early in life, which stunted her growth and left her with a hunchback. Because of her unattractiveness Jeanne developed a withdrawn and defensive personality. She automatically considered most people her enemies, and she was quick to mock others.

Jeanne's parents attempted to get rid of their disagreeable child at an early age by sending her to an aunt who was a prioress at a nearby abbey. After about three years, she was sent home. When she was old enough, she was sent to the Ursuline convent. She was careless in her duties and unpleasant in demeanor, but the nuns tolerated her because her family was wealthy. Suddenly, she underwent a marked change of personality and became docile and extremely devout. The prioress, who was retiring, decided to recommend Jeanne, at age 25, as her replacement. Jeanne retained the position of mother superior for all but three years from 1627 until her death in 1665.

In her autobiography, Jeanne gave a much different and mocking account. She said she deliberately made herself indispensable and used ingratiating behavior to gain her advantage. She also became adept at feigning states of ecstasy and rapture. Through her false spirituality, she sought to prove herself better than the other nuns.

The nuns passed much of their time in gossip, and at the center of attention was the handsome curé of Loudun, Father Urbain Grandier, who was well known for his sexual exploits. At some point, Jeanne became sexually obsessed with him from afar, an obsession that grew for about five years. She wrote:

> When I did not see him, I burned with love for him and when he presented himself to me . . . I lacked the faith to combat the impure thoughts and movements that I felt. . . . Never had the demons created such disorder in me.

When the Ursulines' director, Canon Moussant, died, Jeanne wasted no time in inviting Grandier to replace him. He declined, saying he was not worthy of the post, and besides, he was too busy with parish duties. Shocked and insulted, Jeanne became his enemy and began allying herself with a growing list of Grandier's enemies in town. She appointed to her vacancy a cleric, Canon Mignon, who openly detested Grandier.

Meanwhile, Jeanne regaled her nuns with stories of lurid dreams involving Grandier. She had already told of dreams in which the deceased Moussant returned from purgatory to ask for prayers. Now Moussant was transformed into Grandier, who caressed her, told her he loved her, and pressed her to have sex with him. These salacious stories found receptive ears, for some of the other nuns were also having sexual dreams about other clergymen.

Shortly after Moussant's death in 1632, the nuns said they saw shadowy forms of men, including Moussant and Grandier, moving about the convent at night. Canon Mignon did nothing to discourage the talk or the tales of sexual dreaming, which he began to reinforce by characterizing them as incubi sent by SATAN. Rather, he used these episodes as weapons against Grandier. He met with some of the curé's enemies and conceived a plot in which Grandier could be accused of bewitching the nuns. The conspirators enlisted the aid of Carmelite EXORCISTS. Word spread through Loudun that the Ursuline nuns were plagued by demons, and the demons blamed everything on Grandier.

At first, Grandier shrugged off the stories, confident no one would believe he had done those things to women he had never met. But Mignon persisted, and exorcisms went on for months. Jeanne complied, eager to take revenge on Grandier for spurning her invitation to join the convent.

Mignon's next move was to call in new exorcists who had higher standing, and who firmly believed the Devil was at work: Pierre Rangier, the curé of Veniers, and M. Barre, the curé of Saint-Jacques. The exorcisms were made public, and townspeople poured into the convent to witness them. On October 6, 1632, in his third exorcism, Barre sent Jeanne into convulsions, in which she rolled on the floor, growled and howled, and ground her teeth. Seven devils claimed to have hold of her. The crowd was entertained.

Two days later, Barre battled ASMODEUS, who said he was residing in Jeanne's belly. It took the curé two hours to expel the demon, who finally parted after Jeanne, pinned down to her bed, was administered an enema of a quart of holy water. Jeanne later claimed that she was so confused that she barely knew what was happening to her.

Although Mignon and Barre assured her that she was infested with demons, Jeanne privately doubted that she could be, according to her autobiography, since she had entered into no demonic PACT. She became angry when people talked to her about being possessed and felt that if demons were influencing her, they were quite subtle about it. Nonetheless, she performed as a demoniac during the public exorcisms. Most of the educated people who witnessed the exorcisms did not believe the nuns were genuinely possessed, and physicians believed their conditions had natural causes. The most gullible witnesses were uneducated Catholics.

Mignon lent her his book on the Marseilles Possessions and the death of Father Louis Gaufridi in the AIX-EN-PROVENCE POSSESSIONS, which may have influenced Jeanne and spurred her on in her performances as a demoniac. She allowed herself to believe she was indeed possessed.

Jeanne wrote later in her autobiography that when her possession started, she was plunged into "continual disturbance of mind" for almost three months. She was in constant "rages and fits of madness" and could hardly remember what happened to her. She excused her performances as a weakness of mind and spirit that made her susceptible to suggestion—although she clung to the claim that the suggestion had been from "the demon":

> In most cases I saw quite clearly that I was the prime cause of my turmoil and that the demon only acted according to the openings I gave him.
>
> When I spoke of that to my exorcists, they told me it was the demon who gave me those feelings in order to hide within me, or to cast me into a little despair at seeing myself in so much malignancy. I was not the more satisfied for that, for although I submitted to believing what they were telling me at the time, nevertheless my conscience, which was my judge, gave me no peace. Thus all their assurances blinded me. I think the fact is that it was difficult for them to believe that I was so wicked, and that they believed the devils were giving me these scruples.
>
> To make myself better understood, I must give a few examples, both in important things and light matters, so that those who may read this will know how necessary it is that souls beleaguered by demons should hold firmly to God and greatly beware of themselves.
>
> It so happened, to my great embarrassment, that during the first days when Father Lactance was given to me to be my director and exorcist, I disapproved of his way of conducting many small matters, although it was a very good way; but it was because I was wicked.
>
> One day he undertook to have us all take communion at our grille.
>
> At that time, since we were for the most part sorely afflicted with the inner turmoil and great convulsions, for the reception of the Eucharist the priest would either come into our chancel or have us go out to take communion in the church. I was angry that he wanted to introduce a different practice. I began to murmur about in my heart, and thought within myself that he would do better to follow the way of the other priests.
>
> As I dwelled negligently on that thought, it entered my mind that, to humiliate that father, the demon would have committed some irreverence toward the Very Holy Sacrament. I was so miserable that I did not resist that thought strongly enough. When I went to take communion, the devil seized my head, and after I had received the holy host and had half moistened it, the devil threw it into the priest's face. I know perfectly well that I did not perform that act freely, but I am very sure, to my great embarrassment, that I gave the devil occasion to do it, and that he would not have had this power had I not allied myself with him.

When she took communion, the demon within her forced her to fling the wafer in the face of the priest. Her mind was filled with blasphemies, which she uttered without control. She hated God and the spectacle of his goodness and looked for ways to displease him.

The demon, she said:

> Beclouded me in such a way that I hardly distinguished his desires from mine; he gave me, moreover, a strong aversion for my religious calling, so that sometimes when he was in my head I tore all my veils and such of my sisters' as I could lay hands on; I trampled them underfoot, I chewed them, cursing the hour when I took the vows. All this was done with great violence, I think I was not free.

The exorcists invited two magistrates to witness the possessions for themselves, and they did. Jeanne went into violent contortions and grunted like a pig. Mignon stuck two fingers in her mouth and performed exorcisms. The demons in her revealed that she was indeed under the influence of two diabolical pacts: one made of three hawthorn prickles and one a bunch of roses that she found on the convent stairs and stuck into her belt. Supposedly, Grandier had tossed the roses over the convent wall. Upon "accepting" the roses, Jeanne was bewitched with obsessive love for Grandier that interfered with her ability to think of anything else.

Mignon, pleased at this performance, suggested to the magistrates that this case bore all the hallmarks of a similar case 20 years earlier, the Aix-en-Provence possessions of Ursuline nuns that resulted in the execution by burning of Father Louis Gaufridi, for his alleged demonic pact.

The chief magistrate, M. de Cerisay, believed the case to be one of natural sickness and fraud, and he attempted to stop the exorcisms. But Mignon persuaded the bishop to order them to continue. Legal jockeying ensued, with Grandier seeking a restraining order and the exorcisms continuing, albeit in private. Mignon reinforced daily to the nuns that they had been bewitched by Grandier. Eventually the archbishop intervened and sent his personal physician to investigate. Scared, the nuns dropped their possession fits.

The cessation of the fits caused supporters of the nuns to turn against them, for now it appeared that they were indeed playing out a deception. Even friends and families deserted them, and they fell on hard times financially.

In autumn 1633, King Louis XIII's commissioner, Baron Jean de Martin Laubardemont, investigated and favored putting Grandier on trial. Grandier was advised by friends to flee, but he remained in town, confident that his innocence would allow him to prevail.

Grandier was accused of SORCERY and of consorting with the Devil and his demons and witches at SABBATs. At his preliminary hearings, all of the witnesses who had recanted their testimonies in 1630 came forward and swore that they had in fact told the truth. Grandier's defense was not allowed; his mother protested with petitions against the illegal hearings, and her petitions were destroyed. She appealed to the Parlement of Paris, but the king barred the parlement from becoming involved in the case.

Beelzebub, the principal demon possessing Jeanne des Anges (© RICHARD COOK)

At the hearings, the nuns screamed and screeched at Grandier, claiming his specter roamed the convent at night seducing them. The prosecution produced "pacts" that appeared mysteriously in the nuns' cells or were allegedly vomited up by them. One pact was a piece of paper stained with three drops of BLOOD and containing eight orange seeds. Another was a bundle of five straws and another was a package containing worms, cinders, and hair and nail clippings. On June 17, while possessed by LEVIATHAN, Jeanne vomited up a pact containing—according to her possessing demons—a piece of the heart of a child who had been sacrificed in 1631 at a witches' sabbat near Orléans, the ashes of a eucharist, and some of Grandier's blood and semen.

Countering these shocking spectacles was the nuns' obvious lack of command of previously unlearned foreign languages, a test of demoniacs. Jeanne displayed little knowledge of Latin and made poor attempts to speak it. Some of the other possessed nuns did not even try to understand or speak Latin, Hebrew, or Greek. Often, the nuns resorted to howling and contorting to avoid answering questions. Other times, they claimed that the pacts they had with Grandier forbade them to speak in certain languages.

The nuns also failed the test for clairvoyance. And they claimed that Grandier's magical books were kept in the home of one of his mistresses—but none were found there.

After the death of Grandier, the nuns fell into states of remorse and guilt, but they were subjected to continuing exorcisms before crowds. They performed as if they were circus animals. In December 1634, four new Jesuit exorcists arrived, including Father JEAN-JOSEPH SURIN, to whom Jeanne took an immediate dislike. Whenever approached by him, she went into fits, howled, stuck out her tongue, and ran away. She laughed and mocked him, and her jokes seemed to energize one of the demons, BALAAM, who urged her to continue and thus undermine the progress made by Surin. The priest wrote:

> I saw that this spirit was wholly opposed to the seriousness with which one ought to take the things of God, and that it fostered in her a certain glee which destroys the compunction of heart indispensable to a perfect conversation with God. I saw that in a single hour of this kind of jocularity was enough to ruin everything I had built up in the course of many days, and I induced in her a strong desire to rid herself of this enemy.

Jeanne diverted attention with a false pregnancy. She claimed ISACAARON began tempting her anew; she said "he performed an operation upon my body, the strangest and most furious that could be imagined; thereafter he persuaded me that I was great with child, in such sort that I firmly believed the fact and exhibited all signs."

Jeanne's belly became greatly distended and she stopped menstruating. She vomited frequently and secreted milk from her breasts. She was in a state of extreme agitation nearly constantly and only experienced relief when Isacaaron visited her nightly and sexually assaulted her. Refusals resulted in beatings.

Jeanne considered trying to abort herself with herbs and drugs but abandoned the idea. She considered cutting the baby out of her womb with a knife but could not carry out the deed. Isacaaron once offered her a magic plaster that would terminate the pregnancy, but she refused it.

A physician pronounced her pregnancy to be genuine, but Isacaaron, speaking at an exorcism, claimed it was all deception created by the demons in Jeanne. She threw up a large quantity of blood and the pregnancy symptoms vanished. For Jeanne and Surin, a miracle had taken place.

Surin persisted in trying to rid Jeanne of devils, if not by exorcisms alone, then by spiritual instruction that would elevate her soul. He offered to take on her demons himself and soon became obsessed, and then possessed.

Jeanne continued to revile and resist Surin and then suddenly had a turnabout. She decided she wanted to become a saint; in fact, she wanted to imitate St. Teresa of Avila. She increased her prayer time and took on severe austerities: a hair shirt, a bed of boards, wormwood poured onto her food, and a belt spiked with nails. She beat herself up to seven hours a day. Surin, a great believer in discipline, encouraged her.

Jeanne became more receptive to Surin, and by summer 1635, they were meeting privately in the convent's attic, where he expounded on mystical theology and they prayed together. These private sessions raised gossip in Loudun, which the two ignored.

Whenever Jeanne objected to the mortifications prescribed by Surin, which were private instead of public, she let the demons out to howl and complain. Surin ordered the demons to whip themselves—and they did, making Jeanne scream.

In February 1635, Isacaaron announced that three anonymous magicians had three consecrated wafers, which they intended to burn. Surin ordered Isacaaron to fetch the wafers. At first, the demon refused and then relented. The three wafers mysteriously appeared in a niche at the convent. The feat appeared to be a miracle.

Surin had transformed himself from exorcist to Jeanne's spiritual director, displeasing the Jesuit authorities. In October 1635, he was ordered to return to Bordeaux and be replaced by another exorcist. Distressed, Jeanne fell ill for several days and then asked to be exorcized. On November 5, in front of a large crowd, Surin expelled Leviathan from her and was allowed to stay on at the convent.

A bloody cross appeared on her forehead and remained for three weeks. Then Balaam announced he was ready to go and would write his name on Jeanne's left hand when he did so. Jeanne prayed mightily that the demon would inscribe the name of St. Joseph, not his own. The demon departed on November 29, leaving Jeanne marked with the name *Joseph*. Surin viewed this as an extraordinary grace from God. Others believed it to be the product of autosuggestion. But the crowds saw her as a saint. Later, the names of Jesus, Mary, and St. Francis de Sales were added to her arm. The names would fade after a few weeks and then be renewed by Jeanne's good angel.

Isacaaron left Jeanne on January 7, 1636. Surin took on BEHEMOTH, but 10 months went by with no progress. In October, he broke down and was recalled to Bordeaux. He was replaced by Father Resses.

As she had with Surin, Jeanne resisted Resses, but he forced exorcisms on her anyway. She fell ill and vomited blood. Her condition deteriorated and extreme unction was given. She had a vision in which God told her she would be taken to the point of death but would not die. She reached a point where doctors felt she had only hours to live, and then she had a vision of her good angel in the form of a beautiful youth, followed by St. Joseph, who anointed her with oil, and she miraculously recovered. Later, she revealed her chemise had an oil stain of five drops. She probably faked the evidence, but it took on the status of a relic.

Behemoth announced that he would not depart without Jeanne's making a pilgrimage to the tomb of St. Fran-

cis of Sales at Annency, accompanied by Surin. The priest was recalled to Loudun in June to comply. He and a companion, Father Thomas, accompanied Jeanne on part of her pilgrimage, and then Surin's job with her was done.

Jeanne's five-month pilgrimage was a triumphal march through France in 1638. She visited major cities, including Paris, Lyon, Orléans, Grenoble, Blois, and Annency. Tens of thousands turned out to see her and view her relics, the names on her arm, and the stained shirt. At Annency, a possessed girl was cured by touching the stained shirt.

Jeanne had audiences with royalty, including Queen Anne, wife of Louis XIII; archbishops; and the dying Cardinal Richelieu (who privately thought the Loudun affair was a fraud). Her stained chemise was used as a blanket in the birth of Louis XIV. Everywhere she went, she was hailed and admired.

On October 15, Behemoth kept his end of the bargain and departed from Jeanne, and Surin returned again to Bordeaux.

After the pilgrimage, Jeanne returned to the Loudun convent, never to leave it again. She was bored and hungry for the limelight, but now there were no devils and no miracles to use to gain attention. She fell seriously ill and miraculously recovered, but this time the "miracle" was barely noticed.

A few times, the demons reappeared, to beat her and harass her. Jeanne, however, was more interested in producing heavenly miracles than engaging in fights with the infernal. She claimed her heart split in two and was marked invisibly with the instruments of the Passion. Souls in purgatory appeared to her and spoke. Increasingly, she developed a relationship with her guardian angel and prayed for "true lights" to be revealed to her. Her angel complied, dispensing even personal advice to visitors of the most petty nature.

Jeanne began to write her autobiography in 1644. Her account of events reveals a personality self-absorbed and unconcerned about the consequences of her actions. She made little reference to the unfortunate Grandier, even though at the height of the drama, she had confessed her guilt and remorse at framing him with lies. Rather, she saw her life as a spiritual quest, in which she had allowed demons to act against her as a consequence of her own defective will. Twice during the depths of her spiritual darkness, she had tried to commit suicide.

For years, she wrote to Surin, but she received no reply until 1657, when he resumed serving as her spiritual director until his death in 1665. She enjoyed a correspondence and close friendship with him, confessing the state of her soul, still seeking to be the center of attention to the end of her life.

By 1662, her "miracles" were at an end. Despite her saintliness, she was still the object of criticism and was called a witch and magician even in the last years of her life.

Jeanne died in January 1665. Her head was cut off and placed in a silver and gold reliquary. The stained chemise was already in its own reliquary. These relics were the objects of popular devotion.

The convent commissioned an artist to paint a huge image of the expulsion of Behemoth. In the center, Jeanne knelt before Surin, Tranquille, and a Carmelite, a look of ecstasy on her face. Royalty and commoners looked on. A radiant St. Joseph, accompanied by cherubim, floated overhead with three thunderbolts intended for the demons leaving Jeanne's mouth.

The painting hung in the chapel for more than 80 years, when a bishop ordered it removed. The nuns hid the painting by covering it with another one. In 1772, the convent was suppressed. The painting, chemise, and mummified head were sent into hiding and disappeared.

FURTHER READING:

Certeau, Michel de. *The Possession at Loudun.* Translated by Michael B. Smith. Chicago: University of Chicago Press, 2000.

Ferber, Sarah. *Demonic Possession and Exorcism in Early Modern France.* London: Routledge, 2004.

Huxley, Aldous. *The Devils of Loudun.* New York: Harper and Brothers, 1952.

Jesus   The fight against evil, the DEVIL, and DEMONs are central in the life and purpose of Christianity's Son of God. "The reason the Son of God appeared was to destroy the devil's work," affirms 1 John 3:8. Accounts in the New Testament tell of Jesus' ability to overcome evil forces and to cast out demons afflicting people.

Baptism and Temptation in the Desert

Jesus' BAPTISM by John the Baptist marked the beginning of his ministry. Shortly after that, he spent 40 days in the wilderness, where he was tempted by SATAN. He fasted for 40 days and 40 nights. Then Satan appeared and ordered him to turn stones into loaves of bread to prove that he was the Son of God. Jesus answered, "It is written, 'Man shall not live by bread alone, but by every word that proceeds from the mouth of God'" (Mt. 4:4).

The Devil then took him to the holy city (Jerusalem) and set him on the pinnacle of the temple. He told Jesus to throw himself down and demonstrate that God's ANGELs would protect him. Jesus answered, "Again it is written, 'You shall not tempt the Lord your God'" (Mt 4:6).

Finally, Satan tried a third time to tempt Jesus. He took him to a high mountain, where they could see all the kingdoms of the world. "All this I will give you, if you will fall down and worship me," said the Devil (Mt. 4:9). Jesus rejected him, answering, "Begone, Satan! for it is written, 'You shall worship the Lord your God and him only shall you serve'" (Mt. 4:10).

Satan departed, and angels appeared to minister to Jesus.

The offer of glory in exchange for worship implies a PACT with the Devil, a concept that more than 1,000 years later weighed heavily in the WITCHCRAFT trials of the Inquisition.

Casting Out of Demons

The Gospels of Matthew, Mark, and Luke refer to many instances when Jesus "cast out demons" or "unclean spirits." Such acts are differentiated from healing diseases or defects. Some of the descriptions of the EXORCISMs hint that epilepsy or seizures may have been responsible for what were assumed at the time to be the effects of demons.

The term *exorcize* is from the Greek word *exousia,* meaning to "put under oath and command," invoking a higher authority to force compliance. To exorcize, then, is to adjure (in Latin, *adjuro*) the spirits to depart in the name of God. As such, Jesus was not technically an EXORCIST, for he needed no higher authority.

The first instance of Jesus' casting out demons occurred after his return from the wilderness. Jesus began selecting his disciples and went into Capernaum to teach. Both Mark (1:23–27) and Luke (4:33–36) tell the story; the text appears in the Authorized (King James) Version translation in Mark:

> And there was in their synagogue a man with an unclean spirit; and he cried out, saying, "Let us alone; what have we to do with thee, thou Jesus of Nazareth? Art thou come to destroy us? I know thee who thou art, the Holy One of God." And Jesus rebuked him, saying, "Hold thy peace, and come out of him." And when the unclean spirit had torn him, and cried with a loud voice, he came out of him. And they were all amazed, insomuch that they questioned among themselves saying, "What thing is this? What new doctrine is this? For with authority commandeth he even the unclean spirits, and they do obey him."

The man's POSSESSION and exorcism follow the traditional pattern. First, the demon recognized Christ. Second, the spirit's departure caused great pain to the possessed, coupled with loud voices and cries. Third, the demon ultimately yielded to Jesus' higher power.

Jesus' method of simple command over the demons differed greatly from that practiced by other holy men of his time. Most exorcists of the period relied on ritual, chants, signs, and artifacts to expel evil spirits. Jesus used only his word as the source of ultimate power. Not long after the episode in Capernaum, Mark and Luke describe Jesus' healing the sick and casting out more demons in Galilee (Mark 1:32–34, as follow; Luke 4:38–41):

> That evening, at sundown, they brought to him all who were sick or possessed with demons. And the whole city was gathered together about the door. And he healed many who were sick with various diseases, and cast out many demons; and he would not permit the demons to speak, because they knew him.

After naming his 12 disciples—to whom he gave the power to cast out demons also—Jesus returned home, welcomed by great crowds of the faithful and curious. Some of his friends believed he was temporarily insane, and some of the Jewish scribes considered him possessed by BEELZUBUB. Matthew (12:24–29), Mark (3:22–27, as follows), and Luke (11:14–22) recount the incident:

> And the scribes who came down from Jerusalem said, "He is possessed by Beelzebul, and by the prince of demons he casts out the demons." And he called them to him, and said to them in parables, "How can Satan cast out Satan? If a kingdom be divided against itself, that kingdom cannot stand. And if a house is divided against itself, that house will not be able to stand. And if Satan has risen up against himself, and is divided, he cannot stand but is coming to an end. But no man can enter into a strong man's house, and plunder his goods, unless he first binds the strong man; then indeed he may plunder his house."

The name Beelzebub, or "Lord of the Flies," is a distortion of *Baal-zebul*, referring to the chief Canaanite or Phoenician god, meaning "lord of the divine abode" or "lord of the heavens." In the prophet Elijah's day, the god Baal was the main rival to the Israelite god Yahweh (Jehovah), and his name would represent Satan to the Jews (1 Kings 18; 2 Kings 1:3). This incident also presents the idea of binding Satan to the will of God before he can be thrown out of the "house," or the body of the possessed victim.

The episode most often told about Jesus' casting out demons concerns the Gerasene or Gadarene demoniac, according to Mark (5:1–13) and Luke (26–33), and the two demoniacs in Matthew (8:28–32). Although identified differently, the story is the same. After delivering the Sermon on the Mount, Jesus and his disciples traveled by boat to the country of the Gerasenes, or Gadarenes. There they met a man possessed of an unclean spirit, as told in Mark:

> And they came over unto the other side of the sea, into the country of the Gadarenes. And when he was come out of the ship, immediately there met him out of the tombs a man with an unclean spirit, who had his dwelling among the tombs; and no man could bind him, no, not with chains: Because that he had been often bound with fetters and chains, and the chains had been plucked asunder by him, and the fetters broken in pieces; neither could any man tame him. And always, night and day, he was in the mountains, and in the tombs, crying, and cutting himself with stones. But when he saw Jesus afar off, he ran and worshipped him, And cried with a loud voice, and said, "What have I to do with thee, Jesus, thou Son of the most high God? I adjure thee by God, that thou torment me not." For he said unto him, "Come out of the man, thou unclean spirit." And he asked him, "What is thy name?" And he answered, saying, "My name is Legion: for we are many." And he besought him much

that he would not send them away out of the country. Now there was there nigh unto the mountains a great herd of swine feeding. And all the devils besought him, saying, "Send us into the swine, that we may enter into them." And forthwith Jesus gave them leave. And the unclean spirits went out, and entered into the swine and the herd ran violently down a steep place into the sea, (they were about two thousand;) and were choked in the sea.

As did other possessed souls, the Gerasene demoniac suffered great physical pain and spiritual anguish. He ran to Jesus for help, but the demon within denied Jesus' power and adjured Jesus not to cast him out. Another important part of this story is the naming of the demon, a vital point in the exorcism ritual. A legion is a major unit in the Roman army (who were considered demons by many) consisting of 4,000–6,000 men. An estimate of 2,000 may be low. Finally, however, the demons could not stand up to Jesus any longer and begged to enter the herd of swine. Because pigs were already deemed unclean animals in Jewish law, the choice was appropriate. People in Jesus' day believed that demons hated water, so when the pigs drowned, the demons were destroyed.

Jesus continued to cast out demons during his ministry, even cleansing the unclean spirit from the daughter of a Gentile woman who accepted him as the messiah (Mark 7:25–30, which follows; Mt. 15:21–28).

> But immediately a woman, whose little daughter was possessed by an unclean spirit, heard of him, and came and fell down at his feet. Now the woman was a Greek, a Syrophoenician by birth. And she begged him to cast the demon out of her daughter. And he said to her, "Let the children first be fed, for it is not right to take the children's bread and throw it to the dogs." But she answered him, "Yes, Lord; yet even the dogs under the table eat the children's crumbs." And he said to her, "For this saying you may go to your way; the demon has left your daughter." And she went home, and found the child lying in bed, and the demon gone.

Such acts were crowd pleasers, and the disciples told Jesus of an exorcist who claimed to cast out demons in his name (Luke 9:49–50):

> John answered, "Master, we saw a man casting out demons in your name, and we forbade him, because he does not follow with us." But Jesus said to him, "Do not forbid him; for he that is not against you is for you."

Later, 70 other followers, sent out as disciples but not specifically given the power to exorcise, found they were also able to cast out demons. Jesus reminded them that the joy was not that they were able to exorcise, but that God had found them worthy (Luke 10:17–20):

> The seventy returned with joy, saying, "Lord, even the demons are subject to us in your name!" and he said unto them, "I saw Satan fall like lightning from heaven.

Jesus exorcizing demons from a young man (AUTHOR'S COLLECTION)

Behold, I gave given you authority to tread upon serpents and scorpions, and over all the power of the enemy; and nothing shall hurt you. Nevertheless, do not rejoice in this, that the spirits are subject to you; but rejoice that your names are written in heaven."

After Jesus' death, the power of his name grew, and exorcists used it to quell demons. However, the name of Jesus was not always a guarantee of success, as demonstrated in Acts 19:13–16:

Then some of the itinerant Jewish exorcists undertook to pronounce the name of the Lord Jesus over those who had evil spirits, saying, "I adjure you by the Jesus whom Paul preaches." Seven sons of a Jewish high priest named Sceva were doing this. But the evil spirit answered them, "Jesus I know, and Paul I know; but who are you?" And the man in whom the evil spirit was leaped upon them, mastered all of them, and overpowered them, so that they fled out of the house naked and wounded.

This example shows the dangers of exorcism to the exorcist. It also drove home the power of Jesus' name, influencing some to burn their books of "magical arts."

These stories in the Gospels provided proof to medieval thinkers that Satan not only was real, but took possession of innocent souls at will. If not only Jesus Christ but his disciples—even those not specifically chosen but only devoutly faithful—were able to cast out demons, then holy men of the Church everywhere had the same power to exorcise in the name of the Lord.

John Bosco (1815–1888)   Saint and founder of the Society of St. Francis De Sales, known as the Salesians. John Bosco was known as the "Dreaming Saint" because of his frequent lucid dreams, more like out-of-body travels, in which he encountered angels, JESUS, Mary, and other religious figures and journeyed to heaven and HELL. His visit to hell was particularly detailed, and he used this and other lucid dream experiences to teach his students religious lessons. At the request of Pope Pius IX, he kept detailed records of his dreams.

Bosco was born in Becchi, Piedmont, Italy, to a peasant farmer family. His father died when he was two, and he was raised by his mother. He had his first lucid dream when he was about nine years old, in which a man, possibly Jesus, and a woman, possibly Mary, revealed his life purpose and destiny. He dedicated himself to his spiritual work with great and unwavering seriousness. His lucid dreaming increased in frequency as he grew older.

At age 16, he began studying for the priesthood and was ordained on June 5, 1841, at age 26. He went to Turin and enrolled at the Convitto Ecclesiastico, a theological college that trained young priests for the pastoral life. He began a Sunday catechism for poor boys and soon was taking in and housing them. He constructed a church, placing it under the patronage of his favorite saint, Francis de Sales. By 1856, he had 150 resident boys, plus four workshops and some 500 children in oratories. This became the Society of St. Francis de Sales in 1859. John died on January 31, 1888, and was canonized in 1934 by Pope Pius XI. The Salesians work around the world.

Dreams
John's unusual dream life attracted the interest of Pope Pius IX, who instructed him to record his dreams. More than 150 of John's unusual dreams were collected and recorded by his followers. Many of the dreams were prophetic and concerned his boys and the Salesian order. Other dreams were in harmony with his religious training and beliefs, couched in symbols of his religious life, and concerned the need to follow Catholic doctrine in order to attain salvation.

John's lucid dreams were quite long and involved much specific detail. Unlike most ordinary dreams, they were logical and followed a complete story line from beginning to end. He was usually accompanied by a guide figure, either an angel, St. Francis de Sales, St. Dominic Savio, or a mysterious man he referred to as "the man with the cap." The dreams seemed more like real experiences than dreams. His sensory impressions were so strong that sometimes he would clap his hands or touch himself in the dream to try to ascertain whether he was dreaming or was awake. This is a technique used today by lucid dreamers to verify that their experience is real.

Sometimes physical phenomena followed him out of the dream and into waking consciousness. He would awaken exhausted. In one dramatic dream where he was shown the horrors of hell, the putrid smell of evil remained after he awakened. This bleed-through between worlds is characteristic of shamanic journeys and belongs to Carl G. Jung's "psychoid unconscious," a level in the unconscious that is not accessible to consciousness, but that has properties in common with the physical world.

Visit to Hell

Among the many dreams recorded by John, one of his longest and most vivid concerns a frightfully realistic visit to the bowels of hell. John is accompanied by "the man with the cap." John sometimes protested in his dream and tried to resist the guide, but he could not put off whatever business was intended for him in the night.

As with all of John's lucid dreams, this one follows a religious theme, conforms to Catholic doctrine, and provides John with guidance and instructions for running his oratory program for boys. The visit to hell took place over two nights:

No sooner had I fallen asleep than I dreamed that I saw a most loathsome toad, huge as an ox, enter my room and squat at the foot of my bed. I stared breathlessly as its legs, body and head swelled and grew more and more repugnant; its green body, fiery eyes, red-lined mouth and throat, and small bony ears presented a terrifying sight. Staring wildly, I kept muttering to myself: "But a toad has no ears." I also noticed two horns jutting from its snout and two greenish wings sprouting from its sides. Its legs looked like those of a lion, and its long tail ended in a forked tip.

At the moment, I seemed not a bit afraid; but when that monster began edging closer to me, opening its huge, tooth-studded jaws, I really became terribly frightened. I thought it was a demon from Hell, because it looked like one. I made the Sign of the Cross, but nothing happened. I rang the bell, but no one responded. I shouted, but in vain. The monster would not retreat. "What do you want of me, you ugly devil?" I asked. As if in answer, it just crept forward, ears fully stretched out and pointing upward. Then, resting its front paws on the top of the bedstead and raising itself on its hind legs, it paused momentarily, looked at me and crawled forward on by bed until its snout was close to my face. I felt such revulsion that I tried to jump out of bed, but just then the monster opened its jaws wide. I wanted to defend myself and shove the monster back, but it was so hideous that, even in my predicament, I did not dare to touch it. I screamed and frenziedly reached behind me for the small holy water font, but I only hit the wall. Meanwhile, the monstrous toad had managed to mouth my head, so that half of my body was inside its foul jaws. "In the name of God," I shouted, "why are you doing this to me?" At these words, the toad drew back and let my head free. Again, I made the Sign of the Cross, and since I had now dipped my hand in the holy water

font, I flung a few drops of water at the monster. With a frightening shriek it fell backward and vanished, while a mysterious voice from on high clearly said: "Why don't you tell them?"

I turned in that direction and saw a distinguished person standing by my bed. Feeling guilty about my silence, I asked: "What should I tell my boys?"

"What you have seen and heard in your last dreams and what you have wanted to know and what you shall have revealed to you tomorrow night!" He then vanished.

I spent the whole next day worrying about the miserable night in store for me, and when evening came, loath to go to bed, I sat at my desk browsing through books until midnight. The mere thought of having more nightmares thoroughly scared me. However, with great effort, I finally went to bed.

Lest I should fall asleep immediately and start dreaming, I set my pillow upright against the headboard and practically sat up, but soon in my exhaustion I simply fell asleep. Immediately the same person of the night ["the man with the cap."] before appeared at my bedside.

"Get up and follow me!" he said.

"For heaven's sake," I protested, "leave me alone. I am exhausted! I've been tormented by a toothache for several days now and need rest. Besides, nightmares have completely worn me out." I said this because this man's apparition always means trouble, fatigue and terror for me.

"Get up," he repeated. "You have no time to lose."

I complied and followed him. "Where are you taking me?" I asked.

"Never mind. You'll see."

John is led to a lifeless desert, vast in expanse. He and his guide trudge across it. A road appears, beautiful, wide, and neatly paved. Flowers and greenery grow along the sides. The road begins to slope downward. Suddenly, John notices that boys from the oratory are following him. Without warning, one by another falls to the ground and is dragged toward a drop in the distance, which slopes into a furnace. The guide explains that the boys fall because they are ensnared in traps—traps they have made themselves out of sin. The boys who are stricter in their religious observances are able to walk without becoming ensnared.

As they continue along the downward-sloping road, the scenery changes. The lush roses and flowers give way to hedges of thorns. The road becomes gutted and filled with boulders. Most of the boys leave to follow other paths.

The descent becomes so arduous that John falls repeatedly and finally he complains to the guide that he cannot go another step. The guide merely continues on. John realizes he has no choice but to follow.

We continued our descent, the road now becoming so frightfully steep that it was almost impossible to stand erect. And then, at the bottom of this precipice, at the entrance of a dark valley, an enormous building loomed into sight, its towering portal, tightly locked, facing our road. When I finally got to the bottom, I became smothered by a suffocating heat, while a greasy, green-tinted smoke lit by flashes of scarlet flames rose from behind those enormous walls which loomed higher than mountains.

"Where are we? What is this?" I asked my guide.

"Read the inscription on that portal and you will know."

I looked up and read these words: *Ubi non est redemption*—"The place of no reprieve." I realized that we were at the gates of Hell. The guide led me all around this horrible place. At regular distances, bronze portals like the first overlooked precipitous descents; on each was an inscription, such as: *Discedite, maledicti, in ignem aeternum qui paratus est diabolo et angelis eius*—"Depart from Me, you cursed into everlasting fire which was prepared for the devil and his angels" (Matt. 25:41). *Omnis arbor quae non facit fructum bonum excidetur et in ignem mittetur*—"Every tree that does not bear good fruit is cut down and thrown into the fire" (Matt. 7:19).

I tried to copy them into my notebook, but my guide restrained me: "There is no need. You have them all in Holy Scripture. You even have some of them inscribed in your porticoes."

At such a sight I wanted to turn back and return to the Oratory. As a matter of fact, I did start back, but my guide ignored my attempt. After trudging through a steep, never-ending ravine, we again came to the foot of the precipice facing the first portal. Suddenly the guide turned to me. Upset and startled, he motioned to me to step aside. "Look!" he said.

John is startled to see one of his boys dashing down the road out of control. He has a wild look about him, and his arms windmill as though he's trying to resist a great force. John wants to help him, but the guide restrains him. The boy is fleeing from God's wrath. He tumbles into a ravine and hits a bronze portal at the bottom.

As the boy crashed into the portal, it sprang open with a roar, and instantly a thousand inner portals opened with a deafening clamor as if struck by a body that had been propelled by an invisible, most violent, irresistible gale. As these bronze doors—one behind the other, though at a considerable distance from each other—remained momentarily open, I saw far into the distance something like furnace jaws spouting fiery balls the moment the youth hurtled into it. As swiftly as they had opened, the portals then clanged shut again.

Many more boys, screaming in terror, follow. They are all swallowed through the portal. Is there no way to save them? John asks. The guide replies that they have their rules and sacraments—let them observe them.

The guide then instructs John to enter the portal, saying he will learn much. John shrinks back in horror. Then he realizes that he is in no danger, for he cannot be condemned to hell without being judged, and he has not yet been judged. John agrees to go forward.

We entered that narrow, horrible corridor and whizzed through it with lightning speed. Threatening inscriptions shone eerily over all the inner gateways. The last one opened into a vast, grim courtyard with a large, unbelievably forbidding entrance at the far end. [John pauses to read various biblical verses about the certain tortures of hell for the wicked.] "From here on," [the guide] said, "No one may have a helpful companion, a comforting friend, a loving heart, a compassionate glance, or a benevolent word. All that is gone forever. Do you just want to see or would you rather experience these things yourself?"

"I only want to see!" I answered.

"Then come with me," my friend added, and, taking me in tow, he stepped through that gate into a corridor at whose far end stood an observation platform, closed by a huge, single crystal pane reaching from the pavement to the ceiling. As soon as I crossed its threshold, I felt an indescribable terror and dared not take another step. Ahead of me I could see something like an immense cave, which gradually disappeared into recesses sunk far into the bowels of the mountains. They were all ablaze, but theirs was not an earthly fire, with leaping tongues of flames. The entire cave—walls, ceiling, floor, iron, stones, wood, and coal—everything was a glowing white at temperatures of thousands of degrees. Yet the fire did not incinerate, did not consume. I simply cannot find words to describe the cavern's horror. *Praeparata est enim ab heri Thopeth, a rege praeparata, profunda et dilatata. Nutrimenta eius, ignis et ligna multa; flatus Domini sicut torrens sulphuris succendens eam*—"For in Topheth there has been prepared beforehand . . . a pit deep and wide with straw and wood in plenty. The breath of Yahweh, like a stream of brimstone, will set fire to it" (Is. 30:33).

I was staring in bewilderment around me when a lad dashed out of a gate. Seemingly unaware of anything else, he emitted a most shrilling scream, like one who is about to fall into a cauldron of liquid bronze, and plummeted into the center of the cave; instantly, he too became incandescent and perfectly motionless, while the echo of his dying wail lingered for an instant more. . . .

As I looked again, another boy came hurtling down into the cave at break-neck speed. He too was from the oratory. As he fell, so he remained. He too emitted one single heartrending shriek that blended with the last echo of the scream that had come from the youth who had preceded him. Other boys kept hurtling in the same way in increasing numbers, all screaming the same way and then all becoming equally motionless and incandescent. I noticed that the first seemed frozen to the spot, one hand and one foot raised into the air; the second boy seemed bent almost double to the floor. Others stood or hung in various other positions, balancing themselves on one foot or hand, sitting or lying on their backs or on their sides, standing or kneeling, hands clutching their hair. Briefly, the scene resembled a large statuary group of youngsters cast into ever more painful postures. Other lads hurtled into that same furnace. Some I knew; others were strangers to me. I then recalled what is written in the Bible to the effect that as one falls into Hell, so he shall forever remain. *Lignum, in quocumque loco ceciderit, ibi erit*—"Where the tree falls, there it shall lie" (Eccles. 13:3).

More frightened than ever, I asked my guide: "When these boys come dashing into this cave, don't they know where they are going?"

"They surely do. They have been warned a thousand times, but they still choose to rush into the fire, because they do not detest sin and are loath to forsake it. Furthermore, they despise and reject God's incessant, merciful invitations to do penance. Thus provoked, Divine Justice harries them, hounds them, and goads them on, so that they cannot halt until they reach this place."

"Oh, how miserable these unfortunate boys must feel in knowing they no longer have any hope," I exclaimed.

"If you really want to know their innermost frenzy and fury, go a little closer," my guide remarked.

I took a few steps forward and saw that many of those poor wretches were savagely striking at each other like mad dogs. Others were clawing their own faces and hands, tearing their own flesh and spitefully throwing it about. Just then the entire ceiling of the cave became as transparent as crystal and revealed a patch of Heaven and their radiant companions safe for all eternity.

"Why do I hear no sound?" I asked my guide.

"Go closer!" he advised.

Pressing my ear to the crystal window, I heard screams and sobs, blasphemes and imprecations against the Saints. It was a tumult of voices and cries, shrill and confused. . . .

"Such are the mournful chants which shall echo here throughout eternity. But their shouts, their efforts and their cries are all in vain. *Omnis dolor irruet super eos!*—'All evil will fall upon them'" (Job 20:22).

"Here time is no more. Here is only eternity.". . .

He led me away and we went down through a corridor into a lower cavern, at whose entrance I read: *Vermis eorum non morietur, et ignis non extinguetur*—"Their worm shall not die and their fire shall not be quenched" (Is. 66:24). *Dabit Dominus omnipotens ignem et vermes in carnes eorum ut urantur et sentiant usque in sempiternum*—"He will give fire and worms into their flesh, that they may feel for ever" (Judith 16:21).

Here one could see how atrocious was the remorse of those who had been pupils in our schools. What a torment was theirs to remember each unforgiven sin and its just punishment, the countless, even extraordinary means they had to mend their ways, persevere in virtue and earn Paradise, and their lack of response to the many favors promised and bestowed by the Virgin Mary. What a torture to think that they could have been saved so easily, yet now are irredeemably lost, and to remember the many good resolutions made and never kept. Hell is indeed paved with good intentions!

In the lower cavern, I again saw those Oratory boys who had fallen into the fiery furnace. Some are listening to me right now; others are former pupils or even strangers to me. I drew closer to them and noticed that they were all covered with worms and vermin, which gnawed at their vitals, hearts, eyes, hands, legs and entire bodies so ferociously as to defy description. Helpless and motionless, they were a prey to every kind of torment. Hoping I might be able to speak with them or to hear something from them, I drew even closer, but no one spoke or even looked at me. I then asked my guide why, and he explained that the damned are totally deprived of freedom. Each must fully endure his own punishment, with absolutely no reprieve whatsoever.

"And now," he added, "you too must enter that cavern."

"Oh no!" I objected in terror. "Before going to Hell, one has to be judged. I have not been judged yet, and so I will not go to Hell!"

"Listen," he said, "What would you rather do: visit Hell and save your boys, or stay outside and leave them in agony?"

For a moment I was struck speechless. "Of course, I love my boys and wish to save them all," I replied, "but isn't there some other way out?"

"Yes, there is a way," he went on, "provided you do all you can."

John and the guide then have a long conversation about what makes a good confession, and about the need to cultivate the virtues and obedience to the church. The guide tells John which boys are guilty of what crimes. He gives permission to John to discuss anything of the dream with the boys. John thanks him and asks to leave.

Encouragingly, he took my hand and held me up because I could hardly stand on my feet. Leaving that hall, in no time at all we retraced our steps through that horrible courtyard and the long corridor. But as soon as we stepped across the last bronze portal, he turned to me and said, "Now that you have seen what others suffer, you too must experience a touch of Hell."

"No, no!" I cried in terror.

He insisted, but I kept refusing.

"Do not be afraid," he told me; "just try it. Touch this wall."

I could not muster enough courage and tried to get away, but he held me back. "Try it," he insisted. Gripping my arm firmly, he pulled me to the wall. "Only one touch," he commanded, "so that you may say you have both seen and touched the walls of eternal suffering and that you may understand what the last wall must be like if the first to so unendurable. Look at this wall!"

I did intently. It seemed incredibly thick. "There are a thousand walls between this and the real fire of Hell," my guide continued. "A thousand walls encompass it, each a thousand measures thick and equally distant from the next one. Each measure is a thousand miles. This wall therefore is millions and millions of miles from Hell's real fire. It is just a remote rim of Hell itself."

When he said this, I instinctively pulled back, but he seized my hand, forced it open, and pressed it against the first of the thousand walls. The sensation was so utterly excruciating that I leaped back with a scream and found myself sitting up in bed. When I got up this morning I noticed that it was swollen. Having my hand pressed against the wall, though only in a dream, felt so real that, later, the skin of my palm peeled off.

The dream so upset John that for several nights he had difficulty falling asleep. As vivid as his description is, John assured others that he gave them only a watered-down, abbreviated version of what really transpired in the dream. "Bear in mind that I have not tried to frighten you very much, and so I have not described these things in all their horror as I saw them and as they impressed me," he said. "We know that the Lord always portrayed Hell in symbols, because, had He described it as it really is, we would not have understood Him. No mortal can comprehend these things. The Lord knows them and He reveals them to whomever He wills."

FURTHER READING:
Forty Dreams of St. John. Rockford, Ill.: TAN Books and Publishers, 1996.

Johnson, Carl Leonard (1954–); Johnson, Keith Edward (1954–); Johnson, Sandra Ann Hutchings (1963–) Paranormal investigators, especially of cases involving demonic activity. Carl and Keith Johnson (identical twin brothers) have worked as demonologists with paranormal investigators and have appeared on reality television shows featuring demonic cases. Keith and Sandra Johnson (husband and wife) founded the New England Anomalies Research organization.

Keith and Carl were born on December 9, 1954, in Providence, Rhode Island, and grew up in North Scituate, Rhode Island. The Johnson family was the first to occupy the new house in North Scituate. Family members, including the children, soon experienced paranormal phenomena, such as disembodied voices and knockings at the walls and windows. Once, water in a glass held by the boys' mother suddenly vanished with a loud "slurping" sound. By the time Keith and Carl were five, the sounds of animated human conversation could be heard outside their bedroom window. Although the conversation sounded close enough to be clearly heard, no specific words could be distinguished. This and other odd experiences led the boys to become intensely interested in spirit phenomena at an early age.

While in school in Scituate, Carl and Keith began serious study of the paranormal, including ghosts, ANGELs,

DEMONs, and other inhuman spirits. Carl was especially interested in the demonic and the darker side of both human and spirit nature. He began concentrating on the works of ALEISTER CROWLEY and Anton Szandor LaVey (see SATANISM), among others.

When Carl and Keith were 17, they attended a lecture at Rhode Island College given by ED AND LORRAINE WARREN. They struck up a lifelong friendship with the famed paranormal investigators and demonologists. This meeting, especially with Ed, was a turning point for Keith, inspiring him to pursue the field of demonology.

The two participated in paranormal investigations with Rhode Island groups and worked occasionally with the Warrens, assisting in an EXORCISM.

Sandra Ann Hutchings was born in Warwick, Rhode Island, on May 17, 1963. She was the seventh child of a seventh child, a birth order that in folklore indicates supernatural powers such as psychic abilities. She attended high school in Warwick and received her college degree in human services in Warwick as well. Sandra also became actively involved in local theater in Warwick, where she met Keith. They married in 1991 and live in Warwick with their son, Keith Edward Johnson, Jr.

In the 1990s, Carl also moved to Warwick. They became involved for a time with The Atlantic Paranormal Research Society, whose members have starred in a popular reality television show, *Ghost Hunters.* In 2004, Keith and Sandra branched off to found their own group, New England Anomalies Research, which Carl joined. They have worked with lay demonologists such as JOHN ZAFFIS and ADAM BLAI and have appeared on other reality shows besides *Ghost Hunters.*

Keith and Sandra teach classes and lecture on the paranormal, specializing in inhuman hauntings. They host a weekly television talk show, *Ghosts R NEAR,* aired in New England. Carl serves as alternate cohost.

The Johnsons estimate that approximately 15 percent of hauntings involve nonhuman entities. Such cases have been on the rise since about the 1990s. One significant factor is the overall rise in global tensions and feelings of insecurity and vulnerability, due in part to terrorism and the World Trade Center attacks in 2001.

FURTHER READING:
Near England Anomalies Research Web site. URL: http://www.nearparanormal.com.

Jonah   See LEVIATHAN.

Kabbalah (Cabala, Kabala, Qabalah) The mysticism of classical Judaism, and part of the foundation of the Western magical tradition.

Kabbalah is derived from the Hebrew word *QBL (Qibel)*, meaning "to receive" or "that which is received." It refers especially to a secret oral tradition handed down from teacher to pupil. The term *Kabbalah* was first used in the 11th century by Ibn Gabirol, a Spanish philosopher, and has since become applied to all Jewish mystical practice. The Kabbalah is founded on the Torah, but it is not an intellectual or ascetic discipline. It is a means for achieving union with God while maintaining an active life in the mundane world.

Branches of the Kabbalah
There are four main, overlapping branches of the Kabbalah:

1. *The Classical, or Dogmatic, Kabbalah* concerns the study of the Torah and the central texts of the Kabbalah, such as the Sefer Yetzirah and the Sefer Zohar (see later discussion).
2. *The Practical Kabbalah* concerns MAGIC, such as the proper ways to make TALISMANS and AMULETs, and lore about ANGELs and DEMONs.
3. *The Literal Kabbalah* concerns the relationship between the letters of the Hebrew alphabet and numbers. It features the deciphering of relationships and correspondences through *gematria,* a system for determining the numerical values of

words and names; the finding of acronyms through *notarikon,* in which the first letters of words are used to make new words; and an encryption system called *temurah,* in which letters are transposed into code. *Temurah* plays a role in interpreting the Torah and in making talismans.
4. *The Unwritten Kabbalah* concerns the study of the Tree of Life (discussed later).

Of the four branches, the Practical Kabbalah, Literal Kabbalah, and Unwritten Kabbalah are the most important to the Western mystery tradition. Joined with Hermetic principles and philosophy, these parts of the Kabbalah create a philosophical, mystical, and magical system for the practice of ceremonial magic. This system, sometimes called the "Western Kabbalah" or "Western Qabalah," also plays a role in practical magic for the casting of spells.

History of the Kabbalah
According to lore, God taught what became the Kabbalah to ANGELS. After the Fall, angels taught the knowledge to Adam in order to provide humans a way back to God. The knowledge was passed to Noah, then to Abraham and Moses, who in turn initiated 70 elders. Kings David and SOLOMON were initiates. Influenced by Gnosticism and Neoplatonism, the oral tradition was passed on into the tradition and literature of the Merkabah mystics (ca. 100 B.C.E.–1000 C.E.).

Merkabah means "God's Throne-Chariot" and refers to the chariot of Ezekiel's vision. The goal of the Merkabah mystic was to enter the throne world and perceive God sitting upon his throne. The throne world was reached after passing through seven heavens while in an ecstatic trance state. The passage of the mystic was dangerous, impeded by hostile angels. Talismans, SEALs, the sacred names of angels, and incantations were required to navigate through the obstacles.

The historical origin of the true Kabbalah centers on the Sefer Yetzirah (Book of Creation), attributed to Rabbi Akiba, whom the Romans martyred. The book's exact date of origin is unknown. It was in use in the 10th century, but it may have been authored as early as the third century.

The Sefer Yetzirah presents a discussion on cosmology and cosmogony and sets forth the central structure of the Kabbalah. It also is reputed to contain the formula for creation of a golem, an artificial human.

In 917, a form of practical kabbalism was introduced by Aaron ben Samuel in Italy; it later spread through Germany and became known as German kabbalism or Early Hasidim. It drew upon the Merkabah practices, in that it was ecstatic, had magic rituals, and had as primary techniques prayer, contemplation, and meditation. The magical power of words and names assumed great importance and gave rise to the techniques of *gematria, notarikon,* and *temurah.*

The Classical Kabbalah was born in the 13th century in Provence, France, and moved into Spain, where it was developed most extensively by medieval Spanish Jews. The primary work from which Classical Kabbalah developed is the Sefer Zohar (Book of Splendor), attributed to a second-century sage, Rabbi Simeon bar Yohai, but actually written between 1280 and 1286 by the Spanish kabbalist Moses de Leon. According to lore, the book comprises the teachings given to Rabbi Simeon by divine revelation.

The teachings of the Zohar became known as the Spanish Kabbalah and spread into Europe in the 14th and 15th centuries. After the expulsion of Jews from Spain in 1492, Kabbalah study became more public. Isaac Luria Ashkenazi (1534–72), called the Ari Luria, a student of the great kabbalist Moses Cordovero (1522–70), conceived of bold new theories, which gave the Kabbalah a new terminology and complex new symbolism. Luria emphasized letter combinations as a medium for meditation and mystical prayer.

In the 14th century, a Practical Kabbalah developed, involving magical techniques for making amulets and talismans and for invoking spirits. The Practical Kabbalah is complex and features the use of magical alphabets, secret codes of communication with angels.

The Hasidic movement emerged from the Lurianic Kabbalah and made Kabbalah accessible to the masses. The Hasidim are the only major branch of modern Judaism to follow mystical practices. Interest in the Kabbalah among Jews declined after the 18th century. The reconstructionist movement, founded in 1922 by Rabbi Mordecai M. Kaplan, borrows from Hasidic traditions and espouses a more mystical Judaism. Interest in Kabbalah enjoyed a cross-cultural renewal that began in the late 20th century as part of a broad interest in esoteric subjects.

Western occult interest in the Kabbalah grew first out of German kabbalism and then Lurianic kabbalism. Christian occultists were attracted to the magical amulets, incantations, demonology, angelology, seals, and letter permutations, and they used these as the basis for ritual magical texts (see GRIMOIRES). The Tetragrammaton (*YHVH, Yod He Vau He,* or *Yahweh,* the sacred name of God) was held in great awe for its power over all things in the universe, including DEMONs, a subject of intense fear and interest.

In the late 15th century, the Kabbalah was harmonized with Christian doctrines, which supposedly proved the divinity of Christ. Cornelius Agrippa von Nettesheim included Kabbalah in his monumental work, *Occult Philosophy* (1531). Also in the 16th century, alchemical symbols were integrated into the Christian Kabbalah.

Interest in the Kabbalah received renewed attention in the 19th century from non-Jewish occultists such as Francis Barrett, Eliphas Levi, and Papus. Levi's works were especially important in the occult revival that spread through Europe in the 19th century. As did some of his contemporaries, Levi related the Kabbalah to the Tarot and numerology and drew connections to Freemasonry, in which he saw a fusion of Judaic kabbalism and Neoplatonic Christianity. The Kabbalah, he said in *The Book of Splendors,* is one of three occult sciences of certitude; the other two are Magic and Hermeticism. Of the Kabbalah, Levi said:

> The Qabalah, or traditional science of the Hebrews, might be called the mathematics of human thought. It is the algebra of faith. It solves all problems of the soul as equations, by isolating the unknowns. It gives to ideas the clarity and rigorous exactitude of numbers; its results, for the mind, are infallibility (always relative to the sphere of human knowledge) and for the heart, profound peace.

The Kabbalah formed a central part of the teachings of the Hermetic Order of the Golden Dawn, one of the most significant esoteric orders in the Western mystery tradition, which flourished in England during the late 19th and early 20th centuries. In 1888, the Golden Dawn founder, Samuel Liddle Macgregor Mathers, published the first English translation of a Latin translation of the Kabbalah, *Kabbala Denuda,* by Knorr von Rosenroth. In his introduction, Mathers describes the Kabbalah as the key that unlocks the mysteries of the Bible.

Central Concepts of the Kabbalah
God is Ain Soph (without end or unending), who is unknowable, unnamable, and beyond representation. God

created the world out of himself but is not diminished in any way through the act of creation; everything remains within him. The aim of human beings is to realize union with the divine. All things are reflected in a higher world, and nothing can exist independently of all else. Thus, humans, by elevating their soul to unite with God, also elevate all other entities in the cosmos.

One of the mysteries of the Kabbalah is why God chose to create imperfect, lower worlds, though it is held that he did so because he wished to show the measure of his goodness. He created the world by means of 32 secret paths of wisdom, which are formed of letters and numbers: the 22 letters of the Hebrew alphabet and 10 *sephirot* (from the Hebrew word for sapphire), which are vessels bearing the emanations of God, or are expressions of God. They form a language that substitutes for God. The *sephirot* are the source from which all numbers emanate and by which all reality is structured.

The *sephirot* comprise the sacred, unknowable, and unspeakable personal name of God: *YHVH* (*Yahweh*), the Tetragrammaton. So sacred is the Tetragrammaton that other names, such as *Elohim*, *Adonai*, and *Jehovah*, are substituted in its place in Scripture. The letters *YHVH* correspond to the Four Worlds that constitute the cosmos:

- Atziluth is the world of archetypes and emanation, from which are derived all forms of manifestation. The *sephirot* themselves exist here. Atziluth is the realm of contemplation.
- Briah (also Beriyah) is the world of creation, in which archetypal ideas become patterns. The Throne of God is here, and God sits upon it and lowers his essence to the rest of his creation. It is the realm of meditation.
- Yetzirah is the world of formation, in which the patterns are expressed. It is the world of speech and the realm of ritual magic.
- Assiah is the world of the material. It is the realm of action in daily life.

Demonology in the Kabbalah

Most of the demon lore is part of the Practical Kabbalah, a syncretic blend of Talmudic and Midrashic lore, and adapted Arabian, Christian, and Eastern European demonologies and folk beliefs. As in most demonologies, there are contradictions about demons, their nature and duties. Various texts have long lists of individual demons and types of demons.

Demons are made of fire and air and live in wastelands. They are associated with cold and the north. They have subtle bodies that allow them to fly through the air; they occupy the space between the Moon and Earth. They have life spans and die, but they live much longer than human beings, especially their kings and queens. Some, such as LILITH and Naamah, will live until Judgment Day.

Demons are often described as under the direction of SAMAEL. Demons gather at nocturnal revelries, where they have intercourse with Samael, similar to the SABBATs attended by witches in Christian demonology.

Other demons are under the direction of Ashmedai (ASMODEUS), whose name in *gematria* means "pharaoh." Demons also are linked to the left-hand, or evil, side of the *sephirot* of the Tree of Life (see later discussion).

Sexual activities between demons and humans are prominent. Demons cannot reproduce on their own. Through sex, demons can multiply and take on physical form. Adam spawned a hybrid human-demon race, which has continued on down through the ages through the sexual intercourse between humans and demons. Adam and Eve's sons, Cain and Abel, were tainted with the impurity of the SERPENT who slept with Eve and spawned demonic children as well.

The hybrid demon-human children who continue to be born are *banim shovavim* (mischievous sons). When a man dies, they attend his funeral, lament him, and claim their inheritance. They will even injure the legitimate sons in order to get what they want. In the 17th century, folk customs arose to repel these demons. Sometimes legitimate sons were forbidden to accompany the corpse of their father to the cemetery. The illegitimate demons also were repelled by circling a grave.

Demons are assigned to all things in creation, with angels as their counterparts. They can be summoned, commanded, and repelled in magical rituals according to their hours, days, months, planetary aspects, fumes, and SEALS.

The Tree of Life

The *sephirot* form the central image of kabbalistic meditation, the Tree of Life, a ladder map that depicts the descent of the divine into the material world, and the path by which humans can ascend to the divine while still in the flesh. The *sephirot* channel streams of divine light that become denser and coarser as they near the material plane. The divine light flows both down to the material world and up to God along these paths.

Organization of the Tree Each *sephirah* is a state of consciousness and a level of attainment in knowledge: mystical steps to unity with God. The 10 *sephirot* are arranged in different groups, which facilitate the understanding of their meanings. The first *sephirah*, Kether (Crown), is the closest to Ain Soph and is the source of all life and the highest object of prayer. Malkuth (Kingdom) penetrates the physical realm and is the only *sephirah* in direct contact with it. The lower seven *sephirot* are associated with the seven days of creation. Another division splits them into two groups of five, the upper ones representing hidden powers and the lower five representing manifest powers.

In another division, the top three—Kether, Chockmah (Wisdom), and Binah (Intelligence)—are associated with the intellect; the middle three—Chesed (Love), Geburah (Strength), and Tipareth (Beauty)—are associated with the soul; and the lower three—Netzach (Victory), Hod (Splendor), and Yesod (Foundation)—are associated with nature.

Each *sephirah* is governed by angels and demons. The demonic forces represent chaos and turbulence and are used in black magical practices.

The *sephirot* are ineffable, and descriptions of them cannot begin to approach their true essence. They can be reached only through the second *sephirah*, Chockmah (Wisdom), which is nonverbal consciousness. Binah (Intelligence) is verbal consciousness. One must learn to oscillate between Chockmah and Binah states of consciousness in order to grasp the *sephirot*.

The tree is split into three pillars. The Right Pillar, masculine, represents Mercy and includes the *sephirot* Chockmah, Chesed, and Netzach. The Left Pillar, feminine, represents Severity and includes Binah, Geburah, and Hod. The Middle represents Mildness or Moderation and includes Kether, Tipareth, Yesod, and Malkuth. The Middle Pillar alone also is called the Tree of Knowledge.

Sometimes an 11th *sephirah* is included, Daath (Knowledge), located on the Middle Pillar below Chockmah and Binah, and mediates the influences of the two; it is also considered to be an external aspect of Kether. Daath made its appearance in the 13th century. When represented on the Tree, it is depicted as a sort of shadow sphere. Daath cannot be a true *sephirah,* for the Sefer Yetzirah, the key text of kabbalistic philosophy, states that there can be only 10 *sephirot,* no more, no less.

The pathways linking the *sephirot* have become more complex over time. Illustrations in the early 16th century, for example, depict only 16 pathways. By the 17th century, there were 22 pathways, each of which was assigned a letter of the Hebrew alphabet. Thus, God's Creation is made through the essences of numbers and letters.

Together the *sephiroth* of the Tree of Life compose a unity and create a five-dimensional continuum: the three dimensions of the physical world, plus time, plus the spiritual realm. As do the Akashic Records, they serve as a permanent record of everything that has ever taken place and ever will take place—the memory of God. The *sephirot* also serve as a means of communication with the unknowable God. The totality of the *sephirot* is expressed in the Tetragrammaton, the sacred and unspeakable name of God, given as YHVH (Yahweh), or "the Lord."

Following are the names and associations of the *sephirot*, as given in Agrippa's *Occult Philosophy:*

KETHER
> *Number:* One
> *Titles:* The Crown, The Ancient One, The Aged, The Most Holy Ancient One, The Ancient of the Ancient Ones, The Ancient of Days, The Concealed of the Concealed, The Primordial Point, The Smooth Point, The White Head, The Inscrutable

Height, The Vast Countenance (Macroprosopus), The Heavenly Man
> *Divine Name:* Eheieh (I Am)
> *Archangel:* Metatron
> *Angelic Order:* Hayyoth (The Holy Living Creatures)
> *Archdemons:* Satan, Moloch
> *Demonic Order:* Thamiel (The Two Contenders)
> *Heavenly Sphere:* Primum Mobile
> *Part of Man:* Head

CHOCKMAH
> *Number:* Two
> *Titles:* Wisdom, Divine Father, The Supernal Father
> *Divine Names:* Jah, Jehovah (The Lord), Yod Jehovah (given by Agrippa)
> *Archangel:* Raziel
> *Angelic Order:* Ophanim (The Wheels)
> *Archdemon:* Beelzebub
> *Demonic Order:* Ghogiel (The Hinderers)
> *Heavenly Sphere:* Zodiac
> *Part of Man:* Brain

BINAH
> *Number:* Three
> *Titles:* Intelligence, The Mother, The Great Productive Mother
> *Divine Names:* Elohim (Lord), Jehovah Elohim (The Lord God)
> *Archangel:* Tzaphkiel
> *Angelic Order:* Aralim (The Thrones)
> *Archdemon:* Lucifuge
> *Demonic Order:* Ghogiel (The Concealers)
> *Heavenly Sphere:* Saturn
> *Part of Man:* Heart

CHESED
> *Number:* Four
> *Titles:* Love, Greatness
> *Divine Name:* El (The Mighty One)
> *Archangel:* Tzadkiel
> *Angelic Order:* Hasmallim (The Shining Ones)
> *Archdemon:* Ashtaroth
> *Demonic Order:* Agshekeloh (The Smiters or Breakers)
> *Heavenly Sphere:* Jupiter
> *Part of Man:* Right arm

GEBURAH
> *Number:* Five
> *Titles:* Strength, Judgment or Severity, Fear
> *Divine Names:* Eloh (The Almighty), Elohim Gabor (God of Battles)
> *Archangel:* Camael
> *Angelic Order:* Seraphim (The Fiery Serpents)
> *Archdemon:* Asmodeus
> *Demonic Order:* Golohab (The Burners or Flaming Ones)
> *Heavenly Sphere:* Mars
> *Part of Man:* Left arm

TIPHARETH

> *Number:* Six
> *Titles:* Beauty, Compassion, The King, The Lesser Countenance (Microprosopus)
> *Divine Names:* Eloah Va-Daath (God Manifest), Elohim (God)
> *Archangel:* Raphael
> *Angelic Order:* Malachim (Kings or Multitudes)
> *Archdemon:* Belphegor
> *Demonic Order:* Tagiriron (The Disputers)
> *Heavenly Sphere:* Sun
> *Part of Man:* Chest

NETZACH

> *Number:* Seven
> *Titles:* Firmness, Victory
> *Divine Name:* Jehovah Sabaoth (Lord of Hosts)
> *Archangel:* Haniel
> *Angelic Order:* Elohim (Gods)
> *Archdemon:* Baal
> *Demonic Order:* Nogah (The Raveners)
> *Heavenly Sphere:* Venus
> *Part of Man:* Right leg

HOD

> *Number:* Eight
> *Titles:* Splendor
> *Divine Name:* Elohim Sabaoth (God of Hosts)
> *Archangel:* Michael
> *Angelic Order:* Bene Elohim (Sons of Gods)
> *Archdemon:* Adrammelech
> *Demonic Order:* Samael (The False Accusers)
> *Heavenly Sphere:* Mercury
> *Part of Man:* Left leg

YESOD

> *Number:* Nine
> *Titles:* The Foundation, Eternal Foundation of the World
> *Divine Names:* Shaddai (The Almighty), El Chai (Mighty Living One)
> *Archangel:* Gabriel
> *Angelic Order:* Cherubim (The Strong)
> *Archdemon:* Lilith (The Seducer)
> *Demonic Order:* Gamaliel (The Obscene Ones)
> *Heavenly Sphere:* Moon
> *Part of Man:* Genitals

MALKUTH

> *Number:* Ten
> *Titles:* The Kingdom, The Diadem, The Manifest Glory of God, The Bride (of Microposopus), The Queen
> *Divine Names:* Adonai (Lord), Adonai Malekh (Lord and King), Adonai he-Aretz (Lord of Earth)
> *Archangel:* Metatron in manifest aspect; also Sandalphon
> *Angelic Order:* Issim (Souls of Flame)
> *Archdemon:* Nahema (The Strangler of Children)
> *Demonic Order:* Nahemoth (The Dolorous Ones)
> *Heavenly Sphere:* Elements
> *Part of Man:* Whole body

Magical work with the Tree of Life The pathways between the *sephirot* are avenues of navigation on the astral plane. Communication with the tree is accomplished through prayer, meditation, contemplation, and ritual magic. Some traditional meditations of arrays of numbers and Hebrew letters take days to complete.

The *sephirot* are contemplated by visualizing them vibrating with colors (which represent various qualities), together with images of their corresponding Hebrew letters of the divine names of God and the planets, angels, metals, parts of the body, and energy centers. Breath and sound also are utilized to raise consciousness. Mantras of arrays of Hebrew letters, having specific numerical properties, are employed.

FURTHER READING:

Fortune, Dion. *The Mystical Qabalah.* York Beach, Me.: Samuel Weiser, 1984.
Gray, William G. *The Ladder of Lights.* York Beach, Me.: Samuel Weiser, 1981.
Kraig, Donald Michael. *Modern Magick: Eleven Lessons in the High Magickal Arts.* 2nd ed. Paul: Llewellyn, 2004.
Scholem, Gershom. *Kabbalah.* New York: New American Library, 1974.

Kakabel (Kabaiel, Kochab, Kochbiel, Kokbiel) ANGEL who is both good and evil. In 1 Enoch, Kakabel is a FALLEN ANGEL who commands 365,000 DEMONS and teaches astrology. In the Sefer Raziel, Kakabel is a high angel and prince who rules over stars and constellations.

kelippah In Jewish demonology, a type of demon or demonic force not distinguished by individual names. *Kelippah* means "shell," "husk," or "skin." The *kelippot* (plural) are forces and the root of all evil, the clinging demons of sin found in early Jewish mysticism and kabbalistic lore. They were created as shards or residues of the light cast down from the spiritual lights that formed the *sephirot* of the Tree of Life (see KABBALAH). They became gross matter, the shadow side of the Tree of Life. The *kelippot* are intermediaries between the upper and lower worlds.

kesilim In Jewish demonology, DEMONS who play tricks, misguide people, and make fun of them. *Kesilim* means "fooling spirits." The *kesilim* appear in a 17th-century book, *Emek ha-Melekh.* Related to them is a type of low demon, the *lezim* (jesters), who act as poltergeists and throw things about a house.

kitsune In Japanese lore, a wild fox DEMON that causes POSSESSION. The *kitsune* also appears in the form of a beautiful maiden, who vampirizes her victims sexually as a SUCCUBUS. The *kitsune* appears in many Japanese folktales and in the literature about possession. It originated in the lore of China, where it is described as a lewd creature, the HULI JING.

Possession

Possession by the fox demon is called *kitsune-tsuki*. Cases have been recorded in Japan since the 12th century. Some are believed to be revenge for a family's former offenses against a *huli jing*.

Most possession victims are female. The fox spirit enters the body either through the breast or under the fingernails. It resides on the left side of the body or in the stomach. The victim hears the fox spirit speak inside her head; when she talks out loud, the fox spirit takes on a different voice. The victim exhibits cravings for certain food, especially beans or rice demanded by the demon, sometimes as a condition of its departure. The victim also suffers insomnia, restlessness, and aberrant behavior.

The following case concerned a teenaged girl described as "nervous from birth," who was recovering from typhus. Her weakened condition, plus strong belief in the *kitsune*, seemed to make her highly suggestible or vulnerable to possession:

> A girl of seventeen years, irritable and capricious from childhood, was recovering from a very bad attack of typhus. Around her bed sat, or rather squatted in Japanese fashion, female relations chattering and smoking. Everyone was telling how in the dusk there had been seen near the house a form resembling a northern fox. It was suspicious. Hearing this, the sick girl felt a trembling in the body and was possessed. The fox had entered into her and spoke by her mouth several times a day. Soon he assumed a domineering tone, rebuking and tyrannizing over the poor girl.

After several weeks of this behavior, the family consulted an EXORCIST from the Nuhiren sect, specialists in dealing with *kitsune-tsuki*. The exorcist commenced a "solemn exorcism." The fox resisted all efforts until food was provided:

> Neither excommunication nor censing nor any other endeavor succeeded, the fox saying ironically that he was too clever to be taken in by such maneuvers. Nevertheless, he consented to come out freely from the starved body of the sick person if a plentiful feast was offered to him. . . . On a certain day at four o'clock there were to be placed in a temple sacred to foxes and situated twelve kilometers away two vessels of rice prepared in a particular way, of cheese cooked with beans, together with a great quantity of roast mice and raw vegetables, all favorite dishes of magic foxes: then he would leave the body of the girl exactly at the prescribed time. And so it happened. Punctually at four o'clock when the food was placed in the distant temple the girl sighed profoundly and cried: "He has gone!" The possession was cured.

Not all cases of *kitsune-tsuki* are resolved. An account from the early 20th century tells of a 47-year-old Japanese woman who became permanently possessed. She was a peasant, sad-looking (and thus perhaps suffering from depression), not intelligent, but in good physical health. She sought out help in a university clinic in Tokyo. She related that one day eight years earlier, she had been with friends when one of them said that a fox had been driven out of a woman from a nearby village and was seeking a new home. This made quite an impression on her. The same evening, the door was opened unexpectedly at her home, and she felt a prick in the left side of her chest—the traditional entry point for a fox demon. She knew it was the fox, and immediately she became possessed:

> In the beginning the sinister guest contented himself with occasional stirrings in her bosom, and mounting into her head, criticized by her mouth her own thoughts and made mock of them. Little by little he grew bolder, mingled in all conversations, and abused those present.

The woman went to a succession of exorcists, including the *hoiny,* mendicant monks from the mountains who specialized in EXORCISM. None could help her.

The clinicians witnessed the appearance of the fox, who first showed with twitching of her mouth and arm on her left side where the demon had entered. These became more violent, and she repeatedly struck her left side with her fist. The fox spoke and called her a "stupid goose" and said he could not be stopped. There followed a fit in which the woman and the fox argued. It lasted about 10 minutes. The speech of the fox deteriorated, and then the spirit left her. The woman said that these fits occurred six to 10 times a day and even awakened her at night.

The clinicians put her in a glass room for round-the-clock observation. The pattern was consistent. Any emotional excitation brought on a fit.

The fox spoke far more intelligently than the woman and even taunted the clinicians:

> "Look here, Professor. You might do something more intelligent than trying to entice me by your questions. Don't you know that I am really a gay young girl, although I live in this old frump? You should rather pay court to me properly."

The *kitsune* said he would depart with the proper offering of food but never did so. Efforts to cast him out with chloroform, verbal orders, and "other suggestion" (perhaps hypnotism) also failed. The woman was released without a cure, having been diagnosed as suffering from a chronic condition of "periodic delusion."

Shape Shifting

To accomplish its shape shifting to human form, the *kitsune* flicks its fire-shooting tail once, puts on a human skull, turns around, and bows to the Big Dipper constellation. If the skull remains in place and does not fall, the transformation is successful.

Kitsune hide in forested areas and use human voices to lure victims and cast spells over them. They also frequent eating and drinking establishments and prey upon people who eat and drink too much. If they eat and drink too much themselves, they vanish without harming the victim. In addition to sexually ravaging victims, the *kitsune* love to cut women's hair and shave men's heads as pranks.

According to lore, whenever it rains when the Sun is shining brightly, a *kitsune* bride is going through the woods in a procession to the home of her groom. Marsh lights are fireballs breathed by the foxes or created by their fire-shooting tails, or the lights are the torches carried by the foxes who lead a wedding procession.

In the mountainous areas of Japan where *kitsune* lore is strong, annual rites traditionally are held to ward off *kitsune* troubles. Processions of people take straw foxes and dolls to a mountain outside the village, where they are buried.

FURTHER READING:
Mack, Carol K., and Dinah Mack. *A Field Guide to Demons, Fairies, Fallen Angels, and Other Subversive Spirits.* New York: Henry Holt/Owl Books, 1998.
Oesterreich, Traugott K. *Possession and Exorcism.* Secaucus, N.J.: University Books, 1966.

Klingenberg Possession   See MICHEL, ANNELIESE.

Kokabiel (Kabiel, Kakabiel, Kochab, Kochbiel, Kokbiel)
FALLEN ANGEL also described as a good angel. *Kokabiel* means "star of God." In 1 Enoch Kokabiel is a fallen angel who commands 365,000 DEMONS.

In 3 Enoch he is prince of the stars, commanding 365,000 myriads of ministering angels who make the stars run from city to city and from state to state in the Raqia' of the heavens. In the Sefer Raziel, Kokabiel is a high-ranking angel.

Kunda   In ZOROASTRIANISM, the DEMON of drunkenness. Kunda becomes drunk without drinking. He also is associated with helping wizards in their magic.

Kunopegos (Kunopaston)   DEMON in the shape of a sea horse. Kunopegos is a cruel spirit who raises himself up like great waves in the open seas, causes seasickness among sailors, and sinks ships in order to claim the bodies of men and their treasures. He consults the prince of demons, BEELZEBUB. He can go to shore as waves and shape shift into the form of a man. He is thwarted by the angel Iameth.

In the Testament of Solomon, Kunopegos tells King SOLOMON that he can shape shift into a man. Solomon confines Kunopegos by casting him into a broad flat bowl filled with 10 receptacles of seawater. The top is fortified with marble and the bowl's mouth is covered with asphalt, pitch, and hemp rope. The vessel is sealed and stored in the Temple of Jerusalem.

FURTHER READING:
The Old Testament Pseudepigrapha. Vols. 1 & 2. Edited by James H. Charlesworth. 1983. Reprint, New York: Doubleday, 1985.

Labartu Mesopotamian goddess with demonic characteristics, associated with Lilitu, the prototype of LILITH. Labartu carries a SERPENT in each hand and attacks young children, mothers, and nurses.

Lactance, Father Gabriel (d. 1634) Franciscan priest who was a principal EXORCIST in the LOUDUN POSSESSIONS in France from 1630 to 1634. Father Gabriel Lactance earned the nickname of "Father Dicas" because he kept shouting, "Dicas, Dicas!" at URBAIN GRANDIER, the priest accused of bewitching the nuns.

Lactance was one of three exorcists sent to the Ursuline convent at Loudun when the POSSESSIONs and bewitchments of the nuns seemed to be getting out of control. He was joined by a Jesuit, FATHER JOSEPH SURIN, and a Capuchin, Father Tranquille.

Lactance was especially zealous in his persecution of Grandier. As the condemned priest, badly broken by torture, was carted about town on his way to be burned at the stake, Father Lactance prevented supporters from helping him. He was the first to light the execution fire.

Later, when the priests continued their EXORCISMs of the principal DEMONIAC, Mother Superior JEANNE DES ANGES, he was obsessed to know precisely how Grandier was suffering in HELL. One of the DEMONs possessing Jeanne, ISACAARON, tried his best to satisfy the priest, but Jeanne went into convulsions to avoid further answers.

Lactance immediately suffered psychological and physical ailments. The evening of the execution, while the exorcists were at the convent, Lactance became pale and distant. He worried that he had prevented Grandier from making his confession by tearing him away from one of his supporters as he was taken to the stake. Perhaps this had been a sin. Reassured that it was not by his colleagues, Lactance remained ill at ease. He passed a sleepless night and by morning was in a fever. He repeated, "God is punishing me; God is punishing me."

A physician, Mannoury, bled him, a customary remedy at the time. He worsened and began hallucinating and hearing things. He relived Grandier's screaming under torture and asking God to forgive his enemies as he was strapped to the stake. He saw swarms of demons. The demons entered him and made him rave and contort. He spouted blasphemies.

On September 18, 1634, exactly one month after Grandier's execution, Lactance was on his deathbed. A priest was summoned to give him extreme unction. He knocked the crucifix from the priest's hand and died.

Lactance was given a fine funeral. Father Tranquille preached the sermon and said Lactance was a model of holiness who was killed by SATAN.

Shortly thereafter, Mannoury had a vision of the naked Grandier when he was pricked for DEVIL'S MARKS. The doctor fell to the ground, screaming for pardon. Within a week, he was dead.

FURTHER READING:
Certeau, Michel de. *The Possession at Loudun*. Translated by Michael B. Smith. Chicago: University of Chicago Press, 2000.
Ferber, Sarah. *Demonic Possession and Exorcism in Early Modern France*. London: Routledge, 2004.
Huxley, Aldous. *The Devils of Loudun*. New York: Harper and Brothers, 1952.

Lahmu   Benevolent Assyrian god who protects against evil DEMONs. *Lahmu* means "hairy," a description of the god's long hair and beard. Statues of Lahmu were placed in house and building foundations to ward off evil.

Lam   See CROWLEY, ALEISTER.

Lamastu   Babylonian and Assyrian goddess who practices evil for its own sake. *Lamastu* is usually translated as "demonness." She is hideous in appearance, having the head of a lion, the teeth of a donkey, a hairy body, naked breasts, blood-stained hands with long fingers and fingernails, and the feet of a bird. Sometimes she is shown with donkey ears. She suckles pigs and holds SERPENTs. She floats in a boat in the river of the underworld.

Lamastu causes disease in all humans. As does LILITH, she especially preys upon pregnant women, women in childbed, and newborn infants. Lamatsu goes into homes at night. She kills pregnant women by tapping on their bellies seven times. She steals infants from their wet nurses.

The DEMON god PAZUZU has power over her and can force her back into the underworld. Women protected themselves against her by wearing AMULETs made of bronze and fashioned as the head of Pazuzu. Offerings of centipedes and brooches were made to tempt her away.

FURTHER READING:
Black, Jeremy, and Anthony Green. *Gods, Demons and Symbols of Ancient Mesopotamia*. London: British Museum Press, 1992.

lamiae   Monstrous female birth DEMONs found in Middle Eastern and Greek lore. The lamiae are named after Lamme, a destroyer deity in Babylonian and Assyrian lore, and Lamia, who was the mistress of Zeus.

Lamia was the beautiful daughter of Belus, the king of Libya, who caught Zeus' eye. In exchange for her sexual favors, Zeus gave her the power to pluck out the eyes of people and replace them. She had several children. Hera, the wife of Zeus, was so enraged by the liaison that she killed all the offspring who resulted from the union. She condemned Lamia to give birth only to stillborn infants.

In revenge, Lamia became a demon and swore to kill the children of others. She joined the EMPOUSAI, female demons similar to the SUCCUBUS. Lamia bore a large family of children, all female demons, who became known as the lamiae. They have deformed lower limbs (often depicted as SERPENTs) and the face and breasts of beautiful women. They prey upon newborns, drinking their BLOOD and consuming their flesh.

In Hebrew lore, lamiae are the *lilim*, the demonic children-killing offspring of LILITH, Adam's first wife.

JOHANN WEYER used the term *lamia* to describe female witches who had entered into a deceptive or imaginary PACT with the DEVIL in order to perpetrate evil.

larvae   In Roman lore, evil spirits that harm and frighten the living. *Larvae*, also known as *lemurs*, are demonic ghosts of the dead who, because of their misdeeds in life, are punished in the afterlife by being sentenced to exile and eternal wandering without a home. They do not bother good men, but they harass men of evil intent. The counterpart of the *larvae* are *lares*, benevolent ghosts of the dead who guard people, homes, and places.

Apuleius described both of these types of spirits in *De deo Socratis*:

> There is also another species of daemons, according to a second signification, and this is a human soul, which, after its departure from the present life, does not enter into another body. I find that souls of this kind are called in the ancient Latin tongue Lemures. Of these Lemures, therefore, he who, being allotted the guardianship of his posterity, dwells in a house with an appeased and tranquil power, is called a familiar [or domestic] Lar. But those are for the most part called Larvae, who, having no proper habitation, are punished with an uncertain wandering, as with a certain exile, on account of the evil deeds of their life, and become a vain terror to good, and are noxious to bad men.

Romans observed a festival in May called Lemuria, for appeasing the spirits of the dead, exorcising them from households, and preventing them from causing trouble. Businesses and temples closed. The most important ritual took place on the last night of the festival, when the *larvae* or *lemures* were exorcised. The homeowner or head of the household washed his hands three times, placed black beans in his mouth, and walked barefoot through the house, making the sign of the horns with his hands (see EVIL EYE), tossing black beans over his shoulder, and saying, "With these beans I do redeem me and mine." This incantation was repeated nine times without looking backward. The evil ghosts who followed would pick up the beans and depart, leaving the residents alone until the following year's festival.

The Greeks had a similar festival, observed in February or March.

In *The City of God*, St. Augustine commented on *larvae*, believing them to be wicked demons, in reference to comments made by Plotinus:

> He [Plotinus] says, indeed, that the souls of men are demons, and that men become Lares if they are good, Lemures or Larvae if they are bad, and Manes if it is

uncertain whether they deserve well or ill. Who does not see at a glance that this is a mere whirlpool sucking men to moral destruction?

For, however wicked men have been, if they suppose they shall become Larvae or divine Manes, they will become the worse the more love they have for inflicting injury; for, as the Larvae are hurtful demons made out of wicked men, these men must suppose that after death they will be invoked with sacrifices and divine honors that they may inflict injuries. But this question we must not pursue. He also states that the blessed are called in Greek eudaimones, because they are good souls, that is to say, good demons, confirming his opinion that the souls of men are demons.

FURTHER READING:
Augustine. *The City of God.* Translated by Marcus Dods, George Wilson and J. J. Smith; introduction by Thomas Merton. New York: Modern Library, 1950.
Guiley, Rosemary Ellen. *The Encyclopedia of Ghosts and Spirits.* 3rd ed. New York: Facts On File, 2007.
Ogden, Daniel. *Magic, Witchcraft, and Ghosts in the Greek and Roman Worlds: A Sourcebook.* New York: Oxford University Press, 2002.

LaVey, Anton Szandor   See SATANISM.

legion   A unit of DEMONs. There are 6,666 demons per legion. JOHANN WEYER cataloged demons, listing 72 princes who commanded legions totaling 7,405,926 underlings. The legions are organized in military fashion, with ranks and specific duties assigned to each demon. The legions attend their princes when summoned by a magician. They are dispatched by SATAN to infest, oppress, and possess victims.

Legion   See JESUS.

lemures   See LARVAE.

Lerajie (Leraie, Lerayou, Oray)   FALLEN ANGEL and 14th of the 72 SPIRITS OF SOLOMON. Lerajie is a marquis who appears as an archer, dressed in green and carrying a bow and quiver. He causes great battles and makes arrow wounds putrefy. He commands 30 LEGIONS of DEMONS.

Leviathan   In Hebrew lore, primordial monster DEMON of the seas and king of beasts.

Leviathan is described in the book of Job as a huge whalelike creature who is nearly invulnerable; spears do no more than tickle him:

His back is made of rows of shields,
Shut up closely as with a seal. . . .
His sneezings flash forth light,
And his eyes are like eyelids of the dawn.

Out of the mouth go flaming torches;
Sparks of fire leap forth. . . .
In his neck abides strength,
And terror dances before him.

The book of Jonah tells about Jonah, who flees from God's wrath across the sea toward the city of Tarshish. Along the way, God sends a tempest, and the ship's crew find out that Jonah is the cause. They throw him overboard and he is swallowed by Leviathan. For three days, he is imprisoned in the belly of the beast, and then God forces Leviathan to vomit him up on land.

John Milton, in his epic poem *Paradise Lost,* describes Leviathan as "the Arch-Fiend," who lurks about the seas around Scandinavia. He would rise to the surface and fool sailors into thinking his huge bulk was actually land. When the ships were close, he would drag them down and sink them.

Leviathan was one of the possessing demons named in the LOUDUN POSSESSIONS. He is ruler of Envy, the fourth of the SEVEN DEADLY SINS.

In Hebrew lore, Leviathan has two aspects, male—Leviathon, the Slant Serpent—and female—LILITH, the Tortuous Serpent.

See BEHEMOTH.

FURTHER READING:
Hyatt, Victoria, and Joseph W. Charles. *The Book of Demons.* New York: Simon & Schuster, 1974.
Koltuv, Barbara Black. *The Book of Lilith.* Berwick, Me.: Nicolas-Hays, 1986.

leyak   In Balinese lore, a sorcerer who has the ability to shape shift into a DEMON, causing death and destruction to people, animals, and crops. The leyak also is the cause of all bad events and misfortunes.

While the sorcerer sleeps, the leyak flies in the night skies in the form of a mysterious light, a monkey, or a bird. If the leyak is destroyed, its human form dies instantly along with it. A leyak can remain disguised to fellow human beings indefinitely. Usually, it is unmasked only when it is killed in its shape-shifted form.

lezim   See KESILIM.

liderc   Hungarian DEMON that shape shifts into three guises: an INCUBUS, a household spirit, and a death omen light.

The incubus liderc takes advantage of loneliness, masquerading as long-absent lovers and dead husbands. Once in its victim's bed, it returns night after night and fornicates with the victim, who has a wasting death. A giveaway to the demon's true nature is that it has one goose leg and foot, which it keeps hidden in trousers and boots.

The household liderc takes the form of a featherless chicken that suddenly appears or is hatched from an egg carried in the armpit. It can never be banished once it has entered a home. The only solution is to keep it busy with tasks; otherwise, it will destroy the occupants.

The flickering light liderc is a ball of light (*ignis fautis*) that hovers over the household where someone will soon die.

FURTHER READING:
Mack, Carol K., and Dinah Mack. *A Field Guide to Demons: Fairies, Fallen Angels, and Other Subversive Spirits.* New York: Owl Books/Henry Holt, 1998.

ligature   A knotted loop of thread used by witches to cause demonic castration or impotence in men, as well as barrenness in women and unhappiness in marriage. The ligature also served to bind couples in illicit amatory relationships.

Belief in impotence caused by SORCERY with DEMONS was not widespread until about the 14th century, when SABBATS, PACTS with the DEVIL, and the evil acts of witches gained prominence in witch trials. Fear of ligature increased in the witch hysteria of the Inquisition, when witches were believed to use powers bestowed by the Devil to interfere in the sexual acts of people.

Thomas Platter, a physician in the Montpellier region of France in 1596, described how ligature happened to newlyweds: At the instant when a priest blessed a new marriage, a witch went behind the husband, knotted a thread, and threw a coin on the ground while calling the Devil. If the coin disappeared, it meant that the Devil took it to keep until Judgment Day, and the couple was doomed to unhappiness, sterility, and adultery.

Platter believed fully in ligatures, noting that couples living in Languedoc were so fearful of demonic castration that not 10 weddings in 100 were performed publicly in church. Instead, the priest, the couple, and their parents went off in secret to celebrate the sacrament. Only then, Platter reported, could the newlyweds enter their home, enjoy the feasting, and go to bed. He concluded that the panic was so bad that there was a local danger of depopulation.

Other means could cause ligature: a nut or acorn split in two and placed on either side of a bed; a needle used to sew a corpse's shroud, placed beneath a pillow; or three or four beans placed beneath the bed, on the road outside a house, or around the door.

Folk magic remedies could remove a ligature. The victim would be cured by eating a woodpecker or by smelling the scent of a dead man's tooth. Another remedy called for rubbing the entire body with raven's bile and sesame oil. Quicksilver (mercury) enclosed in a reed sealed with wax or sealed in an empty hazelnut shell could be placed beneath the afflicted person's pillow or under the threshold of the house or the bedroom. The bile of a BLACK DOG sprinkled on a house would neutralize a demon, and the BLOOD of a black dog sprinkled on the walls would clear all evil spells. Wormwood or squill flowers hung at the bedroom door would keep out a demon.

FURTHER READING:
Lea, Henry Charles. *Materials toward a History of Witchcraft.* Philadelphia: University of Pennsylvania Press, 1939.

lightning   In folklore, the mark of the DEVIL. Lightning strikes leave streaks and ragged, hooked, charred marks on objects. According to lore, these are claw marks of the Devil.

NICHOLAS REMY, a 16th-century demonologist, said that DEMONS mingle with lightning and determine where it strikes. Remy said that when he was a boy, his house at Charmes, France, was struck by lightning and marked with "deep claw marks." Further evidence of the presence of the Devil was the "most foul smell of sulphur."

FURTHER READING:
Remy, Nicholas. *Demonolatry.* Secaucus, N.J.: University Books, 1974.

Lilith   A female DEMON of the night and SUCCUBUS who flies about searching for newborn children to kidnap or strangle and sleeping men to seduce in order to produce demon children. Lilith is a major figure in Jewish demonology, appearing as early as 700 B.C.E. in the book of Isaiah; she or beings similar to her also are found in myths from other cultures around the world. She is the dark aspect of the Mother Goddess. She is the original "scarlet woman" and sometimes described as a screech owl, blind by day, who sucks the breasts or navels of young children or the dugs of goats.

In addition to Jewish folklore, Lilith appears in various forms in Iranian, Babylonian, Sumerian, Canaanite, Persian, Arabic, Teutonic, Mexican, Greek, English, Asian, and Native American legends. She is sometimes associated with other characters in legend and myth, including the queen of Sheba and Helen of Troy. In medieval Europe, she was often portrayed as the wife, concubine, or grandmother of SATAN.

Lilith appears in different guises in various texts. She is best known as the first wife of Adam, created by God as twins joined in the back. Lilith demanded equality with Adam and, failing to get it, left him in anger. Adam complained to God that his wife had deserted him. God sent three angels, Sanvi, Sansanvi, and Semangelaf, to take Lilith back to Eden. The angels found her in the Red Sea and threatened her with the loss of 100 of her demon children every day unless she returned to Adam. She refused and was punished. Lilith took revenge by launching a reign of terror against women in childbirth, newborn infants—particularly males—and men who slept alone. She was forced, however, to swear to the three angels that whenever she saw their names or images on an amulet, she would leave infants and mothers alone.

After the Fall, Adam spent 130 years separated from Eve, during which Lilith went to him and satisfied him during sleep. They had a son, who became a frog.

The earliest account of Lilith appears in a midrash, *Alpha Bet Ben Sira,* which attempts to resolve the discrepancies in the Torah about the creation of Lilith in Genesis, followed by the creation of Eve just a few passages later. In the midrash, God created Lilith in the same way as he did Adam, but he used filth and impure sediment instead of dust from the earth. Adam and Lilith were at odds with each other from the beginning, and she refused to lie beneath him during intercourse. When she saw that Adam would gain power over her, she uttered the ineffable name of God and flew off to a cave in the desert near the Red Sea. There, as queen of Zemargad or queen of the desert, she engaged in promiscuity, including with demons, and gave birth to 100 demonic offspring called *lilim* every day. The daughters all practice SORCERY, seduction, and strangling.

She became the bride of SAMAEL, the DEVIL (in some accounts called Ashmodai, or ASMODEUS), in a union arranged by the Blind Dragon, an entity who has been castrated so that his offspring will not overcome the world. The *lilim* are hairy beings, having hair everywhere on their faces and bodies except their heads.

In a text preceding the Zohar, Lilith and Samael are born joined as androgynous twins from an emanation beneath the throne of glory. They are the lower aspects of another androgynous twin, Adam and Eve.

In the Zohar, Lilith arises from an evil shell or husk, a KELIPPAH, that is created in the waning of the Moon. In the beginning, the Sun and Moon were equal, and this created a rivalry. To end it, God diminished the Moon and made it rule the night. Lilith's powers are at their peak when the Moon is dark. She is the seducer of men and the strangler of children; the latter role is sometimes attributed to NAAMAH.

Lilith, who has the upper body of a beautiful woman and a lower body of fire, carries the fiery resentment of the Moon. Lilith lurks under doorways, in wells, and in latrines, waiting to seduce men. She is adorned with the "ornaments for seduction":

> Her hair is long and red like the rose, her cheeks are white and red, from her ears hang six ornaments, Egyptian cords and all the ornaments of the Land of the East hang from her nape. Her mouth is set like a narrow door comely in its decor, her tongue is sharp like a sword, her words are smooth like oil, her lips are red like a rose and sweetened by all the sweetness in the world. She is dressed in scarlet and adorned with forty ornaments less one.

Men who sleep alone are especially vulnerable to Lilith.

The Zohar also describes Lilith as a female aspect of LEVIATHAN, who has a SERPENT body. She is Leviathan, the Tortuous Serpent, the counterpart to the male aspect, Leviathon, the Slant Serpent. Lilith is the serpent who tempts Eve with the apple of forbidden knowledge in paradise and thus instigates the Fall. She also persuades Eve to seduce Adam while she is menstruating and impure.

The numerical value of Lilith's name equals the Hebrew word for "screech." Thus, Lilith is the "demon of screeching" and "the princess of screeching" and is personified as a screech owl. In legend, on the Day of Atonement, Lilith spends the day in a screeching battle with MAHALATH, a concubine to Samael. They taunt each other so much that the very earth trembles. Also on the Day of Atonement, Lilith goes forth into the desert with 420 LEGIONS of her demons, and they march about while she screeches.

Lilith is also known as Lady of the Beasts, who rules the wilderness and all beasts, the animal side of human nature.

In her guise as the queen of Sheba, she attempted to seduce King SOLOMON. He discovered her true nature by having the DJINN build a throne room with a floor of glass. Lilith mistook it for water and raised her garments in order to cross it to his throne. Her hairy, bestial legs were revealed in the reflection of the glass.

AMULETs and INCANTATION BOWLS traditionally protected new mothers and infants against Lilith. Common amulets were knives and hands inscribed with CHARMs; some had bells attached. Frogs also protect against her. Male infants were vulnerable for the first week of life, girls for the first three weeks. Sometimes a magic circle was drawn around the lying-in bed, with a charm inscribed with the names of the three angels, Adam and Eve, and the words *barring Lilith* or *protect this newborn child from all harm.* Sometimes amulets with such inscriptions were placed in all corners of and throughout the bedchamber. If a child laughed in its sleep, it was a sign that Lilith was present. Tapping the child on the nose made the demon go away.

According to lore, men who had nocturnal emissions believed they had been seduced by Lilith during the night and had to say incantations to prevent the offspring from becoming demons. Any seed spilled during sex, even marital sex, is at risk for becoming *lilim.*

FURTHER READING:
Koltuv, Barbara Black. *The Book of Lilith.* Berwick, Me.: Nicolas-Hays, 1986.
Scholem, Gershom. *Kabbalah.* New York: New American Library, 1974.

lilitu A family of Babylonian DEMONs, composed of a male *lilu* and two females, *lilitu* and *ardat-lili.* The demons have associations with LILITH.

The *lilu* and *lilitu* haunt deserts and threaten pregnant women and infants. The *ardat-lili* is incapable of sex and takes out her frustrations upon young men by rendering them impotent. She also makes women sterile. The *ardat-lili* is thought have the form of a scorpion-tailed she-wolf.

lion-demon Babylonian hybrid DEMON, usually in the shape of a bare-chested man with a lion head and tail, donkey ears, and bird feet. Lion-demons hold a dagger upraised in one hand and a mace in the other. Lion-demons are benevolent and protect against evil demons that cause misfortune and disease.

Lion-Shaped Demon   FALLEN ANGEL in the shape of a roaring lion, who commands LEGIONs of DEMONs.

In the Testament of Solomon, the Lion-Shaped Demon appears before King SOLOMON and says he cannot be bound. He sneaks up to people who are lying in their sickbeds and makes it impossible for them to recover. He says he is of Arab descent.

Solomon invokes the name of "the great God Most High" and forces the demon to reveal that he is thwarted by Emmanuel (JESUS). Emmanuel has bound the Lion-Shaped Demon and his legions and will torture them by driving them off a cliff into water. Solomon sentences the demon's legions to carrying woods from a grove of trees and sentences the Lion-Shaped Demon to use his claws to saw it into kindling and throw it under a perpetually burning kiln.

FURTHER READING:
The Old Testament Pseudepigrapha. Vols. 1 & 2. Edited by James H. Charlesworth. 1983. Reprint, New York: Doubleday, 1985.

Lion-demon of disease and evil (AUTHOR'S COLLECTION)

Lix Tetrax   FALLEN ANGEL and DEMON of the wind. In the Testament of Solomon, Lix Tetrax is summoned to the presence of King SOLOMON by BEELZEBUB, at the king's orders. The demon appears with his face high in the air and his body crawling like a small snail. He raises up clouds of dust and wind and hurls them at Solomon, who watches, unharmed and in amazement at this display. At last, the king spits on the ground and seals the demon with his magical ring.

Lix Tetrax claims he is "the direct offspring of the Great One," perhaps a reference to Beelzebub, the Prince of Demons. He lives in the constellation near the tip of the horn of the Moon when it is in the south. He says he divides men, creates whirlwinds, starts fires, sets fields on fire, and renders households nonfunctional. He is especially busy during the summertime. He slithers into houses at the corners night and day (see INCANTATION BOWLS).

He has the power to heal the "day-and-a-half fever" if invoked to do so with the three names of Baltala, Thallal, and Melchal. He is thwarted by the angel Azael.

Solomon sentences Lix Tetrax to throw stones up to the workmen at the heights of the Temple of Jerusalem, under construction.

FURTHER READING:
The Old Testament Pseudepigrapha. Vols. 1 & 2. Edited by James H. Charlesworth. 1983. Reprint, New York: Doubleday, 1985.

loogaroo   In West Indies lore, an old woman who has made a PACT with the DEVIL and must supply him with large quantities of warm BLOOD. The term *loogaroo* was coined by French colonists and is a corruption of the French term for werewolf, *loup-garou.*

In order to satisfy the Devil's demand for blood, the loogaroo preys as a vulture during the day. At night, she goes to a cottonwood tree, where she removes her own skin and hides it in the tree. She shape shifts into a blob of light and flies about, attacking people and animals and sucking their blood as a vampire.

If the loogaroo is injured while in her shape-shifted form, she will show her wound when she changes back to human form, thus revealing her true identity. Another way of exposing her is to find her skin and grind it up with pepper and salt. This will force her to be naked in the daytime, and she will die of exposure.

Loudun Possessions (1630–1634)   Mass POSSESSION of Ursuline nuns of Loudun, France, who accused Father URBAIN GRANDIER as the source of their demonic afflictions. The Loudun Possessions were probably the most famous case of mass possession in history. Vividly described in Aldous Huxley's *The Devils of Loudun* (1952), the torments of Mother Superior JEANNE DES ANGES (Joan of the Angels) and the sisters by the handsome Grandier resulted in not only the priest's fiery death but great debate on the veracity of the nuns' sufferings, the theological probability of witchcraft, and the possibility that Grandier had been sacrificed for his political missteps.

A total of 27 nuns claimed to be possessed, obsessed, or bewitched. The EXORCISMS became a circus of public spectacles conducted at the Ursuline convent, local chapels, and even private homes. Though the case had generally ended by 1634 with the execution of Grandier, exorcisms continued until 1637.

The Ursuline Convent

The Ursuline convent was new, established in 1626 by 17 nuns, most of them of noble birth. They were not particularly pious but were sent to the convent because their families could not afford dowries large enough to attract suitors of comparable rank. Most were resigned to their fate and lived lives of boredom at the convent.

The only place they could afford to rent for their quarters was a gloomy house no one would live in because it was notoriously haunted. There was no furniture and the nuns slept on the floor. They did menial work and did not eat meat. Soon the locals realized that the nuns were well connected by blood to important people, and so they sent their daughters to the convent for education.

In 1627, a new superior was appointed: Jeanne des Anges, formerly Jeanne de Belciel, a baron's daughter. Contemporaries of Jeanne des Anges described her both as a living saint and as a strange, ambitious woman. She was arrogant, mean, rich, and extravagant in her secular life as the daughter of a baron. Sent to the convent because her hunchback and unattractive appearance made her marriage prospects poor, Jeanne nursed secret resentments. She feigned piety in order to become mother superior.

Grandier's Rise and Fall

In 1617, Grandier was appointed parish priest of St.-Pierre-du-Marche in Loudun, a town in Poitiers, France. He cut quite a figure. Handsome, urbane, wealthy, and eloquent, he had no trouble finding women willing to help him bend his priestly vows. He inspired admiration and adoration and at the same time resentment and envy. Everything he did was successful, and he enjoyed the support of powerful people.

Grandier reveled in his popularity and often acted arrogantly. He quarreled with people and did not care whether they became enemies. Townspeople suspected him of fathering a child by Philippa Trincant, the daughter of the king's solicitor in Loudun, and he openly courted Madeleine de Brou, daughter of the king's councilor, to whom he composed a treatise against the celibacy of priests. Most assumed Madeleine was Grandier's mistress.

Grandier's first serious setback occurred June 2, 1630, when he was arrested for immorality and found guilty by his enemy, the bishop of Poitiers. But Grandier's own political connections restored him to full clerical duties within the year. Next, Grandier's enemies approached

Father Mignon, confessor to the Ursuline nuns at their convent and a relative of Trincant. The plan was for Father Mignon to persuade a few of the sisters to feign possession, swearing that Father Grandier had bewitched them, causing his removal and downfall. The mother superior, Jeanne des Anges, and another nun readily complied, falling into fits and convulsions, holding their breath and speaking in hoarse voices.

Jeanne became sexually obsessed with Grandier and had strange dreams in which he appeared to her as a radiant angel but spoke more as a devil would, enticing her to sexual acts and vices. Her hysterical dreams and ravings disturbed the peace of the convent, and after flagellation and penance, Jeanne was no quieter, and more nuns had succumbed to hallucinations and dreams. At this point, some accounts report Jeanne called for Father Mignon's help, not the other way around.

Father Mignon and Father Pierre Barre, his aide, saw an opportunity for revenge against Grandier. There was no shortage of other enemies of Grandier, for he had made many, especially concerning his seductions of women in town.

When word circulated that the Ursuline nuns were bewitched and possessed and Grandier was responsible, the curé shrugged off the gossip. It was a foolish mistake, for the revised Witchcraft Act of 1604 called for the death penalty upon conviction of sorcery, WITCHCRAFT, and diabolical PACT. The development of sorcery accusations against Grandier had grave implications.

The two priests began exorcizing the nuns, while Jeanne and the others shrieked, cavorted, and suffered convulsive fits. Whether the rituals added to the performance or caused Jeanne's mind to snap, she swore that she and the others were possessed by two DEMONS, ASMODEUS and ZABULON, sent by Father Grandier via a bouquet of roses thrown over the convent walls.

Now realizing his peril, Grandier appealed to the bailiff of Loudun to have the nuns isolated, but the bailiff's orders were ignored. In desperation, Grandier wrote to the archbishop of Bordeaux; the archbishop sent his doctor to examine the nuns and found no evidence of possession. The archbishop ended the exorcisms on March 21, 1633, and ordered the nuns to confinement in their cells. Peace returned for a while, but the hysteria began again later that year.

Still convinced he could not be convicted of such imaginary crimes, Grandier was thrown into prison at the castle of Angiers on November 30, 1633. DEVIL'S MARKS were quickly found by lancing him in one part of the body, causing pain, and lightly touching him elsewhere, causing none. Observers such as Dr. Fourneau, the physician who prepared Grandier for torture, and the apothecary from Poitiers protested the examiner's hoax and found no such marks. Other voices were raised in Grandier's defense, even from the possessed nuns themselves.

Grandier's enemies continued their efforts against him. A relative of Jeanne's, Jean de Laubardemont, and a crony of the powerful Cardinal Richelieu, along with a Capuchin monk, Father Tranquille, called to the cardinal's attention a libelous satire on Richelieu that Grandier was supposed to have written in 1618 and reports of the unsuccessful exorcisms. Eager to prove his power in the church and in France, and aware of his relative, Sister Claire, in the convent, the cardinal appointed Laubardemont head of a commission to arrest and convict Grandier as a witch. The exorcisms resumed publicly under Mignon, Barre, Father Tranquille, and FATHER GABRIEL LACTANCE, a Franciscan.

Experts continued to doubt that the possessions were genuine. Most of the nuns failed the test of knowledge of foreign languages not known to them prior to their possession. Nuns who did not know Latin were conveniently possessed by demons who did not know Latin. Sometimes when given commands in Latin or Greek, the nuns had to be coached to respond correctly. Similarly, the nuns repeatedly failed tests for clairvoyance, levitation, and superhuman strength. To make up for their shortcomings in crucial areas, the nuns resorted to contortions and gymnastics, revealing their legs, much to the delight of onlookers.

Even more glaring were other gaffes. Sister Agnes said repeatedly she did not believe herself to be possessed but was convinced by Jeanne and the exorcists. On another occasion, during an exorcism, some burning sulfur accidentally fell on the lip of Sister Claire. She burst into tears and said she was ready to believe that she was possessed as she had been told, but she did not deserve to be treated in this manner. On another occasion, Claire said tearfully that her possession and the accusations against Grandier were all lies she had been forced to tell by Mignon, Lactance, and the Carmelites. Agnes attempted to escape the convent but was captured and returned.

Jeanne made a deranged appearance in the convent yard one day, dressed only in her shirt, and stood for two hours in pouring rain with a rope around her neck and a candle in her hand. She then tied herself to a tree, threatening to hang herself, but was rescued by other sisters. This was witnessed by the chief magistrate, de Laubardemont. The exorcists said Jeanne's actions and the retractions were lies of SATAN.

Despite these problems, the case against Grandier continued full force. In part, the case was also being used against the Protestant Huguenots in general, for the nuns all said that the Huguenots were disciples of Satan. After the Protestant Reformation, Catholics and Protestants battled each other in possession and exorcism cases to try to demonstrate who had the greater spiritual authority.

Besides the accusations of the nuns, Grandier's former mistresses came forward with stories of adultery, incest, sacrilege, and other sins committed not only by a priest but in the holiest places of the church. The dreams and

physical responses of the nuns were overtly sexual, providing shocking evidence of Grandier's diabolical nature. Jeanne added a new possessor, ISACAARON, the devil of debauchery, and even went through a psychosomatic pregnancy.

Pillet de la Mesnardiere, one of Cardinal Richelieu's personal physicians, determined exactly where some of demons resided in the bodies of the possessed nuns, among them:

- Jeanne des Anges: Leviathan in the center of the forehead, Beherit in the stomach, Balaam under the second rib on the right side, Isacaaron under the last rib on the left
- Agnes de la Motte-Barace: Asmodeus under the heart and Beherit in the stomach
- Louise of Jesus: Eazaz under the heart and Caron in the center of the forehead
- Claire de Sazilly: Zabulon in the forehead, Nepthali in the right arm, San Fin (Grandier of the Dominions) under the second rib on the right, Elymi on one side of the stomach, the enemy of the Virgin in the neck, Verrine in the left temple, and Concupiscence of the Order of the Cherubim in the left rib
- Seraphica: A bewitchment of the stomach consisting of a drop of water guarded sometimes by Baruch and other times by Carreau
- Anne d'Escoubleau: A magic bayberry leaf in her stomach guarded by Elymi

Among the lay demoniacs and their resident demons were:

- Elizabeth Blanchard: A devil under each armpit, the Coal of Impurity in the left buttock, and devils under the navel, below the heart, and under the left breast nipple
- Françoise Filatreau: Ginnillion in the forebrain, Jabel throughout the body, Buffetison below the navel, and Dog's Tail of the Order of Archangels in the stomach

The nuns' accusations escalated. Madeleine de Brou was accused of witchcraft, arrested, and imprisoned. Because of her father's political connections, she was released, rearrested, and released again. This time, she disappeared into a convent.

Gentlemen in town were accused of consorting with the Devil, and even the chief magistrate, de Cerisay, was accused of practicing black magic. Other priests were accused of rape.

Finally, Father Grandier was forced to exorcize the nuns himself, since he was the apparent cause of their sufferings. To test their knowledge of languages previously unknown to them—a sure sign of possession—Grandier spoke in Greek, but the nuns had been coached, replying that one of the terms of their pact had been never to use Greek. Of course, Grandier failed.

One of the most interesting items from the exorcisms and trial was the alleged written PACT between the Devil and Grandier, allegedly stolen from Lucifer's cabinet of devilish agreements by Asmodeus and presented to the court as proof of Grandier's complicity. Purportedly written backward by Grandier in Latin and signed in BLOOD, the pact outlined Grandier's duties to the Devil and the benefits he accrued thereby. Cosigners were SATAN, BEELZE-BUB, LUCIFER, ELIMI, LEVIATHAN, and ASTAROTH, and it was notarized by "signature and mark of the chief devil, and my lords the princes of hell." The recorder, BAALBERITH, countersigned the pact. Asmodeus also accommodatingly wrote out a promise to leave one of the nuns he was possessing, as reported by an earlier exorcist, Father Gault:

> I promise that when leaving this creature, I will make a slit below her heart as long as a pin, that this slit will pierce her shirt, bodice and cloth which will be bloody. And tomorrow, on the twentieth of May at five in the afternoon of Saturday, I promise that the demons Gresil and Amand will make their opening in the same way, but a little smaller—and I approve the promises made by Leviatam, Behemot, Beherie with their companions to

sign, when leaving, the register of the church St. Croix! Given the nineteenth of May, 1629.

The message is written in Jeanne des Anges hand. Other demonic "evidence" was that of Astaroth, a devil of the angelic order of seraphim and chief of the possessing devils; from Easas, Celsus, Acaos, Cedon, Alex, Zabulon, Naphthalim, Cham, and Ureil; from Asmodeus of the angelic order of thrones; and from Achas of the angelic order of principalities.

As the circus escalated, skeptics and defenders of Grandier came forward to protest. On July 2, 1634, they were officially silenced, forbidden to speak out against the nuns, the exorcists, or any others assisting in the exorcisms, under pain of stiff fines and physical punishment.

Jeanne des Anges appeared in court with a noose around her neck, threatening to hang herself if she could not expiate her previous perjury. Such efforts were ignored, and other defense witnesses were either pressured to keep silent or threatened with arrest as accessory witches or traitors to the king. Many had to flee France.

Grandier believed almost to the end that he would be exonerated. He appeared before the 14 judges only

The Devil's pact allegedly signed by Father Urbain Grandier (AUTHOR'S COLLECTION)

three times. Inevitably, the Royal Commission passed sentence on August 18, 1634: After the first and last degrees of torture, Grandier was to be burned alive at the stake. Even under extreme torture, Grandier maintained his innocence, refusing to name accomplices, so angering Father Tranquille and the others that they broke both his legs and claimed that everytime Grandier prayed to God, he was really invoking the Devil. Grandier had been promised he could make a last statement and be mercifully strangled before burning, but the friars who carried him to the stake deluged him with holy water, preventing him from speaking. And the garotte was knotted so that it could not be tightened, leaving Grandier to be burned alive. One monk who witnessed the execution reported that a large fly buzzed about Grandier's head, symbolizing that Beelzebub, the Lord of the Flies, had appeared to carry Grandier's soul to HELL.

But Grandier had the last word. As he struggled, Grandier told Father Lactance that he would see God in 30 days. The priest died accordingly, reportedly crying, "Grandier, I was not responsible for your death." Father Tranquille died insane within five years, and Dr. Mannoury, the fraudulent witch pricker, also died in delirium. Father Barre left Loudun for an exorcism at Chinon, where he was finally banished from the church for conspiring to accuse a priest of rape on the altar; the bloodstains turned out to be from a chicken. Louis Chavet, one of the judges who was skeptical of the possessions and who was denounced by Jeanne as a sorcerer himself, fell into depression and insanity and died before the end of the winter.

FATHER JEAN-JOSEPH SURIN, who arrived as an exorcist in 1634 after the death of Grandier, succumbed to possession by Jeanne's devils. For years after Grandier's death, Surin was haunted by the exorcisms, eventually becoming unable to eat, dress himself, walk, read, or write. He no longer prayed to God and continually saw visions of devils, black wings, and other terrors. In 1645, he tried to kill himself. Only after Father Surin received tender care from Father Bastide, the new head of Surin's Jesuit College at Saintes, in 1648, did he begin to recover. Surin finally wrote again in 1657 and walked in 1660. He died at peace in 1665.

Grandier's death did not stop the possessions at Loudun. Public appreciation of the exorcisms had been so great that the convent continued the performances as a type of tourist attraction, led by Mignon and three other Jesuit exorcists who arrived in December 1634 (one was Surin). Twice a day except Sundays, the afflicted nuns were exorcised for the amusement of the crowds. They lifted their skirts and coarsely begged for sexual relief. They beat their heads, bent backward, walked on their hands, stuck out blackened tongues, and used language that, according to one account, "would have astonished the inmates of the lowest brothel in the country." Such shows continued until 1637, when the duchess d'Aiguillon,

niece to Cardinal Richelieu, reported the fraud to her uncle. Having satisfied his original aim—to demonstrate his considerable power—Richelieu righteously cut off the performers' salaries and put the convent at peace. Jeanne des Anges, convinced of her saintliness by Father Surin, died in 1665.

Huxley's account of the madness at Loudun forms the basis of Ken Russell's film version, *The Devils* (1971). Vanessa Redgrave plays Jeanne des Anges, portrayed as a deformed, bitter, and sexually repressed woman. Oliver Reed plays the unfortunate Grandier.

FURTHER READING:
Ferber, Sarah. *Demonic Possession and Exorcism in Early Modern France.* London: Routledge, 2004.
Huxley, Aldous. *The Devils of Loudun.* New York: Harper and Brothers, 1952.

Louviers Possessions (1647) Mass demonic POSSESSIONS at a convent chapel of the Hospitaller sisters of St. Louis and St. Elizabeth in Louviers, France. The Louviers Possessions have similarities to the AIX-EN-PROVENCE POSSESSIONS and the LOUDUN POSSESSIONS. Conviction of the priests involved hinged mainly on the evidence of the possessed DEMONIACS.

On the promptings of Sister Madeleine Bavent, 18 nuns were possessed, allegedly as a result of bewitchment by Mathurin Picard, the nunnery's deceased director, and Father Thomas Boulle, vicar at Louviers. According to Bavent, Picard was bewitching the nuns from his grave and causing them to become possessed. This, in turn, was due to certain questionable spiritual practices previously associated with the convent. The bishop of Evreaux ordered Picard's body to be exhumed.

Bavent confessed to authorities that the two clergymen had taken her to a witches' SABBAT, where she married the DEMON Dagon and committed horrible and obscene acts with him on the altar. (See BLACK MASS.) During the orgy, she told, babies were strangled and eaten, and two men who had attended out of curiosity were crucified and then disemboweled. Dagon disturbed the peace of some of the other nuns as well, and all showed the classic signs of possession: contortions, unnatural body movements, glossolalia (talking in unknown languages), insults, blasphemies, and the appearance of strange wounds, which just as quickly vanished.

One writer who observed the exorcisms tells that one young nun "ran with movements so abrupt that it was difficult to stop her. One of the clerics present, having caught her by the arm, was surprised to find that it did not prevent the rest of her body from turning over and over as if the arm were fixed to the shoulder merely by a spring."

Besides seducing the nuns to unspeakable sexual acts, SATAN tried to lead the nuns of Louviers down heretical roads as well. According to the account of the proceedings at Louviers published in 1652 by Father Bosroger, the Devil, appearing as a beautiful ANGEL, engaged the nuns in theological conversations, cleverly spoken and so charming that the nuns began to doubt what they were taught, meekly protesting that what the Devil told them had not been revealed by their teachers. Satan replied that he was a messenger of heaven, sent to speak the divine truth and reveal the errors in established dogma. PACTs with the Devil were made.

As in Loudun, the exorcisms were public and became more of a circus than a holy ritual. Nearly everyone was questioned and harassed by the inquisitors, and the whole town of Louviers exhibited hysteria as the cries of the nuns rose with the tortured screams of Father Boulle. In the end, the parliament at Rouen passed sentence: Sister Madeleine was imprisoned in the church dungeon, and Father Boulle was burned alive. The dead Picard was convicted and his decomposing corpse was burned.

Boulle became the model for a character in *La-bas*, J. K. Huysmans' 1891 novel about satanic decadence in Paris.

FURTHER READING:

Certeau, Michel de. *The Possession at Loudun.* Translated by Michael B. Smith. Chicago: University of Chicago Press, 2000.

Ferber, Sarah. *Demonic Possession and Exorcism in Early Modern France.* London: Routledge, 2004.

Lucifer   FALLEN ANGEL sometimes equated with SATAN. In Latin, *Lucifer* means "light bringer," and he originally was associated with Venus, the morning star. Lucifer's identity as a prideful angel cast out of heaven with his followers—who became DEMONS—rests mainly on legend and poetic literature, such as in the works of Dante and John Milton.

The sole biblical reference to Lucifer occurs in Isaiah 14:12: "How you are fallen from heaven, O Day Star, son of Dawn!" The reference is probably to the boastful king of Babylon, a prediction of the fall of Babylon and its king.

Lucifer (AUTHOR'S COLLECTION)

Jerome's translation of the Bible, the Latin Vulgate, made Lucifer the chief fallen angel. His rebellion against God with the sin of pride caused him and his followers to be cast from heaven. The fallen angels lost their beauty and power and became demons.

2 Enoch, also called the Slavonic Apocalypse of Enoch, names the leader of the fallen as SATANAEL (Satanail). The text may date to the late first century, although some scholars believe it to be of medieval origin, because it exists only in Slavonic.

According to the text, God creates the ranks of angels on the second day of creation, shaping them out of a great fire cut off from rock. He gives them clothing of burning flames and fiery weapons. He gives orders that each one should stand in his own rank. God tells the prophet Enoch:

> But one from the order of the archangels deviated, together with the division that was under his authority. He thought up the impossible idea, that he might place his throne higher than the clouds which are above the earth, and thus he might become equal to my power.

> And I hurled him out from the height, together with his angels. And he was flying around in the air, ceaselessly, above the Bottomless.

Lucifer has received most attention in Christianity. In the early years of Christianity, the name was sometimes applied to Christ as the light bearer. The early church father Origen, who lived in the second and third centuries, equated Lucifer and Satan; later, Augustine and Jerome were among those who followed suit. By the Middle Ages, both *Lucifer* and *Satan* were used as names for the DEVIL. Lucifer could apply to the Devil in either his prefall or postfall state. Milton's *Paradise Lost* and Dante's *Inferno* strengthened the connection of Lucifer to Satan.

In Mormonism, Lucifer (*Helel* in Hebrew) is a brilliant and powerful archangel, a son of Elohim (God the Father) and brother to Yahweh (God the Son, Jehovah, or Jesus) and to all of the children of Elohim including all of the souls of humanity. Lucifer became obsessed with pride and attempted to take over Elohim's family and subvert the Father's plan for his children. A struggle of wills ensued, and Lucifer and his followers lost. They are exiled to Earth and are permitted to tempt people. When Elohim's purpose has been fulfilled, Lucifer and his demons will be exiled to the "Outer Darkness," completely cut off from divine light and love.

In the hierarchies of demons in magical lore, Lucifer is emperor of HELL and ranks above Satan, one of his lieutenants. When conjured, he appears as a beautiful child. Lucifer rules Europeans and Asiatics.

In the 19th century, Leo Taxil, a Frenchman who excelled in occult hoaxes, perpetrated the fraud that Freemasonry was associated with worship of Lucifer. Although the hoax was thoroughly exposed, Taxil continues to be cited by opponents of Freemasonry.

Lucifer and the souls of sinners (AUTHOR'S COLLECTION)

Some modern occultists and satanists see Lucifer as an archangel of light who will incarnate in human form at key times to confer enlightenment and redemption.

FURTHER READING:
Kelly, Henry Ansgar. *A Biography of Satan*. New York: Cambridge University Press, 2006.
The Old Testament Pseudepigrapha. Vols. 1 & 2. Edited by James H. Charlesworth. 1983. Reprint, New York: Doubleday, 1985.
Russell, Jeffrey Burton. *Lucifer: The Devil in the Middle Ages*. Ithaca, N.Y., and London: Cornell University Press, 1984.

Luciferian witchcraft   See WITCHCRAFT.

Lucifuge Rofocale   The prime minister of LUCIFER. Lucifuge Rofocale is featured only in one text, the *Grand Grimoire*, a French magical handbook of black magic written in the 17th or 18th century (see GRIMOIRES). The book is especially significant for its feature of a specific PACT between a magician and Lucifuge Rofocale for the purpose of securing the services of DEMONs. *Rocofale* may be an anagram of *Focalor,* a demon named in the *Lemegeton,* a major grimoire.

The *Grand Grimoire* states that if the magician cannot master a magic circle and a blasting rod for controlling demons, then a pact is necessary. A pact cannot be made with the three highest demons—Lucifer, BEELZEBUB, and ASTAROTH—but only with one of their lieutenants. It provides a Grand Conjuration for summoning Lucifuge Rofocale, who is a reluctant and obstinate spirit who must be forced to appear with the use of the blasting rod and threats of CURSES.

According to the *Grand Grimoire,* when Lucifuge Rofocale appears, he demands that in exchange for his services, the magician "give thyself over to me in fifty years, to do with thy body and soul as I please." After more bargaining that involves threats from the magician to send him into eternal fire with the blasting rod, the demon agrees to appear twice a night except on Sundays and makes a written conditional pact with the magician. He recognizes the authority of the magician and his grimoire, agrees to grant requested services if properly summoned, and demands certain services and payment in return, on penalty of forfeiture of the magician's soul:

> I also approve thy Book, and I give thee my true signature on parchment, which thou shalt affix at its end, to make use of at thy need. Further, I place myself at thy disposition, to appear before thee at thy call when, being purified, and holding the dreadful Blasting Rod, thou shalt open the Book, having described the Kabbalistic circle and pronounced the word Rocofale. I promise thee to have friendly commerce with those who are fortified by the possession of the said Book, where my true signature stands, provided that they invoke me according to rule, on the first occasion that they require me. I also engage to deliver thee the treasure which thou seekest, on condition that thou keepest the secret for ever inviolable, art charitable to the poor, and dost give me a gold or silver coin on the first day of every month. If thou failest, thou art mine everlastingly.
>
> LUCIFUGE ROFOCALE IMPRIMATUR

The reference to the "Book" is the spurious *Fourth Book,* a grimoire attributed to Henry Cornelius Agrippa.

The *Grand Grimoire* tells how to make a pact with Lucifuge Rofocale, which must be signed by the magician with his own BLOOD. The magician collects the following tools: a wand of wild hazel (not a blasting rod), a bloodstone, and two blessed candles. He goes to an isolated place either indoors or outdoors—the depths of a ruined castle are ideal. He makes a magic triangle with the bloodstone and enters it, holding his written pact, the Grand Conjuration of the Spirit, the hazel wand, the grimoire, and the discharge for dismissing the demon once business is concluded. He first conjures Lucifer, Beelzebub, and Astaroth to ask them to send Lucifuge Rofocale for the purpose of entering into a pact. When the demon finally appears, this exchange takes place:

Lucifuge Rofocale (AUTHOR'S COLLECTION)

Manifestation of the Spirit
> Lo! I am here! What dost thou seek of me? Why dost thou disturb my repose? Answer me.
>
> LUCIFUGE ROFOCALE

Reply to the Spirit
> It is my wish to make a pact with thee, so as to obtain wealth at thy hands immediately, failing which I will torment thee by the potent words of the Clavicle.

The Spirit's Reply
> I cannot comply with thy request except thou dost give thyself over to me in twenty years, to do with thy body and soul as I please.
>
> LUCIFUGE ROFOCALE

Thereupon throw him your pact, which must be written with your own hand, on a sheet of virgin parchment; it should be worded as follows, and signed with your own blood: —I promise the grand Lucifige to reward him in twenty years' time for all the treasures he may give me. In witness thereof I have signed myself

N.N.

Reply of the Spirit
I cannot grant thy request.

LUCIFUGE ROFOCALE

In order to enforce his obedience, again recite the Supreme Appellation, with the terrible words of the Clavicle, till the spirit reappears, and thus addresses you: —

Of the Spirit's Second Manifestation

Why dost thou torment me further? Leave me to rest, and I will confer upon thee the nearest treasure, on condition that thou dost set apart for me one coin on the first Monday of each month, and dos not call me oftener than once a week, to wit, between ten at night and two in the morning. Take up thy pact; I have signed it. Fail in thy promise, and thou shalt be mine at the end of twenty years.

LUCIFUGE ROFOCALE

FURTHER READING:
Waite, Arthur Edward. *The Book of Black Magic and of Pacts*. 1899. Reprint, York Beach, Me.: Samuel Weiser, 1972.

Luther, Martin (1483–1546) Founder of Protestantism and the Protestant Reformation. For much of his life, Martin Luther was concerned with the influence and action of evil and the DEVIL in the world.

Luther was born on November 10, 1483, in Eiselben, Germany, the oldest son of Johan and Margarita (Margarethe) Luther, a wealthy Catholic couple. He was given the name *Martin* because the feast of St. Martin occurred on the day after he was baptized. In 1484, the family moved to Mansfeld. Martin was given a good education as his father hoped that he would become a lawyer. Luther tried to follow that path and studied law at the University of Erfurt but felt no heart in it and left. He joined the Augustinian order in Erfurt in 1505 and devoted himself to an austere monastic life.

Luther became increasingly disenchanted with Catholicism, especially the church's practice of selling indulgences. In 1516, the church undertook a major campaign to sell indulgences to raise money to refurbish St. Peter's Cathedral in Rome. Luther felt strongly that forgiveness for sins could not be purchased; it could be obtained only directly from God.

Luther developed his arguments and on October 31, 1517, supposedly posted them as Ninety-five Theses by nailing them to the door of Castle Church in Wittenberg. The story may be more legend than fact, for Luther never commented about nailing anything to a church door, and

the story arose after his death. However, he did write a letter to his superiors on that date, denouncing the sale of indulgences. The letter included the Ninety-five Theses.

The document aroused instant sensation, and quickly spread throughout Germany, and was translated into other languages. He was in demand as a public speaker, and he spoke out against the corruption he saw in the church.

The church, under Pope Leo X, was slow to respond. Leo dismissed Luther as "a drunken German" and thought the fuss would soon die down. Instead, a movement grew. In 1519, Leo demanded an explanation from Luther of his theses. Luther responded, and the pope summoned him to Rome. Frederick III, the Saxon elector, intervened and attempted to arrange a compromise.

In 1520, Leo issued a bull demanding that Luther recant 41 points in his writings, including the Ninety-five Theses, or be excommunicated. On December 20, 1520, Luther publicly burned the bull in defiance. Leo excommunicated him on January 3, 1521. The Diet of Worms declared him an outlaw, banned his works, and called for his arrest. Luther disappeared into exile, sheltered at the castle of Frederick III at Wartburg. He secretly returned to Wittenberg in 1521 and preached several sermons about trust in God and Christian values. He opposed the use of violence to spread the gospel and to further the ends of the church. At the time, the Inquisition was gaining force, witchcraft was considered a heresy, and fears about demonic interference and PACTS were rampant.

In 1523, Luther helped a group of nuns to escape from a Cistercian convent in Nimbschen by hiding them in herring barrels. He fell in love with one of them, Katharina von Bora, and married her in 1525. He was 42 and she was 26. They made a former monastery their home and tilled the land to earn a living. They had five children and enjoyed a happy marriage.

Despite Luther's opposition to violence, Protestantism became embroiled in other factors of social and political unrest. In 1524, the Peasants' War broke out, with lower classes revolting against the upper classes, many of them believing that religious reform would lead to other reforms as well. Luther refused to support the revolt, and the peasants were quelled in 1525.

Luther was opposed to Jews throughout his life, calling them "the Devil's people" and worse. His anti-Semitism is believed by some scholars to have influenced the Nazi movement centuries later. The Lutheran Church repudiates his anti-Jewish views today.

During his later years, Luther suffered from a variety of health problems, and his health steadily declined. He preached his last sermon, against the Jews, on February 15, 1546, and died three days later, after suffering chest pains and a stroke.

In developing his reformist ideas, Luther devoted more attention to the Devil than had been seen in Christianity since the early days of the religion. He believed firmly in predestination, that a human being has no free will but can follow only the will of God for good or the will of SATAN for evil. God embraces both good and evil. God is good but allows, even wills, evil. God uses the Devil to weed out the unworthy; therefore, the Devil is actually the servant of God. Even though God allows evil, God fights evil at every opportunity.

From childhood, Luther felt attacked by DEMONS and evil spirits; attacks increased as he grew older and reached great intensity while he was exiled at Wartburg and was at work on translating the Bible into German. He attributed his mood swings and depressions to the operations of demons, as well as his ongoing health problems. He said he combated them with prayer and "happy song." Reportedly, he was pestered one night by the Devil and drove him away by throwing his inkwell at him. An ink stain remained in his room at the castle for a long time. He also said that he drove the Devil away with ink, which may have been a reference to his writings.

He was completely believing of the evil nature and powers of witches and their allegiance to the Devil, stating, "I should have no compassion on these witches; I would burn all of them. We read in the old law that the priests threw the first stones at these malefactors. . . . Does not witchcraft, then, merit death, which is a revolt of the creature against the Creator, a denial to God of the authority which it accords to the demon?"

Luther said his mother had been harassed by a witch, who had cursed him and his siblings to cry themselves to death. The CURSE was broken by a preacher who collected the witch's footprints and threw them into a river.

Luther believed that witches shape shifted into animal forms and flew through the air to SABBATS. The Devil caused diseases, he said, by making them appear to have natural causes. Many physicians do not realize this, he said, and should add faith and prayer to their medical treatments. All mentally ill people are under POSSESSION by the Devil, Luther said, and are possessed with God's permission. They are capable of blasting crops, brewing tempests and storms, and causing pestilence, fires, fevers, and severe diseases.

He said people do engage in pacts with the Devil to further their selfish gains, but there is always a heavy price to pay. He related a case of a sorcerer in Erfurt who tried to escape his poverty by making such a pact. The Devil gave him a crystal for divination, which the sorcerer used to become rich. But he accused innocent people of theft and was arrested. He confessed to his pact and repented but was burned at the stake anyway.

Luther also said the Devil raped maidens bathing in water and impregnated them, then took their infants and exchanged them for others, much as in lore of the FAIRIES and their changelings. The changelings never lived beyond 18 or 19 years of age.

According to one story, the Devil himself visited Luther while he was studying at the University of Wittenberg. He arrived disguised as a monk and asked for Luther's advice on "papal errors." The "monk" continued interrogating Luther, who grew impatient. Then Luther saw that his visitor had hands like bird talons, and he ordered him to depart. The Devil gave out a great stinking fart and left. The stench lasted for days.

Luther performed at least one EXORCISM, on a pastor from Torgau who went to him for advice. The Devil had been tormenting him for a year, the pastor said, by throwing around pots and dishes, breaking them, and laughing at him while remaining invisible. The pastor's wife and children wanted to move. Luther told him to have patience and to pray. He ordered the demon to depart.

Luther also believed that as one advances in faith, the Devil increases attacks upon him. He felt this in his own life, enduring physical distress, poltergeist disturbances, and mental interferences that he attributed to the Devil. He considered the pope to be the ANTICHRIST.

After the start of the Reformation, tales circulated that Luther had been born of the Devil, a common accusation levied against religious and political enemies of all kinds. According to one, the Devil disguised himself as a merchant of jewelry and went to Wittenberg, where he encountered Margarita, his mother, and seduced her. After Luther's birth, the Devil counseled him in how to advance himself in the world. He did well at school, became a monk, ravished a nun, and then rejected his monastic life. He went to Rome, where he was treated poorly by the pope and his cardinals. He asked his father how to exact revenge and was told to write a commentary upon the Lord's Prayer. The commentary vaulted him into the spotlight, and he became the chief purveyor of the heresy that became Protestantism.

FURTHER READING:
Bainton, Ronald. *Here I Stand: A Life of Martin Luther.* New York, Penguin, 1995.
Lea, Henry Charles. *Materials toward a History of Witchcraft.* Philadelphia: University of Pennsylvania Press, 1939.
Russell, Jeffrey Burton. *Mephistopheles: The Devil in the Modern World.* Ithaca, N.Y., and London: Cornell University Press, 1986.
Weyer, Johann. *On Witchcraft (De praestigiis daemonum).* Abridged. Edited by Benjamin G. Kohl and H. C. Erik Midelfort. Asheville, N.C.: Pegasus Press, 1998.

lutin   French name for a hobgoblin common in French folklore and fairy tales. The lutin is either male or female; a female is called a lutine. The lutin is comparable to house spirits such as brownies, and to elves, fairies, gnomes, imps, leprechauns, pixies, and sprites.

The lutin has a trickster nature. It can choose to be invisible. In some tales, it becomes invisible by donning a red cap with two feathers.

French immigrants to Quebec, Canada, spread lutin lore there. Lutins are fond of taking animal forms, especially pets and common animals such as rabbits, and also especially white animals. Lutins can control the weather and be either good or bad. Good lutins will perform personal services, while bad lutins will cause domestic upsets, misplace objects, and make messes.

Salt spilled on the ground or floor will prevent lutins from crossing it.

See SINISTRARI, LODOVICI MARIA.

Macariel DEMON and wandering duke of the air. Macariel has 12 chief dukes, who have 400 servants, all good-natured and willing to obey an EXORCIST. They appear in many forms, most commonly a dragon with a virgin head. The 12 chief dukes are Claniel, Drusiel, Andros, Charoel, Asmadiel, Romyel, Mastuet, Varpiel, Gremiel, Thuriel, Brufiel, and Lemodac.

magic A superior power created by the combining of inner power with supernatural forces and beings such as ANGELs and DEMONs. The term *magic* is derived from Greek, either from *megus,* which means "great" (as in "great" science); from *magein,* referring to Zoroastrianism; or from *magoi,* referring to a Median tribe in Iran recognized for its magical skills and known to the Greeks. Many systems of magic exist, each with its own procedures, rules, and proscriptions.

Magic lies at the heart of all esoteric and occult traditions and is found in mystical and religious teachings. Through magic, a person can cause inner change and change in the physical world. High magic has a spiritual nature. Low magic, such as spell casting, is a form of SORCERY.

Magic had its beginnings in humankind's earliest attempts to control its environment, survival, and destiny, either by controlling natural forces or by appealing to higher powers for help. The anthropologist Bronislaw Malinowski defined magic as having three functions and three elements. The three functions are to produce, to protect, and to destroy. The three elements are spells and incantations, rites or procedures, and altered states of consciousness accomplished through fasting, meditating, chanting, visualizing symbols, sleep deprivation, dancing, staring into flames, inhaling fumes, taking drugs, and so forth.

Magic is practiced universally by skilled individuals who either are born into their powers or train themselves to acquire powers. Magic is not inherently good or evil but reflects the intent of the magician. The ethical and moral uses of magic have always been ambiguous. Evil magic is associated with sorcery and WITCHCRAFT. Throughout history, people and authorities have had an uneasy relationship with magic, depending on it and tolerating its practice and at the same time condemning it. Magic is both part of religion and a competitor of religion. It has been regarded as a science and has been discredited by science. In modern times, however, science is providing evidence in support of magic.

Magical phenomena exist in a realm of liminality, a blurred borderland that is neither in the material world nor in the spiritual world but in both simultaneously. *Liminality* is a term coined by the anthropologist Arthur van Gennup to refer to the condition of being "betwixt and between." The word is from *limen,* or "threshold." Change, transition, and transformation are conditions that are conducive to psi and the supernatural. Magic ritual—and ritual in general—exposes the ordinary, predictable world to the instability of the liminal world.

Strange things happen. The liminal realm is considered to be a dangerous, unpredictable one. Individuals such as magicians thus are dangerous because they work in this uncertain world. As adepts, they are themselves the agents of change and even chaos.

Magic Influences

The Western magical tradition is rich and complex, evolving from a mixture of magical, mystical, philosophical, and religious sources. It incorporates the low magic of spells and divination, the dark magic of sorcery and witchcraft, and the high magic of spiritual enlightenment that is closer to mysticism than to spell casting. There are several major streams of influence.

Egyptian magic Magic played an important role in ancient Egypt, and the magic of the Egyptians became important in the development of Western ritual magic. Egyptian priests were skilled in magical arts of spell casting, divination, necromancy, making of amulets and talismans, procuring and sending of dreams, use of magical figures similar to poppets, and use of magic in the practice of medicine. Illnesses were believed to be caused by a host of demons who controlled various parts of the human body; thus cures involved EXORCISMs. The mummification of the dead was done according to precise ritual magic to ensure safe passage to the afterlife. The Egyptian Book of the Dead is a magical handbook of preparation for navigation through judgment into Amenti, the underworld domain of Osiris, lord of the dead. In Hellenistic times, Egyptian magic was mixed with classical magic.

Especially important to Egyptian magic was the proper use of words and names of power. Some incantations involved strings of names, some incomprehensible, borrowed from other cultures.

Greek and Roman magic The Greek and Roman worlds teemed with magic. Power was channeled from a host of sources: deities, spirits called DAIMONes, celestial intelligences, and the dead. Everything was connected by sympathetic bonds, which allowed magical action at a distance. The Hermetic principle that the microcosm reflects the macrocosm ("As above, so below") was espoused in variations by Pythagoreans, Platonists, and Stoics.

All magical arts were practiced; the Greeks were especially interested in destiny and devoted great attention to the prophecy of oracles and to the fate forecast by the stars in a horoscope. Both Greeks and Romans practiced numerous forms of divination, especially lot casting and the examination of signs in nature. Dreams were consulted, especially for healing. Cursing one's competitors and enemies was routine in daily life. Incantations involved long strings of magical words, often nonsensical, which had to be precisely pronounced along with the correct gestures.

An exalted form of magic, *theurgia*, had religious overtones and was akin to ritual magic. The Neoplatonists favored *theurgia*, believing they could summon divine powers to Earth and enable their souls to ascend to heaven.

In *Natural History,* Pliny asserts that all magic originated in medicine, in the search for cures. The magical workings of the heavens, especially the Moon, both caused and cured illnesses. In addition, demons flying through the air and shooting arrows stirred up poisonous vapors that caused plagues and pestilence.

Jewish magic The early Jews were steeped in magical lore, much of which was borrowed and adapted from the magical practices of the Canaanites, Babylonians, Egyptians, and, later, Hellenistic-Gnostic influences. Magic was not organized into systems; rather, it was a collection of beliefs and practices chiefly concerning protection from demons and the procuring of blessings. As early as the first century C.E., magical lore was attributed to the wisdom of King SOLOMON. This lore provided the basis for the later GRIMOIRE the *Key of Solomon,* the most important of the old handbooks of Western magic.

According to Jewish lore, the magical arts were taught to human by ANGELS, chiefly the WATCHERS, who fell from God's grace when they departed heaven to cohabit with human women. The gift was dubious, for the Tanakh—the Old Testament—condemns sorcery, the use of spirits and various forms of magic, such as enchantment, shape shifting, divination, mediumship, and necromancy.

Talmudic law reinterpreted sorcery. Magic requiring the help of demons was forbidden and was punishable by death. Magic that did not require the help of demons was still forbidden but received lesser punishments. The distinction between the two often was not clear. Later, the use of mystical names of God and angels and verses of Scripture were incorporated into incantations.

Magic was organized into systems around 500 C.E., about the same time as the development of Merkabah mysticism, a precursor to the KABBALAH. Merkabah mystics performed elaborate rituals of purification, contemplation of the sacred and magical properties of letters and numbers, the recitation of sacred names, and the use of AMULETs, SEALs, and TALISMANs. The trance recitation of long incantations of names was similar to the Egyptians' "barbarous names," in that many were corruptions of names of deities and angels.

By the Middle Ages, Jewish magic depended almost entirely on the use of names and interventions of spirits. The Kabbalah, a body of esoteric teachings dating to about the 10th century and in full bloom by the 13th century, does not forbid magic but warns of the dangers of it. Only the most virtuous persons should perform magic and do so only in times of public emergency and need, never for private gain. How strictly these admonitions were followed is questionable. A practical Kabbalah of magical procedures developed from about the 14th century on. Kabbalists were divided on the issue of whether or not one could invoke demons as well as angels.

Black magic is called "apocryphal science" in the Kabbalah. It is strictly forbidden, and only theoretical knowledge is permitted. Those who choose to practice it become sorcerers in the thrall of FALLEN ANGELS.

By the Middle Ages, Jews were renowned among Christians as magical adepts. These adepts were not professional magicians but were rabbis, doctors, philosophers, teachers, and students of oral transmission of mystical and esoteric knowledge.

Christian magic As did Judaism, Christianity held paradoxical attitudes toward magic. In general, magic was looked upon with disfavor, as the practices of non-Christians that interfered with the new religion. Manipulative "low" magic was forbidden, but helpful magic, such as for healing, was practiced within certain limits. Jesus performed magical acts, but they were cast as miracles made possible by his divine nature. The early church fathers especially opposed divination, which took one's destiny out of the hands of God.

Christian magic emphasized nature, such as herbal lore, and placed importance on mystical names. But the body of Christ, as represented by the Eucharist, held the greatest magic, as did the name of Jesus and relics (body parts and possessions) of saints.

Medieval Europe was rife with magic of all sorts: folk practitioners, wizards, cunning men and women, alchemists, and others. The practical Kabbalah, Hermetic principles, Gnostic and Neoplatonic lore, Christian elements, and pagan elements joined in syncretic mixtures. A Western Kabbalah emerged that became the basis for Western ritual magic. Magical handbooks called grimoires circulated.

The medieval church frowned upon magic of all sorts:

- divination of all kinds
- conjuration of spirits
- necromancy
- weaving and binding magic, in which spells were imbued into knots and fabric
- love magic and any other magic involving potions, poppets, and so forth
- magical medical remedies

The populace relied on the folk magic of local practitioners, called by many names, such as *cunning men, witches,* and *wizards.* Many possessed natural healing and psychic abilities and practiced homegrown magic passed down orally through generations. The church tolerated magic that was adequately Christianized, such as through the substitution of the names of Jesus, Mary, and angels for those of pagan deities and spirits; the use of the cross, holy water, and the Eucharist; and incantations that were more like prayers.

Folk magicians were often feared, and if their spell casting or divination failed, they were persecuted. Any bad luck was liable to be blamed on the black magic or witchcraft of a rival or enemy.

The Inquisition capitalized on fear. In 1484, Pope Innocent VIII declared witchcraft heretical, making the persecution of any enemy of the church easy. Witchcraft was not merely black magic, but was DEVIL worship, service to SATAN's grand plan to subvert souls. A "witch craze" swept Europe and reached across the Atlantic to the American colonies. Thousands of persons were executed.

The witch hysteria died in the advance of the scientific revolution of the 17th century. Though many great scientists of the day were versed in alchemy and the principles of magic, the importance of the latter two declined.

The occult revival and modern magic In the 19th century, a revival of interest in occultism and magic occurred, centered in and spreading out from France through Eliphas Levi, Papus (Gerard Encausse), and others. Levi's works were particularly influential and were translated into English by Arthur Edward Waite. Levi drew together the Kabbalah, Hermeticism, and magic as the three occult sciences that lead to truth. He described the Kabbalah as the "mathematics of human thought," which answers all questions through numbers. Magic is the knowledge of the secret laws and powers of nature and the universe.

In the late 19th century, magical fraternities and lodges rose in prominence, the best known of which was the esoteric Hermetic Order of the Golden Dawn in England. The Golden Dawn was founded by Rosicrucians and Freemasons who were also familiar with the Eastern philosophy taught by the Theosophical Society. It was not originally intended to be a magical order. It taught only theoretical magic in its outer order, but eventually its inner order taught and practiced the magical arts as well as rituals of high magic. The rituals systematized by the Golden Dawn influenced much of the magical work that was yet to unfold.

A considerable contribution to ritual magic was made by ALEISTER CROWLEY, who was already well versed in the subject by the time he was initiated into the Golden Dawn in 1898. The Golden Dawn could not contain Crowley's oversized personality, and he was expelled two years later.

His most significant magical innovation is his Law of Thelema: "Do what thou wilt shall be the whole of the Law." The Thelemic law was dictated to an entranced Crowley in 1909 in Egypt by a spirit named Aiwass, an emissary of the god Horus. *The Book of the Law* lays out the emergence of the New Aeon of Horus, for which Crowley was to be the chief prophet. Everything springs from the Thelemic law, and magic is the "art and science of causing change to occur in conformity with Will." The individual is sovereign and responsible only to himself or herself. The proper use of will raises the individual to the highest purpose, not a selfish purpose.

Crowley had numerous dealings with spirits, including demons (see CHORONZON).

From the 20th century on, there have been cycles of revival of popular interest in magic. Influences are fiction, television (especially reality TV) and film, the growth of Wiccan and Pagan spiritual traditions (which emphasize working with positive spirits for benevolent purposes), and popular fascination with paranormal investigations of haunted places. Practitioners engage in a wide variety of magical activities. Some are derived from folk magic and involve spell casting; others involve the conjurations of spirits; some are paths of spiritual development.

Types of Magic

Though magic itself is neutral, practitioners often distinguish between good, or white, magic and bad, or black magic, though such distinctions are subjective. The occultist Franz Bardon divided magic into three types:

- Lower magic, which deals with the laws of nature and control of forces in nature, such as the elements
- Intermediate magic, which deals with the laws of human beings in the microcosm and how the microcosm can be influenced
- Higher magic, which deals with the universal laws of the macrocosm and how they can be controlled

Other types of magic are known by their distinguishing characteristics.

Folk magic Folk magic comprises local traditions of simple magic for the purposes of casting spells for healing, luck, protection, and so forth. Folk magic blends other forms of magic, often with mixed religious elements. Folk magic remedies and prescriptions are handed down in oral traditions and in small handbooks.

Natural magic Natural magic is based on nature, such as herbs, stones, crystals, the commanding of the elements and the influences of planets and stars. Natural magic draws on the inherent magical properties of things. Philters, potions, powders, ointments, and so forth, are based on natural magic recipes, combined with folk magic incantations and CHARMs.

Sympathetic magic Sympathetic magic is spell casting through associations that establish a sympathetic connection for the flow of power. One of the best-known sympathetic magic tools is the poppet, a doll that substitutes for a person. The connection is strengthened by attaching photographs, hair, or personal objects of the victim to the doll. Whatever is done to the doll happens to the person.

Anything can be used to establish a sympathetic connection. The best items are from a person's body, such as hair and nail clippings. Personal possessions or any object handled by a person can be used. A gift can be magically charged and enter into a home or place as a magical Trojan horse.

Australian aborigines put sharp pebbles or ground glass in the footprints of enemies as sympathetic magic to weaken and destroy them. The Ojibwa use a straw effigy to drive evil spirits away from their communities. If a member has a dream of disaster, a straw man is erected that substitutes for the trouble. The people eat, smoke tobacco, and ask for blessings. They attack the straw effigy, shooting it and clubbing it until it is in pieces. The remains are burned.

Ceremonial magic Ceremonial magic, also called high magic and ritual magic, involves systems of spiritual development. Practitioners learn to access and travel in other-dimensional realities, including the astral plane, and to experience spirits and otherworldly beings. The emphasis is on self-mastery and union with the godhead. The initiate must develop inner plane contacts with gods, angels, and other entities. Some modern branches of ceremonial magic incorporate scientific principles and elements, such as chaos theory, which attempts to identify the system or pattern behind seemingly random occurrences.

Composite magic Composite magic, also called practical magic, combines various religious influences, for example, Christian and Jewish elements, with folk magic. Composite magic is found in grimoires. Composite magic has practical purposes, such as conjuring and spell casting for information, healing, attainment of goals and objectives, and even hexes and CURSES.

Black magic Black magic is used for malevolent purposes, to harm or kill. According to tradition, black magic is accomplished with the aid of demonic entities. Another term for it is goetic magic, or *goetia.*

Levi said in *The History of Magic,* "Black Magic may be defined as the art of inducing artificial mania in ourselves and in others; but it is also above all the science of poisoning."

Arthur Edward Waite termed black magic as the utterance of words and names of power for "unlawful purposes" and "the realm of delusion and nightmare, though phenomenal enough in its results." It involves communing with demons and evil spirits for material gain or harmful purpose.

Black magic is associated with sorcery and witchcraft. The Christian Church associated all pagan and folk magic with "black magic."

White magic White magic is used for positive goals: healing, blessings, good luck, abundance, and so forth. White magic can involve any form of magic when used for beneficence.

FURTHER READING:

Bardon, Franz. *Initiation into Hermetics: A Course of Instruction of Magic Theory and Practice.* Wuppertal, Germany: Dieter Ruggeberg, 1971.

Butler, E. M. *Ritual Magic.* Cambridge: Cambridge University Press, 1949.

Flint, Valerie I. J. *The Rise of Magic in Medieval Europe.* Princeton, N.J.: Princeton University Press, 1991.

Gray, William G. *Western Inner Workings.* York Beach, Me.: Samuel Weiser, 1983.

Hall, Manly P. *The Secret Teachings of All Ages.* Los Angeles: Philosophic Research Society, 1977. First published 1928.

Hansen, George. *The Trickster and the Paranormal.* New York: Xlibris, 2001.

Knight, Gareth. *The Practice of Ritual Magic.* Albuquerque: Sun Chalice Books, 1996.

Kraig, Donald Michael. *Modern Magick: Eleven Lessons in the High Magickal Arts.* 2nd ed. St. Paul, Minn.: Llewellyn, 2004.

Levi, Eliphas. *The History of Magic.* 1860. Reprint, York Beach, Me.: Samuel Weiser, 2001.

Luck, Georg. *Arcana Mundi: Magic and the Occult in the Greek and Roman Worlds.* Baltimore: Johns Hopkins University Press, 1985.

Malinowski, Bronislaw. *Magic, Science and Religion.* Garden City, N.Y.: Doubleday Anchor Books, 1948.

Regardie, Israel. *The Golden Dawn.* 6th ed. St. Paul, Minn.: Llewellyn, 1989.

Thomas, Keith. *Religion and the Decline of Magic.* New York: Scribners, 1971.

Maid of Orlach Possession (1831) The most remarkable POSSESSION case from the files of the German mesmerist Justinus Kerner. The Maid of Orlach was a dairymaid over whom a White Spirit and a Black Spirit fought for control. The spirits were those of a sinning nun and a murderous monk. In the end, a house had to be destroyed to get rid of the possessing DEMON. The account of the maid is in Kerner's 1834 book *Geschichten Besessener neurer Zeit (Histories of Modern Possession).*

Strange events began in February 1831 at the farm home of a Lutheran peasant named Grombach, who lived in the tiny village of Orlach, Wurtemberg, Germany. The activity centered in the cowhouse and involved his daughter, Magdalene, the "maid." First, the cows were affected and poltergeist phenomena occurred. The cows would be mysteriously tied to new spots, and their tails were braided. Grombach kept watch but caught no visible person in the act.

Magdalene one day received a sharp blow to one of her ears that sent her cap flying. From February 8 through February 11, mysterious fires broke out in the cow house. Then, Magdalene heard a child whimpering in the cottage house, but none could be seen.

A shadowy gray apparition of a woman appeared to Magdalene against a wall in the cow house. The spirit, which became known as the White Spirit, said the fires had been caused by an evil spirit, but that she had protected the family. She said that 400 years earlier, she had been a 14-year-old girl who was sent against her will to a convent, where she had committed a sin she could not reveal. She told Magdalene that the house must be destroyed by March 5 the following year. It told her, "Flee from the house! Flee from the house! If it is not pulled down before the fifth of March of the coming year a misfortune will happen to you . . . promise me that you will do it!" The girl agreed.

The White Spirit appeared frequently to the maid until May. It also spoke in religious language and prayed the 112th Psalm. It read Magdalene's thoughts and accurately predicted future events. No one but she could see it.

In May, the White Spirit announced that she would not be able to visit for some time, and Magdalene would be persecuted by the Black Spirit, her evil companion. Magdalene should never answer him, no matter what happened.

The Black Spirit took various guises, such as frogs, a black cat, dogs, a headless horse, and disembodied male voices that followed the maid, mocking her. Then, it began showing up as a monk, tempting her with questions. The Black Spirit sometimes imitated the voices of neighbors in order to trick the girl into answering, but she held fast in her silence to him.

A bag of coins mysteriously appeared in the barn, and the Black Spirit said he put it there to compensate the maid for the box on the ear. Soon, the White Spirit appeared and told the maid that the money must be given to the poor. It was.

After this, the Black Spirit intensified his attacks on Magdalene. He appeared as a bear on July 15 and threatened to plague her if she would not answer him. From then on, he appeared in various monstrous, animalistic shapes, promising her money and threatening her with torture.

On August 21, the Black Spirit appeared as a horrible animal with its neck in the middle of its body. The maid fainted and was unconscious for several hours. The fainting episodes happened again on the following days. She could answer questions while entranced but could not remember anything when she awakened. She said that the Black Spirit came upon her and then disappeared when the White Spirit arrived.

On August 23, the White Spirit said she would protect Magdalene from harm but urged her to proceed with demolishing the family's house, to end her suffering. The spirit said that the Black Spirit would take complete possession of her, but that she, the White Spirit, would take Magdalene away to a place of safety when that happened. These developments finally prompted Magdalene's father to begin tearing down the house.

Beginning on August 25, Magdalene fell under intensified attacks from the Black Spirit, who was able to take over her body and speak through her mouth. A description of the manner of possession is as follows:

> In the midst of her work she would see the figure of a man clothed in a monk's frock, which seemed to be made from black mist, approach and say, when she refused to answer his questions: "Now I will enter thy body in spite of thee." Then she always felt him tread on her left side, seize her with five cold fingers at the back of the neck and then enter her body. She lost consciousness and individuality. Her voice was no longer her own, but that of the monk's. The speeches which she uttered when in this state were worthy of a demon. Magdalene lay during the whole time with her head sunk towards her left side, and her eyes firmly closed; if the eyelids were raised the pupils would be discovered upwards. The left

foot constantly moved up and down upon the ground throughout the attack, which frequently lasted four or five hours.

TRAUGOTT KONSTANTIN OESTERREICH stated of these occurrences:

> He (the possessing spirit) speaks of her, he knows quite well that she is alive, but he pretends *that she is not there, but it is he who is there,* and he pours out abuse and calumnies against the girl herself, whom he never calls anything except "the sow.". . . During these fits the spirit of darkness now utters through her words worthy of a mad demon, things which have no place in this true-hearted maid, curses upon the Holy Scriptures, the Redeemer, and all the saints.

Her transformation of personality was so marked, said Oesterreich, that it was "exactly as if a stronger man drove the owner from his house and looked out of the window at his ease, making himself at home."

Magdalene's head would move from side to side while the Black Spirit was in her and then flop to the right when it left. If a Bible was placed nearby, the Black Spirit hissed like a SERPENT and tried to spit on it.

Magdalene remembered nothing from the attacks, except a faint memory of having attended church, presumably the way she perceived the protection of the White Spirit. Her left foot always went cold during the attacks, while her right foot stayed warm. But upon awakening, she could walk normally and felt nothing wrong with either foot.

Magdalene was taken to doctors, who said she had a natural illness and prescribed pills or medications, but none helped her. Finally Grombach took her to see Kerner. He tried magnetic passes two or three times, but the Black Spirit immediately neutralized them with countermovements of the girl's hands. Kerner recommended prayer and a sparse diet. Magdalene did not respond to those, either, but Kerner was confident the matter would resolve itself according to the White Spirit's promise of a cure by March 5.

Word spread about the girl's afflictions, and crowds would gather to watch her when she was possessed.

On March 4, the day before the White Spirit's deadline, the White Spirit appeared to the maid at six in the morning. She confessed her sins: She had been seduced by the monk who was now the Black Spirit and had lived with him. When she tried to reveal his wickedness, he had murdered her. While the spirit spoke, a phantom black dog appeared and spit fire. The White Spirit reached her hand toward the maid, who touched it with a handkerchief. The cloth sparkled and then exhibited holes that matched a palm print.

The White Spirit said she was now freed from earthly concerns and said farewell. The maid was taken to a neighbor's house, where the Black Spirit took possession, during which the girl ate no food. A huge crowd gathered

to witness this and to question the demon, which gave accurate answers.

DELIVERANCE occurred when the Black Spirit prayed during the night of March 4 and for the first time could say the words JESUS, Bible, church, and heaven. He confessed all of his crimes, including murders. He said there is a reckoning after death, and he must appear at the judgment seat a second time after he departed the maid.

The last wall of the Gromlach cottage was destroyed at 11:30 on the morning of March 5. The Black Spirit left Magdalene in an astounding transformation back to radiant health. She was never troubled again.

Old bones were found in the debris of the house, including those of children, who people assumed were the victims of the monk.

FURTHER READING:
Oesterreich, Traugott K. *Possession and Exorcism.* Secaucus, N.J.: University Books, 1966.
Stead, W. T. *Borderland: A Casebook of True Supernatural Stories.* Hyde Park, N.Y.: University Books, 1970.

Maillat Possession (1598)   Case of Loyse Maillat, a young French DEMONIAC whose story of POSSESSION led to a mass witch hunt in the Burgundy region of France, presided over by one of the most ruthless judges and witch hunters, Henri Boguet.

Eight-year-old Loyse Maillat was the daughter of Claude and Humberte Maillat, who lived in the village of Coyrières, Perche. On June 5, 1598, Loyse suddenly lost the use of her arms and legs and had to move about on all fours with her mouth twisted in a strange way. When the condition did not clear up, her parents assumed her to be possessed and took her on June 19 to the Church of Our Savior for EXORCISM. Five DEMONS called Wolf, Cat, Dog, Jolly, and Griffon identified themselves. Asked by the priest who caused her problem, Maillat pointed to a woman, Françoise Secretain, who was among those in attendance. The demons did not depart.

Back home, Loyse asked her parents to pray for her, to deliver her from the demons. They complied, and after a period of praying, Loyse said that two of the demons were dead, and the others would follow if they kept praying. The parents prayed all night.

In the morning, Loyse's condition was worse. She foamed at the mouth and had seizures. She fell to the ground, and the devils emerged from her mouth in the form of fist-size balls. Four of them were red as fire, and Cat was black. Three issued forth with great violence, and the two that Loyse had said were dead emerged with less force. The demons danced three or four times around the fire and departed, and, from then on, Loyse's health improved.

Loyse and her parents told judges, including Boguet, how and why Loyse came to be possessed. For her young age, Loyse was quite convincing in her testimony. Her parents backed up her account. Secretain, a poor woman of good repute, had gone to the Maillat home on June 4 asking for lodging. Humberte was alone, and she refused at first, but Loyse persuaded her to change her mind. After Secretain was admitted, Humberte went out to tend to their cattle. Loyse and her two sisters sat by the fire. Secretain gave Loyse a crust of bread the color of dung and told her to eat it, and not speak of it to anyone, or Secretain would kill her and eat her. The next day, the child was possessed.

Secretain was imprisoned and for three days vehemently maintained her innocence. She prayed incessantly with a rosary, which Boguet said later was "defective," and thus usable by a witch. Boguet observed that she shed no tears, a certain sign of witches, according to prevailing belief. He had her tortured. She was stripped naked and shaved of body hair to search for a DEVIL'S MARK, but none was found. When the inquisitors started to cut off the hair from her head, she broke down and began confessing. For days, she added to her confessions as the pressure continued. Her seven principal confessions were the following:

- She had sent five devils into Loyse Maillat.
- She had for a long time served the DEVIL, who appeared to her in the form of a black man.
- She had copulated with the Devil four or five times. Sometimes, he was in the form of a dog, a cat, or a fowl. His semen was very cold.
- She had attended SABBATs countless times at a place called Combes, near the water, and near Coyrières. She traveled to them through the air on a white staff she placed between her legs.
- She danced at the sabbats and beat water to cause hail.
- She and an accomplice, a man named Groz-Jacques Boquet, had murdered a woman, Loys Monneret, by making her eat a piece of bread dusted with a powder given to them by the Devil.
- She had caused several cows to die by touching them with her hand or a wand and uttering certain words.

Secretain named others, thus enabling Boguet to launch a mass witch hunt. She and many of the accused were sent to the stake to be burned alive.

For Boguet, the Maillat case served his purpose to demonstrate that witches had the ability to send demons into the bodies of victims. In his book *Discours des Sorciers (An Examen of Witches)*, he cites a long list of supporting cases in which people sent demons into others. Even God and St. Paul had done this. In Psalm 78, God sent "evil angels" among people to punish them. St. Paul sent SATAN into several heretics.

Boguet commented that God allowed such innocents to become possessed in order for his works and justice to shine more gloriously. The case, he said, "led to the discovery of countless witches who have been punished as the gravity of their crimes deserved."

FURTHER READING:
Boguet, Henri. *An Examen of Witches: Discours Excrable des Sourciers.* London: John Rodker, 1929.

Maillot, Thomas (16th century)   French official who resisted entering into a PACT with the DEVIL in order to procure love, according to the French demonologist NICHOLAS REMY. The account of Thomas Maillot is related in Remy's book *Demonolatry* (1595) and is retold by the demonologist FRANCESCO-MARIA GUAZZO in *Compendium Maleficarum* (1608).

In youth, Maillot fell in love with a girl of high nobility, far above his social station. He was the son of a tradesman and had no wealth. For all practical purposes, he had no hope of even declaring his love for her, let alone winning her hand in marriage.

Maillot heard about a German fellow servant who had the services of a DEMON and sought out his help. The German was elated; he was in need of a victim, for part of his pact with the demon was to recruit someone to take over his demonic debt or have his neck broken. He told Maillot to meet him at twilight the next day in a secret chamber.

When Maillot arrived, a beautiful and seductive young woman (the demon in disguise) met him and promised to deliver the marriage he desired in exchange for some promises. The requirements sounded innocent and pious on the surface: Maillot should avoid all thieving, drunkenness, lust, wrongdoing, blasphemy, and vices. He should practice devotion, help the poor, fast twice a week, observe all holy days, pray daily, and be a good Christian. If he would bind himself by oath to this, the demon said, then he would win the noble girl as a bride. Maillot was given a few days to consider this offer and make his answer.

At first, Maillot thought this to be the perfect deal: love in exchange for piety that he should practice anyway. But the more he thought about it, the more he doubted the reliability of a demon. Demons were known to trick people in order to claim their souls.

A priest Maillot knew sensed his trouble and inquired about his visible distress. Maillot told him and was persuaded by the priest to drop all communication and dealings with the demon. He complied and declined the pact.

Shortly thereafter, the German, having failed to find a substitute for his debt to the demon, fell off his horse, hit his head, and was killed instantly, thus experiencing the consequences of his failure.

Maillot, who presumably gave up his love for the noble girl, later in life became governor of a province in Lorraine. Remy swore that the story was true and that it was confirmed to him by Maillot himself.

FURTHER READING:
Remy, Nicholas. *Demonolatry.* Secaucus, N.J.: University Books, 1974.

Makhlath   In Jewish demonology, a powerful female DEMON. Makhlath (dancer) and her daughter, AGRATH, are in constant warfare with LILITH. Makhlath commands 478 hosts of evil spirits. She and Agrath meet Lilith and battle on the Day of Atonement. While they quarrel, the prayers of Israel are able to rise to heaven.

Malgaras   DEMON among the 31 AERIAL SPIRITS OF SOLOMON. Malgaras rules in the west and has dozens of dukes serving him both day and night. His servants are courteous and appear in pairs, along with their own servants. His 12 major servants of the daytime are Camiel, Meliel, Borasy, Agor, Casiet, Rabiel, Cabiel, Udiel, Opriel, Masiel, Barfas, and Arois. His 12 major dukes of the nighttime are Aros, Doiel, Cubi, Liblel, Raboc, Aspeil, Caron, Zamor, Amiel, Aspara, Deilas, and Basiel.

Malleus Maleficarum (Witch Hammer)   The most influential and important witch hunter's guide of the Inquisition. Published first in Germany in 1487, the *Malleus Maleficarum* was translated into dozens of editions throughout Europe and England and was the leading reference for witch trials on the Continent for about 200 years. It was adopted by both Protestant and Catholic civil and ecclesiastical judges. It was second only to the Bible in sales until John Bunyan's *Pilgrim's Progress* was published in 1678. The book gives instructions for interrogating, trying, and punishing accused witches and details the nature, characteristics, and behavior of DEMONs and the DEVIL.

Fourteen editions were published by 1520; another 16 editions appeared by 1669. By the end of the 17th century, there were more than 30 editions. The book became the definitive guide by which inquisitors and judges conducted themselves and that subsequent writers used as a foundation for their own works. The book was important in the way it linked witchcraft to heresy. It has been described in the centuries since as a vicious and cruel work, the most damaging book of its kind during the Inquisition.

Authorship
The *Malleus Maleficarum* is credited to the authorship of two Dominican inquisitors, Heinrich Kramer and James Sprenger, though historians now believe that it was written by Kramer, by far the more zealous of the two and one of the most zealous participants in the entire Inquisition. Kramer and Sprenger were empowered by Pope Innocent VIII in his bull of December 9, 1484, to prosecute witches throughout northern Germany. The papal edict was intended to quell Protestant opposition to the Inquisition and to solidify the case made in 1258 by Pope Alexander IV for the prosecution of witches as heretics. It was the opinion of the church that the secular arm, the civil courts, were not punishing enough witches solely on the basis of their evildoing.

Both Kramer and Sprenger were prolific writers. Kramer, also known as Institoris, the latinized version of his name, rose to power as an inquisitor and was known to have framed some of his victims. He was violently op-

posed to witchcraft and seemed also to harbor hatred against women, whom he viewed as inherently weak and evil. He sought to establish a direct connection between women and diabolic witchcraft. Some historians also think that Kramer was reacting to broader sentiments of the time that were responses to the influences of holy women and mystics such as St. Catherine of Siena, a powerful figure consulted by royalty and heads of state. He did praise the saintliness of certain holy women who were able to resist the lustful temptations indulged in by witches, in his view.

Sprenger was a distinguished friar, and he may have allowed Kramer to use his name in Kramer's virulent antiwitch treatise, *Apologia auctoris in* Malleus Maleficarum, written by 1485. He had some association with Kramer in trials of accused witches.

Kramer's treatise was absorbed into the *Malleus Maleficarum*. After its publication, evidence surfaced that Kramer may have fabricated one of the official letters authorizing the work. Relations between Kramer and Sprenger became strained. After Sprenger died in 1496, his colleagues attempted to distance his legacy from Kramer.

Little is known about Kramer's activities after publication of the *Malleus* in 1487 until his death in 1505. He remained an inquisitor. In 1500, Pope Alexander VI appointed him papal nuncio and inquisitor of Bohemia and Moravia. He was pursuing witches and heretics in Bohemia at the time of his death.

Contents
The *Malleus* is based on the biblical pronouncement "Thou shall not suffer a witch to live" (Exodus 22:18) and draws on Scripture and the works of Aristotle, St. Augustine, and St. Thomas Aquinas as support. It maintains that because God acknowledged witches, to doubt witchcraft is heresy. The book is divided into three parts and organized as questions answered by opposing arguments.

Part 1 concerns how the Devil and his witches, with "the permission of Almighty God," perpetrate a variety of evils upon men and animals, including succubi and incubi, instilling hatred, obstructing or destroying fertility, and causing the metamorphosis, or shape shifting, of human beings into beasts. God permits these acts; otherwise, the Devil would have unlimited power and destroy the world.

Part 2 describes how witches cast spells and bewitchments and do their evil and how these actions can be prevented or remedied. Particular emphasis is given to Devil's PACTs, a key to proving heresy. The existence of witches and their *maleficia* is treated as unassailable fact, and wild stories of SABBATs and other abominations are presented as truth. Most of the stories are from the inquisitions conducted by Sprenger and Kramer and from material of other ecclesiastical witchcraft writers.

Part 3 sets forth the legal procedures for trying witches, including the taking of testimony, admission of evidence, methods of interrogation and torture, and guidelines for sentencing. Judges are instructed to allow hostile witnesses because everyone hates witches. Torture is to be applied if the accused do not confess voluntarily. Judges are permitted to lie to the accused, promising them mercy if they confess, a tactic readily employed by Kramer. This, the text argues, is all done in the best interest of society and the state. The *Malleus* allows for light sentences of penance and imprisonment in certain cases but urges execution of as many witches as possible. Most of the instructions on sentencing pertain to death.

Some questions are not answered clearly and contradictions abound. For example, the authors say that the Devil, through witches, mainly afflicts good and just people, then says only the wicked are vulnerable. At one point, judges are said to be immune to the bewitchments of witches; at another, witches cast spells over judges with the glance of an eye, and judges are admonished to protect themselves with salt and sacraments.

The *Malleus Maleficarum* was refuted by JOHANN WEYER.

FURTHER READING:
Herzig, Tamar. "Witches, Saints and Heretics." *Magic, Ritual, and Witchcraft.* Summer 2006, 24–55.
The Malleus Maleficarum of Heinrich Kramer and James Sprenger. New York: Dover, 1971.

Malphas (Malpas)   FALLEN ANGEL and 39th of the 72 SPIRITS OF SOLOMON. Malphas is a powerful president in HELL who appears first as a crow and then, when commanded, as a human who speaks in a hoarse voice. He skillfully builds houses and high towers and brings down the temples and towers of enemies. He will bring deceivers together quickly. He destroys the desires, thoughts, and accomplishments of anyone's enemies. Malphas gives good FAMILIARS. He will receive a sacrifice kindly but then deceive the one who offers it. Malpas commands 40 legions of DEMONS.

Mammon   FALLEN ANGEL who rules in HELL as an archdemon and prince of tempters. The name *Mammon* in Aramaic means "riches." He embodies the second of the SEVEN DEADLY SINS, avarice. Mammon is equated with LUCIFER, SATAN, and BEELZEBUB. He serves as hell's ambassador to England.

mandragora   DEMON who appears in the shape of a little man with no beard and thin hair. Mandragoras also are small poppets, or dolls, that are inhabited by the DEVIL and used in spell-casting. According to lore, mandragoras can predict the future by nodding their head, and can converse with their owners. They bestow good health, curing of disease, and protection of homes against evil.

Marbas (Barbas)   FALLEN ANGEL and fifth of the 72 SPIRITS OF SOLOMON. Marbas is a president in HELL who rules 36 legions of DEMONS. He appears first as a lion but will change into a man. He knows about hidden and secret things. He causes and cures diseases. He imparts wisdom and knowledge of the mechanical arts. He can change men into different shapes.

Marchosias   FALLEN ANGEL and 35th of the 72 SPIRITS OF SOLOMON. Marchosias is a marquis ruling 30 LEGIONS of DEMONS. He appears as a cruel she-wolf with griffin wings and a serpent's tail, with fire spewing from his mouth. He will take a human form if commanded to do so. He is a strong fighter. He faithfully serves the magician and gives true answers to all questions. Once a member of the angelic order of dominions, Marchosias holds the futile hope that he will return to the Seventh Throne in Heaven after 1,200 years.

Marie des Vallees (1590–1656)   French girl of Coutances, France, whose lifelong struggle with POSSESSION led to her cult recognition as a local mystic. Marie des Vallees was possessed for 44 of her 66 years and was called the Saint of Coutances.

Marie was born to a peasant family in Saint-Sauveur-Landelin in the diocese of Coutances in Lower Normandy. Her father, Julien, died when she was 12. Her mother, Jacquelin Germain, married a butcher, who beat Marie with a stick. The abuse forced her to leave home, and she wandered for two years living with different people. In 1609, she was living with a female tutor when the symptoms of demonic possession manifested.

According to Marie, who shared details of her life with St. Jean Eudes, who was inspired by her, the cause of her possession was a witch's CURSE. A young man proposed to her and she turned him down. He sought the help of a witch to force her to love him. Soon after, he pushed against her while they were in a procession for the feast of St. Mercouf, and she felt lustful stirrings within her. When she went home, she fell down and uttered "terrible cries." From then on, Marie was in the grip of DEMONS. She found it difficult to pray or attend church.

Marie never disclosed the name of the young man but said that he left the parish permanently. The witch, known as "La Grivelle," was later burned at the stake on unrelated charges of WITCHCRAFT.

Another version of the possession cause was publicized by one of Marie's critics, who said that her problem started after she indulged in a "lascivious and sacrilegious dance" with a young man in a cemetery on a feast day.

Regardless, once Marie was afflicted, her problems increased. After three years of unrest and near-sleepless nights, her adopted family took her to Bishop Briroy, the bishop of Coutances, to seek his advice. Doctors could not help her. The bishop tried for three years to exorcise the demons but failed.

In 1614, Marie went to Rouen, to undergo EXORCISMS by the archbishop and several doctors. The demons promised to leave at a certain time but did not. When asked why, they said that a local gentleman was using witchcraft to prevent them from leaving. Outraged at this accusation, the nobleman denounced Marie as a witch, and she was arrested.

Marie was held in prison for six months. She was shaved and searched for a DEVIL'S MARK by being pricked with needles. She was "matroned," a test for virginity. It was believed that witches had intercourse with demons and the DEVIL, and so if she were indeed a witch, she would not be a virgin. Marie passed the virginity test and was released.

She turned the situation to her advantage by expressing compassion for witches and desiring to take on the punishments for all their crimes. She wore a pigskin shirt with bristles and a horsehair ceinture and fasted. From 1617 to 1619 she said she descended into a state of HELL during which she suffered all the tortures inflicted upon witches. She said that witches gathered around her and accused her of sins she did not commit and added to her suffering.

Marie displayed common signs of possession, such as revulsion toward holy objects and the inability to take communion. She tried to commit suicide by stabbing herself with a knife but said that God stopped her by stiffening her arm.

Marie never expressed a desire to be free of demons and used her possession to advance herself as a saintly person. She enjoyed great patronage but also was controversial and was severely criticized. She operated outside the church. In 1651, a local church tribunal declared that she had been fooled by the Devil and had entered into a PACT with him.

In 1655, Marie's possession left her. For the first time in 30 years, she was able to take communion. She died in 1656.

FURTHER READING:
Ferber, Sarah. *Demonic Possession and Exorcism in Early Modern France.* London: Routledge, 2004.

Martin, Malachi Brendan (1921–1999)   Catholic theologian and EXORCIST. Malachi Martin, a former Jesuit, gained popular fame with book about POSSESSION and EXORCISM, *Hostage to the Devil* (1976). In all, he wrote more than 60 religious books, including fiction.

Martin was born on July 23, 1921, in Ballylongford, county Kerry, Ireland. He was educated at Belvedere College in Dublin and became a Jesuit novice in 1939. He received a bachelor's degree in Semitic languages and Oriental history from the National University of Ireland and studied Assyriology at Trinity College Dublin. He studied theology at the University of Louvain in Belgium and earned a doctoral degree there. In addition, he studied at Oxford in England and at the Hebrew University in Jerusalem.

Martin was ordained a Jesuit priest on August 15, 1954, and served the Holy See in Rome from 1958 to 1964. He

was also professor at the Pontifical Biblical Institute of the Vatican. Martin was gravely concerned about corruption within the church. In 1964, Pope Paul VI released Martin from his vows of poverty and obedience, but not chastity, and ordered him to report directly to the pope or one of his designates. He continued as a lay priest and did not wear a collar in public.

Martin pursued a literary career. He also participated in several exorcisms and became an expert on possession. He went to live in Paris and then New York City, where he lived with a wealthy Greek-American family by the name of Livanos.

In the late 1970s, the New York City serial killer David Berkowitz ("son of Sam") invited Martin to write his autobiography, but Martin declined.

In 1990, Martin published a nonfiction book, *Key of This Blood,* in which he referred to diabolic rites and activities in the Vatican. More on papal satanic forces was included in his 1996 novel, *Windswept House,* which describes a BLACK MASS ritual called "The Enthronement of the Fallen Archangel Lucifer." Martin said the ceremony had actually occurred prior to the election of Pope Paul VI. The pope later made a comment that "the smoke of Satan has entered the Sanctuary."

Martin is best known for *Hostage to the Devil.* He believed that forces of evil are at work in the world, manifesting in possession and in satanic child abuse. His book acquainted the general public with the signs and stages of possession, and the manner in which formal exorcisms are undertaken. During the 1990s, Martin was an occasional guest on Art Bell's *Coast to Coast AM* radio show.

Martin died at age 78 on July 27, 1999, after a second stroke and fall in his apartment in Manhattan. His funeral wake took place in St. Anthony of Padua Roman Catholic Chapel of West Orange, New Jersey. He is buried in Gate of Heaven Cemetery, in Hawthorne, New York.

At the time of his death, he was working on a book about the Vatican's involvement in the New World Order.

Mary of Nemmegen   A 16th-century fictional tale of a woman's seduction by the DEVIL and her ultimate redemption and triumph over him.

Mary of Nemmegen was published at the beginning of the 16th century in Antwerp. The identity of the author is uncertain, but is believed to be Ann Binns or Byns. The story appeared at a time when women were seen as weak vessels easily used by demonic forces. The triumph of Mary is a female version of FAUST, but she stands in stark contrast to the equally weak but doomed male counterpart in the Christopher Marlowe drama *Dr. Faustus,* written in the same period, and later in Johann Goethe's *Faust.*

According to the story, Mary lives in the land of Gelders. One day, while shopping in Nemmegen, she is caught by encroaching darkness and does not have enough time to return home before nightfall. She calls at the home of her uncle and aunt for shelter. The aunt refuses to let her in. Mary, loaded with heavy parcels, is in despair. She cries out that she cares not whether God or the Devil will help her.

The Devil answers her call. He appears in the guise of an ugly, one-eyed young man. The Devil cannot embody perfection but must be defective in some way. He introduces himself to Mary as a "man of many sciences." If she will promise to be his paramour, he will teach her all his knowledge, as well as shower her with gifts of gold and silver and love her above all women. In addition, she must give up her name, because "for one Mary [the Blessed Virgin] I and all my fellowship fare the worse," he tells her.

Mary agrees, effectively making a PACT with the Devil. She asks also to be taught magic and spell casting so that she can raise spirits, but the Devil dissuades her from this.

She becomes known as Emmekyn. She takes up with the Devil, and they go to different cities, including Antwerp. Emmekyn dazzles people with the knowledge she has been given, and men vie for her favor, even killing each other in their rivalries. Emmekyn enjoys it all, but she never loses her connection to her namesake, the Blessed Virgin Mary.

Meanwhile, the aunt, in a fit of temper influenced by the Devil, self-administers punishment for turning her niece away and cuts her own throat and dies.

After seven years of a dissipated lifestyle, Emmekyn grows bored and persuades the Devil to leave Antwerp and return to Nemmegen. They arrive on the day of a traditional procession and pageant for the Blessed Virgin. The sight of it causes Emmekyn to repent.

The Devil carries her high up into the air and casts her down, hoping to break her neck. But God does not allow it. Emmekyn falls into the street before many people, including her uncle, a priest, to whom she makes confession. He tells her, "There is nobody lost without the fall in despair." She then has an audience with the pope to seek absolution. Interestingly, she confesses only to her material sins and not to the desire to have learning and knowledge.

The pope gives her a heavy penance: She must wear three iron rings around her neck and arms. After two years, the rings miraculously fall away, showing that God has indeed forgiven her.

In a Dutch dramatic version of the story, an inset of the PROCESSUS SATHANE play is added. Masscheroen, the advocate for the Devil, petitions God for justice, arguing that the sinfulness of humankind should be judged the same as that of the FALLEN ANGELS. He says that God has become too lenient, and people have become increasingly wicked. God acknowledges that he may be right, and Masscheroen claims the right for the Devil to act as God's avenger. The Virgin Mary intervenes and makes a compassionate appeal to God for mercy. Mary wins the case.

Mary of Nemeggen shows that no matter how far one falls from grace, there is always the hope of redemption and God's forgiveness. Faust, on the other hand, is doomed to HELL beyond all hope once he makes his pact and falls into sin.

FURTHER READING:
De Bruyn, Lucy. *Woman and the Devil in Sixteenth-Century Literature.* Tisbury, England: Bear Book/The Compton Press, 1979.

Maseriel   DEMON among the 31 AERIAL SPIRITS OF SOLOMON. Maseriel serves CASPIEL and rules in the west. He has a great number of servants both day and night, each of whom has 30 servants. Maseriel's 12 major daytime dukes are Mahue, Roriel, Earviel, Zeriel, Atniel, Vessur, Azimel, Chasor, Patiel, Assuel, Aliel, and Espoel. The 12 major nighttime dukes are Arach, Maras, Noguiel, Saemiet, Amoyr, Bachile, Baros, Ellet, Earos, Rabiel, Atriel, and Salvor.

maskim   Seven Sumerian DEMONs who are great princes of HELL or princes of the abyss, considered to be among the most powerful of all. *Maskim* means "ensnarer" or "layers of ambush." Azza, AZAZEL, and MEPHISTOPHELES are among the *maskim.*

Sumerian descriptions of the *maskim* say they are neither male nor female, they take no wives and have no children, they are "strangers to benevolence," and they pay no attention to prayers or wishes. They live either on mountaintops or in the bowels of the earth.

The *maskim* have the power to affect the earth and the cosmic order. They can cause earthquakes and alter the courses of the stars in the sky. They do not like humans and attack them with the most severe evil and spells.

Masscheroen   See *PROCESSUS SATHANE.*

Mastema (Mastemah, Mansemat)   ANGEL of evil, hostility, adversity, and destruction; the accuser; a prince of DEMONs and injustice. The proper name *Mastema* has the same root as the Hebrew noun that means "hostility," its use in two references in the Old Testament (Hosea 9:7–8).

According to lore, Mastema once was the Angel of the Lord who delivered the punishments of the Lord and became demonized.

In 10 references in Qumran texts, Mastema is equated with BELIAL, whose purpose is to destroy. He also is described as existing between the Prince of Light and the Angel of Darkness and ruling the children of falsehood. He leads the children of righteousness astray.

In Jubilees, Mastema is the only angel named and is equated with the Angel of Hostility. His origins are not explained, though he is equated with SATAN and is the prince of evil beings who menace and harass humankind. As a SATAN, Mastema urges God to test Abraham with the sacrifice of his son, Isaac. Mastema also aids the Egyptians in opposition to Moses and tries to kill him. He helps the pharaoh's magicians compete with Moses and

Aaron. His demons lead the sons of Noah astray to commit sin, idolatry, and pollution.

One legend holds that Mastema asked God to give him some demons so that he might have power over humankind; God gave him one-tenth of the fallen ones to be under his command.

FURTHER READING:

Dictionary of Deities and Demons in the Bible. 2nd ed. Edited by Karel van der Toorn, Bob Becking, and Pieter W. van der Horst. Grand Rapids, Mich.: William B. Eerdmans, 1999.

mazziqin   In Jewish lore, evil spirits who injure. The *mazziqin* are divided into two classes. One class comprises FALLEN ANGELs who are led by SATAN. The second class are half-spirit and half-human hybrids, divided into two subclasses. One subclass includes the night terrors such as LILITH and her hordes. The second class is the SHEDIM, the offspring of Lilith or a SUCCUBUS and men.

McKenna, Bishop Robert (1927–)   Dominican bishop at Our Lady of the Rosary Chapel in Monroe, Connecticut. Bishop Robert McKenna has performed EXORCISMs, including at the haunted house known as the SMURL HAUNTING in Pennsylvania, and in Warren, Massachusetts, featured in the book *Satan's Harvest* (1990). He has worked with ED AND LORRAINE WARREN, JOHN ZAFFIS, and other lay demonologists. McKenna was ordained a priest in 1958 and a bishop in 1986. He has said that many officials in the church do not wish to believe that the DEVIL exists, or, if they do believe, they do not want to become involved with him. McKenna has retired from performing exorcisms.

Menadiel   DEMON and wandering duke of the air. Menadiel has 20 dukes and 100 companions under his command, plus many other servants. The demons must be summoned according to planetary hours. Six chiefs dukes are Larmol, Drasiel, Clamor, Benodiel, Charsiel, and Samyel. The six lesser dukes are Barchiel, Amasiel, Baruch, Nedriel, Curasin, and Tharson.

Menghi, Girolamo (1529–1609)   Franciscan friar and leading EXORCIST of the Italian Renaissance. Girolamo Menghi wrote extensively on demonology and EXORCISM prior to the codification of exorcism rites in Pope Paul V's RITUALE ROMANUM in 1614.

Menghi was born in 1529 in Viadana, Mantua, Italy. At age 20, he entered the Franciscan order of the Frati dell'Osservanza in Bologna, where he studied theology. He became famous as a preacher and was named superior of a Franciscan province in 1598.

An excellent scholar and writer, he authored numerous theological books, the most famous of which were on DEMONs and exorcism: *Flagellum daemonum* (*The Devil's Scourge*), 1576; *Compendio dell'arte essorcistica,* 1576; *Remedia probatissima in lamignos spiritus expellendos* (1579);

and *Fustis daemonum* (Club against demons), 1584. His books were immediately successful, especially *Compendio* and *Flagellum.* Menghi considered the battle against demons to be extremely important.

Characteristics of Demons

Menghi supported the view that the DEVIL was originally created good and chose evil. However, the Devil was not the principle of evil itself. The Devil and demons were created as beings superior to humans, with perfect intellect, memory, and will. They are able to see into humans, know their weaknesses, and know their future actions. Demons are clever and crafty and know the truth of all things by experience, revelation, and nature. However, they cannot force humans into sin but only tempt and persuade them to make sinful choices.

Demons can dominate matter through possession and can appear in human form, even in the guise of beautiful men and women and saints. They engage in sexual intercourse with humans and are capable of producing children from such unions. They will eat and drink as humans, but they do not digest any of it; whatever they consume dissolves into its preexisting matter.

Orders of Demons

Menghi was influenced by the works of MICHAEL PSELLUS and envisioned a hierarchy of demons according to functions, spheres of activity, and habits, in much the same way that angels were arranged in hierarchies.

The lowest types of demons are elflike demons (*l'infimo choro*) who appear at night to play tricks to harm people and the incubi and succubi who tempt people into sexual activities. All of these demons are harmful but not malevolent.

According to Menghi, the first order of demons are the "fiery ones" (*Leliureon*), who inhabit the air near the Sun. The second order is that of demons of the air (*Aerea*), who live in the air nearest to humans. The *Aerea* are vain and constantly compare themselves to God. They push people to be conceited and vain. The third order is that of earth demons (*Terreo*), who tempt people to immorality and put filthy thoughts into their heads.

The worst and most dangerous demons are in the fourth through sixth orders. The fourth order is that of water demons (*Acquatile* or *Marino*), who live in lakes, seas, and rivers, where they like to cause storms and sink ships. The fifth order includes subterranean demons (*Sotterranei*), who torment miners, cause earthquakes, destabilize the world, and throw stones. They are cruel and enjoy tormenting people. The *Sotterranei* disguise themselves as servants of magicians and sorcerers (see FAMILIAR). Last and most deadly are the *Lucifogo,* who are dark and mysterious and avoid light. They will kill people in cold blood and should be avoided at all costs.

Demonic Pacts

Menghi wrote extensively on demonic pacts made by witches, or LAMIAE. The witches had sex with demonic incubi and succubi and swore fidelity to the Devil. Candidates for initiation worshipped the Devil as if he were God. They were assigned a familiar demon, called Martinetto, disguised as a ram, who trained them and always accompanied them. The witches killed and ate babies, especially those who were unbaptized. They used their Devil-given magical powers to predict the future and persuade others to follow the Devil. They caused abortions and killed with the EVIL EYE.

Demonic Possession and Exorcism

Menghi called possession victims *fetoni,* or "stinkers." Even the most holy persons could become possessed. When demons possess a person, they put on great shows of magical tricks. Menghi lamented the lack of skilled exorcists in his time. Exorcisms were essential to the mission of the church, he said, and had to be carried out with great pity.

Exorcists must be aware of their own unworthiness and have great humility. They must have great purity of heart and be morally sound. The playing of sacred music is especially effective against demons. Exorcists must use harsh words and CURSEs in their attacks against the demons. Great care should be taken in the use of saints' relics and crucifixes, for if they are not genuine, the demons will mock them and render them useless.

Anything touched by a DEMONIAC must be blessed. Sometimes it may be necessary for a demoniac to abandon his or her house, if the demons have thoroughly contaminated everything in it. Menghi said it is best to perform exorcisms in a sacred place, such as a church, and before an audience, after the acts of Jesus, who performed exorcisms before crowds.

FURTHER READING:

Menghi, Giolamo. *The Devil's Scourge: Exorcism during the Italian Renaissance.* York Beach, Me.: Samuel Weiser, 2002.

Mephistopheles (Mephistophilis, Mephistophilus, Mephostophiles)

DEMON and representative of the DEVIL who is a principal figure in the legend of FAUST. Mephistopheles is more of a literary figure than one belonging to mythology and demonology. He is usually described as a tall man wearing black clothing.

The origin of the name *Mephistophiles* is uncertain. The name was known to the German occultist Johannes Trithemius (1442–1516), who described him as "a mysterious kind of demon, dark through and through, malicious, restless, stormy." "Mephistophiles" appears in 1527 in a Renaissance magical text, *Praxis Magia Faustiana,* and later as "Mephostophiles" in the Faust chapbook *Historia von D. Johann Fausten,* first published in 1587 by an anonymous author.

The chapbook tells the story of Dr. Johann Georg Faust, who bargains his soul to the Devil. Mephistophiles is invisible to others but can be seen by Faust in various shape-shifted guises, including as a grey friar monk. *Dr*

Mephistopheles, right, with Faust and Margaret. (AUTHOR'S COLLECTION)

Fausts Hollenzwang describes "Mephistophiel" as one of the seven great princes of HELL, who "stands under the planet Jupiter, his regent is named Zadkiel, an enthroned angel of the holy Jehovah . . . his form is firstly that of a fiery bear, the other and fairer appearance is as of a little man with a black cape and a bald head." The demon also manifests as an invisible ringing bell.

Mephistopheles is a trickster and practical joker, who serves the lusts and desires of Faust. In the end, he is a shrewd negotiator who has the last laugh by trapping Faust into damnation. In some accounts, however, Faust manages to redeem himself and escape eternal punishment in hell.

The chapbooks inspired Christopher Marlowe's play *The Tragic History of Doctor Faustus* and Johann Wolfgang von Goethe's drama *Faust.* Shakespeare mentioned Mephistophilus in *The Merry Wives of Windsor.*

mezuzah   See AMULET.

Michel, Anneliese (1952–1976)

German woman who died during prolonged EXORCISMS for demonic POSSESSION. In a sensational trial, the parents of Anneliese Michel and the two priests who conducted the exorcisms were convicted of negligent homicide. The case was the basis for a film, *The Exorcism of Emily Rose* (2005).

Michel was born on September 21, 1952, in Klingenberg, Bavaria, to a conservative, middle-class Catholic family. She was the second of five girls; the first child, Martha, died at age eight of a kidney ailment. Michel's parents were Josef and Anna Michel; Josef worked as a carpenter. As a child, Michel was frail and sickly but did well in school. She exhibited signs of being hypersensitive and was overcome sometimes during Mass at church. Her parents envisioned a career as a schoolteacher for her, and they sent her to study at the Gymnasium in Aschaffenberg.

In 1968, Michel suffered her first blackout, while sitting in class. That night, she experienced a terrifying seizure of paralysis, suffocation, and uncontrolled urination. A year passed before these episodes repeated. Her mother took her to a neurologist in Aschaffenberg, Dr. Siegfried Luthy, who diagnosed probable epilepsy but prescribed no medication because of the infrequency of episodes. Michel's health declined and she contracted tonsillitis, pleurisy, pneumonia, and tuberculosis. She was also diagnosed with heart and circulatory problems. She was hospitalized in a sanatorium in Mittelberg.

Michel was still in the hospital on June 3, 1970, when she suffered another nighttime seizure. She was sent to a neurologist in Kempten, who ordered an electroencephalogram an (FEG) The results showed abnormal brain waves, and he prescribed anticonvulsant medication. Michel was returned to the sanatorium, where she grew increasingly depressed. About one week after her visit to Kempten, she experienced her first demonic vision. While praying, she saw a huge, grimacing, cruel face that loomed before her for a brief moment. Michel was in the habit of praying intensely, but after this, she was afraid to pray, lest the demonic face intrude again. She began to wonder whether the demon was inside her, perhaps causing her illness. She had thoughts of suicide.

On August 29, 1970, she was sent home, but family members observed that she seemed changed: She was depressed and withdrawn. She resumed school, but her grades were only average. She had a hard time studying. She suffered another seizure.

Michel was sent back to doctors, who confirmed her circulatory problems and prescribed more anticonvulsants. She may not have taken them, at least for long.

Her health and mental state continued to decline, and she lost all interest in school. She made an effort to study to please her mother. Her seizures, sometimes severe, continued. Her mother sent her back to Dr. Luthy in Aschaffenberg. He prescribed an anticonvulsant and recommended regular checkups. Michel dutifully returned at several-month intervals into 1973. She did not inform her doctor of her increasing seizures and blackouts or tell him that she now smelled a horrible stench that others did not. She felt the medication was contributing to her apathy and listlessness.

Michel had increasing visions of ghastly, horned demonic faces. There were more stenches of something burning, feces, or rotting flesh. Knocking noises sounded in her bedroom; her mother told her she was dreaming them. However, Anna soon began to think that her daughter was being plagued by demons. She told her skeptical husband that she had caught Michel staring at a statue of the Virgin Mary in the house, and her eyes were jet black and her hands looked like paws with claws. Josef recommended prayer and said he would take her to a saint shrine, the Mother of God of San Damiano.

Michel had a terrible time at the shrine. She could not enter the chapel and said the ground burned her feet. So did the miraculous water there. She tore her rosary and refused to wear a saint medal bought by her father, saying it suffocated her. She spoke with a man's voice and exuded a stench.

Michel's bouts grew worse. She had periods of seeming to feel fine and then suddenly had seizures, visions, or deep depression. She became convinced that demons were inside her, and she felt empty, torn in two, or believed that she was someone else. She gave more thought to suicide. She acquired a boyfriend, Peter, but was unable to be sexually responsive to him.

Anna returned her to Dr. Luthy. According to Anna and Michel, he recommended that they consult a Jesuit priest. Later, after Michel was dead, Dr. Lithy denied this, stating he would have only recommended another medical professional.

At any rate, while Michel was shuttling around among various physicians, she did consult various priests, including Father Roth at the parish at San Damiano. He referred her to Father Ernst Alt. Also, Father Adolf Rodewyk of Frankfurt, an expert on possession, opined in a letter that she showed symptoms of possession, but he declined to see her in person, because of his age and distance.

Alt became involved in the case. He seemed to possess psychic ability or sensitivity and had an empathic connection to Michel even before meeting her. He was inclined to see her as suffering from *circumsessio* (surrounded by evil forces) at the least and possibly from possession.

Michel had sessions with Father Alt in which they talked and prayed, and she seemed better, temporarily, after the visits. Alt wrote to his superior, Bishop Stangl, on September 30, 1974, asking for permission to say the prayer of exorcism over her. Stangl refused, telling Alt to monitor her. The bishop thought she needed more medical help.

In 1975, Michel was unbalanced by the death of her grandmother and the departures of sisters from the household. Studying became harder than ever. She told Peter that she felt she was eternally damned, although she did not know why. She developed an aversion to holy objects and stopped going to church. She could barely walk. She suffered episodes in which her face and body contorted. Peter told others she was possessed. When she starting throwing things uncontrollably at Peter and others, she begged Alt to come to her aid.

Alt arrived on July 1 and found her in a hysterical state. Mentally, he said the prayer of *exorcismus probativus*, which caused her to jump up and tear off her rosary.

After Alt departed, Michel's condition worsened dramatically. She went home from school and lay stiff in bed. When she finally got up, she walked as though her legs were sticks. She fell into rages, cursing and attacking, growling like an animal, and exuding a horrible stench. Josef Michel summoned Father Roth, who witnessed one of these episodes himself.

Alt appealed again to Stangl for permission to perform an exorcism. Stangl agreed to the small rite. On August 3, 1974, Alt and Roth performed the small rite on Michel. She moaned and whimpered and said she felt as though she were burning. They were convinced they were dealing with genuine possession.

At home, Michel was out of control. Her body swelled in odd places, she raced around bucking like a goat, screamed incessantly, went rigid and catatonic, and exhibited superhuman strength. She tore off her clothes, complaining of burning up inside. She stuck her head in icy water and in the toilet. She ate flies, spiders, and coal; urinated on the kitchen floor and tried to lick it up; and chewed on panties soaked in urine. She destroyed religious objects. She was worst on Sundays and holy days. She attacked priests who arrived to see her with verbal abuse and blows. She required constant surveillance from her family.

Clouds of flies suddenly appeared in the house and vanished just as suddenly. Shadowy animals were seen scurrying about.

The extreme nature of the case finally made Father Rodewyck agree to see Michel in person. During one of her fits, he asked for her name and she replied, "Judas." This identified the name of the demon. Further evidence was her repeated attempts to kiss people, her face twisted into grotesque hostility.

In Rodewyck's assessment, Michel was possessed by a demon named Judas, with subsidiary demons participating as well. Thus far, they were mute, not speaking through her themselves. In order for the two-hour RITUALE ROMANUM to be performed, the demons must speak through the mouth of the possessed and truthfully answer certain questions put to them.

Michel and her family were convinced she was possessed, and they desired the exorcism to be performed. Rodewyck met with Roth and Alt and gave them his opinion. Stangl gave permission for the *Rituale Romanum* to be performed. The man selected for the job was Father Arnold Renz, a Salvatorian superior at a monastery in Ruck-Schippach. Renz had never before performed an exorcism, though he was knowledgeable on the subject.

The first rite was performed at the Michel home on September 24, 1975. In attendance were Michel's family, some friends, her boyfriend Peter, and Fathers Alt, Roth, and Hermann, the latter of whom also had attended and counseled the afflicted girl.

Michel was held by three of the men while she struggled, kicked, and attempted to bite. She swore, howled like a dog, and screamed when she was sprinkled with holy water. Still, her actions of the first exorcism were relatively mild compared to her earlier behavior.

The second exorcism took place on September 28. From then on, the sessions were recorded. The demons—for more than one had been present—said that Michel was possessed because she was cursed by a jealous neighbor woman before she was born. The family attempted to verify this, but the suspect had died.

The exorcisms proceeded. People in attendance felt physically affected, as though the demons were making it difficult for them to participate.

After Judas, LUCIFER appeared, and then Nero. After a time, the demons named three others, Cain, Hitler, and a fallen priest named Fleischmann. Cain and Hitler had little to say. Judas remained the primary mouthpiece for the demons, followed by Lucifer.

Alt found records of the fallen priest, who had lived in Ettleben in the 16th century. He was a womanizer, a batterer, and a drunkard and had killed a man. The demon, through Michel, gave details of his life that were in the records but unknown to the girl. Michel referred to him as "The Black One."

The demonic activity ebbed and flowed and seemed to increase sometimes when Michel had medications renewed. She suffered stigmata. Jesus communicated to Michel that she would be purified by her ordeal, would become a saint, and would marry.

On October 31, 1975, the exorcists believed they had achieved complete success. They expelled the six demons one by one, and each departed with great vomiting and protests before it surrendered by saying, "Hail Mary full of grace." But just when they thought the ordeal was over, a new demon announced itself with a growl. It identified itself only as "I" and said it had been secretly lurking in Michel all along. The demon told Renz that "they," meaning the other demons, "really pulled a fast one on you." On November 9, Renz was able to goad the demon into admitting that it was Judas, who had returned immediately upon being exorcized on October 31, in spite of the priests' taking the steps to seal the door against the demons by singing the *Te Deum* and a prayer to Mary. Judas said he returned with the permission of Mary and would remain until her triumph, upon which all demons would be cast out.

After Christmas 1975, the character of the exorcisms changed. The demon has less and less to say and refused to state when he would depart. In January, Judas suggested that he might be Lucifer. Michel had episodes of violence, including growling, contorting, and striking out against others, that happened outside the exorcisms.

By March 1976, Michel was showing signs of physical deterioration. On March 7, Renz carried out an exorcism with Michel in bed, seemingly unconscious and barely responsive. In April, before Easter, Michel predicted another great trial was ahead of her. She seemed exhausted and at Eastertide went through pain that she likened to the death agony of Jesus. She had more frequent episodes of severe rigidity and spent more time in bed.

In early May, Alt decided that Michel should go to Etteleben. She told her boyfriend Peter that she would suffer until July, and then her ordeal would be over. Upon arrival in Ettelben, Michael spent much of her time rigid, screaming, and exhausted in bed, unable to eat. She said the demons were choking her.

On May 9, her parents decided to take her home. She remained in bed, in pain and screaming. She hit and bit herself and banged herself against the wall. She bit the wall so harshly that her teeth chipped. She smashed her head through a glass door without injury. She slept only one to two hours a night. She was unable to eat except at rare intervals, when she would order specific foods that she could gulp down in a hurry. During exorcisms, the demons were unresponsive. The old demons had been replaced by new ones, who refused to talk or give their names.

On May 30, Alt visited Michel and told a physician friend, Dr. Richard Roth, who had listened to some of the exorcism tapes, to be present as well. Michel was emaciated, and her face was swollen and bruised. Roth gave her no medical treatments.

Michel continued to deteriorate. Her screams became unearthly. June 8 was the last day that Alt saw Michel alive. She was severely emaciated. Her family said she would only consume a little fruit juice and milk. They awaited July because Michel had said her trials would be over then. The demons remained uncommunicative.

The only explanation that made sense to Alt was that she was suffering a "penance possession" to atone for someone else's sins, perhaps those of a member of her family. Penance possession was extremely difficult for an exorcist to treat. Renz continued his exorcisms two or three times a week. Michel's screaming degraded into monotonous moaning. She tried to exorcize herself, without success.

Michel was asked repeatedly whether she wanted a doctor, but she declined, saying there was nothing a doctor could do for her. On June 9 and June 30, she asked for absolution, and Renz complied on June 30. She was running a high temperature. After the exorcism on that date, Michel went to bed, telling her mother she was afraid. She died in her sleep on the morning of July 1. Just as the demons had predicted, her ordeal was over in July 1976.

Roth was summoned but could not write out a death certificate because he did not have the proper forms. Michel's family physician, Dr. Kehler, wrote the certificate and said her death was not due to natural causes. Alt con-tacted the state attorney general's office in Aschaffenberg. An autopsy revealed that Michel had died of starvation. Her brain showed no signs of damage characteristic of epileptic seizures. Nor was her body covered with sores typical of starvation. Her pupils were greatly dilated, a characteristic of people who are in a religious altered state of consciousness.

The case caused a great deal of controversy. People refused to accept the idea that Michel was killed by demons, for that meant that evil could triumph over good. Rather, according to gossip, she had chosen to die as a sacrifice. People made pilgrimages to Klingenberg to pray at Michel's grave. Renz became a media hero, giving interviews and playing the exorcism tapes, until his superiors told him to stop.

The state attorney's office initiated a criminal investigation and spent a year gathering evidence. Indictments for negligent homicide were issued in July 1977 against Alt, Renz, and Michel's parents. Charges were dropped against Stangl and Rodewyck.

Popular veneration of Michel elevated her to practical sainthood. A Carmelite nun came forward and said Michel was communicating from beyond the grave to her. Michel wished her body to be exhumed on February 25, 1978, prior to the start of the trial in March. Renz was to see to it that this was done, the nun said. Furthermore, the nun said that, according to Michel, her body would not be putrefied, and the exhumation would yield proof of the existence of demons, God, the Mother of God, other spiritual beings, eternal life, resurrection, and hell. The nun said that Michel had died as a penance to benefit Germany, its youth and priests. God would resurrect Michel.

Michel's parents succeeded in having the body disinterred on the requested date, on the excuse that they wished to transfer her remains to a better coffin. The event was a media frenzy. But the mayor informed Michel's parents and the audience that the girl's remains were badly decomposed, and he advised against seeing them. The parents agreed. Renz wished to view them but said he was turned away at the door of the mortuary.

Gossip immediately spread. Stories were told that the remains were incorrupt, and officials were keeping it a secret.

The trial began on March 30, 1978. There was much conflicting testimony over what had transpired and whether or not Michel had suffered from epilepsy and mental illness. One medical expert opined that she should have been immobilized with tranquilizers, force-fed, and administered electroshock therapy.

The verdict of the court was that all four defendants were guilty of negligent homicide. The court's opinion held that Michel was incapable of helping herself, and medical help should have been provided. The exorcisms and her environment aggravated her condition. The guilty were sentenced to six months in prison, suspended for three years, and given responsibility to pay court costs.

In the aftermath, efforts were made by critics of the case to have exorcism banned or at least changed.

Seers throughout Europe continue to deliver messages from Michel about judgment and other religious matters. Her grave continues to be visited by pilgrims. Adding to the legend surrounding her are stories of deaths and accidents related to people who attacked her or the priests who tried to help her.

In her analysis of the case, the anthropologist Felicitas D. Goodman opined that the anticonvulsant medications prescribed to Michel, all of which had serious side effects, had interfered with her own ability to regain control of herself, interfered with the exorcism process, and thus probably contributed to her death.

Michel's story was made into a film, *The Exorcism of Emily Rose,* released in 2005. The film was directed by Scott Derrickson and stars Jennifer Carpenter as Emily Rose and Tom Wilkinson as Father Moore, a Catholic priest.

Rose dies after Moore performs an exorcism on her, and Moore is charged with negligent homicide. The prosecutor, Ethan Thomas (Campbell Scott), bases his case on the argument that Rose's affliction had a medical explanation, and Moore killed the girl by preventing her from taking her necessary medication. The defense counsel, Erin Bruner (Laura Linney), claims that Rose's condition and death were due to supernatural causes.

The trial becomes a stage for the debate of religion, philosophy, and supernatural beliefs. The principals suffer events of an apparent supernatural nature during the course of their arguments. Whether or not Rose actually suffered from demonic possession is never declared in the film; it is left to the viewer.

A German film purporting to follow the true story more closely, *Requiem,* was released in 2006.

FURTHER READING:
Goodman, Felicitas D. *The Exorcism of Anneliese Michel.* Garden City, N.Y.: Doubleday, 1981.

Mictantecutli   Aztec lord of the underworld and king of DEMONS. Mictantecutli is the only Aztec deity besides the Sun god, Tonacaecutli, who wears a crown. He is depicted as a skeleton on a throne and keeps with him an owl, a clump of desert grass, a corpse, and a dish of human hearts.

Mictantecutli tortures the souls of those who are imprisoned in his dark kingdom, Mictlampa. He occasionally travels to the realm of the living in search of new victims. He rules the dreaded hour of midnight, when he releases all his demons upon the world. They have free reign until daybreak.

Miracle of Laon (1566)   Sensational POSSESSION case in Laon, France. The Catholic Church used the daily EXORCISMS of Nicole Obry (also Aubry) before huge crowds as examples of the church's power over the DEVIL to sup-

port it in religious struggles with the French Huguenots. Through Obry, BEELZEBUB claimed the Huguenots as his own people, gleefully noting that their supposed heresies made them even more precious to him. The demon was exorcised through repeated administration of holy wafers, a precedent in exorcism, and proved to the faithful the danger of the threat of Huguenot reform.

The central issue dividing French Catholics and Huguenots was transubstantiation, or the Real Presence: whether or not, during communion, the bread and wine actually became the body and blood of Christ. This miracle occurred for Catholics, whereas Huguenots considered such an interpretation to be idolatry. By exorcising Beelzebub with the help of holy wafers, the Catholic Church declared a victory for the power of the presence.

Obry had a troubled past with problems of fits before she showed signs of possession in 1565, at age 15 or 16. The daughter of a butcher in Vervins, near Laon in Picardy, she had spent eight years in a convent at Montreuil-les-Dames. She was a dull-witted student but learned to read. Her fits probably had physical causes, not hysteria, unlike those of many other female demoniacs. She had suffered two severe head injuries, one from a dog bite and one from a falling tile. As a result, she suffered from chronic headache until she was exorcised. At the time of her possession, she had been married for a short time to a merchant, Louis Pierret. Despite her history, she was a stunning and convincing demoniac and exhibited uncanny and genuine clairvoyance via the possessing demons.

One day, while Obry prayed alone in church, the spirit of her maternal grandfather, Joachim Willot, visited her. Willot entered the girl and explained that since he died suddenly after supper and had not confessed his sins nor accomplished certain vows, his soul was in purgatory. He asked for her help to enable him to ascend to heaven: Obry should have masses said in his name, give alms to the poor, and make holy pilgrimages, especially to the shrine of St. James of Compostela.

Obry's family complied but evaded the pilgrimage to St. James, perhaps because of the expense involved. Her convulsive fits, present since Willot's possession, did not improve, and Obry blamed her family's failure to visit St. James. The family arranged a fake departure for the pilgrimage, but Obry was not deceived. At this point, the family asked the local priest, the schoolmaster, and a Dominican monk to conjure the spirit, who admitted he was not the soul of Willot but his good ANGEL. Knowing this to be heresy, the priests finally made the spirit admit he was a devil.

For two months, Obry was exorcized daily in front of ever-growing crowds. The first exorcisms were done in Vervin, where inexperienced priests first used a handbook on baptismal exorcism, then obtained a book of demonic exorcisms. They followed instructions to find out the name of the demon and, when they succeeded in getting Beelzebub's name, did as the manual directed

The exorcism of Beelzebub at Laon (AUTHOR'S COLLECTION)

and wrote it on a piece of paper and burned it. Beelzebub shrieked but did not depart. The demon quickly became immune to this procedure and even remarked that it was a waste of paper and ink.

Obry was moved to the cathedral in Laon when Beelzebub complained that a prince of his rank could be expelled only by a bishop in a suitable location. The exorcisms continued on stage in the cathedral for two days but moved to a private chapel to prevent mob chaos. But Beelzebub protested again. In the account of Obry's exorcism by the Hebrew professor Jean Boulaese in 1578, Beelzebub told the priests that "it was not right to hide what God wanted to be manifested and known to all the world," and that he would only leave Obry in "that great brothel" (the cathedral), and on stage.

The exorcisms grew to two times a day, during which Obry gave an impressive demoniacal performance, with contortions, horrible noises, blackened tongue, rigidity, and levitation. Beelzebub commanded center attention, but 29 other demons also made appearances.

During the rituals, the priests tried to use more traditional methods, such as holy water, relics, the sign of the cross, and prayers to the Virgin Mary, but these only succeeded in angering Beelzebub. Only the host, or Eucharist—the body and BLOOD of Christ—tamed him. By submitting to the host, Beelzebub confirmed the power of the Real Presence. On one occasion, Beelzebub called the Eucharist "Jack the White." Before this, the Eucharist had not been used as a principal weapon in exorcisms, making this case unusual.

Obry occasionally suffered repossessions as often as 50 times a day, leading to mass consumption of holy wafers. The host began to be regarded as medicine for her spiritual sickness. Although he admitted that he was the father of lies, Beelzebub taunted Huguenot doubters about Obry's possession, gleefully noting that their doubts of faith made them all the more precious to him. Through Obry, Beelzebub also pointed out sinners in the masses watching the exorcisms, revealing their secret, unconfessed sins. Many went to receive confession, and some rejoined the church. On some days, thousands confessed out of sheer fear of exposure by Beelzebub; priests were stationed everywhere in the cathedral to handle the demand. As propaganda for the Catholics, Obry's sufferings were unparalleled.

French theologians did not use the accusations of demoniacs against the accused witch until the 17th century. But it may have been the possession of Obry at Laon that planted the seeds of such evidence. As well as identifying secret sinners, Beelzebub, through Obry, accused some women of witchcraft while still in Vervins. According to the account by Barthelemy Faye, a magistrate, Obry claimed that a gypsy woman, not a man, as some claimed, had bewitched her early in her possession. In addition, the Huguenots continually claimed SORCERY and MAGIC against Obry's mother, one of the exorcists, and a priest,

Despinoys, who accompanied Obry after her expulsion from Laon.

Beelzebub finally left Obry at 3:00 P.M. on Friday, February 8, 1566. After his expulsion, Obry and her husband remained in Laon until, fearing outright religious war, the Huguenots succeeded in barring Obry from the city. Still weak, Obry survived only on communion wafers. She made one last bid for celebrity in 1577, when she became blind and was cured, not by the host, but by the holy relic of John the Baptist's head.

The Catholic Church, rejoicing in this miraculous affirmation of transubstantiation, used the accounts of it to their greatest advantage. Future cases of possession and exorcisms relied on the happenings at Laon, and even certain Huguenots, including Florimond De Raemond, the historian of 16th-century heresy, were converted. Obry's redemption was celebrated at the Cathedral of Laon on February 8 until the French Revolution at the close of 18th century.

FURTHER READING:
Calmet, Dom Augustin. *The Phantom World: Concerning Apparitions and Vampires*. Ware, England: Wordsworth Editions in association with the Folklore Society, 2001.
Walker, D. P. *Unclean Spirits: Possession and Exorcism in France and England in the Late Sixteenth and Early Seventeenth Centuries*. Philadelphia: University of Pennsylvania Press, 1981.

mirror According to folklore, a doorway or portal through which spirits, including ghosts and DEMONs, can gain access to the physical world. Mirrors are problems in some cases of demonic infestations and hauntings.

Since ancient times, any shiny surface has been regarded as a spirit doorway and can be used deliberately to summon spirits into the world. They also are used for seeing visions of the future. Much of the folklore about mirrors is negative. In widespread belief, they are "soul stealers" with the power to suck souls out of bodies. In the Greek myth of Narcissus, he sees his own reflection in water, pines away, and dies. The DEVIL and demons can enter through mirrors to attack people, according to some beliefs.

There also are numerous beliefs about mirrors and the dead. When a person dies, all the mirrors in a house should be turned over, for if a corpse sees itself in a mirror, the soul of the dead will have no rest or will become a vampire. Corpses seeing themselves in mirrors also will draw bad luck upon the household. Such beliefs hark back to days when the corpses were laid out in homes, and people believed that souls lingered about the body until burial.

Another folk belief holds that if a person sees his or her own reflection in a room where someone has died, it is a death omen. Mirrors also should be covered in sick rooms in the folk belief that the soul is weakened and more vulnerable to possession during illness.

Mirrors in Problem Hauntings

If a home is plagued with unpleasant spirit activity, investigators, including lay demonologists, may recommend the removal or covering of mirrors. In bedrooms, mirrors should never be placed at the foot of a bed or at the head of a bed. It is considered a negative influence for a person to be able to see himself or herself from any angle in a mirror while in bed. Mirrors should never reflect into each other; this creates unstable psychic space.

A folk remedy calls for positioning a mirror so that it faces outward toward a door or window. The reasoning goes that a spirit who looks in a window or attempts to cross a door threshold will see its own reflection and be scared away. Mirrors can be closed as portals by rubbing the edges of them or washing the surfaces in holy water.

Conjuring Mirrors

One of the cases of ED AND LORRAINE WARREN involved a conjuring mirror, which the Warrens said invited demonic trouble into the life of the user. Oliver B., a 45-year-old man of New Jersey, purchased a mirror in an ornate frame for the purpose of casting spells and CURSES on others.

First, Oliver learned to see images clearly in the mirror by spending long periods gazing into the mirror with intense concentration. After months of practice, he could state whatever he wanted to see, and the image would appear. He learned how to see future situations for himself. Then, he began conjuring images of people he did not like or who had wronged him. He projected an image of a person into the future and willed something bad to happen, with the help of demons he summoned. The scene played out in the mirror, and then it came to pass in physical reality.

Eventually, Oliver's magic backfired on him. The misfortunes he conjured for others began happening to him. In addition, demons invaded his home and created unpleasant disturbances, such as footsteps, heavy breathing, doors opening by themselves, levitations of objects, and unearthly howlings in the night.

After a week of terrifying phenomena, Oliver contacted the Catholic Church and was referred to the Warrens, who investigated. Ed Warren undid the ritual that Oliver had done repeatedly by performing it backward. This stopped the demonic OPPRESSION, Warren said, and nullified the mirror magic spells. Oliver gave the Warrens the mirror to be placed in their museum of POSSESSED POSSESSIONS.

FURTHER READING:

Brittle, Gerald Daniel. *The Demonologist: The Extraordinary Career of Ed and Lorraine Warren.* Englewood Cliffs, N.J.: Prentice-Hall, 1980.

Guiley, Rosemary Ellen. "Mirrors: Do You Know What's Looking Back at You?" *TAPS Paramagazine,* September 2007, 12–13.

Molitor, Simon (d. 1564)

German EXORCIST murdered by his wife.

Simon Molitor, of Hesse, Germany, made his living driving out DEMONs in Westphalia and neighboring areas and had a shady reputation for fraud. He moved to Osbnabruck, and after three years of questionable activities, the magistrate there decided to expel him.

On February 9, 1564, Molitor quarreled with his wife over some stolen money. She went upstairs and called to him to look for the missing money with her. When he arrived upstairs, she pushed him through the trapdoor and attacked him with an ax, cutting off his head and left arm. She threw the head and arm into the fire and intended to burn the rest of the body as well.

Neighbors, hearing the noise and noticing the awful smell of burning flesh, went to investigate and discovered Molitor's grisly remains. His wife was arrested and jailed. Her fatal punishment consisted of having her body torn with red-hot pincers, followed by being lashed to a wheel and broken.

FURTHER READING:

Weyer, Johann. *On Witchcraft (De praestigiis daemonum).* Abridged. Edited by Benjamin G. Kohl and H. C. Erik Midelfort. Asheville, N.C.: Pegasus Press, 1998.

Moloch

Ammonite god demonized in Hebrew lore. Moloch was probably identified with BAAL, and with the Assyrian/Babylonian Malik. King SOLOMON was said to have built a temple to Moloch.

To the Ammonites, Moloch was a Sun god and personified the detrimental effects of the Sun's rays. He also was the cause of plagues. He was depicted as a bull-headed man with long arms sitting on a brass throne. Huge

Moloch (DICTIONNAIRE INFERNAL)

bronze statues of him were erected in his honor, and he was worshipped with human sacrifice rites in the belief that the people would be protected from disaster. The victims were thrown into fires built in hollow bellies of the bronze statue.

Moloch was called "the prince of the valley of tears," a reference to Topheth in the Valley of Hinnom, where the sacrificial rites were said to take place. King Jeremiah defiled Topeth, and the sacrificial practices declined.

The Hebrews called Moloch "the abomination of the Ammonites" (1 Kings 11:7). In Kabbalistic lore, he is, with SATAN, the first of the evil DEMONs of the Tree of Life.

The ancient Greeks associated Moloch with Cronos, the god of time, who devoured his own children in order to prevent them from challenging his rule.

money   In folklore, money from FAIRIES, witches, sorcerers, DEMONs and the DEVIL is worthless.

Many tales exist of victims accepting payment for goods or services and discovering, after it is too late, that the gold coins or currency are actually toads, animal claws, shells, lead, or other worthless objects. For example, the Devil gives a purse filled with gold to a victim, who later finds it contains nothing but embers and smoke.

In one tale, a 15-year-old youth met a strange man who was passing through a village. The man inquired whether the youth would like to be rich. When the youth agreed, the man gave him a folded piece of paper and told him it would produce as many gold coins as he wished as long as he did not unfold the paper. If he managed to contain his curiosity, the youth would then meet his true benefactor. The youth took the paper home and was amazed when it spilled out gold coins. But he was unable to resist the temptation to unfold it. When he did, he saw, to his horror, that it contained bear's nails, cat's claws, toad's feet, and other awful items. He threw the paper on the fire, but it refused to burn for an hour. The gold pieces vanished.

Demons supposedly guard all the vast treasures of the earth but can never draw upon them. NICHOLAS REMY told in his witch-hunting handbook *Demonolatry* (1595) that false riches offered by a demon deceived a man in Nuremberg in 1530. The demon revealed a hiding place of a great treasure. The man found a vault containing a chest guarded by a black dog. But when the man attempted to seize the chest, the vault collapsed and crushed him to death. The tragedy was witnessed by one of the man's servants, who fled and spread the story.

Remy also related several cases of women being deceived by gifts of money and gold coins from demons. The riches were in purses or wrapped in paper and proved to be bits of brick and coal, swine dung, leaves of trees, and a rusty-colored stone that crumbled to dust. Remy said he tried one woman, Catharina Ruffa of Ville-sur-Moselle, on a capital charge in 1587 because she claimed that a demon gave her three genuine gold coins.

According to legend, Paracelsus, the 16th-century Swiss alchemist, roamed about Europe penniless during his last years, paying innkeepers with gold coins that turned into seashells after he departed.

Illusory money parallels another folk belief that livestock purchased unwittingly from witches and fairies disappears or turns into something undesirable. For example, cows dissolve in running water, horses turn into pigs, and so forth.

FURTHER READING:
Collin de Plancy, Jacques. *Dictionary of Witchcraft*. Edited and translated by Wade Baskin. Originally published as *Dictionary of Demonology*. New York: Philosophical Library, 1965.
Remy, Nicholas. *Demonolatry*. Secaucus, N.J.: University Books, 1974.

moonlet   See AMULET.

Morax (Foraii, Forfax)   FALLEN ANGEL and 21st of the 72 SPIRITS OF SOLOMON. Morax is an earl and president in HELL and rules 36 legions of DEMONs. He appears as a bull, and, if he takes on a man's head, he will impart knowledge of astronomy and all liberal sciences. He knows the virtues of herbs and precious stones. He gives good FAMILIARS.

Mot   In Jewish lore, a DEMON of death who hovers around dying people. *Mot* means "death" in Hebrew. Passages in the Old Testament refer to him as Death. In Greek lore, he is the son of Kronos, the god of time. The Phoenicians called him "Death" and "Pluto," lord of the underworld.

Mot is also the name of a Canaanite warrior deity-demon found in Ugaritic literature. He is described as both the beloved of El and the son of El, and he is completely evil, without redeeming features. He was not worshipped as a deity but was associated with death and the underworld. His underworld abode is dank and dangerous. Mot has a voracious appetite for gods and humans. He crushes them in his enormous jaws and mouth. He literally swallows the dead into the underworld. He carries a scepter of bereavement or widowhood.

Mot is the enemy of BAAL, god of the sea and fertility, his opposite. Mot conquers him, forcing him into the underworld. Baal revives to battle him into at least temporary submission. Baal tricks Mot into eating his own brothers.

Mot has associations with the agricultural cycles of growth and harvest. He undergoes ritual dismemberment and dissolution, and resurrection. The huntress Anat attacks Mot and vanquishes him, scattering his body to the fields. In sympathetic magic rituals, he is pruned as a vine is.

FURTHER READING:
Davies, T. Witton. *Magic, Divination and Demonology among the Hebrews and Their Neighbors*. First published 1898.

van der Toorn, Karel, Bob Becking, and Pieter W. van der Horst, eds. *Dictionary of Deities and Demons in the Bible.* 2nd ed. Grand Rapids, Mich.: William B. Eerdmans, 1999.

Mottlingen Possession (1836–1843)   German peasant woman possessed by a ghost and more than 1,000 DEMONS. The case was published in English for the first time by the spiritualist medium W. T. Stead in his book *Borderland: A Casebook of True Supernatural Stories* (1891–92). The victim was a single woman identified only by her initials, G. D., born around 1816 in Mottlingen, Wurtemberg, Germany. She was a servant who was by all accounts pious, so her friends and neighbors were mystified at the sudden onset of supernatural attack followed by complete demonic POSSESSION.

Between 1836 and 1838, G. D. had a serious illness that weakened her overall health and left her with one leg shorter than the other. The same side of her body was affected as well, making it impossible for her continue work as a servant. She went to live with two sisters and a nearly blind brother, who lived on the ground floor of a house in Mottlingen. The illness may have made G. D. vulnerable to spirit invasion.

G. D. immediately felt that a strange presence was in the house. On her very first day there, she was in the midst of saying grace at dinner when she had a seizure and fell unconscious. At night, weird sounds were heard in the house: a swishing, trailing noise and the sound of objects being rolled around on the floor. Even the family who lived on the second floor heard the noises and was alarmed by them.

G. D. saw shadowy figures and moving lights, which were not visible to others. She felt an invisible force seize her hands at night and move them. G. D. underwent a change in personality, becoming unpleasant to others.

By 1841, the nightly visitations and phenomena had become so distressing to G. D. that she sought out a clergyman, Pfarrar Blumhardt. He was at a loss to explain what was happening to her. That winter, she became ill again, but she was extremely unpleasant to Blumhardt when he paid visits to her.

The disturbances escalated. By April 1842, the entire neighborhood could hear the noises at night. G. D. frequently saw the specter of a woman who had died two years prior in the village, holding a dead child in her arms. The ghost said she wanted rest.

One night, a mysterious light in the house revealed a loose floorboard. A paper with writing was found underneath, but the dirt on it was so heavy that the writing could not be read. Two weeks later, another mysterious light and a noise emerged from behind the stove. Underneath the floor, there were hidden objects: money wrapped up in paper, packets of a strange powder, bird bones, and other items. G. D. and her siblings believed these to be magical objects used for spell casting.

Blumhardt persuaded G. D. to move, and she went to live with another relative. The previous house continued to be haunted until 1844. Meanwhile, the activity also followed G. D. to her new residence. Now, she started having convulsions. Her possessions began.

The dead woman kept appearing to her, and simultaneously G. D. would feel tapped and even struck sharply by invisible blows. G. D. said the woman had confessed to grievous sins on her deathbed and could find no peace. G. D. would fall unconscious, during which times "unearthly sounds" would fill the house.

Blumhardt described the first time he saw her become possessed:

> Suddenly, something seemed to enter into her, and her whole body began to move. I said a few words of prayer, mentioning the name of Jesus. Immediately she rolled her eyes, threw out her hands, and spoke in a voice that was at once recognized as that of a stranger—not only on account of the sound, as of the expression and choice of words. The voice cried, "I cannot endure to hear *that* name!" All shuddered. I had never heard anything of the kind, and offered a silent prayer for wisdom and discretion.

Blumhardt questioned the spirit, who said she had no rest in death because she had killed two children and buried them in fields. She could not pray and could not endure the name of JESUS. She said she was not alone; "the worst of all beings" was with her. She also said that she had practiced magic, which made her "the devil's bondswoman." She had been cast out of people seven times, and she was not about to be cast out again. Blumhardt told her she could not remain in the body of G. D., but the spirit was defiant. At last, it left after being sternly ordered out by the minister.

Subsequently, G. D. suffered frequent possessions, with an increasing number of demons entering into her. Blumhardt cast out as many as 14 at one time. Onlookers often felt blows, but the minister was never harmed. The demons told him they could not harm him.

The possessions intensified. G. D. felt invisible blows day and night. Sometimes, she was knocked down while walking on the street. One night, she awakened feeling a burning hand seize her neck. The skin blistered, and the wound festered for weeks.

On July 25, 1842, G. D. suffered a particularly bad possession, lying unconscious "like dead" while more than 1,000 demons passed out of her through her mouth. According to Blumhardt, they exited in groups of 12, 14, and 28 at a time. After this, G. D. had some peace for a few weeks, but then the possessions returned, worse than ever. Every Wednesday and Friday night, the demons arrived. Her health declined.

Others in the village urged the minister to use remedies of sympathetic magic, but he refused, believing that magic would only strengthen SATAN against him. He believed such folk magic practices, as well as fortune telling and divining the location of lost property, were the type of thing the Devil used to ensnare people.

Instead, Blumhardt relied solely on prayer, even when he was not present with G. D. It always afforded her relief, but when he stopped, the attacks started again.

Once, the demons said there were 1,067 of them, the largest of the attacks. They spoke in French, Italian, and "unknown" tongues as well as G. D.'s native German. Whenever Blumhardt cast them out, they stayed in the room for a long time, visible to G. D. but no one else. One of the demons, she said, dressed in rich, ancient clothing and always carried a book. This demon seemed to be the leader.

Eventually, Blumhardt succeeded in casting them out and keeping them out of G. D. Some of them said they were delivered from servitude to the Devil by his prayer and were being sent to a place of rest until Judgment Day. Others were in despair, presumably because they had to go back to HELL. Among the first to leave G. D. was the spirit of the dead woman, who asked to haunt the village church. She was later seen there by G. D.

The last demon was expelled on February 8, 1843. G. D. lay unconscious for hours. When she awakened, she said she had been to a foreign country, the description of which seemed to be the West Indies. A terrible earthquake had happened there, she said, and many of her tormenting demons were cast into the crater of a volcano, including the leader with the book. A few days later, a real earthquake struck the West Indies.

Despite the expulsion of the demons, G. D.'s troubles were not over. She repeatedly vomited sand, pieces of glass, nails, shoe buckles, live grasshoppers, a frog, and a snake. Pins, needles, and knitting needles were drawn out of her body. The worst were two large nails, one of them bent, that were removed from her head and caused copious bleeding from her ears, nose, and eyes. Blumhardt removed many of these pins, nails, and needles himself. First, he would feel them under the skin, working their way out; then, they would pierce the skin. He opined that the Devil had the ability to dematerialize real objects and reassemble their atoms inside the body.

G. D. was still visited at night by spirits, who touched her and forced something like bread into her mouth. However, they did not possess her. She attempted suicide. Her final struggle against the demons took place just before Christmas 1843, and her brother and one sister were affected as well. All three recovered. G. D. moved into Blumhardt's house.

Blumhardt believed that G. D. underwent these afflictions because as a child, she had a relative who was a witch, who promised to teach her the arts when she turned 10. The woman died when G. D. was eight, but Blumhardt said the Devil evidently considered her his property because of the witch's intentions.

FURTHER READING:
Stead, W. T. *Borderland: A Casebook of True Supernatural Stories.* Hyde Park, N.Y.: University Books, 1970.

Murder Headless DEMON who sees through his breasts and speaks with the voice taken over from his victims.

In the Testament of Solomon, Murder is summoned to appear before King SOLOMON. He says that he has no head and he tries to get one by devouring the heads of his victims. Murder grabs hold of heads, cuts them off, and attaches them to himself. A fire (heat) that continually burns within him consumes the heads through his neck. He longs for a head to do what the king does. He takes the voices of the dumb by "closing up" their heads.

Murder is like one of the hordes of LILITH, in that he attacks infants at night. He harms premature infants, and if one 10 days old cries at night, he rushes in and attacks it through its voice. Murder causes quartan fever and inflames limbs, inflicts feet, and creates festering sores. He is thwarted by fiery flashes of lightning.

See SCEPTER.

FURTHER READING:
The Old Testament Pseudepigrapha. Vols. 1 & 2. Edited by James H. Charlesworth. 1983. Reprint, New York: Doubleday, 1985.

Murmur FALLEN ANGEL and 54th of the 72 SPIRITS OF SOLOMON. Murmur is a duke and earl with 30 LEGIONs of DEMONs under his command. He appears as a soldier wearing a duke's crown and riding on a griffin, preceded by two ministers sounding trumpets. He teaches philosophy and makes souls of the dead appear and answer questions. Murmur once was partly a member of the angelic orders of thrones and ANGELs.

Naamah   In kabbalistic lore, one of four angels of prostitution, a DEMON, and a partner of SAMAEL. *Naamah* means "pleasing." Naamah is the mother of the great demon ASMODEUS and other demons. She seduces men and spirits and, with LILITH, causes epilepsy in children.

Naberius (Cerberus)   FALLEN ANGEL and 24th of the 72 SPIRITS OF SOLOMON. Naberius is a marquis who commands 19 LEGIONS of DEMONS. He appears as a crowing cock and flutters about the magic circle. In a hoarse voice, he imparts skill in arts and sciences, especially rhetoric. He also restores lost dignities and honors.

Nancy Possession (1620)   Case of demonic POSSESSION of a young woman in Lorraine, France. Elizabeth de Ranfaing, the DEMONIAC, was exorcized in Nancy. The DEMON possessing her demonstrated a remarkable command of several foreign languages.

De Ranfaing was a virtuous woman who was widowed in 1617. A doctor named Povoit proposed marriage to her, but she declined. Povoit attempted to force her to fall in love with him by slipping her herbal love philters. The ingredients damaged her health. The doctor then tried other magical concoctions, which worsened her condition. The concoctions must have had a psychological effect, for symptoms of possession manifested. The doctor soon was accused of SORCERY, convicted and burned at the stake.

De Ranfaing consulted other physicians but none could relieve her symptoms. As a final recourse, they rec-

ommended that she seek EXORCISM. The exorcisms began on September 2, 1619, in Remiremont. When no relief was obtained, de Ranfaing was sent to Nancy, the capital of Lorraine, where she was interviewed and examined by more physicians. They affirmed that her symptoms were caused by diabolical possession.

The EXORCISTs included church officials, theologians, monks, physicians, and representatives of the royal court. They interrogated the demon in various languages, including Hebrew, Greek, Italian, and Latin, and the demon responded accordingly. Once an attempt was made to trip up the demon with incorrect Greek; the demon pointed out the grammatical error. Sometimes the demon's answers were split in languages, with part of a sentence in French and part in Latin.

Using different languages, the exorcists gave various instructions to the demon, which it understood and carried out. The demon forced de Ranfaing to make signs of the cross, carry holy water, kiss the feet of the bishop of Toul, and make body movements and postures. The demon gave correct answers to questions about Catholic theology and revealed secret sins of those present. Sometimes the exorcists did not even have to speak out loud; the demon understood movements of their lips and even movements of their hands. The demon also pointed out Calvinist and Puritan witnesses who were present to watch the exorcisms.

Critics of the possession were reprimanded. Claude Pithoy, a Minimite monk, declared that he should become possessed himself if the case were real. Pithoy was silenced by his superiors.

De Ranfaing was finally exorcized of the demon and founded an order of nuns. The exorcists signed statements attesting to the validity of her possession, and the case was documented in 1622 by a respected physician named Prichard.

FURTHER READING:
Calmet, Dom Augustin. *The Phantom World: Concerning Apparitions and Vampires.* Ware, England: Wordsworth Editions in association with The Folklore Society, 2001.

Nantes incubus (12th century)
DEMON who had sex with a woman for at least six years, before being exorcized by St. Bernard.

When St. Bernard traveled to Nantes, Brittany, France, in 1135 to visit monks, he learned of a woman who was said to have enjoyed sexual intercourse with an INCUBUS. The supernatural affair had lasted six years before she apparently felt guilty and confessed her sin to priests. They prescribed for her almsgiving, pilgrimages, and intercessory prayer to saints. None of the remedies expelled the incubus. The woman's husband learned of the matter and left her. The incubus became more sexually aggressive.

The woman went to St. Bernard and appealed for his help. She said the demon had told her that her appeal would be useless. Bernard comforted her and told her to return the next day. She did and relayed the demon's terrible threats to her. St. Bernard gave her his staff and told her to take it to bed with her. As long as the staff was in the bed, the incubus could not approach her. Enraged, the demon made threats of what he would do once the saint left town with his staff.

On the next Sunday, St. Bernard told all the townspeople to go to church with lighted candles. He took the pulpit, told about the case, and then anathematized the demon, forbidding him in the name of Christ to assault the victim or any other woman. When the candles were extinguished, the demon's powers were ended. The woman was troubled no more.

FURTHER READING:
Lea, Henry Charles. *Materials toward a History of Witchcraft.* Philadelphia: University of Pennsylvania Press, 1939.

Nemesis
Greek goddess of vengeance, divine justice, and retribution against evil deeds. Nemesis, whose name means "dispenser of dues," was called upon by ancient Greeks and Romans to exorcise and avert DEMONs and POSSESSION.

In mythology, Nemesis is the daughter of either Oceanus or Zeus. She is usually portrayed as a somber winged maiden with a whip, rein, sword, or scales in her left hand. Sometimes she is portrayed as holding a cubit ruler in her left hand and a staff in her right, with one foot on a wheel. She personifies resentment against men who commit callous crimes, those who are wicked and insolent, and those who have too much good fortune. Her job is to be the "leveler," to effect equilibrium by making sure that wrongdoers get their due.

The Romans called Nemesis Invidia (Jealousy) and Rivalitas (Jealous Rivalry). In modern terms, a "nemesis" is one's worst enemy.

Nemesis-stone rings were AMULETs against evil. A Nemesis stone was a stone taken from an altar to Nemesis and engraved with her image. Placed under the stone were the tip of a duck wing and a piece of a mullein, called "death plant." When this ring amulet was given to a person who was possessed, it caused the demon to confess himself and flee. When worn around the neck, the ring warded off nightmares caused by demons and protected children against LAMIAE. The ring also cured "moonstruck" conditions (insanity). In order for the ring to work properly, the wearer had to avoid everything abominable and wicked. Lore also held that the ring would reveal the length of someone's life and the manner of his or her death.

FURTHER READING:
Ogden, Daniel. *Magic, Witchcraft, and Ghosts in the Greek and Roman Worlds: A Sourcebook.* New York: Oxford University Press, 2002.

Nephilim
A race of giants spawned by the cohabitation of ANGELs (see WATCHERS) and human women. *Nephilim* means "fallen," "those who have fallen," or "those who were cast down." The Nephilim sometimes are called the SONS OF GOD, as are their angel parents. Helel is their chief. The Nephilim displeased God.

Genesis 6:4 implies that the Nephilim were already present upon the earth when the Sons of God began their relations with mortal women: "The Nephilim were upon the earth in those days, and also afterward, when the sons of god came into the daughters of men, and they bore children to them. These were the mighty men that were of old, the men of renown." The corruption brought by the mingling of angels and humans caused God to regret that he had created human beings on Earth. He decided to blot out not only the human race but every living thing on Earth. He selected Noah and his family to survive this disaster, the great flood, and repopulate the world.

Evidently not all the Nephilim perished, however, for a later reference in Numbers refers to the Anakim, the sons of the Nephilim: "And there we saw the Nephilim (the sons of Anak, who come from the Nephilim); and we seemed to ourselves like grasshoppers and so we seemed to them" (13:33). The Anakim were later destroyed.

1 Enoch presents a more descriptive picture of the Nephilim as monstrous beings:

> And the women became pregnant and gave birth to great giants whose heights were 300 cubits. These (giants) consumed the produce of all the people until the people detested feeding them. So the giants turned against the

(people) in order to eat them. And they began to sin against birds, wild beasts, reptiles and fish. And their flesh was devoured the one by the other, and they drank blood. And then the earth brought an accusation against the oppressors. (7:3–7)

Meanwhile, the Watchers spread more corruption by teaching people secret and magical arts they are not supposed to know. From the heavens above, the angels Michael, Gabriel, and Surafal observe in horror the bloodshed and oppression upon the earth. They hear the prayers of the people begging for help. They petition God to intervene, saying that the giants have filled Earth with blood and oppression. God declares that he will punish these transgressions with complete destruction in the flood. He tells Gabriel:

> Proceed against the bastards and the reprobates and the children of adultery; and destroy the children of adultery and expel the children of the Watchers from among the people and send them against one another (so that) they may be destroyed in the fight, for length of days have they not. They will beg you everything—for their fathers on behalf of themselves because they hope to live an eternal life. (They hope) that each one of them will live a period of 500 years. (10:9–11)

The Nephilim also are the subject of a Qumran text referred to as the Enochic Book of Giants (4Q532). The text tells that two Nephilim sons of SEMYAZA (leader of the Watchers), named Ahya and Ohya, have a shared dream vision in which they visit a world garden and see 200 trees being cut down by angels. They do not understand the dream and so they take it to the Nephilim council. The council appoints one of their members, Mahawai, to consult Enoch in paradise and ask him what it means. Mahawai rises up into the air like the whirlwinds and flies with the help of his hands like an eagle until he reaches Enoch. Enoch says that the 200 trees symbolize the 200 Watchers who are going to be destroyed in the coming flood.

Later in the text, Mahawai transforms into a bird again to make another journey. He flies too close to the Sun and is threatened with incineration. He is saved by Enoch, whose voice descends from heaven to tell him to turn back and not die prematurely.

FURTHER READING:
The Old Testament Pseudepigrapha. Vols. 1 & 2. Edited by James H. Charlesworth. 1983. Reprint, New York: Doubleday, 1985.
Collins, Andrew. *From the Ashes of Angels: The Forbidden Legacy of a Fallen Race.* London: Signet Books, 1996.
Eisenman, Robert, and Michael Wise. *The Dead Sea Scrolls Uncovered.* London: Element Books, 1992.

Nisroc   Assyrian deity who became both a good ANGEL and a FALLEN ANGEL. As a fallen angel in HELL, Nisroc rules cuisine in the House of Princes. As a holy angel, he rules the order of principalities.

Niyaz   In ZOROASTRIANISM, the DEMON of want, distress, and scarcity. Niyaz is often paired with AZ, the demon of avarice, insatiability, gluttony, and lust. Niyaz is powerful and haughty and is behind the evil deeds and disasters of people's lives and their ill-omened deaths.

Obry, Nicole   See MIRACLE OF LAON.

obsession   A state of being besieged by DEMONs. *Obsession* is derived from the Latin *obsidere* and refers to a state of siege or an attack on a person or personality from without. Sometimes the term is used interchangeably with *OPPRESSION* or even *POSSESSION*; however, this is not accurate, for *possession* entails being completely taken over within.

The literature of saints, monks, and hermits describes numerous cases of obsession as part of a holy person's spiritual challenges. The *Life of St. Hilary* describes how the saint's "temptations were numerous; . . . how often when he lay down did naked women appear to him." St. Anthony endured the most famous obsession during his withdrawal into the desert. When he tried to sleep, the DEVIL assumed the form of a woman and tried to seduce him with feminine gestures. (See SUCCUBUS.) Other holy or biblical figures, such as Saul, also suffered obsessive spirits.

In the 17th century, a young Spanish nun, Doña Micaela de Aguirre, was obsessed by the Devil. Irritated by Doña Micaela's perfection, the Devil began tormenting her, appearing one night in the shape of a horse. He stood on Micaela with his full weight, kicking and trampling her and leaving her severely bruised. Sometimes the Devil immersed Doña Micaela in the convent well up to her neck, leaving her there all night. In the end, according to her biographer, Doña Micaela triumphed. "Mocking his

cunning she bade him fetch an ax and chop wood. And the enemy could not disobey her [for she was a saint]; he took the ax and chopped the wood up with all haste and departed in confusion, roaring with anger at being defeated by a young nun."

In modern psychiatry, obsession refers to total domination by a fixed idea, which controls or affects all other actions, such as constantly checking to see whether a door is locked or believing that deadly germs are everywhere.

Obyzouth   Female DEMON whose principal acts of evil are to kill newborn infants and cause others to be stillborn, making her comparable to the LAMIAE and the offspring of LILITH.

In the Testament of Solomon, Obyzouth appears with disheveled hair and arrogantly refuses to answer questions until King SOLOMON has purified himself by washing his hands and has sat on his throne. The king complies. Obyzouth describes how she travels about every night, visiting women as they give birth and strangling their newborns. She is successful every night, going to even the remotest parts of Earth. She also injures eyes, condemns mouths, destroys minds, and makes bodies feel pain.

Obyzouth says Solomon cannot give her orders. However, she is thwarted by the archangel Raphael (see THWARTING ANGELS) and admits that she will flee to the "other world" (the realm of demons) if women who are in labor write her name on a piece of parchment.

185

The horrified king has Obyzouth bound by her hair and hung in front of the Temple of Jerusalem, so that everyone who passes through will glorify the God of Israel, who has given Solomon command over the demons.

FURTHER READING:
The Old Testament Pseudepigrapha. Vols. 1 & 2. Edited by James H. Charlesworth. 1983. Reprint, New York: Doubleday, 1985.

Oesterreich, Traugott Konstantin (1880–1949)
German professor of philosophy and author of a classic work on POSSESSION and EXORCISM.

Traugott Konstantin (T. K.) Oesterreich was born in Germany in 1880. Little is known of his personal life. In 1910, he took a philosophy teaching post at a university in Tubingen, Germany, and he became professor there in 1922.

In 1933, the Nazi government dismissed him from his university post, apparently because of his marriage in 1912 to a Jewish woman and his political writings in 1919, which later provoked the dislike of the Nazis. He was forced into retirement on a severely limited pension.

After the defeat of the Nazis in 1945 in World War II, he was reinstated at the university but soon was dismissed again, allegedly because he was near retirement age. He may have been terminated because of his deep interest in psychical research and in cases of possession.

Oesterreich is the author of *Possession: Demoniacal & Other,* a comprehensive examination of states of possession, both voluntary and involuntary, since ancient times, and in various cultures, and the exorcisms applied for relief. The book has been reprinted as *Possession and Exorcism.*

FURTHER READING:
Oesterreich, Traugott K. *Possession and Exorcism.* Secaucus, N.J: University Books, 1966.

Omen, The (1976)
Horror film about the birth of the ANTICHRIST. The film, scripted by David Seltzer and directed by Richard Donner, features the birth of the son of SATAN to fulfill biblical prophecies of Armageddon.

The film stars Gregory Peck and Lee Remick as the unwitting adoptive parents of the Antichrist, whom they name Damien (Harvey Stephens). Peck and Remick are Robert (Jeremy in the novel) and Katharine Thorn, a prosperous American couple living in Italy, where Robert is the U.S. ambassador. They want to start a family. Tragedy strikes when Katharine gives birth in a hospital, and Robert is informed that the child was stillborn. Before she realizes what has happened, Robert is approached by a priest and offered a newborn child whose mother has just died in childbirth. Desperate to save his wife a crisis, Robert takes the child and presents it to Katharine as their own son.

The family relocates to London. As the child grows, strange things happen in the household, including the apparent suicide of the nanny and a bizarre impaling of a priest who knows the real secret, that Damien is the son of the DEVIL, the Antichrist.

Robert realizes the awful truth with the help of a photographer, Keith Jennings (David Warner). He reveals it to Katharine. They return to the hospital and learn from the priest the location of the grave of Damien's real mother. The priest dies. The couple find the grave and disinter the woman. They are horrified to find the skeleton of a jackal where the woman should be buried and that of a newborn whose skull has been smashed. The murdered child is the real son of the Thorns. The priest deceived them in order to pass Damien on to them.

Deaths of people involved with Damien continue. Katharine dies when she is thrown over a railing by their new nanny, Mrs. Baylock (Billie Whitelaw). Robert and Jennings travel to Tel Megiddo, Israel, and find an archaeologist, Carl Bugenhagen, who knows how to kill the Antichrist, with seven special daggers. Robert acquires the daggers but is emotionally unable to kill the child. Jennings tries to take over the job but is killed himself in a gruesome accident of decapitation by a pane of glass atop a runaway truck.

Robert returns to London, where the nanny's demonic Rottweiler attacks him. He removes the last bit of doubt about the true identity of his adopted son when he snips away some of Damien's hair and discovers 666, the "Mark of the Beast," on his scalp (see SIX-SIX-SIX). Robert fights the nanny and manages to stab her to death.

Robert seizes Damien and takes him to a church, intending to lay him on the altar and stab him to death in a sacrificial manner. He pulls out a dagger and then hesitates. He is shot by police who pursued him and Damien into the church.

The film ends with the double funeral of Robert and Katharine. Damien, the Antichrist, has triumphed and is shown holding the hand of the president of the United States.

Selzter wrote a novelization of the film, which became a best-seller.

The Omen was remade in 2006 in a film directed by John Moore and starring Liev Schrieber as Robert Thorn, Julia Stiles as Katharine, and Seamus Davey-Fitzpatrick as Damien. Seltzer declined to write the screenplay.

A sequel to the original film, *The Omen II,* was released in 1978. Directed by Don Taylor, it stars William Holden and Lee Grant as Richard and Ann Thorn, Damien's aunt and uncle, and Jonathan Scott-Taylor as Damien. Damien, living with his wealthy relatives in Chicago, is now 13 and knows his true identity. He is enrolled in a military academy along with Mark, Richard's son by his first marriage. Damien is not well liked.

An industrialist, Richard invests in Third World countries. Unbeknownst to him, secret allies of Damien help

Jonathan Scott-Taylor as Damien, the Antichrist, in Damien: The Omen II *(1978)* (AUTHOR'S COLLECTION)

him buy up land as part of the fulfillment of the Anti-christ's 10 kingdoms on Earth. People who refuse to sell to Thorn Industries are murdered.

Meanwhile, a journalist, Joan Hart, investigates the strange earlier death of Carl Bugenhagen, who knew Damien's secret. She tries to warn Richard but is neutralized when a satanic crow pecks out her eyes.

Others who learn Damien's secret also are dealt with in grisly ways. Damien even kills his stepbrother, Mark. Richard tries in vain to stop Damien, but he is stabbed to death by Anne, who reveals herself as the Whore of Babylon. She herself is killed when Damien causes a boiler to explode and she bursts into flames. Damien is left once again triumphant, this time heir to a fortune that will enable him to pursue his plans freely.

Omen III: The Final Conflict was released in 1981. Directed by Graham Baker, the film stars Sam Neill as the now-adult Damien Thorn; Lisa Harrow as the journalist Kate Reynolds, and Rossano Brazzi as the priest Father DeCarlo, who has the divine assignment to kill the Antichrist. Damien is a charismatic figure with slavish followers, the U.S. ambassador to England, and a favorite to

run for president of the United States. He is romantically involved with Reynolds.

An unusual alignment of stars in the sky creates a new Star of Bethlehem and tells Damien that the Second Coming of Christ is at hand. He secretly orders the murders of all male infants in England. Those who try to thwart the plan die. Father DeCarlo, who has the Seven Daggers of Megiddo, hunts for Damien with a band of priests. All but DeCarlo are killed.

DeCarlo knows that Christ will reappear as an adult, not as an infant, but he remains intent on slaying Damien. Tragically, Damien uses Reynolds' teenage son as a shield, and DeCarlo kills him instead. But Reynolds sneaks up behind and fatally stabs Damien in the back. He calls out for Christ to appear, and he does, telling Damien, "You have won nothing."

Onoskelis   Female DEMON. In the Testament of Solomon, Onoskelis is summoned by BEELZEBUB to the presence of King SOLOMON, when the king asks whether there are any female demons and says he wants to see one.

Onoskelis appears in the form of a beautiful woman with a fair complexion and the legs of a mule. She says she lives in caves, cliffs, and ravines and perverts men and strangles them. They think they will obtain gold through her, but she gives little to those who worship her. She travels by the full Moon and is associated with the constellation of Capricorn. She is thwarted by the name *Yahweh* (Holy One of Israel).

Solomon uses the name of Yahweh and his magical ring to bind Onoskelis in a standing position to work day and night spinning hemp for ropes used in the construction of the Temple of Jerusalem.

FURTHER READING:
The Old Testament Pseudepigrapha. Vols. 1 & 2. Edited by James H. Charlesworth. 1983. Reprint, New York: Doubleday, 1985.

oppression   Demonic influence over a person that involves total domination of the victim's will, either through a horrendous bombardment of external terrors or through an internal, psychological breakdown. Oppression follows INFESTATION and can progress to full demonic POSSESSION. It is also referred to as "vexation."

Oppressed victims are terrorized by demonic bloodcurdling screams; heavy breathing and footsteps; knockings, rappings, and poundings; hellish moans and inhuman voices through televisions or telephones; nightmares and disturbed sleep; putrid and disgusting smells, such as sulfur, rotting flesh, and excrement; extremes of hot and cold, often in succession; levitation of people or large objects and furniture; and, finally, materializations of a black form that personifies evil.

Internally, the demon causes the victim to believe he or she is insane. There are dramatic personality changes and mood swings and deep depression. The victim becomes argumentative and makes heavy use of foul or obscene language. Friends and family feel the victim has undergone a marked personality change.

Oppression is relieved by rites of EXORCISM, accompanied by the spiritual reform of the victim.

Orias   FALLEN ANGEL and 59th of the 72 SPIRITS OF SOLOMON. Orias is a marquis who has 30 LEGIONS of DEMONS. He appears as a lion with a serpent's tail that rides a horse and holds two huge, hissing snakes. He teaches the virtues of the planets and stars. He transforms men; grants dignities, prelacies, and confirmations; and confers the favor of friends and enemies.

Ornias   One of the FALLEN ANGELS, who is bested by King SOLOMON. According to the Testament of Solomon, Ornias is an annoying, vampirizing DEMON who lives in the constellation Aquarius. He has shape-shifting ability: He strangles men born under the sign of Aquarius because they have passion for women born under the sign of Virgo; he becomes a man who likes boys and

causes them pain when he touches them; he turns into a heavenly winged creature; and he can assume the form of a lion.

During the construction of Solomon's Temple of Jerusalem, Ornias appears at sunset and takes half the wages and food of the master workman's boy—Solomon's favorite—and sucks out his soul through his right thumb. The boy grows thin. Solomon asks him why he is losing weight, and the boy tells him about Ornias. Incensed, Solomon begs God for help to have authority over the demon. The archangel Michael gives him a magical ring with a seal engraved upon it that will bestow the power upon Solomon. Michael tells Solomon, "You shall imprison all the demons, male and female, and with their help you shall build Jerusalem when you bear this seal of God."

Solomon gives the ring to the boy and instructs him to fling it at the demon's chest when he next appears and order him to go to Solomon. When Ornias next appears, as a flaming fire, the boy does so and shouts, "Come! Solomon summons you!" Ornias screams and promises to give the boy all the gold and silver on Earth if he will give the ring back to Solomon. But the boy binds the demon and delivers him to the king.

Solomon finds the demon trembling at his gates and goes to interrogate him. Ornias says that he is descended from an archangel and is thwarted by the archangel Uriel (see THWARTING ANGELS). He says he resides in the constellation Aquarius, where he strangles "those who reside in Aquarius because of their passion for women whose zodiacal sign is Virgo." Ornias says that while in trance, he undergoes three transformations: "Sometimes I am a man who craves the bodies of effeminate boys, and when I touch them, they suffer great pain. Sometimes I am a creature with wings (flying) up to the heavenly regions. Finally, I assume the appearance of a lion."

Solomon binds the demon with his ring and sets him to work cutting stone from the quarry. Terrified by IRON, the demon begs for a measure of freedom, promising to call up other demons. Solomon summons Uriel, who forces Ornias to cut stones by terrorizing him. Uriel calls up sea monsters and withers them, casting them to the ground.

When that work is done, Solomon orders Ornias to fetch the Prince of Demons. He gives Ornias the magical ring, and the demon goes to BEELZEBUB. The Prince of Demons is unimpressed by the name of Solomon, so Ornias throws the ring at his chest and commands him to go to the king. Beelzebub cries out like one burned by fire and does as commanded.

Ornias has the gift of prophecy, explaining to Solomon that demons fly up to heaven, where they overhear God's plans. Those who are exhausted by doing so become FALLING STARS.

FURTHER READING:
The Old Testament Pseudepigrapha. Vols. 1 & 2. Edited by James H. Charlesworth. 1983. Reprint, New York: Doubleday, 1985.

Orobas FALLEN ANGEL and 55th of the 72 SPIRITS OF SOLOMON. Orobas is a prince in HELL, where he governs 20 LEGIONS of DEMONS. He makes his first appearance as a horse but then changes to a man upon command. He discovers all things past and present and bestows great favors. He gives true answers to questions about the past, present, and future; divinity, and the creation of the world. Orobas is faithful to magicians and does not like them to be tempted by any other demon. Prior to his fall, he was in the angelic order of thrones.

Ose FALLEN ANGEL and 57th of the 72 SPIRITS OF SOLOMON. Ose is a president in HELL, who appears first as a leopard and then as a human. He teaches all liberal sciences and gives true answers to questions about divine and secret things. He can change people into any shape desired by the magician; the victims will not know they have been changed. He commands three LEGIONS of DEMONS. According to JOHANN WEYER, Ose also will make people insane and delusional, so that they will believe they are kings and such. The delusions only last for an hour.

Ouija™ A patented game consisting of a board printed with letters and numbers, and the words *yes, no, goodbye*, over which players slide a three-legged triangular pointer, used by many people for divination and attempts to contact the dead and spirits. The users place fingertips on the pointer and ask questions, and the pointer spells out the answers. *Ouija* is a trademarked name owned by Parker Brothers. A generic term for devices similar to the Ouija is "talking board."

As an interface between worlds, the Ouija is neutral, neither good nor evil. It is said to be dangerous by authorities in the Christian Church, who claim it provides a doorway for evil DEMONS to possess the users. Advocates of the Ouija say the device reveals the subconscious of the user or is an interface to genuine spirit communication.

History
Precursors to the Ouija date to Greece around 540 B.C.E. Pythagoras was said to have a divination tool that was a table that rolled on wheels. Pythagoras or a pupil placed his hands on the table, and it rolled toward signs and symbols.

Ouija-like instruments were used through the Middle Ages. The forerunner of the modern Ouija was the planchette (French for little board), a triangular or heart-shaped pointer on three legs, which appeared in Europe in 1853. Its invention is usually attributed to a French spiritualist named M. Planchette. One leg was a pencil, which wrote out words and drew pictures. The planchette was popular with spiritualists and was used in séances for automatic writing.

A type of talking board used by Native Americans was called a *squdilatc*.

The Ouija board itself has had a turbulent history. The origin of the board is murky: No one knows exactly where the inspiration originated and even who was the first to produce it. The Ouija seems to blend the characteristics of the planchette, minus the pencil, and dial plates, which were circular boards with letters painted along the bottom rim. Two persons concentrated on a rocking T-bar that spelled out messages by pointing to letters.

The Ouija may have been the idea of a coffin maker, E. C. Reiche, who lived in Maryland in the 19th century. According to lore, Reiche had an interest in table tilting, in which a group of people sit around a table with hands lightly touching its surface and ask questions of spirits. The answers are given in the manner in which the table moves, shakes, and rocks. Reiche desired to create a device for communicating with the dead, and he was impressed that heavy tables seemed to be easily manipulated by spirits. He teamed up with two friends, Elijah Bond and Charles Kennard. At some point, Reiche dropped out of the picture.

The Kennard Novelty Company began manufacturing the Ouija in 1890. It is not clear whether Kennard or Bond founded the company or if they worked together. But later, each claimed to have been the founder. The patent for the Ouija was registered in Bond's name in 1891.

Also unclear is the origin of the name *Ouija*. According to one story, Kennard was given the name by a spirit while he was using the board himself. The spirit claimed it meant "good luck" in ancient Egyptian. Another story says that Reiche thought of the name.

The Ouija was sold initially as a device for talking to spirits, which angered mediums, who feared they would lose business. The early success of the company was short-lived, however, for in 1892 it was lost in a hostile takeover by two of Kennard's own financial supporters, the brothers Isaac and William Fuld. The patent for the Ouija was reregistered the same year in the name of William Fuld, and the company's name was changed to the Ouija Novelty Company. William Fuld also reinvented some of the board's history, claiming credit himself for its invention. He said the name *Ouija* really was from the French and German words for "yes," *oui* and *ja*, respectively.

The new company had a difficult time. Competitors jumped into the market. Isaac manipulated the financial books and was fired by William, who then changed the company name again, to the Baltimore Talking Board Company. Isaac set up a rival company called Oriole and began marketing a near-duplicate board. In 1910, William added a clear plastic window to his planchette.

The brothers engaged in a legal battle for control of the patent; William won. "Ouija, the Mystifying Oracle" soared in popularity during and after World War I, as thousands of bereaved persons attempted to contact the spirits of soldiers killed in the war. Fuld publicly claimed not to use the board himself, but many people believed that he did.

The company ran into federal tax trouble. Fuld had tried to avoid paying taxes on the grounds that the Ouija was a scientific device for mediumship and therefore qualified for religious status tax exemption. The federal government considered it a "sporting game." A federal court ruled in favor of the government. Fuld appealed to the U.S. Supreme Court, which in 1922 upheld the lower court ruling. The Ouija has been a game or toy ever since.

By the late 1920s, the Ouija fad was in decline. In 1927, Fuld, 54, was on the roof of his company when he fell three stories to his death. His company was taken over by his sons, William and Hubert. In 1966, Parker Brothers, of Salem, Massachusetts, the maker of Monopoly and other games, bought the company. Parker Brothers purchased the trademark and rights in 1966 and markets the Ouija as entertainment.

Pros and Cons of the Ouija

Until the 1960s, the Ouija was considered to be mostly benign in nature. People used it to try to contact the dead, for divination of the future and for entertainment, to obtain messages from spirits. Clergy have criticized and denounced it, as they might any popular device or method used by people for do-it-yourself spirit contact.

There are two theories as to the sources of answers derived from a Ouija board. One school of thought holds that the subconscious prompts the hands to spell out the answers most desired. The second holds that real entities are contacted, many of which are negative, earthbound spirits who have not accepted their deaths and are bent on possessing living human beings. A person who uses a Ouija invites entities to communicate, providing an opening through which evil beings gain a foothold.

The Ouija is credited with helping users discover spiritual insights and self-truths and aiding in creativity. In 1913, Pearl Curran, a St. Louis homemaker, began receiving communications from "Patience Worth," a 16th-century English woman, via the Ouija. Worth, speaking in an old English dialect, dictated an astounding volume of poetry and novels. In 1919, Betty and Stewart Edward White were using a Ouija as a lark with friends, when suddenly Betty was instructed to "get a pencil" and take dictation. Thus began a long relationship with the "Invisibles," who seemed to be higher entities, who dispensed metaphysical wisdom. Stewart compiled it into *The Betty Book.* In 1963, Jane Roberts was using the Ouija when she met Seth, who purported to be a highly developed entity, who dictated highly regarded books on metaphysics. The Pulitzer Prize–winning poet James Merrill composed his epic *The Changing Light at Sandover* from two decades of spirit communications via the Ouija. The New Age author Ruth Montgomery began her channeling with a Ouija then moved to automatic typing.

The Ouija has not been without problems, however. Throughout its history, people have claimed to be instructed to commit crimes—even murder—via the Ouija

and have blamed cases of insanity on the board. However, it is possible that such unstable individuals were already so inclined and were not "forced" by "spirits" to do anything beyond their inclinations and control.

Sexual assaults, beatings, torment, OBSESSION, and POSSESSION also have been blamed on spirit contacts initiated via Ouija boards. At first, users think they are talking with dead people they know or friendly spirits. After benign beginnings, the communications turn dark and threatening as malicious and evil demons reveal their true selves. The demons engage in vicious attacks such as physical injury, rape, nightmares, visions of monsters, poltergeistlike disturbances, and even levitation of victims. Some victims must seek psychiatric help. Some psychiatrists and psychologists say the "possession" is not caused by entities but by material dredged up from the subconscious. The "evil spirit" may be only the prankster archetype.

Since some people expect problems from Ouija use, it is difficult to ascertain how many problems are genuine versus self-fulfilled expectations. Some problems may arise from open-ended use without control or discernment: People ask for any spirit to manifest. The great English magician and occultist ALEISTER CROWLEY was critical of this approach and once stated, "When you use the Ouija board, you give permission for any unknown spirit to communicate with you. Would you open the front door to your house and let in anybody who felt like it? Of course not."

ED AND LORRAINE WARREN, demonologists, called the Ouija "a notorious passkey to terror, even when the intent of communication is decidedly positive in nature." Of the thousands of demonic and negative cases the Warrens claimed to have investigated in their careers, they said four of 10 involved problems resulting from the Ouija. Ed said that all doors to the supernatural—the Ouija, séances, conjuring and candle rituals, and automatic writing devices—"lead down a road of misfortune, terror, and ruin."

One of the Warrens' most sensational cases involved a Ouija board. In March 1974, they were consulted by the Donovan family, whose daughter, Patty, had been using a Ouija board for months to talk to a spirit who said he had died as a teenager. Patty asked the spirit to manifest, and the Donovan household began experiencing unpleasant phenomena of destruction, rains of rocks, levitation of objects, the manifestation of black forms, and noises. The Warrens investigated, and the case was turned over to Catholic clergy for exorcism. A successful rite was performed on May 2, 1974, during which a demon manifested as a seven-foot-tall being with horns, cloven feet, and a tail, according to the Warrens.

Responsibilities of Users

Many paranormal investigators and occultists say they have no problem using the Ouija, and the key is responsible use. Any spirit interface device should not be used for entertainment or for open calls to the spirit world; nor should participants use alcohol or drugs prior to or during sessions. Boards should never be used to contact or conjure demonic entities.

FURTHER READING:

Brittle, Gerald Daniel. *The Demonologist: The Extraordinary Career of Ed and Lorraine Warren.* Englewood Cliffs, N.J.: Prentice-Hall, 1980.

Cornelius, J. Edward. *Aleister Crowley and the Ouija Board.* Los Angeles: Feral House, 2005.

Covina, Gina. *The Ouija Book.* New York: Simon & Schuster, 1979.

Guiley, Rosemary Ellen. "Why Are We Bashing the Ouija?" *TAPS Paramagazine,* July 2007, 7–9.

Hunt, Stoker. *Ouija: The Most Dangerous Game.* New York: Harper & Row, 1985.

Taylor, Troy. *The Devil Came to St. Louis: The True Story of the 1949 Exorcism.* Alton, Ill.: Whitechapel Productions Press, 2006.

pact A binding agreement with a DEMON or the DEVIL for gain and services beyond the power of nature, usually in exchange for one's soul.

The Devil's pact is implied in biblical passages. In the book of Isaiah, the prophet Isaiah says, "For you have said: We have entered into a league with death; we have made a covenant with hell" (28:15). Matthew 4 tells about the temptations of JESUS in the wilderness, and the Devil's promises of glory and power in return for worship: "Again, the devil took him to a very high mountain, and showed him all the kingdoms of the world and the glory of them; and he said to him, 'All these I will give you, if you will fall down and worship me'" (4:8). Jesus refuses and the Devil leaves.

Legendary Pacts

Informal pacts with demons and the Devil exist in legend and folklore tales about individuals seduced into selling their souls, often to obtain treasure, love, or power. The Devil's pact is based on a long history of assumption among theologians that any practice of magic, or even divination had to involve a demonic pact. (See SIMON MAGUS.) Such assertions were made by Origen (185–254), who condemned divination. St. Augustine (354–430), one of the most important fathers of the early church, gave weight to the concept of Devil's pacts in *De Doctinia Christiana*. Formal pacts with the Devil appeared for the first time in the writings of St. Jerome in the fifth century.

Jerome's story involves St. Basil. A man who wishes to seduce a pretty girl goes to a magician for help. For payment, he agrees to renounce Christ in writing. The magician writes a letter to the Devil to advise him of his conquest. The magician tells the man to take his renunciation and go out at night and thrust it up into the air.

The man does as told and calls upon the powers of darkness. He is taken to the presence of LUCIFER and undergoes a parody of a BAPTISM in which he reaffirms his renunciation of Christ. Lucifer insists that he sign a pact in writing. The man does so, and the Devil causes the girl to fall in love with the man. Her father refuses to allow her to marry him, for he desires his daughter to become a nun. The girl gives in to her lover. St. Basil learns about the pact, helps the man repent, and saves the girl from going to HELL.

Another of the earliest Christian stories of a pact with the Devil concerns THEOPHILUS, treasurer of the church of Adana, who allegedly sold his soul to the Devil around 538 in order to become a bishop. The story of Theophilus was told in many variations throughout Europe and became the basis for the legend of FAUST. It also boosted the cult of the Blessed Virgin Mary, for it is she who often appears in the stories to save the person.

In the 13th century, St. Thomas Aquinas (ca. 1227–74), the church's greatest theologian, stated in *Sententiae*, "Magicians perform miracles through personal contracts made with demons."

Stories of Devil's pacts were common in the Middle Ages, and particularly in the 16th and 17th centuries during the witch hysteria. The victim usually was not a witch, but an ordinary person who was vulnerable to temptation. (See MAILLOT, THOMAS.) Satan or a demon would appear, sometimes as a man and sometimes as an animal, and offer to help. The pact would last for a specified number of years, at which time Satan would collect: The victim would die and his soul would go to HELL. In the legend of Faust, a scientist and alchemist sells his soul to MEPHISTOPHELES in exchange for youth and lust. A female version of the Faust legend is MARY OF NEMMEGEN. These moralistic stories were publicized through pamphlets and portrayed Satan as a trickster. The victim, despite supernatural favors, usually had a dreadful demise. Sometimes the Virgin Mary would intercede for the victims and snatch the pacts away from the Devil.

According to JACQUES COLLIN DE PLANCY, "The angel of darkness is not hard to deal with, provided of course that he receives the soul as a pledge."

Pacts in Witchcraft and Possession

During the Inquisition, Devil pacts became a deadly matter. European witch hunters believed that all witches entered into a Devil's pact, pledging to serve the Devil or one of his satellite demons, not so much for their personal gain but expressly for the power to harm others. The pact was said to be sometimes oral but traditionally was written on virgin parchment and signed in BLOOD. If witches bewitched people into becoming possessed, their victims also might enter into Devil pacts.

The first appearance of a Devil's pact in WITCHCRAFT trials occurred in Toulouse, France, in 1335. The trials also were significant for being the first to feature the diabolical SABBAT. The accused witch Catherine Delort, a married woman, said a shepherd with whom she had a tryst had forced her into a Devil's pact. According to her deposition quoted by Julio Caro Baroja in *The World of Witches*:

> This loathsome ceremony took place at midnight at the edge of a wood at a place where two roads meet. She let some blood from her left arm and allowed it to flow on to a fire made of human bones which had been stolen from the parish cemetery. She pronounced certain strange words which she no longer remembers and the Devil Berit appeared to her in the form of a violet flame. Since then she has made certain harmful concoctions and potions which cause men and beasts to die.

After that, Delort said, she attended obscene sabbats every Friday night.

Demonologists said there are two types of diabolical pacts: explicit and implicit. The explicit pact is a solemn vow of fidelity and homage made to a visible form of the Devil in the presence of witnesses. The implicit pact involves a written petition offered to the Devil, either in person or through a proxy such as a witch.

The MALLEUS MALEFICARUM (1487), the leading inquisitors' handbook, emphasized the importance of the Devil's pact in recruiting witches and coercing them to

Two Dominican monks are executed for signing pacts with the Devil. (AUTHOR'S COLLECTION)

evil acts. Sometimes pacts were made in lewd rites at SABBATs, at which the initiates cooked and ate babies, kissed the anus of the Devil, signed his book in their own blood, copulated with him and his demons, and promised fealty to him. The pact required them to renounce Christianity, trample on the cross, and deny the Eucharist.

The *Malleus* describes other ways pacts were made, according to tortured accused witches. One man from Berne said that the Devil required him to go to church and before Mass was said, in the presence of the priests, deny his faith, Christ, baptism, and the church. Then he pledged himself to the "Little Master," as the Devil was called. He was burned at the stake.

If pacts were not made at sabbats or in public displays, they were made privately. The Devil, usually in the form of a man dressed in black, approached a candidate with an offer he could not refuse. The enticements started with a small price, such as fealty for a certain number of years, but always had a catch, such as the cost of one's soul, according to the *Malleus*.

Sometimes, pacts were made spontaneously, according to witchcraft trial testimonials. The Devil, it seems, seldom passes up an opportunity. NICHOLAS REMY, a French demonologist, wrote of a case in 1587 in which a woman told of a demonic pact made by her mother and her. They were out gathering rushes one day when a shoemaker appeared. His belt was stained with pitch. The mother seemed to be expecting him, according to the daughter. He made the women swear allegiance to him and marked them on the brow with his nail. He had sex with the daughter and then the mother and then danced in a ring with them, holding hands. He gave them money and vanished into the air. The money crumbled to dust.

FRANCESCO-MARIA GUAZZO, a leading Italian demonologist of the 17th century, said that people who enter into any pacts, explicit and implicit, share the same 11 characteristics:

1. They deny the Christian faith, withdraw allegiance from God, repudiate the protection of the Blessed Virgin Mary, and deny their BAPTISM. The Devil places a claw on their brow to rub off the Holy Chrism and destroy the mark of their baptism.

2. They undergo a mock baptism administered by the Devil.

3. They forswear their old name and are given a new name.

4. The Devil forces them to deny their godfathers and godmothers, both of baptism and of confirmation, and assigns them new ones.

5. They give the Devil a piece of their clothing as a symbol of the acquired goods that now belong to him.

6. They swear allegiance to the Devil within a circle traced upon the ground. The circle is a symbol of divinity, and the earth is "God's footstool." This demonstrates that the Devil is their God of heaven and Earth.

7. They pray to the Devil to strike them out of the book of life and write their names in the book of death.

8. They vow to sacrifice to him on a regular basis, such as offering up children they murder.

9. They make annual gifts to their demons in order to avoid being beaten by them. The gifts must be black.

10. The Devil brands them with his mark on some part of their body, especially those he suspects will lose their faith in him.

11. After being marked, they make many vows. In return, the Devil promises to stand by them, fulfill all their prayers in this world, and award them happiness after death. The vows are

    • never to adore the Eucharist
    • to insult and revile in both word and deed the Blessed Virgin Mary and the saints continually
    • to abstain from making the sign of the cross and from using anything consecrated by the church, including holy water and blessed salt and bread
    • never to make confessions again to a priest
    • to maintain silence concerning their pact with the Devil
    • to participate in sabbats when they can
    • to recruit others into the service of the Devil

Guazzo agreed with other demonologists that these elaborate pacts were empty, for the Devil never keeps his word.

Inquisitors tortured accused witches to force confessions of devil's pacts, which were important to securing convictions. There was no need to produce an actual document; an oral confession was sufficient to sentence the accused to death, often by burning at the stake. In two famous trials in 17th-century France, Devil's pacts were produced, one orally and one in writing.

In 1611, Father Louis Gaufridi was tried in the AIX-EN-PROVENCE POSSESSIONS involving bewitched nuns. Under torture he recited his pact verbally for the inquisitors:

> I, Louis Gaufridi, renounce all good, both spiritual as well as temporal, which may be bestowed upon me by God, the Blessed Virgin Mary, all the Saints of Heaven, particularly my Patron St. John-Baptist, as also S. Peter, S. Paul, and S. Francis, and I give myself body and soul to Lucifer, before whom I stand, together with every good that I may ever possess (save always the benefits of the sacraments touching those who receive them). And according to the tenor of these terms have I signed and sealed.

One of Gaufridi's victims was a woman named Madeleine de la Palud, who also confessed orally to making a Devil's pact:

> With all my heart and most unfeignedly and with all my will most deliberately do I wholly renounce God, Father, Son and Holy Ghost; the most Holy Mother of God; all the Angels and especially my Guardian Angel, the Passion of Our Lord Jesus Christ, His Precious Blood and the merits thereof, my lot in Paradise, also the good inspirations which God may give me in the future, all the prayers which are made or may be made for me.

Father Gaufridi was convicted and burned alive at the stake. Sister Madeleine was convicted and banished from the parish.

In 1633, Father URBAIN GRANDIER, a parish priest of St.-Pierre-du-Marche in Loudun, France, in 1633, was brought to trial in the LOUDUN POSSESSIONS, also involving bewitched nuns. A written pact was introduced as evidence. It was written backward in Latin and signed in blood. It read:

> We, the all-powerful Lucifer, seconded by Stana, Beelzebub, Leviathan, Elimi, Astaroth, and others, have today accepted the pact of alliance with Urbain Grandier, who is on our side. And we promise him the love of women, the flower of virgins, the chastity of nuns, worldly honors, pleasures, and riches. He will fornicate every three days; intoxication will be dear to him. He will offer to us once a year a tribute marked with his blood; he will trample under foot the sacraments of the church, and he will say his prayers to us. By virtue of this pact, he will live happily for twenty years on earth among men, and finally will come among us to curse God. Done in hell, in the council of the devils.
>
> (Signed by) Satan, Beelzebub, Lucifer, Elimi, Leviathan, Astaroth.
>
> "Notarized the signature and mark of the chief devil, and my lords the princes of hell.
>
> (Countersigned by) Baalberith, recorder.

Grandier was convicted and burned alive at the stake.

In England in the mid-17th century, the famous "witch finder" Matthew Hopkins tortured many accused witches into confessing Devil pacts.

JOHANN WEYER, an influential physician and writer on demons and witchcraft in the 16th century, acknowledged in his work *De praestigiis daemonum* (*On the Illusions of Demons*) that there were witches who made pacts with Satan but said that Satan, not the witches, caused harm. If such a witch killed cattle, she did so by poison, not by supernatural means. He acknowledged that there were sorcerers who entered into demonic pacts for their own personal gain, but they were not the same as those who were being persecuted by the church. He argued for forgiving accused witches if they renounced Satan and repented.

As for the pacts themselves, Weyer said they were "illusory," a fabrication of mind that had "no weight." Legally, there could be no contract between a human and a demon, he said: "The deception occurs when an apparition of Satan's choice is cunningly imposed upon the optic or visual nerves by the disturbing of the appropriate humors and spirits, or when whistling, or whispering, or murmuring, corresponding in form to the corrupt image, is aroused in the organs of hearing by the evil spirit's art. . . . Satan needs the help of no second creature in displaying his power and declaring his actions, he who is constrained by the will or command of none but God and God's good ministers."

Weyer was one of the first authoritative voices to speak out against the witch hysteria and Devil pacts.

Pacts in Satanism

In some practices of modern SATANISM, followers pledge to serve Satan, a form of pact. The Church of Satan holds that a formal pact is not necessary to become a satanist. The church founder, Anton Szandor LaVey, states in *The Satanic Bible* (1969) that the Devil's pact was a threat "devised by Christianity to terrorize people so they would not stray from the fold."

Pacts in Magic

Magical GRIMOIRES give instructions for making pacts with demons for procuring favors. There are two types of pacts: a unilateral pact, in which a demon agrees to serve without condition, and a bilateral pact, in which a demon agrees to conditional service, on penalty of forfeiture of one's body and soul. According to grimoires, some spirits bind easily and some do not; the latter are dangerous and not to be trusted.

The most important grimoire, the *Key of Solomon*, mentions "penal bonds" and "pacts" only in connection with magic for love and favors. It states that pentacles—magical inscriptions of words and symbols—are sufficient to protect the magician from demons.

The *Grand Grimoire* states that if the magician cannot master a magic circle and a blasting rod, a magical wand feared by every demon, then a pact is an absolute neces-

sity. Even with those two instruments of magic, a pact is advisable. A pact cannot be made directly with major demons such as LUCIFER, BEELZEBUB, and ASTAROTH, but only with one of their lieutenants. The grimoire provides a lengthy pact for commanding LUCIFUGE ROFOCALE, the prime minister of Lucifer.

One magical formula for conjuring the Devil for a pact calls for sacrificing a cock at the center of a CROSSROADS and letting its blood drip into the center while reciting a spell. The Devil will appear and offer a pact to be signed in the blood of the magician.

Another formula calls for composing a pact and signing it in one's own blood. The pact must be written on virgin parchment, which is made from the first calf borne by a cow, while standing or sitting in a magic circle. The pact should read, "I promise GREAT DEMON to repay him in seven years for all he shall give me. In witness thereof, I sign my name."

The pact is held while the following incantation in recited:

LUCIFER, Emperor, Master of All Rebellious Spirits, I beseech thee to be favorable to me in calling upon thy GREAT MINISTER which I make, desiring to make a pact with him.

BEELZEBUB, Prince, I pray thee also, to protect me in my undertaking.

ASTAROTH, Count, be propitious to me and cause that this night the GREAT DEMON appear to me in human form and without any evil smell, and that he grant me, by means of the pact which I shall deliver to him, all the treasures of which I have need.

GREAT DEMON, I beseech thee, leave thy dwelling, in whatever part of the world you may be, to come speak with me; if not, I shall thereto compel thee by the power of the mighty words of the Great Key of Solomon, whereof he made use to force the rebellious spirits to accept his pact.

Appear then instantly or I shall continually torment thee with the mighty words of the Key: *AGLON, TETRAGRAMMATON, VAYCHEON, STIMULAMATHON, EROHARES, RETRASAMMATHON, CLYORAN, ICION, ESITION, EXISTIEN, ERYONA, ONERA, ERASYN, MOYN, MEFFIAS, SOTER, EMMANUEL, SABAOTH, ADONAI. I call you.* AMEN.

Breaking Pacts

Pacts with the Devil are not necessarily irrevocable, and redemption is always possible. In moral tales, appeals are made to the Virgin Mary or Jesus, who intercede. (In some versions of the Faust legend, however, there is no salvation once the pact is made).

St. Alphonso Maria de Liguori, who founded the Redemptorist order in the 18th century, gave advice for breaking demonic pacts. He said that one must renounce and abjure the pact, burn it if in writing, or declare it to be rejected; destroy all CHARMS, talismans, and writings connected with black magic; and make whatever restitution is possible.

According to modern demonologists, humans always have free will to revoke a diabolic pact. Repenting will render a pact useless.

See HAIZMANN, CHRISTOPHER.

FURTHER READING:

Baroja, Julio Caro. *The World of the Witches.* Chicago: University of Chicago Press, 1975.

Butler, E. M. *Ritual Magic.* Cambridge: Cambridge University Press, 1949.

Fortea, Fr. José Antonio. *Interview with an Exorcist: An Insider's Look at the Devil, Diabolic Possession, and the Path to Deliverance.* West Chester, Pa.: Ascension Press, 2006.

Guazzo, Francesco-Maria. *Compendium Maleficarum.* Secaucus, N.J.: University Books, 1974.

LaVey, Anton Szandor. *The Satanic Bible.* New York: Avon Books, 1969.

Lea, Henry Charles. *Materials toward a History of Witchcraft.* Philadelphia: University of Pennsylvania Press, 1939.

The Malleus Maleficarum of Heinrich Kramer and James Sprenger. New York: Dover Publications, 1971.

Remy, Nicholas. *Demonolatry.* Secaucus, N.J.: University Books, 1974.

Russell, Jeffrey Burton. *Lucifer: The Devil in the Middle Ages.* Ithaca, N.Y., and London: Cornell University Press, 1984.

Summers, Montague. *The History of Witchcraft and Demonology.* London: Kegan Paul, Trench, Trubner, 1926.

Waite, Arthur Edward. *The Book of Black Magic and of Pacts.* 1899. Reprint, York Beach, Me.: Samuel Weiser, 1972.

Weyer, Johann. *On Witchcraft (De praestigiis daemonum).* Abridged. Edited by Benjamin G. Kohl and H. C. Erik Midelfort. Asheville, N.C.: Pegasus Press, 1998.

Padiel   DEMON among the 31 AERIAL SPIRITS OF SOLOMON. Padiel is the second-ranking spirit of the east and rules the south as king. He governs 10,000 spirits by day and 20,000 by night, and several thousand more in addition. The lower spirits can be trusted. According to Solomon, the only powers they have are those conferred upon them by Padiel. They can be conjured only with Padiel's permission.

Paimon   FALLEN ANGEL and ninth of the 72 SPIRITS OF SOLOMON. Prior to his fall, Paimon was in the angelic order of dominations. He was conceited with his own knowledge and fell with LUCIFER. In HELL, he rules as a king and has 200 LEGIONS of DEMONs under his command. He appears as a crowned man seated on a camel, preceded by many musicians with trumpets, cymbals, and other instruments. He has a roaring voice. He teaches all arts, sciences, and secrets; subjugates people to the will of the magician; and gives good FAMILIARs. He will give the answer to any question. He is observed in the northwest.

Pairikas   In Persian lore and ZOROASTRIANISM, a class of DAEVA or DEMON of beautiful seductresses who have the power to bewitch in malevolent ways. The Pairikas exert their baleful influences on the elements, cattle, and all vegetation. AHRIMAN uses them to bewitch the stars in order to prevent rain and cause bad harvests, famine, and sterility. They also cause meteor showers.

palis   In Arabian lore, a desert DEMON that vampirizes people by licking the soles of their feet until their BLOOD is drained. There is no known description of the *palis*.

The *palis* waits until desert travelers are asleep and then licks their feet. To prevent attack, travelers should sleep with the soles of their feet touching the soles of another person's feet. Salt sprinkled around will repel the demon.

Pamersiel   DEMON among the 31 AERIAL SPIRITS OF SOLOMON. Pamersiel is the chief of the east and serves under CARNESIEL. He has 1,000 spirits under his command, which must be called only during the daytime and with great care, for they are stubborn and arrogant. Pamersiel's primary dukes are Anoyr, Madriel, Ebra, Sotheano, Abrulges, Ormenu, Itules, Rablion, Hamorphiel, Itrasbiel, and Nadrel. Pamersiel and his dukes are evil and false, and not to be trusted. However, they can be commanded to drive away other evil spirits who haunt any place or house.

The *Lemegeton,* a GRIMOIRE, gives instructions for summoning Pamersiel and his dukes. The ritual must be done in the most secret room of a house, or a hidden grove, wood, or occult place. Other persons must not be able to observe the ritual. The place should be airy. The spirits can be summoned into a stone or glass and bound into the objects. A crystal stone must measure four inches in diameter and be set on a table consecrated to King Solomon. The SEAL of Pamersiel must be worn upon the breast.

Seal of Pamersiel (AUTHOR'S COLLECTION)

Pazuzu Assyrian and Babylonian DEMON god of the first millennium B.C.E., who sends diseases, pestilence, and plagues into households. Pazuzu has the feet of an eagle, the paws of a lion, the head of a dog, the tail of a scorpion, bulging eyes, and four wings.

Pazuzu rules the hot desert winds of Arabia that wither and kill and is sometimes called upon to provide protection against airborne diseases. Figures of the head of Pazuzu were placed in windows facing outward to ward off his own effects.

Pazuzu vanquished the childbirth demon LAMASTU to the underworld. AMULETs of his head were worn around the necks of pregnant women.

In William Peter Blatty's novel *THE EXORCIST*, Pazuzu plays a role as a reawakened demon who possesses a girl, Regan.

FURTHER READING:
Black, Jeremy, and Anthony Green. *Gods, Demons and Symbols of Ancient Mesopotamia.* London: British Museum Press, 1992.

Pearce-Higgins, Canon John D. Anglican clergyman and spiritualist known for his "depossession" work. Canon John D. Pearce-Higgins was former vice provost of Southwark Cathedral in London, and one of the founders of the Anglican Church's Fellowship for Psychical and Spiritual Studies. He chaired its Psychic Phenomena Committee. He was knowledgeable about psychology and took care to rule out psychiatric disorders in cases that seemed to involve spirit interference.

Pearce-Higgins preferred not to use the term *EXORCIST*. He said his religious service has no relation to the ideas of binding and adjuring present in other Christian exorcisms. He did not damn the entity to eternal hellfire, believing the discarnate needs as much counseling and help as the victim. In Pearce-Higgins' view, even the most intractable spirits may someday repent.

As did DR. CARL A. WICKLAND, Pearce-Higgins persuaded rather than forced possessing entities to leave their living victims and enter the next realm of consciousness. He disagreed with the orthodox Christian notion of evil spirits and possessing DEMONs, stating that if the DEVIL and his minions really tormented the living, then dualism, not monotheism, exists. The concept of Christian demonic EXORCISM—to bind and place the Devil under oath by the power of God, sending it to everlasting damnation—does not take into account the idea that some people die but do not realize it. Pearce-Higgins preferred to think that even the Devil is a FALLEN ANGEL, who, along with human sinners, may be redeemed. In his view, the possessing spirit needs as much help as the victim.

Many cases of possession are caused by souls confused by the transition to the afterlife and thus earthbound, he said. He argued for a more serious attitude toward spirit POSSESSION and a gentle guiding of both the possessed and the possessing spirit into better understanding of death and afterlife. He believed that there are more haunted people and haunted places than anyone realizes, because of these earthbound souls.

Pearce-Higgins wrote a ritual to release earthbound souls and send them to heaven, or the White Light. He called the process "soothing" rather than exorcising.

He "soothed" or depossessed both people and places, using the services of mediums. His ritual, a combination of Anglican liturgy and special prayers, has been distributed worldwide to those in need.

Phoenix (Phenix, Pheynix) FALLEN ANGEL and the 37th of the 72 SPIRITS OF SOLOMON. Phoenix reigns as a marquis in HELL with 20 LEGIONs of DEMONs. He appears as a phoenix bird and sings sweetly in a child's voice. It is really a siren's voice, and so the magician must take precautions not to be seduced by it. Upon command, Phoenix will assume a human shape and then speak on all the sciences and deliver excellent poetry. He fulfills all commands well. Phoenix has the futile hope that he will return to the seventh throne in 1,200 years. He formerly was in the angelic order of thrones.

Pirichiel DEMON and a wandering duke of the air. Pirichiel has no dukes or princes under his command, but he has dukes beneath him, each with 2,000 servants. The spirits must be summoned at the right planetary hour, and when they appear, they are good-natured and obedient. The eight chief knights are Damarsiell, Cardiel, Almasor, Nemariel, Menariel, Demediel, Hursiel, and Cuprisiel.

Pithom In Jewish lore, a SERPENT DEMON summoned for prophecy. Pithom is mentioned in the Talmud. The demon is human in form, with his head resting on his breast between his shoulders. He utters oracular pronouncements from his armpits or with his hands raised and his head lying between his armpits.

planoi In Greek lore, a type of DEMON that assaults travelers and taunts them. *Planos* (singular) means "vagabond" or "deceiver."

According to JOHN CASSIAN, a father of the church in the fourth century, most *planoi* are tricksters, but some attempt greater harm, including the incitement of bloodshed. In his work *Conferences*, Cassian described the *planoi* as

> . . . so seductive and sportive that, when they have taken continual possession of certain places or roads, they delight themselves not indeed with tormenting the passers by whom they can deceive, but, contenting themselves merely with laughing at them and mocking them, try to tire them out rather than to injure them: while some spend the night merely by harmlessly taking possession of men, though others are such slaves to fury and ferocity that they are not simply content with hurting the

bodies of those, of whom they have taken possession, by tearing them in a dreadful manner, but actually are eager to rush upon those who are passing by at a distance, and to attack them with most savage slaughter: like those described in the gospel, for fear of whom no man dared to pass by that way. And there is no doubt that these and such as these in their insatiable fury delight in wars and bloodshed.

FURTHER READING:
Cassian, John. "Conference 7." In *The Conferences of John Cassian*. Translated and notes by Edgar C. S. Gibson. Available online. URL: http://www.osb.org/lectio/cassian/conf/book1/conf7.html#7.0. Downloaded February 3, 2008.

possessed possessions   Objects attached by spirits. Any object can become possessed by a spirit, which may cause disturbances in an environment. The term *possessed possessions* was coined by Ed Okonowicz, a Delaware paranormal researcher.

Objects can become possessed through a CURSE, magical spell, or use in magical rituals. Some objects seem to take on personalities of previous owners. In lore, objects can be used to imprison entities, such as King SOLOMON did when he imprisoned the DJINN in vessels and rings.

Possessed objects can remain dormant and then become activated if brought into the right environment by the right person. Problems include poltergeist disturbances; apparitions and dark, shadowy figures; demonic INFESTATION; nightmares; illness; and so on.

Remedies include spiritual cleansing of the object and premises, EXORCISM, or removal or destruction of the object. Usually the paranormal problems stop after remedial measures are taken.

FURTHER READING:
Okonowicz, Ed. *Possessed Possessions: Haunted Antiques, Furniture and Collectibles*. Elkton, Md.: Myst and Lace Publishers, 1996.
Okonowicz, Ed. *Possessed Possessions 2*. Elkton, Md.: Myst and Lace Publishers, 1998.

possession   The takeover and control of a person's mind and body by a DEMON, condemned soul, ghost, spirit, or deity. There are different forms of possession; most are not demonic. While possession is a universal and ancient belief, the approaches to it differ widely. In Christianity, possession is associated with malevolent spirits under the direction of the DEVIL that threaten not only a person's health and life but his or her afterlife as well.

Since ancient times, there have been beliefs that gods and other spirits interfere in human affairs on a daily basis. The spirits may possess a person's mind and/or body and cause him or her to carry out certain acts for the possessing entity's own purpose. While possession usually is regarded as undesirable, some traditions hold that it shows the favor of the gods. Mediums, channelers, and trance prophets undergo a type of temporary and voluntary possession, in which they become a vehicle for discarnate entities to communicate through them. Another type of voluntary possession is spirit, such as the Holy Spirit or Holy Ghost experienced as a religious altered state of consciousness.

Anything might be blamed on or credited to a possessing entity. Most possessions are temporary and end when the goal of the possessing entity is accomplished, but sometimes the entities present an ongoing problem that requires stronger measures. If possession creates problems, remedies of EXORCISM, the expulsion or banishing of the entity, are sought from a trained practitioner, such as a priest, magician, or other expert. Some forms of possession are more psychiatric in nature, causing mental disturbances and personality changes.

Demonic Possession

In demonic possession, a demon takes up residence in a person's body and influences or controls his or her thoughts, words, and actions. A possessed person can seem normal for periods of time and then exhibit bizarre, uncontrolled behavior attributed to the demon. During the demonic episodes, the victim is entranced, and, when they end, there is a transition period of a return to normalcy.

Possessed persons usually are under the influence of more than one demon. Unless they are exorcised, the demons cause extreme deterioration of health to the point of death, sometimes by suicide.

According to Catholic theology, demons cannot possess a person's soul, but they can influence a person to take actions that jeopardize his or her status in the afterlife, so that the soul goes to HELL. Souls of the damned already in hell are capable of possessing a living person in much the same way as demons.

Christian History of Demonic Possession

There are few references to evil spirits in the Old Testament. In each case, the evil spirit was sent by God to punish and torment people. 1 Samuel 16:14–16 describes how an indwelling evil spirit was sent by the Lord tormented Saul, who was relieved when David played his harp:

> Now the Spirit of the LORD had departed from Saul, and an evil spirit from the LORD tormented him.
>
> Saul's attendants said to him, "See, an evil spirit from God is tormenting you. Let our lord command his servants here to search for someone who can play the harp. He will play when the evil spirit from God comes upon you, and you will feel better."

Demons and possession play a more prominent role in the New Testament. The Gospels and Acts tell how JESUS healed by casting out "unclean spirits," a customary practice for healers at the time. Demons were believed to cause

Asmodeus one of the principal demons in many cases of possession (AUTHOR'S COLLECTION)

illness as well as their own torments. One who consulted Jesus was a deranged man who was possessed by demons who identified themselves as LEGION, after the unit of Roman soldiers numbering 6,000. Seeing that their possession of the man was at an end, the demons begged Jesus to send them into a nearby herd of swine, and he did. The pigs went berserk and plunged over a cliff to their deaths, taking the demons with them (Luke 8:30).

In no case in Scripture was a possessed person considered responsible for his or her condition on account of sin. As with Legion, most of the cases cited involve problems and illnesses caused by the possessing spirits. Luke 9:38–43 describes a case of apparent epilepsy in a boy who experiences convulsions believed to be caused by a demon. Luke 11:14 describes a person who is rendered mute because of a demon:

> Jesus was driving out a demon that was mute. When the demon left, the man who had been mute spoke, and the crowd was amazed. But some of them said, "By Beelzebub, the prince of demons, he is driving out demons."

Luke 13:10–13 tells of a woman who was crippled for 18 years by a demon:

> On a Sabbath Jesus was teaching in one of the synagogues, and a woman was there who had been crippled by a spirit for eighteen years. She was bent over and could not straighten up at all. When Jesus saw her, he called her forward and said to her, "Woman, you are set free from your infirmity." Then he put his hands on her, and immediately she straightened up and praised God.

Faith makes a woman worthy of having her demon-possessed daughter exorcised in Matthew 15:21–28:

> Leaving that place, Jesus withdrew to the region of Tyre and Sidon. A Canaanite woman from that vicinity came to him, crying out, "Lord, Son of David, have mercy on me! My daughter is suffering terribly from demon-possession."
>
> Jesus did not answer a word. So his disciples came to him and urged him, "Send her away, for she keeps crying out after us."
>
> He answered, "I was sent only to the lost sheep of Israel."
>
> The woman came and knelt before him. "Lord, help me!" she said.
>
> He replied, "It is not right to take the children's bread and toss it to their dogs."
>
> "Yes, Lord," she said, "but even the dogs eat the crumbs that fall from their masters' table."
>
> Then Jesus answered, "Woman, you have great faith! Your request is granted." And her daughter was healed from that very hour.

By the end of the New Testament period, demons were equated with the wicked FALLEN ANGELS cast out of heaven with LUCIFER. Early Christian theologians considered possession to be orchestrated by the Devil and carried out by the demons who served him. Demons plagued the holy, such as saints, and fooled the innocent.

In the Middle Ages, demonic possession became a major concern of the church. Anyone found showing signs of unusual behavior or change in personality was assumed to be possessed by the Devil. During the Inquisition, possession became a heresy—a reason to be arrested, tried, and, if found guilty, executed. Theologians said that the Devil worked through the agency of witches; the practice of WITCHCRAFT also became a heresy. Witches were accused of using black MAGIC or animal FAMILIARS to send demons into people. Demons also preyed upon the weaknesses of people—their lust, greed, anger, and so forth—to find an entry point for possession.

Even eating certain foods, such as APPLES, could result in possession, for demons rode along into the body on the food. The apple was considered a favorite demonic vehicle because it was the fruit involved in the fall of Adam and Eve. In 1585, the townspeople of Annecy, Savoy, France, became alarmed over an apple that gave out a "great and confused noise." Believing it to be full of demons, they pushed the apple into a river.

In 1614, the Catholic Church issued the *RITUALE ROMANUM* to standardize procedures. Part of the *Rituale Romanum* was especially intended for demonic possession, an all-out spiritual battle between the forces of good and evil. Revisions have been made to the text since then, and it continues in modern use. Only a priest, preferably one who is trained in exorcism, can perform it. The Protestant Reformation rejected the idea of demonic possession, although in the 16th and 17th centuries, there were famous possession cases, many in France, which served as exorcism power contests between Catholics and Protestants to sway the faithful and win converts.

Demonic possession cases continue in present times. Church attention to possession cases dropped in the 20th century. In the 1970s, public attention was renewed by William Peter Blatty's novel and film *The Exorcist,* based on a real case in 1949 (see ST. LOUIS EXORCISM CASE). The numbers of reported possession cases began to rise. A sharp increase was seen at the turn of the 21st century, perhaps in response to the 9/11 terrorist attacks on the World Trade Center in New York City, and rising global fears over terrorism and war. The church increased the training of exorcists (see INTERNATIONAL ASSOCIATION OF EXORCISTS).

Catholic clergy dealt with most cases, but some Protestant and evangelical ministers perform varying types of exorcism. Lay demonologists also investigate cases and work with clergy in exorcisms, usually as assistants or witnesses.

Causes of Demonic Possession

According to the Catholic Church, the chief causes of possession are the following:

- making a PACT with the Devil or demons
- participating in occult or spiritualist rites, including playing with divination devices such as a OUIJA™ or doing automatic writing
- offering or dedicating a child to SATAN
- being the victim of a witchcraft spell or CURSE

Engaging in these activities, as well as leading a deliberately sinful life, give demons the right and license to take up residence, according to the church.

Mental illnesses such as schizophrenia and multiple personality disorder are not considered to be caused by demonic possession.

The church teaches that God allows possession to happen for a variety of reasons:

- to demonstrate the truth of the Catholic faith
- to punish sinners
- to confer spiritual benefits through lessons
- to produce teachings for humanity

Signs of Demonic Possession

The Catholic Church defines the true signs of possession as

- displaying superhuman strength and levitation, often accompanied by fits, convulsions, and contortions
- having knowledge of the future or other secret information
- being able to understand and converse in languages previously unknown to the victim
- exhibiting revulsion toward sacred objects or texts

Exorcists develop discernment that enables them to determine whether or not a person is truly possessed, rather than suffering from mental illness or stress. A DEMONIAC's eyes will be rolled back into his head and his or her voice will be altered to an evil, mocking tone. The person will scream insults, profanities, and blasphemies at the exorcists and witnesses.

How a possessed person behaves depends on the type of demon involved, and the exorcist's skill at recognizing the signs. There are three types of possessing demons, *clausus* (Latin for shut), *apertus* (Latin for open), and *abditus* (Latin for hidden). If a demon is *clausus,* it can resist prayer for a short time before eventually revealing its presence in an entranced condition and rolled-back eyes. The possessed person does not move or speak out but is still possessed.

If a demon is *apertus,* it will keep the possessed person's eyes open and will laugh at and mock the exorcist, claiming that the person's condition is only psychological.

An *abditus* demon is capable of hiding deep within a person's interior and can show no signs for hours in an exorcism.

In all cases, a possessed person will not recall his or her behavior during possessed episodes.

Stages of Demonic Possession

Demonic possession can progress through stages:

- INFESTATION, the actual entry point, when the demon first enters the victim and begins to exert an influence in the environment, such as unpleasant phenomena.
- OPPRESSION or vexation, in which the victim weakens and makes unethical or immoral choices or serious mistakes on vital matters. As oppression worsens, the victim voluntarily yields control to the demon, even though he or she knows it is alien to his or her personality.
- Full-blown demonic possession. The demon tries to cause the victim to commit heinous acts, such as murder or suicide. The victim's appearance and behavior alter in radical ways. A host of unpleasant phenomena manifest: lewd and obscene acts and thoughts; cursing and swearing; screaming in rage; spitting, vomiting, and urinating; foul smells; horrible facial expressions; physical contortions; unusual strength; speaking in tongues; prophesying; emaciation through rapid weight loss; levitation; and so forth. If presented with holy objects or splashed with holy water, a victim recoils.

Remedies for Demonic Possession

Exorcisms can be performed at any stage, and sometimes the offending entity can be expelled before full possession is reached. Some cases require repeated exorcisms and last for years before a person is liberated. In addition to the exorcism rites, the possessed person and his family must pray and make an effort to regain a spiritual life. Once demons are expelled, they stay out, but they can return if invited back through a relapse of sin and behavior.

Dangers of Demonic Possession

Severely possessed people are in danger of dying (see MICHEL, ANNELIESE). According to the church, if they die before their demons are expelled, they are not necessarily condemned to hell. If they die in a state of grace, they will go to heaven. Once a victim is dead, the demons depart.

Those present at an exorcism—the exorcists, assistants, and witnesses—are in danger of suffering possession from departing demons, who may seize an opportunity to occupy a new host. At the very least, the demon, speaking through the victim, may hurl their secret fears and vices in their faces. Exorcists and demonologists also can suffer mishaps, such as strange accidents, while they are working on cases. Good health and a virtuous life are important defenses in dealing with possession cases.

Nonetheless, some untrained paranormal investigators, attracted by the danger, have involved themselves in the field, thus opening themselves and their families to unpleasant problems. Exorcists stress that amateurs should not meddle in possession.

Possession of Animals

In the Catholic tradition, animals have the potential to become possessed, but reported cases are not common. The best biblical example is that of Jesus driving demons out of a man and into a herd of swine, which then commit suicide by drowning themselves in the sea (Mark 5:1–13). Animals that become possessed by demons act strangely and may exhibit self-destructive behavior, such as running in front of vehicles. If a possessed animal dies or is sacrificed, the demon departs.

Possession by Djinn

According to Islam, there are two principal causes of possession by DJINN, and both are forbidden by Allah. The djinn can possess a person out of lewdness, desire, love, capriciousness, trickster horseplay, and whim. It will attack the weak, vulnerable, and insane; "under Satan's touch" describes madness. Sometimes possession of this sort is permitted by the victim, but it is still forbidden. Without permission, the possession becomes a grave offense of oppression, and the djinn must be rebuked and informed that it has broken the laws of Allah.

In the second case, djinn may possess a person out of revenge, if they feel they have been wronged or injured. Humans may inadvertently urinate on them, pour water on them, or kill them, causing the djinn to react by punishing the humans. In that case, the djinn should be informed that the harm was accidental, and the djinn are not permitted to occupy the person's home, property, or body.

In possession, djinn can make people speak in unintelligible languages, have supernormal strength, and run unnaturally fast. The djinn will rain blows upon people and make them have fits.

Minor djinn called ZAR possess women and cause sickness, marital discord, and rebelliousness.

Other Demonic Possession outside of Christianity

Beliefs in the ability of negative, interfering spirits to possess people are universal. Views on possessing demons and their purposes vary, as do remedies against them. In Hinduism, possession permeates every facet of daily life. The victim is most often a woman, who attributes her personal problems—menstrual pain, barrenness, the death of children, miscarriage, abuse by husbands or fathers, the husband's infidelities—to the intervention of evil spirits. Exorcism techniques include blowing cow-dung smoke, pressing rock salt between the fingers, burning pig excreta, beating the victim herself or pulling her hair, using copper coins as an offering, reciting prayers or mantras, and offering gifts of candy or other presents.

In Japanese tradition, fox fairies cause similar negative conditions (see HULI JING; KITSUNE). The spirits communicate their requirements for departure, usually offerings of special foods.

Elsewhere, negative spirits and even mischievous deities are held responsible for all bad things that happen. Sometimes, the possessed victims gain social status by becoming possessed, which entitles them to privileges, attention, and gifts.

Possession by the Holy Ghost

Voluntary possession by the divine presence is accepted in traditions of Christianity. The word *enthusiastic* originally meant being filled with the Holy Ghost or Holy Spirit, or the supreme state of oneness with God.

After the Crucifixion and Resurrection of Jesus, on the first day of Pentecost (the date seven weeks after Passover, in the Jewish calendar), the apostles became possessed with the Holy Ghost. Acts describes how flames appeared above their heads and they spoke in tongues previously unknown to them. Speaking in unknown tongues, called glossolalia, and other ecstatic communion with God characterized early Christian worship but by the Middle Ages had come to signify the work of the Devil instead.

In modern Christianity, the Pentecostal movement has revived interest in ecstatic religious practices. The movement began on January 1, 1901, when a group of worshippers at Bethel College, Topeka, Kansas, reportedly received the Holy Spirit. Members of Pentecostal churches may speak in tongues, engage in long prayer revivals, perform faith healing, and even roll and writhe on the floor as the spirit fills them.

Such voluntary and temporary possessions are a "religious altered state of consciousness." Their phenomena are similar to cases of demonic possession, in which the possessed person exhibits rigidity of limbs, speaking in foreign languages or tongues, dilation of pupils, visions, insomnia, fasting, self-infliction of pain, sensations of a burning death, and catatonia. These states of consciousness can have 40-day cycles, imitating the 40-day withdrawal of Jesus into the desert.

Voluntary Spirit Possession

In some non-Western cultures, including shamanic traditions, voluntary possession as a means to communicate with spirits and deities serves as the centerpiece of religious worship and is used to obtain beneficial help in solving problems, divining the future, curing illness, and restoring happiness and harmony in life. Possession by a god shows the possessed to be worthy of the god's notice and protection.

In the Caribbean and South America and lands where tribal Africans were taken to be slaves, worship of the religions of their ancestors—now practiced as Vodun, Santeria, candomblé, or Umbanda—involves the possession of the faithful by the gods to obtain true communion and protection. Black slaves transported to Brazil by the Portuguese in the 1550s found their tribal religion had much in common with the spiritual practices of Indian tribes along the Amazon River. Forced to syncretize the worship of the gods, or *orishas,* into the veneration of Catholic saints to escape persecution, the blacks continued to follow the old ways and rituals in secret. By the time the slaves won their independence in 1888, more than 15 generations of Brazilians—black, white and Indian—had heard the stories of the *orishas* and how their magical intervention had snared a lover, saved a marriage or a sick baby, or eliminated a wicked enemy.

Worshippers, entranced by rites of chanting and drumming, are temporarily possessed or "mounted" by a god or spirit, becoming the entity's "horse." They take on that spirit's personal characteristics, such as facial expressions, body postures and gestures, preferences for certain foods or colors, perfumes, patterns of speech, use of profanity, smoking, and so forth.

Under possession, the worshipper may endure great extremes of heat and cold, dance unceasingly for hours, suffer from cuts and bruises with no pain, and even tear off the heads of live chickens used for sacrifice with his or her own teeth. Often the possessed issue prophesies and deliver pronouncements about local affairs. The worshipper becomes the deity and is accorded all appropriate rights and honors. Once possession subsides, the special treatment ends and the worshipper resumes his or her ordinary life.

Candomblé Candomblé closely resembles the ancient Yoruban practices from Africa. The term *candomblé* probably derives from *candombe,* a celebration and dance held by the slaves on the coffee plantations. The first candomblé center was organized in 1830 in Salvador, the old capital city of Brazil and now the capital of the state of Bahia, by three former slaves who became the cult's high priestesses. The slave women inherited the formerly all-male ceremonial duties when the men spent their time in slave field labor. Also serving as mistresses to the white Portuguese, the women claimed the exercise of their magi-

cal rites helped maintain their sexual skill and prowess. These "Mothers of the Saints" trained other women, called the "Daughters of the Saints," ensuring that the men were excluded from major responsibilities.

Candomblé ceremonies involve invocations to the gods, prayers, offerings, and voluntary possession. Healing is emphasized. Devotees believe the moment of greatest spiritual healing occurs when a person becomes one with his or her *orisha* during initiation into the cult. Such possession is often intense, requiring constant aid from the other worshippers. The priest may beg the *orisha* to treat the initiate gently, offering a pigeon or other sacrifice to the *orisha* in return for his or her mercy. The stronger the *orisha* the more violent the possession.

Umbanda Umbanda was founded in 1904 and has its roots in Hinduism and Buddhism in addition to African tribal religions. The teachings of spiritism—that communication with discarnate spirits is not only possible but necessary for spiritual healing and acceptance of one's earlier incarnations—also plays a large part in the practices of umbanda.

The term *umbanda* probably derives from *aum-gandha,* a Sanskrit description of the divine principle. Umbanda incorporates the worship of the Catholic saints with the beliefs of the Brazilian Indians. The *orishas* go by their Catholic names and personae.

In addition to the *orishas,* possessing entities include the *exus* and *pomba giras, caboclos, pretos velhos,* and *criancas.*

The *exus* are the spirits of the wicked and dangerous dead and of suicides. Their female counterparts are the *pomba giras.* Their light is diminished. They are sometimes equated with demons by outsiders, but their nature is not evil and satanic, more that of a trickster.

The *caboclos* are the spirits of dead Indians. They possess good herbal knowledge, pride, and strength and are valued when decisiveness is needed.

The *pretos velhos* are the spirits of dead Afro-Brazilian slaves. They have a gentle nature and are good for personal matters and healing, especially concerning herbal remedies.

The *criancas* are the spirits of children who died between ages three and five. They are consulted for personal matters and healing.

Quimbanda, formerly called Macumba, involves black magic in which lower spirits are contacted.

Vodun Vodun entered the Caribbean islands of Jamaica and Saint-Domingue, now divided into the nations of the Dominican Republic and Haiti, with the millions of black African slaves, encompassing members of the Bambara, Foula, Arada (or Ardra), Mandingue, Fon, Nago, Iwe, Ibo, Yoruba, and Congo tribes. Their religious practices perhaps first amused white masters, but soon fearful whites forbade their slaves not only from practicing their religion but gathering in any type of congregation. Penalties were sadistic and severe, including mutilation, sexual disfigurement, flaying alive, and burial alive. Any slave found possessing a fetish (a figurine or carved image of a god) was to be imprisoned, hanged, or flayed alive.

To save the blacks from the "animal" natures that they were believed to have, masters baptized their slaves as Catholic Christians. In front of whites, blacks practiced Catholicism, but among each other, the gods of their ancestors were not forgotten. Rites held deep in the woods, prayers transmitted in work songs, and worship of saints while secretly praying to the gods preserved the old traditions while giving them a new twist.

The syncretic practices that evolved featured worship rites in which voluntary possession was invited of the *loas* or *mystères*, the old gods and ancestral spirits. The priest or priestess, called *houngan* and *mambo,* respectively, acts as intermediary to summon the *loas* and help them to depart when their business is finished. The *houngan* and *mambo* receive total authority from the *mystères*. The possessed lose all consciousness, totally becoming the possessing *loas* with all their desires and eccentricities. Young women possessed by the older spirits seem frail and decrepit, while the infirm possessed by young, virile gods dance with no thought to their disabilities. Even facial expressions change to resemble that of the god or goddess. Although sacred, possession can be frightening and even dangerous, causing mental imbalance and deterioration of health.

Santeria Similar in practice to Vodun, Santeria centers around the worship of the ancient African gods (mostly Yoruban) who were blended with Catholic saints. *Santeria* is derived from the Spanish word *santo,* or "saint"; practitioners are called *santeros* and *santeras*.

The *orishas* who possess worshippers have complex human personalities, with strong desires, preferences, and temperaments. When possessed, the devotees assume the *orishas*' supernatural characteristics, performing feats of great strength, eating and drinking huge quantities of food and alcohol, and divining the future with great accuracy.

The *santeros* wield enormous power, having knowledge that can change a person's life either through their own skill or by the help of the *orishas*. To use that power for good or evil rests with the *santeros* alone.

Voluntary Possession in Mediumship and Channeling

During the 19th century, belief in diabolical possession declined in the West, while belief in spirit possession increased. Mediumship involves communicating with the dead and other spirits. In physical mediumship, the medium allows a form of temporary possession to take place, in which the spirits use the medium's body and voice to communicate directly. In mental mediumship, communication is impressed on a medium's thoughts.

In order for the temporary possession to take place, mediums enter into altered states of consciousness that range from dissociated states, in which they are fully aware of what happens, to deep trance, in which they have no awareness of events. Entranced mediums may exhibit physical symptoms similar to religious altered states of consciousness. Once the trance is ended, there is a period of transition in the return to normal awareness. Mediumship takes a physical and sometimes mental toll and can adversely affect health.

Though mediumship is voluntary, it sometimes begins as involuntary episodes in which spirits take over a person. Over time, a medium learns how to control spirit access. There are many ways of inducing entranced states for mediumistic possession, including drugs, fasting, meditation, and prayer.

Channeling is essentially the same as mediumship and is a newer term, usually applied to contact with highly evolved human spirits or nonhuman spirits, angels, and extraterrestrials, rather than the dead.

Religious critics of both mediumship and channeling contend that the true identities of the possessing spirits are demons intent on deception and demonic possession. Catholics and others are counseled not to consult psychics and mediums.

Voluntary Possession in Spiritualism and Spiritism

Life everlasting for the spirit and the ability to contact such spirits through mediums, proving their survival, underlie spiritualism, a religious movement that began in the mid-19th century and swept both sides of the Atlantic. It declined in popularity in the 20th century but still continues today.

A central feature of spiritualism is communication with the dead through mediums. One of the purposes of mediumship is to validate the tenets of spiritualism: belief in an immanent God as the active moving principle in nature, the affirmation of the essential goodness of human beings, a denial of the need for salvation, and the repudiation of HELL. Rather, the dead go to Summerland, a place of perpetual summer where the departed spirits spend eternity.

Spiritism evolved from spiritualism in the mid-19th century. Its chief proponent was a French writer and physician named Hippolyte-Léon-Denizard Rivail, who knew Latin and Greek and wrote under the pseudonym *Allan Kardec.*

Trained as a doctor, Kardec believed that certain illnesses have a spiritual cause and can be treated psychically through communication with spirit guides. Specifically, he said that persons suffering from epilepsy, schizophrenia, and multiple personality showed signs of spirit interference or possession, either from the dead or from remnants of the patients' own past lives. Kardec theorized that within each person's personality are what he called "subsystems" of past lives inherited with each new incarnation. Sometimes, these subsystems dominate the present life, blocking out reality and controlling the body for extended periods. Successful treatment depends not only on counseling and therapy but on communication with these spirits to understand their presence and persuade them to depart the victim.

Kardec's theories were fashionable in France for a while but did not catch on in the rest of Europe. They found enthusiastic audiences in Brazil.

Possession as Physical or Mental Illness

In ancient times, demons and spirits were held to be the cause of diseases and illnesses, both physical and psychological. The oldest extant text on epilepsy, *On the Sacred Disease,* attributed to the Greek physician Hippocrates (ca. 460–ca. 370 B.C.E.), but probably authored by several of his students, states that bizarre emotions, behavior, and sensations commonly believed to be due to demonic possession were instead due to a brain disease. It is likely that some cases of alleged demonic possession were either cases of epilepsy or of Tourette's syndrome, a rare neurological disorder.

According to Catholicism, the New Testament distinguishes between illness and possession, in descriptions of Jesus both performing the casting out of unclean spirits *and* healing the sick. However, some physicians and medical professionals even into modern times have postulated demonic interference as a cause of certain health problems.

Epileptic seizures are characterized by unconsciousness, violent behavior, vomiting, and visual, auditory, and olfactory hallucinations that may seem supernatural. Epileptics report feeling the presence of God, angels, or other spirits, including the dead. They may smell terrible stenches resembling brimstone or rotting flesh. Tourette's syndrome, often misdiagnosed as schizophrenia, starts in childhood and manifests with facial contortions, upward eye rolling, bizarre growls, barks, and grunts, and verbal outbursts of a sexual, blasphemous, or scatological nature—all characteristics of demonic possession.

Schizophrenia sufferers, who also experience altered states of consciousness and various hallucinations, may project fragments of their own personality as external "demons" or spirits. A theory about multiple personality sufferers, however, holds that the repression of a great deal of hatred, common in the disorder, acts as a magnet for evil influences. Obsession always represents an abnormal condition, and once one admits the existence of spirit influence, the idea of spirit obsession cannot be ignored. Severe physical or psychological trauma may so upset the victim that a "window" in the mind opens, allowing spirit influences to enter. In many cases of multiple personality, some psychiatrists find that only exorcism, perhaps simply invoking the Lord's name, eliminates one or more of the troubling personalities so that the patient can eventually become one person.

DR. JAMES HERVEY HYSLOP, an American psychologist famous for his research of obsession cases, states in his book *Contact with the Other World* (1919) that if people believe in telepathy, then invasion of a personality over distance is possible. And if that is true, he found it unlikely that sane and intelligent spirits were the only ones able to exert influence from beyond. Hyslop also stated that persons diagnosed as suffering from hysteria, multiple personality, dementia praecox, or other mental disturbances showed, in his view, unmistakable signs of invasion by discarnate entities. He called on medical practitioners to take such situations into account during treatment.

The American psychiatrist Dr. M. Scott Peck, a graduate of Harvard University, claims that two of his patients suffered from possession in addition to their other symptoms of multiple personality. In both cases, Peck found the spirits to be evil, actively working to destroy the mind of the host patients.

In *People of the Lie* (1983), Peck describes these patients, their awareness from the beginning of an alien presence, and the exorcisms that eventually cleared the way for spiritual healing. When the demonic entities finally revealed themselves, the patients' faces were completely transformed into masks of utter malevolence. One patient became a SERPENT, with writhing body, hooded reptilian eyes, and darting efforts to bite the exorcism team members. But what really overwhelmed Peck was not the performance but the feeling that a tremendous weight—an ageless, evil heaviness, or the true Serpent—was in the room. He reports that everyone present felt such a presence, only relieved when the exorcism succeeded.

Peck's experiences have corroborated those of the California psychiatrist Dr. Ralph Allison, trained at the University of California at Los Angeles School of Medicine and Stanford Medical Center. According to Allison, some cases of multiple personality may be the result of spirit possession, both nonthreatening and demonic. His controversial book *Minds in Many Pieces* (1980) discusses some of these patients and the inexplicable paranormal occurrences surrounding them. At least one personality in each patient—sometimes the primary but usually a secondary one—displayed striking psychic abilities.

One case cited by Allison was that of a young man who began hearing a voice in his head after being struck on the head by a heavy object. He had convulsive seizures that could not be explained neurologically. The voice told him he was about to die. Under hypnosis, the voice identified itself as the Devil and said it had entered the man when he was on military duty in Japan. The man had rushed into a burning house to rescue someone and was blown out by an explosion. The Devil entered him at that time and was the cause of all his physical and mental problems. Allison consulted a religious expert, who opined that the spirit was not the Devil but a stupid but evil entity who thought it was the Devil. He performed an exorcism, and the man was relieved of all symptoms.

In the 1920s and 1930s, Dr. Titus Bull, a well-respected physician and neurologist in New York City, treated many of his patients spiritually as well as physically. With the assistance of a medium, Mrs. Carolyn Duke (a pseudonym), Bull claimed to treat and sometimes cure schizophrenics, manic-depressives, and alcoholics. As had his predecessor DR. CARL A. WICKLAND, a pioneer in the spiritual exorcism of unwanted spirits as treatment for mental disorders, Dr. Bull believed that the possessing spirits were not necessarily evil but merely confused. With help from either the doctor or other spirits, the entities could pass on to their proper plane, leaving the victim in peace and finding happiness themselves. On the basis of his experiences, Bull found that spirits enter the victim through the base of the brain, the solar plexus, or the reproductive organs. He also postulated that pains suffered by the living might be pains produced by the obsessing dead spirit, especially if that spirit suffered in life.

FURTHER READING:

Blai, Adam. "Demonology from a Roman Catholic Perspective." Available online. URL: http://www.visionaryliving.com/ghosts.html. Downloaded August 14, 2006.

Crabtree, Adam. *Multiple Man, Explorations in Possession and Multiple Personality.* New York: Praeger, 1985.

Ebon, Martin. *The Devil's Bride, Exorcism: Past and Present.* New York: Harper & Row, 1974.

Eliade, Mircea. *Shamanism.* Princeton, N.J.: Princeton University Press, 1964.

Fortea, Fr. José Antonio. *Interview with an Exorcist: An Insider's Look at the Devil, Diabolic Possession, and the Path to Deliverance.* West Chester, Pa.: Ascension Press, 2006.

Goodman, Felicitas D. *The Exorcism of Anneliese Michel.* Oreg.: Garden City, N.Y.: Doubleday, 1981.

———. *How About Demons? Possession and Exorcism in the Modern World.* Bloomington: Indiana University Press, 1988.

Ibn Taymeeyah's Essay on the Jinn (Demons). Abridged, annotated and translated by Dr. Abu Ameenah Bilal Philips. New Delhi: Islamic Book Service, 2002.

Kapferer, Bruce. *A Celebration of Demons.* Bloomington: Indiana University Press, 1983.

Kelly, Henry Ansgar. *The Devil, Demonology, and Witchcraft: The Development of Christian Beliefs in Evil Spirits.* Eugene, Oreg.: Wipf & Stock, 1974.

Martin, Malachi. *Hostage to the Devil.* New York: Harper & Row, 1987.

Oesterreich, T. K. *Possession: Demonical and Other among Primitive Races, in Antiquity, the Middle Ages and Modern Times.* New Hyde Park, N.Y.: University Books, 1966.

Peck, M. Scott. *Glimpses of the Devil: A Psychiatrist's Personal Accounts of Possession, Exorcism and Redemption.* Detroit: Free Press, 2005.

———. *People of the Lie.* New York: Simon & Schuster, 1983.

Wickland, Carl. *Thirty Years among the Dead.* 1924. Reprint, N. Hollywood, Calif.: Newcastle, 1974.

Wilkinson, Tracy. *The Vatican's Exorcists: Driving Out the Devil in the 21st Century.* New York: Warner Books, 2007.

Zaffis, John, and Brian McIntyre. *Shadows of the Dark.* New York: iUniverse, Inc., 2004.

Prince of Darkness   Title given to SATAN and BELIAL. In the Dead Sea Scrolls, Belial is appointed by God to corrupt and to serve as "the prince of the dominion of wickedness." He is followed by the children of falsehood. The Prince of Darkness also is the Angel of Death.

***Prince of Darkness* (1987)**   Horror film written and directed by John Carpenter, about the attempt of SATAN to release the ultimate evil into the world. In writing the script, Carpenter sought to merge the idea of evil with the physics of matter and antimatter. The film is regarded as one of the creepiest good-versus-evil horror films.

Donald Pleasance stars as Father Loomis, who, with other priests, has discovered a mysterious large glass cylinder in the basement of an abandoned church in Los Angeles. The cylinder contains a swirling green liquid. Loomis invites a college professor, Howard Birack (Victor Wong), to investigate. Birack arrives with a team of students, who tackle the problem via physics. They learn from a text that the liquid is actually Satan himself, and he is the son of an even more evil force, an anti-God, who is trapped in another dimension. If released from the cylinder, Satan will seek an interdimensional portal to draw his father through into the world.

The liquid begins spilling out of the cylinder, enabling Satan to take POSSESSION of the students one by one. Once possessed, they turn on the others. There are swarms of insects. The students are prevented from fleeing the church, which comes under siege by an army of possessed people outside. In addition, they share a chilling dream, a warning sent back in time from the year 1999, in which a fragment of video shows a dark figure emerging from the church. A voice repeats, "Warning, this is not a dream."

One possessed student tries to draw the anti-God through a MIRROR portal, but the mirror is too small and the attempt fails. The student finds a larger mirror and begins to draw the hand of Satan's father through it. He is tackled by Catherine Danforth (Lisa Blount), another student, and both fall into the mirror and the portal. The priest shatters the mirror, trapping everyone, including the satanic Father, inside.

The evil is dispelled. The possessed students die, the unpossessed recover, and the possessed crowd disperses.

Later, Danforth's lover, Brian Marsh, also one of the investigators (Jameson Parker), has the recurring dream again, except that the dark figure that emerges from the church is recognizable as a possessed Danforth. Still dreaming, he rolls over in bed to find Danforth in the form of Satan lying beside him. He awakens screaming and goes to his bedroom mirror, touching it as the film ends.

Procel (Crocell, Pucel)   FALLEN ANGEL and 49th of the 72 SPIRITS OF SOLOMON. Procel is a duke who appears in the form of an ANGEL. He speaks mystically of hidden and secret things and teaches geometry and the liberal sciences. Upon command, he will make a commotion and make the sound of roaring water. He also warms waters and tempers thermal spring baths. Before his fall, he was in the angelic order of powers. He rules over 48 LEGIONS of DEMONS.

Processus Sathane   Devil's advocate drama in which a representative of SATAN appeals to God for his right to lead humanity astray. The *Processus Sathane,* or "play of Masscheroen," as it is also known, dates to the 12th century, a time when mariolatry, or devotion to the Blessed Virgin Mary, was at a peak.

The earliest known version of the *Processus Sathane* dates to 1260 in Jacob van Maerlant's *Merlijn,* a translation of Robert de Boron's *Merlin.* The original form of the *Processus Sathane* was that of a debate. Over time, citations from canonical law were added. It was produced as a pageant by the 14th century in a variety of languages.

The general story line is as follows:

Now that mankind can be forgiven for sins, Satan and his DEMONS worry that they will be cheated out of their right to tempt people into sin. The devils decide to elect a representative to go to the Court of Heaven to plead their case. Masscheroen, the elected one, asks God to summon mankind before the court and plead against him. God agrees, deciding that Good Friday shall be the day. Masscheroen objects, but God assures him that he will be given dispensation.

Masscheroen appears early on Good Friday and susses out the court for the best place to make his case as the accuser. He is armed with the Bible for reference. Nothing happens—no representative of the accused arrives—and, by noon, Masscheroen is impatient. God tells him to have patience. Masscheroen snaps, "I have spent all this day in the kingdom of justice, but there is no justice." God adjourns court until the following day.

Meanwhile, Mary finds out about the situation and offers herself as the advocate of humankind. The next day, she arrives in court with a retinue of ANGELS, patriarchs, and prophets, much to Masscheroen's dismay. Mary sits at the side of JESUS, the judge. Masscheroen protests, but Mary is allowed to remain.

Masscheroen pulls out his Bible and reads a verse God spoke to Adam and Eve: "This thou shalt know: thou mayest eat from all the fruits except this one and thou shalt regret the hour thou eatest thereof, for thou shalt die the one after the other."

Masscheroen demands that these words be executed at all times. Mary counters that the DEVIL is guilty of falsehood for beguiling Adam and Eve, and she blames him for the Fall. Masscheroen is laughed at by the court.

He says that offenses should be punished even if there is no accuser. Mankind sinned publicly, and neither he, Masscheroen, nor Mary can have any bearing on the case.

This worries Mary, and she makes a compassionate appeal to the court. She tears off her clothes and exposes her breast, reminding Jesus how she bore and fed him. Weeping, she asks him to choose between her and Masscheroen. Jesus denies Masscheroen.

Masscheroen replies: "Flesh and blood have counseled thee and not the justice of heaven. I knew this would happen. It is hard to have the Judge's mother as opponent." But he does not give up and refigures his strategy. He advocates dividing up mankind. He should get the lion's share, for good people are only a mustard seed.

Mary answers by addressing Jesus, "This was done long ago, when thou didst hang on the cross, and bought mankind. We shall, therefore, have no further weighing."

Masscheroen roars in fury. He demands two advocates, and Justice and Truth are given to him. The angels advise Mary to choose advocates, and she selects Mercy and Peace. The four advocates continue the debate. Eventually, all four side with Mary, and Masscheroen makes a humiliating retreat.

FURTHER READING:
de Bruyn, Lucy. *Woman and the Devil in Sixteenth-Century Literature.* Tisbury, England: Bear Book/The Compton Press, 1979.

Psellus, Michael (1018–ca. 1078)   Byzantine scholar, philosopher, author, and statesman, who undertook a classification of DEMONS in his work *On the Work of Demons.*

Michael Psellus was born in Constantinople, where he rose to prominence in the royal court as a lawyer and philosopher. He became imperial secretary under Emperor Michael V in 1041–42. He taught philosophy at the Academy at Constantinople, where he advocated the ideas of Plato over those of the more popular Aristotle.

Psellus' book *On the Work of Demons* was translated into Latin by Marsilio Ficino, and then into Italian by a mid-16th-century scholar. He said the DEVIL was the artificer of all evils, the lord of subcelestial things, and the counterpart to God.

In the Neoplatonic view, demons were more like the Greek DAIMONES, morally ambivalent intermediary beings rather than FALLEN ANGELS. Psellus' demonic classes are

- *leliouria,* shining or glowing ones who live in the ether, a rarified sphere beyond the Moon
- *aeria,* demons of the air below the Moon
- *chthonia,* demons who live on the land
- *hydraia* or *enalia,* demons who live in the water
- *hypochthonia,* demons who live beneath the earth
- *misophaes,* blind and nearly senseless demons who hate the light and live in the lowest parts of HELL

Demons swarm everywhere. Higher demons act on the intellect, imagination, and senses, and lower demons are animalistic, causing disease and bad luck and engaging in POSSESSION. Lower demons can speak, and they utter false prophecies.

Demons can be repelled by sacred words and objects in Christianity, Psellus said, and by holy women and men, who can cause them great pain.

Purson (Curson) FALLEN ANGEL and 20th of the 72 SPIRITS OF SOLOMON. Purson once was in the angelic order of virtues and partly in the order of thrones. In HELL, he is a great king. He appears as a lion-headed man, riding on a bear and carrying a viper. He is preceded by many trumpeters. Purson hides and reveals treasure; discerns the past, present, and future; provides good FAMILIARS; and gives true answers about matters both human and divine. He commands 22 LEGIONS of DEMONS.

rabisu A type of Babylonian DEMON who lurks at the thresholds of homes, waiting to attack humans. *Rabisu* means "the ones that lie in wait."

The *rabisu* were deeply feared in Babylonian times. Inverted bowls inscribed with magical charms were placed at the corners of foundations in an effort to trap and contain them. (See INCANTATION BOWL.) An ancient inscription about them says that doors and bolts will not stop them. They can glide into doors as SERPENTs do and enter through windows as the wind does. *Rabisu* also perch on rooftops waiting to devour newborn infants.

Not all *rabisu* are evil; some are good.

See BAR EGARA.

Rais, Gilles de. See GILLES DE RAIS.

rakshasas The most powerful and numerous DEMONs of the Indian underworld, feared as cannibals, vampires, night stalkers, assassins, "dark faces," and biters. *Rakshasa* means "to guard" and refers to the demons' task of guarding the elixir of immortality found on the floor of the ocean.

The *rakshasas* are ruled by RAVANA and live on the island of Lanka. They haunt burial grounds, reanimate dead bodies, and cannibalize people. They have a multitude of grotesque shapes, with the heads of SERPENTs or animals, two to four crooked legs, and long sharp teeth. Some are beautiful, however, and go about in magnificent clothing.

Ranfaing, Elizabeth de See NANCY POSSESSION.

Raum (Raym) FALLEN ANGEL and 40th of the 72 SPIRITS OF SOLOMON. Raum is an earl who appears as a crow but will shift to human form when commanded to do so. He steals treasure, even from kings, and carries it anywhere. He destroys cities and the dignities of men. Raum also discerns the past, present, and future and makes friends and enemies love each other. Before his fall, he was in the angelic order of thrones. He governs 30 LEGIONs of DEMONs.

Ravana Powerful Indian DEMON who is lord and master of the fearsome *RAKSHASAS*. Ravana's parents are Visravas and Nikasha, descendants of the first demons created. Ravana is equal in stature to SATAN. He and his hordes of demons live on the island of Sri Lanka (formerly Ceylon).

Ravana has 10 heads, 20 arms, copper-colored eyes, bright teeth, and a huge form. His body is covered with the scars of battle wounds. He can stand as tall as a mountain and with a single look stop the Sun and Moon in their paths. He breaks all laws and ravishes any woman of his choice. He has a regal bearing.

The *Ramayana* tells a great deal about Ravana. The city of Lanka, solid gold, was built by Visva-Karma for Ravana's half brother, Kuvera. Ravana overthrew him and stole his magical chariot, which he uses to leave the island and stir up trouble in the world.

Ravana has a trickster side to him. He spent years in penance to Brahma, then forced the great god to repay him by making him invulnerable to all the gods. Then he declared war on the gods, who could not defeat him. He captured many of them, forcing them into servitude on Lanka. Eventually they escaped and plotted their revenge.

Ravana went next to Siva and did penance, hoping for the favor of immortality. He stood on one of his heads for 1,000 years. Siva was unmoved. Ravana cut off the head and stood on another one for 1,000 years. This went on until Ravana had exhausted all of his heads, and it seemed that he would have to cut off the last one. Siva at last granted Ravana immortality, the most beautiful woman in the world, and the sacred phallus, Atmalingham, for his mother. The boons were short-lived, however, for Siva tricked Ravana on his return to Lanka and forced him to return all the favors.

Ravana declared war on the gods again. Still unable to defeat him because of his invulnerability, they appealed to Vishnu for help. Vishnu cut himself into quarters, each of which became mortal. The strongest and purest was Rama, who had the power to kill Ravana.

Ravana kidnapped Rama's wife, Sita, and imprisoned her on Lanka. He threatened to eat her unless she agreed to marry him. Sita held him off long enough for Rama to build a bridge to Lanka, where Rama engaged in battles with Ravana. Finally, Rama shot an arrow clean through the demon, killing him.

Raysiel DEMON among the 31 AERIAL SPIRITS OF SOLOMON. Raysiel serves under DEMORIEL and rules as a king in the north, attended by 50 dukes during the day and 50 more at night. Each duke has 50 servants. The daytime demons are good-natured; the nighttime demons are evil, stubborn, and disobedient. The 16 major dukes of the day are Baciar, Thoac, Sequiel, Sadar, Terath, Astael, Rarnica, Dubarus, Armena, Albhadur, Chanael, Fursiel, Baetasiel, Melcha, Tharas, and Vriel. The 14 of the night are Thariel, Paras, Arayl, Culmar, Lazaba, Aleisi, Sebach, Betasiel, Belsay, Morael, Sarach, Arepach, Lamas, and Thurcal.

Remy, Nicholas (Nicholas Rémy, Remigius) (1530–1616) French lawyer, demonologist, and witch hunter. Nicholas Remy claimed to have sent 900 witches to their deaths over a 15-year period in Lorraine, France. Remy's book, *Demonolatry,* served as a leading guide for witch hunters.

Remy was born in Charmes to a Roman Catholic family of distinguished lawyers. His father was mayor of Charmes. He followed the family tradition and studied law at the University of Toulouse. He practiced in Paris from 1563 to 1570, when he was appointed lieutenant general of Vosges, filling a vacancy created by his retiring uncle. He held chairs in law and literature at several French universities. Remy also was a historian and poet and wrote several works on history. He was married and had "numerous" children, including three sons.

As a youth Remy had witnessed the trials of witches, which shaped his later opinions that witches were thoroughly evil and must be exterminated. He believed that France was riddled with secret covens of witches plotting malicious acts in league with DEMONS and the DEVIL. He even believed that everything unexplained and not normal is in the "cursed domain of demonology."

In 1575, Remy was appointed secretary and privy councillor to Duke Charles III of Lorraine and went to live in Nancy. The duke also made him a provost of Nancy. There were four to six provosts, and they constituted a ducal court that judged all criminal cases, including those involving sorcery and witchcraft. Remy was zealous in pursuing the latter cases and, if he could not judge them himself, had detailed reports submitted to him. He earned the title of "scourge of the witches." His dedication impressed the duke, who conferred a noble title upon him as a reward.

In 1582, Remy took up his own personal crusade against witches in greater earnest. Several days after refusing to give money to a beggar woman, his eldest son died. Remy was convinced the woman was a witch and successfully prosecuted her for bewitching his son to death. He controlled all the courts within his jurisdiction and ordered all the magistrates to prosecute witches. He even took to the road himself to make certain that his orders were followed. No village was too small for his inspection.

As did his contemporary Jean Bodin, Remy believed in Devil's PACTs, wild SABBATs, and *maleficia* against people and beasts. He believed fantastic stories about demons raising mountains in the blink of an eye, making rivers run backward, extinguishing the stars, and making the sky fall. As did Bodin and other authorities, he advocated the torture of witches and their execution by burning.

In 1592, after a decade of prosecuting witches, Remy retired to the countryside to escape the plague. There, he compiled *Demonolatry,* which was published in 1595 in Lyons. The book is divided into three parts: a study of SATANISM, accounts of the activities of witches, and Remy's conclusions, based on confessions and evidence obtained in the 900 trials.

Remy discussed the powers, activities, and limitations of demons. He asserted that witches and demons were inextricably linked. He described witches' black magic and spells, the various ways in which they poisoned people, and their infernal escapades with demons and the DEVIL. Demons prepared ointments, powders, and poisons for witches to use against human beings and beasts.

He devoted much space to describing satanic pacts and the feasting, dancing, and sexual orgies that took place at sabbats. He described how the Devil drew people into his service, first with cajoling and promises of wealth, power, love, or comfort, then with threats of disaster or death, such as the following:

> At Guermingen, 19th Dec., 1589, Antoine Welch no longer dared oppose the Demon in anything after he threatened to twist his neck unless he obeyed his commands, for he seemed on the very point of fulfilling his threat. . . . Certainly there are many examples in pagan histories of houses being cast down, the destruction of the crops, chasms in the earth, fiery blasts and other such disastrous tempests stirred up by Demons for the destruction of men for no other purpose than to bind their minds to the observance of some new cult and to establish their mastery more and more firmly over them.
>
> Therefore we may first conclude that it is no mere fable that witches meet and converse with Demons in very person. Secondly, it is clear that Demons use the two most powerful weapons of persuasion against the feeble wills of mortals, namely, hope and fear, desire and terror; for they well know how to induce and inspire such emotions.

Remy believed that ghosts of the dead could not remain on Earth and could not be summoned from the grave through necromancy. Such entities, he said, were demons masquerading as souls of the dead, and he cited similar statements by St. Justin Martyr, one of the early fathers of the church. Remy said the body is completely dissolved by death and cannot be reconstituted in any way. Ghosts were in reality "foul and unclean spirits" inhabiting "stinking corpses."

Remy's claim of sending 900 witches to their deaths cannot be corroborated by existing records; he cites only 128 cases himself in his book. Nevertheless, his arguments impressed others as reasoned and beyond refute. *Demonolatry* was an immediate success and was reprinted eight times, including two German translations. It became a leading handbook of witch hunters, replacing the *MALLEUS MALEFICARUM* in some parts of Europe.

Remy continued in the service of the duke until his death in Charmes in April 1612, secure in the righteousness of his work.

FURTHER READING:

Finlay, Anthony. *Demons! The Devil, Possession and Exorcism.* London: Blandford, 1999.

Remy, Nicholas. *Demonolatry.* Secaucus, N.J.: University Books, 1974.

Revelation   The last book of the New Testament, which portrays a final conflict between the forces of good and evil. Also called the book of the Apocalypse and the Apocalypse of John, Revelation portrays the Second Coming of Christ, the final triumph of the kingdom of God, and the destruction of all evil. The opening verse presents the book's title as meaning either "the

Revelation (© RICHARD COOK)

revelation that Christ possesses and imparts" or "the unveiling of the person of Christ." It is a message sent by God through the celestial Jesus to an angel and then to the author, John.

Revelation is the only book of the New Testament whose character is exclusively prophetic. The text has been the subject of criticisms and commentaries for centuries and was even controversial in the early times of Christianity.

The book officially became part of the Christian canon by the fourth century C.E. The identity of the author, John, an exile on the island of Patmos, remains in doubt. Even some of the church fathers assumed he was John the Evangelist, the author of the Gospel of John. It is more likely that the text was written by various authors who blended Christian and Jewish symbolism.

There are four main schools of interpretation of the book. The preterists (from the Latin term *praeter*, meaning beyond or past) hold that the book tells the story of the contemporary condition of the state of Rome and the church, told in a mystical code that hides the meaning from hostile pagans. Those of the historical school hold that the symbolic form tells the story of the entire historical life of the church, not just its contemporary condition.

The futurists hold that some passages refer to the contemporary scene, and some to the return of Christ at the end of time. The symbolic school sees the book as a dramatic picture of the war between good and evil, which exists in varying degrees in every historical age.

The four great visions presented in Revelation are each introduced with the phrase "in the spirit," near the beginning of the first, fourth, seventh, and 21st chapters. Each of the four visions presents the seer in a different location, each paints a distinctive picture of Christ, and each advances the previous vision.

The book is written in three parts. Part 1 features letters addressed to seven of the groups of Christians of the Roman province of Asia. The letters of the churches (chapters 1–3) are thought to have originally existed as a separate text. They depict Christ's continuing relationship with his followers. The seven local churches may have been chosen to represent successive periods in the life of the church as a whole.

Part 2 features the visions of judgment and the victory of God over the forces of evil. By extensive use of the number 7 and other mystical numbers and symbols, the book foretells (or "reveals") a violent end of the world. First, seven seals are broken on a scroll that reveal visions of what is to come.

The first four seals reveal the Four Horsemen, often called the Four Horsemen of the Apocalypse. These are symbols of the evils to come at the Second Coming: a white horse (conquest), a red horse (war), a black horse (famine), and a pale horse (plague).

The fifth seal concerns the vengeance of the saints, who have been "killed on account of the Word of God." They are given white robes and told to be patient a little longer while more of their fellow servants and brothers will be killed.

The sixth seal reveals a cosmic catastrophe caused by the "wrath of the Lamb." There is a violent earthquake, the Sun goes black, the Moon turns red as BLOOD, and stars fall from the sky. All the people of the earth, including the mighty, hide.

The seventh seal tells how ANGELs are ordered to wreak destruction upon the land, to strike and kill everyone save for 144,000 people marked with a cross on their foreheads. The angels blow their trumpets, and the earth burns, the seas turn to blood, fire falls from the sky, and water turns to wormwood. One-third of everything, including the celestial bodies, is destroyed. The Abyss opens and belches smoke and pours out locusts with scorpion tails upon the earth, demonic forces that torture people.

Signs appear in heaven: a woman clothed with the Sun and standing on a crescent Moon, who gives birth to a boy who is taken into heaven; and a seven-headed red dragon with 10 horns and crowns of coronets. A war—Armageddon—breaks out in heaven. Michael and his angels attack the dragon, known as the DEVIL or SATAN, who fights back with his own army of DEMONs. The satanic forces are defeated, driven out of heaven, and hurled to the earth. But it is not yet the end for evil, for Satan rises anew as beasts from the land and sea. The beast that rises out of the sea is like a leopard with bear paws and a lion's mouth, and the dragon's seven heads and 10 horns. The beast that emerges from the earth has two horns like a lamb and makes noise like a dragon.

The beast worshippers are marked with the number equivalent to its name, 666 (see SIX-SIX-SIX), while Jesus and his special 144,000—those who will ascend to heaven—are marked with the name of God. An angel warns that beast worshippers will be condemned to eternal torture and punishment (HELL). The faithful are exhorted to fear God and glorify him.

God's wrath has not ended, however. Seven angels unleash seven plagues upon the earth, including demon spirits who look like frogs and are able to work miracles. The whore of Babylon, the "mother of all the prostitutes and all the filthy practices on the earth," appears riding the Satanic seven-headed, 10-horned beast. The dead are summoned to the throne of God and are judged.

Part three features a vision of heaven. John is taken to a high mountain, where he looks down on the perfect holy city of Jerusalem, constructed on the number 12. God and the Lamb are in radiant glory. There are a river of life and trees of life. John sees a new heaven and a new

Revelation (© RICHARD COOK)

Jerusalem. Creation is made anew. The book concludes with a call to all those who listen to "come."

The immediacy of the Last Day is a belief of many Christian groups. Even the first-century Christians interpreted the New Testament, especially the closing two verses of Revelation, to mean these events were to happen in their lifetime. St. Augustine believed that the Second Coming of Christ would happen in the year 1,000. Ever since, some religious leaders have prophesied a specific time for the final day.

Possession by the Apocalypse Archetype
The Apocalypse presented in Revelation is deeply embedded in the Western collective psyche as an archetype, one capable of possessing people and dramatically influencing their behavior, according to the Jungian analyst Edward F. Edinger. Such individuals become religious zealots and exhibit the traits of both criminals and the insane, Edinger said. Two notable examples of "possession by Apocalypse archetype" he cited are David Koresh and the Heaven's Gate cult.

Koresh, born in 1959 as Vernon Howell, became convinced that God had revealed to him total understanding of Revelation. He identified himself with the "apocalyptic Lamb" and established a cult in Waco, Texas, the Branch Davidians, ruling it with an iron hand. In 1993, the compounded was raided by federal agents of the Bureau of Alcohol, Tobacco and Firearms and was set on fire. Koresh was among those killed in the blaze.

Heaven's Gate, under the leadership of Marshall Applewhite and Bonnie Nettles, believed in the coming end of the world as described in Revelation and thought that they and their followers would be martyred by the beast of the abyss and would ascend to heaven. Applewhite and Nettles had identified themselves since 1972 with the "two witnesses" described in Revelation 11, the two lampstands and two olive trees in attendance to the Lord, who would prophesy for 1,260 days.

Nettles died of cancer in 1985. By 1997, the group grew tired of waiting for biblical martyrdom and contemplated provoking the government to speed events along. They also believed that the resurrection cloud described in Revelation would manifest as a UFO or spaceship full of aliens. The appearance of the comet Hale-Bopp in 1997 was seen as a sign that Nettles was approaching in a ship behind the comet to collect her flock for the Rapture to heaven. The entire group of 39 persons committed mass suicide by drinking poison.

FURTHER READING:
Edinger, Edward F. *Archetype of the Apocalypse: A Jungian Study of the Book of Revelation.* Chicago: Open Court, 1999.

Rimmon   FALLEN ANGEL. *Rimmon* means "exalted" or "roarer" in Hebrew. Originally, Rimmon was an Aramaic deity and Syrian idol. In Babylonian and Semite lore, he was the god of thunder and storms. As a DEMON, he is infernal ambassador to Russia.

Rituale Romanum   Catholic priest's service manual that includes the only formal EXORCISM rites sanctioned by an established church. First written in 1614 under Pope Paul V, the *Rituale Romanum* remained untouched until 1952, when two small revisions were made in the language. More revisions were done by the Second Vatican Council (1962–65), and the rite was reissued in 1999.

The *Rituale* includes rites for BAPTISM, confirmation, the Holy Eucharist, penance, anointing the sick, marriage, the holy orders of priesthood, the seven pentential psalms and liturgy of the saints, death and burial, blessings, processions, and litanies, besides exorcism.

As early as its 17th-century publication, the *Rituale* strongly cautions the priest against exorcism when no true POSSESSION exists. As medical science further defines illnesses previously thought to be the result of demonic interference—hysteria, epilepsy, multiple personality disorder, schizophrenia, paranoia, sexual dysfunction, and other neuroses brought on by childhood terrors and obsessions—determining true possession has become increasingly difficult. The 1952 revisions change the wording that symptoms of possession "*are* signs of the presence of a demon" to "*might be.*" Those in alternative states to possession, originally described as "those who suffer from melancholia or any other illness," became "those who suffer from illness, particularly mental illnesses." Many devout Christians have turned away from the idea of possessing DEMONS at all.

More revisions were undertaken by the Second Vatican Council. Since 1999, the exorcism portion has been reissued in a new 90-page document, *De Exorcismus et Supplicationibus Quibusdam (Concerning Exorcisms and Certain Supplications).* The rite includes prayers and passages from the Bible and calls upon the demons, in powerful Latin, to depart in the name of Jesus Christ.

The new version eliminates some of the rough medieval language used to describe the Devil. And instead of having the exorcist command the demons or Devil to leave the victim, the exorcist now calls on God to command the demons to leave.

Guidelines also were issued stating that exorcisms should not be performed as part of healing services or masses, especially any involving hysteria, theatrics, or sensationalism.

However, if the victim exhibits paranormal capabilities, shows superhuman strength, and, most importantly, manifests knowledge of previously unknown languages, then he or she is a possible candidate for demonic exorcism. If such symptoms accompany extreme revulsion toward sacred texts and objects, then the church may deem the victim possessed. With permission from a bishop, the exorcist begins the ancient ritual.

Exorcism is not a sacrament but a rite and is not dependent on rigid adherence to a set of actions. Rather, exorcism relies on the authorization of the church and the faith of the exorcist. The exorcist is free to vary the procedure, substituting his own favorite prayers, altering the sequence of events, or speaking in his own language. Most exorcists have found, however, that Latin particularly bothers evil spirits.

The *Rituale* exhorts the exorcist to make sure that the victim is possessed and not suffering from mental illness. Even during exorcism, the priest should continue to question the victim about his or her mental and spiritual state. Under no circumstances should the exorcist offer medicine to the victim, leaving such work to the medical practitioner. If the possessed is a woman, the exorcist should be assisted by a strong woman, preferably from the possessed's family, to prevent any hint of scandal. The possessed should hold a crucifix during the exorcism, and the exorcist is encouraged to use holy water and relics, recite passages from the Bible, and liberally make the sign of the cross over the victim. Finally, the exorcist should speak in a commanding voice, only questioning the Devil about his name, the number of demons in possession, where they are from, and how they got there.

Before beginning, the priest should make confession. Then, donning a surplice and purple stole (required of an exorcising priest), the exorcist stands before the possessed and recites the Litanies of the Saints, the Pater Noster (the Lord's Prayer), and Psalm 53. He calls upon the demon to state why it is possessing the victim and when it intends to depart. The demon is asked to name itself, giving the exorcist an advantage. The exorcist gives more Scripture readings, then does a laying on of hands. He calls upon God to command the demon to leave, then enjoins the spirit to succumb to JESUS and depart back to HELL, the depths of *gehennam*.

Each recitation is accompanied by more prayers, including the Ave Maria (Hail Mary), the Gloria Patri (Glory Be to the Father), the Anima Christi (Body of Christ), the Salve Regina (Save us, merciful Mary), the sign of the cross, and Scripture readings. The demon is enjoined a second time; the exorcist repeats each of these acts until the demon leaves permanently.

The victim, released from evil, is then encouraged to profess faith in Christ and refrain from evil thoughts and actions so as to provide no haven for devils in the future. More prayers are said, and then, finally, the exorcist asks the Lord's help in protecting the victim from further harm.

Exorcising demonic infestation of a place rather than a person follows a shorter ritual. The priest invokes the archangel Michael to intercede with Christ on behalf of the church and to crush the serpent. This call is followed by a formal announcement of the exorcism, prayer, then an address to Satan and his legions to leave the place and harm it no longer. The priest offers more prayers, always accompanied by the sign of the cross, and blesses the place with holy water.

FURTHER READING:
Martin, Malachi. *Hostage to the Devil*. New York: Harper & Row, 1976.
Oesterreich, Traugott K. *Possession and Exorcism*. Secaucus, N.J.: University Books, 1966.
Wilkinson, Tracy. *The Vatican's Exorcists: Driving Out the Devil in the 21st Century*. New York: Warner Books, 2007.

Roche Rock   Three-pointed outcropping of rock in the Bodmin Moor in Cornwall, England, said to be haunted by demonic spirits. Roche Rock, several miles south of the town of Bodmin, was formed millions of years ago out of gray quartz and black tourmaline, distinctly different from the surrounding granite and clay. Numerous legends are associated with it.

Roche Rock juts up from the boggy moor and cuts a striking, brooding figure on the landscape. It has been associated with sacred and supernatural lore. St. Conan, the first bishop of Cornwall, was said to have lived atop the largest of the three peaks as a hermit prior to becoming bishop. In 1409, a brick chapel was built there, supposedly by the last male heir of Tregarrick, and was dedicated to the archangel St. Michael. A man suffering from leprosy took up residence there as a hermit and was attended by his daughter, St. Gundred, until he died.

The area around Roche Rock was said to be the hunting grounds of King Arthur. Another hermit said to have lived there was Ogrin, who gave refuge to the legendary lovers Tristan and Iseult when they were trying to escape King Mark of Cornwall.

According to lore, JAN TREGEAGLE tried to find refuge at Roche Rock when he was being pursued across the moor by the DEVIL and his hellhounds. Tregeagle's head became stuck in the east window of the chapel. His ghost haunts the rock, especially when winds howl around the moor.

Roche Rock is also said to be haunted by DEMONS, mine spirits, a phantom monk, and the ghost of the leper hermit.

FURTHER READING:
Bird, Sheila. *Haunted Places of Cornwall: On the Trail of the Paranormal*. Newbury, England: Countryside Books, 2006.

Ronove (Roneve, Ronobe)   FALLEN ANGEL and 27th of the 72 SPIRITS OF SOLOMON. Ronobe is an earl and marquis who appears as a monster. He teaches rhetoric and art, as well as knowledge and understanding of languages. He gives the favor of friends and enemies. He has 19 LEGIONS of DEMONS.

***Rosemary's Baby* (1967)**   Ira Levin's novel about Devil-worshipping witches who conspire to have a woman bear the ANTICHRIST.

Rosemary's Baby was made into a film in 1968, starring Mia Farrow as the victim mother, John Cassavetes as her opportunistic husband who sells her out to the DEVIL, and Ruth Gordon and Sidney Blackmer as the ringleader witches of a coven. Ralph Bellamy stars as a doctor and member of the coven. Much of the shooting was done at the Dakota, New York's brooding Gothic residence of the rich and famous and the site where, in 1980, John Lennon was fatally shot.

Levin's plot deals with Devil worshippers who call themselves witches. They follow the Devil's instructions to arrange for him to rape the woman the Devil has chosen to conceive and deliver the Antichrist.

The story takes place in New York City in 1966. Rosemary and Guy Woodhouse are young newlyweds in search of a new apartment. Guy is a mediocre actor struggling to succeed but barely making it in bit parts and commercials. At the sinister-looking Branford building, Rosemary falls in love with an apartment and persuades Guy to rent it. The apartment belonged to a mysterious old woman who grew herbs and died in a coma.

After taking the apartment, the Woodhouses learn from a writer friend, Edward Hutchins ("Hutch"), that the Branford has a long and dark history of crime and strange happenings, including cannibal sisters and a dead

Mia Farrow as Rosemary Woodhouse, whose husband sells her to Satan in order to give birth to his demonic son in Roman Polanski's film Rosemary's Baby *(1968)* (AUTHOR'S COLLECTION)

baby found in the basement. It was home to the notorious Adrian Marcato, a self-proclaimed witch of the late 19th century, who claimed to be able to conjure up the Devil. The Woodhouses laugh it off.

The Woodhouses meet their odd neighbors, Minnie and Roman Castevet, following the suicide of a young girl who was living with them. Unbeknownst to Rosemary, the Castevets seduce Guy with promises of professional success in exchange for the satanic rape of Rosemary. Rosemary is drugged by a chocolate mousse dessert made by Minnie but remains conscious enough during her hideous ordeal to know that it is not a dream. The naked witches stand around her chanting while an inhuman monster with animal eyes, reptilian skin, and a huge penis rapes her. The following morning, she uncomfortably decides it was a dream, after all. Guy tells her he made love to her while she was asleep.

Rosemary becomes pregnant, and the Castevets convince her to see Dr. Abraham Saperstein. Saperstein prescribes a daily "vitamin" drink made by Minnie, supposedly containing fresh herbs. The true ingredient is a mysterious and vile-smelling "tanis root." This root, which is more like a fungus, also is contained in a silver amulet necklace the Castevets give Rosemary to wear—the same necklace worn by the suicidal girl.

The pregnancy does not go well. Rosemary loses weight and suffers constant pain, which Saperstein tells her is not unusual. When Hutch visits and hears of the tanis root, he becomes alarmed and does research. He attempts to tell Rosemary of his findings but is felled by a coma and dies before he is able to do so, murdered by a CURSE cast by the witches. At his funeral, a woman gives Rosemary a book that Hutch had wanted her to have, along with the message that "the name is an anagram."

The book, *All of Them Witches*, tells of a fungus known as "Devil's pepper" used in rituals, and profiles various infamous witches, among them Adrian Marcato. Rosemary gets out her Scrabble set to try to decipher the anagram in the book's title, but nothing makes sense. Then she notices that the name of Marcato's son, Steven, is underlined in the book. *Steven Marcato* rearranges to *Roman Castevet*. Rosemary buys books on witchcraft, which tell her that witches cast malevolent spells upon people to maim and kill them and use BLOOD in their rituals—particularly baby's blood—as well as human flesh. She surmises the witches want her baby to use in their rituals.

The dark forces close in on Rosemary, despite her attempts to save herself. She appeals to Guy, then discovers he is part of the conspiracy. The same thing happens with Saperstein. She attempts to escape, but the witches trap her in her apartment, and she is delivered of the baby. She is told the baby was stillborn, but she discovers the witches are keeping it in the Castevets' apartment.

The coven convenes to hail the birth of the Antichrist, who has been named Adrian Steven. Rosemary, armed with a knife, appears. She is told how the Devil chose her for her role. When she first sees the infant, swaddled in black in a black bassinet, she is horrified and can hardly bear to look upon the golden-yellow animal eyes, the orange-red hair, the tail, and the budding horns. His little hands, which have "tiny, pearly" claws, are encased in black mittens so that he does not scratch himself. Rosemary decides she will kill the creature and commit sui-cide, but then becomes fascinated with it; it is, after all, hers. With the witches' encouragement, she begins to mother it, holding on to a naive hope that she will be able to exert a good influence over it. The Antichrist gains a foothold in the world.

Rosemary's Baby influenced other coming-of-the-Anti-christ films, such as *The Omen* (1976), about an adopted child Devil who escapes destruction.

sabbat A wild party of witches, heretics, DEMONS, and the DEVIL in a remote location. The participants supposedly indulge in obscene behavior, orgies, gluttony, blasphemy, worship of the Devil, and the cannibalism of roasted infants. Use of the term *sabbat* or *sabbath* to describe these rites may derive from the Hebrew term *sabbath*, or synagogue.

During the witch hysteria of the Inquisition, lurid confessions were tortured out of accused witches and were recorded by zealous demonologists. However, no historical evidence exists that such rites ever really took place. Rather, they were probably degraded, contorted descriptions of pagan seasonal festivals, as well as the Inquisition's stance that heretics practiced obscene rites.

The idea of demonic revelry was well in place in Christianity long before the Inquisition, however, in the increasing demonization of pagan deities, and in folklore such as the WILD HUNT. For example, the 10th-century Benedictine abbot Regino of Prum wrote in his *De ecclesiasticis disciplinis*:

> This too must by no means be passed over that certain utterly abandoned women, turning aside to follow Satan, being seduced by the illusions and phantasmical shows of demons firmly believe and openly profess that in the dead of night they ride upon certain beasts along with the pagan goddess Diana and a countless horde of women, and that in those silent hours they fly over vast tracts of country and obey her as their mistress, while on

certain other nights they are summoned to do her homage and pay her service.

The first appearance of a sabbat in trials of the Inquisition occurred in Toulouse in 1335. Anne Marie de Georgel and Catherine Delort confessed to a having a PACT with the Devil for about 20 years to serve him in life and after death. On Friday nights, they attended sabbats held in various locations. Georgel said that the Devil appeared in the form of a goat and had sex with her and taught her how to use poisonous plants. Delort said that she, too, copulated with the goat. The witches ate newborn infants stolen from their nurses during the night and drank vile brews.

The term *sabbat* (also *sabbath*) for these meetings was not used with consistency until about the mid-15th century, but after the Toulouse trials, descriptions of the rites were always similar. The sabbat played a more prominent role in Europe during the witch hunts than it did in England, where there is no record of a witch sabbat prior to 1620, except for an innocuous feast that was termed a "sabbat" in the Lancashire witch trials of 1612.

Sabbats sometimes took place during the day, but most usually occurred at night in remote locations, such as mountains, caves, and deep forest areas. The favored beginning time was midnight, after a dance. The best-known gathering place for sabbats, according to demonologists, was the Brocken in the Harz Mountains of Germany, where the greatest activity took place on Walpurgisnacht (Beltane), April 30. Witches testified at their trials that hundreds of them would gather at these sabbats. They wore masks to protect their identities.

The frequency of sabbats varied with testimonies at witch trials. Witches were said to participate in them frequently, once to several times a week. In the AIX-EN-PROVENCE POSSESSIONS trials of 1614, Maria de Sains said they took place daily, with special sabbats of blasphemy and the BLACK MASS on Wednesdays and Fridays. Other reports were tied to pagan observances, such as the previously mentioned Walpurgisnacht and Lammas Day (August 1), Midsummer (June 22), and Samhain (October 31).

To travel to a sabbat, witches left their homes by rising up through the chimney and flying through the air, sometimes on the backs of demons that had metamorphosed into animals or astride broomsticks, poles, reeds, or farm tools. The witches themselves sometimes shape shifted into animals and were accompanied by their FAMILIARS. They left behind them demons in their forms in their beds to fool their spouses. When asked by inquisitors how they

could get their bodies through narrow chimneys, some witches said the Devil removed all obstacles so that they had enough room. As payment for their transport, witches said, they were defiled by the demons in animal form. Sometimes witches said they walked to sabbats, usually to a wooded area outside their village.

The Devil usually appeared in the shape of a goat, ugly and smelly, though at times he was said to arrive as a toad, crow, or black cat. He presided over the sabbat while sitting on a throne. The Devil turned into a foul-smelling goat, and the witches took off their clothes and paid homage to him by falling to their knees and kissing his anus.

Witches were forced to confess their latest crimes of evil. If they had committed none since the previous sabbat, they were beaten by demons.

Unbaptized infants were offered up as sacrifices. New witches were initiated by signing the Devil's BLACK BOOK in BLOOD, renouncing Christianity, taking an oath, and trampling upon the cross. The Devil marked his initiates

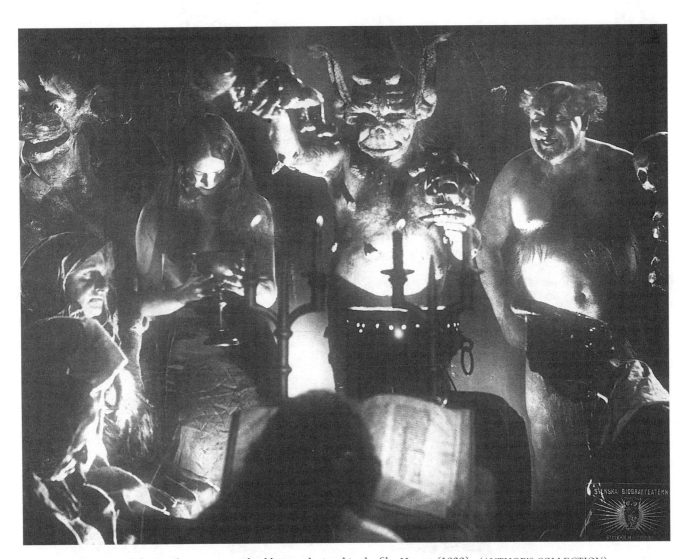

Witches gather around the Devil at a nocturnal sabbat, as depicted in the film Haxan *(1922).* (AUTHOR'S COLLECTION)

with his claw (see DEVIL'S MARK). There followed a great feast, with much drinking and eating, although demonologists often noted that the food tasted vile, and that no salt was present, for nothing evil could abide salt. If infants had been sacrificed, they were cooked and eaten by roasting or made into pies. Witches ate disinterred corpses and drank wine that looked and tasted like clotted black blood. If they refused to eat and drink or spat it out, they were beaten by demons.

After the feasting—which always left people hungry and never satisfied—were dancing and indiscriminate copulation among the witches and demons. Witches danced with their backs to one another as an additional precaution to prevent being recognized. They did ring dances, moving widdershins, or counterclockwise. One example cited by both FRANCESCO-MARIA GUAZZO and NICHOLAS REMY was that of Johann von Hembach, a German youth who lived in the late 16th century. His mother allegedly was a witch and took him one night to a sabbat. Von Hembach was a skilled flute player, and his mother told him to climb up into a tree and play for the assembly. He did so and was aghast at the revelry that he watched while he played. He exclaimed, "Good God! Where did this crowd of fools and madmen come from?" As soon as he uttered the words, he fell out of the tree and injured his shoulder. When he called for help, the witches vanished.

Von Hembach talked freely about this experience, which some believed and others said was an imaginative vision. In 1589, a witch who supposedly was present at that sabbat, Catharina Prevotte, was arrested on charges of witchcraft in Freissen. Prevotte told the same story. Two other women found guilty of witchcraft in 1590, Otilla Kelvers and Anguel Eysartz, also told the same story and said that the sabbat had taken place at Mayebuch.

The witches also conducted obscene religious masses (see BLACK MASS). On occasion, the witches would go out into the night and raise storms or cause other trouble. The witches flew home before dawn and the crow of the cock.

The nights of the sabbats varied. Some witches said they attended weekly sabbats, some at the traditional pagan seasonal festival times, and others only once or twice a year.

In 1459–60, accused witches tried at Arras, France, confessed to sabbats, described by the inquisitor Pierre le Broussard:

When they want to go to the *vauderie*, they spread an ointment, which the Devil has given them, on a wooden stick and rub it on their palms and all over their hands also; then they put the stick between their legs and fly off over towns, woods and stretches of water, being led by the devil himself to the place where their assembly is to be held. There they meet together and the also they find tables loaded with wines and things to eat, and there the devil appears to them, sometimes in the form of a he-goat, sometimes as a dog or monkey; never in

human form. They make oblations and pay homage to the Devil, worshiping him. Many of them give him their souls or at least part of their bodies. Then with candles in their hands they kiss the hind parts of the goat that is the Devil. . . .

. . . When the paying of homage was over, they all walked over a cross spitting on it, scorning Christ and the Holy Trinity. Then they exposed their hinder parts to the sky and the heavens above as a sign of their disregard for God, and, after eating and drinking their fill, they all had sexual intercourse; and the Devil appeared in both the form of a man and of a woman, and the men had intercourse with him in the form of a woman and the women in the form of a man. They also committed sodomy and practiced homosexuality and other vile and monstrous crimes against god and nature.

In 1659, a French shepherdess gave this description of a sabbat that occurred on the summer solstice, observed by her and some companions:

[They] heard a noise and a very dreadful uproar, and, looking on all sides to see whence could come these frightful howlings and these cries of all sorts of animals, they saw at the foot of the mountain the figures of cats, goats, serpents, dragons, and every kind of cruel, impure and unclean animal, who were keeping their Sabbath and making horrible confusion, who were uttering words that were most filthy and sacrilegious that can be imagined and filling the air with the most abominable blasphemies.

Sabbat accounts even appeared in witchcraft cases in the American colonies. In the 1692–93 hysteria in Salem, Massachusetts, accused witches participated in "Diabolical Sacraments," according to the Puritan minister and witch hunter Cotton Mather.

Heretics as well as witches indulged in these rites. For example, the Fratricelli, a sect that broke away from the Franciscan order, were said to hold orgiastic sabbats. Children born from the orgies were sacrificed and burned, and their ashes were mixed into the wine drunk by the priests. Similarly, the Waldenses, whom the church eventually eradicated, were said to turn to the Devil and make pacts with him because they were excluded from the church.

Demonologists debated whether people attended sabbats in physical reality or in flights of imagination. The *MALLEUS MALEFICARUM* (1487), the leading inquisitors' handbook, insisted that witches could be transported bodily, although some did have imaginary experiences. Henri Boguet was among demonologists who believed in literal rites.

Remy said that both real and imaginary sabbats occurred. He cited the confessions of witches such as Prevotte, mentioned earlier, that sometimes witches were fully awake and present, and sometimes they visited in their sleep. Their demons either transported them bodily or impressed images upon their sleeping minds.

Remy gave examples of supposed genuine sabbats. On July 25, 1590, a woman named Nicolette Lang-Bernhard was traveling from a mill at Guermingen to Assencour. She was walking along a forest path at high noon when she came upon a group of men and women dancing in a ring in a field. They were dancing strangely, with their backs to one another. There were also demons in disguise, given away by their cloven feet like those of goats and oxen. Stricken with fear, Lang-Bernhard called out the name of JESUS for protection. Immediately all the dancers vanished, except one man, whom she recognized, Petter Gross-Petter, who rose into the air and let go of a mop. Lang-Bernhard herself was swept up into a violent, suffocating gale. She managed to go home, where she lay deathly ill in bed for three days.

Lang-Bernhard told her story, and Gross-Petter was arrested and tortured. He confessed and named others present, who also confessed. A herdsman, Johann Michel, said he had been taken from his flock and transported to the dance, where he had been forced to climb a tree and play his shepherd's crook. When Lang-Bernhard called out the name of Jesus, he fell out of the tree and found himself back with his flock.

The final proof of this event was the actual appearance of trodden soil, as though people had danced in a ring. Mingled with the human footprints were cloven hoof prints, according to court records. The imprints remained until the soil was plowed the following winter.

It is doubtful that such organized, malevolent activities ever took place. Probably the witches' sabbat was a fabrication of the witch hunters, who tortured victims to make the most outrageous confessions in order to appease the public fear of witchcraft and the church's political agenda against heretics, Protestants, rivals, and undesirables. It is plausible that seasonal festivals and other gatherings, along with traditional stories and superstitions, were twisted into diabolic sabbats by the manipulations of inquisitors. Victims who confessed were pressed to name others who had attended the sabbats. In this manner, entire villages sometimes became implicated in Devil worship.

Wiccans and Pagans use the term *sabbat* to describe their religious ceremonies, which are recreations of ancient pagan rites to observe seasonal festivals and changes. They have no connection to the diabolical rites described by earlier demonologists.

FURTHER READING:
Baroja, Julio Caro. *The World of the Witches*. Chicago: University of Chicago Press, 1975.
Guazzo, Francesco-Maria. *Compendium Maleficarum*. Secaucus, N.J.: University Books, 1974.
Lea, Henry Charles. *Materials toward a History of Witchcraft*. Philadelphia: University of Pennsylvania Press, 1939.
Monter, E. William. *Witchcraft in France and Switzerland*. New York: Cornell University Press, 1976.
Remy, Nicholas. *Demonolatry*. Secaucus, N.J.: University Books, 1974.
Russell, Jeffrey Burton. *Witchcraft in the Middle Ages*. Ithaca, N.Y., and London: Cornell University Press, 1972.
Summers, Montague. *The History of Witchcraft and Demonology*. London: Kegan Paul, Trench, Trubner, 1926.

Sabnack (Sabanack, Sabnach, Salmac) FALLEN ANGEL and 43rd of the 72 SPIRITS OF SOLOMON. Sabnack is a marquis who appears as an armed soldier with a lion's head, riding on a pale horse. He builds and fortifies towers, camps, and cities. Upon command, he torments people with wounds and maggot-filled putrid sores. He also gives good FAMILIARs at the command of an EXORCIST. He rules 50 LEGIONs of DEMONs.

Salem witchcraft hysteria Trials and executions of accused witches in Salem, Massachusetts, from 1692 to 1693. In all, 141 people were arrested as suspects, 19 were hanged, and one was pressed to death. The principal accusers were girls who claimed that witches in league with the DEVIL were attacking them and sending their DEMON FAMILIARs to attack them. Adding to the hysteria were widespread Puritan fears of demonic influences in New England, as well as political and social tensions.

Tensions were already high between Salem Village and Salem Town when the witch panic erupted, starting in the home of the Reverend Samuel Parris, who had arrived to be the fourth minister in Salem Village in 1689. Before becoming a minister, Parris had worked as a merchant in Barbados; when he returned to Massachusetts, he took back a slave couple, John and Tituba Indian (*Indian* was probably not the couple's surname but really a description of their race). Tituba cared for Parris' nine-year-old daughter, Elizabeth, called Betty, and his 11-year-old niece, Abigail Williams. Tituba probably regaled the girls with stories about her native Barbados, including magic, divination, and spell-casting.

The girls were joined by other young girls in Salem Village—Susannah Sheldon, Elizabeth Booth, Elizabeth Hubbard, Mary Warren, Sarah Churchill, Mercy Lewis, and Ann Putnam, Jr. (Ann Putnam, Sr., was her mother). Dabbling in the occult was fun in the beginning, but it soon frightened them to the point of having fits.

In January 1692, Betty Parris and others began having fits, crawling into holes, making strange noises, and contorting their bodies. It is impossible to know whether the girls feigned witchcraft to hide their involvement in Tituba's magic, or whether they believed they were possessed. In the climate of the times, they were declared by experts to be bewitched.

Seventeenth-century Puritans believed in witchcraft as a cause of illness and death and thought that witches derived their power from the Devil. So, the next step was to find the witch or witches responsible, exterminate them, and cure the girls. After much prayer and exhortation, the frightened girls, unable or unwilling to admit their own complicity, began to name names.

Tituba made a witch cake out of rye meal mixed with the urine of the afflicted girls. Taken from a traditional English recipe, the cake was then fed to the dog. If the girls were bewitched, one of two things should happen: Either the dog would suffer torments, too, or he would identify the witch as her familiar. The Reverend Parris furiously accused Mary Sibley of "going to the Devil for help against the Devil," lectured her on her sins, and publicly humiliated her in church. But the damage had been done: "The Devil hath been raised among us, and his rage is vehement and terrible," said Parris, "and when he shall be silenced, the Lord only knows."

The first accused, or "cried out against," were Tituba herself, Sarah Good, and Sarah Osborne. Warrants for their arrest were issued, and all three appeared before Salem Town magistrates John Hathorne and Jonathan Corwin on March 1. The girls, present at all interrogations, fell into fits and convulsions as each woman stood up for questioning, claiming that the woman's specter was roaming the room, biting them, pinching them, and often appearing as a bird or other animal someplace in the room, usually on a particular beam of the ceiling. Hathorne and Corwin angrily demanded why the women were tormenting the girls, but both Sarahs denied any wrongdoing.

Tituba, however, beaten since the witch cake episode by Parris and afraid to reveal the winter story sessions and conjurings, confessed to being a witch. She said that a black dog—a favored form of the Devil—had threatened her and ordered her to hurt the girls, and that two large cats, one black and one red, had made her serve them. She claimed that she had ridden through the air on a pole to "witch meetings" (see SABBAT) with Good and Osborne, accompanied by the other women's familiars: a yellow bird for Good, a winged creature with a woman's head, and another hairy one with a long nose for Osborne. Tituba cried that Good and Osborne had forced her to attack Ann Putnam, Jr., with a knife just the night before, and Ann corroborated her statement by claiming that the witches had menaced her with a knife and tried to cut off her head.

Tituba revealed that there was a coven of witches in Massachusetts, about six in number, led by a tall, white-haired man dressed all in black, and that she had seen him. During the next day's questioning, Tituba claimed that the tall man had approached her many times, forcing her to sign his devil's book in BLOOD, and that she had seen nine names already there.

All three women were taken to prison in Boston, where Good and Osborne were locked in heavy iron chains to prevent their specters from traveling about and tormenting the girls. Osborne, already frail, died there. Tituba joined the ranks of the accusers.

Complicating the legal process of arrest and trial was the loss of Massachusetts Bay's colonial charter. The colony was established as a Puritan colony in 1629 with self-rule, the English courts revoked the charter in 1684–85,

Title page of a witch-hunting pamphlet by Cotton Mather
(AUTHOR'S COLLECTION)

restricting the colony's independence. Massachusetts Bay had had no authority to try capital cases, and for the first six months of the witch hunt, suspects merely languished in prison, usually in irons.

The loss of Massachusetts' charter represented to the Puritans a punishment from God: The colony had been established in covenant with God, and prayer and fasting and good lives would keep up Massachusetts' end of the covenant and protect the colony from harm. Increasingly, the petty transgressions and factionalism of the colonists were viewed as sins against the covenant, and an outbreak of witchcraft seemed the ultimate retribution for the colony's evil ways. Published sermons by Cotton Mather and his father, Increase Mather, and the long-winded railings against witchcraft from the Reverend Parris' pulpit every Sunday convinced the villagers that evil walked among them and must be rooted out at all cost.

In May 1692, the new royal governor, Sir William Phips, established a Court of Oyer and Terminer ("to hear and determine") to try the witches. By May's end, approximately 100 people sat in prison on the basis of the girls' accusations. Bridget Bishop was first to be found guilty and was hanged on June 10.

The court had to deal with the issue of spectral evidence. The problem was not whether the girls saw the specters, but whether a righteous God could allow the Devil to afflict the girls in the shape of an innocent person. If the Devil could not assume an innocent's shape, the spectral evidence was invaluable against the accused. If he could, how else were the magistrates to tell who was guilty? The court asked for clerical opinions, and on June 15 the ministers, led by Increase and Cotton Mather, cautioned the judges against placing too much emphasis on spectral evidence alone. Other tests, such as "falling at the sight," in which victims collapse at a look from the witch, or the touch test, in which victims are relieved of their torments by touching the witch, were considered more reliable. Nevertheless, the ministers pushed for vigorous prosecution, and the court ruled in favor of allowing spectral evidence.

Of the executions, that of George Burroughs, formerly minister of Salem Village, stood out. Burroughs and several others were sent to be hanged at Gallows Hill on August 19. Before Burroughs died, he shocked the crowd by reciting the Lord's Prayer perfectly, creating an uproar. Demands for Burroughs' freedom were countered by the afflicted girls, who cried out that "the Black Man" had prompted Burroughs through his recital of the prayer. It was generally believed that even the Devil could not recite the Lord's Prayer, and the crowd's mood grew darker. A riot was thwarted by Cotton Mather, who told the crowd that Burroughs was not an ordained minister, and the Devil was known to change himself often into an angel of light if there were profit in doing so. When the crowd was calmed, Mather urged that the executions proceed, and they did. As before, the bodies were dumped into the shallow grave, leaving Burroughs' hand and chin exposed.

Samuel Wardwell, completely intimidated, confessed to signing the Devil's book for a black man who promised him riches. He later retracted his confession, but the court believed his earlier testimony. Wardwell choked on smoke from the hangman's pipe during his execution, and the hysterical girls claimed it was the Devil preventing him from finally confessing.

Giles Corey, a wealthy landowner, was pressed to death September 19 for refusing to acknowledge the court's right to try him. He was taken to a Salem field, staked to the ground, and covered with a large wooden plank. Stones were piled on the plank one at a time, until the weight was so great his tongue was forced out of his mouth. Sheriff George Corwin used his cane to poke it back into Corey's mouth. Corey's only response to the questions put to him was to ask for more weight. More stones were piled atop him, until finally he was crushed lifeless. Ann Putnam, Jr., saw his execution as divine justice, for she claimed

that when Corey had signed on with the Devil, he had been promised never to die by hanging.

The hysteria subsided when the girls began accusing more and more prominent people, including the wife of the governor, Lady Phips. On October 29, Governor Phips dissolved the Court of Oyer and Terminer, and spectral evidence became inadmissible. The trials came to an end.

Eventually, the prosecutions were seen as one more trial of God's covenant with New England—a terrible sin to be expiated. Those who had participated in the proceedings—Cotton and Increase Mather, the other clergy, the magistrates, even the accusers—suffered illness and personal setbacks in the years after the hysteria. Samuel Parris was forced to leave his ministry in Salem.

By 1703, the Massachusetts colonial legislature began granting retroactive amnesties to the convicted and executed. Even more amazing, they authorized financial restitution to the victims and their families. In 1711, Massachusetts Bay became one of the first governments ever voluntarily to compensate persons victimized by its own mistakes.

In 1693, Increase Mather acknowledged in his *Cases of Conscience Concerning Evil Spirits Personating Men* that finding a witch was probably impossible, because the determination rested on the assumption that God had set humanly recognizable limits on SATAN, but Satan and God are beyond human comprehension.

In 1957, the legislature of Massachusetts passed a resolution exonerating some of the victims. Still, citizens felt they should do more. In 1992, a memorial was erected to all the victims of the 1692 trial. It was dedicated by Elie Weisel, a Nobel laureate known for his work concerning the victims of Nazi concentration camps. The memorial is located at the Old Burying Point in Salem and is a park-like square with stone benches engraved with the names of the victims.

Saleos FALLEN ANGEL and 19th of the 72 SPIRITS OF SOLOMON. Saleos is a duke who appears as a gallant soldier wearing a duke's crown and riding on a crocodile. He promotes love between men and women and speaks authoritatively about the creation of the world. He governs 30 LEGIONS of DEMONS.

salt See AMULET.

Samael (Sammael) In Hebrew lore, the prince of DEMONS known as "the venom of God" and the executioner of death sentences decreed by God. Samael is linked to ADRAMELECH, another demon of death.

In rabbinical lore, Samael is a demon of a desert wind called Samiel or Simoon. He flies through the air like a bird, and the dark spots on the Moon are his excrement.

Samael was the SERPENT who tempted Eve in the Garden of Paradise. He was an uncircumcised sexual partner and husband of LILITH and created with her a host of de- mon children, including a son, SARIEL. Fearful that Samael and Lilith would flood the world with their offspring, God castrated Samael.

When God ordered the patriarch Abraham to kill his son, Isaac, Samael tried to persuade Abraham not to do it, in order to disobey God. When Abraham refused, Sa- mael went to Abraham's wife, Sarah, and told her Isaac was sacrificed to God, the news of which killed her instantly.

In kabbalistic lore, a Spanish kabbalist of the 15th cen- tury tried unsuccessfully to capture and control Samael. The kabbalist summoned him in the name of God and bound him by placing a crown upon his head that said "Thy Master's Name Is Upon Thee." But Samael tricked the kabbalist by convincing him to burn incense—an act of idolatry—in order to seal his victory. When the incense was burned, Samael was instantly freed.

Samael is the chief of the 10 evil demons of the *sephi- rot* of the Tree of Life.

See KABBALAH.

FURTHER READING:
Hyatt, Victoria, and Joseph W. Charles. *The Book of Demons.* New York: Simon & Schuster, 1974.

Sariel (Sarakiel, Saraqael, Saraqel, Suruquel, Suriel, Uriel, Zerachiel)

Good and FALLEN ANGEL. In the Eno- chian writings, Sariel is Saraqel, not the same as Uriel. Sariel rules Aries and is one of the nine ANGELs who pre- side over the summer solstice. As a fallen angel, he teaches the course of the Moon.

In Hebrew lore, Sariel is the son of LILITH and SAMAEL (in some accounts, Ashmodai or ASMODEUS), the "Sword of Samael." Sariel's face flames like fire. In the middle of the night of Yom Kippur, the prayers and acts of sages and elders can call him forth. Sariel appears reluctantly, fly- ing through the air with 130 warriors, all of whom have flaming faces. Sariel gives enlightenment to all who call him forth. A scribe, Pifiron, carries all the secrets of the firmament that have been sealed by Sariel. These secrets are revealed to the elders.

In the War of the Sons of Light and the Sons of Dark- ness (also known as the Triumph of God), one of the Qum- ran texts, Sariel is one of the four leaders of the forces of good. The human warriors are given exact instructions on who is to fight where, with weapons described care- fully. There are four subdivisions (towers), and each is to have the name of their archangel inscribed on their shield. Sariel is on the third tower.

Satan

The personification of evil and the head of all DEMONs. He is equated with the DEVIL. *Satan* is a Hebrew word meaning "adversary" and originally was not a proper name. Satan has evolved over the centuries to become the opposite and the opponent of God, the Prince of Darkness, and the subverter of souls. His goal is turn

to human beings away from God so that they become condemned to eternal torment in HELL.

Satan, as the proper name of a being, makes scant ap- pearance in religious texts prior to the New Testament. There is no mention of "the" Satan, or even "a" satan in Genesis. The SERPENT who tempts Eve is not equated with Satan. The Old Testament features a variety of satan ad- versaries, including an angel adversary in the story of Balaam and the ass in the book of Numbers; lying spirits; and, in the book of Job, a satan, who is one of the SONS OF GOD, and who walks the earth looking for people to test concerning their devotion to God. In the case of the pious and devout Job, God gives the satan permission to test him, and he suffers years of setbacks, disasters, and losses. A satan, as an accuser, is mentioned in the book of Zechariah. In 1 Chronicles, a satan stands up and chal- lenges David to take a census of the people. Psalm 109 refers to wicked men as satans, and they should be pun- ished by Yahweh.

In the New Testament, Satan becomes more personi- fied as a particular, single entity, and the terms *Devil* and *Satan* are used interchangeably. The Gospels tell of Sa- tan's testing JESUS in the wilderness. In Mark, he is named as Satan; in Matthew and Luke, he is "the tester" or "the Devil." In Luke, the Devil promises Jesus earthly glory if he will pay the proper homage. In Luke 10, Jesus com- ments that he has seen Satan "fallen like lightning from the sky," a reference similar to the fall of LUCIFER in Isaiah that is probably a prophecy of a fall to come, not one that occurred in the past. Luke also states that Satan entered into Judas to induce him to betray Jesus.

The Gospel of John makes references to the Devil. In the first, he is the "man-killer from the beginning" who does not stand for Truth, a reference often taken to refer to the serpent in the Garden of Eden. Jesus refers to him as the Ruler of the World. The Devil and Satan are both men- tioned in reference to entering into the heart of Judas.

The Epistles refer to both the Devil and Satan. Paul refers to Satan by name as obstructing his efforts to spread the gospel, as a tester of men's morals and faith, and as an agent of punishment for the wicked. In 2 Corinthians 2.10–11, Paul indicates that Satan has his own designs on the world, and that forgiveness will outwit Satan. In the same letter, Paul urges people to be on guard against Sa- tan, who can disguise himself as an angel of light. He also says that an "angel of Satan" has been sent to batter him, to prevent him from becoming too puffed up with his own pride. Paul did not see Satan as marshaling an army of demons; rather, he said that demons were the lifeless idols of the pagans. In Ephesians, Paul gives advice for spiritual armaments against Satan and warns that committing sins will make room for him. In Hebrews, Satan has the power of death, and it is Christ's mission to overcome him.

In Revelation, Satan is synonymous with the dragon and serpent. He tests people, battles angels, and is pun- ished and bound.

The early church fathers did more to cement the identity of Satan with the Devil and the tempter in the Garden of Eden, and with Lucifer. In the second century, Justin Martyr was the first to identify Satan with the serpent. He said the fall of Satan at the hands of Christ was predicted in Isaiah in the description of the fall of Lucifer. Justin also linked Satan with the Sons of God, or WATCHERS, and associated the powers and principalities (two orders of angels) of the Epistles with pagan gods and demons.

Other church fathers, such as Theophilus and Tertullian, also placed Satan as tempter in the Garden. According to Cyprian, the Devil was once a beloved and intimate angel of God, who perished at the beginning of the world out of envy over humanity. In losing his own immortality, he took away the immortality of humans. Irenaeus echoed this view.

Origen (ca. 185–250) was the first church father to reinterpret Satan within the context of Lucifer.

The Life of Adam and Eve, a pseudepigraphal text written around 100 A.D., states that the angel Satan was ordered by the archangel Michael to bow down and worship Adam, made in the image of God, but he refused because Adam was inferior, saying that Adam ought to worship him. The angels under Satan also refused, and God cast them all out of heaven. Muhammad was influenced by this text and retells the story in the Qur'an 10 times; the Devil is named IBLIS, who is head of the DJINN.

The idea that Satan was cast down because of his refusal to worship Adam did not take hold in Christianity, however. Satan is jealous of humans, but only after his fall.

Satan later became identified with gods of paganism. The idea was developed that Satan had rights over humanity and the world because of the sin of Adam and Eve; redemption was made through Christ, who paid off the debt with his own life. According to St. Augustine, Adam's sin meant that the whole of humanity fell under the servitude of Satan.

In the Middle Ages, legends and hagiographies of the saints were popular, offering many stories of saints besting the Satan and his demons and curing DEMONIACS of their POSSESSION.

St. Thomas Aquinas, one of the greatest and most influential theologians of the church, saw only one Devil, Satan, and never referred to "devils" in the plural unless he was quoting other writers. Aquinas said that the only two sins angels can commit are pride and envy, for all other sins are related to physical appetites. According to Aquinas, demons have no possibility of redemption and can only go to hell (where they torment the dead) or Smoggy Air (where they torment the living). He said human beings deserved to be turned over to Satan because of Adam's sin.

At some point—the origins are unclear—Satan became the ruler of hell and the chief tormenter of souls of the dead. From the 16th century on, his primary role was tempter of humanity.

The artist William Blake saw Satan as the imagination, a view also held in Sufism.

Even by the 18th century, Satan seemed an outdated superstition to some theologians, among them the influential Daniel Ernst Schleiermacher (1768–1834), a minister in the Reformed Church. The concept of the Devil was unenlightened, he argued, pointing out that Jesus and the disciples made few direct references to Satan. Schleiermacher argued that Satan does not exist and is used as a convenient metaphor for evil.

Since the mid-20th century, belief in Satan has risen, in part the result of the rise of fundamentalism, and of interest in demonic POSSESSION.

FURTHER READING:
Kelly, Henry Ansgar. *A Biography of Satan.* New York: Cambridge University Press, 2006.
Pagels, Elaine. *The Origin of Satan.* New York: Random House, 1995.
Russell, Jeffrey Burton. *Mephistopheles: The Devil in the Modern World.* Ithaca, N.Y., and London: Cornell University Press, 1986.
———. *Satan: The Early Christian Tradition.* Ithaca, N.Y., and London: Cornell University Press, 1981.

Satan and Jesus (AUTHOR'S COLLECTION)

Satanael (Satanail)   FALLEN ANGEL. *Satanael* is a name for SATAN or the DEVIL.

Satanael in Bogomilism

In Bogomilism, a Gnostic dualistic sect that flourished in Europe in the 10th through 15th centuries, Satanael is the older of two sons of God; the other is Christ. Satanael existed before Christ and was created good along with all the other ANGELs. He was held in the highest esteem and sat at the right hand of God as his steward. Soon, however, he grew dissatisfied with his station and rebelled. He persuaded other angels to join him, promising them freedom from boring liturgical duties. God reacted by casting them all out of heaven. Satanael wandered in the void and then decided to make a new world for himself—a second heaven over which he could become like a second God. The universe became this second heaven.

Satanael created the physical world, with all of its misery and suffering. He inspired the Old Testament. He created Adam out of earth and water. But Adam was defective, and he had life trickling out of his right foot and forefinger in the shape of a SERPENT. Satanael breathed spirit into Adam, but it trickled out and became the serpent. Satanael appealed to God for help, promising that God would be able to help govern humankind. God agreed because he wanted to replenish the ranks of angels depleted by the Fall.

Another version of the story says that Satanael could not animate Adam, and Adam lay lifeless for 300 years. Satanael wandered about the world, eating unclean animals. He returned to Adam's body and vomited his food into his mouth. Thus, the soul is imprisoned in a defiled and corrupt physical house.

After Adam was created, Satanael created Eve with God's help. He assumed the form of a serpent and had sexual intercourse with Eve with his tail, begetting the twins Cain and his sister Calomena (Abel was conceived by Adam and Eve). God punished Satanael for defiling Eve by making him dark and ugly and taking away his power to create and his divine form. God left Satanael to have dominion over the world for seven ages.

Satanael gave the law to Moses in order to retain his control. He keeps humankind oppressed and strives to make people worship him instead of the true God. Humanity was unable to rise to the ranks of angels as God intended.

After 5,500 years, God sent Christ to Earth to tell people about their true condition and to help them unite with him. Christ/Michael defeated Satanael and took his place at the right hand of God, sending him out of heaven for a second time. He lost the *-el* suffix on his name, becoming *Satan*.

The Bogomils said the world of matter must be rejected and despised. They rejected the sacraments of the church and the cross, for they maintained that Christ never died on the cross. Miracles and the acts of saints are deceits by the Devil. The only salvation is gained through asceticism.

The Bogomils believed that Satan will be loose in the world at the end of time but will be defeated by Christ/Michael.

Satanail in Enoch

In 2 Enoch, Satanail is an archangel and the leader of the WATCHERS. He is cast from heaven on the second day, the day in which God creates all angels from a great fire he cuts off from the rock (foundation) of the heavens:

> But one under the order of the archangels deviated, together with the division that was under his authority. He thought up the impossible idea that he might place his throne higher in the clouds which are above the earth, and that he might become equal to my power.
>
> And I hurled him from out of the height, together with his angels. And he was flying around in the air, ceaselessly, above the Bottomless. (29:4–5)

Satanail is imprisoned in the fifth heaven along with the Watchers and NEPHILIM.

FURTHER READING:
Russell, Jeffrey Burton. *Lucifer: The Devil in the Middle Ages.* Ithaca, N.Y., and London: Cornell University Press, 1984.
The Old Testament Pseudepigrapha. Vols. 1 & 2. Edited by James H. Charlesworth. 1983. Reprint, New York: Doubleday, 1985.

satanism   Devotion to SATAN, the DEVIL, or forces of darkness. Satanism is not structured as a single, unified organization or movement. Some forms of it are religious and involve worship of Satan, while other forms involve high magic or are philosophies and lifestyle choices.

As early as the seventh century, the Catholic Church was condemning priests who subverted the magical powers of the Holy Mass for evil purposes, a policy that can be seen as a precursor to the development of ideas about satanism.

Beliefs about satanism as Devil worship solidified during the Inquisition, when witch hunters and demonologists promoted the ideas that witches worshipped the Devil and were in PACTs with him to wreak havoc in the world. Enemies of the Christian Church, such as the Order of the Knights Templar and rival religious sects, were accused of Devil worship and witchcraft, crimes of heresy. Many of the accused confessed under the duress of severe torture.

The extent of genuine satanism is not known. There is little evidence of it as an organized activity prior to the 17th century, when it became fashionable to participate in BLACK MASSes. The most notorious of these took place in France during the reign of Louis XIV under the direction of the king's mistress, Madame de Montespan. The rituals were led by an occultist named La Voisin and a 67-year-old libertine priest, the abbé Guiborg.

There is no reliable evidence of satanic activity in the 18th century. In England, the HELL-FIRE CLUB, a society founded by Sir Francis Dashwood (1708–81), often described as satanic, was little more than a club for young men to indulge in drinking, sexual play with women called "nuns," and outrageous behavior. The club, or the "Medmenham Monks," as they called themselves, met regularly between 1750 and 1762 in Dashwood's home, Medmenham Abbey. They were said to conduct Black Masses, but it is doubtful that these were serious satanic activities. Similar groups were the Brimstone Boys and Blue Blazers of Ireland.

One of the most famous satanists of the 19th century was Abbé Boullan of France, who became the head of an offshoot of the Church of Carmel and allegedly practiced black magic and infant sacrifice. The Church of Carmel was formed by Eugene Vintras, the foreman of a cardboard box factory in Tilly-sur-Seule. In 1839, Vintras said he received a letter from the archangel Michael, followed by visions of the archangel, the Holy Ghost, St. Joseph, and the Virgin Mary. He was informed that he was the reincarnated prophet Elijah, and he was to found a new religious order and proclaim the coming of the age of the Holy Ghost. The true king of France, he was told, was a man named Charles Naundorf.

Vintras went about the countryside preaching this news and acquiring followers, including priests. Masses were celebrated that included visions of empty chalices filled with blood and bloodstains on the Eucharist. By 1848, the Church of Carmel, as the movement was known, was condemned by the pope. In 1851, Vintras was accused by a former disciple of conducting Black Masses in the nude, homosexuality, and masturbating while praying at the altar.

Shortly before his death in 1875, Vintras befriended Boullan, who formed a splinter group of the Church of Carmel upon Vintras' death. He ran the group for 18 years, until his death, outwardly maintaining pious practices, but secretly conducting satanic rituals.

Boullan seems to have been obsessed with satanism and evil since age 29, when he took a nun named Adèle Chevalier as his mistress. Chevalier left her convent, bore two bastard children, and founded with Boullan the Society for the Reparation of Souls. Boullan specialized in exorcising DEMONS by unconventional means, such as feeding possessed victims a mixture of human excrement and the Eucharist. He also performed Black Masses. On January 8, 1860, he and Chevalier reportedly conducted a Black Mass in which they sacrificed one of their children.

By the time Boullan met Vintras, Boullan was claiming to be the reincarnated St. John the Baptist. He taught his followers sexual techniques and said the original sin of Adam and Eve could be redeemed by sex with incubi and succubi. He and his followers also were said to copulate with the spirits of the dead, including Anthony the Great.

Boullan's group was infiltrated by two Rosicrucians, Oswald Wirth and Stanislas de Guaita, who wrote an exposé, *The Temple of Satan.* Supposedly Boullan and de Guaita engaged in magical warfare. Boullan and his friend, the novelist J. K. Huysmans, claimed to be attacked by demons. When Boullan collapsed and died of a heart attack on January 3, 1893, Huysmans believed it due to an evil spell from de Guaita and said so in print. De Guaita challenged him to a duel, but Huysmans declined and apologized.

In his novel, *Là-bas* (*Down There*), Huysmans included a Black Mass, which he said was based on his observations of one conducted by a satanic group in Paris, operating in the late 19th century. He said the mass was recited backward, the crucifix was upside down, the Eucharist was defiled, and the rites ended in a sexual orgy.

By the early 20th century, ALEISTER CROWLEY was thought to be involved in satanism. Although he called himself "the Beast"; used *Life, Love,* and *Light* to describe Satan; and once baptized and crucified a toad as JESUS, he was not a satanist, but a magician and occultist.

Modern Satanism

The largest movement of modern satanism began in the 1960s, in the United States, led by Anton Szandor LaVey, a shrewd, intelligent man with a charismatic persona and an imposing appearance. In 1966, LaVey founded the Church of Satan in San Francisco, the activities of which became the object of great media attention.

Born April 11, 1930, in Chicago, LaVey claimed an ancestry of Alsatian, Georgian, and Romanian blood, including a Gypsy grandmother from Transylvania. As a child, he studied music and became interested in the occult. He learned to play the piano at 10, and, at 15, became an oboist for the San Francisco Ballet Symphony Orchestra. He dropped out of high school in his junior year and joined the Clyde Beatty Circus as a cage boy. He had a gift for working with the big cats and became assistant trainer. It was in the circus, working with lions, he later said, that he learned about inner power and magic. On the side, he investigated haunted houses. At 18, he left the circus and joined a carnival, as a magician's assistant and a calliope player. In 1948, he met Marilyn Monroe and played as her accompanist.

He married his first wife, Carole, in 1951; they had one daughter, Karla. He studied criminology at City College in San Francisco and spent three years as a crime photographer with the San Francisco Police Department. Disgusted with the violence he saw, he quit and returned to playing the organ in nightclubs and theaters. He began holding classes on occult subjects. From these classes evolved a Magic Circle, which met to perform rituals LaVey had devised or discovered from historical sources on the Knights Templar, Hell-Fire Club, Hermetic Order of the Golden Dawn, and Aleister Crowley. LaVey apparently enjoyed the theatrics of the rituals; he dressed in a scarlet-lined cape and kept skulls and other odd objects about. Magic Circle members included the actress Jayne Mansfield and the filmmaker Kenneth Anger.

LaVey divorced Carole in 1960 and married Diane, 17, who worked as an usher at his Friday night occult sessions. They had a daughter, Zeena. From 1960 to 1966, he developed his elitist satanic philosophy. He viewed the Devil as a dark force hidden in nature, ruling earthly affairs. Humans' true nature is one of lust, pride, hedonism, and willfulness, attributes that enable the advancement of civilization. Flesh should not be denied, but celebrated. Individuals who stand in one's way of achieving what one wants should be cursed.

On Walpurgisnacht (April 30) in 1966, LaVey shaved his head and announced the founding of the Church of Satan. He shrewdly recognized the shock value in using the term *church* for worshipping the Devil and recognized people's innate need for ritual, ceremony, and pageantry. He performed satanic baptisms, weddings, and funerals, all of which received widespread media coverage. He used a nude woman (partially covered by a leopard skin) as an altar. His wife, Diane, became high priestess of the church. He baptized Zeena. Karla began giving lectures on satanism at universities and colleges.

LaVey preached antiestablishmentarianism, self-indulgence, all forms of gratification, and vengeance. Enemies were to be hated and smashed. Sex was exalted. He opposed the use of drugs, saying they were escapist and unnecessary to achieving natural highs. He also deplored the use of black magic in criminal activity. He did not include a Black Mass in his rituals, because he considered it outdated.

The Church of Satan organized into grottoes. A reversed pentacle containing a goat's head, called the Baphomet, was chosen as the symbol. LaVey used Enochian as the magical language for rituals and espoused the Enochian Keys used by Crowley.

LaVey composed Nine Satanic Statements, Eleven Satanic Rules of the Earth, and Nine Satanic Sins.

The following are the Nine Satanic Statements:

1. Satan represents indulgence instead of abstinence.
2. Satan represents vital existence instead of spiritual pipe dreams.
3. Satan represents undefiled wisdom instead of hypocritical self-deceit.
4. Satan represents kindness to those who deserve it instead of love wasted on ingrates.
5. Satan represents vengeance instead of turning the other cheek.
6. Satan represents responsibility to the responsible instead of concern for psychic vampires.
7. Satan represents man as just another animal—sometimes better, more often worse than those that walk on all fours—who, because of his "divine spiritual and intellectual development," has become the most vicious animal of all.
8. Satan represents all of the so-called sins, as they all lead to physical, mental, or emotional gratification.
9. Satan has been the best friend the church has ever had, as he has kept it in business all these years.

The following are the Eleven Satanic Rules of the Earth:

1. Do not give opinions or advice unless you are asked.
2. Do not tell your troubles to others unless you are sure they want to hear them.
3. When in another's lair, show him respect or else do not go there.
4. If a guest in your lair annoys you, treat him cruelly and without mercy.
5. Do not make sexual advances unless you are given the mating signal.
6. Do not take that which does not belong to you unless it is a burden to the other person and he cries out to be relieved.
7. Acknowledge the power of magic if you have employed it successfully to obtain your desires. If you deny the power of magic after having called upon it with success, you will lose all you have obtained.
8. Do not complain about anything to which you need not subject yourself.
9. Do not harm little children.
10. Do not kill nonhuman animals unless you are attacked or for your food.
11. When walking in open territory, bother no one. If someone bothers you, ask him to stop. If he does not stop, destroy him.

The Nine Satanic Sins are the following:

1. Stupidity
2. Pretentiousness
3. Solipsism
4. Self-deceit
5. Herd conformity
6. Lack of perspective
7. Forgetfulness of past orthodoxies
8. Counterproductive pride
9. Lack of aesthetics

The church attracted an international following. Most were middle-class and included occultists, celebrities, thrill seekers, the curious, racists, and political right wingers. At its peak, it was said to have about 25,000 members (years later, former members said the figures were exaggerated).

The film director Roman Polanski hired LaVey for his film version of Ira Levin's novel of Devil worshippers, ROSEMARY'S BABY, released in 1968. LaVey portrayed Satan and advised Polanski on satanic ritual details.

LaVey turned many of his organizational activities over to others in the church and began writing books. *The Satanic Bible* was published in 1969, followed by *The*

Satanic Rituals in 1972. A third book, *The Compleat Witch*, was published in Europe.

In 1975, the church lost members, who left to form a new satanic organization, the Temple of Set. The Church of Satan reorganized as a secret society and dissolved its grottoes. LaVey retired from the scene and went into seclusion. He reappeared in the media in the 1990s and published another book, *The Devil's Notebook*, in 1992. He died on October 30, 1997, at age 67, having suffered from heart problems for years. The "Black House" in San Francisco where he founded the church was torn down to make way for an apartment complex. A new Black House was established in a secret location.

The Church of Satan is presently run by Peter Gilmore. Members do not all believe in Satan, demons, or ANGELS. As do the principles espoused by LaVey, the church emphasizes personal freedom and swift action against persistent enemies.

Key founders of the Temple of Set were Michael A. Aquino, Lilith Sinclair (Aquino's wife), and Betty Ford. It is an initiatory society devoted to the Egyptian god Set (also known as Seth), whom members do not consider evil, but the prototype of Satan. According to the temple, Set has over the millennia altered human genetics in order to create people of superior intelligence for the next level of evolution. Three major phases have occurred: the first in 1904, when Crowley received *The Book of the Law*, dictated via mediumship by the spirit AIWASS; the second in 1966, when the Church of Satan was formed; and the third in 1975, when the Temple of Set was formed.

In his writings, Aquino has prophesied an apocalypse in which only the "elect," or members of the Temple of Set, will survive. Aquino has an interest in Nazi Pagan rituals practiced during World War II but has stated he does not sympathize with Nazi politics.

Other satanic groups have formed; some become defunct after a period of activity. The extent of satanism is impossible to gauge, because of the secrecy of many organizations. There is evidence of "family traditions" of satanism, passed down from one generation to another.

FURTHER READING:
Barton, Blanche. *The Church of Satan*. New York: Hell's Kitchen Productions, 1990.
———. *The Secret Life of a Satanist: The Authorized Biography of Anton LaVey*. Los Angeles: Feral House, 1990.
LaVey, Anton Szandor. *The Satanic Bible*. New York: Avon Books, 1969.

Scepter DEMON who appears in the form of a gigantic dog and who causes quartan fever.

In The Testament of Solomon, Scepter tells King SOLOMON that before the king's time he was a man, not a dog, and he accomplished many unlawful deeds in the world. He is so strong that he restrains the stars of heaven, and he is planning many more evil deeds. He deceives men who follow his star closely and leads them into stupid-

ity. He also subdues the hearts (thoughts) of men through their throats and destroys them.

Solomon asks Scepter why he is so prosperous. The demon tells him to turn over his manservant, whom he will spirit off to a place in the mountains where he will be shown an emerald stone. The stone will adorn Solomon's temple.

Solomon agrees, but he gives his servant his magical ring, with which he can quell the demon. The servant retrieves the emerald, which is shaped like a leek. He uses the ring to bind Scepter. Solomon extracts 200 shekels from the stone and has it carried about day and night as a light for the artisans. Then he locks it up. He commands Scepter and the headless demon MURDER to cut marble for the temple.

Scepter is thwarted by the ANGEL Briathos.

FURTHER READING:
The Old Testament Pseudepigrapha. Vols. 1 & 2. Edited by James H. Charlesworth. 1983. Reprint, New York: Doubleday, 1985.

scorpion-people Assyrian and Babylonian supernatural, semidivine beings who protect against evil DEMONS. The scorpion-people have a human body and head with a beard, the hindquarters and talons of birds, a snake-headed penis, and a scorpion's tail. They wear a horned cap that denotes divinity. They are powerful protectors, and figurines of them were used in homes and buildings.

Scot, Reginald (ca. 1538–1599) English writer who was one of the few outspoken critics of witch hunts. Reginald Scot was openly derisive of prevailing beliefs that witches were servants of the DEVIL and committed abominable acts in his name. He was skeptical of the ability of DEMONS and spirits to interfere in the lives of the living.

Scot was not a DEMONOLOGIST, clergyman, or lawyer, but rather an outraged citizen. He was born in or around 1538 in Kent. His father was Richard Scot, the youngest of three sons of Sir John Scot, a wealthy landowner. Young Scot was sent to Oxford at age 17, but he left without earning a degree and returned to Kent, settling in Smeeth. He worked as a subsidies collector for the government, served a year in Parliament, and tended to hop gardening. He was supported by a wealthy cousin, Sir Thomas Scot, whose estate he managed.

He married twice. His first wife was Jane Cobbe, whom he married on October 11, 1568. They had one daughter, Elizabeth. Jane died (the date is unknown), and Scot married a widow named Alice, who had a daughter, Marie, by her first marriage.

Scot spent much of his time reading, and he especially enjoyed obscure topics such as the occult and superstitions. On his own, Scot studied law, superstitions, folklore, and the contemporary literature of antiwitch demonologists. He grew increasingly angry at the tortures and executions of witches, who in his view were innocent people falsely accused. He wrote a refutation of the assertions of the witch hunters, *The Discoverie of Witchcraft,* and published it in 1584, during a time of intense anti-witch activity. His opening statement reflects his disdain for witch hunters: "The fables of Witchcraft have taken so fast hold and deep root in the heart of man, that few or none can (nowadays) with patience endure the hand and correction of God." Many of his comments were directed against the demonologist Jean Bodin and the MALLEUS MALEFICARUM, the leading inquisitors' handbook, written by two Dominican priests.

In composing *Discoverie,* Scot drew upon his knowledge of superstition, the law, and literature. He also drew upon the writings of numerous scholars, theologians, and experts in various fields, even those who disagreed with his own views. He was influenced by the writings of JOHANN WEYER, a German physician who also was a strong opponent of the witch hunts. However, unlike Weyer, who at least believed in the supernatural, Scot denied the supernatural altogether.

Scot defined four categories of witches: innocents who were falsely accused; deluded people who imagined themselves to be in PACTs with the Devil; evil people who did harm others, but not by SORCERY; and frauds and imposters who pretended to cast spells and make prophecies. Storms and crop failures were not caused by witches, but by God, he said.

Scot believed that it is not possible for a pact to be made between a living person and a spirit. "Confessions" of pacts were made under torture and in desperate attempts to avoid execution. There is nothing about satanic pacts in the Bible, he observed.

In particular, Scot believed that the appearances of demons and spirits were delusions caused by mental disorders, and that sexual encounters with incubi were a "natural disease." Stories of incubi covered up all-too-human lecheries, he said. Spirits were incapable of physical lust. Some experiences of incubi were due to nightmares, or "the mare," a physical condition caused by a thick vapor that arose from the "crudity and rawness" of the stomach and rose to the brain, oppressing it. Again, he cited a lack of references in Scripture to prove the existence of the INCUBUS and SUCCUBUS.

Scot derided the use of CHARMs against the Devil, witches, and evil and pointed out that there is no evidence that JESUS or the apostles ever had need of holy water, inscriptions and Bible verses on parchment, objects hung about the neck or in a house, and so forth, in order to drive away evil.

One section of *Discoverie* delves into an inventory of demons, their appearances and duties, and how they are conjured and commanded through the use of magical ritual. Detailed instructions are given for how to capture a demon in a crystal stone for the purpose of doing one's bidding. Scot called these magical activities "notorious blasphemy" and "blind superstitious ceremonies"

that were nothing but falsehood. Only the gullible and credulous believe the lies of conjurors and necromancers who claim they could summon demons out of HELL, he said. He questioned the difference between magical conjurations and the "popish conjurations" of Catholic ritual, as well as the difference between conjurations and charms. According to the church, charms were lawful because they contained nothing superstitious, whereas magical conjurations were said to be based on false superstition.

Scot was not alone in his condemnation of the witch persecutions; his writing was part of a continuing skepticism about witchcraft that persisted in England. Despite its lack of originality, *Discoverie* was well received by the clergy in England. King JAMES VI of Scotland (who became James I of England) was violently opposed to it and ordered copies to be burned. He wrote his own refutation, *Daemonologie.*

Montague Summers described Scot as a "myopic squireen" who was "utterly without imagination, a very dull, narrow, and ineffective little soul."

Scot died in Smeeth on October 8, 1599. There are different accounts of where he was buried. According to one, he was interred in a family plot in the churchyard at Smeeth; in another, he was buried beside Sir Thomas Scot's tomb in Brabourne Church.

FURTHER READING:
Scot, Reginald. *The Discoverie of Witchcraft.* Mineola, N.Y.: Dover Publications, 1989.

seal   In MAGIC, a symbol unique to a DEMON, ANGEL, or other occult force, used in rituals such as the summoning of specific spirits. Seals are also called sigils, a term derived from the Latin word for seal, *sigillum.*

Seals can be likened to a form of shorthand that enable a magician to set in motion forces or summon spirits into awareness and control them. Seals alone do not call forth spirits, however, but serve as a physical focus through which the practitioner achieves a desired state of mind. Their primary purpose is to stimulate the imagination of the magician in accordance with the purpose of a ritual. A seal is given energy via visualization, chanting, and intensity of will and then is "sent." The correct use of seals is one of the factors that determine the success of the ritual. According to the *Lemegeton,* one of the principal GRIMOIRES, a seal must be worn on the breast; otherwise, the spirit will not obey.

Seals of demons are symbols. Other seals are created from the numbers in magic squares. They also can be symbols, astrological signs, runes, and even designs created by a magician. They can contain the entire essence of a spell or the magical properties of celestial forces, spirits, or deities.

Seere   One of the FALLEN ANGELS and 70th of the 72 SPIRITS OF SOLOMON. Seere is a prince under Amaymon, the King of the East. He appears as a beautiful man riding a strong winged horse. He makes things happen instantly, transports himself anywhere instantly, and discovers all thefts. Seere is good-natured, will follow commands, and is indifferent to good or bad. He governs 26 LEGIONS of DEMONS.

Sej   See DRUJ.

Semyaza (Semiaza, Semjaza, Shemhazi, Shamayza, Shemyaza)   A leader of the FALLEN ANGELS, one of the SONS OF GOD, or WATCHERS, who cohabit with women. *Semyaza* probably means "meaning the name of Azza, or Uzza," which in turn means "strength."

According to the Zohar, Semyaza cohabits with one of Eve's daughters and produces two sons, Hiwa and Hiya, who eat every day 1,000 each of camels, horses, and oxen. As punishment for his sins, he hangs upside down in the constellation Orion, suspended between heaven and Earth.

In 1 Enoch, he is identified as the leader of the Watchers and is warned of their punishment by the archangel Michael.

serpent   Ancient symbol of wisdom and fertility, but in Christianity turned into a symbol of evil, the DEVIL, and SATAN. The serpent is a favorite shape-shifted form of the Devil and the DJINN.

The serpent is one of the oldest, most universal, and most revered symbols in mythology. Although negative associations exist, the serpent is predominantly associated with wisdom, enlightenment, immortality, healing, renewal, magic, and the guardianship of hidden treasure. Numerous deities have been associated with serpents. The Aztecs' Quetzacoatl is the "Plumed Serpent" and is prophesied to return as a great teacher. The "Rainbow Serpent" in Australian mythology is a creator deity. Asklepios, the Greek god of healing, has a totemic serpent entwined on a staff. Hermes, the Greek god of learning and magic, carries a caduceus wand entwined by two serpents. Athena, the Greek goddess of wisdom, has a serpent on her shield. The Nagas of Vedic lore are human/serpent beings who possess a high level of wisdom. In yoga, the kundalini, the energy of enlightenment, is likened to a coiled serpent that sleeps at the base of the spine and rises to the crown of the head when awakened by spiritual study and discipline.

Serpent in the Bible
The book of Genesis tells how a clever talking serpent convinces Eve to eat forbidden fruit from the Tree of Knowledge. She gives the fruit also to Adam. Angry, God casts them out of the Garden of Eden and condemns the serpent to travel upon its belly.

The appearance of the biblical serpent is controversial. Genesis does not give an exact description. Some illustrations of the serpent, in Eden, depict a reptilian-humanoid being. The serpent talks to Eve and exhibits intelligence and wile. In some older Jewish legends, the Genesis serpent is a tall, extremely intelligent creature with human arms and legs. He was created by God to be king of all creatures and eat the same food as humans. But his envy of humans, which was the evil within him, caused him to bring about the Fall.

Genesis does not equate the serpent with the Devil or Satan; the associations were made later by early church fathers, such as Justin Martyr and Tertullian. The serpent later symbolized lies, treachery, and evil, serving as the inspiration for the forked tongue and serpent-tailed representations of the Devil.

In Christian art and literature, the Devil took on snakelike and reptilian features, such as scaly skin, a forked tongue, and a long tail. Dragons also became symbols of evil and the Devil.

At the opposite end, the highest-ranking order of ANGELS, the seraphim, have serpent associations. Their name is thought to be derived from the Hebrew verb *saraf*, which means to "burn," "incinerate," or "destroy" and probably refers to the ability of seraphim to destroy by burning.

The seraphim may have evolved from the uraeus, the gold serpent (specifically a cobra) worn by Egyptian pharaohs on their foreheads. Uraei without wings and with two or four wings were depicted in iconography throughout the Near East. They protected by spitting their poison or fire. The seraphim who became angels in lore perhaps originally had serpent forms with human characteristics.

In the Old Testament, the term *saraf* is applied to fiery serpents. Numbers 21:6–8 refers to fiery serpents sent by the Lord to bite and kill sinning Israelites. After Moses prayed for forgiveness, he was instructed to set a fiery serpent atop a pole. Whoever was bitten by it, when he looked upon it, would live. Moses made a bronze serpent, which may have been a representation of a seraph angel. Deuteronomy 8:15 refers to the "fiery serpents" and scorpions in the land of Egypt.

3 Enoch, one of the most important works in the pseudepigrapha, says that the seraphim are so named because they burn the tablets of Satan. Every day Satan sits down with SAMAEL, prince of Rome, and Dubbiel, prince of Persia, to write down the sins of Israel on tablets. Satan gives the tablets to the seraphim to take to God so that God will destroy Israel. But the seraphim know that God does not wish to do so, and so they take the tablets and burn them.

In the New Testament, JESUS acknowledged the wisdom of the serpent in his statement "Be ye therefore wise as serpents and harmless as doves" (Matthew 10:16).

Serpent in Gnosticism
Gnosticism, a dualistic sect, considered the serpent as the Son of Man, the Savior himself, who initiates humankind into consciousness and raises them up out of a primitive, nature-identified unconsciousness. Gnostic teachings

Angels fly over the Serpent of Eden. (AUTHOR'S COLLECTION)

identify Jesus with the serpent in Eden because they were both condemned for giving humans more godlike status.

Serpent in Mythology

In mythology, serpents are powerful, magical, and mystical creatures. They are universal symbols of renewal and rebirth because of their unique ability to shed their old skin for new. The ouroboros, the serpent that forms a circle by biting its own tail, symbolizes the eternal cycle of life, death, and rebirth. In its carnal aspect, the serpent represents a phallus and its associations of the life force, sexuality, and sensuality. As a phallic symbol, the serpent often is associated with pregnancy in imagery and mythology.

As a creature that crawls along the earth and lives in holes in the ground, the serpent has connections to the underworld, the unconscious, and humankind's instinctual drives. Mythical serpents guard the sleep of both the living and the dead; thus, they are creatures at the gateway to new consciousness. The serpent also is a universal companion to goddesses and thus can symbolize the feminine, the anima, the womb, the dark, intuition, emotion, and all the aspects of the Great Mother.

The coils of the serpent represent the cycles of manifestation: life and death, good and evil, wisdom and blind passion, light and dark, healing and poison, protection and destruction. In kundalini yoga, a psychic force called the "serpent power" resides coiled near the base of the spine. In spiritual transformation, the energy rises up the spine to the crown chakra. The appearance of serpents in one's life can presage or accompany the rising of kundalini energy.

The dark aspect of serpents rules chaos, night, and death. Deities that wear serpents are depicted with headdresses of crescent Moons.

Serpent in Alchemy

In alchemy, the serpent is the *serpens Mercurii,* the quicksilver that represents the constant driving forward of psychic life forces: living, dying, and being reborn. The serpent is the *prima materia,* the unformed and dark chaos, from which order and life spring. Alchemical art often shows the serpent wearing a gold crown, gem, diadem, or light to depict its expanded spiritual consciousness. This is another way of expressing the activated kundalini or serpent power.

Serpent in Healing

The serpent is a potent symbol of healing, which also is part of the transformation process. Asclepius, the Greek god of healing, appears in the form of a serpent, and domesticated serpents were kept at the sacred healing temples of the classical world. Dream experiences were an integral part of the healing therapies at these temples; it was especially good to dream of serpents, because it portended healing. The healing power of serpents is cited in Numbers 21:8, in which Moses is instructed to set a fiery serpent upon a pole, so that all who look upon it shall live.

Serpent in Dream Symbolism

To be bitten by a serpent in a dream can represent an initiation or an infusion of wisdom—being "bitten" by a new awareness, a gift from the gods. It is the equivalent of an injection administered by a doctor: One is forcibly administered a substance that will bring about some kind of healing or new spiritual awareness. To be stalked or pursued by a serpent intent on biting indicates that the unconscious is attempting to introduce something into waking awareness.

Serpent as Archetype

The serpent represents great power indicating change, renewal, and transformation. Carl G. Jung considered the serpent to represent a potent archetype of psychic energy, power, dynamism, instinctual drive, and the entire process of psychic and spiritual transformation. When serpents appear, they may indicate a transformative process that already is under way, or they call attention to the need to move to a new level of consciousness.

Serpents also are associated with water, the symbol of the unconscious, and trees, the symbol of wisdom and knowledge. A serpent climbing up a tree represents the process of becoming conscious or going through psychic transformation. Two serpents twine up the caduceus staff of Hermes (Mercury or Quicksilver), the classical god who escorts the souls of the dead and delivers messages to the gods. The caduceus is a symbol of enlightenment and of healing.

Seven Deadly Sins   In Christianity, seven moral transgressions of divine law that damn a soul to HELL. The Seven Deadly Sins each have an associated DEMON that is a special agent of tireless temptation.

The Seven Deadly Sins are not mentioned as a group in the Bible, though they are dealt with separately in many passages. They were collected together around the time the Bible was translated into a single language. More than a dozen groupings of deadly sins exist. JOHN CASSIAN, a father of the church in the fourth century, wrote a treatise on eight deadly sins: Gluttony; Fornication; Covetousness (avarice); Anger; Dejection; "Accidie," or heaviness or weariness of heart; Kenodocila, or foolishness or vainglory; and Pride. The list was refined in the sixth century by St. Gregory the Great. In the 13th century, St. Thomas Aquinas wrote about them in more detail in *Summa Theologica,* a defining work of Christian dogma. Aquinas referred to the sins as "appetites."

In 1589, the demonologist and witch hunter PETER BINSFELD published a list of demons and sins and paired the Seven Deadly Sins with demons. His pairings are given in the following, along with the opposing virtues recognized by the Catholic Church.

The most common grouping of the Seven Deadly Sins lists a specific order. Five are spiritual in nature and two are carnal. Each of the seven spawns more sins, and each has an opposing virtue and a symbolic animal.

The seven sins and their demons are as follows:

1. Pride—Lucifer: Pride led to the fall from heaven of the angel LUCIFER (equated with SATAN and IBLIS) and his followers, who became demons. Pride leads to arrogance and a desire for glory, which blocks God and others from one's heart. It destroys all virtues.

   Pride is symbolized by the lion. Humility is the opposing virtue.

   Pride can be countered by taking credit for nothing but placing the credit for everything with God.

2. Avarice—Mammon: Avarice is about greed and obsession, for a greedy person never has enough of anything. Greed leads to cheating, fraud, thievery, murder, and miserliness. Aquinas called MAMMON "the devil who is Lord of Money." Avarice is symbolized by the wolf. Sufficiency is the opposing virtue.

3. Lust—Asmodeus: Lust is the first carnal deadly sin and leads to infidelity, deceit, betrayal, and uncleanliness. ASMODEUS is a major demon who figures in many POSSESSION cases and in the story of Tobit. Lust is symbolized by either the goat or the ass. Chastity is the opposing virtue.

Representation of the demons of the Seven Deadly Sins (AUTHOR'S COLLECTION)

4. Envy—Leviathan: One of the Ten Commandments is "Thou shalt not covet," characterizing envy as a "sin of the Devil." Jealousy leads to an obsession with possessions, with having more and better things than others. St. Paul called covetousness the root of all evils, because those who desire above all else to be rich fall into temptation and the Devil's traps. It is possible to commit the sin of envy even when one has no money or possessions but still has the desire for them.

   LEVIATHAN is the monster SERPENT creature from the depths that swallows its victims whole. Envy is symbolized by the dog. Charity is its opposing virtue.

5. Gluttony—Beelzebub: This deadly sin concerns eating and drinking that never satisfy but go on to excess. BEELZEBUB (Lord of the Flies) is the Prince of Demons and is often equated with Satan. In hell, the gluttonous are forced to eat toads and drink putrid water.

   Gluttony generates wantonness and a loss of reason. The remedy is fasting and prayer.

   Sobriety is the opposing virtue.

6. Anger—Satan: Anger leads to rage, vengeance, war, bloodshed, violence, cruelty, irrationality, and all of humanity's baser actions. It is easy to spark, and

Satan quickly fans its flames. Uncontrolled anger lays waste to all landscapes, physical, emotional, and spiritual. Anger is symbolized by fanged animals such as a leopard or a raging wild boar.

Cassian said that anger clouds discretion and right judgment and must be rooted out from the "inmost corners of the soul."

Patience is the opposing virtue.

7. Sloth—Belphegor: The second carnal sin is sloth, which spawns laziness, carelessness, apathy, and negligence. Aquinas said that sloth breeds ignorance, which in turn creates a host of other sins. BELPHEGOR, who is worshipped with offerings of excrement, rules this sin. Sloth is symbolized by a donkey. Diligence is the opposing virtue.

FURTHER READING:

Cassian, John. *On the Training of the Monk and the Eight Deadly Sins.* Available online. URL: http://www.thenaz areneway.com/Institutes%20of%20John%20Cassian/the_eight_deadly_sin s.htm. Downloaded December 27, 2007.

Mack, Carol K., and Dinah Mack. *A Field Guide to Demons: Fairies, Fallen Angels, and Other Subversive Spirits.* New York: Owl Books/Henry Holt, 1998.

Thomas Aquinas. *Summa Theologiae.* Edited by Timothy McDermott. Allen, Texas: Christian Classics, 1989.

Seven in Lancashire Possessions (1595–1597)   English case of possessed children and adults, involving John Dee and the Puritan minister the REVEREND JOHN DARREL. The case bears similarities to the children in the THROCK-MORTON POSSESSIONS, in that the children probably faked fits in order to avoid religious studies and attending church and perhaps to gain attention. An accused witch was executed. Accounts of the case were written by Darrel and another minister who performed the EXORCISMS, George More, and were published in 1600.

The Seven in Lancashire case began in 1595 in the household of Nicholas Starkie of Cleworth, Lancashire. His two children, Ann, 10, and John, 12, began having fits and convulsions. Starkie spent 200 pounds—a huge sum of money—trying to cure the children, to no avail. He consulted a priest—his wife had been a Catholic—but the priest had no instructions for exorcism.

Starkie then turned to a cunning man, Edmund Hartley, and hired him at the annual salary of two pounds. Hartley was skilled in herbal remedies and charms. Shortly after the arrival of Hartley in the household, three other children who were being raised by Starkie became possessed. So did a maid, Jane Ashton, and a poor relative, Margaret Byrom, 33.

The behavior of the DEMONIACs conformed to that of other demoniacs. They screamed, howled, and writhed. They went into fits whenever Scripture was read, and they burst out with foul language during church services. John

Starkie ranted for hours on sin and the wrath of God. One of the girls made a hole in her wall to let her DEMON enter.

Hartley successful calmed the demoniacs for about 18 months, using CHARMs and herbs. Oddly, he was subject to fits himself.

By autumn 1596, Starkie, perhaps wishing for more dramatic results, consulted Dee, who was famous for his contact with spirits and who had had an experience with a possessed woman in his employ. Dee recommended calling in some "godly preachers" and treating the children with fasting and prayer, common Protestant remedies for POSSESSION.

Starkie then consulted Darrel and More. Darrel interviewed Hartley and criticized his approach. The children had no fits for three weeks.

Hartley fell under suspicion. Dee's curate, Matthew Palmer, identified him as a witch because he could not say the Lord's Prayer without stumbling—a common test for discovering witches that was employed in witch trials. Hartley was accused of bewitching the demoniacs by kissing them. He was brought to trial in March 1597 and was found guilty. However, the court had no grounds for execution. Conjuring spirits was against the law and punishable by death, but there was no evidence that Hartley had done so.

Then Starkie "remembered" an incident. He said that prior to his consulting Dee—and the reason for it—he had been with Hartley in a wood. The cunning man had made a circle on the ground with "crosses and partitions" and asked Starkie to walk it. He allegedly said, "Now I shall trouble him that troubled me, and be meete with him that sought my death."

Hartley denied this, but it was all the court needed to dispatch him, and he was hanged for conjuring. The rope broke, giving Hartley a chance to make a confession and repent, but the court had him hanged again, this time successfully.

The demoniacs seemed mollified by his death, but Starkie called in Darrel and More to exorcise them just the same. When the preachers arrived, the demoniacs resumed their fits and even rejoiced in the death of Hartley. They made a terrific show of screaming blasphemies and convulsing for a day. Then, all were dispossessed. All but one were never to be troubled so again. The maid, Jane Ashton, continued to suffer fits and went to live with a Catholic uncle, who sent her to priests to be exorcised.

FURTHER READING:

Walker, D. P. *Unclean Spirits: Possession and Exorcism in France and England in the Late Sixteenth and Early Seventeenth Centuries.* Philadelphia: University of Pennsylvania Press, 1981.

Shamsiel   FALLEN ANGEL who is by some accounts a good ANGEL. *Shamsiel* means "light of day" or "mighty son of God."

As a fallen angel, Shamsiel is one of the WATCHERS, according to the book of Jubilees. In 1 Enoch he is a fallen angel who teaches the signs of the Sun.

As a good angel, Shamsiel is a prince of paradise, guardian of Eden, and ruler of the fourth heaven. According to the Zohar, he is chief of 365 LEGIONS of angels and is one of two aids to the archangel Uriel in battle. He crowns prayers and takes them to the fifth heaven. Shamsiel guided Moses when he visited paradise in the flesh.

Shax (Chax, Scox) FALLEN ANGEL and 44th of the 72 SPIRITS OF SOLOMON. Shax is a marquis who has the form of a stork and speaks with a hoarse voice. He destroys the eyesight, hearing, and understanding of any person upon command. He steals money from kings and then returns it in 1,200 years. After he is commanded into the magician's triangle, Shax will transport anything; otherwise, he will be deceptive. Upon command, he will steal horses. He will find all hidden things, unless they are being kept by evil spirits. He sometimes gives good FAMILIARS. He commands 30 LEGIONS of DEMONS.

shaytan (mazikeen, shaitan, shedeem, shedim, sheytan) In Islamic lore, a type of djinn, thoroughly evil, created by Allah from smokeless fire. In Hebrew and Arabic mythology, they are evil spirits who have cock's feet.

The *al-shaytan* (plural) work under the direction of IBLIS and try unceasingly to tempt people into sin. They create illusions of pleasure in the mind that lead to desires. They can shape shift into the forms of beautiful women (see SUCCUBUS) to tempt men sexually. They can also shape shift into animals, inhabit corpses, and take POSSESSION of people.

The *al-shaytan* eat dirt and excrement. If a person forgets to wash his or her hands after supper, the DEMONS will lick the hands to bloody stumps during the night. According to lore, they have an aversion to water and cannot open the lids of vessels and jars, because King SOLOMON once imprisoned them in bottles. A folktale tells that a huge number of *al-shaytan* were accidentally released into the world by Moroccan fishermen who found bottles with the red seal of Solomon upon them and opened them.

White cocks will repel the *al-shaytan*. They can be kept out of a house by keeping all doors tightly closed.

Shaytan is a name for Iblis.

See SATAN.

FURTHER READING:
Frieskens, Barbara. *Living with Djinns: Understanding and Dealing with the Invisible in Cairo.* London: Saqi Books, 2008.
Mack, Carol K., and Dinah Mack. *A Field Guide to Demons: Fairies, Fallen Angels, and Other Subversive Spirits.* New York: Owl Books/Henry Holt, 1998.

shedim In Hebrew demonology, evil spirits created by the union of a succubus or Lilith and a man. The *shedim* are a man's "demonic children." When a man dies, they go to the grave to weep. Tradition called for a man's legitimate offspring to stay away from the graveside at burial in order to avoid dangers from the *shedim*.

A 17th-century account of beliefs of German Jews describes them:

> They [Jews] firmly believe that if a man's seed escapes him, it gives rise, with the help of *mahlath* [a female demon] and Lilith, to evil spirits, which however die when the time comes. When a man dies and his children begin to weep and lament, these *shedim*, or evil spirits, come too, wishing, along with the other children, to have their part in the deceased as their father; they tug and pluck at him, so that he feels the pain, and God himself, when He sees this noxious offspring by the corpse, is reminded of the dead man's sins.

One custom called for 10 men to dance in a circle around a man's body seven times before it was lowered into the grave, reciting the 91st Psalm or other prayers to ward off the *shedim*. Then a stone was laid on the bier while Genesis 25:6 was recited: "But unto the sons of the concubines, which Abraham had, Abraham gave gifts, and sent them away."

In later lore, the *shedim* were hairy, wild DEMONS who lived in the woods and danced. They were known for their tricks, such as leaving human beings with grotesque deformities if they were displeased.

The *shedim* are ruled by ASMODEUS.

See SHAYTAN.

FURTHER READING:
Davies, T. Witton. *Magic, Divination and Demonology among the Hebrews and Their Neighbors.* First published 1898.
Mack, Carol K., and Dinah Mack. *A Field Guide to Demons: Fairies, Fallen Angels, and Other Subversive Spirits.* New York: Owl Books/Henry Holt, 1998.
Scholem, Gershom G. *On the Kabbalah and Its Symbolism.* New York: Schocken Books, 1965.

Simon Magus (first century) Gnostic wonder-worker and sorcerer. Simon Magus' Christian opponents said that he was a DEMON or had obtained his powers from the DEVIL. Simon Magus became the prototypical heretic and black magician.

Simon came from Samaria. He was attracted to Christianity and the miracles associated with it, and he was converted to the faith by Philip the Deacon, whose magic impressed Simon.

According to Acts 8:9–24, the apostles Peter and John were sent to Samaria to deliver the Holy Spirit into the population by a laying on of hands. When Simon witnessed their supernatural work, he offered the apostles money: "Give me this power, that any one on whom I lay my hands shall receive the Holy Spirit." The apostles, angry that Simon should expect to buy holy power, had him thrown out of the church. Peter told him, "Your silver perish with you, because you thought you could obtain the gift of God with money." Simon's name gave rise to the term *simony,* the sin of buying or selling a church office.

Simon traveled to Rome, where he impressed people with his occult ability, and then to Egypt, where he allegedly learned how to make himself invisible, levitate, move objects with his mind, handle fire unharmed, and shape-shift into an animal. He may have accomplished some of these feats through illusion and hypnosis. The Roman emperor Nero was impressed, however, and named him court magician.

According to the Acts of Peter, an apochryphal text, the apostle Peter went to Rome to challenge Simon and expose him of fraud. They tried to outdo each other in magical feats. Simon is said to have died after he attempted to levitate off the top of the Roman Forum and fell to earth, breaking his legs.

Simon is credited with founding a Gnostic sect that became known as the Simonians.

See PACT.

Sinistrari, Lodovico Maria (1622–1701)   Franciscan theologian whose contribution to demonology is his work *Demoniality,* in which he examines sexual acts with DEMONS. Lodovico Sinistrari likened demons more to the LUTIN, or mischievous hobgoblin, than to evil servants of SATAN.

Sinistrari had an illustrious career as a theologian. He was born on February 26, 1622, in Ameno, a small town in Piedmont, Italy. He was educated at the esteemed University of Pavia, and in 1647 he entered the Order of Reformed Minors of the Strict Observance of St. Francis. He became a professor of philosophy at Pavia and taught theology. Students from all over Europe traveled to hear him lecture. Sinistrari also was popular as a preacher throughout Italy. Good-looking and personable, he was well liked by royalty and the general public.

Sinistrari served as consultant to the Supreme Tribunal of the Most Holy Inquisition; as vicar-general to the archbishop of Avignon, France; and as theologian to the cardinal-archbishop of Milan. By 1688, Sinistrari was in retreat at the Franciscan sanctuary of Sacro Monte, where he wrote poetry. He compiled the statutes of the order and wrote other works. He died on March 6, 1701, at age 79.

His manuscript *Demoniality (De Daemonialitate, et Incubis et Succubis)* remained unknown until 1872, when the original was discovered in a London bookshop by Isidore Lisieux, a bibliophile. The shop had acquired part of the collection of a man who had died in Florence; *Demoniality* was among the manuscripts. It was only 86 pages in length, handwritten in Latin on Italian parchment. Lisieux translated it into French and published it in 1875. It was then translated into English. A 1927 edition includes an introduction and notes by Montague Summers.

Demoniality concerns the nature of demons. Sinistrari uses the term INCUBUS to describe spirits that are more lutinlike rather than evil. He confirms opinions of his con-temporary demonologists, especially FRANCESCO-MARIA GUAZZO. Witches and wizards are physically present at SABBATs and copulate with the DEVIL and demons as part of their infernal PACT. Demons also have intercourse with people, appearing to them at night and impersonating human lovers. Some of these copulating demons are different from the antireligious demons who possess people, according to Sinistrari; they simply want to satisfy carnal lusts and harass people.

The Incubus of Hieronyma

Sinistrari relates one such case he was involved in himself. About 25 years prior to the time he wrote the manuscript, he was a lecturer on theology in the convent of the Holy Cross in Pavia. A married woman named Hieronyma, of "unimpeachable morality," was pestered by such an incubus. Her problems started with a mysterious cake. One day she kneaded bread and took it to a baker for baking. When he gave her back her loaves, there was a large cake of peculiar shape among them, made of butter and Venetian paste. Hieronyma said it was not hers, but the baker insisted it was, and she had just forgotten about it. She took it home and shared it with her husband, three-year-old daughter, and maid.

The next night, she was awakened by a hissing voice that asked whether "the cake had been to her taste." The voice went on, "Be not afraid, I mean you no harm; quite the reverse: I am prepared to do anything to please you; I am captivated by your beauty, and desire nothing more than to enjoy your sweet embraces." Hieronyma then felt kisses upon her cheeks. She crossed herself and invoked JESUS and Mary repeatedly, and after about half an hour, the invisible tempter departed.

The following morning, she went straight to her confessor, who advised her to continue resistance and surround herself with relics. The incubus returned night after night, wearing her down. She had herself exorcised in case she was possessed. But the priests could find no evidence of an evil spirit in her, so they blessed the house, the bedroom, and the bed and ordered the incubus to stop pestering her.

The demon started appearing to her in the form of a handsome young man with golden hair and beard, sea-green eyes, and beautiful Spanish clothing. He approached her even when she was with others, and no one else could see him. He attended her as an ardent lover, cooing and kissing her hands.

After months of rejection, the incubus became angry. He spirited away her silver cross and Agnus Dei, which she always wore. Silver and gold jewelry went missing from her locked jewelry box. The incubus also started beating Hieronyma, causing ugly bruises on her face, arms, and body that mysteriously disappeared after a day or two. He snatched her daughter away from her and hid the child. He upset furniture and smashed crockery and in an instant restored everything to its original condition.

The demon continued to visit Hieronyma at night. Enraged at her resistance, one night he took huge roofing flagstones to the bedroom and built a wall around the bed that was so high, Hieronyma and her husband could not get out without a ladder.

One evening, when the couple had guests for dinner, the dining room table, set with plates and utensils and loaded with food, abruptly disappeared. Just as the guests were leaving—without their meal—a crash sounded in the dining room. They found the table restored, and on it a huge array of fine foods and foreign wines that had not been there before. Everyone sat down and enjoyed the meal. They adjourned to sit by the fire, and the table once again disappeared, then reappeared with the original food that had been prepared.

After months of these wearying annoyances, Hieronyma went to the Church of St. James and prayed to Blessed Bernadine of Feltre whose body was incorrupt. She promised to wear a shapeless frock with a cord, like those worn by the Franciscans, for an entire year, if the saint would intercede and expel the incubus.

The day after she donned the frock was Michaelmas Day, and Hieronyma went to mass. As soon as she set foot on the threshold of the church, a gust of wind hit her and her clothing fell off and disappeared, leaving her naked and embarrassed. Two cavaliers covered her with their cloaks and took her home. Six months went by before the incubus returned the clothing.

Sinistrari wrote that the incubus harassed Hieronyma for years. She never gave in, and at last he gave up and went away for good. Such are many incubus attacks: The demons attempt no act against religion but merely assail chastity. "Consequently, consent is not a sin through ungodliness, but merely through incontinence," he said. It is on the same level as bestiality and sodomy. These acts differ, he said, from intentional intercourse with demons, such as attributed to witches at sabbats and those who had made pacts with the Devil.

Traits of Incubi and Succubi

Sinistrari agreed with his peers that demons could be invisible and take corporeal form for the purpose of intercourse, and women could become impregnated by them. However, he argued, their passion had to spring from the senses, and one could not have senses without physical organs through a combination of body and soul. Therefore, incubi are perfect, rational animals with rational souls. They are not the same as the possessing evil spirits, who flee at the signs of holiness or entice witches into pacts, he said. Their behavior indicates they only desire sex, and, as any rational animal does, they become frustrated and angry when they do not get it.

As further evidence to support this argument, Sinistrari pointed to the case of animals sexually harassed by incubi. Since animals do not have souls, he said, the incubi cannot have a purpose of ruining and damning their souls. Again, the only purpose is sex.

Incubi do not cause illness but mistreat people by beating them. They do not require the direction of a witch or wizard to harass people; they undertake it of their own choice and volition.

As evidence to support his assertions, Sinistrari cites two cases of incubus attacks. One, related to him by a confessor of nuns whom he trusted, concerned a young noble maiden who lived in a convent. An incubus began appearing to her day and night, making earnest and impassioned pleas for sex with her. She resisted and, as the attacks continued, sought help from EXORCISMS, relics, blessings, prayer, and candles kept lit all night long. The incubus persisted and kept appearing in the form of a handsome young man.

The solution was discovered by an unnamed but eminent theologian, who observed that the young woman had a watery humor. Since like attracts like, according to the prevailing views at the time, the demon had to be watery in nature as well. The theologian prescribed a continual suffumigation of the girl's room. An earthenware and glass vessel was filled with sweet calamus, cubeb seed, roots of both aristolochies, great and small cardamom, ginger, long-pepper, caryophylleae, cinnamon, cloves, mace, nutmeg, calamite storax, benzoin, aloes-wood and roots, one ounce of fragrant sandal, and three quarts of half-brandy and half-water. The vessel was set on hot ashes to cook, and the room was sealed.

When the incubus arrived, he would not enter the room, repelled by the fumes. However, he still assaulted the maiden if she went elsewhere, such as for a walk in the garden. He hugged her and kissed her and remained invisible to others.

The theologian prescribed that she carry on her person pills and pomanders made of perfume from musk, amber, civet, Peruvian balsam, and other exotic essences. This threw the incubus off, and he permanently departed in a black rage.

Sinistrari himself was involved in the second example he cites. In the Carthusian monastery in Pavia, a deacon named Augustine was attacked by a demon. All spiritual remedies, including exorcism, failed. Sinistrari prescribed the same fumes and perfumes that had been effective in the earlier case. The demon continued to appear, taking the forms of a skeleton, pig, ass, angel, bird, another monk, and even the prior of the monastery.

As the prior, the demon completely fooled Augustine. It heard his confession, genuflected, blessed his room and bed with holy water, ordered the demon to desist, and then vanished into thin air, betraying his real identity. He then went to the vicar, appeared as the prior, and asked for musk and brandy, saying he was very fond of them.

Sinistrari deduced the demon had a fiery nature and so prescribed the opposite, herbs that were "cold": water lily, agrimony, spurge, mandrake, house-leek, plantain, henbane, and others. These were knit into two bundles, one hung in the window of Augustine's cell and one hung in the door. Herbs were strewn on the floor. When the incubus next appeared, he would not enter the cell. He grew angry, hurled abuse, and left, never to return.

Sinistrari said that incubi are on a spiritual path and, like humans, capable of salvation and damnation. They are born, live, and die. They, have their own sperm and can reproduce themselves and impregnate human women on their own, he said, refuting the prevailing view that in order to impregnate a woman, a demon had to become a succubus to seduce a man and then change into an incubus to seduce a woman. However, the offspring of incubi and humans are barren, he said, and do not reproduce on their own.

Sinistrari would have been in a minority in his time concerning his views on copulating demons. By the 17th century, there were other skeptics about sabbats, Devil pacts, and other infernal activities; REGINALD SCOT had been vocal in the century before. It is not known why Sinistrari's manuscript remained unknown for 171 years after his death. There is no record of his attempting to publish it.

FURTHER READING:
Sinistrari, Lodovico Maria. *Demoniality*. New York: Dover, 1989.

Sitri   FALLEN ANGEL and 12th of the 72 SPIRITS OF SOLOMON. Sitri is a great prince who appears first with a leopard's face and griffin wings. He then assumes the shape of a beautiful human. He inflames men and women to fall in love with each other and take off all their clothes. He commands 60 LEGIONS of DEMONS.

Six-six-six (666)   The number of "the Beast," or Antichrist, according to interpretations of the book of REVELATION in the Bible. Six-six-six is associated with the DEVIL and SATANISM.

Revelation is based on a series of apocalyptic visions John of Patmos experienced during his exile on the island of Patmos in the Aegean Sea. In one vision, a beast rises up from the sea. It has seven heads, 10 horns, and 10 crowns; the heads bear the name of blasphemy. One of the heads had a fatal wound but had healed. A voice in the vision says, "Let him that hath understanding count the number of the beast: for it is the number of a man; and his number is Six hundred threescore and six."

The number would be marked on the forehead or right hand of worshippers. An ANGEL tells John, "If anyone worships the beast and its image, and receives a mark on his forehead or hand, he also shall drink the wine of God's wrath, and shall be tormented with fire and sulphur in the presence of the holy angels and of the Lamb. And the smoke of their torment goes up for ever and ever; and they have no rest, day or night."

The number 666 has been projected onto many enemies throughout history. Names have been manipulated to add up to the numerical value of 666. Revelation makes reference to Roman emperors who claimed deity, and "Nero Caesar" adds up to 666. The Gnostics were considered great enemies of the church, and some church fathers said the Gnostic Ogdoad was the Number of the Beast. During the Reformation, Protestants called the Catholic Church the *Italika Ekklesia* and referred to the pope by the Greek word *papeiskos* in order to arrive at 666, and the Catholics did the same to MARTIN LUTHER. Similarly, the number has been applied to Muhammad, and even to political villains such as Napoleon Bonaparte and Adolf Hitler.

ALEISTER CROWLEY often signed his name as "The Beast 666" or "TO MEGA THERION," which equals "The Great Beast" in Greek, or 666. He associated 666 with the powers of the Sun, not evil. In the KABBALAH, the Sun is the sixth emanation from God. A magical square expressing the Sun adds up to 666. A square composed of 36 squares (6 times 6) contains the numbers 1 through 36 so that any line connecting the numbers, horizontal, vertical, or diagonal, adds up to 111. The sum of all the squares is 666.

In 1934, Crowley testified in a lawsuit and was asked about his self-designations of "The Beast 666" and "Mega Therion." *Therion* means "great wild beast," he said, and 666 is the number of the Sun. Crowley said, "You can call me Little Sunshine."

Throughout history, people look for the Beast in names or things that add up to 666. However, languages and numbers can be manipulated to arrive at 666 for any name. Crowley was able to make his own name add up to 666 by using Hebrew letters and adding his middle initial, *E,* which he never used otherwise. The number 666 has been so stigmatized that people avoid using it for legitimate purposes.

Because of its associations with the Antichrist, 666 is feared and avoided by many people, especially for addresses and telephone exchange numbers. Fear of 666 is called *hexakosioihexakontahexaphobia.*

FURTHER READING:
DuQuette, Lou Milo. "666: What's in a Number?" *FATE,* October 2005, 10–17.
Edinger, Edward F. *Archetype of the Apocalypse: A Jungian Study of the Book of Revelation.* Chicago: Open Court, 1999.
Godwin, David F. "The Number of the Beast." *FATE,* October 2005, 18.

Smith, Helene (19th century)   Swiss medium who underwent a spirit POSSESSION and was overtaken by the discarnate Count Cagliostro. Smith, whose real name was Catherine Elise Muller, never worked as a paid medium but gave séances to friends and admirers for entertainment. She earned a living holding a high position in a large store in Geneva, Switzerland.

Smith's séances were characterized by trances, automatic writing in Arabic, and glossolalia, or speaking in tongues. She hypnotized herself into a trance and allowed her control, Leopold, to speak and write through her.

Smith claimed she had been a Hindu princess and Marie Antoinette in previous lives. Her present humble life was repayment of a karmic debt for her transgressions as Antoinette. One of the spirits she channeled in trances was Cagliostro. When he appeared, Smith exhibited signs of temporary spirit possession. Her appearance changed markedly to drooping eyelids and a double chin. The spirit used her vocal cords, speaking in a deep bass voice. She also underwent marked physical changes when Leopold spoke through her.

Leopold, who controlled a bevy of spirits around Smith, said he had been transported to Mars. The spirits were able to take Smith to Mars while she was in a trance. The results of these journeys were crude pictures of Martian landscapes, including plants, houses, and city streets, and automatic writing of a Martian language. Many spiritualists believed her.

In the late 1890s, Smith was studied by a number of leading investigators, most notably Theodore Flournoy, a Swiss professor of psychology. Flournoy, using psychoanalytic techniques, spent five years sitting in on séances, researching Smith's personal history, and corroborating historical information she provided at her séances.

Flournoy described the takeover of Cagliostro as a gradual process. First, Smith felt as though an invisible force seized her arms and she could not move them. Then, pain arose in her neck at the base of her skull. Her eyelids drooped, and her chin dropped and formed what appeared to be a double chin, giving her a resemblance to portraits of Cagliostro. She took on a pompous bearing, made Masonic signs with her hands, and spoke in a slow, deep, masculine bass voice with an Italian accent. Cagliostro addressed everyone as "thou" and acted as though he was "the grand master of secret societies," according to Flournoy.

Flournoy concluded that Smith had a fantastic imagination, perhaps complemented with telepathy and psychokinesis. The Martian language that she produced was a childish imitation of French; a Sanskrit expert declared that 98 percent of the words could be traced to earthly languages. "Leopold," who was pompous, dignified, and sensible, was probably her most highly developed secondary personality.

Flournoy published his findings in 1900 in *From India to the Planet Mars*. Smith's supporters stood by her, and Flournoy was banished from her life. The exposé served to increase her popularity, and Smith enjoyed comfortable wealth and fame.

FURTHER READING:

Flournoy, Theodore. *From India to the Planet Mars: A Study of a Case of Somnambulism with Glossolalia*. New York: Harper & Bros., 1900.

Gauld, Alan. *Mediumship and Survival*. London: William Heinneman, 1982.

Myers, F. W. H. *Human Personality and Its Survival of Bodily Death*. Abridged ed. Edited by Susy Smith. New Hyde Park, N.Y.: University Books, 1961.

Oesterreich, Traugott K. *Possession and Exorcism*. Secaucus, N.J.: University Books, 1966.

Smurl Haunting (1986–1987)   Demonic activity in a private residence in West Pittston, Pennsylvania. The phenomena at the home of Jack and Janet Smurl at 328–330 Chase Street received wide attention in the media, primarily due to the investigations of ED AND LORRAINE WARREN, lay demonologists. Three EXORCISMS were performed, but the DEMON refused to leave. Skeptics said the case was a prank or hoax. The events were the subject of a best-selling book, *The Haunted* by Robert Curran, and a film by the same title.

The afflicted house was a duplex, built in 1896 on a quiet street in a middle-class neighborhood. The Smurls were a close-knit Catholic family living in Wilkes-Barre, Pennsylvania. A Navy veteran, Jack worked as a neuropsychiatric technician. The Smurls were forced to move by the devastation caused by Hurricane Agnes in 1972. Jack's parents, John and Mary Smurl, bought the house in West Pittston in 1973 for $18,000. They lived in the right half, and Jack, Janet, and their first two daughters, Dawn and Heather, moved into the left half. The Smurls did their own redecorating and remodeling and enjoyed a close relationship with Jack's parents. For 18 months, their new life seemed idyllic.

Then strange things occurred. In January 1974, a mysterious stain appeared on new carpet. Jack's television set burst into flame. Water pipes leaked even after repeated soldering. The new sink and bathtub in the remodeled bathroom were found severely scratched, as if a wild animal had clawed at them. Freshly painted woodwork in the bathroom showed scratches, as well. In 1975, their older daughter, Dawn, repeatedly saw people floating around in her bedroom.

The Smurls tolerated the annoyances. Life went on, and they had two more children, the twins Shannon and Carin in 1977. By then, something was obviously wrong in the house. Toilets flushed without anyone using them. Footsteps were heard on the stairs; drawers opened and closed when no one was in the room. Radios blared even when unplugged. Empty porch chairs rocked and creaked. Strange sour smells filled the house. Jack felt ghostly caresses.

In 1985, the annoying disturbances became frightening experiences. The house was often ice cold. John and Mary Smurl heard loud, abusive, obscene language from Jack and Janet's side of the duplex when they were not even arguing. Then in February, Janet heard her name called several times when she was alone in the basement.

Two days later, icy cold announced the arrival of a black human-shaped form, about five feet nine inches tall, with no facial features. First, it appeared to Janet in her kitchen, then it dematerialized through the wall and appeared to Mary Smurl.

From that point on, the haunting increased. A large ceiling light fixture crashed down on Shannon, nearly killing her, on the night 13-year-old Heather was to be confirmed. Jack levitated. In June, Janet was violently pulled off her bed after making love to her husband, while Jack lay paralyzed, gagging from a foul odor. The family German shepherd, Simon, was repeatedly picked up, thrown around, or whipped. Terrible rapping and scratching noises were heard in the walls. Phantom dogs ran through the duplex. Shannon was tossed out of bed and down the stairs. Invisible snakes hissed, bedspreads were shredded, and heavy footsteps crossed the attic. Even neighbors were not spared; several heard screams and strange noises from the house when the Smurls were not home, and others detected the presence in their own homes. Most of the neighbors were sympathetic. The Smurls vowed to fight.

In January 1986, Janet heard about the Warrens, and the couple decided to call them. The Warrens arrived with Rosemary Frueh, a registered nurse and psychic, and began the investigation by quizzing the Smurls about their religious beliefs, the happiness of their family life, and whether they had ever practiced SATANISM, used a OUIJA™ board, or in any way invited the supernatural into their home. The Smurls said they had not. Then, the Warrens and Frueh walked the house, identifying the bedroom closet as the crossover point between the two sides of the duplex. The team said they detected the presence of four evil spirits. Three were minor, but the fourth was a demon.

Without any evidence of family discord, occult invitation, or tragedy, the Warrens could only surmise that the demon must have been dormant, probably for decades, and had risen to draw on the emotional energy generated by the girls' entrance into puberty.

The Warrens tried twice to induce the demon to expose itself through religious provocation, by playing tapes of religious music and confronting it with prayer. The demon reacted by shaking the MIRROR and dresser drawers; another time by spelling out "You filthy bastard. Get out of this house." The portable television emitted an eerie, silvery white glow. Only prayer and holy water seemed to stop the manifestations.

Phenomena continued. The eerie glow returned, the pounding in the walls worsened, and Jack and Janet were slapped, bitten, and viciously tickled. Small items disappeared. One day, Janet tried to talk to the demon, asking it to rap once for *yes* and twice for *no*. When she asked the demon whether it were there to harm them, it rapped once. Two phantom women dressed in colonial clothing appeared to Jack.

Even more horrifying, Jack was raped by a scaly SUC-CUBUS posing as an old woman with a young body. Her eyes were red and her gums green. Ed Warren was choked

and suffered terrible flu symptoms. An INCUBUS sexually assaulted Janet. Pig noises were heard in the walls.

The Smurls said they tried several times to obtain support and action from the Catholic Church. The Roman Catholic Diocese of Scranton said it would consult experts, but official involvement seemed unlikely. At one point, Janet thought she was getting help from a Father O'Leary but discovered he did not exist: Allegedly it was the demon impersonating a priest.

The Warrens called in BISHOP ROBERT McKENNA, a traditionalist priest who refused to abide by the changes in ritual mandated by the Second Vatican Council. He said Mass in Latin and had performed more than 50 EX-ORCISMS for the Warrens. He conducted the ancient rite, infuriating the DEMON.

The infestation intensified. Their daughter Carin fell seriously ill from a strange fever and nearly died. Dawn was nearly raped by the presence. Janet and Mary had slash marks and bites on their arms. Everyone was depressed. Ed Warren explained they had moved into the second demonic stage, OPPRESSION, which follows infestation and is followed by POSSESSION and death.

McKenna performed a second exorcism in late spring, to no avail. The demon even accompanied the family on camping trips in the Poconos and harassed Jack at work. The family could not move to another house since the demon would simply follow. After repeated refusals by the church to help, the Smurls decided to appear on television.

Remaining anonymous behind a screen, the Smurls were interviewed by Richard Bey on a Philadelphia talk show, *People Are Talking.* Later at home, the demon retaliated. It levitated Janet, then hurled her against the wall. It appeared to Jack as a monstrous creature resembling a pig on two legs. A human hand rose up through the mattress and grabbed Janet by the back of the neck. Jack was raped again.

In August 1986, the Smurls felt that the risk of ridicule did not outweigh the need to tell their story to a wider audience and granted an interview to the Wilkes-Barre *Sunday Independent* newspaper. Their home became a tourist attraction for the press, curious onlookers, and skeptics who wished to investigate. Some skeptics, who included some of the Smurls' neighbors, said they believed the family was concocting a story in order to profit from book and movie contracts.

Paul Kurtz, chairman of a skeptical organization, the Committee for the Scientific Investigation of Claims of the Paranormal (CSICOP) in Buffalo, New York, sought to investigate but was rebuffed by the family and the Warrens. Kurtz proposed to pay for the family to spend a week in a hotel with a private security guard while a team of investigators examined the house. Kurtz also offered free psychiatric and psychological examinations, which might have provided clues to the alleged activity. The Smurls said CSICOP had already made up its mind that their story was a hoax, and they preferred to work with the Warrens and the church.

Two CSICOP investigators went to the Smurl house but were denied entrance. Kurtz later opined in an article he wrote for *Skeptical Inquirer,* CSICOP's journal, that the case was not paranormal, and the Smurls had denied CSICOP access because they were afraid of what the organization would discover. He cited discrepancies in Dawn Smurl's accounts of her experiences and was critical of the Warrens. Kurtz suggested natural explanations for some of the phenomena experienced by the Smurls:

- abandoned mine voids in the area, settling and creating strange noises
- delusions by Jack Smurl that he was raped by a ghost
- a broken sewer pipe causing foul smells
- pranks by teenagers

Kurtz also pointed out that there were no police records of complaints of the haunting by Mrs. Smurl, though she said she had contacted police. Kurtz also wondered about motivation to make money on the case, since the Smurls began talking with Hollywood film companies shortly after the story broke in the press. The Smurls denied any interest in money.

Ed Warren raised more doubts of reporters and skeptics during a press conference he called in late August 1986. Warren said they had recorded paranormal sounds—groanings and gruntings—and had videotaped an unclear image of a dark mass moving about the house. Asked by journalists and CSICOP to produce the tapes, he declined. He told one journalist he had given the tapes to a TV company, the name of which he could not remember, and told Kurtz and other reporters they were in the exclusive possession of the church. However, church authorities later said nothing had been turned over to them.

Warren also declined reporters' requests to stay in the house, saying no one had paid attention when the Smurls first begged the media to spend a night to witness phenomena, and such requests were now out of the question. Warren said the Smurls would no longer deal with the press, and he was in charge of the case.

The Smurls contacted a medium, Mary Alice Rinkman, who examined the house and corroborated the Warrens' finding of four spirits. She identified one as a confused old woman named Abigail and another as a dark mustachioed man named Patrick who had murdered his wife and her lover and then been hanged by a mob. She could not identify the third, but the fourth was a powerful demon, she said.

Press coverage finally pushed the Scranton diocese into action, and they reluctantly offered to take over the investigation. The Warrens, meanwhile, planned a mass exorcism with several priests. Prayer groups went to the house to give comfort. The Reverend Alphonsus Travold

of the St. Bonaventure University, asked by the diocese to investigate, said he believed the Smurls were sincere and disturbed by the events but could not say whether demonic presence was the true cause.

McKenna arrived a third time to exorcise the house in September 1986; this time, the ritual seemed to be effective. There were no disturbances for about three months.

Prior to Christmas 1986, Jack again saw the black form, beckoning him to the third stage of possession. He clutched his rosary and prayed, hoping this was an isolated incident. But the banging noises, terrible smells, and violence started again.

The Smurls moved to another town immediately before the book about their ordeal, *The Haunted,* went to press in 1988. The church performed a fourth exorcism in 1989, which finally seemed to give them peace. A film version of *The Haunted* was released in 1991.

FURTHER READING:
Curran, Robert. *The Haunted: One Family's Nightmare.* New York: St. Martin's Press, 1988.
Kurtz, Paul. "A Case Study of the West Pittston 'Haunted' House." *The Skeptical Inquirer,* Winter 1986–1987, 11, 2: 137–146.

sneezing   According to a European folk belief, the soul flies out of the mouth whenever a person sneezes. A blessing should be said immediately to prevent the soul from being captured by a DEMON before it can return to the body. In Islam, Allah instructs people to wish one who sneezes well. Folklore also holds that sneezing expels a demon. Saying "Bless you" prevents the demon from immediately reentering the person and protects him or her from evil.

Soissons Possessions (1582)   The POSSESSION of four persons in Soissons, France, used by the Catholic Church in their campaign against the Protestant Huguenots. The Soissons Possessions resembled in many respects the MIRACLE OF LAON case and demonstrated the Real Presence. The overall mediocrity of the demoniacs and their EXORCISM, however, diminished the propaganda value. Nonetheless, audiences of thousands turned out to witness the exorcisms, and in one case a huge stage was built for the purpose.

One of the DEMONIACS was a 13-year-old boy, Laurent Boissonet, possessed by a DEMON named *Bonnoir.* The demon praised the Huguenots, damned the priests and friars, and said the Huguenots would go to a fine paradise where good beds awaited them. Relics of blessed virgins placed on the boy's stomach caused it to swell and the boy to convulse.

Boissonet was handed over to two Franciscans, one of whom had been present at the exorcisms of Nicole Obry in the Miracle of Laon case. The Franciscans tested the boy for fraud by sprinkling him during fits alternately with ordinary water and then holy water. The ordinary water produced no reaction, but the holy water increased his convulsions.

Bonnoir was finally expelled after he challenged the priests to administer a holy wafer to the boy, saying it would leave if Boissonet took it. The boy went into such convulsions that the the exorcist, Jean Canart, could not insert it into his mouth. Finally, he put the two sacred fingers—the index and middle—into Boissonet's mouth, causing it to open. He inserted a wafer and then clamped the jaws together and put his fingers over the boy's nostrils. There followed an internal struggle in the boy between JESUS and Bonnoir, with sounds like a shrieking pig being stifled or "a little dog being flayed."

Three times, Canart called out to the demon to give glory to God, honor Jesus and his body, and finally yield to God, Christ, and "His Catholic and Roman Church."

The demon replied in anger, "You're stifling me—how on Earth do you think I can get out?"

Canart released his hold on the boy's nostrils, and immediately a puff of wind and smoke emerged. Boissonet fell to his knees, crying, "Praise be to God; now I am healed."

Boissonet was possessed a second time by another demon named Bolo, who said he was on good terms with the saints and took his direction from St. James. Alternately, he said his superior was Ergon but explained that Ergon and St. James were one and the same. Bolo said he was not really a demon: "You can expel devils all right, but not us." This assertion concerned the exorcists, but they succeeded in making Bolo admit that he was evil and depart the boy.

Another of the demoniacs was Marguerite Obry (no mention is made in accounts whether or not she was related to Nicole Obry, associated with the Miracle of Laon). As Nicole, Marguerite was possessed by BEELZEBUB. The Franciscans tested her for fraud as well, giving her ordinary wafers and holy wafers. They secretly put holy water into her wine, and she refused to drink it.

The other notable demoniac in the case was a 50-year-old married man, Nicolas Facquier, an artisan. Facquier was possessed twice, first, by a demon named Cramoisy and, second, by an unnamed demon. Cramoisy claimed to be the same kind of spirit as Bolo: an order that lived in the limbo of unbaptized infants. He said he visited paradise three times a year.

Cramoisy announced that he was possessing Facquier in order to persuade three of his Huguenot cousins to return to Catholicism. Two of the cousins quickly converted. The third did so only after a long session with the demon, a bishop, and Charles Blendec, a monk who performed some of the exorcisms. After the third converted, Cramoisy departed Facquier.

All of the demoniacs were successfully exorcised, but they had no real impact on other cases or on public opinion. A year later, in 1583, the church's national synod at

Reims warned against performing exorcisms before making certain the victims were not in need of a medical doctor instead of an exorcist.

FURTHER READING:
Walker, D. P. *Unclean Spirits: Possession and Exorcism in France and England in the Late Sixteenth and Early Seventeenth Centuries.* Philadelphia: University of Pennsylvania Press, 1981.

Solas (Stolas)   FALLEN ANGEL and 36th of the 72 SPIRITS OF SOLOMON. Solas is a powerful prince who appears first as a raven or an owl and then as a man. He teaches astronomy and the virtues of herbs, including prophecy through plants and the uses of precious stones. He governs 26 LEGIONS of DEMONS.

Soleviel   DEMON and wandering duke of the air. Soleviel commands 200 dukes and 200 companions, who also have many servants and who wander from place to place. The 12 chief dukes have 1,840 servants who are obedient and good-natured. The 12 dukes are Inachiel, Praxeel, Moracha, Almodar, Nadrusiel, Cobusiel, Amriel, Axosiel, Charoel, Prasiel, Mursiel, and Penador.

Solomon (10th century B.C.E.)   Legendary king of the Israelites, son of David, builder of the Temple of Jerusalem, and commander of an army of DEMONS or DJINN.

The actual existence of Solomon and his father, David, remains unproved, but they are among the most important figures of the Old Testament. Solomon is granted great wisdom and understanding by God, far surpassing the wisdom of any other man. He knows the lore of plants, animals, and everything in the natural world. Men from far away seek him out for his counsel. In legend, his wisdom expands to include formidable magical knowledge, and his name (including *Son of David*) is used to control both good and bad spirits.

In 1 Kings, Solomon takes the throne upon his father, David's, death. The Lord goes to him in a dream and says, "Ask what I shall give you" (3:5). Solomon replies that he wishes to be given an understanding mind for governing and for discernment between good and evil. Pleased that he has not asked for riches, God says, "Behold, I give you a wise and discerning mind, so that none like you has been before you and none like you shall arise after you" (3:12). God also grants him incomparable riches. Thus does Solomon become famed for his wisdom.

In the fourth year of his reign, Solomon builds his famed Temple of Jerusalem, and his palace and administrative complex. In the temple, he places two gilded olivewood cherubim in the innermost part of the sanctuary. He positions them so that a wing of one touches one wall and the wing of the other touches the other wall, and their other wings touch each other in the middle of the house. When the temple is dedicated, priests place the ark of the covenant, containing the two stone tablets of

Moses upon which are written the Ten Commandments, underneath the wings of the cherubim.

Solomon has another vision, in which the Lord promises that his house will prosper as long as the commandments are kept and no other gods are worshipped. If there are any transgressions, God will cause the ruination to the kingdom.

For most of the 40 years of his reign, Solomon prospers: "Thus King Solomon excelled all the kings of earth in riches and in wisdom. And the whole earth sought the presence of Solomon to hear his wisdom, which God had put into his mind" (10:23–24). He rules over the natural world as well as people.

By his later years, he has acquired 700 wives and 300 concubines. Some of his wives convince him to turn away from God and worship pagan deities, especially the goddess Ashtoreth. Angry, God sends adversaries against him. In the end, God decides not to wrest his kingdom away from Solomon but instead to take it away from all but one of his sons.

One day, Solomon went to a person described as "the Jebusite" and fell in love with his daughter, who is called the Shulamite (Soumanitis). The priests of MOLOCH, however, said, "Thou canst not have her to wife except thou worship the great gods Remphan and Moloch." Solomon refused, but they gave him five locusts and said, "Crush these upon the altar of Moloch, and it will suffice."

Solomon said, "And so I did, and immediately the Spirit of God departed from me . . . and I became a laughingstock unto the idols and to the demons. Therefore have I written this my Testament that ye which come on it may pray and take heed to your latter end and not to your beginning, that ye may find grace perfectly for ever."

Other texts expand upon Solomon's wisdom; he becomes the greatest of magicians, a ruler over the realm of nature, able to summon angels and command demons. Such details are found in the Testament of Solomon, Odes of Solomon, and Psalms of Solomon, all part of the pseudepigrapha, and in the Wisdom of Solomon, part of the apochrypha. Josephus' *Antiquities* credits Solomon with writing 1,500 books of odes and songs and 3,000 books of parables and similitudes and knowing how to exorcize demons. The Sefer Raziel, a magical text, says that Solomon was heir to the famed book (also called the Book of Mysteries), which enabled him to become the source of all wisdom.

From the time of Origen, Solomon becomes more prominent in Christian lore than in Jewish lore, appearing on AMULETs, talismans, and lintels and in numerous incantations for protection against and removal of demons. His magical seal is a pentagram or hexagram.

In Islamic lore, Solomon becomes the greatest of world rulers, a true apostle and messenger of Allah, and the prototype of Muhammad. His magical powers against demons, the djinn, are famous. Solomon acquired his power over the djinn by asking for "soverignity not allowed to anyone after me" (sura 38:35). Allah responds by granting him unique power: "Then We subjected the wind to his power, to flow gently by his order wherever he wished, and also the evil Jinns, every builder and diver as well as those bound together in chains" (sura 38:36–38). Solomon alone was given the power to bind the djinn; however, much later, the prophet Muhammad repelled IBLIS by invoking Solomon's prayer request for sovereignty (see EXORCISM).

According to tradition, after Solomon died, the djinn wrote books of magic filled with acts of disbelief, or disinformation, and put them under his chair. When the books were discovered, the djinn claimed that Solomon had used the magic in them to control the djinn. As a result, Solomon was discredited by some Christians and Jews. Others took the books and began practicing the magic. Both groups erred, according to scholars, one by practicing magic, which earns no happiness in the afterlife, and the other by discrediting Solomon, whose power was directly from Allah. The Qur'an says:

> When a messenger from Allah came to them conforming what was revealed to them, a group of those given the scripture cast the book behind their backs as if they did not know about it. They followed what the devils claimed about Sulaymaan's dominion. However, Sulaymaan did not disbelieve, but the devils did by teaching men magic and what was revealed to the two angels Haaroot and Maaroot in Babylon. Though neither of them taught anyone without first saying, "We are only a trial, so do not commit disbelief," they learned from them means to separate a man from his wife. But, they could not harm anyone with it except by Allah's will. They learned what would harm themselves and not what would benefit them, though they knew that the buyers of (magic) would have no share in the happiness in the next life. They sold their souls for an evil price if they only knew. (Sura 2:101–102)

Despite the warnings of Islam, the allure of Solomonic magic proved irresistible. Numerous magical handbooks, or GRIMOIRES, attributed to the authorship of Solomon were popular in the early centuries of Christianity. By the 12th century, at least 49 texts were in existence. The most famous was the *Greater Key of Solomon,* quoted often in the magical books of the 17th–19th centuries.

Testament of Solomon

The Testament of Solomon, a text in the pseudepigrapha probably written between the first and third centuries C.E., is a legendary tale about how Solomon built the Temple of Jerusalem by commanding demons. The text is rich in demonology, angelology, and lore about medicine, astrology, and MAGIC. The author is unknown and may have been a Greek-speaking Christian who was familiar with the Babylonian Talmud. The magical lore related to demons, which dominates the text, shows Babylonian influences.

The demons are described as FALLEN ANGELS or the offspring of fallen angels and human women, and they live in stars and constellations. They can shape shift into beasts and forces of nature. They lurk in deserts and haunt tombs, and they dedicate themselves to leading people astray. They are ruled by Beelzeboul (BEELZEBUB), the Prince of Demons.

The stellar bodies themselves are demonic, wielding destructive power over the affairs of humanity. The 36 decans, or 10-degree portions of the zodiac, are called heavenly bodies and likewise are ruled by demons, who cause mental and physical illnesses. There are seven "world rulers," who are equated with the vices of deception, strife, fate, distress, error, power, and "the worst," each of whom is thwarted by a particular angel (with the exception of "the worst").

The testament considers angels as God's messengers but does not describe their origin or hierarchy. The main purpose of angels is to thwart demons and render them powerless. Each angel is responsible for thwarting specific demons. Humans must call upon the right angel by name in order to defeat a demon; otherwise, demons are worshipped as gods. Among the angels named are the archangels Michael, Raphael, Gabriel, and Uriel.

When the demon ORNIAS vampirizes Solomon's favorite boy by sucking out his soul through his thumb, Solomon begs God for power over the demon. While he prays, Michael appears and gives Solomon a ring with a seal engraved upon a precious stone. Michael tells Solomon that this magical ring will give him power over all demons, male and female, and that they will help him build the temple. The demons are subdued when the ring is thrown at their chests with the command "Solomon summons you!" Solomon interviews the demons and demands from them the names of their thwarting angels. When they are subdued, they are made to construct his temple.

One of demons interrogated by Solomon gives no name but describes himself as "a lecherous spirit of a giant man who died in a massacre in the age of giants." He lives in "inaccessible places." When someone dies, he sits in the tomb near the body and assumes the form of the dead man. If anyone visits, he tries to seize him or her, and, if he can, he kills that person. If he cannot kill the person, the demon causes him or her to become possessed by a demon and to gnaw his or her own flesh and drool at the mouth. The demon admits to Solomon that he is thwarted by the Savior, and if anyone bears the cross, the mark of the Savior, on his forehead, the demon flees. Solomon binds the demon and locks him up as he has the others.

The Testament of Solomon also describes the demons of the decans of the zodiac, the 36 degrees dividing the 12 zodiacal signs. The decans are ruled by ANGELs, but in the Testament, they are reduced to lower-level demons who cause disease and strife.

Solomon summons them to appear before him for interrogation to learn what they do and the names of the angels who thwart them. They appear with heads of formless dogs and as humans, bulls, dragons with bird faces, beasts, and sphinxes. The demons are, by order of decan:

1st—Ruax (also Rhyx), or "the Lord": He causes headaches and is dispatched by the words "Michael, imprison Ruax."

2nd—Barsafael: He causes those who live in his period to have pains in the sides of their heads. He is repelled by the words "Gabriel, imprison Barsafael."

3rd—Artosael: He damages eyes and is sent away by the words "Uriel, imprison Artosael."

4th—Oropel: He causes sore throats and mucus and is thwarted by the words "Raphael, imprison Oropel."

5th—Kairoxanondalon: He causes ear problems and is dispatched by the words "Ourouel (Uriel), imprison Kairoxanondalon."

6th—Sphendonael: He causes tumors of the parotid gland and tetanic recurvation (the body bent backward rigidly) and is quelled by the words "Sabael, imprison Sphendonael."

7th—Sphandor: He paralyzes limbs, deadens the nerves in hands, and weakens shoulders. He is subdued by the words "Arael, imprison Sphandor."

8th—Belbel: He perverts the hearts and minds of men and is dispatched by the words "Karael, imprison Belbel."

9th—Kourtael: He causes bowel colic and pain and retreats when he hears the words "Iaoth, imprison Kourtael."

10th—Methathiax: He causes kidney pains and is sent away by the words "Adonael, imprison Methatiax."

11th—Katanikotael: He causes domestic fights and unhappiness. To dispel him, write on seven laurel leaves the names of the angels who thwart him: "Angel, Eae, Ieo, Sabaoth."

12th—Saphthorael: He causes mental confusion. To get rid of him, write down the words "Iae, Ieo, sons of Sabaoth" and wear the AMULET around the neck.

13th—Phobothel: He causes loosening of the tendons and retreats when he hears the word "Adonai."

14th—Leroel: He causes fever, chills, shivering, and sore throats and retreats when he hears the words "Iax, do not stand fast, do not be fervent, because Solomon is fairer than eleven fathers."

15th—Soubelti: He causes shivering and numbness and is dispatched by the words "Rizoel, imprison Soubelt."

16th—Katrax: He causes fatal fevers. He can be averted by rubbing pulverized coriander on the lips and saying, "I adjure you by Zeus, retreat from the image of God."

17th—Ieropa: He causes men to collapse and creates stomach problems that cause convulsions in the bath. He retreats if the words "Iouda Zizabou" are repeated three times in the right ear of the afflicted person.

18th—Modebel: He causes married couples to separate but will retreat if the names of the eight fathers are written down and posted in doorways.

19th—Mardeo: He causes incurable fevers and is sent away by writing his name down in the house.

20th—Rhyx Nathotho: He causes knee problems and is repelled if the word "Phounebiel" is written on a piece of papyrus.

21st—Rhyx Alath: He causes croup in infants and is dispelled if the word "Rarideris" is written down and carried on a person.

22nd—Rhyx Audameoth: He causes heart pain and is dispatched by the written word "Raiouoth."

23rd—Rhyx Manthado: He causes kidney disease and is thwarted by the written words "Iaoth, Uriel."

24th—Rhyx Atonkme: He causes rib pain. If a person writes "Marmaraoth of mist" on a piece of wood from a ship that has run aground, the demon retreats.

25th—Rhyx Anatreth: He causes bowel distress and is quelled by the words "Arara, Arare."

26th—Rhyx, the Enautha: He alters hearts and "makes off" with minds. He is thwarted by the written word "Kalazael."

27th—Rhyx Axesbuth: He causes diarrhea and hemorrhoids. If he is adjured in pure wine given to the sufferer, he retreats.

28th—Rhyx Hapax: He causes insomnia and is subdued by the written words "Kok; Phedisomos."

29th—Rhyx Anoster: He causes hysteria and bladder pain and is thwarted when someone mashes laurel seeds into oil, massages it into the body, and calls upon Mamaroth.

30th—Rhyx Physikoreth: He causes long-terms illnesses but retreats when the sick person massages his or her body with salted olive oil while saying, "Cherubim, seraphim, help me."

31st—Rhyx Aleureth: He causes choking on fish bones. If one places a fish bone into the breasts of the afflicted one, the demon retreats.

32nd—Rhyx Ichthuron: He detaches tendons and retreats when he hears the words "Adaonai, malthe."

33rd—Rhyx Achoneoth: He causes sore throats and tonsillitis. He is sent away by writing "Leikourgos" on ivy leaves and heaping them into a pile.

34th—Rhyx Autoth: He causes jealousy and fights between people who love each other. He is subdued by writing the letters *alpha* and *beta.*

35th—Rhyx Phtheneoth: He cast the evil eye on everyone and is thwarted by the "much suffering eye" amulet.

36th—Rhyx Mianeth: He holds grudges against the body, causes flesh to rot, and demolishes houses. He flees when the words "Melto Ardad Anaath" are written on the front of the house.

King Solomon orders the demons of the decans to bear water and prays that they will go to the Temple of God (Jerusalem).

Magical Handbooks

The *Testament* provides a significant contribution to the legends of Solomon's magical powers and the magical handbooks attributed to Solomon. The two most important magical handbooks, or GRIMOIRES, are the *Key of Solomon*, also called the *Greater Key of Solomon*, and the *Lemegeton*, or *Lesser Key of Solomon*, said to be based on Solomonic wisdom. Many other grimoires borrow from these texts.

FURTHER READING:
The Old Testament Pseudepigrapha. Vols. 1 & 2. Edited by James H. Charlesworth. 1983. Reprint, New York: Doubleday, 1985.

Sons of God   FALLEN ANGELS known as the WATCHERS.

Genesis 6:1–4 states, "The sons of God, looking at the daughters of men, saw they were pleasing, so they married as many as they chose." The cohabitation produces a race of giants called NEPHILIM (also sometimes called the Sons of God) and leads to great corruption among humans. Yahweh is not pleased at the mixture of his spirit with flesh and casts the offending angels out of heaven. The corruption leads to God's decision to destroy life on the Earth with the flood.

In other biblical references, Sons of God are good angels shouting for joy when the morning stars sing (Job 38:7), and the Chosen People (Exodus 4:22; Wisdom 18:33), individual Israelites (Deuteronomy 14:1; Hosiah 2:1), and their leaders (Psalms 82:6).

FURTHER READING:
Godwin, Malcolm. *Angels: An Endangered Species.* New York: Simon & Schuster, 1990.
Graves, Robert, and Raphael Patai. *Hebrew Myths.* New York: Doubleday Anchor, 1964.
Ibn Taymeeyah's Essay on the Jinn (Demons.) Abridged, annotated, and translated by Dr. Abu Ameenah Bilal Philips. New Delhi: Islamic Book Service, 2002.

Sorath   DEMON angel who is the spirit of the Sun and whose number is 666.

RUDOLF STEINER said Sorath is the Sun-demon of Revelation, a great evil power far mightier than LUCIFER and AHRIMAN. He predicted that after the turn of the millennium, spiritual people would be able to see the Sun-Genius, the etheric vision of Christ. In response, Sorath will foment opposition through men who are possessed by him, who have strong natures, raving tongues, destructive fury in their emotions, and faces, which outwardly appear like those of animals. They will mock that which is of a spiritual nature. The mystery of Sorath and his number 666 holds the secret of black MAGIC. The power by which the Sun-Genius overcomes Sorath is the archangel Michael, who has the key to the abyss and the chain in his hand.

See SIX-SIX-SIX.

sorcery   A magical art involving spell casting with the help of spirits, including DEMONS, and often associated with WITCHCRAFT. *Sorcery* is derived from the French word *sors*, which means "spell."

Sorcery is engaged to influence one's lot in the world: love, fertility, luck, health, and wealth; protection against disaster, outsiders, and enemies; redress of wrongs and the meting out of justice; control of the environment; and explanations of frightening phenomena. Sorcerers have the power to harm, curse, and kill and to counteract spells cast by other sorcerers or practitioners of magic. They make use of FAMILIARS, sending them on magical errands to fulfill their spells. They have shape-shifting powers.

Goetic sorcery in Western magic is based on the 72 SPIRITS OF SOLOMON, also called FALLEN ANGELS. Details of their duties, characteristics, and SEALS are given in the *Lemegeton,* a grimoire attributed to Solomon but probably written much later than his time.

Spare, Austin Osman (1888–1956)

English magician who expressed his occult vision in strange and sometimes frightening art. Austin Osman Spare's talent for art was widely acknowledged and even called genius. He could have pursued a conventional artist's career but instead chose to devote himself to creating images of DEMONS and spirits raised up from deep levels of consciousness.

Spare was born on December 31, 1888, in London; his father was a City of London policeman. He left school at age 13 and worked for a time in a stained glass factory. He obtained a scholarship to the Royal College of Art in Kensington and enjoyed success as an artist by 1909.

The seeds for Spare's occult life were sewn early in childhood. Alienated from his mother, he gravitated toward a mysterious old woman named Mrs. Paterson. She claimed to be a hereditary witch descended from a line of Salem witches who escaped execution during the witch trials in 1692—an unlikely claim, considering that the Salem incident was perpetrated by hysterical children. The young Spare referred to her as his "witch-mother." Later, he said that she possessed great skill in divination and had the ability to materialize her thoughts.

Mrs. Paterson taught Spare how to visualize and evoke spirits and elementals and how to reify, or interpret, his dream imagery. Information was transmitted in dreams with the help of Mrs. Paterson's FAMILIAR, Black Eagle. She also initiated Spare in a witches' SABBAT, which he described as taking place in another dimension, where cities were constructed of an unearthly geometry. Spare said he attended such sabbats several times.

Under further tutelage of Mrs. Paterson, Spare developed his own system of MAGIC, based heavily on will and sex—his own sex drive was quite intense—and the works of ALEISTER CROWLEY.

When Mrs. Paterson died, Black Eagle was passed to Spare. For practitioners of the Left Hand Path, Black Eagle is seen as a "vampyre spirit" of the dream or astral plane.

Black Eagle can be summoned by ritual involving intense concentration of will, desire, and belief. It manifests in different forms, including bestial and demonic.

Spare believed that the power of will is capable of fulfilling any deeply held desire. The formula, simpler than ceremonial magic, was in his unpublished grimoire, "The Book of the Living Word of Zos." The formula called for creating sigils, or talismans, in an "alphabet of desire." The desire is written down in full. Repeating letters are crossed out, and the remaining letters are combined into a sigil like a sort of monogram. The sigil is impressed upon the subconscious by staring at it. The original desire is then let go so that the "god within" can work undisturbed toward the desired end.

According to one story, Spare once told a friend he would conjure freshly cut roses to fall from the air. His magic involved creating some symbolic drawings, which he waved in the air while repeating "roses." He got results, but they were unexpected. The plumbing in the room overhead burst, and Spare and his friend were dowsed by sewage.

In his art, Spare is best known for his atavisms, the reifying of primal forces from previous existences, drawn from the deepest layers of the human mind. This, too, was a product of his education from Mrs. Paterson. According to another story, one of his atavisms caused the suicide of one witness and the insanity of another.

Despite his ability to paint the spirits and images he saw, Spare was occasionally at a loss for words to describe some of his more bizarre experiences. Some of his visions put him into a place that he was able only to describe as "spaces beyond space."

In 1956, the English Witch Gerald B. Gardner (see WITCHCRAFT) contacted Spare for his help in a magical war with Kenneth Grant. Gardner believed that Grant was stealing his witches for his own New Isis Lodge, and he decided to launch a magical attack on him and reclaim his witches. In particular, Gardner wanted back a self-proclaimed "water-witch" named Clanda. It was the last year of Spare's life, and by then he was living in dire poverty and obscurity, eking out a living by painting portraits in local pubs.

Using his "alphabet of desire," Spare created a talisman for Gardner that would "restore lost property to its rightful place," which Spare himself described as "a sort of amphibious owl with the wings of a bat and talons of an eagle." Gardner did not give Spare specific information as to the exact nature of the "lost property"; he knew that Spare and Grant were on friendly terms.

During a Black Isis rite at the New Isis Temple, Clanda experienced the apparent negative effects of the talisman. Her role was to lie passively on the altar. Instead, she sat up, sweating and with a hypnotized and glazed look in her eyes. She behaved as though in the grip of terror, convulsing and shuddering. Later, she described what she experienced: the appearance of a huge bird that gripped her in its talons and carried her off into the night. She struggled and broke free, falling back onto the altar. The attending magicians saw none of this, but they did hear what sounded like the talons of a large bird scrabbling against the wind, and they felt a cold wind rush about the room. Physical talon marks were found on the window frame, and the windowsill was covered with a strange, gelatinous substance that seemed to breathe on its own. A strong odor of the sea permeated the temple for days.

As for Clanda, she failed to return to Gardner. Instead, she moved to New Zealand, where she drowned.

Some of Spare's work appears in two quarterly art review magazines he edited, *Form* and *Golden Hind*. He wrote three books that were published: *The Book of Pleasure (Self-love), the Psychology of Ecstasy* (1913) and *The Focus of Life* (1921), both of which dealt with his magic system, and *A Book of Automatic Drawing*, published posthumously in 1972. *The Book of Ugly Ecstasy* (1996) includes Spare's drawing of demonic beings and automata he discovered on the astral plane, formed by astral semen and stored sexual energy.

Spare spent most of his life as a recluse, living in poverty in London. He was remote and detached, preferring the company of his cats to that of human beings. He is considered a source of modern chaos magic.

FURTHER READING:
Cavendish, Richard, and Brian Innes, eds. *Man, Myth and Magic*. Rev. ed. North Bellmore, N.Y.: Marshall Cavendish, 1995.
Ford, Michael W. *Luciferian Witchcraft*. Lulu.com, 2005.
Guiley, Rosemary Ellen. *The Encyclopedia of Witches and Witchcraft*. 3rd ed. New York: Facts On File, 2008.
King, Francis. *Megatherion: The Magickal World of Aleister Crowley*. London: Creation Books, 2004.

Spirit of Orléans (1534)   Fraudulent EXORCISM plot perpetrated by Franciscan monks in Orléans, France, for money.

In the 16th century, it was customary to follow certain procedures in funeral rites that gave employment to mendicant monks. Soon after a person's death, funeral criers were hired to go about a town and proclaim the death, urge people to pray, and announce the time and place of the burial. Monks were hired for the funeral procession to carry lights. An elaborate procession, with many hired monks, enhanced the importance of the deceased and the family.

In 1534, the wife of the mayor of Orléans died. She had specified in her will that she did not wish to have an elaborate funeral and burial with a large procession and huge crowd. Her husband honored her wishes, and so no monks were hired. Instead, the woman was buried at the Franciscan church with only her husband and father in attendance. Her husband paid the monks six gold pieces, far less than they had hoped to earn.

The monks might have let it pass, save for another insult. Not long afterward, the mayor had some trees cut down to sell as logs. The Franciscans asked for free wood, and he refused. They decided to get revenge by convincing him that the soul of his wife was damned and required exorcisms.

A novice monk was stationed above the vault of the church. Late at night, when the monks arrived to pray, he made a great racket. Adjurations and exorcisms were to no avail. Instead, he made noises to indicate that he was a mute spirit.

With this fiction established by performance, the monks went to prominent citizens who were supporters of the Franciscans and said that a terrible thing was happening at their church. They invited people to go and see for themselves during evening prayers.

The novice performed again, indicating that he could not speak but could answer questions with signs—making loud rapping noises. Through a secret hole, he could hear the questions to the "spirit" posed by the EXORCIST. Thus, the novice indicated that he was the spirit of the mayor's dead wife, and her soul was condemned because of the heresy of her Lutheranism, and her body should be dug up and transferred to another place.

The monks asked the witnesses to sign a record to this effect. However, the citizens refused out of fear of offending the mayor. Nonetheless, the monks moved house to conduct their masses elsewhere, a practice they were entitled to do if a church had been profaned and needed purification.

The bishop sent a judge and committee of noted persons to investigate. The judge ordered that the exorcisms be performed in his presence and that someone climb up into the vault to see whether any spirit could be detected. The monks objected, saying that the spirit of the dead woman should not be disturbed. Nor would they perform the exorcisms in the presence of the judge.

The mayor reported all of this to the king of France, who sent members of the Parisian senate to investigate. Other investigators were sent by Chancelor Anton du Prat, a cardinal and papal legate to France.

The monks were summoned to Paris and interrogated, but they refused to cooperate, hiding behind religious privileges and immunities. The novice kept his silence, fearing death at the hands of the monks if he betrayed them, until the king promised him immunity and said he would not be sent back to the Franciscans if he told the truth. The novice confessed all and repeated his confession in the presence of his fellow conspirators.

The monks were returned to Orléans and sent to jail. They were paraded through town and forced to confess their crime in public.

The incident became the basis for a proverb whenever a lie was told: "It's the spirit of Orléans."

FURTHER READING:
Weyer, Johann. *On Witchcraft (De praestigiis daemonum)*. Abridged. Edited by Benjamin G. Kohl and H. C. Erik Midelfort. Asheville, N.C.: Pegasus Press, 1998.

spirits of Solomon   Seventy-two DEMONS or DJINN captured by the legendary King SOLOMON, who imprisoned them in a brass vessel and cast it into the sea. The vessel was discovered by Babylonians, who believed it contained a great treasure. When they broke open the vessel, the demons and their legions were set free, and they returned to their home. One exception was BELIAL, who entered an image and delivered oracles in exchange for sacrifices and divine honors.

The *Lemegeton*, or *Lesser Key of Solomon*, is a grimoire that gives instructions for the evocation of the 72 spirits. They are also known as the Spirits of the Brazen Vessel and the False Monarchy of Demons. Combined, the spirits accomplish "all abominations."

The 72 spirits are, in the order they were commanded into the brazen vessel (see individual entries):

Bael	Glasyalabolas	Perocel
Agares	Bune	Fureas
Vassago	Ronove	Balam
Gamagin	Berith	Alloces
Marbas	Astaroth	Caim
Valefor	Forneus	Murmur
Amon	Foras	Orobas
Barbatos	Asmoday	Gemory
Paimon	Gaap	Ose
Buer	Furfur	Amy
Gusion	Marchosias	Orias
Sitri	Stolas	Vapula
Beleth	Phoenix	Zagan
Lerayou	Halpas	Valac
Eligor	Malpas	Andras
Zepar	Raum	Flauros
Botis	Focalor	Andrealphus
Bathin	Vepar	Cimeies
Saleos	Sabnack	Amduscias
Purson	Shax	Belial
Morax	Vine	Decarabia
Ipos	Bifrons	Seere
Aim	Vual	Dantalion
Naberius	Haagenti	Andromalius

FURTHER READING:
Waite, Arthur Edward. *The Book of Black Magic and of Pacts.* 1899. Reprint, York Beach, Me.: Samuel Weiser, 1972.

Stanton Drew   Standing stones in Somerset, England, associated with a legend of the DEVIL. The Stanton Drew stones consist of three stone circles, two stone avenues, a cove, and a fallen stone called Hautville's Quoit.

According to lore, a wedding was held one Saturday, and the guests danced late into the night. At midnight, the fiddler stopped and said he could not play on the sabbath. A mysterious dark man appeared and continued the fiddling, and the guests danced faster and faster, unable to stop. At dawn, the music suddenly stopped, and

the mysterious man was revealed to be the Devil himself. The guests were unable to flee. The Devil told them that one day he would return to play for them again. Until that day, the guests are frozen in place as the standing stones.

FURTHER READING:
Bord, Janet, and Colin Bord. *Mysterious Britain.* London: Granada, 1974.

Steiner, Rudolf (1861–1925)   Philosopher, artist, scientist, and educator who developed the spiritual science of Anthroposophy, blending occultism, esoteric Christianity, and elements of ZOROASTRIANISM. At one point in his life, Rudolf Steiner faced a serious inner struggle with the forces of darkness.

Steiner was born to Austrian parents on February 27, 1861, in Kraljevic, Hungary. His father, a railway clerk, hoped Rudolf would become a railway civil engineer, but an early manifestation of psychic gifts set him on a different path. Steiner began to experience clairvoyance at the age of eight. When he was 19, an adept whose identity was never revealed initiated him into the occult.

Steiner joined the Theosophical Society and was active for about a decade before becoming disillusioned with internal rivalries and pettiness and with its emphasis on Eastern mysticism.

In 1913, Steiner formed the Anthroposophical Society, taking some members with him from the Theosophists. He described his path as one leading to spiritual growth on four levels of human nature: the senses, imagination, inspiration, and intuition. In Dornach, near Basel, Switzerland, he established the Goetheanum, a school for esoteric research, where he intended to produce Goethe's dramas and his own mystery plays. The building burned down in 1920 but was rebuilt in 1922 and now serves as the international headquarters for the organization.

For the last 25 years of his life, Steiner traveled around Europe and Great Britain, giving more than 6,000 lectures. His published works include more than 350 titles, most of which are collections of lectures. His key works outlining his occult philosophy are *Knowledge of the Higher Worlds and Its Attainment* (1904–05), *Theosophy: An Introduction to the Supersensible Knowledge of the World and the Destination of Man* (1904), and *An Outline of Occult Science* (1909).

Spiritual Philosophy

Up to age 40, Steiner devoted himself to pursuing his inner development and forming his spiritual science and philosophy. He developed his inner abilities to experience spiritual realms and beings. He spent time exploring the Akashic Records, the repository of all information in creation.

He was greatly influenced by Johann Willhelm von Goethe, the author of a version of FAUST.

At 40, Steiner felt he was ready to speak publicly about his spiritual philosophy, his clairvoyant experiences, and what he learned from them. By this time, he had gained much experience in the nonphysical realms through profound meditation. He said that at one time humankind was more spiritual and possessed supernormal capabilities but lost them on the descent to the material plane. At the lowest point of human descent, JESUS arrived and provided the opportunity to reascend to higher spiritual levels. For Steiner, the life, death, and Resurrection of Christ were the most important events in the history of humankind and the cosmos. However, the Gospels did not contain the complete story.

Steiner envisioned humanity as following a path of higher consciousness, guided by ANGELS, intelligences, and a host of spiritual beings. One of the most important is the archangel Michael, who guides the way to cosmic enlightenment, through which humanity will respiritualize the earth.

The old Christian spirituality will fall apart. Without a new spiritual vision, humanity will be overpowered and numbed by technology. Higher beings will help humanity form the new spiritual vision by sending impulses, but only if humans ask for help and cooperate. Meanwhile, Luciferic and Ahrimanic beings—forces of darkness and chaos—will constantly challenge angelic forces in human thought, sense, and will, thus making it crucial to learn a discerning spiritual science.

Steiner remarked in a lecture on April 4, 1912, that without new spiritual impulses, technology will not only dominate our outer life, but overpower and numb us. It will drive out the religious, philosophical, artistic, and ethical interests and turn us into "living automata." Many people today, even highly educated ones, are already unwitting slaves of outer material conditions, he said. FALLEN ANGELS—active in the information and computer technologies and economic networks—spread evil over the earth through racism and nationalism, though their approach is so subtle and intimate that people think they are not influenced by them.

Luciferic and Ahrimanic Beings

Steiner called beings that encourage destruction through vices Luciferic spirits. Still other spirits wish people to remain mired in a materialistic, mechanistic world. These spirits Steiner called "Ahrimanic" beings, after AHRIMAN, the Persian personification of evil. He links LUCIFER with air and warmth, and Ahriman with earth and cold. The changes of seasons reveal the eternal struggle between the two forces.

Steiner faced serious inner battles with evil forces and felt that his ultimate victory over them was his immersion in the esoteric mysteries of Christ. He warned that the spiritual path to higher consciousness entails such battles. He noted that people strongly resist taking responsibility to fight on the inner plane, preferring to project the battle out onto imagined enemies. Every thousand years as a new millennium approaches, Luciferic and Ahrimanic beings make particularly strong attacks on human progress. Our fear and projections make us increasingly susceptible to spiritual debasement, mental slavery, and mass hysteria.

Steiner thought that the greatest challenge of the modern age is to understand the polarity between Lucifer and Ahriman. Modern consciousness understands the polarity between God and the DEVIL and heaven and HELL. To strive toward either extreme is not good. Humanity must find balance in the middle.

Chaos, in which Luciferic and Ahrimanic forces participate, is necessary for human evolution, but highly antisocial. Steiner's commitment to "higher civility" spurred his reappraisal of human relations. At Dornach, a sculpture shows the *Representative of Man* standing between Lucifer and Ahriman. People can achieve this balance by paying attention to those who have educated, befriended, and even injured them. Steiner said on October 10, 1916, that, as a rule, people do not encounter anyone they have not met in previous incarnations. Likes and dislikes are great enemies of real social relations. Condemning a person obliterates a karmic relationship entirely, postponing it to a next incarnation, and no progress can be made.

Steiner explains that Ahrimanic beings are highly intelligent, extraordinarily clever, and wise. They act behind the veil of nature and work to destroy the human physical organism by fomenting destruction and hatred. Sensuous urges and impulses are enhanced. They replace thinking by all kinds of lower organism powers, especially the impulse to lie.

The Luciferic beings do everything to foster egoism within people and a passion for creating and bringing things into existence. Steiner insists that future evolution will be endangered if the Luciferic and Ahrimanic beings are not recognized and counteracted by spiritual science.

See SORATH.

FURTHER READING:
McDermott, Robert A., ed. *The Essential Steiner.* San Francisco: Harper & Row, 1984.
Sheperd, A. P. *Rudolf Steiner: Scientist of the Invisible.* 1954. Reprint, Rochester, Vt.: Inner Traditions International, 1983.
Steiner, Rudolf. *An Autobiography.* New trans. Blauvelt, N.Y.: Rudolf Steiner, 1977.
———. *The Four Seasons and the Archangels.* Bristol, England: Rudolf Steiner Press, 1992.
———. *Planetary Spheres and Their Influence on Man's Life on Earth and in the Spiritual Worlds.* London: Rudolf Steiner Press, 1982.

St. Louis Exorcism (1949)   Complex POSSESSION case that inspired the novel and movie *The Exorcist*, variously interpreted as one of demonic possession, POLTERGEIST activity, and delusion. Many of the details of the case remain secret, and all of the principal EXORCISTS involved in it have died.

Some experts believe that there was no demonic possession and that the events could be explained by poltergeist activity, Tourette's syndrome, or even mental illness.

The DEMONIAC was a 13-year-old boy, pseudonymously known as Robbie Doe. He was born in 1935 to a family in Cottage City, Maryland, a suburban community near Washington, D.C. He had a troubled childhood. His mother was Lutheran, and his father was a lapsed Catholic.

In January 1949 the family began to be disturbed by scratching sounds coming from the ceilings and walls of their house. Thinking that they had mice, the Does called an exterminator. This man could find no signs of rodents, and his efforts failed to end the scratching, which only became louder. Noises that sounded like someone walking about in squeaky shoes began to be heard in the hall. Dishes and furniture moved for no evident reason.

Then Robbie began to be attacked. His bed shook so hard that he could not sleep. His bedclothes were repeatedly pulled off the bed, and once, when he tried to hold on to them, he was pulled off onto the floor after them.

The Does made a connection to the recent death on January 26, 1949, of Robbie's Aunt Tillie in St. Louis, which had devastated the boy. Tillie, a Spiritualist, had interested Robbie in the paranormal, and they had used the OUIJA™ board together. Robbie may have used the Ouija™ to try to communicate with his dead aunt.

Convinced that an evil spirit was behind the disturbances, the Does consulted their Lutheran minister, Luther Schulze. Schulze prayed with Robbie and his parents in their home and then with Robbie alone in his home. He led prayers for Robbie in church. Schulze ordered whatever was possessing the boy to leave him in the name of the Father, the Son, and the Holy Ghost, but the affliction continued.

Robbie's torments increased. He could not sleep because of the weird noises and movements of objects day and night. In February, Schulze offered to let Robbie spend a night in his house, to which his parents agreed.

That night, Mrs. Schulze went to a guest room, while Robbie and the Reverend retired to twin four-poster beds in the master bedroom. Some time in the night, Schulze heard Robbie's bed creaking. He grasped the bed and felt it vibrating rapidly. Robbie himself was wide awake but was lying absolutely still.

Schulze put Robbie to sleep in an armchair, and before long, the heavy chair began to move. It scooted backward several inches and then slammed into a wall. It turned in slow motion and sent Robbie to the floor. Schulze noticed that Robbie appeared to be in a trance and made no effort to move out of the chair.

Schulze persuaded Robbie's parents to send him to Georgetown Medical Hospital, where he underwent medical and psychological evaluation from February 28 to March 3. Robbie acted wildly and, according to some reports, the message "Go to St. Louis!" appeared scratched on his skin in blood-red letters.

Robbie's parents took him by train to St. Louis, where they stayed with relatives. There they consulted Jesuits. Father Raymond J. Bishop came to the house to bless Robbie but quickly saw that the situation was far worse than INFESTATION. Bishop consulted Father William Bowdern, and the two went to Archbishop Joseph E. Ritter and requested an EXORCISM. The request was granted.

Exorcisms

Robbie's exorcisms began on March 16 at the home of his relatives on Roanoke Drive. More and more, Robbie acted like someone suffering from full demonic possession. He coughed up phlegm and drooled. Painful, bloody welts and scratches mysteriously appeared on his body. He cursed, vomited, spit, urinated, and made physical attacks on the exorcists, exhibiting unusual strength. He appeared to be cured and then relapsed into vile and violent behavior. When the episodes were over, he had no recall of them.

On March 21, Bowdern had Robbie taken to the Alexian Brothers Hospital and placed in a room in the security ward. The exorcism resumed in tight secrecy over the course of several weeks. It is not known how many people participated. Among the witnesses were Father William Van Roo and Father Charles O'Hara. Also present at various times were hospital staff and seminarians, among them Walter Halloran, whose help Bowdern had requested.

On April 1, Robbie was taken to the St. Francis Xavier Church (no longer in existence) to be baptized into the Catholic faith, a move that Bowdern thought would help the progress. However, Robbie went berserk on the way to the church, and Bowdern decided not to let him enter, lest he desecrate the premises. The boy was taken to the rectory instead. Despite his vomiting of BLOOD and mucous, and his struggling and shouting of obscenities, the baptism proceeded, followed eventually by a successful communion.

After several weeks of repeated progress and relapse, Robbie's behavior changed for the better. The turning point was a dream Robbie had of a fierce, sword-bearing ANGEL who made snarling DEMONs vanish. In April, the exorcism was declared a success.

Robbie returned to Maryland with his parents and resumed a normal life with no further episodes of any paranormal or supernatural phenomena. His father rededicated himself to Catholicism, and his mother converted. Robbie lives in the suburbs of Washington, D.C.

Aftermath

Bishop recorded details of the exorcisms in a diary. The church never intended for the case to be made public, but it was leaked to the media by Schulze. William Peter Blatty was a student at Georgetown University in Washington in August 1949 when he read an Associated Press account of the case in the *Washington Post*. Intrigued, he compiled as much information as he could about it. Twenty years later, he used it as the basis for his best-selling novel *The Exorcist,* changing many details and adding fictional ones.

The Exorcist was published in 1971 and was made into a film directed by William Friedkin and released in 1973. Blatty wrote the screenplay. During the filming, most of the cast and crew had strange experiences and misfortunes, including the news of nine deaths of people they knew. The movie terrified audiences, some of whom consulted medical and spiritual help out of fear of possession. Critics said the film itself was evil. The movie led to two sequels, the second of which was directed by Blatty.

In 2000, a new film version of *The Exorcist* was released, written and directed again by Blatty and Friedkin. Friedkin decided to show the face of the possessing demon, an effect which ruined the horror for many viewers.

Divided Opinions

Numerous inaccurate stories and legends have arisen around the case, and opinions still are divided as to what really happened. Critics have said that Robbie failed to meet criteria of possession set by the Catholic Church: prophecy and speaking in foreign languages. In addition, his feats of unusual strength were not thought to be characteristic of the supernormal strength usually exhibited by demoniacs.

During his involvement, Schulze had contacted parapsychologists J. B. and Louisa Rhine of Durham, North Carolina. The Rhines drove to St. Louis, but the phenomena had ceased by the time they arrived. Nonetheless, Rhine thought the case was one of "recurrent spontaneous psychokinesis," a type of poltergeist activity caused by unwitting psychokinetic outbursts from a living person. Rhine suggested that the phenomena were expressions of Robbie's own unconscious ability to influence objects in his environment and his own body through the power of his mind.

Bowdern never spoke about the case except to acknowledge that he believed it to be a true case of demonic possession. He died in 1983 at age 86. Bishop died in 1978 at age 72. Halloran, who burned his copy of Bishop's diary, stated that he did not believe that Robbie was possessed, but later said he was not enough of an expert to know. Toward the end of his life, he said mental illness probably could not explain all of the phenomena put together. Halloran died in 2005 at age 83.

Robbie himself has remained quiet about his experiences. With the principal exorcists dead and no further testimony from Doe himself, the case remains controversial.

FURTHER READING:

Allen, Thomas B. *Possessed: The True Story of an Exorcism.* New York: Doubleday, 1993. Revised edition, iUniverse, 2000.

Blatty, William Peter. *William Peter Blatty on* The Exorcist. New York: Bantam, 1974.

Chorvinsky, Mark. "Return to the Haunted Boy: The Exorcist Case Update." *Strange Magazine* 21. Available online by subscription only. URL: http://www.strangemag.com/. Downloaded October 7, 2006.

Opsasnick, Mark. "The Haunted Boy of Cottage City." *Strange Magazine* 20 (1999): 4–27.

"Report of a Poltergeist." *Parapsychology Bulletin* 15 (1949): 2–3.

Taylor, Troy. *The Devil Came to St. Louis: The True Story of the 1949 Exorcism.* Alton, Ill.: Whitechapel Productions Press, 2006.

succubus   A DEMON who takes the form of a beautiful woman in order to seduce men.

The succubus, along with its male counterpart, the INCUBUS, appears in ancient mythologies. Succubi appear in the flesh as beautiful, voluptuous women. They visit men in their sleep—especially men who sleep alone—and cause erotic dreams, nightmares, and nocturnal emissions. During the European witch hunts, succubi were agents of the DEVIL, who continually tempted men to commit sexual sins, sometimes by promising them immortality in return.

Succubi were not as prevalent as incubi in witch hunt cases. The prevailing belief of the time was that women were more licentious than men and, therefore, offered more opportunity for incubi. If a succubus assaulted a man, it was probably not his fault, according to demonologists of the day.

NICHOLAS REMY wrote in *Demonolatry* of a succubus case that happened in 1581. A man named Petrone Armenterious of Dalheim was persuaded by a succubus, Abrahel, to murder his son. He was so overcome with grief and guilt that he contemplated suicide. Abrahel told him that if he worshipped her, he would restore the boy to life. He complied, and his son returned to the living. But it was all an illusion, for the boy suddenly died again and immediately stank abominably.

The sex act itself with a succubus was said to be an awful experience, like penetrating a cavern of ice. Sometimes, a succubus was really an incubus in disguise, who collected a man's semen and used it to impregnate a woman. Some believed that sex with succubi could produce demon children. The Hebrew night demon, LILITH, bore an infinite number of demon sons this way.

Men accused of witchcraft were tortured until they confessed having sex with demons, among other demonic crimes. In 1468, in Bologna, Italy, a man was executed for allegedly running a brothel of succubi.

The *MALLEUS MALEFICARUM* (1487), the chief inquisitors' handbook, set forth five ways to get rid of a succubus:

- by reciting the Ave Maria
- by making a sacramental confession
- by making the sign of the cross
- by moving to a new home
- by having a priest or holy man excommunicate the demon

The Lord's Prayer and holy water also were said to work a cure.

FRANCESCO-MARIA GUAZZO wrote of one alleged succubus incident in *Compendium Maleficarum* (1608), in which a succubus forced herself on a young man near Aberdeen, Scotland. The succubus visited him in bed every night and stayed until dawn. The young man claimed that he tried to get rid of the succubus, but to no avail. Finally, the local bishop ordered him to go away to another place and devote himself to prayer and fasting. After several days, the young man said the succubus left him.

At the end of the 17th century, an odd lawsuit was tried in court in Posen, Germany. A young man forced his way into the cellar of a locked home and was later found dead on the threshold. Demons then set up housekeeping inside and created severe disturbances. The owners of the home were frightened into leaving.

Local exorcists failed to expel the demons, and so an expert was summoned, Rabbi Joel Baal Shem of Zamosz. He was able to induce the demons to disclose their identity. They claimed the house belonged to them, and they demanded the opportunity to prove it in a court of law. The case was tried with Rabbi Joel and an invisible demon advocate, who could be heard.

According to the demons, the previous owner of the home had engaged in intercourse with a succubus, who had borne hybrid children. The man was persuaded by a rabbi to break off his affair, but the demon demanded that the cellar be given to it and the offspring as inheritance. The man and all his heirs were now dead, and the demon children demanded possession of the house.

The new homeowners said they had lawfully purchased the house. The demon children were not legitimate "seed of men" and so had no legal rights. In addition, the demon had forced the previous owner into sexual relations.

The court decided against the demons, saying that their abodes were deserts and wastelands, not the homes of men. Rabbi Joel performed EXORCISMs that drove away the demons.

FURTHER READING:

Guazzo, Francesco-Maria. *Compendium Maleficarum*. Secaucus, N.J.: University Books, 1974.

The Malleus Maleficarum of Heinrich Kramer and James Sprenger. New York: Dover, 1971.

Remy, Nicholas. *Demonolatry.* Secaucus, N.J.: University Books, 1974.

Surin, Jean-Joseph (1600–1665) French priest and mystic who became involved in the LOUDUN POSSESSIONS of Ursuline nuns during 1630–34. Father Jean-Joseph Surin became possessed himself, and his health was adversely affected for the rest of his life.

Surin was unsuited to deal with DEMONIACs because of a neurotic temperament brought on by years of ascetic practices. He probably should have avoided the case, but

he felt compelled, even obsessed, to do battle with DEMONS. He spent his entire life as a virgin.

Surin was drawn to the religious life at an early age. He was reared in a cloister and attended the College of Bordeaux, where he was a contemporary of Father URBAIN GRANDIER, who left the school in 1617. Grandier was burned at the stake during the Loudun Possessions. Surin practiced self-denial during his early years as a priest, denying himself food, sleep, and social contact. He served in Rouen and then spent four years in the fishing village of Marennes, where he was director to two women who had remarkable visions and ecstasies that captured his attention.

By the time he arrived in Loudun on December 15, 1634, Grandier had been executed. Surin, at age 34, was in poor health, suffering severe headaches, muscle pain, melancholy, and attacks of depression and confusion. He had numerous psychosomatic complaints, and the slightest physical activity brought on severe pain. He constantly perceived himself as beset by all sorts of spiritual agonies and pressures. Perhaps most problematic was his credulity: He believed everything he was told, especially about people's spiritual experiences. Thus, he was inclined never to doubt the claims of the possessed nuns at Loudun.

Unlike many of his fellow Jesuits, Surin was indeed convinced that JEANNE DES ANGES and other nuns were genuinely possessed. He wrote that he had engaged in combat with "four of the most potent and malicious devils in hell" and that God "permitted the struggles to be so fierce and the onslaughts so frequent that exorcism was the least of the battlefields, for the enemies declared themselves in private both day and night in a thousand different ways."

Surin wrote candidly of the sexual temptations he himself felt working closely with demoniacs who convulsed in suggestive ways and spoke frankly of their demonic copulations.

At first, Jeanne did her best to avoid him and his attempts at EXORCISM. Surin was convinced he could help Jeanne and tried to force spiritual instruction upon her. Day after day, he tolerated the most wretched and insulting behavior from her.

Finally, he made a fatal mistake: he prayed to suffer in Jeanne's stead and to take on her POSSESSION. His prayers were answered, and on January 19, 1635, he began to feel the effects of OBSESSION. By Good Friday, April 6, he was exhibiting signs of possession. He felt that the demons had passed from Jeanne and into him. He was both elated at his success and plunged into the deepest despair over his fate.

In May 1635, Father Surin wrote of his torments to Father D'Attichy, a Jesuit in Rome, saying:

> Things have gone so far that God has permitted, for my sins, I think, something never seen, perhaps, in the Church: that during the exercise of my ministry, the

Devil passes from the body of the possessed person, and coming into mine, assaults me and overturns me, shakes me, and visibly travels through me, possessing me for several hours like an energumen. . . . Some say that it is a chastisement from God upon me, as punishment for some illusion; others say something quite different; as for me, I hold fast where I am, and would not exchange my fate for anyone's, being firmly convinced that there is nothing better than to be reduced to great extremities.

Surin asked D'Attichy to pray for him and to keep his letter confidential, but the priest had it copied and widely circulated.

Jeanne continued to exhibit signs of possession until October 1635, when Surin succeeded in expelling LEVIATHAN, followed by BALAAM on November 29 and ISACAARON on January 7, 1636. Next, he struggled with Behemoth, but after 10 months of failure, he broke down. Behemoth said he would leave if Jeanne made a pilgrimage to the tomb of St. Francis de Sales, and Surin went with her.

He accompanied her on part of the trip. He was by then struck dumb by the devils, and he prayed for deliverance at the tomb, without success. He was given a dried clot of the saint's blood to eat, but it enabled him to speak only for a moment. Surin left to return to Bordeaux and, along the way, regained enough speaking ability to give strained sermons.

Surin said usually there were two demons in him, Isacaaron and Leviathan. The DEVIL told him that he would be deprived of everything, and the Devil had made a PACT with a witch in order to prevent Surin from speaking of God.

The demons tortured the priest. Surin said his possession felt as if he had two different souls within him, fighting over his body. He was subjected to extremes of emotion and action, ranging from great peace at God's good pleasure to rage, aversion to God, and intense and violent desire to cut himself off from God. His attempts at spiritual practice, such as making the sign of the cross, were immediately thwarted by the warring demons within him. Any thoughts of goodness were countered by rage. He was plagued by thoughts of suicide.

Others told Surin that he was being punished by God for some sin. If so, he said, he accepted his fate and was glad to be reduced to extremities and was content to die.

Surin continued ill and tormented throughout 1637 and 1638. He had periods of lucidity and normalcy. By 1639, his afflictions worsened, and he lost the ability to move and speak. He could not converse or preach and was struck completely dumb for seven months. He could not read or write, dress and undress himself, walk, or stand upright. He slept in his clothes. He suffered fever and partial paralysis and fell into a mysterious sickness that defied the diagnosis of doctors and that no medical treatments remedied. He vomited almost everything he ate.

From 1639 to 1657, Surin stopped writing letters and communicating and lived in near-total isolation. He had wild swings of mood, thought, and emotion. He was seized with repeated temptation to burn down the house. Others considered him insane and avoided him. He believed he was a sorcerer who had the power to send demons into others.

Visions of angry saints and an angry Christ tormented him; he believed he was damned to HELL. Visions of the Blessed Virgin Mary scowled at him in disapproval and threw punishing thunderbolts that he felt throughout his body.

On May 17, 1645, Surin attempted suicide at a Jesuit house in Saint-Macaire, near Bordeaux, where he lived. The house was built above a river. Surin threw himself out of his window and landed on the rocks below. He survived with a broken thighbone.

After a few months, Surin was able to walk again, but with a limp, and to read and write. He even attained enough inner strength to preach and hear confession. But for the next three years, he was watched by a brother or was tied to his bed to prevent more suicide attempts.

In 1648, a sympathetic brother, Father Bastide, was appointed rector of the College of Saintes and took Surin with him. Bastide nursed him back to a functioning level of health. Surin felt better mentally if he was in pain physically. He still considered himself damned, completely evil.

He returned to Bordeaux. From 1651 to 1655, he managed to dictate his greatest work, *The Spiritual Catechism*. In 1657, he recovered a limited ability to scrawl words on paper, and, in 1660, he regained an ability to walk. He had profound psychic experiences, and, through his good angel, began dispensing personal advice. He was ordered to stop. (Jeanne did the same thing later in her life but was allowed to continue.)

Surin began functioning as a priest again, visiting the sick, and writing letters. His behavior was odd, however, and his superiors censored most of his letters.

In 1663, he wrote his account of the Loudun affair, *Experimental Science*. He died peacefully in 1665.

Modern commentators have opined that Surin was never really possessed, because he retained his own intelligence, and that he was instead in the grip of a long-lasting obsession.

FURTHER READING:
Huxley, Aldous. *The Devils of Loudun.* New York: Harper and Brothers, 1952.

Swedenborg, Emanuel (1688–1772)

Scientist and mystic who traveled out of body to both heaven and HELL. Emanuel Swedenborg described in great detail the structure and hierarchy of the afterlife. He believed that people make the choice of either heaven or hell. Swedenborg wrote about his experiences, but his views were rejected by his contemporaries. After his death, his works influenced philosophers and theologians from the 19th century on.

Swedenborg was born in Stockholm on January 29, 1688, the second son of the Lutheran bishop of Skara. The family name was then *Swedberg*; the father changed it to *Swedenborg* when they became part of the nobility in 1719. After graduation, Swedenborg traveled to the Netherlands, Germany, and England, where he met the astronomers Edmund Halley and John Flamsteed. By the time of his return to Sweden in 1716, his reputation called him to the attention of King Charles XII, who named him a special assessor to the Royal College of Mines. Fascinated by the mining industry, Swedenborg turned down the opportunity to teach at Uppsala.

Swedenborg never married and devoted himself to work instead. He was a creative inventor, conceiving of a device to carry boats overland for a distance of 14 miles, submarine and air guns that could fire 60 or 70 rounds without reloading, and flying machines. In 1734–44, Swedenborg wrote various treatises on animals, mineralogy, geology, creation, and anatomy. In 1745, he published *Worship and the Love of God*, based on his visionary experiences, and turned his attention completely to the study of religion and God's revelations.

Swedenborg began having ecstatic visions in 1743. Up to that time, he had not given much thought to spiritual matters, although he had argued that the soul existed. Suddenly, he was overcome with revelations about heaven and hell, the work of ANGELS and spirits, the true meaning of Scripture, and the order of the universe.

He was fully conscious during the visions and could remain in a trance for up to three days. During these times, his breathing would be severely slowed, and he would be insensible, but his mental activity remained sharp. He once likened his trances to what happens when a person dies and is resuscitated.

He also had the unusual ability to remain for prolonged periods in the borderland state between sleep and wakefulness, either as he was going to sleep or as he was awakening. In this twilight state of consciousness, he was immersed in vivid images and voices. He called his visionary travels being "in the spirit," and he clearly knew that he was out of his body.

In 1744 and 1745, he had visions that had a profound effect on him and greatly opened his spiritual senses. He later was able to exist simultaneously in the material world and the spiritual realms. He quit his job as assessor in 1747 to devote himself fully to his visionary work.

In his later years, he moved to England, and he died there at age 84. He is buried in London.

After his death in 1772, some of Swedenborg's followers established various churches and societies to study and promulgate the mystic's theories. The Church of the New Jerusalem was founded in England in 1778 and in the United States in 1792. The Swedenborg Society was established in 1810 to publish translations of Sweden-borg's books, create libraries, and sponsor study and lecture. Spiritualists embraced Swedenborg's concept of the spirit's survival after death and the possibility of communication with spirits. As did Swedenborg, they rejected reincarnation.

Swedenborg recorded his visionary experiences in 30 volumes in Latin. Of those, *Heaven and Hell* (1758) describes how souls go to the spiritual world and choose the realm with which they resonate in terms of their earthly interests. It describes societies, cities, life, work, children, and other topics.

According to Swedenborg, people, through free will, create their life and eventually choose heaven or hell. Men and women are completely at liberty to pursue lives devoted to love of the divine and charity toward the neighbor or to glorify self-love and evil. By so doing, they make their own heaven or hell. Choices are final.

Immediately after death, the soul passes to an intermediary state called the spiritual world or world of the spirits, halfway between Earth and heaven and hell. The spiritual world and the material world are separate and distinct but mirror each other through the law of correspondences. The soul awakens to find itself in an environment similar to the one left behind. This "first state" lasts for a few days. Angels, friends, and relatives greet the newcomer. If a spouse has preceded the newly arrived soul, they may reunite.

The first state is followed by the second state, in which the soul enters interior contemplation and judges its true character, which is impossible to hide. One's secret thoughts and intentions in life are more important than actions, for the soul may have acted falsely to impress others or curry favors for itself. This self-examination prepares the soul to move into its permanent home in heaven or hell. In the first state, evil and good souls are together, but they separate in the second state.

Evil souls go on to hell at the end of the second state. Good souls go through a "vastation," or a purification of spiritual impurities. They then enter the third state, in which they receive instruction for becoming angels in heaven.

Swedenborgian hell differs greatly from the eternal fire of damnation propounded by preachers of his day. It is quite a modern place, peopled by those who choose self-love and evil rather than divine love and truth. The Lord casts no one into hell but instead works steadfastly through his angels to save that soul. During life, angels try to replace evil thoughts and intentions with good ones. But those who still embrace evil and falsehood make their own hell after death.

Hell's denizens continue their earthly lives and habits, much as angels do, but with the continual threat of punishment if they exceed acceptable levels of vice and corruption. Retribution is the only restraint on their evil natures. There is no fallen LUCIFER or SATAN leading them. *Lucifer* and *Satan* themselves mean hell, and there is no chief DEVIL, for all the spirits in hell are former human beings. Because they have chosen malice and darkness, their faces are distorted into monstrous, repulsive shapes. They live in gloom yet appear burned by the fire of their own hatred. They speak with anger and vengefulness, they crave each other's company, and they shrink back in loathing and pain from the approach of an angel. The constant clash of their falsehoods and senses produces a sound like the gnashing of teeth. The openings, or "gates," of hell are numerous and everywhere but only visible to those spirits who have chosen that path. Inside, hell resembles cavernous, bestial lairs, with tumbledown homes and cities, brothels, filth, and excrement. Other hells may be barren deserts.

Swedenborg had conversations with evil spirits. Once, a man and woman were given permission to go to heaven from hell. The woman was a siren who served as the man's concubine. That man said that in his hell nature was their God, and religion was only a toy for the lower class. He dismissed angels and heaven as having no significance. On another occasion, Swedenborg was told by devils that they cannot avoid bothering people, and they become enraged when they see angels.

In any of these afterlife worlds, time does not exist as it does on Earth. It is measured by changes of one's interior state. Space also is different; spirits of like mind are "near" each other whatever their actual "location."

Swedenborg places responsibility for the permanent state of the soul squarely upon the individual and not on a judging God or a redeeming savior. The road to heaven or hell begins early in life with thoughts and intentions. Ultimately, each soul is true to its own nature.

FURTHER READING:
Lachman, Gary. "Heavens and Hells: The Inner Worlds of Emanuel Swedenborg." *Gnosis* no. 36 (Summer 1995): 44–49.
Swedenborg, Emanuel. *Heaven and Hell.* Translated by George F. Dole. New York: Swedenborg Foundation, 1976.

Symiel   DEMON among the 31 AERIAL SPIRITS OF SOLOMON. Symiel rules as a king in the northeast, with 10 dukes during the day and 1,000 during the night. The daytime dukes have 720 servants each, and the night dukes have 790 servants each. The daytime dukes are good-natured, but the nighttime dukes are stubborn and resist commands. The 10 major dukes of the day are Asmiel, Chrubas, Vaslos, Malgron, Romiel, Larael, Achol, Bonyel, Dagiel, and Musor. The 10 dukes of the night are Mafrus, Apiel, Curiel, Molael, Arafos, Marlano, Narzael, Murahe, Rhicel, and Nalael.

talisman An object that possesses magical or supernatural powers and transmits the powers to the owner. Talismans are different from AMULETs, which are objects that passively protect wearers from evil and harm. Talismans usually perform a single function and make powerful transformations possible. The magic wand of a sorcerer or FAIRY, the magical lamp or bottle of DJINN lore, King Arthur's sword Excalibur, seven-league boots, and Hermes' helmet of invisibility are all talismans. Talismans draw to their owners luck, success, wealth, love, magical abilities, and cures for illnesses. They also can be used in spell casting.

Any object can become a talisman. It may derive its powers from nature, such as a holed stone, or be imbued with power by acts of ANGELS, spirits, or gods. Talismans can be made in MAGIC. DEMONs and other spirits can be bound to a talisman, such as by the BLOOD and semen of a sorcerer or magician. The magician controls the spirits via the talisman. When the talisman is no longer needed, it should be burned. It is dangerous for a talisman to fall into the wrong hands.

Magical handbooks (see GRIMOIRES) give instructions for making talismans at auspicious astrological times. Talismans for a specific purpose can be created and drawn or engraved on metal or paper. They are consecrated in a ritual. Most Western talismans are based upon the principle of correspondences found in the KABBALAH, which holds that everything in Creation is connected. For example, the planets all have correspondences to aspects of daily life. Thus, a talisman inscribed with the symbol of a planet can be empowered to influence that sphere of life.

FURTHER READING:
Hall, Manly P. *Paracelsus: His Mystical and Medical Philosophy.* Los Angeles: Philosophic Research Society, 1964.
Kraig, Donald Michael. *Modern Magick: Eleven Lessons in the High Magickal Arts.* 2nd ed. Paul: Llewellyn, 2004.

talking board See OUIJA™.

Taru (Tauru) In ZOROASTRIANISM, and Persian lore, the arch-DEMON of evil hunger. Taru is usually paired with another archdemon, ZARIKA (evil thirst). Zarika makes poison, which Taru administers to plants and animals. Taru opposes the good *amesha spenta* Hurdat. He is especially pleased when a person walks around wearing only one boot, considered a sin in this culture.

Tase In Burmese lore, hordes of the demonic dead who prey upon the living and spread disease and pestilence. There are several types of Tase:

- Thaber Tase are the spirits of women who died in childbirth and return as succubi. (See LILITH.)
- Thaye Tase are grotesque giants who were people who died violently. They spread smallpox, cholera, and other deadly diseases. They also appear at the bedsides of dying people to laugh at them.

- Hminza Tase enter the bodies of crocodiles, tigers, and dogs and attack people. They haunt areas where they once lived unhappy lives.

The Tase can be kept away by banging pots and making great rackets of noise or by appeasing them with sacrifices and dances. Sometimes, the dead are buried without grave markers, an attempt to make them forget where they once lived, so they will not return in demonic form.

tefillin   See AMULET.

Temple of Set   See SATANISM.

tengu   Asian GOBLIN or DEMON who acts as a vampire, poltergeist, and trickster.

Descriptions of the *tengu* date to the eighth century. The demon appears in the shape of a man with wings and long, sharp nails on his hands and toes. His nose is either a crow's beak or red and round, and its size indicates the demon's strength. Sometimes, he carries a fan or a stick. The *tengu* is especially known for kidnaping people in remote, mountainous areas. He is fond of stealing children. POSSESSION by a *tengu* is not necessarily diabolical. The possessed acquire supernormal skills and knowledge during their occupation by the spirit.

Tezcatlipoca   Aztec prince of the Underworld, sorcerer, and king of the witches. The name *Tezcatlipoca* means "smoking mirror," in reference to the obsidian MIRROR that he uses to foretell the future and spy on others. He is also known as *Yaomauitl,* which means "dreaded one."

According to the Popul Vuh, Tezcatlipoca wears a star on his forehead as a sign that he is the ruler of darkness. He wears a jaguar skin around his hip, the body of a dead bird on his ear, and a snake's head fixed to one nostril. As a scepter, he carries the amputated arm of a woman who died in childbirth, which he uses in necromantic rites.

Tezcatlipoca and his brothers, the TZITZIMIME, created the world. They were thrown out of paradise, Tamoanchan, when Tezcatlipoca made the mistake of picking the sacred roses of Tamoanchan. Tezcatlipoca entered the underworld by climbing down a giant spider web.

There are many stories about this DEMON god and his activities. He sentences the newly arrived souls of the dead, who stand before him dressed in ocelot skins with yokes around their necks. He makes them run an obstacle course through Mictlan, a region of HELL.

According to lore, the practice of human sacrifice in Mexico began with Tezcatlipoca. He assumed the shape of a rooster to seduce the first woman ever created. Then he killed her, cut out her heart, and offered it to the Sun.

Tezcatlipoca is blamed for the disappearance of the Toltecs, a mythical race of beings. The demon summoned them to a great feast where they danced and sang. A sudden panic gripped them, and they fled across a stone bridge over the river Texcaltlauhco. Tezcatlipoca caused the bridge to collapse, and most of the Toltecs fell into the river and became stones. A few survived but were rendered senseless.

Tezcatlipoca spreads disease and pestilence. He assumes the form of a blob and rolls like a tumbleweed, spreading sickness as he goes. Sometimes, he takes the form of a cock or a coyote and lurks at CROSSROADS in order to ambush travelers. He rides howling winds, especially at night.

FURTHER READING:
Hyatt, Victoria, and Joseph W. Charles. *The Book of Demons.* New York: Simon & Schuster, 1974.

Theophilus (ca. 538)   Legendary monk who made a PACT with the DEVIL. The story of Theophilus was popular during the Middle Ages, especially because of its triumphant ending. It was written in various languages, was read at many churches, and was made into a drama, *Le Miracle de Theophile,* by Ruteboeuf, a 13th-century *trouvere.*

Theophilus was bursar of the church of Adana in northern Cicilia. He was offered a bishopric. A modest man, he declined because he was afraid he could not do the job. The man who did become bishop took a perverse interest in tormenting and harassing Theophilus, even accusing him of sorcery. Theophilus lost his job.

In revenge, he went to see Salatin, an "evil old Jew" who took Theophilus to a CROSSROADS and conjured the Devil in an exotic language. The Devil offered revenge and the bishopric in exchange for Theophilus' soul. Theophilus agreed, renounced Jesus and Mary, and signed a pact in his own BLOOD.

According to *Le Miracle de Theophile,* the pact read:

> To all who shall read this open letter, I, Satan, let know that the fortune of Theophilus is changed indeed, and that he has done me homage, so might he have once more his lordship, and that with the ring of his finger he has sealed this letter and with his blood written it, and no other ink has used therein.

As SATAN promised, the church realized there was no evidence against Theophilus. The bishop was removed from his office and Theophilus installed in his stead. But Theophilus was not happy; he began to worry about spending eternity in HELL. He started praying unceasingly to the Virgin Mary for help. She took pity on him and interceded with God, obtaining God's pardon. The relieved Theophilus burned his pact, made a public confession, and lived the rest of his life piously and in peace.

The moral of Theophilus' story is that repentance and prayer will save a person from the snares of the Devil.

See FAUST.

Thompson/Gifford Obsession   Remarkable spirit OBSESSION case investigated by the psychical researcher JAMES

HERVEY HYSLOP. The case proved to Hyslop, and to many others, the reality of spirit obsession.

Frederic L. Thompson was a 39-year-old metal-worker and weekend artist who first visited Hyslop in January 1907. Thompson claimed he was under the influence of the late R. Swain Gifford, a noted landscape painter in the late 1800s, experiencing tremendous urges to paint and sketch trees and rocky coasts that he had never seen. Although Thompson had met Gifford one summer in New Bedford, Massachusetts, and had contacted him in 1898 to ask for a recommendation to Tiffany Glass Company, the two men were hardly acquaintances, much less friends. In 1900, Thompson moved to New York, where he was employed in metal and jewelry work. He did not know that Gifford died on January 15, 1905.

By the late summer and fall of that year, Thompson was overcome with strong impulses to paint. He did not understand these urges but began to visualize pictures he knew Gifford had painted on the New Bedford coast. He referred to his artist alter ego as "Mr. Gifford," a fact confirmed to Hyslop by Thompson's wife, Carrie.

But, in January 1906, Thompson saw an exhibit of the works of "the late R. Swain Gifford" and realized for the first time that Gifford was dead. Fascinated by the similarities between Gifford's paintings and his own recent efforts, he could almost feel the fresh sea breezes. Then a voice said to him, "You see what I have done. Go on with the work," and he blacked out.

Thompson continued painting, as his private life and finances deteriorated under the ever-increasing compulsions. He believed he was becoming insane—two physicians diagnosed him as a paranoid—and finally visited Hyslop after hearing of the doctor's work in psychical research. Hyslop was intrigued but at first believed Thompson was suffering from personality disintegration. But if there were any truth to Thompson's claims, Hyslop believed consulting a psychic would shed light on the situation. He and Thompson met with Margaret Gaule on January 18, 1907.

Gaule immediately sensed the presence of an artist, although Hyslop had given her no information about Thompson, even introducing him as "Mr. Smith." She described landscape scenes, much as Thompson had detailed them to Hyslop two days earlier. On March 16, Hyslop took Thompson to Boston, to sit with Minnie M. Soule (referred to in Hyslop's papers as "Mrs. Chenoweth"), judged the most talented medium of her day. Her spirit communicator, Sunbeam, gave her information about Gifford's personal habits, even his clothing and rugs—items later confirmed by Gifford's widow—and vividly described a certain scene of gnarled trees overlooking the water that had haunted Thompson for days. The medium's communications convinced Thompson he was not becoming insane, and he left for the New England coast to try and find the pictures in his mind.

Throughout summer and autumn 1907, Thompson traveled over Gifford's favorite island haunts, recognizing scenes he had been compelled to paint, hearing music and even the voice he had heard at the Gifford exhibition. On one of the trees Thompson sought, Gifford had carved his initials, R.S.G., 1902. By early 1908, Thompson was completing large paintings and selling them. Prominent art critics who viewed the works agreed they bore uncanny resemblances to Gifford's works. Hyslop still harbored suspicions that Thompson was merely cultivating long-harbored desires to be an artist, and that his association with Gifford had influenced him more than he realized.

To prove whether Thompson was obsessed with the spirit of Gifford or had merely incorporated his style in his own work, Hyslop decided to establish contact with the dead artist. After an initial sitting with Gaule, Hyslop took Soule down to New York from Boston so that he and Thompson could meet with her regularly. During the séance of June 4, 1908, Soule appeared to be receiving communications from Gifford, and she finally revealed that the artist was elated over his power to return and finish his work through Thompson. Later séances revealed hundreds of communications about scenes and colors that indicated Gifford's influence.

Back in Boston, Soule met with Hyslop alone on July 15. During the séance, the supposed spirit of Gifford revealed he had sent a dream of the angel of death to Thompson. When Hyslop returned to New York, Mrs. Thompson visited Hyslop, worried about a dream of death her husband had recently experienced and then sketched. Hyslop felt he was close to establishing real contact with Gifford's spirit, which had yet to identify himself. Hyslop attended no more séances on the Thompson case until December 1908. At that time, he consulted Mrs. Willis M. Cleaveland as the medium. Cleaveland's first sessions were disappointing, but on the morning of December 9, she sat with Thompson alone. Her communicator addressed Thompson, telling him that he had given his work to him and telling him not to neglect it. Through automatic writing, Cleaveland first tried to write initials, then began sketching scenes of the Massachusetts coast that Thompson had visited the summer before. The spirit reminisced about his childhood and early paintings, then admonished Thompson to continue with the work and not to forget him. Finally, the spirit told Thompson he had to leave and scrawled R.S.G. using Cleaveland's hand.

Hyslop firmly believed that he had found a true case of spirit obsession in Frederic Thompson/R.Swain Gifford. Later investigations, some alleging fraud or supertelepathy, never quite refuted Hyslop's earlier conclusions. Gifford's spirit reportedly never bothered Thompson again, but Thompson left his metalworking career and became a full-time painter, joining the then-prestigious Salmagundi Club for professional painters in 1912. He worked out of New York for a few years then moved to Martha's Vineyard off the coast of New Bedford. Returning to New York in the 1920s, Thompson continued to paint and sculpt, showing his works in various exhibitions and apparently making a good living. He worked out of Miami in the late 1920s and probably died about 1927.

FURTHER READING:
Anderson, Roger I. "The Life and Work of James H. Hyslop." *Journal of the American Society for Psychical Research* 79 (April 1985): 167–200.
Rogo, D. Scott. *The Infinite Boundary.* New York: Dodd, Mead, 1987.

Throckmorton Possessions (1589–1593) The first well-known case of possessed young people and the successful destruction of witches based on the evidence of minors. The story of the five Throckmorton (also Throgmorton) girls in Warboys, Essex, England, foreshadowed by a century the witchcraft hysteria that unfolded in Salem, Massachusetts.

The sole account of the POSSESSIONS of the girls and trials and executions of the accused witches was published in 1593 in London in a book entitled *The Most Strange and Admirable Discoverie of the Three Witches of Warboys, arraigned, convicted, and executed at the last Assizes at Huntington, for the bewitching of the five daughters of Robert Throckmorton, Esquire, and divers other persons, with sundrie Divillish and grievous torments: And also for the bewitching to death of the Lady Crumwell, the like hath not been heard of in this age.* The book may have been written in part by the girls' uncle, Gilbert Pickering.

Squire Robert Throckmorton of Warboys, his wife, and his five daughters—Joan, Elizabeth, Mary, Grace, and Jane—enjoyed a genteel life and were known for their generosity. As a wealthy landowner, Throckmorton supported many of his poorer neighbors, among them the Samuels. Alice Samuel and her daughter, Agnes, frequently visited the Throckmorton household and were well known to the girls.

In 1589, the youngest, Jane, began having sneezing fits and convulsions and fell into a trance. Her frightened parents consulted a Cambridge physician, Dr. Barrow, and a Dr. Butler. Looking only at Jane's urine, both doctors diagnosed bewitchment. When the 76-year-old Alice Samuel visited to offer her sympathies, Jane cried out against her, accusing the old woman of WITCHCRAFT, saying, "Did you ever see one more like a witch than she is? Take off her black thumb'd cap for I cannot abide to look at her."

Within two months, all the other sisters were suffering violent, hysterical fits several times a day. They claimed to have no memory of the fits, but they all were certain that Mother Samuel was the cause.

The eldest daughter, Joan, predicted that there would eventually be 12 DEMONIACs in the house. Soon thereafter, seven maidservants fell victim to the spells. If they were sent away, they recovered. If any left Squire Throckmorton's employ, her successor also became possessed. All pointed to Mother Samuel as the source of their torments. The hysterical behavior of the daughters and the maids continued for more than three years.

As with other demoniacs, the girls shrieked and contorted if the parson attempted prayer or read from the Bible, especially the beginning of the Gospel of John, known to be particularly offensive to the DEVIL. Such actions are generally accepted as the signs of true possession but may also have been a convenient way for the girls to avoid pious exercises. Elizabeth would throw fits to avoid religious lessons, only ending a tantrum if someone played cards with her. She clenched her teeth unless she ate outdoors at a particularly pretty pond, so the family had picnics every day.

Squire and Mrs. Throckmorton doubted the girls' possession, since they had only lived in the area a short time and no one had any motive for bewitching the family. They ignored the girls' accusations and tauntings of Mother Samuel, but the hysterics did not subside. Even as late as autumn 1592, Mrs. Throckmorton thought the "devils" might be lying.

In September 1590, the Throckmortons were visited by Lady Cromwell and her daughter-in-law. Lady Cromwell was the wife of Sir Henry Cromwell (grandfather of Sir Oliver Cromwell), the richest commoner in England. When she saw Mother Samuel, one of the Cromwells' tenants, she angrily ripped the old woman's bonnet from her head, denounced her as a witch, and ordered her hair burned. Horrified, Mother Samuel beseeched Lady Cromwell, "Madame, why do you use me thus? I never did you any harm, as yet."

Back home, Lady Cromwell experienced a terrible nightmare, in which she dreamed that Mother Samuel had sent her cat FAMILIAR to rip the flesh from Lady Cromwell's body. Lady Cromwell never fully recovered; her health gradually declined, and she died a lingering death 15 months later, in July 1592. Mother Samuel was not immediately seen as the cause of her death.

By this time, the girls showed signs of relief only when they were taken to the Samuel house or she went to theirs, and Alice was forced to live with the Throckmortons for several weeks. Alice; her daughter, Agnes; and another suspected witch were also scratched repeatedly by the girls, a custom similar to pricking that was intended to reveal true witches. If the skin was insensitive, it indicated a witch.

The girls constantly exhorted Alice to confess her dealings with the Devil and repent and delivered pious speeches that moved onlookers to tears. Giving in to the constant pressure, Alice confessed just before Christmas 1592.

Not long after Christmas, however, Alice's husband, John, and daughter, Agnes, convinced Alice to recant, and she again claimed her innocence, only to confess again before the bishop of Lincoln and a justice of the peace in Huntington on December 29. All three Samuels were jailed, although Agnes was released on bail to allow the girls to extract incriminating evidence from her through more scratchings. The demons identified were minor ones, with the silly names of *Pluck, Catch,* and *White* and the three cousins, all named *Smackes.* The demons often appeared as chickens.

The Throckmorton children now accused Alice Samuel of bewitching Lady Cromwell to death, a serious accusation that placed Alice in jeopardy of capital punishment as a murderer under the Witchcraft Act of 1563.

The Samuels were tried on April 5, 1593, on charges of murdering Lady Cromwell by witchcraft. The court, under the impressionable Judge Edward Fenner, accepted the testimony of the Throckmorton girls, as well as several other persons who claimed that the Samuels family had bewitched their livestock to death over the years. The jury took only five hours to convict all three.

Alice, Agnes, and John were hanged, and afterward the Throckmorton girls returned to perfect health. Since Lady Cromwell had allegedly died through the black offices of Alice Samuel, her husband, Sir Henry Cromwell, received all the Samuels' forfeited property and goods. He used the money to establish an annual sermon at Queens' College, Cambridge, to "preache and invaye against the detestable practice, synne, and offence of witchcraft, inchantment, charm, and sorcereye." The sermons lasted until 1812.

The Throckmorton case had a significant impact on public belief in witchcraft and the EVIL EYE. The case was widely known through the publication of the account. It also had an impact on the governing class. The Cromwells served in the Parliament of James I, who gained the throne in 1603. In response to public pressure for more stringent actions against witches, Parliament passed a new Witchcraft Act in 1604, which stiffened punishment.

FURTHER READING:
Coverntry, William W. *Demonic Possession on Trial: Case Studies in Early Modern England and Colonial America, 1593–1692.* New York: AuthorHouse, 2003.
Walker, D. P. *Unclean Spirits: Possession and Exorcism in France and England in the Late Sixteenth and Early Seventeenth Centuries.* Philadelphia: University of Pennsylvania Press, 1981.

thwarting angels   ANGELs who nullify the powers of specific DEMONs. All diseases, bad weather, and other misfortunes are caused by certain demons. Each demon has a thwarting angel who can be summoned in prayer and MAGIC to stop or cancel out the demon's mischief. Knowing the appropriate thwarting angel is important in order to invoke the fastest and best help.

The most important thwarting angels are the planetary rulers, six angels who have the sole powers to thwart the demonic HEAVENLY BODIES of the world of darkness responsible for all the misery in the world. The planetary rulers are as follows:

1. Lamachiel, who thwarts Deception
2. Baruchiel, who thwarts Strife
3. Marmaroth, who thwarts Fate
4. Balthioul, who thwarts Distress
5. Uriel, who thwarts Error
6. Asteraoth, who thwarts Power

See AMULET; MAGIC; SOLOMON.

Tregeagle, Jan (John)   A 17th-century Cornish highwayman punished by the DEVIL. The ghost of Jan Tregeagle is known for his howling in protest over his fate.

A historical Jan Tregeagle existed; he was an unpopular magistrate in Cornwall, England. Local lore held that he achieved his success by forgery, fraud, and illegal seizure of estates of orphans. He also was rumored to have made a PACT with the Devil.

According to lore, Tregeagle worried about the fate of his soul as he grew older, and he bribed the clergy to allow him to be buried in consecrated ground, which he believed would prevent the Devil from collecting his soul. He was buried in St. Breock's churchyard, where he rested quietly for seven years.

A legal dispute over landownership arose, and Tregeagle's ghost was summoned from the grave to testify in court. He did, on behalf of the defendant, who won the case. But the man refused to return Tregeagle to his grave, claiming the job was too dangerous. The clergy decided that the only way they could keep Tregeagle out of the clutches of the Devil was to keep him busy for eternity. Tregeagle was bound by spells to bail out DOZMARY POOL with a leaky limpet shell, a task he could never complete.

One night, Tregeagle escaped and dashed across Bodmin Moor, with the Devil and his HELL hounds (see BLACK DOGS) in pursuit. Tregeagle tried to hide in the ruined chapel atop ROCHE ROCK, but his head became wedged in the east window.

He was rescued by a priest and two saints, who took him to Padstow beach and set him to the endless and impossible task of weaving ropes from sand. Every time the tide came in, the ropes were destroyed, and Tregeagle howled in protest. He became such a noisy nuisance that he was sent to Berepper, where he was supposed to empty the beach of sand. Once a DEMON tripped him and made him spill his sack, creating a sandbar.

He was unpopular at Berepper and so was sent on to Land's End, where he was supposed to sweep sand. Once again, he howled in protest. Tregeagle's ghost is said to haunt Roche Rock, especially on windy nights. He still screams and howls at the torment of the hellhounds.

Tzitzimime   Brothers of TEZCATLIPOCA who were cast out of heaven for their acts of sacrilege and desecration against the gods. *Tzitzimime* means "dangerous beings." Prior to their fall, the brothers had the names of stars and constellations.

The Tzitzimime assume the shapes of scorpions, hideous insects, frogs, and toads. At certain times of the year, they have the power to enter households in the form of beams of light. In earlier times, people filled the cracks in their homes on those nights in order to keep the demons out.

One of the brothers, Tacatecutli, was idolized as a walking stick in strange rites. Followers drew BLOOD from their noses and ears and smeared it on walking sticks placed on the altar. It was believed that this would placate the demon and prevent him from troubling people.

Another brother took the form of a donkey skull and terrorized people traveling on roads at night. If people happened to see the skull, it followed his or her relentlessly to their destination.

udugg (utukku) A type of Babylonian DEMON who can be either good or evil. A group of evil ones are known as the Seven; they are offspring of the sky god, An, and the Earth goddess, Ki, and they act as assistants to the underworld god, Nergal. In Akkadian lore, the *utukku* are servants of the underworld, whose task is to fetch the sacrificial offerings made by humans, especially the BLOOD, liver, and organs of animals. The evil *utukku* are the *ekimmu* and the good ones are the *shedu*.

Ukobach Low-ranking DEMON who invented fireworks and the art of frying food. Ukobach appears with an inflamed body. BEELZEBUB assigns him to tend the oil in the cauldrons of HELL. He throws burning coals on the souls of the damned or tortures them with flames. In lore, Ukobach is the lamp oil for the jack-o'-lantern.

Um Es Sibyan Arabian DEMON who, as does LILITH, preys upon newborn children. Um Es Sibyan has the body of a chicken, the face of a human, and the chest of a camel. She flies through the air at night crying, "Warh, warh warh." The sound is a death omen to any child who hears it. Parents can ward off the demon by sounding, "Tchlok, tchlok, tchlok" until it passes by.

Uriel DEMON and wandering duke of the air. Uriel has 10 chief dukes and 100 underdukes with numerous servants. They are evil, false, and deceitful, and reluctant to obey the commands of an EXORCIST. They appear in the form of a SERPENT with a virgin's head and face. The 10 chief dukes are Chabri, Drabros, Nartniel, Frasmiel, Brymiel, Dragon,

Curtnas, Draplos, Hermon, and Aldrusy. *Uriel* is also the name of an archangel.

Usiel DEMON among the 31 AERIAL SPIRITS OF SOLOMON. Usiel rules as a prince in the northwest under the command or AMENADIEL. He has 40 dukes in the daytime and 40 at night, plus their many servants. All are obedient. According to King SOLOMON, Usiel and his demons have more power to hide and discover treasure than any other spirits. His main 14 dukes of the day are Abariel, Ameta, Amen, Heme, Saefer, Potiel, Saefam, Magni, Amandiel, Barsu, Gamasu, Hissain, Fabariel, and Usiniel. His main dukes of the night are Ansoel, Godiel, Barfos, Burfa, Adan, Saddiel, Sodiel, Ossidiel, Pathier, Marae, Asuriel, Almoel, Las Pharon, and Ethiel.

Usiel (Uziel, Uzziel) FALLEN ANGEL who is also good. In kabbalistic lore, Usiel is a fallen angel who married women and begat giants. (See WATCHERS.) In the Sefer Raziel, Usiel is a good angel who is among the seven who stand before the throne of God and the nine who are set over the four winds.

Uzza (Ouza, Semyaza, Uzzah) FALLEN ANGEL. *Uzza* means "strength." In 3 Enoch, Uzza is named as one of three primary ministering angels with Azael and Azza, who live in the seventh (highest) heaven (probably prior to their fall). The three object to the elevation of the prophet Enoch into the great angel Metatron and are cast out of heaven as punishment.

Uzza also is a tutelary spirit of Egypt.

See SEMYAZA.

Valac FALLEN ANGEL and 62nd of the 72 SPIRITS OF SOLOMON. Valac is a president who appears as a small boy with ANGEL wings riding on a two-headed dragon. He gives true answers about hidden treasures. He reveals where SERPENTs can be seen and delivers them

Valac (*DICTIONNAIRE INFERNAL*)

harmless to the magician. He governs 30 LEGIONs of DEMONs.

Valefor (Malaphar, Malephar) FALLEN ANGEL and sixth of the 72 SPIRITS OF SOLOMON. Valefor is a duke who rules 10 LEGIONs. He appears either as a many-headed lion or as a lion with the head of a human thief. He leads people into thievery and leaves them at the gallows.

Vapula FALLEN ANGEL and 60th of the 72 SPIRITS OF SOLOMON. In HELL, Vapula is a duke with 36 legions of DEMONs under his command. He appears as a lion with griffin wings. He confers skill in handicrafts, philosophy, and all science contained in books.

Vassago FALLEN ANGEL and third of the 72 SPIRITS OF SOLOMON. Vassago is a prince who has the same nature as AGARES. He discerns past, present, and future. He discovers all things lost or hidden. Good-natured, he is invoked in divination rituals. He rules 26 LEGIONs of DEMONs.

Veltis One of the DEMONs imprisoned by King SOLOMON in his brazen vessel.

Veltis is mentioned in the lore of the life of St. Margaret of Antioch, who was executed by beheading in Christian persecutions in 304. While in prison, Margaret prayed to have a face-to-face confrontation with the DEVIL. Upon arising from prayer, she saw a terrible dragon, which threatened to devour her. She made the sign of the cross and the dragon burst into flames.

Then, she saw a black man sitting with his hands bound to his knees. She took him by the hair and cast him to the ground, holding his head down with her foot. She prayed, and a light shone down from heaven, illuminating her cell. She saw in heaven the cross of Christ with a dove on it. The dove said, "Blessed art thou o Margaret, the gates of paradise attend thy coming."

Margaret demanded that the demon give his name, and he asked her first to remove her foot from his head. She did, and he gave the name *Veltis*. He said that he and other demons had been locked up in the brazen vessel. Babylonians found it and, thinking that it contained gold, smashed it and thus freed the demons. Ever since, Veltis and the others have lain in wait to annoy the just.

REGINALD SCOT, a skeptic about the powers of the DEVIL and demons, dismissed the legend as a fiction, saying Margaret could not have possibly had the eyesight and hearing to perceive anything as far away as heaven. Surely, the demons could have used their fiery nature and breath to melt the brazen vessel at any time. "The devils carry hell and hell fire about with them always; insomuch as (they say) they leave ashes evermore where they stand," he noted.

Scot opined that anyone who burned a candle in the name of St. Margaret "shall never be the better, but three pence the worse."

FURTHER READING:
Scot, Reginald. *The Discoverie of Witchcraft*. 1886. Reprint, Yorkshire, England: E. P. Publishing, 1973.

Vepar (Separ)   FALLEN ANGEL and 42nd of the 72 SPIRITS OF SOLOMON. In HELL, Vepar is a duke with 29 LEGIONS of DEMONS under his command. He appears as a mermaid and has jurisdiction over certain things pertaining to the sea: He guides the waters and battleships and causes the sea to seem full of ships. When commanded, he will raise storms at sea. He can cause a person to die in three to five days of wounds that putrefy and become filled with maggots. According to JOHANN WEYER, a person so afflicted can be healed "with diligence."

Vienna Possession (1583)   Teenaged girl possessed of more than 12,000 DEMONS, allegedly sent by her grandmother. The Vienna Possession case has political overtones of anti-Protestant propaganda.

In 1583, a 16-year-old girl in the village of Manx near Vienna, Austria, began suffering from severe cramps. She was determined by local authorities to be possessed and was sent to Vienna to the Jesuit chapel of St. Barbara for EXORCISM. After eight weeks of intense daily exorcisms, the priests succeeded in expelling 12,652 DEMONS, one of the highest numbers on record in demonic possession cases.

The thousands of demons who had possessed her made her so heavy that she could scarcely be carried from place to place. The wagoner who transported her every day from the hospital to the chapel said that she seemed to be made of lead and iron, and the horses sweated profusely in pulling her cart.

The priests, of course, sought to assign blame. The girl told them that she was often in the company of her grandmother, Elisabeth Pleinarcher, who took her to Lutheran weddings and church services. The priests pressured her to state that Pleinarcher kept demons in the forms of flies in a bottle, and she had used these against the girl.

The confession enabled Kaspar Neubeck, the bishop of Vienna, to arrest Pleinarcher. The 70-year-old woman was imprisoned and tortured until she said that her granddaughter's story was true that she had accomplished the possession by sending the DEVIL into an APPLE that she had given the girl to eat. Pleinarcher also confessed to attending SABBATs for 50 years. She had copulated with the Devil in the forms of a cat, a goat, and even a ball of thread.

Pleinarcher was tied to the tail of a horse and dragged through Vienna to the Richplatz, where she was burned alive.

Not long after the execution, a Jesuit priest, Georg Scherer, preached a lengthy sermon about the case, urging Viennese officials to increase their diligence against WITCHCRAFT.

FURTHER READING:
Lea, Henry Charles. *Materials toward a History of Witchcraft*. Philadelphia: University of Pennsylvania Press, 1939.

Vine   FALLEN ANGEL and 45th of the 72 SPIRITS OF SOLOMON. In HELL, Vine is a king and earl. He appears either as a monster or as a lion seated on a black horse, holding a viper. When commanded, he assumes human form. Vine discerns hidden things, reveals witches, and knows the past, present, and future. Upon command, he will build towers, demolish walls, and make seas stormy. He governs 35 LEGIONS of DEMONS.

Vual   FALLEN ANGEL and 47th of the 72 SPIRITS OF SOLOMON. Once a member of the angelic order of powers, Vual is a duke in HELL with 37 LEGIONS of DEMONS under his command. He appears first as an enormous dromedary camel, then changes into human form and speaks in imperfect Egyptian. He procures the love of women; knows the past, present, and future; and makes enemies become friends.

Warren, Ed (1926–2006) and **Lorraine (1927–)**
American DEMONOLOGISTS and ghost investigators. Ed
and Lorraine Warren, husband and wife, were involved
in thousands of cases of spirit identification, hauntings,
and demonic INFESTATION, OPPRESSION, and POSSESSION of
both people and property. They acted as consultants on
some of America's most famous paranormal cases, such
as the SMURL HAUNTING in West Pittston, Pennsylvania,
in the 1980s, and the AMITYVILLE HAUNTING of the Lutz
family on Long Island, in the 1970s. During his lifetime,
Ed Warren achieved the rare distinction of being a lay-
person recognized as a demonologist by the Catholic
Church.

Background
Both Ed and Lorraine were born in Bridgeport, Connecticut, but did not meet until they were teenagers. Ed was
born on September 7, 1926; his father was a state trooper
and a devout Catholic and enrolled Ed in parochial school.
The Warren family lived in a big old house rented out by
an unmarried landlady who did not approve of dogs or
children, always throwing things at them in annoyance.
Ed was five when the landlady passed away, and he saw
his first apparition when she materialized in his bedroom
closet a few days later, as sour as she had been in life. His
father always told Ed that there must be a logical explanation for the paranormal behavior his son experienced, but
the elder Warren never produced one. Young Ed would
choose to stay outside in freezing or rainy weather rather

than be in the house alone. One of Ed's supernatural visitors was a nun, his father's sister. Ed had expressed a
desire to become a priest, but the nun told him that he
would not; rather, he would consult priests and would do
more work than 100 of them.

When Ed was 12, his family moved out of their
haunted home. Although he had come to terms with the
spirits there, his exposure to the paranormal just fueled
his desire for more investigation and confrontation.

Three blocks away, Lorraine Rita Moran was born on
January 31, 1927, to a fairly affluent Irish family. She attended Laurelton Hall, a Catholic girls' school in nearby
Milford, and it was while at school that young Lorraine,
age 12, discovered that her gift of clairvoyance was not
shared by everyone. On Arbor Day that year, the nuns
had organized a tree planting, and as soon as the sapling
was set in the ground, Lorraine began staring at the sky,
seeing the tree in its full-grown splendor. Once she told
a nun that her "lights," or aura, were brighter than the
lights around the mother superior. The nuns considered
her psychic ability to be sinful and packed her off to a
weekend retreat of prayer and silence.

At age 16, Ed met Lorraine while working as an usher
at the Colonial Theater in Bridgeport, on June 23, 1943.
She knew immediately that they would spend the rest of
their lives together. He was the only boy she ever dated.
On his 17th birthday on September 7, 1943, Ed enlisted in
the U.S. Navy, and he served with the armed navy guard
aboard a merchant marine vessel. He and Lorraine married

on May 22, 1945, on survivors' leave in Bridgeport. They were both 18. Their only child, Judy, was six months old before Ed left the navy. After the war, Ed attended the Perry Art School, affiliated with Yale University, but left to travel around New England painting landscapes and searching for haunted houses. His favorite pastime was to hear of a haunted house in a community, paint a portrait of the home, and give it to the house's owners. He also earned income from his paintings.

But what Ed particularly liked was to be invited inside the haunted house by its owners and allowed to look around. Eventually, Ed's experiences as a ghost hunter and the wealth of information he had collected led the Warrens away from itinerant art to the full-time pursuit of paranormal consultation. Frequently, they had been the only ones in whom the frightened owners of a haunted house had confided the strange occurrences happening there; more and more, the Warrens found themselves giving advice and consolation not only to the homeowners but to interested strangers. Finding that negative energy associated with teenagers and young adults attracted spirit activity, the Warrens began giving lectures at colleges in order to encourage their listeners to avoid unwittingly inviting trouble into their lives and family homes.

In 1969, an exhibit of Ed's artwork attracted the attention of the media and a literary agent, which significantly boosted their public profile.

Paranormal Investigations
The Warrens amassed a large archive of detailed interviews and reports from afflicted families and from other investigators; photographs; audio and video recordings of paranormal activity, including the voices of the spirits; a museum of spirit-infested clothing, dolls, and other objects; and myriad letters of gratitude from government officials, clergy, and ordinary people for the couple's intervention in horrible, unbelievably evil situations. From their research, they identified different types of spirits requiring different remedies. They investigated abroad, as well as throughout America.

After an invitation to investigate a site, the Warrens arranged a visit as quickly as possible. Once at the site, they usually split up, with Ed conducting careful and thorough interviews of all persons involved, and Lorraine walking the house to see whether she could discern spirit activity through her psychic sense. Lorraine usually detected spirit presence almost immediately and knew also whether the spirits were earthbound human ghosts or apparitions or inhuman, demonic influences.

Demonology Work
The Warrens stressed that God does not let evil visit humans, but that humans must in some way invite the malevolence into their lives: by toying with the supernatural (conjuring, OUIJA™ boards, séances, black WITCHCRAFT, and satanic rituals); by sinking into negative, depressive states; or by becoming obsessed with a person or place.

Ed referred to these "permissions" as the Law of Invitation and the Law of Attraction. Once allowed to enter, the demonic takes control in three stages: infestation, oppression, and possession. In severe circumstances, the final outcome can be death.

The Warrens' objective was to document and effect closure through the clergy. They helped identify the manifestations of demonic infestation, oppression, and possession so that trained exorcists could work to rid the victim of evil influence. They helped the afflicted through support, blessing, and prayer. They did not perform exorcisms themselves but worked with exorcists and assisted them. Ed and Lorraine strongly warned against anyone's trying to perform exorcisms independently.

The Warrens estimate that they investigated more than 8,000 cases in more than 50 years of work. Some of these investigations have been sensational, such as "Annabelle," in which spirits infested a large Raggedy Ann doll claiming to be the ghost of a little girl; the Donovan case, which stemmed from a teenage daughter's invitation for infestation through her Ouija™ board; the identification of a ghost at the United States Military Academy at West Point and Lorraine's help to the spirit to pass on to the other side; and the study of cemeteries and how they are gathering points for spirits.

The most famous and controversial case the Warrens encountered was the possession of the Lutz home in Amityville, Long Island, New York. Ed and Lorraine were two of only nine individuals asked to be consultants on the legitimacy of demonic activity in the house. They said that the possession of the Lutz home was authentic.

Besides their demonology rescue work, lectures, and guidance of supernatural tours, the Warrens cofounded the New England Society for Psychic Research, in the early 1950s. They also wrote 10 books based on their experiences: *Deliver Us from Evil*, *The Demonologist*, *The Devil in Connecticut*, *The Haunted* (based on the Smurl case), *Werewolf*, *Satan's Harvest*, *The Ghost Hunters*, *In a Dark Place*, *Graveyard*, and *Ghost Tracks*. *The Haunted* was released as a film in 1991, and the made-for-television movie *The Demon Murder Case* (1983) was based on *The Devil in Connecticut*.

On March 26, 2001, Ed Warren collapsed as a result of heart problems after a trip to Japan to assist in Buddhist exorcism techniques. He was hospitalized for a year and was in a coma for several months. He spent the next four years under the home care of Lorraine, who was at his side when he passed away of natural causes on August 23, 2006. He was buried with full military honors.

Lorraine continues their work, collaborating with her son-in-law, Tony Spera; conducting research and investigations; giving lectures; and participating in media projects.

Ed's nephew, JOHN ZAFFIS, of Stratford, Connecticut, who investigated cases with the Warrens, works independently as a paranormal researcher and investigator;

he founded the Paranormal Research Society of New England in 1998.

FURTHER READING:

Brittle, Gerald Daniel. *The Demonologist: The Extraordinary Career of Ed and Lorraine Warren.* Lincoln, Nebr.: An Authors Guild BackinPrint.com Edition, 2002.

New England Society for Psychic Research. Official Web site of Ed and Lorraine Warren. Available online. URL: http://www.warrens.net. Downloaded January 18, 2006.

Pionzio, Melissa. "Factual Exorcism Book Evokes Past Pain." *Hartford Courant,* October 14, 2007. Available online. URL: http://www.religionnewsblog.com/19688/the-devil-in-connecticut. Downloaded August 6, 2008.

Smith, D. R. "An Interview with the Ghost Hunter: Ed Warren." Left Field-Paranormal Studies & Investigations. Available online. URL: http://www.leftfield-psi.net/ghosts/warren.html. Downloaded January 18, 2006.

Warren, Ed, and Lorraine Warren with Robert David Chase. *Ghost Hunters.* New York: St. Martin's Paperbacks, 1989.

Watchers FALLEN ANGELS. The Watchers cohabited with human women and fell from God's grace. Watchers are also referred to as SONS OF GOD. Their monstrous offspring, the NEPHILIM, and the corruption the Watchers created on Earth so revolted God that he decided to send the great flood to destroy all life on Earth. The cohabitation of the Sons of God and the daughters of men is briefly described in Genesis 6:1–4.

Watchers also describes ANGELS who do not fall but who are close to the throne of God, thus causing some confusion as to whether they are good or bad.

1 Enoch tells in detail the story of the Watchers and their fall. The Watchers, described as angels who are "the children of heaven," see the beautiful daughters of men and desire them. They decide to take them as wives. But their leader, SEMYAZA, expresses the fear that he alone will be held accountable for this great sin. The angels, who are 200 in number, swear an oath binding them all together. Their chiefs (called chiefs of tens) who serve under Semyaza are Arakeb, Rameel, Tamel, Ramel, Danel, Ezeqel, Baraqyal, Asel, Armaros, Batrel, Ananel, Zaqeel, Sasomaspweel, Kestarel, Turel, Yamayol, and Arazyal.

The Watchers descend to Earth and take the women. Many of them commit adultery against their new wives. Their offspring, the giant Nephilim, turn against people, cannibalize them, and drink their blood.

The Watchers teach people secret arts such as magical medicine, incantations, and knowledge of plants and herbs. AZAZEL teaches the art of making weapons of war, jewelry, and cosmetics, and dye making and alchemy. Amasras teaches plant lore and how to perform magic. Baraqiyal teaches astrology, Kokarerel teaches the zodiac, Tamel teaches about the stars, and Asderel teaches about the Moon and the deception of humans.

Later in the text, 1 Enoch gives the names of 21 chiefs of the fallen (some angels are named more than once):

Semyaza	Aristaqis
Armen	Kokbael
Turel	Rumyal
Danyul	Neqael
Baraqel	Azazel
Armaros	Betryal
Besasel	Hananel
Turel	Sipwesel
Yeterel	Tumael
Turel	Rumel
Azazel	

Fallen angels who are known as the Five Satans:

- Yeqon, who misleads all the children of the angels, brings them down upon the earth, and perverts them by the daughters of the people
- Asbel, who misleads holy angels so that they will defile their bodies by the daughters of the people
- Gaderel, who shows the children of the people all the blows of death, who misleads Eve, and who shows the children of the people how to make weapons and all other instruments of war and death
- Pinene, who demonstrates to people the bitter and the sweet, reveals to them all the secrets of wisdom, and teaches them the secret of writing with ink and paper, thus causing them to err through all eternity
- Kasadya, "who reveals the flagellations of all evil including the flagellation of the souls and the DEMONS, the smashing of the embryo in the womb so that it may be crushed, and the flagellation of the soul; snake bites, sun strokes, and the son of the SERPENT whose name is Tabata" according to 1 Enoch 69:4–12

Sin, corruption, and oppression spread across the earth. Horrified, the angels Michael, Surafel (Suriel/Uriel), and Gabriel petition God to take action, for the people on Earth are suffering. God declares that he will wipe out the wicked and all life on Earth in a great flood. He instructs Raphael to bind Azazel hand and foot and to throw him into darkness. Raphael makes a hole in the desert, casts Azazel into it, and covers him with sharp rocks. God tells Gabriel to destroy the children of the Watchers. He tells Michael to inform Semyaza that they will die together with their wives and children in their defilement. He is to bind them for 70 generations beneath rocks until the day of judgment. They will then be led into the bottom of fire, where they will be locked up in prison and in torment forever. All those who collaborated with the Watchers will be similarly punished. Finally, Michael is to eradicate injustice from the face of the Earth.

The Watchers call to the prophet Enoch for help, and he hears them in a dream vision. Upon awakening, he tells Azazel there will be no peace for him, for a grave judgment has come upon him. Enoch then speaks to all the Watchers, who are full of fear and trembling. They beg him to write a prayer of forgiveness for them. Enoch records their prayers and petitions and then reads them until he falls asleep. He has another dream vision in which he sees plagues. When he awakens, he goes to the Watchers and reprimands them for their sins and tells them their petitions will not be heard.

Enoch nonetheless tries to intercede on behalf of the Watchers but is refused by God. God says that their giant offspring shall be called evil spirits upon the earth, for they will dwell on the earth and in the earth. He tells Enoch to inform the Watchers that because they have rejected heaven, they shall have no peace.

1 Enoch also gives the names of "the holy angels who watch," implying that the term *Watchers* was given to angels in heaven, not just the fallen ones. The holy angels are

- Suruel—angel of eternity and trembling
- Raphael—angel of the spirits of man
- Raguel—angel who takes vengeance for the world and for the luminaries
- Michael—angel who is obedient in his benevolence over the people and the nations
- Saraqael—angel who is over the spirits of mankind and who is in the spirit
- Gabriel—angel who oversees the garden of Eden, the serpents, and the cherubim

In 2 Enoch, Enoch sees the "innumerable armies" of the Watchers and Nephilim imprisoned in the fifth heaven. They are dejected and silent. Enoch, who unsuccessfully tries to intercede on their behalf with God, urges them to sing a liturgy to God so that God will not be enraged against them "to the limit." They do so, singing in a piteous and touching way.

3 Enoch describes the Watchers as holy angels. According to the text, four great princes called "Watchers and holy ones" (the terms used in Daniel) reside in the seventh heaven opposite the throne of glory facing God. They are called Watchers and holy ones because on the third day of judgment (after death), they sanctify the body and soul with lashes of fire (a reference to preparing the soul for God's presence).

Each Watcher has 70 names corresponding to the 70 languages of the world, and all of them are based on the name of God. Each name is written with a pen of flame on God's crown. Such sparks and lightning shoot forth from them that no angels, not even the seraphim, can look upon them.

The Watchers are praised with the praise of the Shekinah, and God does nothing without taking their counsel. They function as officers in the heavenly court and debate and close each case that comes up for judgment. They announce the verdicts, proclaim the sentences, and sometimes go down to Earth to carry out the sentences.

A Qumran text called the Testament of Amran (Q543, 545–548), which exists only in several fragments and

Belial, one of the Watchers, from Francis Barrett's The Magus (AUTHOR'S COLLECTION)

manuscripts, concerns the Watchers. In Manuscript B Fragment 1, the anonymous author describes a dream vision in which two Watchers are fighting over him. He asks, "Who are you that you are thus empowered over me?" They tell him that they have been empowered to rule over all humankind, and they ask him to choose which of them he would want as a ruler. One of them has a terrifying appearance, like a serpent wearing a dark cloak of many colors. He has a "visage like a viper."

Fragment 2 identifies BELIAL as one of the Watchers. He has three titles, *Belial, Prince of Darkness,* and *King of Evil,* and he is empowered over all darkness and his every way, and every work are darkness. Fragment 3 mentions the "sons of Light," who are ruled by a being who identifies himself with three names: *Michael, Prince of Light,* and *King of Righteousness.*

Another fragment says that all the sons of Darkness will be destroyed because of their foolishness and evil and the sons of Light will have eternal joy and rejoicing for all peace and truth will be made light.

FURTHER READING:

Collins, Andrew. *From the Ashes of Angels: The Forbidden Legacy of a Fallen Race.* London: Signet Books, 1996.

Eisenman, Robert, and Michael Wise. *The Dead Sea Scrolls Uncovered.* London: Element Books, 1992.

The Old Testament Pseudepigrapha. Vols. 1 & 2. Edited by James H. Charlesworth. 1983. Reprint, New York: Doubleday, 1985.

Weyer, Johann (1515–1588) German physician who argued against the witch hysteria and the alleged workings of the DEVIL through people and PACTs. Johann Weyer accepted the existence of DEMONs and their ability to wreak evil and cause POSSESSION, but he opposed the torture and execution of accused witches during the Inquisition and refuted the belief that the Devil recruited people to cause harm.

Life

Weyer was born the middle of three sons to a Protestant family in Brabant. His father was a hops merchant who could afford to give his sons a good education. Weyer was 15 when he went to study in the household of Heinrich Cornelius Agrippa von Nettesheim, a prominent physician, philosopher, and occult scholar. Agrippa taught Weyer Platonic and Neoplatonic philosophy and introduced him to the occult works of Abbot Johannes Trithemius of Sponheim.

The seeds of Weyer's skepticism about the witch hysteria that gripped the 16th century may have been planted by Agrippa, who once defended an old woman accused of witchcraft, arguing that she was feeble-minded, not diabolical.

Weyer's apprenticeship with Agrippa lasted for about four years. Weyer studied medicine at the University of Paris in 1534, and at the University of Orléans from 1534 to 1537. He learned the prevailing medical doctrine, still in force from ancient times, that health depends on the balance of four humors in the body: BLOOD, phlegm, bile, and black bile, or melancholy.

After graduation, Weyer returned to Brabant and nearby Ravenstein to work as a physician. In 1545, he became the municipal physician for Arnhem, a much bigger city. At about the same time, he married Judith Wintgens, with whom he had four sons and a daughter.

In 1550, Weyer was appointed to a prestigious post that he held for most of the rest of his career, as personal physician to Duke William V of Julich-Berg-Cleves in Dusseldorf. Though Catholic, the duke was liberal-minded, and Weyer enjoyed a comfortable relationship with him. He pursued scholarly studies and writing. In 1578, he retired from his post with the duke. He was succeeded by one of his sons, Galenus, named after the famous Roman physician Galen. Weyer continued to write and practice medicine until his death in Tecklenburg on February 24, 1588.

Works

Weyer wrote on medicine and philosophy; of importance to the subject of demonology is his main work, *De praestigiis daemonum, et incantationibus, ac veneficiis* (On the illusions, spells and poisons of demons), published in 1563, in which he attacked many of the prevailing beliefs

Johann Weyer (AUTHOR'S COLLECTION)

of inquisitors. Weyer revised and added to the work several times up to 1583.

In 1577, he added an appendix, *Pseudo-Monarchia* (The false kingdom of the demons), to *De praestigiis daemonum.* It is an inventory and description of 68 principal demons, their characteristics, and how they may be conjured. The princes rule 7,405,926 demons organized in 1,111 LEGIONs of 6,666 each. Later, the Lutheran Church thought Weyer's estimate too low and raised the census of the demonic population to 2,665,866,746,664, or roughly 2.6 trillion.

REGINALD SCOT, a contemporary who agreed with Weyer, translated *Pseudo-Monarchia* and included it in his book *The Discoverie of Witchcraft* (1584).

The magical grimoire the *Lemegeton,* also called *The Lesser Key of Solomon,* lists the same 68 spirits and adds four more, and it gives SEALs for their conjuration. The 72 are also known as SPIRITS OF SOLOMON.

Weyer wrote *De lamiis liber* (*On Witchcraft*) in 1577. He used the term LAMIAE to describe female witches who thought they had pacts with the DEVIL.

Views on Demons and Witches

Weyer rejected the Aristotelian view that demons did not exist in reality. He believed in the Devil and his legions of demons but did not believe that witches were empowered by the Devil to harm humankind. Nor did he believe stories of their flying through the air and attendance at SAB-BATs in which the Devil was worshipped and babies were eaten. He thought that belief in WITCHCRAFT was caused by the Devil and that the church ironically served the cause of the Devil by promoting belief in the evil power of witches.

In *De praestigiis daemonum,* Weyer refuted the idea of the demonic pact because there was no basis for it in the Bible. He gave a rational analysis of reports of alleged witch activity and concluded that most witches were deluded and mentally disturbed old women, the outcasts of society, who were fools, not heretics. Some might wish harm on their neighbors but could not carry it out. If harm occurred coincidentally, they believed, in their delusion, that they had brought it about. He did believe that some witches served Satan and did harm people, but not through supernatural means. He urged the church to forgive those who repented or, at most, to levy fines upon them.

Weyer believed that demons could possess people; however, he advocated ruling out all medical and natural explanations and causes before looking for the supernatural.

Weyer successfully discouraged witch hunting in much of the Netherlands for a while but was forced out by the Catholic governor, the duke of Alba. His book had almost the opposite effect from the one he intended. He was savagely denounced by critics such as Jean Bodin and King JAMES VI AND I, both of whom favored the extermination of witches. James' authoring of his antiwitch treatise, *Daemonologie,* was in response to the works by Weyer and Scot. Bodin urged that copies of Weyer's book be burned. Others wrote books refuting Weyer, and these helped to stimulate more witch hunts. Weyer himself was accused of being a witch but was not formally charged.

However, his arguments did persuade many witch hunters in Germany to consult physicians more often to rule out medical causes.

FURTHER READING:
Ankarloo, Bengt, and Gustav Henningsen, eds. *Early Modern European Witchcraft: Centres and Peripheries.* Oxford: Clarendon Press, 1990.
Russell, Jeffrey B. *A History of Witchcraft.* London: Thames & Hudson, 1980.
Weyer, Johann. *On Witchcraft (De praestigiis daemonum).* Abridged. Edited by Benjamin G. Kohl and H. C. Erik Midelfort. Asheville, N.C.: Pegasus Press, 1998.

Wickland, Dr. Carl A. (1861–1945)   Physician who with the help of his medium wife, Anna, performed EXORCISMS in cases of POSSESSION caused by dead people.

Using mild electronic current, Dr. Carl A. Wickland said he could force a possessing spirit to leave its victim, enter Anna's body, and then finally depart forever.

A native of Sweden, Wickland emigrated to the United States in 1881. He married Anna in 1896 and moved to Chicago to study medicine at Durham Medical College. After his graduation in 1900, he worked in private practice before turning to psychiatry. He soon believed that spirits played an unrecognized role in psychiatric problems and illness and began research into this uncharted area.

According to Wickland, a possessing spirit often does not realize that its earthly form is dead. Wickland "enlightened" the spirit and sent it on its way. If the spirit resisted, Wickland called on "helper spirits" to keep the possessing spirit in a so-called dungeon, out of the aura (energy field) of the victim or Anna, until the spirit gave up its selfish attitude and departed.

To facilitate the spirit's entrance into Anna and eventual departure, Wickland invented a static electricity machine that transmitted low-voltage electric shock to the patient, causing the possessing spirit great discomfort. The device was a forerunner of low-voltage electric shock treatment used in psychotherapy.

Wickland was not concerned with proving the identities of the possessing spirits. Rather, he believed that they seldom would provide evidential information because of their allegedly confused states of mind. Some spoke only in foreign tongues through his wife.

In 1918, the Wicklands moved to Los Angeles, where Wickland founded the National Psychological Institute for the treatment of obsession. The building is still standing and is occupied by workers in the garment industry.

Wickland wrote of his experiences in *Thirty Years among the Dead* (1924) and *The Gateway of Understanding* (1934). Anna died in 1937, and, in the same year, the medium Minnie M. Soule, prompting Wickland to go to England to find a new mediumistic partner. He approached Bertha Harris, a celebrated platform clairvoyant and trance psychic, but she refused. The psychical research establishment overlooked Wickland's work, in part because of he did not document information that could help prove the identities of the possessing spirits.

FURTHER READING:
Rogo, D. Scott. *The Infinite Boundary.* New York: Dodd, Mead, 1987.
Wickland, Carl. *Thirty Years among the Dead.* 1924. Reprint, N. Hollywood, Calif.: Newcastle Publishing, 1974.

Wild Hunt   A retinue of the ghostly restless dead, who ride through the sky on their phantom horses, accompanied by their spectral DEMON hounds (see BLACK DOGS), shrieking and making wild noises. The hounds and horses are black, with hideous eyes. The Wild Hunt is prominent in Celtic and Germanic folklore. The retinue flies through the skies on pagan holidays associated with evil by Christianity, such as Walpurgisnacht (Beltane, April 30–May 1) and Samhain (Halloween, October 31–November 2).

There are different versions of the Wild Hunt. Witches join the phantoms, and the ghostly train is led by demonized pagan goddesses such as Diana, Holde, Herodias, Hecate, and Berchta. (See CHTHONIC DEITIES.) Diana's night train punished the lazy and wicked but were generous on occasion: If a peasant left out food for them, they ate it and magically replenished it before they left.

In Cornish lore, the Wild Hunt is led by Devil's Dandy Dogs, who hunt the countryside for human souls.

The Sluagh, or the Host of Celtic lore, is a band of the unforgiven dead of the Highland FAIRY folk.

Winged Dragon FALLEN ANGEL and one of the 72 SPIRITS OF SOLOMON. Winged Dragon has the limbs of a dragon, wings on its back and the face, and the feet of a man. His activity is to copulate with certain beautiful women through their buttocks. In the Testament of Solomon, he tells King Solomon that one woman he attacked bore a child that became Eros. The woman was killed by others. While he is speaking, the demon breathes out fire that burns the forest of Lebanon and all the wood intended for the construction of the Temple of God.

Solomon learns that the Winged Dragon is thwarted by the angel Bazazath. He invokes this angel and then condemns the demon to cut marble for the building of the temple.

FURTHER READING:
The Old Testament Pseudepigrapha. Vols. 1 & 2. Edited by James H. Charlesworth. 1983. Reprint, New York: Doubleday, 1985.

***Wishmaster* (1997)** Horror film in which an evil DJINN is unleashed in the world. Directed by Robert Kurzman, the film stars Tammy Lauren as Alexandra Amberson, Robert Englund as Raymond Beaumont, and Andrew Divoff as the djinn, also known as Nathaniel Demerest. Kane Hodder plays a role as a guard.

According to the back story, God created djinn of smokeless fire and pushed them out of the earth to make way for humans, condemning them to the void between the worlds of ANGELS and humans. The djinn wish to reclaim the world, and thus they are at war with humanity. If a human awakens a djinn, it grants three wishes, after which it is free to summon hordes of fellow djinn into the world. In Persia, in 1187, a sorcerer trapped an extremely powerful djinn in a stone and buried it inside a statue of the god Ahura Mazda.

In present times, the statue is taken to New York. Its crate is dropped by a drunken crane operator, and the statue breaks and the stone flies out. It winds up at an auction house, where Amberson and Beaumont attempt to identify and appraise it. Amberson accidentally releases the djinn, who is now freed to wreak havoc.

The djinn disguises himself as a wealthy man, Demerest. He attacks people and kills them for their souls. However, he is obligated to grant Amberson three wishes before he can summon djinn reinforcements into the world. She learns his true identity. He tries to trick her and succeeds in making her waste two wishes.

Her third wish is that the crane operator was not drunk on the day the statue was unloaded from the ship. This wish changes history. The crate does not break, the statue is not shattered, and the stone, entrapping the djinn, remains hidden inside the statue.

Wishmaster 2: Evil Never Dies was released in 1999 and was directed by Jack Sholder. Divoff again plays the djinn. Morgana (Holly Fields) is a not-very-bright thief. With her partner, she attempts to steal a rare statue from a museum. The heist fails, her partner is killed, and the djinn is released. In this plot, the djinn must collect 1,001 human souls before he can start the apocalypse. He also must still grant the three wishes to the one who freed him, Morgana.

Demerest commits a crime that puts him in prison, where he begins his collection of souls. Then, he relentlessly pursues Morgana to fulfill the requirement of the three wishes. Aided by a priest, Morgana manages to defeat the djinn, but not as cleverly as her predecessor heroine in the original film.

Wishmaster 3: Beyond the Gates of Hell was released in 2001, followed by *Wishmaster 4: The Prophecy Fulfilled* in 2002. In *Wishmaster 3*, a college girl, Diana Collins (A. J. Cook), accidentally frees the djinn (John Novak). He goes on a rampage on campus, until she figures out how to send him back to his prison in the stone. *Wishmaster 4* features a painter, Sam (Jason Thompson), and his girlfriend, Lisa (Tara Spencer-Naim). Sam has an accident that leaves him paralyzed. Lisa engages a lawyer, Steven (Michael Trucco), to file a lawsuit. He develops a crush on Lisa. Steven refuses to take money for the case and gives Lisa a jewel he has found hidden in his desk. It imprisons the djinn (Novak), which is now released, and takes POSSESSION of Steven. He tries to win over Lisa. She inadvertently makes three wishes, the third of which is to love Steven as he really is. Knowing that his true djinn form will repulse her, he refuses, but he offers Lisa the choice of ruling with him when the djinn overtake the world or being cast down into HELL. Sam arrives and thwarts the action. He dies and Lisa survives. The djinn fails.

witchcraft A type of SORCERY involving the magical manipulation of supernormal forces through the casting of spells and the conjuring or invoking of spirits. Beliefs about witchcraft are universal, but there is no universal definition of *witchcraft*. Anthropologists define witchcraft as an innate, inborn condition involving the use of malevolent power by psychic means with no need for ritual or CHARM. In most societies, witches are believed to use their supernatural powers more for evil than for good. However, "white witches" practicing folk medicines and spells are consulted for protection and for ensuring good fortunes.

In the West, witchcraft was especially feared during the Middle Ages and during the Inquisition, in conjunction with fears about the DEVIL and demonic influences. Witches were regarded as servants of the Devil, who made PACTs of worship in exchange for FAMILIARs and malevolent supernatural powers.

In 1484, the Catholic Church, in a bull issued by Pope Innocent VIII, declared witchcraft to be a heresy, thus enabling inquisitors to persecute any enemy of the church. The charge of witchcraft was nearly impossible to refute, and the accused usually were severely tortured until they confessed to having familiars, worshipping the Devil, having sex with DEMONs, and casting evil spells. Witch hunting became a profitable pursuit and an effective way to take revenge on one's enemies.

In the 16th-century, the Protestant Reformation continued the campaign against witches; MARTIN LUTHER called them "the Devil's whores." The witch hysteria affected Europe, including Britain, and America. It died down by the end of the 18th century, but prejudices

Satan holds court for new witches. (AUTHOR'S COLLECTION)

against witches and fears of their malevolent powers remained. Nonetheless, "folk witches," people who possessed magical skills, especially for healing, fertility, luck, and divination, continued to function especially in rural areas. "White witchcraft," or good magic, still flourished from the 18th century on.

The stain of the Inquisition was impossible to remove, however, and many people still perceived a "witch" as a malevolent person in league with the Devil, and anti-witch sentiment continued. In England, continental Europe, and even America, there were outbreaks of violence against suspected witches all through the 19th century and into the early 20th century. The worst case in North America was the SALEM WITCHCRAFT HYSTERIA in Salem, Massachusetts, in 1692–93, which led to the imprisonment of hundreds of accused witches and the deaths of 19 people.

Witchcraft the Religion

In the 1950s, witchcraft was reinvented as a religion, a movement that started in England and gained popularity through the efforts of Gerald B. Gardner and others. Gardner followed the work of the British anthropologist Margaret A. Murray, who, in the 1920s and 1930s, had claimed that witchcraft comprised the remnants of an "Old Religion" based on pagan beliefs and practices centered around the Horned God, a Pan-like deity.

Gardner claimed to be initiated by a coven of "hereditary witches," followers of the Old Religion. He feared that Witchcraft, spelled with a capital *W* to distinguish it as a religion, not a sorcery, was in danger of dying out through its lack of young members. Until 1951, witchcraft was still a serious crime in England, according to an old law still on the books. The law was repealed in that year, enabling people to be witches openly.

Gardner formed his own coven. He said his fellow Witches had given him a framework of rituals, including initiations. He obtained additional rituals from ALEISTER CROWLEY, whom he met in 1946. He borrowed additional material from ritual magic practiced by such orders as the Hermetic Order of the Golden Dawn, the Freemasons, and the Rosicrucians, as well as sex magic rituals from the Ordo Templi Orientis, of which Crowley had been a leader in England. Gardner also mixed in Eastern mysticism and magic.

In 1953, he initiated Doreen Valiente, with whom he collaborated in writing and revising the rituals. Under Valiente's influence, the "ancient laws" of Witchcraft took on a more Christian flavor, with an emphasis on using magic only for good and avoiding associations with the demonic. The religion of Witchcraft was an immediate sensation and attracted adherents around the world. Murray's theory of the unbroken existence of an Old Religion was disproved, but that did not discourage potential initiates from joining covens. For many, the new religion was a refreshing change from traditional faiths.

Witchcraft the religion, also called *Wicca,* has become the largest segment of modern Pagan religions. There are numerous traditions, many involving reconstructions of pagan beliefs and practices, as well as shamanic elements.

Luciferian Witchcraft

A tradition of Luciferian Witchcraft, founded by Michael W. Ford, emphasizes the Left Hand Path of magic centered on the Devil, the Adversary, the gnosis of FALLEN ANGELS, and sex magic. The practitioner becomes like Cain, isolated and living outside the natural order of society, in order to focus inward. According to Ford, Luciferian Witchcraft complements the philosophies and works of Crowley; Anton Szandor Lavey, who founded the Church of Satan (see SATANISM); and the English occultist AUSTIN OSMAN SPARE, who created a unique system of sigil MAGIC.

One of the central rites in Luciferian Witchcraft is the Dragon within the Triangle of Darkness, an evocation circle for the meeting of Daemon and Man and Woman, "to uplift and envenom their spirit with the Adversarial Gnosis." The Adversary challenges and tests; the initiate descends into darkness and chaos to emerge as a Luciferian Bringer of Light. The black magick and witchcraft of the Luciferian tradition involve the shadow aspects of the sorcerer's own psyche. A permanent pact is made with the forces of darkness and chaos, and a Sigillium Diaboli is imprinted upon the body, mind, and spirit. The goal is a path of self-development in Light.

FURTHER READING:

Ford, Michael W. *Luciferian Witchcraft.* Lulu.com, 2005.

Guiley, Rosemary Ellen. *The Encyclopedia of Witches and Witchcraft.* 2nd ed. New York: Facts On File, 1999.

Russell, Jeffrey Burton. *A History of Witchcraft.* London: Thames & Hudson, 1980.

Witches of Eastwick, The   A novel (1984) by John Updike about three women in a small Rhode Island town who become involved with a man who is really the Devil. A 1987 film based on the novel with the same title features Jack Nicholson as the Devil.

In the plot, Alexandra Spofford, a sculptress; Jane Smart, a cellist; and Sukie Rougemont, a reporter for the local Eastwick newspaper, have all dabbled in the slightly black arts since losing their husbands through death or divorce. A few spells, such as willing shoes to untie, pearl necklaces to break, or storms to appear; or collecting herbs and animal leavings while "skyclad" (naked); or flying late at night, help relieve the tedium of raising unwanted children and going from one unfulfilling lover to another. Each has found a third teat, possibly a wart, on her body, supposedly a witch's mark or DEVIL'S MARK, and each has a large dog, or FAMILIAR. Just living in New England puts them in the area where American witchcraft beliefs traditionally have been strongest.

Jack Nicholson as Darryl Van Horne, the Devil, who entertains three women of Eastwick, played by Cher, Susan Sarandon, and Michelle Pfeifer, in The Witches of Eastwick *(1987)* (AUTHOR'S COLLECTION)

Drawn to the mischief, a dark, wealthy, mysterious stranger, Darryl Van Horne, moves to Eastwick and occupies a large old estate. No one else lives with him but his servant, Fidel. As in medieval descriptions of the Devil, he is ugly, with a hairy body. He easily seduces Alexandra, Sukie, and Jane into sexual liaisons, both singly and together. Also as in legends of the Devil, his body fluids are cold, and he asks the women to kiss his backside.

The witchy women add Van Horne to their coven, joining him and Fidel for parties with exotic food, plenty of alcohol, and still more sex. Their SABBATS are like the alleged orgies of earlier Devil worshippers, and the women seem to know when to congregate at Van Horne's without being invited. They share with him their opinions about the wives of the other men they sleep with, especially Felicia Gabriel, the wife of Sukie's boss and editor, Clyde. To punish Felicia for her strident, narrow opinions about Sukie and the others, the witches cast a spell on her, causing Felicia to vomit feathers, pennies, thumbtacks, eggshells, and pieces of insects. Their *maleficia,* or evildoing, yields more evil: Clyde can tolerate Felicia's ranting no longer and kills her with a poker before hanging himself.

The longer the witches are influenced by Van Horne, the easier evil becomes. Alexandra wills a barking dog to death. She no longer feels any sexual desire; nor do some of the witches' lovers. They appear victims of the *aiguillette,* or the knot: a device used by witches to draw illicit lovers together, cause impotence in men and barrenness in women, and foment general discontent. Once started in a community, Alexandra notes, witchcraft eventually runs on its own, out of anyone's control.

When Van Horne marries Jenny Gabriel, Felicia and Clyde's daughter, the women take revenge. Like a medieval sorcerer, Jane flies to the Van Horne mansion, shrinks herself, and collects pieces of Jenny (tissues with lipstick stains, hair, used dental floss, hairs left in the tub after shaving her legs) so that the women can make a charm. The wax figurine is given a female shape, adorned with Jenny's hair, and stabbed with tacks. Incantations are recited, and the women ask that Jenny die of cancer. The witches are later struck with some guilt and attempt to undo the spell, but Jenny dies, anyway. Van Horne, for all his sexual encounters and rhetoric on the importance of women, takes Jenny's brother, Chris, as his lover and disappears.

In the film version of *The Witches of Eastwick,* directed by George Miller, the women—played by Cher as Alexandra, Susan Sarandon as Jane, and Michelle Pfeiffer as Sukie—are not witches but merely bored women before Darryl Van Horne, played by Jack Nicholson, arrives in Eastwick. He introduces them to magic and orgies, which the women enjoy immensely until their witchy dabbling culminates in Felicia Gabriel's murder. Before her death, Felicia vomits enormous quantities of cherry seeds, which Van Horne and the women were spitting out of their mouths at a party. The more they eat, the more seeds she excretes.

Jenny Gabriel is not part of the movie plot at all, and this time the wax figurine is of Van Horne himself as the women try to purge the Devil from their lives. He has impregnated all three, and they wish him gone before the babies are born. They succeed, and he leaves with horrifying special effects.

One interesting note about the filming of the movie: The producers originally planned to shoot the outdoor scenes in Rhode Island, as in the novel, but local protest by practicing witches and others forced them to move the location to Cohasset, Massachusetts. The protests were led by Laurie Cabot, prominent Salem witch and cochair of the Witches League of Public Awareness. The league objected to the book for portraying what they said were inaccurate stereotypes about witches; modern practitioners of WITCHCRAFT as a religion (Wicca) do not worship the Devil.

Xipe Totec   Aztec trickster vampire DEMON of the underworld. Xipe Totec is called the "night drinker" because he sucks the BLOOD of souls of the dead who drop off to sleep instead of doing their penance. Enemies of the Aztec feared him as the god of penitence and sacrificed prisoners of war to him.

According to one story, Zipe Totec went to a village and convinced the residents that their sins had taken the form of a huge monster that lurked outside town and cast spells over people. He told them they had to bind the monster and throw it over a cliff. He led the townspeople to a spot where he conjured an imaginary monster. Believing it to be real, the people bound it and took it to the edge of a cliff. Zipe Totec tricked their eyes, and the people fell off the cliff to their deaths.

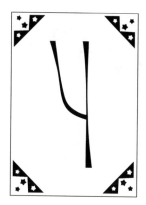

Yacatecutli   See TZITZIMIME.

yawning   In folklore, a means by which DEMONS can enter the body, and the soul can escape. The custom of covering the mouth while yawning has nothing to do with politeness, but with preventing demonic entry and soul loss. In colonial America, it was customary to snap the fingers when yawning in order to scare away demons.

Zaffis, John (1956–) Paranormal investigator and author. John Zaffis is recognized as one of the leading authorities on demonic hauntings and POSSESSION. In more than 30 years, he has worked on more than 7,000 cases internationally, including assisting in more than 90 cases of genuine demonic possession. He has worked with clergy of different faiths and has participated in EXORCISMS. Zaffis does not refer to himself as a DEMON-OLOGIST, a term he says is used too loosely in the paranormal field.

Zaffis was born on December 18, 1956, in Bridgeport, Connecticut, the youngest of three children (two sisters) of John and Babette Warren Zaffis. Zaffis' mother was the twin of the demonologist ED WARREN. As children, the Warrens had experienced haunting phenomena. Unlike Ed, who made the paranormal his career, Babette was frightened of the paranormal and did not want her own children involved in it. John, psychically sensitive, was drawn to it, anyway. At a young age, he became fascinated by the stories Ed and his wife, LORRAINE WARREN, told about their cases.

His interest in the paranormal heightened at about age 15 to 16, when he had a bedside visit from an apparition. The transparent form of a man appeared at the foot of his bed, shaking its head as if to say no. Zaffis's mother thought the apparition was his deceased grandfather. Shortly after the experience, his grandmother died.

When Zaffis turned 18, Ed Warren allowed him to participate in their cases. Warren cautioned him that de-mons always try to destroy those who work in the field and will, through temptation, try to make individuals destroy themselves. Zaffis was determined to become involved, and Ed schooled him on demonology. For about 12 years, he stayed in the background of the Warrens' work, observing and learning. Gradually, he worked more in the forefront on cases of hauntings and demonic possession.

Zaffis studied engineering and quality control at several colleges. On October 13, 1984, he married Cheryl Dimichelle; the couple have three children, two daughters and a son. They live in Stratford.

In 1998, Zaffis founded the Paranormal Research Society of New England (PRSNE) and began working with his own group. The same year, his mother died. She has made two after-death visits to John; the second visit occurred in 2004, just before Zaffis' father died. After her death, Babette sometimes appeared in Ed's dreams prior to significant events.

Demonic cases have been on the rise, especially since about 2000, Zaffis says. He receives requests to investigate several cases a week—sometimes as many as 10 to 15 in a single day. He often works with BISHOP ROBERT MCKENNA, of the Our Lady of the Rosary Chapel in Monroe, Connecticut. The majority of cases do not require exorcisms; for example, places with negative spirit attachments can respond to clearings. Not all malevolent entities in hauntings are demonic; some are bad-tempered ghosts of humans.

275

John Zaffis (COURTESY JOHN ZAFFIS)

Many demonic problems can be traced to misuse of a OUIJA™ or other form of divination that opens a door wide to the spirit world, particularly to deceitful entities who masquerade as dead loved ones, higher spiritual teachers, and so forth, while they gain control. Sometimes one of the first signs of INFESTATION is a knocking on a door or a window; when it is opened, no one is present. However, the opening provides a literal means and invitation for the invisible to enter.

Zaffis acknowledges that demonic cases continue to have frightening aspects, even after so many years of work in the field. The powers of evil work relentlessly, and he has seen many a strong person buckle. He does not describe himself as a devout Catholic but says that the working of evil powers has strengthened his belief in God. Having a strong foundation of religious faith—in any religion—is crucial in the work.

One of the most unsettling experiences Zaffis has had was the materialization of a reptilelike entity in a former funeral home in Southington, Connecticut. The funeral home, turned into a private residence, had negative activity that was plaguing a family who had moved in. Zaffis, the Warrens, and others conducted an investigation that involved 24-hour monitoring of the premises. One night, while Zaffis was a monitor, alone in a room, the temperature dropped, and he had a sensation that something was about to happen. Turning and looking up, he saw a murky-colored reptilian form materialize at the top

of the stairs and descend toward him. Behind it were fluttering movements. It repeated in an audible voice, "You know what they did to us." Zaffis grabbed his car keys and exited the house. It took him three days to return, during which he withdrew from the work and questioned his involvement in it. He ultimately concluded that there are people who need help in dealing with the demonic, and he could not retire from helping them at any cost. As for the funeral home, a full exorcism was performed by Roman Catholic clergy.

Zaffis has experienced a wide range of paranormal phenomena, which often kick up at home before a significant demonic case is under way. Lights going on and off, knockings and rapping, car problems, and so forth, are not uncommon.

Zaffis has collected objects with spirit attachments since the beginning of his paranormal investigations. Bindings and prayers have been said over the objects to neutralize or terminate the attachments. Some of the more troublesome objects are in acrylic cases to prevent people from handling them and being affected by them. One of the most significant pieces is an idol, now in a case, once owned by a young man who was interested in black magic. The youth was adversely affected by the spirit in the idol, which instructed him to kill himself. Fortunately, he did not, but an exorcism was necessary to end his occult problems.

In 2006, Zaffis was involved in a difficult case of demonic possession and encountered a prince of HELL, a high-ranking DEMON. The victim, who had become possessed after practicing black magic, showed the unusual symptom of the eyes changing from their natural brown color to opaque milky white three times; this was captured on videotape.

Zaffis made numerous media and lecture appearances. He is the coauthor, with Brian McIntyre, of *Shadows of the Dark* (2004), about his paranormal career and some of his most notable cases. Some of his collection of POSSESSED POSSESSIONS is featured in *Possessed Possessions Vol. I*, coauthored with ADAM CHRISTIAN BLAI.

The Southington case served as the basis of the film *A Haunting in Connecticut*, released in 2009.

FURTHER READING:
John Zaffis Web site. Available online. URL: http://www. johnzaffis.com. Accessed February 18, 2009.
Zaffis, John, and Brian McIntyre. *Shadows of the Dark*. New York: iUniverse, 2004.

Zagan   FALLEN ANGEL and 61st of the 72 SPIRITS OF SOLOMON. Zagan is a president and king who appears, first as a bull with griffin wings and then as a man. He makes men clever and witty, turns water into wine, blood into oil and oil into water, and wine into water or BLOOD. Zagan can turn any metal into money and can make fools wise. He commands 33 LEGIONS of DEMONS.

zar   In Muslim lore, a possessing DJINN that usually attacks women and refuses to leave until the victim receives lavish gifts of jewelry, perfume, clothes, and dainty foods.

Second-class citizens under male domination, Muslim women rely on the *zar* to give them some measure of power and privilege. Husbands must provide expensive gifts and sweetmeats to create peace in the household. Such appeasement raises suspicions of manipulation, but so ingrained in Islamic culture is the belief in spirit interference that husbands dare not tempt fate. Descriptions of *zar* possessions were recorded in the early 19th century by travelers to the Egypt and the Middle East. The "cult of the *zar*" continues in areas in modern times.

The usual POSSESSION and EXORCISM of the *zar* proceed as follows: The victim, suffering from some minor complaint, blames possession by the *zar,* and other female relatives prevent her from seeing a medical doctor, preferring the services of an old woman who is a female shaman, a *shechah-ez-zar.* For a fee, the *shechah* identifies a *zar* as the source of the woman's troubles and interrogates the *zar,* sometimes in a recognizable language and sometimes in *zar* language, understood only by the *shechah.* After repeated conversations, the *zar* offers to leave once the possessed victim receives specific lavish gifts and attention from her husband.

On the afternoon of the *zar*'s scheduled departure, a "beating the *zar*" ceremony is performed at the victim's home. The victim's female friends and relatives join her for the ceremony, often accompanied by food, coffee, and a flute and drumming performance. The *shechah* and her assistants chant the final exorcism rites, with music, and then often sacrifice a lamb. The lamb's BLOOD is rubbed on the victim's forehead and elsewhere. She then dances madly, sways, and finally faints. The *zar* leaves, satisfied that the victim has been rewarded.

In some ceremonies, the questioning of the *zar* is done after the victim and others dance and enter trance. The *shechah* asks for a remedy to the malady, and the *zar* specifies gifts. The ecstatic dancers may be shown silver rings and bracelets and other objects, which pacify the *zar.*

On a day fixed by the *zar,* another fit can occur, which can be relieved only by the satisfying of a wish.

Zar exorcisms have become part of contemporary urban Islamic culture. In many large cities, such as Cairo, regular exorcisms are held in a public building as often as once a week. The length of the ceremony, from three to seven nights, depends upon the fee that can be paid.

Women from all walks of life participate, whirling and dancing until the spirit leaves them and they return home, exhausted but entertained. Relief from the possession may be only temporary, and it may return with another infraction committed by a husband. Men are expected to believe in the possession, which, in addition to giving women the freedom to ask for gifts, permits them to scold and upbraid their husbands in a manner that would be forbidden under normal circumstances.

Nineteenth-century accounts of *zar* possession in Abyssinia describe a different cult that affected men as well as women, blamed on the *zar,* or *bouddha,* evil spirit. The victim typically was afflicted in the middle of the night. He would run out, roll on the ground, and scream until exhausted and still. The remedy consisted of taking a hen, swinging it around the head, and smashing it to the ground. If the hen died immediately, it meant the *zar* had passed into the body of the fowl and the victim was cleared. If the hen survived, the remedy had to be repeated until a bird died.

FURTHER READING:
Ebon, Martin. *The Devil's Bride, Exorcism: Past and Present.* New York: Harper & Row, 1974.
Lewis, I. M. *Ecstatic Religion: An Anthropological Study of Spirit Possession and Shamanism.* Middlesex, England: Penguin Books, 1971.
Oesterreich, Traugott K. *Possession and Exorcism.* Secaucus, N.J.: University Books, 1966.

Zarika   In ZOROASTRIANISM, the arch-DEMON of evil thirst. Zarika is paired with TARU (evil hunger) and makes poison for Taru to give to plants and animals. Zarika opposes Amurdat, a good *amesha spenta.*

Zepar   FALLEN ANGEL and 16th of the 72 SPIRITS OF SOLOMON. Zepar is a duke who appears wearing red clothing and armed as a soldier. He makes women love men and can transform them into other shapes until they have been enjoyed by their lovers. Alternately, he makes women barren. He commands 26 LEGIONs of DEMONs in HELL.

Zohak   See AZHI DAHAKA.

Zoroastrianism   Religion of ancient Persia based on the teachings of the prophet Zarasthustra (Zoroaster in Greek). Zoroastrianism influenced the development of Western angelologies and demonologies.

Zarathustra may have been born as early as 650 B.C.E. Historical documentation of his life is fragmentary, and documents attributed to him have been dated hundreds of years apart. It may never be known for certain whether the original prophet or one of the followers composed the Gathas, songs or odes of the sacred book of Zoroastrianism, and the Avesta, the religion's central doctrines and creation myth.

Zoroastrianism shares common ground with Hinduism and borrows some of its deities but differs from it in significant ways. Its cosmology is dualistic, and the conflict between the forces of good and evil is played out on a hierarchical scale of spiritual and material spheres. Some Hindu demigods named in the Yashts, a document similar to the song cycle of the earliest Indo-Aryans, the Rig-Veda, are turned into ANGELs. As Zoroastrianism was reformed, the gods and demigods called DAEVAs (devas) in the Veda were demonized, and the class of deity called *ahura* by Iranians and *asura* by the Indians were eliminated. The exception is Ahura Mazda (later called Ohrmazd), who was elevated to the status of the one true God from whom all other divinities proceed.

Evil is a separate principle and substance standing against the good God and threatening to destroy him. Against the God stands Angra Mainyu (in Hinduism, Aryaman), later AHRIMAN, the Destructive Spirit. The duration of this conflict is limited; Ohrmazd will defeat Ahriman. God needs humans' help in his battle with the "Lie," as the principle of evil is frequently called in the ancient documents. Evil is not identified with matter. The material world is the handiwork of God, a weapon fashioned by the Deity with which to smite the Evil One. The world is the trap God sets for the DEVIL, and, in the end, Ohrmazd will deal Ahriman the death blow.

According to the Bundahishn, or Book of the Primal Creation, the two antagonists had always existed in time, but when Ohrmazd first chants the Ahunvar (True Speech), the key prayer of Zoroastrianism, it reveals to Ahriman that his annihilation is certain. Assaulted by this truth, Ahriman falls unconscious for 3,000 years. Ohrmazd creates the universe, the two worlds (spiritual and material), as a weapon with which to defeat Ahriman. An unorthodox text called the Zurvan indicates that early creation myths varied or were altered, for in the Zervanite version, Ahriman creates first the Lying Word (the exact opposite of the Ahunvar) and then Akoman, the Evil Mind, which he could not do if he were unconscious.

The human soul is a spiritual being called *fravashi* or *fravahr,* a concept that encompasses not only individual human souls and guardian angels, but also local genii, the intelligences of places.

Both human body and its *fravashi* are creatures of Ohrmazd and his wife/daughter Spandarmat, the Earth. The soul preexists the human body but is not eternally preexistent as in many Eastern religions. Humankind belongs to Ohrmazd and will return to him. The first Primal Man mates with Ahriman's "Demon Whore." Each individual is free to choose good or evil, but evil is an unnatural act. Life on Earth is a battle between Ohrmazd and his attendant Powers, on one hand, and Ahriman and his demonic hordes, on the other. For Zarasthustra, it was a very real battle, since daeva worshippers were still adherents of the traditional religion; he identified these with all that is evil.

Forces of Good

Ohrmazd is helped by the six *amarahspands* (or Amesha Spenta), the Bounteous Immortals, who are comparable to archangels and serve as Ohrmazd's ministers. After Ohrmazd adopts Man, each of the *amarahspands* adopts one of the material creations. Their names are personifications of abstract concepts or virtues:

- Vahuman: Good Thought, Good Mind
- Artvahisht: Best Righteousness, Truth
- Shahrevar: Choice Kingdom, Material Sovereignty
- Spandarmat: Bounteous Right-Mindedness, Wisdom in Piety; also identified with Earth
- Hurdat: Health, Wholeness, Salvation
- Amurdat: Life, Immortality

Beneath the *ahmarahspands* are the *yazatas* (adorable beings), who are legion and are divided into heavenly (spiritual) and earthly (material) subcategories. Ohrmazd himself leads the spiritual Yazatas, and Zarasthustra the material Yazatas. They have assignments, as do the celestial intelligences and the DAIMONES of water, air, fire, and earth.

Forces of Evil

Ahriman is served by a host of DEMONS, most of which are personified vices, such as concupiscence, anger, sloth, and heresy. There are six archdemons, who oppose the *amarahspands* and try to destroy their good work. According to the Bundahishn, they are assisted by "furies in great multitude," who are "demons of ruin, pain, and growing old, producers of vexation and vile, revivers of grief, the progeny of gloom, and vileness, who are many, very numerous, and very notorious."

The six archdemons are the following:

- Akoman, the Evil Mind, foments vile thoughts and discord and opposes the *amesha spenta,* or good spirit of Vahuman, who opposes Vahuman
- ANDRA, the Slayer, who opposes Artvahisht
- Naoghatya, rules arrogance, presumption, disobedience, insubordination, and contempt and opposes Spandarmat, an *amesha spenta,* or good spirit
- Saru, the Tyrant, opposes the good spirit (*amesha spenta*) of Shahrevar and oversees misgovernment, anarchy, and drunkenness
- TARU, Evil Hunger, opposes Hurdat
- ZARIKA, Evil Thirst, opposes Amurdat

Numerous other demons populate the mythology. Among them are the following:

- Akatasa, who shapes evil and is "the fiend of inquisitiveness" and meddling
- Anaxsti, who sows discord
- Apaosa, who fights the rain god Trishtya and always loses in the end and rides a black bald horse
- Araiti, who encourages stinginess
- Arast (Araska), who spreads falsehood and lies, malice, envy, and jealousy
- Asrusti, who incites disobedience
- Ayasi, who governs the EVIL EYE
- Daiwi daeva, who encourages lying
- Driwi daeva, who rules beggary
- Freftar, who orchestrates deceit and seduction
- Kasvi daeva, who rules spite
- Mahmi, who tried to convince the creator god Ohrmazd that if he had sex with his mother, the Sun would be born, and if he had sex with his sister, the Moon would be born

- Paitisa daeva, who governs counteraction and opposition and is "the most devilish of demons," personifying the power of Ahriman to ruin the world
- Pus, who rules miserliness and hoarding
- Shetaspih, who personifies Christianity
- Spazga, who foments slander, calumny, backbiting, and gossip
- Spenjargak, who raises storms
- Vareno, who incites lust and illicit sex
- Vatya daeva, who battles good winds to create storms
- Vaya, "the merciless one," who plagues the souls of the dead when they arrive at the Chinvat Bridge to the underworld and tries to interfere with their passage
- Vizares, who struggles with the souls of the dead for three days and nights after their passing, binds them, drags them off to torment, and sits at the gates of HELL
- Vyambura daeva, who vampirizes the living
- Xru, who foments murder
- Zamaka, who rules the evils of winter
- Zaurvan, who rules old age, decrepitude, and wasting away

Zoroastrianism in Practice

There are four major arms of Zoroastrianism: the teachings of Zarathustra; the teachings of Mazdaism, which made Ahriman creator and leader of the daevas; the teachings of Zeravanism; and the teaching of the Magi.

The Islamic conquest of Iran in the seventh century scattered Zoroastrian sects and caused a decline in the religion. Many Zoroastrians emigrated east to India, where they are called Parsis. In present times, there are fewer than half a million followers, most of whom live in and around Bombay, India.

Zoroastrians consider their role in this world as to cooperate with nature and to lead a virtuous life; they oppose all forms of asceticism and monasticism. Their duty is to marry and rear children, for human life on Earth is a sheer necessity if Ahriman is to be defeated. Agriculture is honored for making the earth fruitful, strong, and abundant in order to resist the Enemy, who is the author of disease and death. There is a rigid dogmatism preserving the purity of the body, the care of useful animals, agricultural practice, and strict ritual observance. Celibacy is both unnatural and wicked.

On the moral plane, all the emphasis is on righteousness or truth and on good works, for deeds are the sole criterion by which one is judged after parting this life on the "Bridge of the Requiter," the bridge of Rashn the Righteous, who impartially weighs each soul's good and evil deeds. If there is a preponderance of good, the soul proceeds to heaven, but if of evil, it is dragged off to HELL. If good and evil deeds are exactly equal, the soul goes to the "place of the mixed," where it experiences mild correction, and the only pains suffered are those of heat and cold. Zoroastrian hell is like the Christian purgatory in that the punishment is only temporary. The final purgation from sin takes place at the Last Judgment at the end of time. The stain left by sin is purged from all souls, and from this all without exception emerge spotless. None is punished eternally for sins committed in time.

Sin is viewed as perversity; it is a failure to recognize who is your friend and who is your enemy. Ohrmazd is one's friend and Ahriman is the enemy, from whom all evil and suffering proceed. Unlike the Western God, Ohrmazd does not permit evil, for such would give him characteristics of Ahriman. Monotheists have been deceived in this way, and this represents a genuine triumph for Ahriman, for besides being the Destroyer, he is the Deceiver, the Liar, and his deception takes the form of persuading people that evil proceeds from God. But his triumph is short-lived, for in the end all human souls, reunited with their bodies, return to Ohrmazd, who is their creator and father.

FURTHER READING:
Dhalla, Maneckji Nusservanji. *History of Zoroastrianism.* New York and Oxford: Oxford University Press, 1938. Reprint, Brooklyn, N.Y.: AMS Press, 1977.
Jackson, A. V. Williams. *Zoroastrian Studies.* Whitefish, Mont.: Kessinger, 2003.
Zaehner, R. C. *The Dawn and Twilight of Zoroastrianism.* New York: Putnam, 1961.

Zotz   Fearsome Mayan DEMON and a lord of the underworld. Zotz is a huge winged being with the head of a dog, needle-sharp teeth, and a bloody, contorted grin. He is sometimes shown as half-black and half-white, signifying faithlessness. Zotz lives deep within caves. He hides in remote areas at night and ambushes travelers, stealing their goods and wealth to stash in his caves.

In the underworld he has his own area, called the House of Bats. Souls who are condemned must pass by him; he drinks their BLOOD. A Mayan legend tells of two brothers who were condemned. When they passed by Zotz, he bit off the head of one of them. The other brother replaced the head with a nearby tortoise, which restored the boy to life.

❧ BIBLIOGRAPHY ❧

Ahmad, Salim. *Revealing the Mystery behind the World of Jinn.* Booksurge.com: 2008.

Amorth, Gabriele. *An Exorcist Tells His Story.* San Francisco: Ignatius Press, 1999.

———. *An Exorcist: More Stories.* San Francisco: Ignatius Press, 2002.

Ankarloo, Bengt, and Stuart Clark, gen. eds. *The Athalone History of Witchcraft and Magic in Europe.* London: Athlone Press, 1999.

Ankarloo, Bengt, and Gustav Henningsen, eds. *Early Modern European Witchcraft: Centres and Peripheries.* Oxford: Clarendon Press, 1990.

al-Ashqar, Umar Sulaiman. *The World of the Jinn and Devils.* Translated by Jamaal al-Din M. Zarabozo. New York: Al-Basheer Company for Publications and Translations, 1998.

Anson, Jay. *The Amityville Horror.* New York: Prentice Hall, 1977.

Auerbach, Loyd. *ESP, Hauntings and Poltergeists.* New York: Warner Books, 1986.

Augustine. *The City of God.* Translated by Marcus Dods, George Wilson, and J. J. Smith; introduction by Thomas Merton. New York: Modern Library, 1950.

Bainton, Ronald. *Here I Stand: A Life of Martin Luther.* New York, Penguin, 1995.

Bardon, Franz. *Initiation into Hermetics: A Course of Instruction of Magic Theory and Practice.* Wuppertal, Germany: Dieter Ruggeberg, 1971.

Barker, Margaret. *The Great Angel: A Study of Israel's Second God.* Louisville, Ky.: Westminster/John Knox Press, 1992.

Baroja, Julio Caro. *The World of the Witches.* Chicago: University of Chicago Press, 1975.

Barton, Blanche. *The Church of Satan.* New York: Hell's Kitchen Productions, 1990.

———. *The Secret Life of a Satanist: The Authorized Biography of Anton LaVey.* Los Angeles: Feral House, 1990.

Bird, Sheila. *Haunted Places of Cornwall: On the Trail of the Paranormal.* Newbury, England: Countryside Books, 2006.

Black, Jeremy, and Anthony Green. *Gods, Demons and Symbols of Ancient Mesopotamia.* London: British Museum Press, 1992.

Bord, Janet, and Colin Bord. *Mysterious Britain.* London: Granada, 1974.

Brier, Bob. *Ancient Egyptian Magic.* New York: William Morrow, 1980.

Brittle, Gerald Daniel. *The Demonologist: The Extraordinary Career of Ed and Lorraine Warren.* Englewood Cliffs, N.J.: Prentice Hall, 1980.

Bruyn, Lucy de. *Woman and the Devil in Sixteenth-Century Literature.* Tisbury, England: Bear Book/The Compton Press, 1979.

Burr, George Lincoln, ed. *Narratives of the Witchcraft Cases 1648–1706.* New York: Charles Scribner's Sons, 1914.

Butler, E. M. *Ritual Magic.* Cambridge: Cambridge University Press, 1949.

Calmet, Dom Augustin. *The Phantom World: Concerning Apparitions and Vampires.* Ware, England: Wordsworth Editions in association with the Folklore Society, 2001.

Cavendish, Richard. *The Black Arts.* New York: G. P. Putnam's Sons, 1967.

Certeau, Michel de. *The Possession at Loudun.* Translated by Michael B. Smith. Chicago: University of Chicago Press, 2000.

Collin de Plancy, Jacques. *Dictionary of Witchcraft*. Edited and translated by Wade Baskin. Originally published as *Dictionary of Demonology*. New York: Philosophical Library, 1965.

Collins, Andrew. *From the Ashes of Angels: The Forbidden Legacy of a Fallen Race*. London: Signet Books, 1996.

Cornelius, J. Edward. *Aleister Crowley and the Ouija Board*. Los Angeles: Feral House, 2005.

Covina, Gina. *The Ouija Book*. New York: Simon & Schuster, 1979.

Crowley, Aleister. *The Holy Books of Thelema*. York Beach, Me.: Samuel Weiser, 1983.

———. *Magic in Theory and Practice*. 1929. Reprint, New York: Dover, 1976.

Curran, Robert. *The Haunted: One Family's Nightmare*. New York: St. Martin's Press, 1988.

Davies, T. Witton. *Magic, Divination and Demonology among the Hebrews and Their Neighbors*. First published 1898.

Dhalla, Maneckji Nusservanji. *History of Zoroastrianism*. New York and Oxford: Oxford University Press, 1938. Reprint, Brooklyn, N.Y.: AMS Press, 1977.

Dictionary of Deities and Demons in the Bible. 2nd ed. Edited by Karel van der Toorn, Bob Becking, and Pieter W. van der Horst. Grand Rapids, Mich.: William B. Eerdmans, 1999.

Drieskens, Barbara. *Living with Djinns: Understanding and Dealing with the Invisible in Cairo*. London: Saqi Books, 2008.

Ebon, Martin. *The Devil's Bride, Exorcism: Past and Present*. New York: Harper & Row, 1974.

Edinger, Edward F. *Archetype of the Apocalypse: A Jungian Study of the Book of Revelation*. Chicago: Open Court, 1999.

Eisenman, Robert, and Michael Wise. *The Dead Sea Scrolls Uncovered*. London: Element Books, 1992.

Ellis, Bill. *Lucifer Ascending: The Occult in Folklore and Popular Culture*. Lexington: The University Press of Kentucky, 2004.

Elworthy, Frederick Thomas. *The Evil Eye*. Secaucus, N.J.: University Books/Citadel Press. Reprint of 1895 ed.

Ferber, Sarah. *Demonic Possession and Exorcism in Early Modern France*. London: Routledge, 2004.

Finlay, Anthony. *Demons! The Devil, Possession and Exorcism*. London: Blandford, 1999.

Flint, Valerie I. J. *The Rise of Magic in Early Medieval Europe*. Princeton, N.J.: Princeton University Press, 1991.

Fortea, Fr. José Antonio. *Interview with an Exorcist: An Insider's Look at the Devil, Diabolic Possession, and the Path to Deliverance*. West Chester, Pa.: Ascension Press, 2006.

Givry, Emile Grillot de. *Witchcraft, Magic and Alchemy*. 1931. Reprint, New York: Dover Publications, 1971.

Godwin, Malcolm. *Angels: An Endangered Species*. New York: Simon & Schuster, 1990.

Goethe, Johann Wolfgang von. *The Autobiography of Johann Wolfgang von Goethe*. Vols. 1 & 2. Chicago: University of Chicago Press, 1976.

———. *Faust*. Edited by Cyrus Hamlin; translated by Walter Arendt. New York: Norton, 1976.

Goodman, Felicitas D. *The Exorcism of Anneliese Michel*. Garden City, N.Y.: Doubleday, 1981.

———. *How About Demons? Possession and Exorcism in the Modern World*. Bloomington: Indiana University Press, 1988.

Grant, James. *The Mysteries of All Nations: Rise and Progress of Superstition, Laws Against and Trials of Witches, Ancient and Modern Delusions, Together With Strange Customs, Fables and Tales*. Edinburgh: Leith, Reid & Son, n.d.

Graves, Robert, and Patai, Raphael. *Hebrew Myths*. New York: Doubleday Anchor, 1964.

Gray, William G. *Western Inner Workings*. York Beach, Me.: Samuel Weiser, 1983.

Guazzo, Francesco Maria. *Compendium Maleficarum*. Secaucus, N.J.: University Books, 1974.

Guiley, Rosemary Ellen. *The Encyclopedia of Angels*. 2nd ed. New York: Facts On File, 2004.

———. *The Encyclopedia of Magic and Alchemy*. New York: Facts On File, 2006.

———. *The Encyclopedia of Ghosts and Spirits*. 3rd ed. New York: Facts On File, 2007.

Hall, Manly P. *The Secret Teachings of All Ages*. 1928. Reprint, Los Angeles: Philosophic Research Society, 1977.

Hansen, George. *The Trickster and the Paranormal*. New York: Xlibris, 2001.

Henson, Mitch, ed. *Lemegeton: The Complete Lesser Key of Solomon*. Jacksonville, Fla.: Metatron Books, 1999.

Hillyer, Vincent. *Vampires*. Los Banos, Calif.: Loose Change, 1988.

Hoeller, Stephan A. *The Gnostic Jung and the Seven Sermons to the Dead*. Wheaton, Ill.: Quest Books, 1982.

Hunt, Stoker. *Ouija: The Most Dangerous Game*. New York: Harper & Row, 1985.

Huxley, Aldous. *The Devils of Loudun*. New York: Harper and Brothers, 1952.

Huysmans, Joris Karl. *Là-Bas*. New York: Dover, 1972.

Hyatt, Victoria, and Joseph W. Charles. *The Book of Demons*. New York: Simon & Schuster, 1974.

Ibn Taymeeyah's Essay on the Jinn (Demons). Abridged, annotated, and translated by Dr. Abu Ameenah Bilal Philips. New Delhi, India: Islamic Book Service, 2002.

Jackson, A. V. Williams. *Zoroastrian Studies*. Whitefish, Mont.: Kessinger, 2003.

Kelly, Henry Ansgar. *A Biography of Satan*. New York: Cambridge University Press, 2006.

Kesson, H. J. *The Legend of the Lincoln Imp*. Lincoln: J. W. Ruddock & Sons, 1904.

King, Francis. *Megatherion: The Magickal World of Aleister Crowley*. London: Creation Books, 2004.

King James I of England. *Demonology*. Edited by G. B. Harrison. San Diego: Book Tree, 2002.

Kittredge, George Lyman. *Witchcraft in Old and New England*. Cambridge, Mass.: Harvard University Press, 1929.

Koltuv, Barbara Black. *The Book of Lilith*. Berwick, Me.: Nicolas-Hays, 1986.

LaVey, Anton Szandor. *The Satanic Bible*. New York: Avon Books, 1969.

Lea, Henry Charles. *Materials toward a History of Witchcraft*. Philadelphia: University of Pennsylvania Press, 1939.

Lewis, I. M. *Ecstatic Religion: An Anthropological Study of Spirit Possession and Shamanism.* Middlesex, England: Penguin Books, 1971.

Luck, Georg. *Arcana Mundi: Magic and the Occult in the Greek and Roman Worlds.* Baltimore: Johns Hopkins University Press, 1985.

Mack, Carol K., and Dinah Mack. *A Field Guide to Demons: Fairies, Fallen Angels, and Other Subversive Spirits.* New York: Owl Books/Henry Holt, 1998.

MacNutt, Francis. *Deliverance from Evil Spirits: A Practical Manual.* Grand Rapids, Mich.: Chosen Books, 1995.

The Malleus Maleficarum of Heinrich Kramer and James Sprenger. New York: Dover, 1971.

Masters, Anthony. *The Devil's Dominion: The Complete Story of Hell and Satanism in the Modern World.* London: Peter Fraser & Dunlop, 1978.

Martin, Malachi. *Hostage to the Devil.* New York: Harper & Row, 1976.

Mather, Cotton. *On Witchcraft.* Mount Vernon, N.Y.: Peter Pauper Press, n.d.

Menghi, Giolamo. *The Devil's Scourge: Exorcism during the Italian Renaissance.* York Beach, Me.: Samuel Weiser, 2002.

Michaelsen, Scott, ed. *Portable Darkness: An Aleister Crowley Reader.* New York: Harmony Books, 1989.

Middlekauff, Robert. *The Mathers: Three Generations of Puritan Intellectuals 1596–1728.* Berkeley: University of California Press, 1999.

Monter, E. William, ed. *European Witchcraft.* New York: John Wiley & Sons, 1969.

———. *Witchcraft in France and Switzerland.* Ithaca, N.Y.: Cornell University, 1976.

Morehouse, David. *Psychic Warrior: Inside the CIA's Stargate Program: The True Story of a Soldier's Espionage and Awakening.* New York: St. Martin's Press, 1996.

Oesterreich, Traugott K. *Possession and Exorcism.* Secaucus, N.J: University Books, 1966.

Ogden, Daniel. *Magic, Witchcraft, and Ghosts in the Greek and Roman Worlds: A Sourcebook.* New York: Oxford University Press, 2002.

Okonowicz, Ed. *Possessed Possessions: Haunted Antiques, Furniture and Collectibles.* Elkton, Md.: Myst and Lace, 1996.

———. *Possessed Possessions 2.* Elkton, Md.: Myst and Lace, 1998.

The Old Testament Pseudepigrapha. Vols. 1 & 2. Edited by James H. Charlesworth. 1983. Reprint, New York: Doubleday, 1985.

Pagels, Elaine. *The Origins of Satan.* New York: Random House, 1995.

Philostratus. *The Life of Apollonius of Tyana.* Translated by F. C. Conybeare. London: Heinemann, 1912.

Remy, Nicholas. *Demonolatry.* Secaucus, N.J.: University Books, 1974.

Rogo, D. Scott. *The Infinite Boundary.* New York: Dodd, Mead, 1987.

Rudwin, Maximilian. *The Devil in Legend and Literature.* La Salle, Ill.: Open Court, 1959.

Russell, Jeffrey Burton. *Witchcraft in the Middle Ages.* Ithaca, N.Y., and London: Cornell University Press, 1972.

———. *The Devil: Perceptions of Evil from Antiquity to Primitive Christianity.* Ithaca and London: Cornell University Press, 1977.

———. *A History of Witchcraft.* London: Thames and Hudson, 1980.

———. *Satan: The Early Christian Tradition.* Ithaca, N.Y., and London: Cornell University Press, 1981.

———. *Lucifer: The Devil in the Middle Ages.* Ithaca, N.Y., and London: Cornell University Press, 1984.

———. *Mephistopheles: The Devil in the Modern World.* Ithaca, N.Y., and London: Cornell University Press, 1986.

———. *The Prince of Darkness: Radical Evil and the Power of Good in History.* London: Thames & Hudson, 1989.

Rustad, Mary S., ed. and trans. *The Black Books of Elverum.* Lakeville, Minn.: Galde Press, 1999.

Scholem, Gershom. *Kabbalah.* New York: New American Library, 1974.

———. *On the Kabbalah and Its Symbolism.* New York: Schocken Books, 1965.

Scot, Reginald. *The Discoverie of Witchcraft.* Mineola, N.Y.: Dover Publications, 1982.

Scott, Sir Walter. *Demonology and Witchcraft.* 1884. Reprint, New York: Citadel Press, 1968.

Sheperd, A. P. *Rudolf Steiner: Scientist of the Invisible.* 1954. Reprint, Rochester, Vt.: Inner Traditions International, 1983.

Sinistrari, Lodovico Maria. *Demoniality.* New York: Dover, 1989.

Stead, W. T. *Borderland: A Casebook of True Supernatural Stories.* Hyde Park, N.Y.: University Books, 1970.

Steiner, Rudolf. *An Autobiography.* New trans. Blauvelt, N.Y.: Rudolf Steiner, 1977.

———. *The Essential Steiner.* Edited and introduced by Robert A. McDermott. San Francisco: Harper & Row, 1984.

———. *The Four Seasons and the Archangels.* Bristol, England: Rudolf Steiner Press, 1992.

Stephenson, P. R., and Israel Regardie. *The Legend of Aleister Crowley.* St. Paul: Llewellyn, 1970.

Stewart, R. J. *The Living World of Faery.* Lake Toxaway, N.C.: Mercury, 1995.

Summers, Montague. *The History of Witchcraft and Demonology.* London: Kegan Paul, Trench, Trubner, 1926.

———. *The Geography of Witchcraft.* London: Kegan Paul, Trench, Truner, 1927.

———. *The Werewolf.* 1933. Reprint, New York: Bell, 1967.

Sutin, Lawrence. *Do What Thou Wilt: A Life of Aleister Crowley.* New York: St. Martin's Griffin, 2000.

Swedenborg, Emanuel. *Heaven and Hell.* Translated by George F. Dole. New York: Swedenborg Foundation, 1976.

Symonds, John, and Kenneth Grant, eds. *The Confessions of Aleister Crowley, an Autobiography.* London: Routledge & Kegan Paul, 1979.

Taylor, Troy. *The Devil Came to St. Louis: The True Story of the 1949 Exorcism.* Alton, Ill.: Whitechapel Productions Press, 2006.

Thomas Aquinas. *Summa Theologiae.* Edited by Timothy McDermott. Allen, Tex.: Christian Classics, 1989.

Thomas, Keith. *Religion and the Decline of Magic.* New York: Charles Scribner's Sons, 1971.

Trachtenberg, Joshua. *Jewish Magic and Superstition: A Study in Folk Religion.* New York: Berhman's Jewish Book House, 1939.

Tyson, Donald. *Familiar Spirits: A Practical Guide for Witches and Magicians.* St. Paul, Minn.: Llewellyn, 2004.

Valiente, Doreen. *An ABC of Witchcraft Past and Present.* 1973. Reprint, Custer, Wash.: Phoenix, 1986.

Vogel, Rev. Carl. *Begone, Satan! A Soul-Stirring Account of Diabolical Possession in Iowa.* Rockford, Ill.: TAN Books and Publishers, 1973.

Waite, Arthur Edward. *The Book of Black Magic and of Pacts.* 1899. Reprint, York Beach, Me.: Samuel Weiser, 1972.

Walker, D. P. *Unclean Spirits: Possession and Exorcism in France and England in the Late Sixteenth and Early Seven-teenth Centuries.* Philadelphia: University of Pennsylvania Press, 1981.

Warren, Ed, and Lorraine Warren, with Robert David Chase. *Ghost Hunters.* New York: St. Martin's Paper-backs, 1989.

Weyer, Johann. *On Witchcraft (De praestigiis daemonum).* Abridged. Edited by Benjamin G. Kohl and H. C. Erik Midelfort. Asheville, N.C.: Pegasus Press, 1998.

Wickland, Carl. *Thirty Years among the Dead.* 1924. Reprint, N. Hollywood: Newcastle, 1974.

Wilkinson, Tracy. *The Vatican's Exorcists: Driving Out the Devil in the 21st Century.* New York: Warner Books, 2007.

Zaehner, R. C. *The Dawn and Twilight of Zoroastrianism.* New York: Putnam, 1961.

Zaffis, John, and Brian McIntyre. *Shadows of the Dark.* New York: iUniverse, 2004.

❧ INDEX ❧

Boldface page numbers indicate major treatment of a topic. *Italic* page numbers indicate illustrations.

Malinowski, Bronislaw 159

Malkuth 138–139, 140

Malleus Maleficarum (Witch Hammer) 120, **166–167**, 193, 218, 249

Malphas (Malpas) **167**

Mammon **167**, 231

mangragora **167**

Manichaeism, Az in 20

Mannoury, Dr. 143, 152

Mansemat. *See* Mastema

Marbas (Barbas) **167**

Marchosias **167**

Mardero 109

Marescot, Michel 34

Margaret of Antioch 261–262

Mariazell 107–108

Marie des Vallees **167–168**

Marino 170

Marlowe, Christopher 89, *89*

Marmaroth 109, 258

Mars, Frederick 8

"Marta" possession 91

Martin, Malachi Brendan 78, 80–81, **168**

Marwood, William 61

Mary (Virgin Mary) 192, 193, 195, 206, 255

Mary, Queen of Scots 60–61, 123

Mary of Nemmegen **168–169**, 193

Maseriel **169**

maskim **169**

Massachusetts Bay Colony 219–221

Masscheroen 169, 206

Mass of St. Secaire 30, 31

Mastema (Mastemah, Mansemat) 57, 62, **169–170**

Mather, Cotton 96–97, *220*, 221

Mather, Increase 42, 58, 221

Mathers, Samuel Liddell Macgregor 44–45, 47, 137

Mathim. *See* Bathin

Mayan lore 279

mazikeen. *See* shaytan

mazziqin **170**

McCambridge, Mercedes 83

McKenna, Bishop Robert **170**, 238, 239, 275

mediumship 203

Medmenham Abbey 114, 225

Megaera (Megara) 41, 74

Memorable Providences (Mather) 96

Menadiel **170**

Menghi, Girolamo **170–171**

Menippus 73

menstrual blood 33

mental illness 157, 204–205

Mephistopheles (Mephistophilis, Mephistophilus, Mephostopiles) 88, 89–91, **171**, *171*

Merkabah mystics 136–137, 160

Merrill, James 190

Mesopotamian lore 62, 143

Metathiax 109

Metatron 118

mezuzah, as amulet 11

Michael 109, 184, 188, 265, 266

Michaelis, Sebastian (grand inquisitor) 5–6

Michel, Anneliese 55, **171–175**

Michel, Johann 219

Mictantecutli **175**

Middle Eastern lore 144

Mignon, Canon 99, 125–126, 149–150, 152

milk, exorcism of 86

Minds in Many Pieces (Allison) 204

Minor, Roddie 45, 48

Mirabilia 1 (Phlegon of Tralles) 73

Miracle of Laon 175–177, *176*

Miron, Bishop Charles 34

mirror **177–178**, 205, 255

misophaes 206

Mithraism, Abraxas in 2

Moabite deities, Belphegor 27

Modebel 109

Modu 61

Molitor, Simon **178**

Moloch *178*, **178–179**, 241

monasticism 14

money **179**

monotheism, evil in xiii

Montespan, marquise de 30, 224

Montgomery, Ruth 190

Moonchild (Crowley) 45

moonlets, as amulet 11

Morax (Foraii, Forfax) **179**

More, George 232

Morehouse, David 68

Mormonism, Lucifer in 154

Moses 2, 113, 229

Mot **179–180**

Mottlingen Possession **180–181**

Moussant, Canon 125

Muhammad, as exorcist 79

Muller, Catherine Elise 236

multiple personality disorder 204

Murder **181**

Murmur **181**

Murray, Margaret A. 270–271

mystères 203

mythology xiii, 17, 33, 230. *See also specific lores*

N

Naamah **182**

Naberius (Cerberus) **182**

Nancy Possession **182–183**

Nantes incubus **183**

National Psychological Institute 268

Native American lore 83

Natural History (Pliny) 160

natural magic 161, 162

Nazis, in *Hellboy* 113

necromancy, in *Grand Grimoire* 102

Nemesis **183**

Nephilim 57, **183–184**, 243, 265

Nestorian heresy 37

Nettles, Bonnie 212

Netzach 140

Neubeck, Kaspar 262

Neuberg, Victor 39–41, 47–48

New Age, and possessions 121

New England Anomalies Research 135

New England Society for Psychic Research 264

New Isis Lodge 244

New York Sunday News 8

Nicodemus, Gospel of 25

night, vulnerability during 59

Night of the Demon (film) 63

Nine Satanic Sins 226

Nine Satanic Statements 226

Ninety-five Theses 156

Ninurta 18

Nisroc **184**

Niyaz 20, **184**

Norse lore 110

North Berwick witches 123–124

notarikon 136

numerology, in Mithraicism 2